W9-BGQ-087

Pension Planning:

Pension, Profit Sharing, and Other Deferred Compensation Plans

Pension Planning:

Pension, Profit Sharing, and Other Deferred Compensation Plans

Ninth Edition

Everett T. Allen, Jr. LLB

Retired Vice President and Principal
Towers Perrin

Joseph J. Melone, Ph.D., CLU, CHFC, CPCU

President and Chief Executive
Officer (RET.)
AXA Financial

Jerry S. Rosenbloom, Ph.D., CLU, CPCU

Frederick H. Ecker Professor of
Insurance and Risk Management
Academic Director, Certified
Employee Benefit Specialist Program
Wharton School, University of
Pennsylvania

Dennis F. Mahoney, CEBS, CFP

Associate Academic Director,
Certified Employee Benefit Specialist
Program
Wharton School, University of
Pennsylvania

Boston   Burr Ridge, IL   Dubuque, IA   Madison, WI   New York   San Francisco   St. Louis
Bangkok   Bogotá   Caracas   Kuala Lumpur   Lisbon   London   Madrid   Mexico City
Milan   Montreal   New Delhi   Santiago   Seoul   Singapore   Sydney   Taipei   Toronto

McGraw-Hill Higher Education

A Division of The **McGraw-Hill** Companies

PENSION PLANNING:

PENSION, PROFIT SHARING, AND OTHER DEFERRED COMPENSATION PLANS

Published by McGraw-Hill/Irwin, a business unit of The McGraw-Hill Companies, Inc., 1221 Avenue of the Americas, New York, NY, 10020. Copyright © 2003, 1997, 1992, 1988, 1984, 1981, 1976, 1972, 1966 by The McGraw-Hill Companies, Inc. All rights reserved. No part of this publication may be reproduced or distributed in any form or by any means, or stored in a database or retrieval system, without the prior written consent of The McGraw-Hill Companies, Inc., including, but not limited to, in any network or other electronic storage or transmission, or broadcast for distance learning.

Some ancillaries, including electronic and print components, may not be available to customers outside the United States.

This book is printed on acid-free paper.

3 4 5 6 7 8 9 0 DOC/DOC 0 9 8 7 6 5

ISBN 0-07-253083-9

Publisher: *Stephen M. Patterson*
Sponsoring editor: *Michele Janicek*
Editorial coordinator: *Barbara Hari*
Executive marketing manager: *Rhonda Seelinger*
Producer, Media technology: *Melissa Kansa*
Project manager: *Catherine R. Schultz*
Production supervisor: *Debra R. Sylvester*
Coordinator freelance design: *Artemio Ortiz, Jr.*
Supplement producer: *Matthew Perry*
Cover design: *Artemio Ortiz, Jr.*
Typeface: *Times New Roman*
Compositor: *Carlisle Communications, Ltd.*
Printer: *R. R. Donnelley & Sons Company*

Library of Congress Cataloging-in-Publication Data

Pension planning : pension, profit-sharing, and other deferred compensation plans/
Everett T. Allen, Jr. ... [et al.]. —9th ed.
  p. cm.
 Includes bibliographical references and index.
  ISBN 0-07-253083-9 (alk. paper)
  1. Old age pension—United States. 2. Pension trusts—United States. 3. Deferred compensation—United States. I. Allen, Everett T.
 HD7105.35.U6 P4485 2003
 658.3'253—dc21

2002070975

Dedicated to the Memory
of
Everett T. Allen, Jr.
A renowned Scholar, True Gentleman,
and Friend

The McGraw-Hill/Irwin Series in Finance, Insurance and Real Estate

Stephen A. Ross
Franco Modigliani Professor
of Finance and Economics
Sloan School of Management
Massachusetts Institute
of Technology
Consulting Editor

FINANCIAL MANAGEMENT

Benninga and Sarig
Corporate Finance: A
Valuation Approach

Block and Hirt
Foundations of Financial
Management
Tenth Edition

Brealey and Myers
Principles of Corporate
Finance
Seventh Edition

Brealey, Myers and Marcus
Fundamentals of Corporate
Finance
Third Edition

Brooks
FinGame Online 3.0

Bruner
Case Studies in Finance:
Managing for Corporate Value
Creation
Fourth Edition

Chew
The New Corporate Finance:
Where Theory Meets Practice
Third Edition

DeMello
Cases in Finance

Grinblatt and Titman
Financial Markets and
Corporate Strategy
Second Edition

Helfert
Techniques of Financial
Analysis: A Guide to Value
Creation
Eleventh Edition

Higgins
Analysis for Financial
Management
Seventh Edition

Kester, Fruhan, Piper and Ruback
Case Problems in Finance
Eleventh Edition

Nunnally and Plath
Cases in Finance
Second Edition

Ross, Westerfield and Jaffe
Corporate Finance
Sixth Edition

Ross, Westerfield and Jordan
Essentials of Corporate
Finance
Third Edition

Ross, Westerfield and Jordan
Fundamentals of Corporate
Finance
Sixth Edition

Smith
The Modern Theory of
Corporate Finance
Second Edition

White
Financial Analysis with an
Electronic Calculator
Fourth Edition

INVESTMENTS

Bodie, Kane and Marcus
Essentials of Investments
Fourth Edition

Bodie, Kane and Marcus
Investments
Fifth Edition

Cohen, Zinbarg and Zeikel
Investment Analysis and
Portfolio Management
Fifth Edition

Corrado and Jordan
Fundamentals of Investments:
Valuation and Management
Second Edition

Farrell
Portfolio Management: Theory
and Applications
Second Edition

Hirt and Block
Fundamentals of Investment
Management
Seventh Edition

FINANCIAL INSTITUTIONS
AND MARKETS

Cornett and Saunders
Fundamentals of Financial
Institutions Management

Rose
Commercial Bank
Management
Sixth Edition

Rose
Money and Capital Markets:
Financial Institutions and
Instruments in a Global
Marketplace
Eighth Edition

Santomero and Babbel
Financial Markets,
Instruments, and Institutions
Second Edition

Saunders and Cornett
Financial Institutions
Management: A Risk
Management Approach
Fourth Edition

Saunders and Cornett
Financial Markets and
Institutions: A Modern
Perspective

INTERNATIONAL FINANCE

Beim and Calomiris
Emerging Financial Markets

Eun and Resnick
International Financial
Management
Second Edition

Levich
International Financial
Markets: Prices and Policies
Second Edition

REAL ESTATE

Brueggeman and Fisher
Real Estate Finance and
Investments
Eleventh Edition

Corgel, Ling and Smith
Real Estate Perspectives: An
Introduction to Real Estate
Fourth Edition

FINANCIAL PLANNING
AND INSURANCE

Allen, Melone, Rosenbloom and
Mahoney
Pension Planning: Pension,
Profit-Sharing, and Other
Deferred Compensation Plans
Ninth Edition

Crawford
Life and Health Insurance Law
Eighth Edition (LOMA)

Harrington and Niehaus
Risk Management and
Insurance

Hirsch
Casualty Claim Practice
Sixth Edition

Kapoor, Dlabay and Hughes
Personal Finance
Sixth Edition

Skipper
International Risk and
Insurance: An Environmental-
Managerial Approach

Williams, Smith and Young
Risk Management and
Insurance
Eighth Edition

Preface to Pension Planning, Ninth Edition

The ninth edition of this book has been completely revised in response to the significant developments in the pension field since publication of the eighth edition. An overview of recent legislation is provided in Chapter 1 placing legislative themes in proper context. Provisions from the Economic Growth and Tax Relief Reconciliation Act (EGTRRA) of 2001 and the Job Creation and Worker Assistance Act (JCWAA) of 2002 enacted into law are reflected throughout the text. For instance, the increases in elective deferral limits for future years as passed by EGTRRA are detailed where applicable throughout the book. Clarifications regarding the allowable deduction for simplified employee pensions (SEPs), as amended by JCWAA, is shown in Chapter 18.

Some restructuring of this ninth edition has occurred because of changes in the law and marketplace practices. Because of the evolution in various types of individual retirement arrangements (IRAs) that has occurred over time, this edition separates IRAs into a separate chapter distinct from plans for the self-employed. Chapter 17 covers IRAs while Chapter 18 details the characteristics of Keoghs, SEPs and savings incentive match plans for employees (SIMPLE plans).

The nature of EGTRRA itself has resulted in additional complexity when planning for pensions. The law indicates that its enacted changes will "sunset" or expire come January 1, 2011 unless forthcoming legislation either extends or makes these amendments to prior law permanent. Although it seems inconceivable to many tax practitioners that all of these legal provisions will be revoked, particularly some provisions that simplify or improve prior law, such an occurrence is within the realm of possibility at this writing. It is very difficult when writing a textbook like *Pension Planning* to attempt to foretell the future. Accordingly, the authors made a conscious decision to attempt to document explicitly those legal changes enacted as part of EGTRRA. Therefore, those using the text are alerted to potential problem areas should future legislative action stall or fail to materialize. This approach has resulted in additional historical coverage that would have been less detailed without the "sunset" provision. For instance, EGTRRA eliminated the application of the maximum exclusion allowance calculation for 403(b) plans beginning in 2002. The intricacies of this calculation, which were formerly very important, were moved to an appendix in Chapter 12. Administrators of these plans will decry the reemergence of this calculation if it occurs. Though its reemergence is considered highly unlikely, at the time of publication such an occurrence was within the realm of remote possibility.

EGTRRA made substantial changes to Section 457 plans. With the de-coupling of the limit on elective deferrals for 457(b) plans from coordination with 401(k) and 403(b) plans, these arrangements may now be used as an additional tool in rewarding executives in tax exempt organizations. Because of their increased significance as an additional executive reward mechanism, Appendix 3 is included explaining the evolution, use, and characteristics of 457 plans.

This edition of *Pension Planning* now covers stock options, an important component of compensation not only for executives, but for a broader range of employees in many organizations. Though not a form of a qualified plan, these rewards often are such an integral part of the compensation package, that they must be contemplated when designing other retirement-related arrangements. Chapter 21 explains Employee Stock Compensation Plans.

Tax regulations continue to clarify possibilities for more innovative retirement plan designs. Though some interest in cash balance plans has ebbed because of the controversy surrounding conversions of traditional defined benefit plans into cash balance plans, there is still interest in hybrid plans combining advantages of both defined benefit and defined contribution approaches. Accordingly, Chapter 19 covers Hybrid Retirement Plans.

The shift from defined benefit to defined contribution plans and the continued expansion in participant-directed investing has resulted in wider investment choice for plan participants. This trend heightens needs of plan sponsors to provide investment education. As a result, Chapter 23 examines Investment of Defined Contribution Plan Assets. Due to the collapse of Enron and the horrific losses which plan participants holding Enron stock suffered in their retirement plans, a variety of legislative initiatives have been introduced to better protect plan participants in the future.

EGTRRA was initially heralded by many as ushering in a new era of positive and expanded pension policy with increased benefit and contribution limits and enhanced opportunities for pension portability. However, the tragic events of September 11, 2001 resulted in a detrimental shock to the economy and a need for resources aimed at a global war on terrorism. Though all of us felt the pain of human suffering related to these terrible events, the economic and tax implications of these events are not immediately clear at this point. Though the government responded with an economic stimulus package when the Job Creation and Worker Assistance Act of 2002 was passed into law, the revitalization of the economy has not yet occurred. If longer-term economic growth is adversely impacted, the need for tax revenues could jeopardize an expansion in favorable tax treatment for retirement plans.

We truly live in turbulent times. Long-term economic security is of vital importance to a growing and prosperous economy. It is hoped that this textbook will be helpful in educating those individuals who administer and design retirement plans. To make this edition useful in this aim, educational learning tools are a part of every chapter including an outline of subject matter, learning objectives, insights into important topic areas and chapter summaries.

Acknowledgments

We want to express our appreciation once again to the many individuals who assisted us in prior editions of the text. Many of their contributions have survived in this ninth edition. We are also very much indebted to the individuals in the insurance, financial, and consulting professions who have reviewed portions of this text and made many valuable suggestions, and to the many teachers and students who over the years have given us extremely constructive comments and have enabled us to improve the readability and quality of the text. Special thanks are also due representatives of The American College, the College for Financial Planning, the International Foundation of Employee Benefit Plans, the Society of Actuaries, the Employee Benefit Research Institute (EBRI), and the Life Office Management Association for their comments and review over the years.

A special debt of gratitude is owed to Robert J. Myers, one of the world's leading authorities on Social Security for writing the appendix on Social Security and Medicare. Similarly, a special debt of gratitude is owed to Cynthia J. Drinkwater, Senior Director of Research, International Foundation of Employee Benefit Plans for the appendix on Multiemployer Plans and to Daniel J. Ryterband, CEBS, Managing Director and David Cole, Consultant, both from Frederic W. Cook & Co., Inc. for the appendix on Section 457 Plans.

In addition we would like to thank the many organizations and publishers that granted permissions to use material provided in "Insights" throughout the book. Also, the authors express their appreciation to G. Victor Hallman, a lecturer in financial and estate planning at the Wharton School of the University of Pennsylvania for his contribution to the chapter on Employee Stock Compensation Plans. This chapter is adapted from the sixth edition of *Personal Financial Planning,* which he co-authored. Thanks also are due to Dawn Bizzell, CEBS Benefit, an Economist with the Pension Guaranty Corporation for her help in reviewing Chapter 16, Plan Termination Insurance. The authors greatly appreciate the cooperation of Towers Perrin in providing material from their books, *The Handbook of 401(k) Plan Management* and *The Handbook of Executive Benefits.*

The authors also would like to express their deep appreciation to Dr. Jack L. VanDerhei, Professor of Risk Management and Insurance, Temple University, for his excellent contributions as a co-author on editions six through eight.

Finally, another major change in this edition is the addition of another name to the masthead, that of Dennis F. Mahoney, Associate Director of the Certified Employee Benefit Specialist Program at the Wharton School of the University of Pennsylvania. Mr. Mahoney brings a new perspective to this text and has extensive experience in the retirement and financial planning areas. We are pleased to have him join us for this ninth edition.

Everett T. Allen, Jr.
Joseph J. Melone
Jerry S. Rosenbloom
Dennis F. Mahoney

Contents

Chapter

Development of Private Pension Plans

After studying this chapter you should be able to:

- Describe the components of the tripod of economic security.
- Explain the economic problems encountered with old age.
- Discuss the factors that have contributed to the historical growth of the private pension system.
- Discuss the changing perceptions that unions have had of pension plans.
- Describe the economic rationales for private pensions.
- Cite the major acts of legislation and their impact in shaping the private pension system.

Individuals generally seek means to enhance their economic security. One cause of economic insecurity is the probable reduction of an individual's earning power at an advanced age. In the United States, this risk is met through one or more of the following means: personal savings (including individual insurance and **annuities**[1]), employer-sponsored pension plans (private plans), and social insurance programs. When combined, these three elements produce a multifaceted approach to economic security sometimes referred to as the **"tripod of economic security,"** the "three-legged stool of economic security," or the "pillars of economic security." The dramatic growth of private plans since the 1940s has focused considerable interest on this form of income maintenance.[2]

---

[1]An annuity is a contract with an insurance company whereby the insurance company pays an income for a specific time period, such as a number of years or for life, in exchange for an initial cash payment.
[2]*Private plans,* as used in this text, refer to plans established by private agencies, including commercial, industrial, labor, and service organizations, and nonprofit religious, educational, and charitable institutions. Social Security is covered in Appendix 1 at the end of the book.

Growth of Private Plans

The beginnings of industrial pension plans in the United States date back to the establishment of the American Express Company plan in 1875.[3] The second formal plan was established in 1880 by the Baltimore and Ohio Railroad Company. During the next half century, approximately 400 plans were established. These early pension plans were generally found in the railroad, banking, and public utility fields. The development of pensions in manufacturing companies was somewhat slower, largely because most manufacturing companies were still relatively young and therefore not confronted with the superannuation problems of the railroads and public utilities.

Insurance companies entered the pension business with the issuance of the first group annuity contract by the Metropolitan Life Insurance Company in 1921.[4] The second contract was issued by the Metropolitan in 1924 to an employer who already had a retirement plan on a "pay-as-you-go" basis.[5] In 1924, The Equitable Life Assurance Society of the United States announced its intention of offering a group pension service, thus becoming the second company to enter the field.[6]

Although the beginnings of private pensions date back to the 1800s, the significant growth in these programs has come since the 1940s. In 2000, the percentage of wage and salary workers ages 21-64 who participated in a pension plan reached 52.3 percent.[7] At year-end 2000, total U.S. retirement assets stood at $11.5 trillion. Of this $11.5 trillion, $2.6 trillion were held in defined contribution plans, $2.1 trillion were held in private defined benefit plans, $2.3 trillion were held in state and local government retirement funds, $0.7 trillion were held in federal defined benefit plans, $2.7 trillion were held in individual retirement accounts, and $1.1 trillion were held in fixed and variable annuities. It is worth noting there has been a significant increase in the relative growth of defined contribution plan assets. A similar evaluation of these relationships in 1983 would have shown defined benefit assets exceeding defined contribution assets by a significant margin.[8]

Economic Problems of Old Age

Longevity is a source of economic insecurity in that individuals may outlive their financial capacities to maintain themselves and their dependents. The extent to

---

[3]Murray Webb Latimer, *Industrial Pension Systems* (New York: Industrial Relations Counselors, Inc., 1932), p. 21.
[4]Kenneth Black, Jr., *Group Annuities* (Philadelphia: University of Pennsylvania Press, 1955), p. 9.
[5]Ibid., p. 11.
[6]Ibid.
[7]*EBRI Notes Executive Summary* 23, no. 3, March 2002.
[8]Investment Company Institute, *Fundamentals: Investment Company Institute Research in Brief* 10, no. 2 (Washington, DC: Investment Company Institute, June 2001), p. 3.

The Tripod of Economic Security: 1
A Voluntary System

Retirement income in the United States is structured on the often-referenced "three-legged" stool of Social Security, employer-sponsored pension plans and personal savings. In addition to the fact that one or two of these "legs" is often missing or woefully inadequate, the matter has been exacerbated by a restructuring of employer-provided retirement income programs over the past decade or so. There has been a massive shift from defined benefit pension plans (DBPs) to defined contribution plans (DCPs). The result has been a transfer of much of the cost and risk of longevity and the attending decision-making requirements from employers to the often-unprepared employee. . . .

No group (human resources and employee-benefits professionals) is in a better position to help educate employees on the importance of retirement savings and to counsel employers on the importance and feasibility of sponsoring retirement income programs. . . .

The bottom line is that some progress has been made in encouraging small employers to sponsor pension plans and more is possible, and when employees have access to a plan, they participate to a high degree. However, under a system based on voluntary pension plan sponsorship by employers and voluntary participation by employees, a significant number of employees will always lack access or elect not to participate.

Source: John G. Kilgour, "Responding to Changing Retirement Savings Programs," *Compensation & Benefits Review*, 33, no. 5, September–October 2001, pp. 25–35. Copyright © 2001 by Sage Publications, Inc. Reprinted by permission of Sage Publications, Inc.

which an aged person will have the financial capacity to meet self-maintenance costs and those of dependents relies upon the standard of living desired during retirement years, employment opportunities, and other resources (e.g., personal savings, social insurance, and inherited assets) available to meet this contingency.

Standard of Living after Retirement

The assumption usually is made that the financial needs of an individual decrease after retirement. To some extent, this assumption is valid. The retired individual may have no dependent children, and a home and its furnishings generally have been acquired by retirement age. However, the actual aggregate reduction in the financial needs of a person upon retirement has probably been overstated. Personal expectations and preferences discourage any drastic change in one's standard of living upon retirement, and an increasing tendency exists for retired persons to remain fairly active, particularly in terms of civic, social, travel, and other recreational activities. Furthermore, urbanization, geographic mobility, demographics, and changing culture minimize the prospect of retired parents moving in with their children.

Another major factor preventing a decrease in the financial needs of retirees is the likely cost of long-term care. It is estimated that a person reaching age 65 will have a 40 percent probability of being in a nursing home before death.[9] Although the federal government briefly experimented with the possibility of assuming a greater portion of this burden through the Medicare Catastrophic Coverage Act of 1988, the manner in which this additional coverage was financed proved to be politically unpalatable and was repealed the following year. The Health Insurance Portability and Accountability Act of 1996 made employer-paid long-term care tax-excludable beginning in 1997. Also, employer premiums became tax deductible to employers and tax-free to employees, although employee premiums cannot be paid from a flexible spending account or by elective pretax contributions under a cafeteria plan. Though this favorable tax treatment is an incentive for some employers to provide long-term care coverage to employees, the expense of this benefit limits its use for many employers. Even if retirees are fortunate enough to have comprehensive health insurance coverage continued by their employers after retirement, recent changes in the accounting standards applied to these plans are likely to cause modifications in the type of coverage, cost sharing, or financing of this benefit.

The authors are not suggesting that retired workers require income benefits equal to their earnings levels immediately preceding retirement, nor even the level of pre-retirement take-home pay. Presumably, at least at the higher income levels, these individuals have been allocating a portion of their take-home pay to individual savings. However, it is suggested that the reduction in standard of living after retirement is not very great; and, more important, the trend in social thinking seems to be in the direction of not expecting retired workers to have to take much of a reduction in standard of living after retirement. The effect of inflation also has militated against a lower standard of living. Therefore, it is questionable whether one should assume any significant decrease in basic financial needs upon retirement, at least for individuals in the low- and middle-income categories.

Employment Opportunities

The proportion of persons age 65 and over with some income from earnings is currently about 18 percent.[10] Obviously, many reasons account for the withdrawal of the aged from the labor force. A large number of older workers voluntarily retire. If workers have the necessary financial resources, they may wish to withdraw from active employment and live out their remaining years at a more leisurely pace. Others find it necessary for reasons of health to withdraw from the labor force. The aging process takes its toll, and many individuals are physically unable to operate at the level of efficiency attainable at a younger age. Disabilities at the older ages tend to be more frequent and of longer duration.

---

[9]Anthony J. Gajda and Morris Snow, "Long-Term Care," *The Handbook of Employee Benefits,* ed. Jerry S. Rosenbloom, 5th ed. (New York: McGraw-Hill, 2001), p. 310.
[10]Deborah Holmes, Lynn Miller, and Maureen Richmond, *EBRI Databook on Employee Benefits* (Washington, DC: Employee Benefit Research Institute, 1997), p. 58.

Voluntary retirement and the physical inability to continue employment are undoubtedly important reasons for the decrease in the percentage of older persons participating in the labor force. However, these are probably not the most important factors affecting employment opportunities for the aged. The effects of industrialization, expansive technological advances, and the development of the federal Old-Age, Survivors, Disability, and Health Insurance (OASDHI) program, private pensions, and other employee benefit programs probably have had a more significant impact on this problem.

The rapid pace and dynamic evolution of industrial employment operated to the disadvantage of older persons. Automation and mass-production assembly lines put a premium on physical dexterity and mental alertness. Employers generally were of the opinion, justifiable or not, that younger workers were better suited to the demands of industrial employment. In an agricultural economy, on the other hand, the able-bodied older person could continue to work, at least on a part-time basis.

Similarly, as organizations adapt to the information systems age and increasingly look to enhance productivity through the use of computers, the Internet, and other technology applications, it appears that older workers will continue to be at risk. In fact, the new millennium has witnessed a significant economic downturn with the bursting of the "Internet bubble" and the collapse of the "dot.com economy" resulting in corporate restructurings and downsizings. Some social philosophers expect that greater labor market dislocations will occur and postulate that the systems age could mean a decreasing need for mass labor.[11]

The OASDHI program and private pension plans, although created to alleviate the financial risk associated with excessive longevity, have actually aggravated the problem. These programs have tended to institutionalize age 65 as the normal retirement age, although the 1986 amendments to the Age Discrimination in Employment Act (ADEA) banned mandatory retirement (at any age) for most employees. The 1983 amendments to The Social Security Act will gradually raise the normal retirement age for Social Security benefits to age 67 by the year 2027.[12] At the time of publication, some Social Security reform proposals suggested that normal retirement age for Social Security benefits be linked to life expectancy and automatically increase as life expectancies rise. Also, some employers may hesitate to hire older workers on the assumption that these employees will increase pension and other employee benefit plan costs. It is difficult to generalize the impact of the older worker on employee benefit plan costs. Nevertheless, it must be recognized that an employer's attitude toward hiring older workers may be influenced by the assumption, justified or not, that employee benefit costs will be adversely affected.

Self-employed members of the labor force have greater control as to the timing of their retirement from active employment. For example, physicians and lawyers frequently continue in practice, at least on a part-time basis, until advanced ages. Owners of businesses also continue to be active in their firms until relatively old

---

[11]Jeremy Rifkin, *The End of Work* (New York: Putnam, 1995), p. 5.
[12]The retirement benefits provided under The Social Security Act are discussed in detail in Appendix I at the end of this book.

ages. The fact remains, however, that employment opportunities for the majority of older workers have become more limited. It is quite likely that this will be a temporary phenomenon for many employees given the expected impact of changing demographics and the potential shortage of certain segments of the workforce projected for the future.

Individual Savings of the Aged

If employment opportunities for the aged are decreasing and financial needs are still substantial at advanced ages, the need for savings becomes quite apparent. However, studies indicate that a substantial proportion of the homes owned by the aged are clear of any mortgage. Home ownership reduces the income needs of the aged insofar as normal maintenance costs and taxes are less than the amount of rent required for comparable housing accommodations. It has been estimated that the maintenance costs for an unencumbered home are about one-third to 40 percent less than the costs of renting comparable facilities. Furthermore, there is the possibility that the home can be used in part as an income-producing asset or that a home equity loan can be used to provide additional cash.

There is growing interest in the concept of a so-called **reverse annuity.** Under this approach, the home owner receives a lifetime monthly income in exchange for the title to the home at the home owner's death. The amount of the monthly annuity payment depends on the equity in the home and the life expectancy of the home owner.

Jacobs and Weissert have analyzed the potential for using home equity to finance long-term care. Their results strongly suggest that a significant number of elderly Americans could use their homes' equity to meet their health care expenses. They also conclude that those in the highest risk group and those with the lowest incomes, who are often the same individuals, also can be significantly helped by the use of reverse annuity mortgages.[13]

Pricing this type of financial instrument has proven to be both extremely difficult and a major obstacle to its widespread use. Another problem faced by private institutions is the possibility that the outstanding balance on the mortgage will eventually exceed the value of the property.

As a result of the Housing and Community Development Act of 1987, the federal government began an experimental program in which the Department of Housing and Urban Development (HUD) insured a maximum of 2,500 reverse annuity mortgages. The experimental program was further extended. On March 28, 1996, the National Housing Act was amended and the mortgage insurance authority of the Federal Housing Authority (FHA) Reverse Mortgage program was extended through September 30, 2000. The maximum number of reverse mortgages was increased to 50,000. Since the early 1990s, more than 38,000 reverse mortgages have been closed. According to HUD Secretary Andrew Cuomo, the number of new

---

[13]Bruce Jacobs and William Weissert, "Using Home Equity to Finance Long-Term Care," *Journal of Health Politics, Policy & Law* 12, no. 1 (Spring 1987), pp. 77–95. However, a more recent study analyzes the potential of reverse annuity mortgages to increase the current income of the elderly and concludes that most low-income elderly also have little housing equity. See Steven F. Venti and David A. Wise, "Aging and the Income Value of Housing Wealth," *Journal of Public Economics* 44, no. 3 (April 1991), pp. 371–97.

reverse mortgages has quadrupled in the past decade.[14] Although the complexity of the HUD program, the inherent risks, and the small profit potential have reduced the number of original lenders, it is anticipated that the reverse annuity concept will become more important in the future.[15]

Personal savings rates have been running at historically low levels in recent years. The distribution of savings by savings media has changed considerably over the years. The change that is most pertinent to this discussion is the relative increase in private pension reserves in relation to purely individual forms of saving. Annual employer contributions to private pension funds now amount to about $60.4 billion.[16] It should be noted that many pieces of legislation in the late 80s and early 90s impacted overall pension contributions by changing the limits on allowable pension contributions for plan sponsors.[17] However, a major shift in tax policy resulted with the passage of the **Economic Growth and Tax Relief Reconciliation Act of 2001 (EGTRRA).** For the first time in several years, limits on allowable pension contributions were actually increased. The tremendous increases in disposable income over the last 50 years previously had not resulted in any increase in the proportion of personal savings. It will be interesting to see whether the expansion of pension contribution limits allowed by EGTRRA has a sustained impact on personal savings. There have been many forces at work that have restricted the growth of savings. Advertising, installment credit, and the media of mass communications encourage individuals to set their sights on a constantly increasing standard of living. This competition from consumption goods for current income dollars results in a lower priority being placed on the need for accumulating savings for old age. Also, the high levels of federal income tax rates reduce an income earner's capacity to save. Though tax rates were reduced by the Tax Reform Act of 1986, they subsequently increased. EGTRRA has reduced income tax rates again, although not as dramatically as TRA '86 did. In the not very distant past, inflation was an additional deterrent to increased levels of saving. Inflation is a particularly serious threat to the adequacy of savings programs of persons who already are retired. For employed persons, increases in the cost of living may be offset, in part or in whole, by increases in current earnings; however, inflation protection is likely to be less comprehensive for most aged persons.[18] Therefore, the aged are faced with the alternatives of accepting a lower standard of living or more rapidly liquidating their accumulated savings. Though the initial years of the new millennium

[14]Ilyce R. Glink, *"The Latest on Reverse Mortgages."* (ThinkGlink.com, Jaunary 31, 2002), p. 1.

[15]Robert J. Pratte, "A Mortgage for the 21st Century," *Mortgage Banking* 50, no. 8 (May 1990), pp. 45–52.

[16]*Employer Spending on Benefits* 1999 (Washington, DC: Employee Benefit Research Institute, June, 2001), p. 2.

[17]This reduction in allowable pension contributions results from the conflict between the social policy objectives of encouraging employers to provide pensions and the federal revenue loss occurring since pensions are afforded preferential tax treatment. At the end of this chapter is a more detailed discussion of legislation affecting pension contribution limits.

[18]Appendix 1 at the end of this book describes the inflation protection inherent in Social Security payments; Chapter 13 analyzes the techniques used by many private plan sponsors to provide partial ad hoc relief.

have experienced low levels of inflation, it is important to realize the threat to purchasing power that an increased rate of inflation can mean.

The proportion of individual (as opposed to group) savings, then, is decreasing at a time when the pattern of living for the aged is becoming increasingly more costly. Under such circumstances, the tremendous importance of pension programs in meeting the economic risk of old age is obvious.

Increasing Longevity

Still another dimension to the overall economic problem of old age is the number of aged in the population. The fact that life expectancy has been increasing is well recognized. However, that this increase in **longevity** is a recent and quite dramatic development often is not appreciated. Since 1900, life expectancy at birth has increased from 47 years to approximately 76.9 years. The rates of mortality at the earlier ages are now so low that further improvements in mortality at these ages would have little impact on further extensions of the average length of life. If additional improvements in longevity are to be realized, reductions in mortality at the older ages are required. This impediment to further extensions in life expectancy may be overcome if medical advances result from the current concentration of research in the areas of the chronic and degenerative diseases. Medical research in fields such as biotechnology and gene therapy may result in such advances.

One effect of the improvements in longevity in the twentieth century has been an absolute and relative increase in the population of persons age 65 and over. In 1900, there were approximately 3 million persons age 65 and over, whereas there were about 35 million such persons in 2000. The proportion of the U.S. population age 65 and over in 2000 was about 12.7 percent, whereas the proportion of the population in these age brackets in 1900 was about 4 percent.

Another important dimension in the analysis of the changing **demography** of the elderly—those age 65 and over—is their age distribution. A generation ago, 68 percent of the elderly were 65 to 74 years old, 27 percent were 75 to 84 years old, and only 5 percent were 85 or older. However, today's elderly population reflects a shift toward the upper end of the age scale: Approximately 12.4 percent are 85 or over; 35.4 percent are 75 to 84; and 52.2 percent are 65 to 74.[19]

The problem of old-age economic security, therefore, is of concern to an increasing number and percentage of the U.S. population.

Reasons for Growth of Private Pensions

From the above discussion it can be seen that the problem of economic security for the aged is a serious and increasingly important one. However, the mere existence of the problem does not explain the phenomenal growth of private pensions. In other words, given the existence of the old-age economic problem, why did employers and

---

[19] *Statistical Abstract of the United States, 2000* (Washington, DC: U.S. Government Printing Office, 2000), p. 15.

employees choose to meet the need, at least in part, through the vehicle of private pension programs? In a broad sense, the major reason is the fact that private pensions offer substantial advantages to both employers and employees. Without this foundation of mutual benefit, the private pension movement could not have achieved the substantial and sustained growth it has enjoyed. In addition, for several decades, government officials have recognized the social desirability of pension programs and have acted to encourage the growth of these plans through favorable treatment under the tax system and by other means. As indicated in Chapter 3, some observers have noted that many legislative initiatives have tended to favor defined contribution over defined benefit approaches. The growth of these different types of plans and the historical impact of favorable legislation are chronicled in that chapter. However, it appears that this attitude of encouraging private pension growth through preferential tax treatment stalled when large federal budget deficits occurred in the 80s and 90s.

The specific factors generally considered as having influenced the growth of private pensions are discussed below. It must be recognized that the reasons giving rise to the establishment of one plan are sometimes quite different from those in the case of another plan. As noted above, a policy shift appeared to occur with the passage of EGTRRA. At the time of publication, given the September 11, 2001, tragedy and resulting economic uncertainties, it is unclear whether this policy shift will be sustained.

Increased Productivity

A systematic method of meeting the problem of **superannuated** employees can be easily justified on sound management grounds. Due to advanced age, an employee may reach a point where he or she experiences a diminishment in productivity. That is, at some advanced age, an employee's contribution to the productivity of the firm may be worth less than the compensation he or she is receiving.

The employer has several courses of action if an employee reaches this point. One, the employee can be terminated without any further compensation or any retirement benefits as soon as the value of the employee's services is less than the salary being paid. For obvious reasons, this course of action is seldom followed by employers. Two, the employer can retain the less-productive, superannuated employee in the employee's current position at the current level of compensation, the difference between the employee's productivity and salary being absorbed by the employer as a cost of doing business. This alternative is also undesirable and would undoubtedly be the most costly method of meeting the problem of less-productive, superannuated employees. Furthermore, the longer range indirect costs that would be incurred from the resultant inefficiencies and poor employee morale among the productive, active workers would be significant. Three, the employer could retain the less-productive, superannuated worker but transfer the employee to a less-demanding job at the same or a reduced level of compensation. In the former case, the direct costs would be similar to alternative two, but the indirect costs would be reduced in that a more capable person would now be staffing the more demanding position. If the employee's salary is reduced, the direct costs of superannuation also would be reduced.

Most employers who do not have a pension plan generally handle the problem of the less-productive, superannuated worker in the latter manner. The effectiveness of this approach to the problem has certain important limitations. First, a firm usually has only a limited number of positions to which such workers can be transferred. For a medium- or even large-sized firm, only a fraction of such employees can be efficiently employed. With automation and the increasingly higher levels of skill required in most jobs, the limitations of this solution are apparent. Furthermore, the less-productive, superannuated employee is generally still overpaid in the less-demanding jobs since, for practical purposes, salary reductions commensurate with the decrease in employee productivity are seldom made. Lastly, this approach does not solve the problem of productivity; it merely defers it, since a point will be reached where the employee's productivity is considerably below even a minimum level of wage.

The fourth alternative available to the employer in meeting the problem of productivity loss with superannuation is to establish a formal pension plan. A pension plan permits employers to provide less-productive, superannuated employees with an acceptable alternative to continued employment in a humanitarian and nondiscriminatory manner, and the inefficiencies associated with retaining employees beyond their productive years are reduced. Furthermore, the sense of security derived from the knowledge that some provision will be made, at least in part, for their retirement income needs should increase the morale and productivity of employees. Also, the systematic retirement of older workers will keep the channels of promotion open, thereby offering opportunity and incentive to the younger employees—particularly those aspiring to executive positions. Therefore, a pension plan should permit an employer to replenish the workforce.

The problem of productivity loss with superannuation, then, exists for most business firms. Any solution, except the unlikely alternative of arbitrary termination of older workers without any retirement benefit, results in some cost, direct or indirect, to the employer. Unfortunately, some employers assume that the pension plan solution is the only approach that carries a price tag, but the hidden costs of the other alternatives must be recognized as well. The decision, therefore, is which solution is best suited to the needs and financial position of the employer. For a large number of employers, the formal pension plan approach has proven to be the superior solution.

Tax Considerations

The bulk of the growth in private pension plans has occurred since 1940. One reason for the growth of these plans during the World War II and Korean War periods was that normal and excess-profit tax rates imposed on corporations during these years were extremely high. Since the employer's contributions to a qualified pension plan are deductible (within limits) for federal income tax purposes, a portion of the plan's liabilities could be funded with very little effective cost to the firm. Furthermore, the investment income earned on pension trust assets is exempt from federal income taxation until distributed.[20]

---

[20]For a complete discussion of the tax aspects of qualified pension plans, see Chapters 4, 5, and 27.

The tax advantages of qualified pension plans are attractive from the standpoint of employees covered under the plan; for example, the employer's contributions to a pension fund do not constitute taxable income to the employee in the year in which contributions are made. The pension benefits derived from employer contributions are taxed when distributed to the employee. In addition, under limited circumstances, distributions from a pension plan may be taxed on a favorable basis.

Therefore, qualified pension plans generally offer significant tax advantages to participants; prior to 1988, employees in high income tax brackets received the greatest advantages.[21] Since the high-salaried senior officers of corporations often make the decision regarding the establishment and design of employee benefit plans, their role as participants under the plans may have influenced their decisions on these matters. However, in the case of large corporations, costs and other considerations minimized or eliminated the personal tax situations of key employees as factors influencing the establishment or design of a pension plan. In the case of a small, closely held corporation, on the other hand, one can readily see how the tax implications for stockholder-employees might have been a decisive factor in the establishment and design of a pension plan. Lastly, tax considerations are certainly one reason, although not the most important, why some labor leaders negotiate for the establishment and liberalization of employee benefit programs in lieu of further wage increases.

The Tax Reform Act of 1986 and subsequent legislative initiatives have diminished the benefits available to highly compensated employees. As a result, there is a much greater interest in nonqualified plans for the highly compensated, and the number of employees covered by such arrangements has increased.[22]

Wage Stabilization

The second wartime development that helped to stimulate the growth of pensions was the creation of a **wage stabilization program** as part of a general price control effort. Employers competing for labor could not offer the inducement of higher wages. Under these conditions, union leaders found it difficult to prove to their memberships the merits of unionism.

Therefore, the War Labor Board attempted to relieve the pressure on management and labor for higher wage rates by permitting the establishment of fringe benefit programs, including pensions. This policy further stimulated the growth of pension plans during the period.

---

[21]Up until 1986, the federal income tax law had 14 progressive tax brackets and a maximum rate of 50 percent. The Tax Reform Act of 1986 reduced the number of tax brackets to two (15 percent and 28 percent), effective in 1988. The maximum tax bracket was subsequently increased to 31 percent. The Omnibus Budget Reconciliation Act of 1993 created a further marginal income tax rate of 36 percent and imposed an additional 10 percent surtax on taxable income over $250,000, while increasing the alternative minimum tax rate. The combination of these changes has resulted in some individuals' experiencing marginal federal tax rates at, or exceeding in some cases, 42 percent. The Economic Growth and Tax Relief Reconciliation Act of 2001 (EGTRRA) reduced tax rates so that when fully phased in for year 2006 and later years, base rates would be 10 percent, 15 percent, 25 percent, 28 percent, 33 percent, and 35 percent.

[22]For a detailed discussion of nonqualified plans, see Chapter 20.

Union Demands

Labor leaders have had differing views over the years regarding the desirability of employer-financed pension plans. In the 1920s, labor generally did not favor such plans for its membership. It held the view that pensions represented an additional form of employer paternalism and were instituted to encourage loyalty to the firm. Labor leaders felt that the need would be best met through the establishment of a government-sponsored universal social security system; in the absence of that solution, unions should establish their own pension plans for their members. The former objective was achieved with the passage of The Social Security Act of 1935. By the 1930s, several unions had established their own plans. However, many of these plans were financed inadequately, a condition that became apparent during the depression years. Recognition of the financial burden of a pension program and enactment of wage controls led some labor leaders, in the early 1940s, to favor the establishment of employer-supported pension plans.

From 1945 to 1949, the rate of growth of new plans fell off markedly. During this postwar period, employee interest centered upon cash wage increases in an attempt to recover the ground lost during the period of wage stabilization. In the latter part of the 1940s, union leaders once again began expressing an interest in the negotiation of pension programs. The renewal of interest in pensions probably came about because of two factors. First, there was increasing antagonism on the part of the public toward what were viewed by many persons as excessive union demands for cash wage increases. The negotiation of fringe benefits was one way of possibly reducing pressures from this quarter. Second, some union leaders argued that Social Security benefits were inadequate, and a supplement in the form of private pension benefits was considered to be necessary. Also, certain labor officials believed the negotiation of employer-supported pensions would weaken the resistance of the latter toward liberalizations of Social Security benefit levels. Thus, pension demands became a central issue in the labor negotiations in the coal, automobile, and steel industries in the late 40s. Although unions had negotiated pension benefits prior to this period, it was not until the late 40s that a major segment of labor made a concerted effort to bargain for private pensions.

Labor's drive for pension benefits was facilitated by a National Labor Relations Board (NLRB) ruling in 1948 that employers had a legal obligation to bargain over the terms of pension plans. Until that time, there was some question as to whether employee benefit programs fell within the traditional subject areas for collective bargaining—that is, wages, hours, and other conditions of employment. The issue was resolved when the NLRB held that pension benefits constitute wages and the provisions of these plans affect conditions of employment.[23] Upon appeal, the court upheld the NLRB decision, although it questioned the assumption that such benefits are wages.[24] These decisions determined that an employer cannot install, terminate, or alter the terms of a pension plan covering organized workers without the

---

[23] *Inland Steel Company* v. *United Steelworkers of America,* 77 NLRB 4 (1948).
[24] *Inland Steel Company* v. *National Labor Relations Board,* 170 F (2d) 247, 251 (1949).

approval of the authorized bargaining agent for those employees. Furthermore, management has this obligation regardless of whether the plan is contributory or non-contributory, voluntary or compulsory, and regardless of whether the plan was established before or after the certification of the bargaining unit.

Labor was quick to respond to these decisions, and the 1950s were marked by union demands for the establishment of new pension plans, the liberalization of existing plans, and the supplanting of employer-sponsored programs with negotiated plans. Undoubtedly, labor's interest in private pensions has been an important factor in the tremendous growth in plans since 1949.

Business Necessity

Employers hire employees in a free, competitive labor market. Therefore, as the number of plans increases, employees come to expect a pension benefit as part of the employment relationship. Employers who do not have such a plan are at a competitive disadvantage in attracting and retaining human resources. Therefore, some employers feel they must install a plan even if they are not convinced that the advantages generally associated with a pension plan outweigh the cost of the benefit. Admittedly, this is a negative reason for instituting a plan. In other words, while these employers believe little evidence exists that pension plans truly result in improved morale and efficiency among their workforce, they feel there would clearly be an adverse employee reaction if they did not offer a pension. Also, in contrast to situations where a plan is established in response to labor demands, an employer may offer a pension plan as part of an employee relations objective aimed at keeping a union out of the firm.

Reward for Service

There is a tendency to argue that employers never provide any increase in employee benefits unless they can expect an economic return in some form. Although this philosophy may generally prevail in a capitalistic system, the fact remains that many employers have established plans out of a sincere desire to reward employees who have served the firm well over a long period of service. Also, some employers may feel a moral responsibility to make some provision for the economic welfare of retired employees.

Efficiency of Approach

Part of the growth of private pensions must be attributed to the belief that a formal group savings approach has certain inherent advantages. The advantages are not such that they eliminate the need for individual savings, but the merits of private pensions as a supplement to Social Security benefits and individual savings programs are indeed significant. First, the economic risk of old age derives from the fact that a point is reached when an employee is unable or unwilling to continue in active employment. A formal plan as an integral part of compensation arrangements and employment relationships, therefore, is quite logical. There is no additional wage cost to the employer to the extent that pension benefits are provided in lieu of other forms of compensation. If pension benefits are provided in addition to prevailing wage rates, the employer's extra wage costs resulting from the pension plan may be able to be passed on to the consuming public in the form of higher prices.

It has been argued that from a broad social point of view, the private pension system is the lowest cost method of providing economic security for the aged. In addition to the administrative efficiency of group savings arrangements, it is argued that the small increase in consumer prices that might be required to provide pension benefits is a relatively painless method of meeting the risk. In other words, the burden of retirement security is spread over a large number of people and over a long period of time. Still another aspect to the argument is the assumption that private pensions increase consumption levels among the aged, which in turn helps to maintain a high level of economic activity.

Last, private pensions constitute a form of forced savings. This advantage is extremely important in view of the apparent desire of many people to maintain a relatively high standard of living during their active employment years. Thus, it may be argued that it is economically more efficient if at least part of the risk is met through a forced savings private pension scheme.

Sales Efforts of Funding Agencies

For all these reasons, there has been a considerable demand over the years for private pensions. However, in many instances, the advantages of these programs have had to be called to the attention of specific employers. This function of creating effective demand for the pension product has been aggressively performed by those parties interested in providing services in this area. Insurance companies, through agents, brokers, and salaried representatives, were undoubtedly instrumental in the growth of pensions, particularly in the decades of the 20s and 30s. The trust departments of banks also are equipped to handle pension funds, and many corporate trustees and asset managers have been actively soliciting pension business, particularly since the early 1950s. Similarly, the sales efforts of mutual fund representatives in recent years, particularly with 401(k) plans, have contributed to the growth of private pension and savings plans.

Rationale of Private Pensions

The growth of private pensions is attributable, as seen above, to a variety of reasons. It is difficult to determine the extent of the growth contributed by each factor, but it seems reasonable to conclude that the dominant reasons leading to the establishment of specific plans have varied depending on the circumstances surrounding each case. In other words, productivity considerations have been dominant forces leading to the creation of some plans, while labor pressures, tax considerations, or other factors have encouraged the establishment of others. With such variety of motivation, it is difficult to characterize private pensions in terms of a single philosophy or rationale. Nevertheless, attempts have been made over the years to explain private pensions in terms of an underlying concept or philosophy.[25]

[25]For an excellent discussion of pension philosophies, see Jonas E. Mittelman, "The Vesting of Private Pensions" (Ph.D. dissertation, University of Pennsylvania, 1959), Chapter 2.

Early industrial pension plans were viewed as gratuities or rewards to employees for long and loyal service to the employer. Closely related to this view is the concept that private pensions constitute a systematic and socially desirable method of releasing employees who are no longer productive members of the employer's labor force. Regardless of the view taken, it is clear that these early plans were largely discretionary, and management made it quite evident that employees had no contractual rights to benefits under the plans. Continuation of the pension plan was dependent upon competitive conditions and management policy. Furthermore, management reserved the right to terminate benefit payments to pensioners for misconduct on the part of the beneficiary or for any other reasons justifying such action in the opinion of the employer.

Thus, the growth of early pensions might be best categorized by a single concept: business expediency. Business expediency, by the very nature of the concept, implies that the establishment of a plan is a management prerogative and that the primary motivation for the creation of such plans is the economic benefit, direct or indirect, that is accrued to the employer. But as the economy became more and more industrialized and pension plans became more prevalent, there was increasing expression of the view that employers had a moral obligation to provide for the economic security of retired workers. This point of view was expressed as early as 1912 by Lee Welling Squier, as follows: "From the standpoint of the whole system of social economy, no employer has a right to engage men in any occupation that exhausts the individual's industrial life in 10, 20, or 40 years; and then leave the remnant floating on society at large as a derelict at sea."[26]

This rationale of private pensions has come to be known as the **human depreciation concept.** It was the point of view taken by the United Mine Workers of America in their 1946 drive to establish a welfare fund:

> The United Mine Workers of America has assumed the position over the years that the cost of caring for the human equity in the coal industry is inherently as valid as the cost of the replacement of mining machinery, or the cost of paying taxes, or the cost of paying interest indebtedness, or any other factor incident to the production of a ton of coal for consumers' bins . . . [The agreement establishing the Welfare Fund] recognized in principle the fact that the industry owed an obligation to those employees, and the coal miners could no longer be used up, crippled beyond repair, and turned out to live or die subject to the charity of the community or the minimum contributions of the state.[27]

This analogy between human labor and industrial machines also was made in the report of the president's fact-finding board in the 1949 steelworkers' labor dispute in support of its conclusion that management had a responsibility to provide for the security of its workers: "We think that all industry, in the absence of adequate government programs, owes an obligation to workers to provide for maintenance of the human body in the form of medical and similar benefits and full depreciation in the form of old-age retirement—in the same way as it does now for

[26]Lee Welling Squier, *Old Age Dependency in the United States* (New York: Macmillan, 1912), p. 272.
[27]United Mine Workers of America Welfare and Retirement Fund, *Pensions for Coal Miners* (Washington, DC, n.d.), p. 4.

plant and machinery."[28] The report continues as follows: "What does that mean in terms of steelworkers? It should mean the use of earnings to insure against the full depreciation of the human body—say at age 65—in the form of a pension or retirement allowance."[29]

The validity of the human depreciation concept of private pensions has been challenged by many pension experts.[30] The process of aging is physiological and is not attributable to the employment relationship. Admittedly, the hazards of certain occupations undoubtedly shorten the life span of the employees involved. In those instances, the employer can logically be held responsible only for the increase in the rate of aging due to the hazards of the occupation. More important, the analogy between humans and machines is inherently unsound. A machine is an asset owned by the employer, and depreciation is merely an accounting technique for allocating the costs of equipment to various accounting periods. Employees, on the other hand, are free agents and sell their services to employers for a specified wage rate. An employee, unlike a machine, is free to move from one employer to another. The differences between humans and machines are so great that one must question the value of the analogy as a basis for a rationale of private pensions. As Dearing notes, "Any economic or moral responsibility that is imposed on the employer for the welfare of workers after termination of the labor contract should be grounded on firmer reasoning than is supplied by the machine-worker analogy."[31]

In recent years, a view of private pensions that has achieved broader acceptance is the **deferred wage concept.** This concept views a pension benefit as part of a wage package that is composed of cash wages and other employee fringe benefits. The deferred wage concept has particular appeal with reference to negotiated pension plans. The assumption is made that labor and management negotiators think in terms of total labor costs. Therefore, if labor negotiates a pension benefit, the funds available for increases in cash wages are reduced accordingly. This theory of private pensions was expressed as early as 1913:

> In order to get a full understanding of old-age and service pensions, they should be considered as a part of the real wages of a workman. There is a tendency to speak of these pensions as being paid by the company, or, in cases where the employee contributes a portion, as being paid partly by the employer and partly by the employee. In a certain sense, of course, this may be correct, but it leads to confusion. A pension system considered as part of the real wages of an employee is really paid by the employee, not perhaps in money, but in the forgoing of an increase in wages which he might obtain except for the establishment of a pension system.[32]

---

[28]Steel Industry Board, *Report to the President of the United States on the Labor Dispute in the Basic Steel Industry* (Washington, DC: U.S. Government Printing Office, September 10, 1949), p. 55.

[29]Ibid., p. 65.

[30]For example, see Dan M. McGill and Donald S. Grubbs, Jr., *Fundamentals of Private Pensions,* 6th ed. (Burr Ridge, IL: Richard D. Irwin, 1989), pp. 18–19. See also Charles L. Dearing, *Industrial Pensions* (Washington, DC: Brookings Institution, 1954), pp. 62–63 and 241–43; and Mittelman, "Vesting of Private Pensions," pp. 28–34.

[31]Dearing, *Industrial Pensions,* p. 243.

[32]Albert de Roode, "Pensions as Wages," *American Economic Review* III, no. 2 (June 1913), p. 287.

The deferred wage concept also has been challenged on several grounds. First, it is noted that some employers who pay the prevailing cash wage rate for the particular industry also provide a pension benefit. Thus, it can be argued that in these cases the pension benefit is offered in addition to, rather than in lieu of, a cash wage increase. Second, the deferred wage concept ignores the possible argument that the employer is willing to accept a lower profit margin to provide a pension plan for employees. Third, it is sometimes argued that if pension benefits are a form of wage, then terminated employees should be entitled to the part of the retirement benefit that has been earned to the date of termination. In practice, one finds that only a small proportion of the plans provide for the full and immediate vesting of all benefits. However, it can be argued that the deferred wage concept does not necessarily require the full and immediate vesting of benefits. Proponents of this concept view pension benefits as a wage, the receipt of which is conditioned upon the employee's remaining in the service of the employer for a specified number of years. This view of the pension benefit is similar, conceptually, to a pure endowment in which the policyholder receives the full face benefit of the policy if he or she lives to the maturity of the policy; however, the beneficiaries receive nothing if the policyholder dies prior to this time period. The consideration of the employee in this case is the reduction in cash wages accepted in lieu of the pension benefit.

In spite of the appeal of the deferred wage theory, it is questionable whether the private pension movement can be explained solely in terms of this concept. Indeed, there is probably no one rationale or theory that fully explains the reason for being of private pensions. This conclusion is not surprising in view of the fact that these plans are private, and the demands or reasons that give rise to one plan may be quite different from those leading to the introduction of another plan.

Legislative History and Recent Legal Changes

Employee benefits in general and pension plans in particular have been the subject of substantial legislative activity in recent years.

After many years of discussion and debate concerning reform of the private pension system, the **Employee Retirement Income Security Act of 1974 (ERISA)** became law on September 2, 1974. ERISA effected some of the most significant changes ever enacted in the private pension movement. These changes affected virtually all aspects of corporate and self-employed pension plans from a legal, tax, investment, and actuarial viewpoint. In addition, ERISA established new reporting, disclosure, and fiduciary requirements as well as a program of plan termination insurance. Another major feature of ERISA was the establishment of the individual retirement account (IRA) concept, which was initially designed for individuals not covered under a qualified retirement plan.

The Economic Recovery Tax Act of 1981 (ERTA) was one of the biggest tax reduction acts in history. It also included several provisions that affected retirement plans. Most notable were the provisions that greatly expanded IRA opportunities to anyone with personal service income, allowed for voluntary contributions to qualified plans, and increased contribution and deduction limits for both simplified employee pension (SEP) programs and Keogh (HR-10) plans. ERTA also made changes that affected stock ownership plans and executive compensation arrangements.

Following on the heels of ERTA came another massive act, the **Tax Equity and Fiscal Responsibility Act of 1982 (TEFRA),** considered by some to be the biggest revenue-raising bill in history. TEFRA probably touched everyone in the United States in some manner and affected retirement plans in many ways. It reduced the maximum limits of pension plan benefits and contributions; brought about parity between corporate plans and plans for self-employed persons; introduced special restrictions on plans that are considered "top heavy," that is, plans that appear to be heavily weighted toward key employees; and provided for federal income tax withholding on pension and annuity payments.

After a one-year hiatus, in 1984 Congress passed two acts with significant implications for qualified retirement plans. The Deficit Reduction Act of 1984 (DEFRA) contained several provisions that substantially modified savings incentives. Cost-of-living adjustments for contribution and benefit limits were frozen for a second time. Estate tax exclusions for distributions from qualified plans and IRAs were repealed. Rules for cash-or-deferred plans, also known as 401(k) plans, were tightened. The Retirement Equity Act of 1984 (REACT) represented an attempt on the part of Congress to provide what was perceived by some as a more equitable distribution of retirement benefits from qualified plans. Young employees and females were the chief benefactors, as REACT required a reduction in the minimum age for mandatory participation, modified rules relating to breaks in service, changed the survivor benefit requirements, and allowed for the assignment of qualified plan benefits in divorce proceedings.

In the most pervasive changes since ERISA, the **Tax Reform Act of 1986** imposed new coverage tests and accelerated vesting requirements for qualified plans, changed the rules under which qualified plans can be integrated with Social Security, lowered limits for retirement benefits that begin before age 65, changed the timing and taxation of plan distributions, and terminated IRA deductions for many qualified plan participants. Substantial changes also were made with respect to employee stock ownership plans and executive compensation. Following the Tax Reform Act of 1986, Congress passed the Omnibus Budget Reconciliation Act of 1987 (OBRA '87), which made significant changes with respect to (1) minimum funding and maximum tax deductions for qualified plans, and (2) plan termination obligations for defined benefit plans.

Under the Technical and Miscellaneous Revenue Act of 1988 (TAMRA), Congress provided the possibility that certain minimum participation requirements enacted in the Tax Reform Act of 1986 may be applied separately with respect to each separate line of business of an employer.[33] TAMRA also added an additional

---

[33]The Small Business Job Protection Act of 1996 modified minimum participation rules as they apply to separate lines of business. The act allowed that fewer than 50 employees could be participants in a defined benefit plan for a separate line of business if it otherwise would meet the requirements to qualify as a separate line of business.

sanction for highly compensated employees, requiring them to include in their gross income for the year in which the minimum participation standard is not met an amount equal to their vested accrued benefit as of the close of that year.

The Omnibus Budget Reconciliation Act of 1989 (OBRA '89) made numerous changes in the statutory provisions that permitted a lender to an employee stock ownership plan (ESOP), or ESOP plan sponsor, to exclude 50 percent of the interest from its income for federal tax purposes.[34] OBRA also amended, among other things, provisions pertaining to the Section 404(k) dividend deduction, the ESOP tax-free rollover, and the ESOP estate tax exclusion.

The Omnibus Budget Reconciliation Act of 1990 (OBRA '90) increased Pension Benefit Guaranty Corporation (PBGC) premiums as well as the excise tax on reversions of excess pension plan assets to the employer on termination of a pension plan. However, OBRA '90 presented an opportunity to increase corporate cash flow and possibly decrease near-term expenses through the use of excess pension assets to pay retiree health benefits. The existence of this opportunity depends on the funded status of a pension plan.

The Older Workers Benefit Protection Act of 1990 amended the Age Discrimination in Employment Act (ADEA) to apply to employee benefits but singled out early retirement incentive plans as allowable if they were voluntary, conformed with the purposes of ADEA, and met certain minimum standards.

The Unemployment Compensation Amendments of 1992 (UCCA) instituted a 20 percent mandatory withholding tax on lump-sum distributions that are not directly transferred to a qualified type of retirement account and provided notification requirements that plan sponsors must distribute to participants requesting lump-sum distributions. Furthermore, these amendments liberalized the rollover rules, affording most taxable distributions eligibility for rollover treatment, and required plan sponsors to provide a direct rollover option by the end of the 1994 plan year.

The Omnibus Budget Reconciliation Act of 1993 (OBRA '93) lowered the allowable compensation limit for computation of qualified plan contributions to $150,000 from the $235,840 it had risen to through indexing. The law also limited the indexing of the $150,000 compensation cap to $10,000 increments, thus slowing its rise. This sharp reduction in the allowable compensation base that could be used in determining contributions to qualified pension, 401(k), and other retirement plans of highly compensated employees, caused increased interest in nonqualified plans for replacing lost benefits. The law uncapped the wage base on which employers would pay the 1.45 percent Medicare portion of the Federal Insurance Contributions Act (FICA) tax. Additionally, OBRA '93 increased the amount of Social Security benefits subject to taxation from 50 percent to 85 percent for middle- and higher-income individuals beginning in 1994.

---

[34]The Small Business Job Protection Act of 1996 repealed the interest income exclusion for ESOP loans that allowed banks, insurance companies, regulated investment companies, and certain corporations to exclude 50 percent of the interest received on ESOP loans. Repeal of the interest income exclusion became effective with loans where a contract for the loan agreement occurred on or after June 10, 1996.

The Uniformed Services Employment and Reemployment Rights Act of 1993 guaranteed a veteran's right to pension benefits that would have accrued during military service and clarified various pension issues that arise with a military leave.

The Retirement Protection Act of 1994 that was part of the General Agreement on Tariffs and Trade (GATT) had a number of provisions directly impacting retirement plans. A number of provisions were instituted to strengthen minimum funding for certain underfunded plans. Premiums to the Pension Benefit Guaranty Corporation (PBGC) were increased. Large underfunded plans were required to engage in additional disclosure to the PBGC and plan participants. Certain limitations were instituted on the use of actuarial assumptions for lump-sum distributions, and rounding rules were instituted for the upward indexing of inflation-indexed pension limits. Essentially, these limits were rounded down until inflation adjustments move them up to the next even multiple of $5,000 ($500 or $50, in some cases). These indexing features affected the cap on included compensation for pension contributions, dollar amounts for determining highly compensated employees in nondiscrimination testing, elective deferral, and Section 415 limits. Section 415 of the Internal Revenue Code (IRC) impacts allowable limits on contributions and benefits through retirement plans. The rounding rules slow the rate of escalation in cost-of-living increases.

Immediately before the 1996 congressional summer recess and the fall 1996 presidential election, several pieces of legislation were passed into law. This legislation included the Small Business Job Protection Act of 1996 and the Health Insurance Portability and Accountability Act of 1996. Within these pieces of legislation and some other enacted laws were considerable tax-related provisions that in combination represented the most sweeping alterations to the tax code since the Tax Reform Act of 1986. Most of the pension-related provisions were included in the **Small Business Job Protection Act,** where these provisions were assembled thematically as pension simplification provisions. Many of these provisions were advanced as a necessary compromise to gain the support of the small business community for an increase in the minimum wage, although, because of bipartisan support for the pension simplification issue, many technical corrections to earlier legislation were included.

Among the major provisions in the Small Business Job Protection Act of 1996 were the following: the creation of the savings incentive match plans for employees (SIMPLE plans); a simplified definition for highly compensated employees (HCEs) for nondiscrimination testing purposes; simplified nondiscrimination testing procedures; the establishment of testing safe harbors for 401(k) plans; the repeal of family aggregation rules; a change in the definition of compensation used for computing the limitations of IRC Section 415; modification of plan distribution rules; an increase in the maximum tax deductible contribution for spousal IRAs, and several provisions of significance to plans for tax-exempt entities (403(b) plans) and state and local governments (457 plans).

The Health Insurance Portability and Accountability Act of 1996, although not primarily dealing with pensions, included some provisions that related to retirement security. For example, this act permitted penalty-free early distributions from an IRA for payment of certain medical expenses and health insurance premiums. The act also provided favorable tax treatment for qualified long-term care (LTC) insurance and noninsured LTC expenses, although long-term care employee premiums were prohibited from being sheltered under cafeteria plans.

In 1997 two major pieces of legislation were passed impacting employee benefits and pension plans. Most of the provisions affecting pensions and employee benefit plans were included in the **Taxpayer Relief Act of 1997,** the tax portion of the budget legislation. The spending portion of the legislation known as the Balanced Budget Act of 1997 included many changes related to the Medicare program.

The Economic Growth and Tax Relief Reconciliation Act of 2001 (EGTRRA) made extensive and far-reaching changes to retirement plans. Among the many changes to be phased in over several years were increased contribution, benefit, and deduction limits for all types of retirement savings vehicles; business credits for the start-up of retirement plans; tax credits to lower- and middle-income employees making contributions to retirement plans; greater parity between plans with elimination of the 403(b) exclusion allowance and various changes to eligible 457 (b) plans; greater contribution limits permitted for retirement plan participants who were age 50 and over; plan loans permitted for sole proprietors; S corporation shareholders and partners; a new provision allowing 401(k) and 403(b) plans to incorporate a feature called a "qualified Roth contribution program"; and greater portability for all types of retirement programs by providing for easier roll over of distributions between various types of plans. However, EGTRRA also introduced an element of uncertainty for these extensive retirement plan changes since the act contained a sunset provision stating that all the rule changes would not apply to taxable, plan, or limitation years after December 31, 2010. Effectively all these retirement plan rule changes that are phased in over the next several years will automatically be eliminated in 2011 unless further legislation is passed to extend or retain these changes. Therefore, EGTRRA created both great promise and great uncertainty concerning the expansion of tax incentives for retirement plans.

The **Job Creation and Worker Assistance Act of 2002** increased the interest rate range for computing a defined benefit plan's current liability; specified that contribution deduction limits applicable to employers that maintain a combination of plans do not apply when only elective contributions are contributed to an employer's defined benefit plan; clarified certain issues for rollovers of after-tax contributions; and conformed the percentage of compensation for allowable contributions to simplified employee pensions (SEPs) to the permissible deduction limit.

Many changes, rulings, and regulations relating to these various pieces of legislation have occurred since their enactment. The legislation and the changes, as well as their impact on retirement plans, are discussed throughout this book.

Chapter Summary

- One cause of economic insecurity is the probable reduction of an individual's earning power at an advanced age. Most often, the problem of economic insecurity is remedied by the "tripod of economic security"—personal savings, employer-sponsored pensions, and social insurance programs.

• Although the assumption usually is made that financial needs decrease after retirement, the actual aggregate reduction in financial needs upon retirement is probably overstated.

• Private pensions have experienced dramatic growth since the 1940s for a number of reasons. Among the economic, sociological, and historical reasons for this growth are the following:
  – A systematic method of meeting the problem of superannuated employees can be justified on sound management grounds. Economists have theorized on the economic rationale of private pensions using the human depreciation concept and the deferred wage concept.
  – Tax considerations provide financial incentives for the provision of qualified pension plans.
  – Union demands and the actions of the War Labor Board when increases in wages were prohibited have contributed to pension growth.
  – Employers may be motivated to provide pensions to compete in recruiting and retaining workers, or they may provide pensions to reward service or forestall unionization. At times employers have been encouraged to implement pensions by the sales efforts of funding agencies.

• Pension plans have been the subject of substantial legislative activity and the development of these plans is better understood when the provisions of these legislative acts are known. One of the most notable pieces of legislation is the Employee Retirement Income Security Act of 1974 (ERISA), which established a major foundation from a legal, tax, investment, and actuarial viewpoint. The Tax Reform Act of 1986 probably provided the most pervasive changes in pension regulation since the passage of ERISA. The Small Business Job Protection Act of 1996 contained many pension-related provisions that were linked as pension simplification initiatives. Within the Small Business Job Protection Act of 1996 were many technical corrections relating to earlier pension legislation. In 1997 the Taxpayer Relief Act and Balanced Budget Act were passed.

• The Economic Growth and Tax Relief Reconciliation Act of 2001 (EGTRRA) made extensive and far-reaching changes to retirement plans. Among the many changes to be phased in over several years were increased contribution, benefit and deduction limits for all types of retirement savings vehicles; business credits for the start-up of retirement plans; tax credits to lower- and middle-income employees making contributions to retirement plans; greater parity between plans with elimination of the 403(b) maximum exclusion allowance and various changes to eligible 457(b) plans; greater contribution limits permitted for retirement plan participants who were age 50 and over; plan loans permitted for sole proprietors; S corporation shareholders, and partners; a new provision allowing 401(k) and 403(b) plans to incorporate a feature called a "qualified Roth contribution program"; and greater portability for all types of retirement programs by providing for easier roll over of distributions between various types of plans. However, EGTRRA also introduced an element of uncertainty for these extensive retirement plan changes since the act contained a sunset provision stating that all the rule changes would not apply to taxable, plan, or limitation years after December 31, 2010. Effectively all these retirement plan rule changes that are phased in over the next several years will automatically be eliminated in 2011 unless further legislation is passed to extend or retain these changes. Therefore, EGTRRA created both great promise and great uncertainty concerning the expansion of tax incentives for retirement plans.

Key Terms

annuities, p. *1*

deferred wage concept, p. *16*

demography, p. *8*

Economic Growth and
Tax Relief Reconciliation
Act of 2001 (EGTRRA),
p. *7*

Employee Retirement
Income Security Act of
1974 (ERISA), p. *17*

human depreciation
concept, p. *15*

Job Creation and Worker
Assistance Act of 2002,
p. *21*

longevity, p. *8*

reverse annuity, p. *6*

Small Business Job
Protection Act (of 1996),
p. *20*

superannuated, p. *9*

Tax Equity and Fiscal
Responsibility Act of
1982 (TEFRA), p. *18*

Taxpayer Relief Act of
1997, p. *21*

Tax Reform Act of 1986,
p. *18*

tripod of economic security,
p. *1*

wage stabilization program,
p. *11*

Questions for Review

1. Describe the basic economic problems facing the aged.
2. Why have private pension plans grown so rapidly since the 1940s?
3. Explain the alternatives that exist for an employer dealing with less-productive superannuated employees. What are the limitations of these alternatives?
4. Briefly describe the principal tax advantages of qualified pension plans.
5. Describe how wage stabilization during World War II affected private pension plans.
6. Explain the role played by the National Labor Relations Board (NLRB) in the development of pension plans.
7. Describe the merits of private pensions as a supplement to Social Security benefits and individual savings programs.
8. Briefly describe the impact of recent legislation on the design process for private pension plans.

Questions for Discussion

1. Economists have often argued that pension benefits are a form of deferred compensation accepted by employees in lieu of higher present wages. Assume that the employees of a firm ask you how much the pension benefit they earned this year is actually worth in current dollars. In general terms, how would you perform this valuation? What types of assumptions would you need to make? If the employees told you that they would forfeit the entire pension attributable to employer contributions if they were terminated within five years of the time they were originally hired, how would you factor this information into your analysis?

2. For several years it has been argued that one of the primary advantages of a pension plan for employees is that it allows them to avoid taxation on a portion of their total compensation during the time they are in a high tax bracket and to postpone the receipt—and consequently the taxation—of this money until after they retire. If, as was usually the case prior to the Tax Reform Act of 1986, the employee expected to be in a lower tax bracket after retirement, the tax savings inherent in this deferral could be substantial. However, if the federal income tax system evolved into a modified form of a flat tax sys-

tem in which many taxpayers expected to be taxed at the same rate, regardless of when their money was received, does this necessarily imply that the tax advantages of private pension plans have ceased to be an important advantage for employees? (Hint: Even if all money received from a pension plan is taxed at the same rate, does the fact that money can accumulate at a before-tax rate of return, instead of an after-tax rate of return, affect the eventual amount of money received by the employee?)

3. The text suggests that a private pension plan allows the burden of retirement security to be spread out over a long period of time. Discuss how this specifically applies in the case of investment risk. Assume that there are only two forms of investments for retirement: a risk-free asset with a known rate of return, and a risky asset with a higher expected rate of return. Unfortunately, the risky asset may experience large decreases as well as increases in any particular year. If employees were to invest for their retirement on an individual basis, why might they be willing to choose the risk-free asset, knowing their expected accumulation at retirement will be smaller? In contrast, if employees allowed the employer to invest for their retirement through a defined benefit pension plan (in which the employee's retirement benefit is guaranteed regardless of the level of the pension assets), would the employer be as likely to choose the lower yielding, risk-free asset for the pension plan? (Hint: What is the relevant investment horizon for a pension plan if it is assumed to be an ongoing operation?)

Resources for Further Study

CCH Editorial Staff. "2002 Tax Legislation: Law, Explanation and Analysis: Job Creation and Worker Assistance Act of 2002." *Commerce Clearing House* (2002).

CCH Editorial Staff. "2001 Tax Legislation: Law, Explanation and Analysis." *Commerce Clearing House Pension Plan Guide* (2001).

Investment Company Institute. *Fundamentals: Investment Company Institute Research in Brief* 10, no. 2. Washington, DC: Investment Company Institute (June 2001).

Kilgour, John G. "Responding to Changing Retirement Savings Programs." *Compensation & Benefits Review,* September/October 2001.

Lurie, Alvin D. "The 2001 Tax Law: A Congressional Vanishing Act, but with Real Magic for Retirement Plans. *Compensation & Benefits Management,* Autumn 2001.

McDonnell, Ken; Paul Fronstin; Kelly Olsen; Pamela Ostuw; Jack Van Derhei; and Paul Yakoboski. *EBRI Databook on Employee Benefits.* 4th ed. Deborah Holmes, Lynn Miller, and Maureen Richmond, eds. Washington, DC: Employee Benefit Research Institute Education and Research Fund, 1997.

Rosenbloom, Jerry S. "The Environment of Employee Benefit Plans." *The Handbook of Employee Benefits.* 5th ed. Jerry S. Rosenbloom, ed. New York: McGraw-Hill, 2001.

Salisbury, Dallas L. "Regulatory Environment of Employee Benefit Plans." *The Handbook of Employee Benefits.* 5th ed. Jerry S. Rosenbloom, ed. New York: McGraw-Hill, 2001.

www.ebri.org—website of the Employee Benefit Research Institute.

www.ifebp.org—website of the International Foundation of Employee Benefit Plans.

www.ici.org—website of the Investment Company Institute.

Chapter 2

Benefit Plan Objectives

After studying this chapter you should be able to:

- Identify important environmental factors an employer should consider when designing a pension plan.

- Describe alternative plan design approaches to achieve employer goals and objectives.

- Explain techniques that may be used to make comparisons between the retirement plans of various employers.

- Identify opportunities to comply with legal requirements by modifying elements of plan design.

- Describe how the entire portfolio of benefits for a retiree may affect the goals and objectives set for the pension plan.

- Explain the purpose of income-replacement objectives, why they are less than 100 percent of preretirement gross income, and why they may vary depending upon salary level.

It is reasonable to speculate that the first employee benefit plans were established to serve specific purposes—for example, to avoid "passing the hat" among employees when someone died. For many years, the design of these plans was influenced largely by the insurance industry's attitude toward underwriting, funding, and administration, since the plans were made available by insurers under the terms and conditions they chose to offer.

Over the years, many factors have influenced the design of employee benefit plans, and a body of law has emerged that affects these plans in terms of minimum requirements and permissible provisions. The taxation of contributions and benefits also has influenced plan design, and the process of collective bargaining and the interests of organized labor have been a major influence, as has the availability of alternate funding mechanisms. These, and other factors, including a growing degree of sophistication and knowledge of the field, have created an environment in which an employer has a wide degree of choice and flexibility in benefit plan design. In recent years, however, the increasing level of federal regulation has caused retirement plans to gravitate toward common plan provisions. For example, plans that have eligibility requirements almost always settle on the use of one year of service and a minimum age of 21, and almost all defined benefit plans use five-year cliff vesting. Cliff vesting involves an employee's receipt of a full 100 percent vested right after five years, rather than earning a portion of a vested right each year, as occurs with seven-year graded vesting.[1]

The cost of employee benefits is significant. A well-rounded program (including paid time off) can easily generate a total cost in the vicinity of 30 percent or more of an employer's base payroll. If the cost of statutory benefits also is included, total cost can easily reach 40 percent of payroll or more. Indeed, some companies have total benefit costs that approach 50 percent of payroll. The amounts accumulated under these plans also are of major importance. For example, the assets accumulated by some companies in their pension plans alone exceed their net worth.

Given the substantial costs involved in employee benefits plans, the importance they have to millions of workers, and the complex legal, tax, and funding environments that exist, it is most important that such plans be designed with particular care, that they be fully supportive of the employer's philosophy, goals, and objectives, and that they at least partially satisfy the perceived needs of the employees. This concept is of equal importance to small employers and to larger organizations.

The major focus of this text is on the various mechanisms that exist for the delivery of retirement benefits and the ways in which a specific retirement plan might be designed. However, matters that influence the design of a retirement plan also influence the design of other employee benefit plans. Thus, while the primary emphasis of this chapter is on retirement plans, the subject matter is broad enough to apply to all employee benefits.

In this chapter, some of the environmental considerations that can influence plan design are described first. Then employer philosophy and attitudes are discussed. The final portion of the chapter deals with specific employee benefit plan objectives.

Environmental Considerations

Before passage of the Tax Equity and Fiscal Responsibility Act of 1982 (TEFRA), the employer's legal status often influenced plan design. Federal tax law dealt differently with sole proprietorships, partnerships, Subchapter S corporations, nonprofit organizations, and regular corporations. For example, defined contribution pension or profit sharing plans generally were adopted by unincorporated organiza-

---

[1]The Economic Growth and Tax Relief Reconciliation Act of 2001 (EGTRRA) accelerated the two alternative minimum vesting schedules for employer matching contributions to three-year cliff and six-year graded. The definition for matching contributions pertains only to defined contribution plans. For all other types of retirement plans the five-year cliff and seven-year graded vesting schedules may be retained.

tions and by Subchapter S corporations because of the deduction limits previously imposed on these organizations. Often, these deduction limits and the potential benefits of a defined benefit pension plan caused such organizations to incorporate either on a regular basis or as a professional corporation or association. While the parity provisions of TEFRA eliminated most of the distinctions in tax law that formerly applied to partnerships and sole proprietorships, precedents established by prior practice and prior law still may continue to influence plan design for some organizations.

Section 501(c)(3) organizations need to take special matters into account when considering employee benefits. One such matter is that contributions are not deductible and will not operate to reduce plan costs. Thus, the "out-of-pocket" costs for a given level of employee benefits will be higher for a tax-exempt organization than they would be for a profit-making corporation under like circumstances. Also, these organizations have frequently used defined contribution concepts because of the availability of tax-deferred annuities under Section 403(b) of the Internal Revenue Code.

The basic characteristics of the employer and its industry are part of the background for designing an employee benefit program. Is the firm a young, growing organization, or is it relatively mature? Is its history of profits stable and predictable, or have profits been, or are they likely to be, volatile? Does the firm anticipate moderate or significant growth, and what will its need for employees be in the foreseeable future? Is the industry highly competitive? Are profit margins narrow? Is the business cyclical? What are the firm's short- and long-term capital needs? The answers to these questions and others like them can be of great importance in structuring benefit plans that will both meet employee needs and offer funding patterns compatible with the employer's objectives and capabilities.

The characteristics of the individuals employed by the employer also play an important role in plan design. The distribution of employees by age, service, sex, and pay can have significant implications in terms of the type of benefit provided, cost levels generated, and similar matters.

An employer with diversified operations has special considerations when it comes to employee benefit plan design. For example, such an employer needs to consider whether the same benefit program is appropriate for all facets of the business. Factors such as cost, profit margins, competitive need, and geographic differences should be taken into account. Another factor related to this issue is the employer's attitude regarding the transfer of employees. A uniform program facilitates such transfers, while different plans at different locations may create impediments. Obviously, the employer's basic policy concerning employee transfers, whether encouraged or discouraged, bears on the matter. One approach used by some employers is to combine a basic or "core" program that applies in all areas of the business with a flexible or varying program of supplemental benefits to accommodate different industry needs.

The communities in which the employer does business also can be an environmental factor in plan design. This is less the case in large, urban areas, but it can become quite meaningful when the company is the dominant or a major employer in a discrete geographical area. In this case, the design and structure of an employee benefit plan could reflect the employer's degree of concern over the image it wishes to create in the communities in which it does business. If such a concern exists, it often indicates the need for liberal benefit provisions—not only by the employer's own industry standards, but by the standards established by different employers involved in the same communities.

The presence or absence of collective bargaining units also can be a significant consideration. The demands of labor, both on a local and a national or "pattern" basis, can influence plan design, even for nonbargaining employees. Many employers follow the practice of extending bargained-for benefits to nonbargaining unit employees, or they make the plans of the nonbargaining unit employees slightly better than those of the bargaining unit employees, to the extent that this does not violate labor laws. Others, however, treat the programs as totally separate, particularly in the context that benefit plans are part of total compensation and that basic salary and wage structures also are quite different between the two groups.

The foregoing is not intended to be an exhaustive discussion of environmental factors that influence plan design. Rather, it is intended to give some indication of the various items that should be considered. With these in mind, it is appropriate to turn to a discussion of employer philosophy and attitudes.

Employer Philosophy and Attitudes

Specific objectives for employee benefit plans should be considered in the context of the employer's philosophy and attitudes for the management of human resources. The following list of questions and observations, again not all-inclusive, is designed to suggest the nature of some of the items that need to be considered.

1. What is the employer's basic compensation philosophy? Many employers believe benefit plans are part of total compensation and that the cost and benefit structure of these plans should reflect the employer's basic attitude toward other compensation elements. Thus, the employer who has adopted a policy of paying high wages and salaries may very well adopt a liberal benefit program. On the other hand, an employer may choose to establish a benefit program that keeps total compensation costs at an acceptable level while presenting one element of compensation on a more favorable basis. For example, an employer may wish to establish highly competitive wages and salaries but, to keep total compensation costs in line, may provide only modest benefits. Such a compensation strategy, of course, can affect the type of employee attracted and also can influence matters such as turnover rates. It also is possible for an employer to adopt a reverse compensation strategy mix and have a liberal benefit program to go along with a cash compensation program that is not fully competitive. This type of compensation mix often is found in governmental units, where cash compensation is fixed by law and where incentive compensation may not be payable. Here, it is common to find liberal benefit programs.

2. Is the employer's basic attitude toward providing employee benefits one that emphasizes the protection and maintenance of income in the event of economic insecurity? Or is its attitude oriented more toward providing additional current, although tax-deferred, compensation? Most employers do not have a clear-cut and total pref-

erence for one or the other of these positions; however, one position might be of greater significance than the other. The employer's leaning toward one or the other of these two concepts can find expression in a number of plan decisions. For example, a preference for the **income-maintenance approach** could suggest the choice of a defined benefit pension plan integrated to the maximum extent with Social Security benefits[2] or the choice of a death benefit that provides an income benefit only to survivors of the employee's immediate family. A **compensation-oriented approach,** though, might suggest the use of a defined contribution plan as the basic program for providing retirement benefits. In recent years, as employers have shifted from "paternalistic" attitudes to ones that emphasize individual responsibility, there has been growing interest in the compensation-oriented approach.

3. Does the employer believe employees should share in the cost of meeting their own economic security needs? Many employers take the position that employees do have such a responsibility; they believe that benefits in the event of medical expense needs, death, disability, and retirement should come from three sources— the government, the employer, and the employee's own savings. Where desired, employee involvement can be in the form of direct employee contributions, or it can be recognized in indirect ways as, for example, when income-replacement objectives in a noncontributory pension plan are consciously set below what might otherwise be desired levels, or through the use of deductibles, coinsurance, or inside plan limitations in a medical expense plan. Also, an employer can view this issue from the perspective of the total employee benefit program, making some specific plans **contributory** and some **noncontributory,** with the overall employee contributions achieving a total level the employer feels is satisfactory.

4. A long-term, advance-funded retirement program involves certain risks. Two of the most important risks relate to the impact of inflation and investment results. The employer's attitude on who should bear these risks—the employer or the employees— can play a significant role in the choice between a defined benefit and a defined contribution pension plan.[3] Under the former, these risks are assumed by the employer, although the risk of inflation can be tempered by the choice of a formula that is

---

[2]The basic concept of integration is that the benefits of the employer's plan are dovetailed with Social Security benefits in such a manner that employees earning over the Social Security taxable wage base will not receive combined benefits under the two programs proportionately greater than the benefits for employees earning less than this amount. Although the benefit formula under the private plan may favor the higher paid employees, the additional amounts provided for them cannot exceed levels allowed under the Internal Revenue Code and supporting regulations. This concept is presented in more detail in Chapter 4.

[3]A defined benefit plan is a pension plan under which the employer provides a determinable benefit, usually related to an employee's service and/or pay. Under this approach, the employer's cost is whatever is necessary to provide the benefit specified. A defined contribution plan is a pension plan under which the employer's contribution is fixed and this contribution is accumulated to provide whatever amount of benefit it can purchase. Thus, an employee's benefit becomes the variable, depending upon factors such as age at entry, retirement age, and investment earnings (or losses). A defined contribution plan can involve a specific contribution or it can take the form of a profit sharing plan.

not pay-related, or by the choice of a career-pay formula; under a defined contribution plan, the employee in effect assumes both of these risks. The growing use of defined contribution plans, along with the transfer of these risks to employees, has caused many employers to take steps to provide investment education for their employees.

5. The selection of specific retirement plan provisions (normal retirement age, early retirement age and subsidies, the treatment of **deferred retirement,** and the benefit levels provided in all these events) and the amount of postretirement life and medical expense insurance provided can influence the pattern of retirements in any organization. Many employers prefer to encourage employees to retire at or before normal retirement age for a variety of reasons, such as keeping promotional channels open. Others prefer to encourage deferred retirements and are reluctant to see skilled workers leave while still capable of making important contributions to the firm's profitability. Still other employers take a neutral position and do not seek to exert any influence on the pattern of retirements in their organizations. In any event, this issue took on added significance after the 1986 amendments to the Age Discrimination in Employment Act (ADEA), which protect employment rights of all employees age 40 and over. This issue was further influenced by the 1983 Social Security amendments, which gradually extend the "normal" retirement age for Social Security benefits to age 67, at the same time reducing the level of benefits available from ages 62 through 66. This issue continues to be influenced by demographic considerations and a general recognition of the fact that the relative size of the workforce—over and under age 65—is changing. With these demographic shifts in mind, many employers might choose to encourage employees to remain in the workforce beyond age 65. This could be accomplished in many ways, including phased retirements, reduced-hour work schedules, part-time employment, and consulting arrangements.

6. A growing number of employers prefer to structure an employee benefit program on a basis that gives employees a wide choice of plans in which to participate and some control over the extent to which they participate in these plans. This can be accomplished on the basis of before-tax credits in the form of **flexible** or **"cafeteria" benefits,** or it can be accomplished by developing various layers of after-tax contributory coverage. Such employers believe this type of flexibility makes the program more meaningful to employees and more efficient, since benefits are delivered only when needed or desired. Other employers prefer not to become involved in the administrative complexities and costs associated with such flexibility, nor do they wish to absorb any additional costs associated with the adverse selection made possible by such choices. Also, those employers who have a paternalistic attitude might feel many employees would not want to make those choices or would not be able to make the right choices. However, the apparent trend in recent years has been toward the creation of individual responsibility and choice and away from paternalism.

7. An employer's position concerning the cost levels it can assume can be a major determinant for a plan's benefit levels and the various ancillary benefits that might be included. The assumption of any given level of cost commitment also involves a

balancing of employee interests with those of the organization's owners or shareholders. Another aspect relates to the employer's attitude about the need for maintaining controls over future cost levels. A high degree of concern in this area, for example, might lead to the selection of alternatives such as a career-pay or a defined contribution pension plan, the use of pay-related deductibles in a medical plan, nonpay-related death benefits, or a medical plan structured using defined contribution concepts.

8. Whether the plan's benefits should be coordinated with Social Security benefits is a most important question. The employer's basic philosophy concerning this issue plays an important role in plan design. A great many employers believe that because of the very nature of Social Security benefits and their relatively larger value for lower-paid employees, it would be impossible to achieve an equitable balancing of benefits and costs for employees at all pay levels without integrating pension and disability income plans in some fashion with the benefits provided by Social Security. Others believe the communication and administrative difficulties associated with integrated plans are such that integration is not desirable.

9. Should an employer provide a benefit program for executives that differs from that provided for its employees in general? Over the years, the majority of benefit programs have been applied across-the-board to all employees, and many employers still believe executives or highly paid employees should be treated the same as all employees. An increasing number of organizations, however, believe the unique needs of executives cannot be met by plans that must meet the nondiscrimination requirements of federal tax law. For example, it may be difficult for a firm to recruit a needed executive in midcareer because of the loss of pension benefits he or she would experience, since a large part of the executive's benefits would be frozen at the pay levels achieved with the prior employer. In such a case, a need may exist for the employer to have a retirement arrangement that restores the benefits that such an executive might potentially lose. Similarly, an employer might find it desirable to provide executives with a supplemental pension that applies the basic pension plan formula to the executive's incentive pay, if the basic pension relates to base compensation only. Due to the **nondiscrimination requirements** described in Chapter 4, special benefits for executives such as those described cannot be provided through a qualified, nondiscriminatory pension or profit sharing plan. Instead, these benefits must be provided through some form of **nonqualified supplemental pension arrangement** (these nonqualified arrangements are described in Chapter 20). Many employers also provide executives with additional death benefits, both before and after retirement, as well as with additional disability income protection.

10. An important question since the passage of the Employee Retirement Income Security Act of 1974 (ERISA) is whether the employer is willing to assume the **plan termination obligations** imposed upon the employer in the event of the termination of a defined benefit plan before all accrued and vested benefits have been funded. The impact this might have on net worth, credit ratings, and the ability to raise capital has caused a good deal of concern—particularly among small

employers.[4] This potential liability can be avoided if a defined contribution pension plan is adopted and, indeed, over 80 percent of all new tax-qualified plans adopted since the passage of ERISA have been of the defined contribution variety. In addition, the annual premium payable for plan termination insurance has become quite substantial—a minimum of $19 per year per covered participant (including retired and terminated vested participants)—and the rate is considerably higher for plans with unfunded liabilities.

Employer Objectives

With the preceding in mind, it is appropriate to consider specific employer objectives. The following discusses major employer objectives, as well as some of the factors relating to such objectives. Obviously, not all of these objectives apply to each employer and, if they do have application, it is likely their relative importance may not be the same for each employer.

Attraction and Retention of Employees

Most employers recognize they must maintain some form of employee benefit program to attract and retain desirable employees. This is particularly so when the employer must compete with other employers for personnel.

Even so, many employers believe the presence of an adequate benefit program is not a positive influence in their efforts to attract and retain employees—at least to any significant extent. Rather, these employers reason the absence of such a program could have a negative effect on their recruiting and retention efforts. Put another way, these employers are of the opinion that an inadequate program can hinder their efforts to recruit and retain employees, while an overly generous program will not produce a corresponding increase in their ability to attract and hold desirable workers.

While this might be true as a general concept, it is worth noting that some benefit plans might have greater impact than others as far as employees are concerned. Thus, for example, the presence of a generous profit sharing plan might make employment with one employer more attractive than employment with another employer who maintains a more conventional benefit program. In the same vein, employees might find the choice and value of a flexible (or cafeteria) benefit plan of more interest than a plan that offers a standard fare of benefits.

Meeting Competitive Standards

While the objective of having competitive employee benefit plans is closely related to the objective of being able to attract and retain good employees, it is somewhat broader in scope and can reflect employers' attitudes about their standing in their own industry and in the communities in which they operate. This objective also rec-

---

[4]The employer's liability on termination of a single-employer plan is quite complex and a detailed discussion of this topic is deferred until Chapter 16. It should be noted that an employer also can be exposed to a liability in the case of a negotiated multiemployer plan.

ognizes that, unlike other forms of compensation, employee benefit plans are highly visible and readily subject to external comparison.

An employer who wishes to have competitive employee benefit plans must establish standards for measuring these plans. Will competitiveness be measured against industry standards, geographic standards, or both? Many employers have a preference for measuring their plans against industry standards. However, it should be recognized that such standards are most appropriate for skilled or professional workers and for management personnel—those whose capabilities are more specific to the employer's own industry. For workers whose capabilities are more readily transferred from one industry to another, a more realistic standard would be those plans maintained by the local companies with which the employer competes for human resources. Thus, as a practical matter, most employers seek to compare their plans both on an industrywide and a geographic basis.

Having identified the standard against which the plans are to be measured, the employer also must decide upon the relative level of competitiveness to achieve. For example, the employer might decide the objective is to have an employee benefit program that meets the average of the companies that form its comparison base (or it can establish different positions for different plans). Conversely, the employer might decide it wishes to be a leader and have a program that is consistently among the best, or it might wish to rank somewhere between the 50th and 75th percentiles. And, of course, the employer might elect to lag somewhat behind other companies because of cost or other considerations.

Even though the comparison base has been identified and the relative ranking within this base established, there remains the important matter of determining the technique to be used to establish the relative standing of the different plans. One method used quite frequently is to make comparisons of the benefits actually payable to representative employees under different circumstances. For example, the benefits payable under a retirement plan at normal retirement age might be projected for several employees with differing pay, service, and age characteristics. This method is relatively simple in concept but should be used with caution. First, it shows benefits only and does not necessarily give any true indication of the relative cost of the plans involved. Also, by isolating a specific benefit, the importance and value of other benefits included in the same plan are not taken into account. For example, a company might be ranked as the highest in terms of benefits payable at normal retirement, but the other companies in the comparison may have much more valuable early retirement or survivor income benefits. Even if other benefits are illustrated and compared in the same way, the aggregate value of all benefits within the same plan may not be readily ascertainable. This method is also sensitive to the assumptions used in making the illustrations. If retirement benefits are being illustrated, for example, and if future pay increases are not taken into account, the benefit differences attributable to **final-pay** and **career-pay**[5] formulas

---

[5]A final-pay provision bases benefits on the employee's earnings averaged, for example, over the last three or five years of employment, or over the three or five consecutive years in the 10-year period immediately prior to retirement during which the employee's earnings are the highest. By contrast, a career-pay provision bases benefits on the employee's earnings averaged over the entire career of employment. This concept is presented in detail in Chapter 13.

will not be apparent (nor will there be any apparent difference between a final three-year average plan and a final five-year average plan).

Another method used is to compare actual costs to the employer for different benefit plans. The material used for this purpose usually is information acquired from both published and private surveys about actual employer cost patterns. A major difficulty with this approach is that there is often inconsistent reporting among different employers of the information requested. Also, actual contribution patterns do not necessarily reflect the real cost or value of the benefit involved. The cost reported, for example, might be the total annual cost of the plan, including employee contributions, and might reflect the specific characteristics of the employee group involved. In the case of retirement plans, significant differences may exist in annual contributions because of the choice of a particular actuarial method and the combination of actuarial assumptions used. For example, two employers with identical plans might report significantly different annual costs because of their different choices of assumptions for future investment earnings and growth in pay.

A third method used for measuring plans uses uniform actuarial methods and assumptions and focuses on the relative value of the different benefits provided. This technique establishes the value of specific plans, specific benefits within a plan, and the aggregate value of all plans. The method also can establish these relative values on the basis of employer cost only or on the basis of combined employer and employee cost. By using uniform actuarial methods and assumptions, and by applying these to a database of employees held the same for all employer plans in the study, the actual differences in the value of different benefits are isolated and their relative values established. It should be noted that this technique does not establish actual costs or cost patterns; it simply establishes whether one particular benefit or plan is more valuable than another and the extent to which this is so.

Cost Considerations

Earlier in this chapter, reference was made to an employer's attitude on costs and how this can play a major role in plan design. Since a retirement plan often represents a major part of an employer's total benefit program cost, it is particularly important that the employer have specific objectives in this area.

It is important to distinguish between ultimate real cost and estimated annual accruals. With this distinction in mind, an employer may establish specific objectives for actual liabilities assumed under a plan and specific objectives for annual accruals. The employer also may establish objectives in terms of the budgeting pattern to be assumed. For example, does the employer desire an accrual cost that remains level, as a percentage of payroll, or would it be preferable to have a pattern that starts with relatively low accruals, gradually building to higher levels in the future?

The employer's objectives for these cost levels influence the choice of retirement plan formula as well as the inclusion and level of ancillary benefits. These objectives also may influence the decision as to whether the plan should be contributory and, if so, the level of employee contributions required.

There are other objectives an employer could have for matters concerning cost. The need for contribution flexibility might be one such objective and, if desired,

Compensation and Benefit Objectives   1

More aware today than ever before of the total monies they have earmarked for employee compensation and benefits, more and more companies are analyzing the competitiveness of their total compensation programs. They are launching communication efforts to educate employees on the total value of their compensation and benefits packages. And some also are going to great lengths to educate their managers on the "Total Portfolio Approach," which views compensation as everything of value the company provides, including salary, short-term incentives, long-term incentives, benefits, and perquisites. They also are grouping all types of rewards and recognition systems under the total compensation "umbrella."

As costs and competitive pressures mount, organizations will need to examine the total cost impact of their compensation and benefits programs more strategically. As a result, the traditional development process for these programs will change: Companies will increasingly require new analyses and new measures of program competitiveness, and the corporate finance department will play a greater role in compensation decision making. . . .

For compensation and benefits managers specifically, four conditions are driving the need to change their focus:

- Compensation and benefit costs are a significant company expense.

- Companies desperately need to control fixed costs.

- Companies need to break the "entitlement mentality" among employees.

- Incremental increases to base salaries over time can be devastating to an organization's cost structure.

Source: Jack Dolmat-Connell, "A New Paradigm for Compensation and Benefits Competitiveness," pp. 52–53. Reprinted by permission of Sage Publications, Inc., from *Compensation & Benefits Review*, Sept./Oct. 1994. Copyright © 1994. Sage Publications, Inc., Thousand Oaks, CA. All rights reserved.

could influence the choice of actuarial funding method and assumptions and could even lead the employer to adopt a profit sharing plan. Another objective could relate to the employer's willingness to assume the costs associated with future inflation. The extent to which the employer wishes to limit its commitment might dictate the choice of a career-pay formula for a defined benefit plan or even the choice of a defined contribution plan of some type.

The need for a cost-efficient retirement program is an obvious objective. Thus, employers wish to avoid excessive or redundant benefits and to fund the plan in the most efficient manner possible. For this reason, many employers choose to coordinate benefits from all sources; for example, they may integrate their retirement plan benefits with those provided by Social Security.

It also is possible that an employer may view a retirement plan as a tax shelter for the benefit of key employees. When this is the case, the employer's objective might be to maximize benefits and contributions within the limits permitted by federal tax law.

Other employee benefit plans also involve cost considerations. If postretirement death and medical expense benefits are to be provided, should these liabilities be prefunded, and, if so, how? Should inflation-sensitive benefits—medical expenses and pay-related death benefits—be subjected to some degree of control through plan design? What type of funding mechanism should be used to gain greater control over cash flow? Clearly, cost considerations are becoming an increasingly important factor in plan design and plan funding.

Compliance with Legal Requirements

Employee benefit plans have almost always been subject to some degree of regulation and other legal requirements. This has become much more the case since the advent of ERISA, nondiscrimination laws, and the like. The enactment of the Tax Reform Act of 1986 also has had a major impact on the design of plans. More recently, the provisions of the Economic Growth and Tax Relief Reconciliation Act of 2001 and the Job Creation and Worker Assistance Act of 2002 now have an effect on the design and administration of plans, as well. Thus, the design and maintenance of employee benefit plans must meet the requirements of federal tax law, nondiscrimination laws, securities laws, labor laws, and state insurance laws. In several areas, state as well as federal laws must be taken into account. Thus, an implicit, if not explicit, objective of any employee benefit plan is that it must comply with these legal requirements.

However, an employer often has a choice regarding the manner in which compliance is achieved. For this reason, it is desirable that the employer formulate specific objectives in this regard. The following examples should give at least some indication of areas where compliance choices are available.

1. The Age Discrimination in Employment Act (ADEA) prevents discrimination in employment for employees age 40 and over. However, this does not require all benefit plans to treat all employees alike regardless of age. It is possible, for example, to reduce life insurance coverage for active employees by reason of age (but only within cost-justified limits). Although it is no longer possible to terminate pension accruals in a defined benefit plan or to discontinue allocations in a defined contribution plan after an active employee has attained age 65, a plan may limit the amount of benefit provided under the plan or the number of years of service or plan participation taken into account. An employer should establish basic objectives regarding how its over-65, active employees will be treated and whether compliance with this law should be at or above the minimum level. The employer's decision is, of course, influenced by other objectives and attitudes, such as whether it is desirable to encourage earlier or deferred retirements, the firm's public relations posture, and the like.

2. Federal tax law permits the exclusion from a defined benefit pension plan of those employees who have less than one year of service or who are under age 21. Employers may include all employees in their plans or may seek to exclude the maximum number possible, depending upon their attitude regarding minimum compliance and other objectives.

3. An employer may wish to establish a defined benefit pension plan that includes incentive compensation for executives as part of the compensation base

used to determine plan benefits, but it may not want to include overtime pay and shift differentials paid to other employees. It is unlikely the Internal Revenue Service would approve such a pay definition in a qualified pension plan. Compliance with the nondiscrimination requirements of federal tax law could be satisfied by designing the qualified plan with a nondiscriminatory definition of compensation that relates to base pay only and then instituting a nonqualified, supplemental executive retirement plan (SERP) that applies the base plan formula to incentive pay.

4. A savings plan can be designed so that some part of both employer and employee contributions can be invested in employer securities. Securities and Exchange Commission (SEC) requirements are such that the plan will have to be registered before employee contributions may be invested in this manner. These requirements can be avoided if employer securities are purchased using only employer contributions.

Achieving Optimum Tax Benefits

Federal tax law is such that some advantages exist for distributions from employee benefit plans. This is particularly so in the case of tax-qualified retirement and profit sharing plans. Indeed, on the one hand, these tax advantages very often are the motivating force behind the adoption of a plan.

If an employer wishes to achieve the maximum tax advantages for a retirement program, this can find expression in many areas; for example, potential tax advantages exist depending upon the choice of benefit formula, the degree to which the plan is integrated with Social Security benefits, the level of funding chosen, the funding instrument chosen, the adoption of both a defined benefit and a defined contribution plan, the use of a **target benefit plan,** and so on.[6]

The desire to maximize tax advantages also may affect other benefits and how they are funded. For example, a preretirement spousal benefit may be included as part of a retirement plan, or it may be funded by a separate group term life insurance program. If funded by life insurance, most of the benefit payments will escape income tax; however, the annual cost of insurance can represent taxable income to the employees under Section 79 of the Internal Revenue Code.[7] If the benefit is provided from retirement plan assets, the payments represent taxable income (except to the extent provided by employee contributions), but there will be no annual cost of

---

[6]A target benefit plan is one that combines the concepts of both defined contribution and defined benefit plans. The target benefit plan uses a defined benefit formula to determine an employee's projected pension at normal retirement date. A contribution to provide this benefit is then determined. This contribution is not adjusted for future experience. Instead, contributions are accumulated for each employee in an individual account and, depending upon actual investment results, can accumulate to provide a greater or smaller benefit than that originally projected. This approach has the advantage of determining the initial amount to be allocated to each employee on a basis that reflects the employee's age as well as compensation, while at the same time preserving the accumulation aspects of a defined contribution plan. This concept is presented in more detail in Chapter 19.

[7]Life insurance death benefits generally are income tax free. However, if paid in installments, the portion representing interest payments will be taxable.

Responding to Financial Accounting   2
Standard 106 (FAS 106)

The advent of FAS 106 caused employers to reexamine the design of their postretirement health care plans, with a view toward reducing and controlling their liabilities for these benefits. This type of analysis recognized that postretirement health care benefits are, in fact, a major form of retirement benefit—with costs, in many cases, being equal to or greater than the cost of conventional retirement income benefits. While in the process of considering design alternatives and cost control mechanisms, many employers recognized that their postretirement health care benefits were, in several key ways, inconsistent with the income benefits being provided by their retirement plans. For example,

- Most retirement plans do not provide for automatic benefit increases to respond to postretirement inflation adjustments. These increases, if any, are made on an "ad hoc" basis. By contrast, postretirement health care benefits usually are "defined benefit" in nature and are provided even though their cost is rising due to inflation. This has the effect of making postretirement health care benefits automatically indexed not only to inflation in general, but to the higher rates of inflation associated with health care.

- While some retirement plans do provide for spousal death benefits at employer cost, most do not, with such protection being provided only on a basis where the employee pays for its full cost. By contrast, a great many health care plans provide that if an employee dies after retirement (or after early retirement eligibility), spousal protection will be provided for life.

- The typical retirement plan requires that an employee complete a career of service—usually 25 to 30 years—in order to receive an optimal level of retirement benefits; the typical health care plan requires only 5 to 10 years.

- The earlier an employee retires under a retirement plan, the greater will be the *reduction* in the employee's income benefits; the earlier an employee retires under a health care plan, the greater will be the *value* of the employee's health care benefits.

These differences in plan provisions and benefits have caused employers to reconsider their attitudes and objectives concerning their overall "retirement" programs, and they have caused some to revise health care benefits to bring them more in line with employer commitments under the retirement income plans.

insurance to be reported by the employee. The emphasis to be placed on these various tax considerations and the characteristics of the employee group involved influence the choice of how the benefit will be funded.

Efficiency of Design

The overall cost of employee benefits is quite substantial and, as noted earlier, can amount to one-third or more of an employer's payroll costs. For this reason, it is important for an employer to structure its employee benefit program so benefits are provided in the most efficient manner possible and overlapping or redundant benefits are eliminated or, at least, minimized.

One of the most effective ways of doing this is to recognize that while any particular benefit plan has a primary focus (e.g., retirement, death, or disability), all benefit plans and some statutory plans must function in some fashion in the case of an event covered primarily by another plan. For example, the primary plan dealing with retirement is, of course, the employer's retirement plan. However, Social Security can be a major source of additional retirement income. Supplemental retirement income also can be provided by the employer's savings or profit sharing plan, if such a plan is in existence. The employer's group life insurance and medical expense plans may be the source of additional benefits for a retired employee. Viewing all these plans as a total retirement program can influence the choice of specific benefits and benefit levels. Thus, the existence of significant amounts of postretirement life insurance might suggest that, except for legally required joint and survivor protection, the normal payment of retirement benefits exclude any form of death benefit, such as a guarantee that benefits will be paid for a minimum period of time; otherwise, excessive or redundant postretirement death benefits might be provided.

The same approach can be applied to the events of preretirement death and disability. In the event of preretirement death, the primary plan is the employer's group life insurance plan. However, additional death benefits may be provided by way of continuation of medical expense coverage for the employee's dependents and, in certain cases, the retirement plan may be required to provide **preretirement survivor benefits.**[8] Social Security also can be a substantial source of survivor benefits, as can a profit sharing or savings plan. In the case of disability, a need exists to coordinate the benefits available from the employer's plan (life insurance, short- and long-term disability income plans, savings and profit sharing plans, and medical expense plans) with those available from Social Security and other statutory plans. Again, efficient plan design suggests the benefits from all these sources be coordinated to ensure overall benefits are in line with employer objectives.

Income-Replacement Ratios

Employer objectives as to **income-replacement ratios** are critical in the design of disability income and retirement plans.

In the case of disability income plans, the issues are not as complex. The benefit usually is not service related (although some plans are), and it is generally designed to replace a percentage of current pay. There are no restrictions on the ability of a plan to integrate with Social Security benefits, and it is customary to offset 100 percent of the employee's primary Social Security disability benefit. In fact, most plans offset 100 percent of the total Social Security benefit payable, including family benefits. In general, the plan formula recognizes that some part or all of the Social Security and plan benefits may be income tax free and that total after-tax income should provide adequate maintenance while at the same time creating an economic incentive for the employee

---

[8]The preretirement survivor benefit requirements for a qualified plan are described in Chapter 5.

to rehabilitate and return to active work. A typical formula might provide for a total, gross before-tax benefit (including Social Security) of 60 percent of current pay.

Establishing income-replacement objectives for a retirement plan is more complex. Before selecting a specific benefit formula, it is important for an employer to identify the amount of an employee's gross income to be replaced by the retirement plan and under what circumstances.

From the employee's viewpoint, it would be desirable to have a situation where total retirement income permits the full maintenance of the standard of living the employee enjoyed just prior to retirement. For most employees, some part of this income consists of Social Security benefits. Indeed, for employees at lower income levels, a substantial portion of a preretirement gross income will be replaced by Social Security benefits. For example, the replacement ratios, defined as Social Security benefits relative to gross pay, exceed 70 percent for an individual whose final pay is $10,000. At a final pay level of $30,000, Social Security can replace over 30 percent. Even at $50,000, the replacement ratio is over 25 percent. As discussed later, the after-tax replacement ratios are even more significant.

An employee's personal savings, including equity in a home, also can be a source of retirement income. Also, many employers maintain supplemental profit sharing and savings plans that can be a source of additional income. In the absence of any such plan, however, it must be recognized that many individuals will not be able to save meaningful amounts of money to assist in meeting their retirement needs.

Another factor that should be considered in setting income-replacement ratios is that some reduction in gross income can take place without causing a significant reduction in a retiree's standard of living. Tax considerations are one reason why this is so. First, a retired employee is no longer paying a Social Security tax (unless he or she is in receipt of earned income). Moreover, Social Security benefits are income tax free for many individuals.[9] In addition, the standard deduction for federal taxes is increased for individuals age 65 or over. For example, the standard deduction for an unmarried taxpayer who is not a surviving spouse and is age 65 or over is increased by an additional standard deduction of $1,100. For a married taxpayer who is age 65 or over, the additional standard deduction is $900. Finally, retirement income is not subject to state or local taxes in many jurisdictions.

Another reason why some reduction in gross income can be tolerated is the removal of work-related expenses, such as commuting costs, the expense of maintaining a second car, lunch and clothing costs, and so on.[10] Also, many retired individuals no longer face the costs associated with child rearing (food, clothing, education, and the like), and many will have reduced housing costs because of the completion of mortgage payments and, in some localities, reduced real estate taxes.

---

[9]Under the Social Security amendments of 1983 and the Omnibus Budget Reconciliation Act of 1993, between 50 and 85 percent of Social Security benefits can become taxable for individuals whose income exceeds threshold amounts. For a detailed discussion of the taxation of Social Security benefits, see Appendix 1.

[10] While it is difficult to estimate work-related expenses in any definitive way, it is interesting to note that the President's Commission on Pension Policy, in its Interim Report of May 1980, estimated these expenses to be 6 percent of after-tax preretirement income.

With factors such as these in mind, most employers establish income-replacement objectives that generate something less than a 100 percent replacement of full pre-retirement gross income. Typically, these income-replacement objectives are set with several factors in mind:

1. They usually take the employee's (but not the spouse's) Social Security benefits into account.[11]

2. The objectives usually are higher for lower-paid employees than for higher-paid employees.

3. The objectives usually are set for the employee's pay level during the final year of employment or over a three- or five-year average just prior to retirement, when the employee's earnings are highest.

4. Full income-replacement objectives are set only for individuals who have completed what the employer considers to be a "career" of employment; individuals who have less than this amount of service with the employer have objectives proportionately reduced.

A few comments are appropriate for each of these points. As indicated earlier, Social Security benefits can be of great importance to individuals at lower income levels, and they take on added significance since all or a portion of the benefits may be income tax free. Further, the employer has shared in the cost of providing these Social Security benefits. Thus, even though the particular pension formula for the employer's plan may not directly reflect Social Security benefits, the accrual rates chosen can be designed to produce a net plan benefit that, when added to the employee's primary Social Security benefit, produces the desired result.

At one time, it was not uncommon for an employer to have a single income-replacement objective for employees at all pay levels. However, it was soon recognized that lower-income employees need a higher level of income replacement simply because of minimum income needs. Moreover, it was reasoned that higher-paid employees could accept lower income amounts without incurring a major reduction in living standards.

Most defined benefit plans use an employee's final average pay to determine benefit amounts. Typically, this is a five-year average, although some plans use a three-year average. It is common for employers who have such a plan to state their income-replacement objectives in terms of the pay base used in the plan. Some employers, however, actually set objectives in terms of the employee's pay in the final year of employment, with the result that the plan benefit, when expressed as a percentage of the final average pay used in the plan, is somewhat higher than the employer's actual objective. It also should be noted that employers who adopt career-pay plans or who adopt defined contribution plans often do so with final-pay

---

[11]It is not customary to take the spouse's Social Security benefit into account in setting objectives. To do so would be difficult since a direct recognition of this benefit would not be permitted by the Internal Revenue Service; to approximate its value on an across-the-board basis would result in inequity between employees who have a spouse and those who do not.

income-replacement objectives in mind. Those who use career-pay plans frequently "update" accrued career-pay benefits to reflect current pay levels and to move benefits closer to objectives. Those with defined contribution plans find it more difficult to make such adjustments but often set contribution levels so that, under reasonable expectations for salary growth and investment return, final-pay objectives might be achieved. Unfortunately, the inherent nature of defined contribution plans is such that, in most situations, these objectives will either be exceeded or not met at all.

Understandably, most employers do not feel an obligation to provide a full level of benefits to short-service employees. Thus, it is common practice to set objectives and design benefit formulas so that proportionately smaller benefits are provided for those individuals who work for an employer for less than what the employer considers to be a reasonable career. The number of years involved, of course, varies from employer to employer and reflects the nature of the employer's business and the degree of maturity it has achieved. However, career periods of from 25 to 35 years are common.

With these factors in mind, Table 2.1 sets forth a typical set of income-replacement objectives. These objectives are merely examples. What is appropriate for one employer may be inappropriate for another and, in any event, what one employer adopts as objectives necessarily reflects that employer's own philosophy and environment.

Other Objectives

The foregoing has discussed some of the major employer objectives associated with employee benefit plans. Other employer objectives also play an important role in plan design. Some of these additional objectives are discussed below.

Social Obligations

Many employers feel a strong sense of social responsibility to their employees and to society in general. The adoption of adequate and meaningful employee benefit plans is a form of meeting this responsibility.

Employee Incentives

It would be a rare employer who is not interested in improving employee productivity. Profit sharing plans and plans that involve ownership of employer securities are

TABLE 2.1
Illustrative Income-Replacement Objectives (Employee with 30 Years of Service)

Final Pay	Retirement Income as a Percentage of Final Pay*
Under $20,000	80–70%
$20,000 to $50,000	75–65
$50,000 to $75,000	70–60
$75,000 to $100,000	65–55
Over $100,000	60–50

*Including primary Social Security benefits.

plans that can create employee incentives and, as a result, improve productivity. Beyond this, employee morale is an important factor that can influence productivity. As noted earlier, the presence of employee benefit plans may not be a positive force in recruiting and retaining employees, and they may not be a positive factor in creating improved morale. However, their absence could be a negative influence and, for this reason, most employers believe a benefit program, along with other positive compensation and personnel practices, is an important factor in maintaining employee morale at a proper level.

Corporate Identification

It may be desirable to have employees identify with overall employer business objectives. This might be accomplished by having employees acquire an ownership interest in the firm. Profit sharing plans, savings plans, and employee stock ownership plans (ESOPs) can achieve this objective. By having all or part of an employee's account invested in employer securities, the employee is made aware of the company's progress and the importance of achieving satisfactory profit results. The employee also can have the opportunity to vote the shares credited to his or her account, and the employer has the additional opportunity of being able to communicate with the employee as a shareholder by sending annual reports, proxy statements, and the like.

Administrative Convenience

Generally, it is desirable that employee benefit plans be designed so that administrative involvement and cost are kept to a reasonable minimum. This objective has become especially important with increasing government regulations and requirements and as design and funding choices become greater and more complex. In this regard, employers should be aware of their own administrative capabilities, as well as those available from external sources.

Chapter Summary

- The design of original pension plans was largely influenced by the insurance industry's attitude toward underwriting, funding, and administration.

- More factors have come to influence the design of pension plans as the field has developed. Primary factors include:
  - A body of law affecting minimum requirements and permissible plan provisions.
  - Issues regarding the taxation of contributions and benefits.
  - Collective bargaining and the interests of organized labor.
  - Availability of alternate funding mechanisms.
  - Growing degree of sophistication and knowledge of the pension field.
  - Plan cost considerations.

- Given their substantial costs, their importance to millions of workers, and the complex legal, tax, and funding environment, pension plans should be designed and operated to be fully supportive of an employer's philosophy, goals, and objectives and the perceived needs of employees.

- An employer's philosophy and goals can be shaped by the environment in which it operates.

- Special objectives are established in the context of employer attitudes on matters such as:
  - Basic compensation philosophy.
  - The desired emphasis on the protection and maintenance of income.
  - Employee cost sharing.
  - Whether the employees or employer should bear the risks of inflation and investing.
  - Influencing retirement patterns.
  - Flexibility of choice.
  - Cost and funding controls.
  - Coordination of plan and statutory benefits.
  - The treatment of executives.
  - The assumption of plan termination obligations.

- Employer objectives may include:
  - Attraction and retention of employees.
  - Meeting competitive standards.
  - Cost and funding controls.
  - Legal compliance.
  - Optimizing tax benefits.
  - Efficiency of design.
  - Income-replacement ratios.
  - Social obligations.
  - Employee incentives.
  - Corporate identification.
  - Administrative convenience.

- Employers can use income-replacement ratios, particularly with defined benefit plans, to establish quantifiable objectives that can be monitored to assess plan effectiveness.

Key Terms

career-pay/final-pay
  (benefit formulas), p. *33*
compensation-oriented
  approach, p. *29*
contributory/noncontributory
  (benefit plans), p. *29*
deferred retirement, p. *30*
flexible or "cafeteria"
  benefits, p. *30*

income-maintenance
  approach, p. *29*
income-replacement
  ratios, p. *39*
nondiscrimination
  requirements, p. *31*
nonqualified supplemental
  pension arrangement,
  p. *31*

plan termination
  obligations, p. *31*
preretirement survivor
  benefits, p. *39*
target benefit plan, p. *37*

Questions for Review

1. Describe some of the environmental factors that should be considered in the pension plan design process.

2. Many employers believe employees should share in the cost of meeting their own economic security needs. This type of employee involvement in a private pension plan may take two alternative forms. Explain.

3. Describe the three techniques that may be used to establish the relative standing of various retirement plans.

4. What are some of the objectives an employer could have for matters concerning the cost of its pension plan?

5. An employer often has a choice in the manner in which compliance with legal requirements for pension plans is achieved. Give four examples of areas where compliance choices are available.

6. What are some of the plan design alternatives available to an employer who wishes to achieve maximum tax advantages for a retirement program?

7. An efficient pension plan design requires the identification of all sources of benefits for a retired employee. What plans should be considered as potential sources of benefits?

8. Why do some employers establish income-replacement objectives that generate something less than 100 percent of full preretirement gross income?

9. Identify the factors that are often considered by employers in setting income-replacement objectives.

10. Describe how retirement plans may be used to provide: (*a*) employee incentives, and (*b*) corporate identification.

Questions for Discussion

1. Assume that an employer wants to provide a reasonable combined replacement ratio (a ratio that combines both Social Security and private pension benefits in the numerator) for high-paid employees without providing an excessive replacement ratio for employees at lower income levels. Illustrate why it may be necessary for the employer to integrate the pension plan. (The mechanics of the integration procedure will be treated in Chapter 4.)

2. Provide a numerical example to explain why an executive might experience a loss of pension benefits under a final average defined benefit plan if he or she were to change jobs in midcareer.

3. The age at which unreduced Social Security retirement benefits may commence is scheduled to gradually increase from age 65 to a maximum of age 67. Assume that you are asked to give advice on how a firm's retirement benefits should be restructured as a result of this change. Discuss how your response will vary depending on the employer's objectives.

Resources for Further Study

CCH Editorial Staff. "2001 Tax Legislation: Law, Explanation and Analysis." *Commerce Clearing House Pension Plan Guide* (2001).

Dolmat-Connell, Jack. "A New Paradigm for Compensation and Benefits Competitiveness." *Compensation and Benefits Review,* September–October 1994.

Hallman, G. Victor, III. "Functional Approach to Designing and Evaluating Employee Benefits." In *The Handbook of Employee Benefits.* 5th ed. Jerry S. Rosenbloom, ed. New York: McGraw-Hill, 2001.

McDonnell, Ken; Paul Fronstin; Kelly Olsen; Pamela Ostuw; Jack Van Derhei; and Paul Yakoboski. *EBRI Databook on Employee Benefits.* 4th ed. Deborah Holmes, Lynn Miller, and Maureen Richmond, eds. Washington, DC: Employee Benefit Research Institute Education and Research Fund, 1997.

Stone, Gary K. "Risk Concepts and Employee Benefit Planning." *The Handbook of Employee Benefits.* 5th ed. Jerry S. Rosenbloom, ed. New York: McGraw-Hill, 2001.

Chapter 3

Defined Contribution versus Defined Benefit Plans

After studying this chapter you should be able to:

- Distinguish the fundamental differences between defined contribution and defined benefit plans.

- Explain the primary advantages of both defined contribution and defined benefit plans.

- Describe when employer objectives would be best served by a defined contribution or defined benefit approach.

- Discuss why certain employers have favored the defined contribution approach.

- Explain how specific federal legislation has tended to encourage the use of defined contribution plans.

- Discuss the possible effects of the 1983 Social Security amendments on retirement patterns and the secondary effects of these amendments on use of a defined benefit approach by employers.

Before discussing specific aspects of retirement plan design, it is important to recognize that an employer has two broad choices in selecting a plan to provide these benefits. One of these is the **defined benefit plan,** under which the employer provides a determinable benefit, usually related to an employee's service and/or pay. Under this approach, the employer's cost is whatever is necessary to provide the benefit specified. The second approach is the **defined contribution plan.** Here, the employer's contribution is fixed and accumulates to provide whatever amount of benefit it can purchase. Thus, an employee's benefit becomes the variable, depending upon factors such as level of contributions, age at entry, retirement age, and investment earnings (or losses). A defined contribution plan can involve a specific contribution (as in a money purchase pension plan), or it can take the form of a profit sharing, thrift or savings, or employee stock ownership plan (discussed in subsequent chapters of this text).

Although only the two polar types of pension plans are discussed in this chapter, it is important to note that in recent years some employers have adopted plans that combine the best features of both approaches. These plans, such as target benefit, cash balance, and other hybrid plans, will be best understood after the reader fully understands each of the specific features of a pension plan. Therefore, the discussion of these plans is deferred until Chapter 19.

The choice between a defined benefit and a defined contribution plan to provide or supplement retirement benefits is of great importance to employers and employees. Legislative developments in recent years have been a major factor influencing this decision. While a detailed discussion of various plan types is found in subsequent chapters of this text, it is important, at this stage, to provide an overview of the factors involved in making a choice between these two different approaches to providing retirement benefits. This chapter reviews the background and broad considerations involved, as well as the legislative activity that bears on this choice.

Background

The majority of employees covered by the private pension system in the United States today traditionally participated in defined benefit plans. There were some notable exceptions. Educational and other nonprofit institutions, for example, have historically favored defined contribution pension arrangements because of the unique tax sanctions granted them under section 403(b) of the Internal Revenue Code. Also, a number of profit-making organizations have opted for deferred profit sharing arrangements to serve as retirement plans. Nevertheless, the defined benefit approach was favored by most employers, both small and large, at least until the passage of the Employee Retirement Income Security Act of 1974 (ERISA). Since that time, however, the majority of all new plans established have been defined contribution in nature. Further, there has been a decline, in recent years, in the total number of defined benefit plans in effect. That is, the number of defined benefit plans terminated in each of these years exceeded the number of new defined benefit plans established during the same period.

This historical preference for defined benefit plans over defined contribution plans is based on many factors:

1. If an employer has specific **income-replacement objectives** in mind, these can be accommodated with a defined benefit plan. The defined contribution approach, on the other hand, may produce plan benefits that fail to meet or that exceed such objectives as they affect individual employees. This depends on a num-

ber of factors, such as length of participation, age at retirement, inflation, investment results, and the like.

2. By the same token, most employers wish to take Social Security benefits into account so that the combined level of benefits from both sources will produce desired results. Although defined contribution plans can be integrated with Social Security benefits by adjusting contribution levels, integration of benefits cannot be accomplished as efficiently as under defined benefit plans.

3. The typical defined contribution plan provides that the employee's account balance is payable in the event of death and, frequently, in case of disability. This, of course, produces additional plan costs or, alternatively, lower retirement benefits if overall costs are held constant. An employer who is interested primarily in providing retirement benefits can use available funds more efficiently for this purpose under a defined benefit plan.

4. Some think a more equitable allocation of employer contributions occurs under a defined benefit plan, since the employee's age, past service, and pay all may be taken into account. Others think just the opposite, that allocations on the basis of pay only produce fairer results. This characteristic of defined contribution plans is one of the reasons they do not lend themselves to achieving consistent income-replacement objectives. It should be noted, however, that defined contribution plans

Employer Use of Income-Replacement Objectives   1

One method of weighing the value, efficiency, and sufficiency of retirement benefits is to examine the ratio of the income from retirement benefits available to a career employee at retirement to that employee's final preretirement wages. This wage replacement ratio should guide employers in determining both the level of benefits and basic plan design features.

Having a plan without a goal means that employers can never really evaluate the effectiveness of their retirement benefits once those benefits are delivered. Wage replacement goals can provide an important beginning step for the entire retirement plan design process. By choos-

ing a wage replacement goal first, the employer can then examine a number of different plan designs to find the retirement plan that meets that goal at the lowest cost to the employer.

Source: Martha Priddy Patterson, "Retirement Benefits in 1995: KPMG's Third Annual Survey Findings," *Journal of Compensation and Benefits,* November–December 1995, pp. 19–20. Reprinted with permission from *Journal of Compensation and Benefits,* Copyright © 1995 by Warren, Gorham & Lamont, Park Square Building, 31 St. James Avenue, Boston, MA 02116-4112. 1-800-950-1211. All rights reserved.

can be structured with allocations weighted by age and service, thus achieving allocation patterns more consistent with those of defined benefit plans.

5. A defined benefit plan can be (and often is) structured to provide a benefit that is related to an employee's final pay, thus protecting the employee against the effects of preretirement inflation. Equivalent protection cannot be provided under a defined contribution plan. Thus, in a defined contribution plan, the risk of inflation is assumed by employees, who must rely primarily on investment results to increase the value of their benefits during inflationary periods.

6. This last comment raises another issue in the comparison of defined benefit plans and defined contribution plans. Investment risk and reward are assumed by the employer under the former, by employees under the latter. Risk can be minimized by use of selected investment media. Absent such protection, however, many people feel that it is inappropriate for the average employee to assume such risk with respect to a major component of his or her retirement security. It also should be noted that employees often make investment choices that are quite conservative, with the result that their investment returns do not provide them with adequate inflation protection. In recent years, many employers have initiated educational programs to inform their employees about basic investment principles, with the hope and expectation that this will make their employees better investors.

7. The incremental value from year to year of a younger employee's **accrued benefit** under a defined benefit plan is relatively small; in the typical final-pay plan, the value of accrued benefits for older employees increases each year at a relatively substantial rate. By contrast, the increase in the amount of an employee's accrued benefit (his or her account balance) attributable to employer contributions under a typical defined contribution plan stays relatively constant from year to year as a percentage of pay. One effect of this is that employees who terminate employment at younger ages will receive greater benefits under a typical defined contribution plan than under a defined benefit plan. As a result, termination benefits can be more costly under the defined contribution approach. As noted earlier, however, it is possible to design defined contribution plans with allocation patterns that are weighted for age and service. If this is done, termination benefits will more closely resemble those of a defined benefit plan.

The defined contribution approach is, of course, not without its advantages. Deferred profit sharing plans, for example, offer employers maximum flexibility in cost commitment as well as opportunities to increase employee productivity. Through the use of employer securities as a plan investment, greater employee identification with the company and its goals also can be achieved. Additionally, if the employee group covered is relatively young, the defined contribution plan is apt to have greater employee relations value than a defined benefit plan. Another possible advantage of the defined contribution plan (unless it is a money purchase plan) is that employee contributions can be made on a **before-tax basis** under Section 401(k); defined benefit plans permit employee contributions only on an **after-tax basis**.

Model Raises Concern on Adequacy of Retirement Income   2

A rapidly growing public policy concern facing the United States is whether future generations of retired Americans, particularly those in the "baby boom" generation, will have adequate retirement income. One reason is that Social Security's projected long-term financial shortfall could result in a reduction in the current-law benefit promises made to future generations of retirees. Another reason is that many baby boomers will be retiring with employment-based defined contribution (DC) plans, as opposed to the "traditional" defined benefit (DB) plans that historically have been the predominant source of employer-provided retirement income.

These factors are likely to reduce the amount of life annuity benefits that future retirees will receive relative to current retirees, raising questions as to whether other sources of retirement income—such as individual account plans (DC plans and individual retirement accounts, or IRAs)—will make up the difference.

The Employee Benefit Research Institute developed a model to project retirement income. Under the model's baseline assumptions, both males and females are found to have an appreciable drop in the percentage of private retirement income

that is attributable to defined benefit plans (other than cash balance plans). In addition, results show a clear increase in the income retirees will receive that will have to be managed by the retiree. This makes the risk of longevity more central to retirees' expenditure decisions.

The implications of these model results for retirees are significant. First, individuals—rather than the pension plan sponsor—increasingly will have to manage their retirement assets and bear the risk of investment losses. Second, since most retirees' non–Social Security retirement income will be distributed as a lump sum or in periodic payments (from a defined contribution plan or IRA) rather than as a regular paycheck for life (from a defined benefit plan), retirees will need either to purchase an annuity from an insurance company or carefully manage their individual rate of spending in order to avoid outliving their assets.

Source: "The Changing Face of Private Retirement Plans," Employee Benefit Research Institute issue brief no. 232, April 2001, Executive Summary. Reprinted with permission of the Employee Benefit Research Institute, © 2001 Employee Benefit Research Institute. All rights reserved.

Another factor to consider concerns the cost of plan administration. At one time, it was thought that defined contribution plans produced higher administrative costs because of the individual account record keeping required and because of the many transactions (e.g., loans, withdrawals, investment changes) that could take place. However, legislative activity, particularly the plan termination insurance provisions of the law, have caused the administrative cost of defined benefit plans to increase to the point where they may, indeed, be more expensive to administer than typical defined contribution plans. **Plan termination insurance premiums,** for example, are currently at a minimum of $19 per year per participant (including retirees and vested terminated participants) and could be much higher depending on the plan's unfunded liabilities. In addition, the defined benefit plan has annual actuarial fees along with expenses associated with maintaining employee records, processing benefit payments, and so forth.

Legislative Factors

Despite the advantages noted, since the passage of ERISA, a defined benefit plan now exposes an employer to significant financial liability if the plan is terminated when there are unfunded liabilities for vested benefits. An employer's net worth is subject to a lien in favor of the **Pension Benefit Guaranty Corporation (PBGC)** if necessary to meet any liabilities assumed by the PBGC in this event (the specifics of the employer's liability are discussed in Chapter 16). The problems of potential employer liabilities were exacerbated by the Multiemployer Pension Plan Amendments Act of 1980, which created substantial liabilities for an employer who wishes to or who must withdraw from a multiemployer plan that has **unfunded vested liabilities.** Here, the employer is liable for its share of unfunded vested liabilities (generally on the basis of the ratio of the employer's contributions to total contributions).

The vast majority of employees who are not covered by a private retirement program work for smaller companies. Clearly, these small employers, as well as newly formed companies, are apt to be reluctant to adopt a defined benefit plan and take on the potential liabilities that are imposed by ERISA. Many such employers will find the defined contribution alternative, which has no such liabilities, to be a more palatable approach—despite the possible advantages offered by a defined benefit arrangement.

In addition to the plan termination provisions of ERISA, which implicitly but significantly encourage the use of defined contribution plans, it is important to note that the federal government—knowingly or unknowingly—has emphasized the defined contribution approach in many other ways. For example,

1. Long-standing provisions of the Internal Revenue Code (IRC) permit and encourage the use of **tax-deferred annuities** (discussed in Chapter 12) for employees of educational and other nonprofit organizations.

2. The basic structure of the IRC, as it is applied to HR 10 or Keogh plans for the self-employed, is strongly oriented toward defined contribution plans. Even though amended to specifically sanction defined benefit plans, the defined contribution approach has proven to be the simplest and easiest way to take advantage of this law. Indeed, almost all such plans have used the defined contribution approach. The parity provisions of the Tax Equity and Fiscal Responsibility Act of 1982 (TEFRA) eliminated most of the distinctions in tax law that formerly applied to different organizations. However, precedents established by prior practice and prior law may still continue to influence plan design for unincorporated organizations.

3. The individual retirement arrangement (IRA) concept (described in Chapter 17) is totally a defined contribution approach.

4. Beginning in 1979, employers were permitted to adopt a **simplified employee pension (SEP).** A SEP uses the IRA concept but has higher contribution limits than an IRA and considerably less paperwork than a conventional retirement plan. Again, the defined contribution approach is mandatory. Similarly, the Small Business Job Protection Act of 1996 instituted savings incentive match plans for employees (SIMPLE plans) for small employers with 100 or fewer employees. SIMPLE plans can be structured either as IRAs or 401(k) plans—again, the defined contribution approach is mandatory. Enhancements made by the Economic Growth and Tax Relief Reconciliation Act of 2001 (EGTRRA) such as a new provision allowing 401(k) and 403(b) plans to incorporate a feature called a "qualified Roth contribution program" to these types of plans increase the appeal of these types of defined contribution plans.

5. **Employee stock ownership plans (ESOPs),** also defined contribution plans, have been the subject of special legislation. As described in Chapter 10, such plans, unlike defined benefit plans, can be instrumental in corporate debt financing. In addition, ESOPs have been the subject of special interest legislation—witness, for example, the Regional Rail Reorganization Act of 1973, the Foreign Trade Act of 1974, the Chrysler Corporation Loan Guarantee Act of 1979, the Small Business Employee Ownership Act of 1980, and the Tax Reform Act of 1986.

6. The Revenue Act of 1978 added **Section 125** to the **IRC.** This section permits the adoption of cafeteria or flexible benefit plans and provides that an employee can choose between taxable and nontaxable compensation elements without problems of constructive receipt if certain conditions are met. One of these conditions is that deferred compensation plans cannot be one of the choices. However, this section has since been amended to allow the inclusion of profitsharing and stock bonus plans that meet the requirements of Section 401(k) of the IRC (described in Chapter 11). Thus, a flexible compensation plan can permit an employee to choose among welfare benefits (e.g., life insurance, disability income, medical expense), cash, deferred profitsharing, or savings plan benefits. This legislation further encourages the defined contribution approach. This area is particularly significant since interest in flexible compensation plans is increasing and these plans have become a major factor in the employee benefit planning process.

Some pressures could develop to expand flexible compensation legislation to include defined benefit pension plans. If this does occur, it is still likely that the emphasis on defined contribution plans will remain because there are very real problems involved in trading defined benefits (particularly if they are pay related) for current cash or welfare contributions. It is possible to do this, but it is necessary to resolve issues of equity and the relative value of choices. In many cases, it would be easier to limit employee elections of how available dollars can be used—for example, to a choice of purchasing current benefits or deferring these dollars under some type of defined contribution program. Indeed, it might be said that flexible compensation plans often apply the defined contribution concept to an employer's entire benefit program.

7. Closely related to flexible compensation plans are the Section 401(k) cash/deferred profitsharing or savings plans. A key feature of these plans is that they permit the use of salary reduction arrangements—an approach that can be highly tax

effective and that has captured the interest of many employers. Consequently, the growth of 401(k) plans in recent years has been dramatic. Employers who do not have pension plans may find the combination of tax savings for employees and the possible lesser financial obligations of the defined contribution approach to be an attractive way of establishing a retirement program. This could be particularly true when integrated with an overall flexible compensation program.

8. The plan termination and funding requirements imposed on defined benefit plans by the Omnibus Budget Reconciliation Act of 1987 and strengthened in 1994 by the General Agreement on Tariffs and Trade (GATT) may foster an even higher level of interest in the relatively unrestricted defined contribution approach.

9. Defined benefit and money purchase pension plans must include both **pre- and postretirement joint and survivor benefits** for the benefit of the employee's spouse. These provisions are complex, and their administration can be cumbersome. By contrast, other defined contribution plans need not include these joint and survivor provisions if the plan provides that the employee's spouse is the beneficiary for 100 percent of the employee's account balance if the employee does not elect an annuity distribution from the plan, and all or any portion of the participant's account balance has not been transferred from a plan subject to the joint and survivor rules. These, and other requirements applicable to defined benefit plans (e.g., the anti-cutback rules), have made the design and administration of defined benefit plans much more complex than is the case for defined contribution plans.

Other Factors

Other legislation also may have an indirect effect that will encourage the growth of defined contribution plans. Some of the changes made by the 1983 Social Security amendments are a good example of how indirect legislation can affect the design of private retirement plans.

These amendments gradually change the normal retirement age for Social Security benefits from 65 to 67. While the earliest age for claiming Social Security retirement benefits has not increased beyond age 62, the reduction for early benefit commencement will be gradually increased as the normal retirement age increases. Moreover, workers will have an additional incentive to remain in the workforce beyond age 65, since delayed retirement credits have been increased and the earnings test has been liberalized (see Appendix 1: "Social Security and Medicare" for details).

These changes could affect the planning process associated with defined benefit plans. Most of these plans are designed to produce a specific amount of replacement income, together with primary Social Security benefits, when an employee reaches age 65. The actual income-replacement objectives may vary, but they usually reflect the employee's pay level and length of service. While replacement ratios generally are expressed in terms of before-tax income, they are often consciously set with reference to their after-tax value.

The fundamental concept of this planning process revolves around the coordination of two income sources—the private plan and Social Security—usually occurring around the time of the employee's 65th birthday. However, the idea that 65 is the typical retirement age has already begun to diffuse with recent trends toward early retirement. This diffusion will become even greater as the Social Security normal retirement age is changed, especially since mandatory retirement is no longer legal. What may emerge is a concept that retirement age will become highly subjective for each employee. Actual retirement age may range over a span that begins when employees are in their late 50s and extends until employees reach their early 70s. If retirement becomes spread over such a wide range, it will become increasingly difficult to maintain a plan design structure that is predicated on the majority of employees retiring at age 65 and the coordination of two income sources at this point. Thus, one of the broad but important implications facing employers is the potential need to rethink their approach to plan design and the basic delivery of retirement benefits. Nonintegrated plans and a greater use of defined contribution plans are examples of approaches that might be considered. These approaches allow an employer to opt for cost control in lieu of finely tuned benefit levels.

A mandatory private retirement system in the United States is still a long way off—if, indeed, it ever becomes a reality. Yet the possibility exists that such a system will become law. The last time this issue was studied was in 1981. At that time, a Presidential Commission on Pension Policy recommended that a mandatory minimum pension system be established. More specifically, the commission recommended that this program be in the form of a defined contribution plan. While the commission did not divulge all of its reasoning in support of this defined contribution recommendation, it is likely that it was perceived as the simplest and most acceptable way of moving into a mandatory system. A mandatory defined benefit program would present a host of issues concerning pay-related benefits, the recognition of prior service, and the imposition of related liabilities.

The prospects of a mandatory private pension system are not clear at this time. Movement in this direction during the next few years is quite unlikely, although the issue may very well be revived as efforts are made to revise the Social Security system—particularly if Social Security is changed to allow employees to divert part of their taxes into individual savings accounts. This concept could be easily expanded to accommodate some type of employer contribution (over and above the employer's share of Federal Insurance Contributions Act [FICA] taxes) made under a mandatory defined contribution plan.

The Future

Despite all the foregoing, defined benefit plans are still a significant part of the private pension system. They are firmly entrenched in major companies and in plans covered by collective bargaining agreements. It is unlikely that many of these plans will be shifted—at least completely—to defined contribution plans. Some employers, for example, might opt to use a hybrid plan, such as a target benefit plan, that attempts to achieve a mix of the perceived advantages of both the defined benefit and defined contribution approaches. What also might happen is that employers with defined benefit plans will hold them at current levels, opting to make benefit improvements via some

Proposals to Privatize a Portion of Social Security

3

A White House Commission offered three options for overhauling the Social Security fund, which experts say will be exhausted by 2038 unless it is revamped.

The three proposals—which the White House wants Congress and the public to debate next year and to vote on in 2003—hinge on the creation of limited private investment accounts "that would permit participants to build substantial wealth and receive higher expected benefits than those paid to today's retirees," the draft report said.

Under the first model, American workers could put 2 percent of their payroll taxes into a personal account. In the second, workers could voluntarily contribute 4 percent of their payroll taxes up to $1,000 to a personal account. The third recommends creating a government match of 2.5 percent of the payroll tax up to $1,000 annually for workers who contribute an additional 1 percent of their wages subject to Social Security payroll taxes.

Regardless of the model that is adopted, the commission recommended a two-tier administrative approach that would ultimately result in private management of the accounts.

In the first stage, workers would choose from a range of funds already offered by the federal government's retirement savings program—the Thrift Savings Plan—plus four additional funds. When workers have accumulated a certain minimum account balance, the commission recommended that they be allowed to move their personal accounts in a second level of "qualified private-sector funds."

This is where the financial services industry would play the largest role, but it would have to adhere to strict rules put in place by a Social Security governing board.

Source: Michele Heller, "Social Security Panel Details Options," *American Banker,* December 12, 2001, p. 4. Reprinted with permission of *American Banker,* © Copyright 2001 American Banker. All rights reserved.

kind of supplemental defined contribution arrangement (e.g., a salary reduction, Section 401(k) savings plan). For employers who do not yet have a pension plan, there has already been and is likely to be greater use of one form or another of the defined contribution approaches referred to in this chapter. IRAs, ESOPs, SEPs, SIMPLE plans, flexible compensation plans, and Section 401(k) plans are all attractive and viable programs to consider. While defined benefit plans will remain a major component in the United States private pension system, the defined contribution plan has to taken on a more significant role. This role is likely to become greater in the years ahead.

Chapter Summary

- An employer has two broad choices in selecting a plan to provide pension benefits:
  - A *defined benefit plan,* under which the employer provides a determinable benefit, usually related to an employee's service and/or pay.

- A *defined contribution plan,* where the employer's contribution is fixed and this contribution is accumulated to provide whatever amount of benefit it can purchase upon the employee's retirement.

• In recent years, some employers have adopted pension plans that combine the best features of both defined benefit and defined contribution approaches. These hybrid plans include cash balance and target benefit plans.

• Traditionally, defined benefit plans have covered the vast majority of employees. Employers creating new plans today tend to prefer defined contribution approaches. Defined benefit and defined contribution plan designs each involve distinct advantages.

• Investment risk and reward are assumed by the employer under a defined benefit plan and by employees under a defined contribution plan.

• Legislative factors have been important determinants impacting the growth of defined benefit and defined contribution plan designs. Since the passage of ERISA, extensive pension legislation has shaped employer preferences for distinct plan designs in many direct and indirect ways.

• Other factors, such as modification of the Social Security system (another component of the "tripod of economic security"), have affected and will continue to affect the design of private pension plans. Recent proposals to privatize a portion of Social Security, if enacted, would constitute an important environmental change impacting pension plan design preferences.

Key Terms

accrued benefit, p. *50*
after-tax basis, p. *50*
before-tax basis, p. *50*
defined benefit plan, p. *47*
defined contribution
    plan, p. *47*
employee stock ownership
    plans (ESOPs), p. *53*
income-replacement
    objectives, p. *48*

Pension Benefit Guaranty
    Corporation (PBGC),
    p. *52*
plan termination insurance
    premiums, p. *51*
pre- and postretirement
    joint and survivor
    benefits, p. *54*

Section 125 of the Internal
    Revenue Code (IRC),
    p. *53*
simplified employee
    pension (SEP), p. *53*
tax-deferred annuities, p. *52*
unfunded vested
    liabilities, p. *52*

Questions for Review

1. Describe the factors that will determine an employee's retirement benefit under the defined contribution approach.
2. Explain the primary advantages of a defined benefit plan.
3. Explain the primary advantages of a defined contribution plan.
4. Explain the ways in which the federal government has encouraged the defined contribution approach.
5. Explain how the 1983 Social Security amendments might affect use of the defined benefit approach.

Questions for Discussion

1. The text states that in the view of some, a more equitable allocation of employer contributions occurs under a defined benefit plan than under a defined contribution plan. Assume that a participant in a defined benefit pension plan, age 25, is currently paid $15,000 per year and he or she will retire at age 65. At that time, he or she will receive a pension benefit equal to 1 percent of his or her average salary in the last five years, times years of service. Compute the present value of the pension benefit accrued from working an additional year, as a percentage of the participant's compensation, at ages 30, 35, 40, 45, 50, 55, 60, and 64. Perform the calculations under two sets of assumptions: (*a*) the participant has no wage growth and the discount rate is 3 percent; and (*b*) the participant's wage growth is 7 percent and the discount rate is 10 percent. Graph the change in the present value of accrued benefits from an additional year's work (expressed as a percentage of compensation) against the participant's age under both scenarios. What conclusions can you draw about the allocation of employer contributions under defined benefit plans? (Notice that the discount rate exceeds the wage growth by 3 percent under both scenarios.)

2. Prepare a graph similar to the ones created in the preceding question for an employee participating in a defined contribution plan providing a contribution of 6 percent of compensation, and compare your results with the previous graphs. What conclusions can you draw about the allocation of employer contributions under a defined contribution plan vis-à-vis those of a defined benefit plan? What implications do these conclusions present for the retention of older employees?

3. Assume that you are an employee, age 25, and you are given your choice of participating either in the defined benefit plan described in Question 1 or the defined contribution plan described in Question 2. Which one would you prefer? Describe how you made the evaluation and any assumptions required.

Resources for Further Study

Allen, Everett T., Jr. "Retirement Plan Design." *The Handbook of Employee Benefits.* 5th ed. Jerry S. Rosenbloom, ed. New York: McGraw-Hill, 2001.

CCH Editorial Staff. "2001 Tax Legislation: Law, Explanation, and Analysis." *Commerce Clearing House Pension Plan Guide* (2001).

McDonnell, Ken; Paul Fronstin; Kelly Olsen; Pamela Ostuw; Jack Van Derhei; and Paul Yakoboski. *EBRI Databook on Employee Benefits.* 4th ed. Deborah Holmes, Lynn Miller, and Maureen Richmond, eds. Washington, DC: Employee Benefit Research Institute Education and Research Fund, 1997.

Perdue, Pamela D. "Going, Going, Gone: The Continuing Decline of the Traditional Defined Benefit Plan." *Journal of Pension Planning & Compliance* 26, no. 4 (Winter 2001).

Salisbury, Dallas L. "The Future of Employee Benefit Plans." *The Handbook of Employee Benefits.* 5th ed. Jerry S. Rosenbloom, ed. New York: McGraw-Hill, 2001.

Summary of Comments on Defined Benefit Plan Received by the PBGC Defined Benefit Working Group, July 14, 1998.—www.pbgc.gov/findings.htm—website of the Pension Benefit Guaranty Corporation.

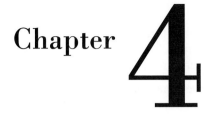

Chapter 4

Tax Qualification Requirements

After studying this chapter you should be able to:

- Summarize the various requirements for a plan to be qualified under the Internal Revenue Code (IRC).

- Determine which plan participants are highly compensated employees.

- Explain the concepts of nondiversion, exclusive benefit, and plan permanency.

- Distinguish between the alternate methods that may be used to satisfy the minimum coverage tests.

- Describe the process involved in the safe and unsafe harbor tests.

- Explain the alternate methods and limitations for integrating a plan with Social Security.

- Explain the remaining tests to comply with the Section 401(a)(4) nondiscrimination requirements.

While an employer may choose to use a nonqualified approach to providing retirement benefits for certain highly paid employees, the requirements of the law are such that a qualified plan is the only tax-effective way to provide these benefits for a large group of employees. Moreover, the tax advantages provided under the Internal Revenue Code (IRC) for qualified plans are most significant—both to the employer and its employees. The principal tax advantages of such plans are as follows:

- Contributions made by the employer, within the limitations prescribed, are deductible as a business expense.

- Investment income on these contributions normally is not subject to federal income tax until paid in the form of benefits.

- An employee is not considered to be in receipt of taxable income until benefits are distributed—even though the employee may be fully vested and even though the employee has the right to receive the amounts involved without restriction.[1]

To obtain these tax benefits, the plan must achieve a qualified status by meeting the requirements of the IRC and appropriate regulations and rulings issued by the Internal Revenue Service (IRS). Many of these provisions are quite complex, and a detailed review of these requirements is beyond the scope of this text.[2] The purpose of this chapter and Chapter 5 is only to provide an overview of these requirements and to give the reader a sense of the general concepts involved. This chapter covers nondiscrimination requirements relating to coverage, benefits and contributions, and other rights and features. Other tax law requirements are discussed in Chapter 5.

Summary of Major Tax Law Provisions

To achieve a tax-qualified status, a plan must conform with the provisions of Section 401(a) and related sections of the IRC. The following is a brief summary of the requirements that must be met in order for a plan to be qualified under the IRC:

- The plan must be created and maintained exclusively for the benefit of employees and their beneficiaries.

- Plan assets cannot be diverted or used other than for the exclusive benefit of employees and their beneficiaries prior to the satisfaction of all plan liabilities.

- Plan coverage must not discriminate in favor of highly compensated employees.

- Defined benefit plans must cover a specified minimum number of employees.

- The plan must not discriminate in favor of highly compensated employees in terms of contributions, benefits, rights, or other features; within limits, however, a plan may integrate its benefits with those of Social Security, thus providing a measure of additional benefits for the highly compensated.

- Limits are imposed on the amount of benefits paid to an employee and/or annual additions made to his or her account, and on the amount of contributions an employee may make on a before-tax basis (elective contributions).

- Employee compensation in excess of a stipulated amount cannot be taken into account for plan purposes.

- Age and service requirements for participation in the plan cannot be more stringent than specified minimums.

---

[1] Until the year 1999 (and thereafter for individuals born before January 1, 1936), certain lump-sum distributions also may qualify for favorable tax treatment.

[2] For a comprehensive discussion of nondiscrimination requirements, see James G. Durfee et al., *A Guide to the Final Nondiscrimination Requirements* (New York: Research Institute of America, January 1994).

- An employee's service must be determined in accordance with specific rules.

- Benefits must vest after an employee completes the prescribed period of service.

- Special vesting and benefit requirements apply to top-heavy plans—those that benefit key employees to a significant extent.

- Distributions must be made according to rules that specify the time by which payments must commence and the period over which they may be paid.

- Qualified joint and survivor annuity (QJSA) rules and qualified preretirement survivor annuity (QPSA) rules must be met for married employees.

- There are limits on the assignment or alienation of benefits other than pursuant to qualified domestic relations orders (QDROs).

- Accrued benefits, to the extent funded, must be protected in case of a plan merger or consolidation or a transfer of plan assets.

- Individual accounts must be maintained for participants under defined contribution plans.

Most of these requirements are discussed in this chapter and Chapter 5. It should be noted, however, that there are still other requirements that apply to specific types of plans—for example, profit sharing and employee stock ownership plans (ESOPs). Additional requirements also apply to plans that include cash or deferred arrangements (CODAs) and plans that include matching employer contributions or after-tax employee contributions. Requirements for these plans are discussed separately in Chapters 7 through 12.

Key Concepts

There are a number of key concepts that must be understood before proceeding to a discussion of specific qualification requirements. These involve the definitions of "compensation" and "highly compensated employees," and the concepts of "controlled groups" and "qualified separate lines of business."

Compensation

Compensation generally determines the amount of an employee's benefits or contributions under a plan. For this purpose, an employer can use any definition of compensation it chooses, provided the definition does not discriminate in favor of highly compensated employees. Thus, for example, a plan definition that uses base pay only would generally be acceptable, while a definition that is limited to base pay plus bonuses would probably be found to be discriminatory since, in most situations, only the highly paid receive bonuses.

Quite apart from what the plan might use as its definition of compensation, the IRC has specific definitions that must be used for limiting benefits and/or contributions and for nondiscrimination testing.

Section 415 Compensation

IRC Section 415 limits the amount of benefits that can be paid to an individual employee under a defined benefit plan and the annual additions that can be made to an employee's account under a defined contribution plan.[3] Limits for both types of plans are restricted to the lesser of a dollar amount or a percentage of compensation. In general, compensation used for purposes of these limits is W-2 compensation less income realized from the exercise of a nonqualified stock option or when restricted stock either becomes freely transferrable or is no longer subject to substantial risk of forfeiture, or from the sale of stock acquired under a qualified stock option or the disqualifying disposition of an incentive stock option. After 1997, Section 415 compensation includes salary reductions under flexible benefit plans, a qualified transportation fringe benefit plan, and elective deferrals under CODAs, simplified employee pension arrangements, savings incentive match plans for employees (SIMPLE plans), and tax-sheltered annuities.

Definition of Highly Compensated Employee

For this purpose, the IRC defines compensation as that used for Section 415 purposes inclusive of salary reductions under flexible benefit plans, a qualified transportation fringe benefit plan, and elective deferrals under CODAs, simplified employee pension plans (SEPs), savings incentive match plans for employees (SIMPLE plans), and tax-sheltered annuities. (Although these items were included in Section 415 compensation beginning in 1998, they were not previously part of this compensation definition.)

Nondiscrimination Testing

The basic **definition of compensation** used for purposes of nondiscrimination testing relates back to the Section 415 definition. An employer can select from among four definitions that are automatically deemed to meet the Section 415 definition. These four safe harbors are:

Traditional 415 Compensation. This is the basic Section 415 definition described above.

Modified 415 Compensation. This is sometimes referred to as the short list definition because it includes only some of the items included in the traditional definition. For example, deductible moving expenses are not included.

W-2 Wages. This is the amount reported in Box 1 on Form W-2.

Wages Subject to Withholding. This is compensation on which an employer must withhold federal income tax.

Employers may modify the four safe harbor definitions for nondiscrimination testing to include or exclude certain elements of compensation. Items that could be included for years prior to 1998 were elective deferrals under CODAs and tax-sheltered annuities and salary reductions under flexible benefits plans. Items that now may be excluded are expense reimbursements or allowances, cash or *noncash fringe benefits,* moving expenses, deferred compensation, and welfare benefits.

---

[3] These limits are discussed at greater length in Chapter 5.

An employer also can use an alternative definition of compensation for nondiscrimination testing if it meets three criteria: (1) it must be reasonable; (2) it must not, by design, favor highly compensated employees; and (3) it must meet an objective nondiscrimination test. This test is satisfied if the ratio of the alternative definition of compensation to total compensation for the highly paid group does not exceed, by more than a *de minimis* amount, the same ratio for the lower-paid employees.

Highly Compensated Employee (HCE)

For years prior to 1997, the tax law contained extremely complicated provisions defining who was to be considered a **highly compensated employee (HCE)** for purposes of various nondiscrimination requirements. These provisions were greatly simplified by the Small Business Job Protection Act of 1996. In 2002, an employee is deemed a highly compensated employee if he or she (1) is a 5 percent owner of the employer during the current or preceding year, or (2) had compensation in the preceding year of $90,000 (indexed for inflation) and (at the election of the employer) was in the top 20 percent of employees in terms of compensation for that year.

If the employer makes this election, the determination of who falls into the top 20 percent of employees is a two-step process. The first step is determining how many employees constitute 20 percent. In making this determination, employers may exclude employees who have not completed six months of service or who have not attained age 21 by year-end, and employees who normally work less than 17½ hours per week or less than six months during any year. Nonresident aliens who have no U.S.-source income also may be excluded as well as employees included in a collective bargaining agreement that does not provide for participation in the plan (but only if 90 percent or more of all employees of the company are covered under such an agreement).

The next step is identifying the specific members of the top 20 percent. To do this, the employer must subtract excludable employees (except for union employees) and then multiply the remaining number by 20 percent. The excluded employees are then added back in to determine which specific employees are in the top-paid group.

Some key points to keep in mind when determining who is an HCE include the following:

- The compensation used must meet the definition set forth in the preceding section.

- The $90,000 dollar amount is adjusted for increases in the consumer price index (CPI); after the new dollar amount is determined, it is rounded down to the next lower multiple of $5,000.

- Family aggregation rules ceased to apply when determining who was an HCE, beginning in 1997.

- The determination of HCEs is made on a "controlled group" basis, as described in the following section.

Controlled Groups

The nondiscrimination requirements of the IRC could be easily circumvented if employers were given complete flexibility in splitting employees among a number of subsidiaries. For example, one subsidiary could contain all the HCEs and cover the entire group while the second subsidiary could contain the vast majority of non-highly compensated employees (NHCEs) and provide no coverage at all. If the subsidiaries could be tested separately, the plan of the subsidiary covering the HCEs would be acceptable since it would exclude no one and would provide benefits that do not discriminate within the group covered.

To eliminate this potential for abuse, the IRC provides that, for nondiscrimination purposes, employees of all corporations who are members of a controlled group of corporations are to be treated as if they were employees of a single employer.

The most common **controlled group** consists of a parent and subsidiary, where one entity owns at least 80 percent of the other entity. A second type is the brother–sister controlled group, where five or fewer "persons" (individuals, estates, or trusts) own (1) at least 80 percent of the entities being examined, and (2) more than 50 percent of the entities being examined, taking into account "identical interests" only (an identical interest meaning the lowest level of ownership he or she has in the entities being examined).

Two or more entities also may be treated as a single entity if they are deemed to be an affiliated service group. However, these rules apply only to service organizations and organizations performing management functions for one organization (or a group of related organizations). The affiliated service group rules look at a combination of very low ownership interests and services between entities.

Qualified Separate Lines of Business (QSLOBs)

The controlled group rules can result in the aggregation of employee groups for qualification testing purposes that would otherwise be considered separate. However, an employer may be able to test a plan in a controlled group separately if it can show that the employees covered by the plan are in a **qualified separate line of business (QSLOB).** These rules are designed to allow employers to structure benefit programs to meet the competitive needs of separate business operations or operating units in separate geographic locations.

The QSLOB regulations issued by the IRS establish stringent requirements that make it difficult for most employers to establish separate lines for testing purposes. In brief, employers must:

- Identify their lines of business.

- Establish that the lines are separate—that is, formally organized as separate units with separate profit centers and separate profit and loss reporting, separate workforces, and separate management.

- Demonstrate that the separate lines are qualified.

- Allocate each employee to a qualified separate line.

- Test plans covering employees of separate lines: first, under the nondiscriminatory classification test on a controlled group basis, and then again under the coverage and nondiscrimination rules on a QSLOB basis.

Tax Qualification Requirements

With the foregoing concepts in mind, the following section discusses the major requirements a plan must meet if it is to achieve and maintain a tax-qualified status.

Nondiversion/Exclusive Benefit Requirements

The plan must specifically provide that it is impossible for the employer to divert or recapture contributions before the satisfaction of all plan liabilities. With certain exceptions, funds contributed must be used for the **exclusive benefit** of employees or their beneficiaries. One exception to this rule may occur at termination of a pension plan when, after all fixed and contingent obligations of the plan have been satisfied, funds remain because of "actuarial error." In this event, such excess funds may be returned to the employer. A second exception makes it possible to establish or amend a plan on a conditional basis so that employer contributions are returnable within one year from the denial of qualification if the plan is not approved by the IRS. It is also possible for an employer to make a contribution on the basis that it will be allowed as a deduction; if this is done, the contribution, to the extent disallowed, may be returned within one year from the disallowance. Further, contributions made on the basis of a mistake in fact can be returned to the employer within one year from the time they were made.

Permanency

The plan must be a **permanent** one. While the employer may reserve the right to amend or terminate the plan at any time, it is expected that the plan will be established on a permanent basis. Thus, if a plan is terminated for any reason other than business necessity within a few years after it is established, this will be considered as evidence that the plan, from its inception, was not a bona fide plan designed for the benefit of employees. This, of course, could result in adverse tax consequences.

In the profit sharing area, it is not necessary that the employer make contributions in accordance with a definite predetermined formula. However, merely making a single or an occasional contribution will not be sufficient to create a permanent and continuing plan. The regulations require that "substantial and recurring" contributions be made when a predetermined contribution formula is not used.

Nondiscrimination in Coverage

A qualified plan must meet specific nondiscriminatory requirements as to employees covered under the plan. This requirement is set forth in Section 410(b) of the IRC, and the tests required by this section often are called the "410(b)" or **coverage tests.** A plan will be considered nondiscriminatory as to coverage if it meets one of the following two tests: (1) the ratio percentage test or (2) the average benefit test.

Ratio Percentage Test

To perform this test, the employer must divide its universe of employees into two groups—HCEs and NHCEs. In doing this, certain employees may be excluded—for example, those who have not met the plan's minimum age and service requirements, certain nonresident aliens, and so forth. The percentage of HCEs benefiting under the plan is then determined by dividing the HCEs who are benefiting by the total number of HCEs in the controlled group. The same procedure is followed for NHCEs. The plan will pass the **ratio percentage test** if the percentage of NHCEs benefiting under the plan is at least 70 percent of the percentage of HCEs who so benefit.

Average Benefit Test

If a plan fails to pass the ratio percentage test, it must pass the **average benefit test.** This test has two parts: the nondiscriminatory classification test and the average benefit percentage test.

Nondiscriminatory Classification Test   To meet the **nondiscriminatory classification test,** a plan must cover a classification of employees that is reasonable and nondiscriminatory under an objective test. To be reasonable, the classification must be established under objective business criteria that identify the category of employees who benefit under the plan—for example, a classification of salaried or hourly employees only. The objective test works like the ratio percentage test described above, but it uses different percentages. The regulations specify both safe and unsafe harbors. A plan is in the safe harbor if the percentage of NHCEs who benefit is at least 50 percent of the percentage of HCEs who benefit. A plan is in the unsafe harbor if the percentage of NHCEs who benefit is 40 percent or less of the percentage of HCEs who benefit. A plan that lies somewhere in between will be subject to a facts and circumstances test. Both the safe and unsafe harbor percentages are reduced if NHCEs make up more than 60 percent of the employer's workforce. The safe and unsafe harbor percentages are shown in Table 4.1. To select the safe and unsafe harbor percentages, first compute the NHCE concentration percentage by dividing the number of NHCEs by the total number of employees.

Average Benefit Percentage Test   Once a plan has satisfied the classification test, it then must satisfy the **average benefit percentage (ABP) test.** This part of the average benefit test is satisfied if the average benefit percentage (ABP) for NHCEs (determined as described below) is at least 70 percent of the ABP for HCEs. To perform this test, the employer must determine a benefit percentage for each nonunion employee, and all qualified plans—including 401(k) plans and ESOPs—must be tested together.[4] Also, only employer-provided benefits are tested. In simple terms, the ABP test works as follows:

1. The employer determines an annual contribution or accrual rate for each employee covered under the plan.

2. This rate is then divided by the employee's compensation to determine a percentage.

---

[4] Plans covering union employees are deemed to satisfy the coverage requirements and are thus excluded when performing this test.

TABLE 4.1 Safe Harbor and Unsafe Harbor Percentages

NHCE Concentration Percentage	Safe Harbor Percentage	Unsafe Harbor Percentage	NHCE Concentration Percentage	Safe Harbor Percentage	Unsafe Harbor Percentage
0–60	50.00	40.00	80	35.00	25.00
61	49.25	39.25	81	34.25	24.25
62	48.50	38.50	82	33.50	23.50
63	47.75	37.75	83	32.75	22.75
64	47.00	37.00	84	32.00	22.00
65	46.25	36.25	85	31.25	21.25
66	45.50	35.50	86	30.50	20.50
67	44.75	34.75	87	29.75	20.00
68	44.00	34.00	88	29.00	20.00
69	43.25	33.25	89	28.25	20.00
70	42.50	32.50	90	27.50	20.00
71	41.75	31.75	91	26.75	20.00
72	41.00	31.00	92	26.00	20.00
73	40.25	30.25	93	25.25	20.00
74	39.50	29.50	94	24.50	20.00
75	38.75	28.75	95	23.75	20.00
76	38.00	28.00	96	23.00	20.00
77	37.25	27.25	97	22.25	20.00
78	36.50	26.50	98	21.50	20.00
79	35.75	25.75	99	20.75	20.00

3. If the plan is integrated with Social Security, the percentage so determined may be increased by an amount representing the employer-provided portion of Social Security. The resulting percentage is added to the percentage for plans that cannot be integrated with Social Security (for example, CODAs and ESOPs), and the result is the benefit percentage for each employee.

4. These percentages are then averaged for both HCEs and NHCEs to determine whether the average benefit percentage for NHCEs is at least 70 percent of the ABP for HCEs.

The ABP may be calculated on a contributions or benefits basis, regardless of the type of plan involved.

Other Provisions of the Coverage Test

The coverage requirements must be satisfied on each day of the calendar year. However, a quarterly testing option is available, taking into account individuals who are employees on the day being tested. An annual testing option also is available, but this requires taking into account all individuals who are or were employees at any time during the year.[5]

---

[5] Employers must use the annual testing option when testing a plan subject to Sections 401(k) and 401(m) and when performing the average benefit test.

NHCEs are not affected when a plan fails to meet the coverage test. HCEs, however, will be taxed on the present value of vested employer-derived benefits and on income earned on any contributions, to the extent that such amounts have not been previously taxed.

Minimum Participation Test

In addition to passing the general coverage test, a defined benefit plan also must benefit at least 50 employees or, in companies with fewer employees, the greater of 40 percent of all employees of the employer or two employees (one employee if the employer has only one employee). As with the general coverage tests, certain employees may be excluded when performing this **minimum participation test**—those who have not met the plan's minimum age and service requirements, nonresident aliens, and so forth. Beginning in 1997, this test no longer applied to defined contribution plans.

Nondiscrimination in Benefits or Contributions

A plan cannot be qualified if it provides benefits or contributions in amounts that discriminate in favor of HCEs. Further, every optional form of benefit, subsidy, or other right or feature under the plan must be available to a nondiscriminatory group of employees. These requirements are found in Section 401(a)(4) of the IRC.

Amount Testing

The regulations provide a limited number of **safe harbors**—formulas that allow a plan to qualify under the amount test without detailed numerical testing. Plans that do not meet a safe harbor must proceed to numerical participant-by-participant testing.

If a plan must be tested numerically, it can be tested on either a benefits or a contributions basis. If a safe harbor is to be used, however, this choice is not available; a defined contribution plan must use a defined contribution safe harbor, and a defined benefit plan must use a defined benefit safe harbor.[6] A plan using a nondiscriminatory definition of compensation that satisfies the integration rules (discussed later in this chapter) will almost invariably meet one of the safe harbor rules.

Defined Contribution Safe Harbors The portion of a plan that consists of a CODA is considered to be nondiscriminatory with respect to contribution amounts if it satisfies the actual deferral percentage (ADP) test under Section 401(k) of the IRC. In addition, the portion of a plan that represents after-tax employee contributions and matching employer contributions not used in passing the ADP test is considered to be nondiscriminatory if it satisfies the actual contribution percentage (ACP) test of Section 401(m). Beginning in 1999, safe harbors were available with respect to the ADP test and the ACP test in regard to matching employer contributions.[7]

---

[6] Exceptions to this rule are provided for hybrid plans. For example, cash balance plans may be tested on a contributions basis and target benefit plans may be tested on a benefits basis, if certain rules are met.

[7] A detailed description of these tests and safe harbors is set forth in Chapter 11.

Other defined contribution plans are deemed to provide nondiscriminatory contributions if they meet one of two design-based safe harbors: (1) a uniform formula; or (2) an age- or service-weighted formula.

A uniform formula is one that allocates contributions using the same percentage of compensation, the same dollar amount, or the same dollar amount per uniform unit of service (not to exceed one week) for every participant. If forfeitures are reallocated among participants, they must be allocated under the same formula. The permitted disparity allowed under the integration regulations may be ignored in determining whether a plan meets this safe harbor.

The safe harbor for plans that use age or service weighting is not really a *safe* harbor—rather, it is closer to a simplified numerical test. Employee-by-employee calculations are required, but testing is performed on an averaging basis. To meet this safe harbor, the plan formula must allocate contributions (and forfeitures, if applicable) based on the relative number of points credited to a participant. Points must be provided on a uniform basis for age or service or both. In addition, points may (but need not) be provided for units of compensation. The unit of compensation used must be a single dollar amount not exceeding $200. Also, the average allocation rate for HCEs must not exceed the average for NHCEs. This safe harbor is *not* available for integrated plans.

Defined Benefit Safe Harbors   There are three safe harbors for defined benefit plans. To qualify for safe harbor treatment, however, a plan must meet some general uniformity requirements. These requirements are as follows:

1. All safe harbor defined benefit plans must provide a uniform normal retirement benefit—that is, the annual benefit under the plan must be the same percentage of annual compensation or the same dollar amount (unrelated to compensation) for all participants with the same number of years of service at normal retirement age. The permitted disparity allowed under integration regulations may be ignored for this purpose.

2. A uniform normal retirement age must apply to all participants under the plan.

3. The plan also must provide uniform post-normal retirement benefits—that is, the annual benefit for a post-normal-retirement-age employee with a given number of years of service must be the same dollar amount or percentage of average annual compensation as would be payable at normal retirement age to an employee with the same number of years of service.

4. Each subsidized optional form of benefit under the plan must be currently available to essentially all participants.

5. A safe harbor plan that bases benefits on compensation must generally use average annual compensation—averaged over a period of at least three consecutive 12-month periods—and this average must be the highest average determined with respect to the employee's compensation history. The "consecutive" requirement does not apply to a nonintegrated plan that uses nonconsecutive pay in determining benefits.

6. A plan must use the same definition of years of service for purposes of applying the benefit formula and meeting backloading requirements.[8]

In addition to the defined contribution and defined benefit safe harbors described above, there is a unit credit safe harbor, a fractional accrual rule safe harbor, and a safe harbor for certain insurance contract plans.

Unit Credit Safe Harbor A unit credit safe harbor plan is one under which an employee's accrued benefit is determined by multiplying the benefit formula by the years of service and, if applicable, an employee's compensation. All employees with the same number of years of service will have an accrued benefit that is the same percentage of compensation or the same dollar amount. The plan must satisfy the 133 1/3 percent rule in meeting the backloading requirements.

Fractional Accrual Rule Safe Harbor A unit credit plan that uses the fractional accrual rule to meet the backloading requirements can meet this safe harbor if no employee accrues normal retirement benefits at a rate that is more than $133\frac{1}{3}$ percent of the rate of any other actual or potential employee, ignoring employees with more than 33 years of projected service at normal retirement age. All participants with the same entry age and the same number of years of service as of any plan year must have an accrued benefit at normal retirement age that is the same percentage of compensation or the same dollar amount.

Insurance Contract Safe Harbor Plans funded exclusively through the use of insurance contracts are provided with a safe harbor if the benefit formula does not recognize service before an employee commences participation.[9] The plan's benefit formula must satisfy the fractional accrual rule safe harbor. Scheduled premiums must be paid as level annual payments to normal retirement age; premiums after normal retirement age must equal the amount necessary to fund the additional benefits that accrue each year under the plan's formula.

The General Test

A plan that does not meet one of the safe harbors must use the general test to determine whether it is discriminatory as to the amount of contributions or benefits it provides. This is one of the more complicated areas of nondiscrimination testing, and the following discussion provides only highlights of the general concepts involved.

The basic goal of the general test is to ensure that, at each benefit level, employees at that level and above constitute a nondiscriminatory coverage group. This test can be done on either a benefits or a contributions basis, at the employer's discretion. Thus, for example, a defined contribution plan can be tested on the basis of the benefits provided, rather than the contributions allocated, to employees, and vice versa.

The first step in testing is to determine an accrual rate (or allocation rate if testing is done on a contribution basis) for each individual covered under the plan. After

---

[8] See the discussion of backloading requirements in Chapter 5.
[9] This restriction does not apply if the plan was in effect on September 19, 1991.

accrual or allocation rates have been established, they are tested against the general nondiscrimination rule. A plan meets this general rule if, for every possible grouping of accrual or allocation rates in the plan, all participants in that grouping or above constitute a nondiscriminatory group under the 410(b) coverage rules.

This grouping of employees is accomplished through the concept of rate groups. A **rate group** for defined benefit testing consists of a highly compensated employee and all employees (highly compensated or not) who have both "normal" and "most valuable" accrual rates equal to or higher than that employee. (Defined contribution testing groups are formed using only normal allocation or accrual rates.) The normal accrual rate is based on the accrued benefit—that is, the benefit accrued at any point in time, payable as of normal retirement age. The most valuable accrual rate is determined based on the qualified joint and survivor annuity that may be paid at any time under the plan, which, in turn, depends on the accrued benefit. Qualified Social Security supplements that meet accrual, vesting, and joint and survivor rules also are taken into account.

Employees are then placed in rate groups that are determined in bands. The range of each band may not be wider than either (1) 0.05 of a percentage point above or below a midpoint, or (2) from 95 to 105 percent of a midpoint for normal accrual rates or 85 to 115 percent for most-valuable accrual rates. All employees within the band are treated as having identical accrual rates.

The general rule states that a plan qualifies if, and only if, every rate group constitutes a nondiscriminatory group under the 410(b) coverage rules.

Other Rights, Options, and Features

The second part of the Section 401(a)(4) test applies to all optional forms of benefits, ancillary benefits, and all other rights and features and requires that these be offered to employees on a nondiscriminatory basis. To meet this test, each benefit, right, or feature must be "currently available" and "effectively available" to a nondiscriminatory group of employees. Actual use of benefits, rights, and features is irrelevant.

Benefits, rights, or features must be currently available to a group of employees that need satisfy only the nondiscriminatory classification test under Section 410(b). It is not necessary that the plan satisfy the ABP test for this purpose; the employer may rely on the nondiscriminatory classification test even if the plan otherwise meets the coverage requirements under the 70 percent ratio test. Generally, age and service conditions may be disregarded for optional forms of benefit; they may not be disregarded in the cases of ancillary benefits or other rights and features. Employers also may ignore certain other conditions, including the attainment of a certain vesting percentage; termination of employment; death; satisfaction of (or failure to satisfy) a specified health condition; disability; hardship; family status; default on a plan loan; execution of a covenant not to compete; application for benefits or election of a benefit form; the application for benefits and other administrative or mechanical acts; absences from service; and the execution of a waiver under the Age Discrimination in Employment Act (ADEA) or other federal or state law.

The effectively available requirement is applied on the basis of all the facts and circumstances. This provision is intended to thwart abusive situations where it is predominantly the highly paid who meet the criteria for a benefit, right, or feature that is nominally available to all participants. This does not require, however, that those who actually use the benefit, right, or feature constitute a nondiscriminatory group.

Integration Rules

The tax law in effect allows a limited form of discrimination by permitting employers to provide additional contributions or benefits for higher-paid employees under a qualified plan so as to compensate for the fact that the relative value of Social Security decreases as pay levels go up. The extent to which additional benefits can be provided for the highly paid is limited by the integration rules of Section 401(l) of the IRC and the general nondiscrimination requirements of Section 401(a)(4). The basic concept of these limitations is that benefits from the employer's plan must be dovetailed with Social Security benefits in a manner such that employees earning above the Social Security taxable wage base will not receive combined benefits under both programs that are proportionately greater than the combined benefits for employees earning under this amount.

Later in this section, an overview of the integration rules is presented. Before beginning this overview, however, the following should be noted:

- An employee stock ownership plan (ESOP) cannot be integrated.

- The CODA portion of a plan cannot be integrated.

- Total integration is available only once. For example, if an employer has a defined benefit plan that takes Social Security benefits into account to the fullest extent permitted by law, it has no more capacity to integrate a defined contribution plan covering the same employees.

- A plan that does not meet the integration rules set forth in Section 401(l) (which are discussed below) may still achieve a qualified status if it can meet the general nondiscrimination tests of Section 401(a)(4); in a sense, the integration rules of Section 401(l) are safe harbors for compliance purposes.

It also will be helpful, before discussing the integration rules, to define some terms that will be used:

• **Excess plan.** This type of integrated plan is one where a higher level of contribution or benefit is provided for a certain level of compensation than is provided for compensation below that level. Both defined benefit and defined contribution plans can be established on an **excess plan** basis.

• **Offset plan.** This type of plan subtracts, or offsets, some amount from a gross plan benefit. Only defined benefit plans use the **offset plan** approach.

• **Social Security taxable wage base.** This is the amount of compensation on which both the employer and the employees pay taxes for old-age, disability, and survivor benefits under the Federal Insurance Contributions Act (FICA). This amount is adjusted annually for changes in the CPI; for 2002, it was $84,900.

• **Integration level.** This is the dollar amount of compensation specified in an excess plan that is the breakpoint at which the contribution or accrual rate is increased. For example, in a plan that provides for a contribution of 5 percent of pay up to $20,000 of compensation plus 8 percent of pay over this amount, $20,000 is the plan's integration level. In general, a plan's **integration level** may be any amount up to the Social Security taxable wage base.

• **Covered compensation.** This is the average (without indexing) of the Social Security taxable wage bases in effect for an employee for each year during the 35-year period that ends with the year in which his or her Social Security full benefit retirement age is attained.

The following sections first discuss the integration rules for defined contribution plans and then those that apply to defined benefit plans.

Defined Contribution Plans

When a plan's integration level equals the Social Security taxable wage base, the contribution percentage for pay above this amount (the excess percentage) may exceed the contribution percentage for pay below this amount (the base percentage) by the lesser of (1) 5.7 percent and (2) the percentage applicable to pay below the integration level. This rule also can be stated as follows:

• When the base percentage is equal to or less than 5.7 percent, the excess percentage cannot be more than twice the base percentage.

• When the base percentage is more than 5.7 percent, the excess percentage cannot be more than the base percentage plus 5.7 percent.

The amount of additional percentage contribution permitted under this rule is called the **permitted disparity.**

This rule applies only if the plan's integration level is set either at the Social Security taxable wage base or at or below an amount equal to 20 percent of the Social Security taxable wage base ($16,980 for 2002). If the integration level falls between these two amounts, the 5.7 percent standard in determining the plan's permitted disparity is reduced. If the plan's integration level is more than 80 percent of the Social Security taxable wage base, it is reduced to 5.4 percent; if the integration level falls between 20 percent and 80 percent of the wage base, it is reduced to 4.3 percent.

Defined Benefit Plans

Excess Plans   The integration rules for defined benefit excess plans work in much the same fashion as they do for defined contribution plans. If the plan's integration level is set at or below covered compensation, the benefit accrual percentage for pay above the integration level—the permitted disparity—is the lesser of

(1) 0.75 percent or (2) the benefit accrual percentage applicable to pay below the integration level. Again, the rule for determining a plan's permitted disparity can be restated as follows:

- When the base percentage is equal to or less than 0.75 percent, the excess percentage cannot be more than twice the base percentage.

- When the base percentage is more than 0.75 percent, the excess percentage cannot be more than the base percentage plus 0.75 percent.

Offset Plans The rules for offset plans are mathematically equivalent to those that apply to excess plans. These rules establish the maximum offset allowance that may be used as the lesser of (1) 0.75 percent or (2) 50 percent of the gross benefit accrual percentage, multiplied by a fraction (not to exceed one) equal to the employee's average annual compensation divided by the employee's final average compensation up to the offset level. To understand this rule, three terms need to be defined: (1) an employee's "average annual compensation" is based on an averaging period of at least three consecutive years during a period that ends with the current year; (2) an employee's "final average compensation" is calculated as an average over the last three years of service; and (3) the plan's "offset level" is covered compensation.

Other Rules for Defined Benefit Plans There are additional requirements for defined benefit plans that do not apply to defined contribution plans. For example, the 0.75 percent factor must be reduced if the plan's integration or offset level exceeds covered compensation; it also must be reduced for benefits payable prior to the employee's having attained age 62.[10] Further, the disparity between percentages must be uniform for all participants with the same years of service.

There is an aggregate maximum on the use of permitted disparities for employees. This is accomplished by determining an annual permitted disparity fraction for each employee. This fraction is the ratio of the plan's actual disparity to its maximum allowance. The cumulative disparity fraction is equal to the sum of the total annual disparity fractions for each year of service over an employee's entire career and may not exceed 35.

Chapter Summary

- A qualified plan is the only tax-effective way to provide benefits for a large group of employees. The tax advantages provided under the Internal Revenue Code (IRC) for qualified plans are most significant—both to an employer and to its employees. The principal tax advantages of such plans are as follows:
  - Contributions made by the employer, within the limitations prescribed, are deductible as a business expense.

---

[10] It also may be increased for benefits that commence after the employee's Social Security full benefit retirement age.

- Investment income on these contributions normally is not subject to federal income tax until paid in the form of benefits.
- An employee is not considered to be in receipt of taxable income until benefits are distributed—even though the employee may be fully vested and even though the employee has the right to receive the amounts involved without restriction.

- An employer can use any definition of compensation it chooses, provided the definition does not discriminate in favor of highly compensated employees (HCEs). Despite what the plan might use as its definition of compensation, however, the IRC has specific definitions that must be used for limiting benefits and/or contributions and for nondiscrimination testing.

- In 2002, an employee is a highly compensated employee if he or she (1) is a 5 percent owner of the employer during the current or preceding year or (2) had compensation in the preceding year of $90,000 (indexed for inflation) and (at the election of the employer) was in the top 20 percent of employees in terms of compensation for that year.

- One of the most important requirements of a qualified plan is that it must be for the exclusive benefit of employees or their beneficiaries. A plan cannot be structured so that it discriminates in any fashion in favor of highly compensated employees.

- A qualified plan must meet specific nondiscriminatory requirements as to employees covered under the plan. This requirement is set forth in Section 410(b) of the IRC, and the tests required by this section often are called the 410(b) or coverage tests. A plan will be considered nondiscriminatory as to coverage if it meets one of the following two tests: (1) the ratio percentage test or (2) the average benefit test.

- In addition to passing the general coverage test, a defined benefit plan also must benefit at least 50 employees or, in companies with fewer employees, the greater of 40 percent of all employees of the employer or two employees (one employee if the employer has only one employee). Beginning in 1997, this test no longer applied to defined contribution plans.

- If an employer is treated as operating qualified separate lines of business, the minimum coverage requirements (including the nondiscrimination requirements) and the minimum participation requirements may be applied separately with respect to the employees of each qualified separate line of business.

- Section 401(a)(4) of the IRC requires that a plan cannot be qualified if it provides benefits or contributions in amounts that discriminate in favor of HCEs. Further, every optional form of benefit, subsidy, or other right or feature under the plan must be available to a nondiscriminatory group of employees.

- The tax law in effect allows a limited form of discrimination by permitting employers to provide additional contributions or benefits for higher paid employees under a qualified plan so as to compensate for the fact that the relative value of Social Security decreases as pay levels go up. The basic concept of integration with Social Security is that benefits from the employer's plan must be dovetailed with Social Security benefits in a manner such that employees earning above the Social Security taxable wage base will not receive combined benefits under both programs that are proportionately greater than the combined benefits for employees earning under this amount.

Key Terms

average benefit percentage (ABP) test, p. *66*
average benefit test, p. *66*
controlled group, p. *64*
coverage tests, p. *65*
definition of compensation, p. *62*
excess plan, p. *72*
exclusive benefit (requirements), p. *65*

highly compensated employee (HCE), p. *63*
integration level, p. *73*
minimum participation test, p. *68*
nondiscriminatory classification test, p. *66*
offset plan, p. *72*

permanent (plan), p. *65*
permitted disparity, p. *73*
qualified separate line of business (QSLOB), p. *64*
rate group, p. *71*
ratio percentage test, p. *66*
safe harbors, p. *68*

Questions for Review

1. Summarize the major tax law provisions necessary for a retirement plan to qualify under the Internal Revenue Code.

2. Who is a highly compensated employee? Explain.

3. Describe when common ownership results in a controlled group of corporations or businesses.

4. Explain the importance of a qualified separate line of business in testing for plan qualification.

5. How does a profit sharing plan demonstrate compliance with the requirement for plan permanency?

6. Explain the minimum participation requirements.

7. Describe the ways a plan administrator can demonstrate that a plan is nondiscriminatory in coverage.

8. Explain the alternate approaches in demonstrating that a plan is nondiscriminatory in benefits or contributions.

9. Are employers allowed to adopt any definition of compensation for purposes of defining benefits and/or contributions for a qualified retirement plan? Explain.

10. What is meant by integration with Social Security?

11. Explain the difference between an excess plan and an offset plan.

Questions for Discussion

1. Explain why it is important to identify the highly compensated employees for purposes of pension plan qualification.

2. What plan design recommendations would you make to an employer initially designing a pension or profit sharing plan who seeks simplicity in meeting nondiscrimination testing requirements as an administrative objective?

3. Explain the economic rationale behind permitting employers to integrate retirement plans with Social Security.

Resources for Further Study

Allen, Everett T., Jr. "Retirement Plan Design." *The Handbook of Employee Benefits.* 5th ed. Jerry S. Rosenbloom, ed. New York: McGraw-Hill, 2001.

CCH Editorial Staff. "2001 Tax Legislation: Law, Explanation, and Analysis." *Commerce Clearing House Pension Plan Guide* (2001).

Donovan, Kevin J. "Proposed New Comparability Regulations Add More Complexity." *Journal of Pension Benefits* 8, no. 2 (Winter 2001).

Durfee, James G.; Russell E. Hall; Christian L. Lindgren; Frances G. Sieller; and John F. Woyke. *A Guide to the Final Nondiscrimination Requirements.* New York: Research Institute of America, January 1994.

McDonnell, Ken; Paul Fronstin; Kelly Olsen; Pamela Ostuw; Jack Van Derhei; and Paul Yakoboski. *EBRI Databook on Employee Benefits.* 4th ed. Deborah Holmes, Lynn Miller, and Maureen Richmond, eds. Washington, DC: Employee Benefit Research Institute Education and Research Fund, 1997.

Chapter 5

Tax Qualification Requirements (Continued)

After studying this chapter you should be able to:

- Summarize the requirements for determining and counting service for plan qualification purposes.
- Describe the minimum vesting standards set by law.
- Explain the significance of the Section 401(a)(17) compensation cap for both defined contribution and defined benefit plans.
- Determine how much a company may contribute to a defined contribution plan on behalf of a participant.
- Determine the maximum annual retirement benefit that a defined benefit plan may provide.
- Explain the legal rights that spouses have to qualified plan benefits.
- Describe the special qualification requirements that apply to top-heavy plans.

There are many requirements, other than those relating to coverage, contributions, and benefits, that a plan must meet if it is to achieve a qualified status under the Internal Revenue Code (IRC). These additional requirements are discussed in this chapter.

Determination of Service

The law establishes specific requirements for the determination of an employee's service in three key areas: (1) initial eligibility to participate; (2) vesting; and (3) the right to a benefit accrual. The law does not mandate how service is to be determined for other purposes (for example, the right to retire early). Any method chosen for these other purposes, however, must not discriminate in favor of highly compensated employees (HCEs).

The basic concept of the law is that an employee must be given credit for a year of service for any "computation period" during which the employee is credited with 1,000 hours of service. A **computation period** is a 12-month period and may be established as a plan year, calendar year, or employment year; however, for eligibility service, the initial 12-month period must begin with the date of employment. The employee also must be given a ratable benefit accrual, if participation has commenced, for any computation period in which he or she is credited with at least 1,000 hours of service.

If an employee is credited with fewer than 1,000 hours of service within a computation period, credit need not be given for a year of service and the employee need not be given any benefit accrual for the period in question. However, if the employee has been credited with at least 501 hours of service in the computation period, this will prevent the employee from incurring a **break-in-service.** Whether the employee has incurred a break-in-service is significant in terms of eligibility and vesting of benefits.

Additional requirements for the determination of service are as follows:

• Service must be determined on a controlled-group basis.

• Service with a predecessor company must be taken into account for eligibility and vesting purposes if the employer maintains the plan of the predecessor. If the employer maintains a plan that is not the plan of the predecessor, service with the predecessor will have to be determined to the extent prescribed in regulations.

• Although an employee's initial computation period for determining eligibility service must begin with his or her employment date, the employer can convert to using another type of computation period after the first 12 months of employment, provided the beginning of the new computation period overlaps with the first employment year.

• Certain service may be excluded for vesting purposes—for example, service prior to the year in which the employee attains age 18, service for any period during which the employee did not elect to contribute under a plan requiring employee contributions, and service prior to the adoption of the plan.

• Years of service before a break-in-service also may be excluded but only if the number of consecutive one-year breaks in service equal or exceed the greater of (1) five or (2) the number of prebreak years of service, and the participant did not have any nonforfeitable right to any part of his or her accrued benefit attributable to employer contributions. Thus, pre- and postbreak service will be aggregated if the employee had any degree of vesting in employer-provided benefits or if his or her break-in-service was shorter than five years.

• A special rule for maternity or paternity absences exists. This rule applies to an individual who is absent from work by reason of the pregnancy of the individual, the birth of a child of the individual, the placement of a child with an individual in connection with adoption, or for purposes of caring for such a child for a period beginning immediately following birth or placement. The law requires that, for purposes of determining whether a one-year break-in-service has occurred, the plan treat as hours of service the lesser of the hours that otherwise would have been credited to the individual, or 501 hours. If the participant would be prevented from incurring a one-year break-in-service solely because the period of absence is treated as hours of service, these hours would be credited only in the year in which the absence began; otherwise, they would be credited in the year immediately following.

Hour of Service

The first step involved in calculating service is to determine what constitutes an hour of service. Depending on the compliance method selected, all or some of these hours of service will have to be taken into account.[1] The regulations define an **hour of service** as an hour for which:

- An employee is paid, or entitled to payment, for the performance of duties for the employer.

- An employee is paid, or entitled to payment, by the employer for a period of time during which no duties are performed (irrespective of whether the employment relationship has terminated) due to vacation, holiday, illness, incapacity (including disability), layoff, jury duty, military duty, or leave of absence.

- Back pay, irrespective of damages, is either awarded or agreed to by the employer.

However, a plan need not credit an employee with more than 501 hours of service for any single, continuous period during which the employee performs no duties, or for any period of nonworking service for which payment is made under workers' compensation, unemployment compensation, or state disability laws.

Compliance Methods

An employer has three methods to choose from in crediting employees with service. The same method may be used for all purposes or, under the decoupling provisions of the regulations, a different compliance method may be used within the same plan for eligibility, vesting, and benefit accrual purposes. Also, if discrimination does not result, a different method may be used for different classes of employees (a particularly helpful factor when distinguishing between part-time and full-time employees). Finally, the regulations permit the use of one compliance method for pre-ERISA service and another for post-ERISA service (again, an important factor in view of the lack, in many instances, of adequate pre-ERISA employment records).

The first method is the **standard hours–counting method,** under which all hours of service must be taken into account. While this method is, in one sense, the

---

[1] Under the elapsed-time method of compliance, the hours of service concept is not relevant since total service is measured from date of employment to date of severance.

simplest to describe, many employers find it difficult to administer—particularly in the case of exempt employees who often do not keep a record of actual hours worked.

The second method involves the use of equivalencies. Under this method, four alternatives exist. The first determines service on the basis of actual hours worked, including overtime and excluding all other nonworked hours for which compensation is paid, such as vacations, holidays, and so forth. The second alternative involves only regular hours worked and excludes overtime hours, along with nonworked hours for which compensation is paid. The third alternative relates service to a time period established by the plan. This time period can be a day, a week, a half-month, a month, or a shift. Under this third alternative, an employee is credited with an imputed number of hours for the time period involved as long as he or she is credited with at least one hour of service during such time period. The fourth alternative involves the employee's earnings, and here hours of service are related to the earnings received by the employee during the period involved.

The third method is the **elapsed-time method.** Under this method, service is measured from the employee's date of employment to date of severance, and the concept of counting hours is not relevant.

An employer who wishes to use an equivalency in lieu of counting hours must pay a "premium." In the case of time-period equivalencies, this premium is measured in terms of the number of hours that must be credited for the time period selected. In essence, the hours credited will exceed a normal work schedule for the period involved to build in a credit for overtime or additional hours that might have been worked. This means that under the time-period equivalencies, an employee will be credited with 1,000 hours of service in a much shorter period of time (in the average situation) than would be the case under the actual standard hours-counting method. The hours that must be credited under each time-period equivalency are as follows:

- One day—10 hours

- One week—45 hours

- Half-month—95 hours

- Month—190 hours

- Shift—actual hours included in the shift

The premium for using the other equivalencies is measured by reducing the 1,000-hour standard for a full year of service and the 501-hour standard for applying the break-in-service rules. The reductions for the different equivalencies are shown in Table 5.1.

Under the elapsed-time method, service credit for eligibility and vesting must begin with the employee's date of hire (except for permissible statutory exclusions, such as service prior to the effective date of the plan). For benefit accrual purposes, service must be credited starting with the date the employee begins participating in the plan. Service must continue to be credited, for all purposes for which the method

TABLE 5.1 Adjustments in Hours of Service Required for Crediting a Year of Service and for Break-in-Service Rules under Certain Equivalencies

Equivalency	Year of Service	Break-in-Service
Hours worked	870	435
Regular hours worked	750	375
Earnings		
Hourly rated employees	870	435
Other employees	750	375

is used, until the employee's date of severance. In the case of quitting, discharge, retirement, or death, the employee's severance date is immediate. In the case of absence from employment for other reasons such as layoff, leave of absence, or disability, the employee's severance date will be 12 months after the beginning of the absence. After the employee's severance date, the plan need not credit service. However, there are two exceptions to this rule. The first exception is if the employee is reemployed within 12 months after quitting, discharge, or retirement, the plan must grant service credit (but only for eligibility and vesting purposes, not for benefit accruals) for the period of absence. The second exception is if an employee quits, is discharged, or retires during a layoff, disability, or leave of absence and is reemployed within 12 months after the absence began, the plan must grant service credit for the period of severance (again, for eligibility and vesting, but not for benefit accruals). Also, under the elapsed-time method, a one-year period of severance is treated the same as a one-year break-in-service.

Eligibility Requirements

As a general rule, a qualified plan cannot require, as a condition of eligibility, that an employee complete more than one year of service. However, a two-year service requirement is acceptable if a plan provides for full and immediate vesting and is not a cash or deferred arrangement (CODA). In addition, a qualified plan cannot require that an employee be older than 21 to participate.[2] A maximum age cannot be used.

The use of entry dates is permissible, but they cannot delay an employee's participation by more than six months. Thus, if it is desirable to use the most stringent minimum age and service requirements possible, the plan should permit entry at least every six months. The use of an annual entry date is permissible only when the minimum age and/or service requirements are at least six months less than those permissible under the law (for example, age 20½ or six months of service).

Other eligibility requirements, such as employment classifications, may be used provided the plan can pass the nondiscrimination tests discussed in Chapter 4.

[2] Tax-exempt educational institutions may use age 26 as a minimum age in a plan that provides full and immediate vesting.

Vesting Requirements

A qualified plan must provide that employees will have a vested right to their benefits under specific rules. The value of after-tax and elective (before-tax) employee contributions must be fully vested at all times.[3] The value of employer contributions must be vested when the employee reaches the plan's normal retirement age, regardless of the employee's service at that time. Otherwise, the value of employer contributions must be vested at least as rapidly as provided under either of the following minimum vesting schedules:

- 100 percent vesting after five years of service.

- Graded vesting, with 20 percent vesting after three years of service, increasing by 20 percent multiples for each year until 100 percent vesting is achieved after seven years.

With passage of the Economic Growth and Tax Relief Reconciliation Act of 2001 (EGTRRA), the minimum vesting schedules were shortened beginning generally in 2002 for employer matching contributions to:

- 100 percent vesting after three years of service.

- Graded vesting, with 20 percent vesting after two years of service, increasing by 20 percent multiples for each year until 100 percent vesting is achieved after six years.

These accelerated vesting schedules apply only to employer matching contributions that match voluntary before- or after-tax employee contributions (as opposed to involuntary contributions made as a condition of employment). Similarly, employer contributions made to noncontributory, employer-pay-all type plans are subject to the previously mentioned five-year cliff and seven-year graded schedules.[4]

Backloading Rules

The IRC also stipulates minimum standards to be followed in determining an employee's accrued benefit for purposes of applying a vesting schedule under defined benefit plans; these rules are not applicable to defined contribution plans.

A plan will be acceptable if it meets any one of the three following rules:

- **The 3 percent rule.** The employee's accrued benefit must be at least equal to 3 percent of the projected normal retirement benefit for each year of participation, to a maximum of 100 percent after 33⅓ years of participation.

---

[3] This does not necessarily require a minimum benefit equal to the amount the employee has contributed. In a defined contribution plan, for example, there may have been investment losses that have resulted in the value of the employee's contributions being less than the amount actually contributed by the employee. In this situation, the plan would not have to return to the employee an amount greater than the value of the employee contributions after taking investment losses into account.

[4] TIAA-CREF, *"Benefit Plan Counselor Special Report,"* (July 2001), pp. 2–3.

- **The 133⅓ percent rule.** The accrued benefit may be the employee's actual benefit earned to date under the plan, provided any future rate of benefit accrual is not more than 133⅓ percent of any prior year's benefit accrual rate.

- **The fractional rule.** The employee's accrued benefit may not be less than the projected normal retirement benefit prorated for years of plan participation.

Most plans are expected to be able to satisfy either or both the 133⅓ percent rule and the fractional rule. Any plan that permits the accrual of benefits for more than 33⅓ years will not be able to satisfy the 3 percent rule.

If a defined benefit plan requires employee contributions, the accrued benefit attributable to employer contributions is determined by subtracting the life annuity value of the employee's contributions.

Other Vesting Requirements

The tax law also establishes a number of other requirements concerning the vesting and payment of an employee's benefits.

1. Vested amounts of less than $5,000 may be paid in a lump sum at termination of employment without employee consent; otherwise, an employee must consent to a lump-sum payment and must have the right to leave his or her accrued benefit in the plan until the later of age 62 or normal retirement age. A plan may not impose a significant detriment on a participant who does not consent to a distribution.[5]

2. If an employee receives payment for his or her accrued benefit and is later reemployed, the service for which the employee received payment may be disregarded in determining his or her accrued benefit after reemployment. The employee, however, must be permitted to "buy back" the accrued benefit attributable to such service by repaying the cash payment with compound interest. (In the case of a defined contribution plan, such a buyback is required only before the employee has incurred five consecutive one-year breaks in service, and interest need not be paid.)

3. Once vested, no forfeitures are permitted—even if termination of employment is due to dishonesty. If a plan has more liberal vesting provisions than the law requires, however, forfeitures are possible up to the time the employee would have to be vested under the law.

4. Any employee who terminates employment must be given written notification of his or her rights, the amount of his or her accrued benefits, the portion (if any) that is vested, and the applicable payment provisions.

---

[5] EGTRRA clarified that a plan may disregard rollovers to the plan in determining the involuntary cash-out threshold. Therefore, if a newly hired employee had accrued a benefit below the cash-out threshold and subsequently terminated her or his new employment, she or he could be cashed out. This could occur even if she or he had transferred retirement benefits from another source, such as an individual retirement account or a plan sponsored by a previous employer. This could be especially troubling to an employee who has secured a loan from the plan because the loan would immediately become due for payment.

5. A terminated employee's vested benefit cannot be decreased by reason of increases in Social Security benefits that take place after the date of termination of employment.

6. If the plan allows an active employee to elect early retirement after attaining a stated age and completing a specified period of service, a terminated employee who has completed the service requirement must have the right to receive vested benefits after reaching the early retirement age specified. However, the benefit for the terminated employee can be reduced actuarially even though the active employee might have the advantage of subsidized early retirement benefits.

7. Any plan amendment cannot decrease the vested percentage of an employee's accrued benefit. Also, if the vesting schedule is changed, any participant with at least three years of service must be given the election to remain under the preamendment vesting schedule (for both pre- and postamendment benefit accruals).

8. The accrued benefit of a participant may not be decreased by an amendment of the plan. This includes plan amendments that have the effect of eliminating or reducing an early retirement benefit or a retirement-type subsidy or eliminating or reducing the value of an optional form of benefit with respect to benefits attributable to service before the amendment. In the case of a retirement-type subsidy, this applies only with respect to a participant who satisfies the preamendment condition for the subsidy, either before or after the amendment. EGTRRA directs the Internal Revenue Service (IRS) to issue regulations providing that the prohibitions against eliminating or reducing an early retirement benefit, a retirement-type subsidy, or optional form of benefit do not apply to "any plan amendment which reduces or eliminates benefits or subsidies which create significant burdens or complexities for the plan and plan participants, and does not adversely affect the rights of any plan participant in a more than de minimis manner." Not later than December 31, 2003, the IRS is directed to issue regulations on plan amendments reducing benefits. The intent of these regulations is to eliminate duplicative benefit options following plan mergers and consolidations while ensuring that meaningful benefit options and subsidies are not eliminated.[6]

Individual Limits

To achieve a tax-qualified status, a plan must observe two statutory limits on contributions and/or benefits.[7] The first is a limit on the amount of an employee's compensation that may be taken into account when determining the contributions or benefits made on his or her behalf. The second is a limit on the annual additions that may be made to an employee's account in the case of a defined contribution plan, or

---

[6] CCH, "2001 Tax Legislation: Law, Explanation, and Analysis," *Commerce Clearing House Pension Plan Guide,* 2001. pp. 271–72.

[7] There is also a limit on the amount an employee may electively defer (contribute on a before-tax basis) under a CODA. This limit is discussed in Chapter 11.

on the benefits payable to an employee in the case of a defined benefit plan. More-over, there is a combined limit on annual additions and/or benefits that applies for years through 1999 in the case of employees who participate in both types of plans.

Limit on Compensation

The Tax Reform Act of 1986 added **Section 401(a)(17)** to the **IRC,** limiting the amount of an employee's compensation that can be taken into account in determin-ing contributions or benefits under a qualified plan. This limit was originally set at $200,000 and was increased for changes in the consumer price index (CPI). By 1993, it had increased to $235,840. However, beginning in 1994, it was rolled back to $150,000. This revised limit also increased with changes in the CPI, but only when the cumulative changes increased the then-effective limit by at least $10,000. For 2001, the limit was $170,000. EGTRRA increased the includable compensation limit to $200,000 in 2002 with indexing in future years in $5,000 increments rather than $10,000 increments.

Limits on Annual Additions and Benefits

As already mentioned, limits on annual additions and benefits are found in Section 415 of the IRC and are often referred to as the **Section 415 limits.** In general, there is one limit for the annual additions that can be made under a defined contribution plan and one limit for the annual benefit that can be paid from a defined benefit plan.[8]

Annual Additions Limit

This limit applies to the total employer and employee contributions that may be added to an employee's account each year under a defined contribution plan. This includes all employee contributions, whether made on a before- or after-tax basis.[9] Any forfeitures that might be reallocated to an employee's account when other employees terminate without full vesting are also included under this limit. If an employer maintains a contributory defined benefit plan, the after-tax employee con-tributions made under that plan are considered to be part of his or her annual addi-tion and will be added to contributions (employer and employee) made to any defined contribution plan.

The basic limit is that the amount added to an employee's account each year cannot exceed the smaller of (1) 100 percent of the employee's compensation and (2) $40,000. This $40,000 amount (in 2002) is adjusted for changes in the CPI. The adjusted

---

[8] In addition, there was a combined plan limit that applied for years through 1999 when an individual participated in both a defined contribution and a defined benefit plan. It should be noted that these limits were applied on a controlled-group basis; for this purpose, however, the controlled-group concept is applied to a parent/subsidiary group on the basis of more than 50-percent ownership or control, rather than 80 percent.

[9] For years beginning before January 1, 1987, the term *annual additions* meant the sum of employer contributions, after-tax employee contributions in excess of 6 percent of compensation (or 50 percent of after-tax contributions if less), and forfeitures. This distinction is important for purposes of the combined limit (described later) because of its cumulative nature.

amount will then be rounded down to the next lower multiple of $1,000. For 2002, the limit was $40,000. For this purpose, the percentage limit applies to compensation in a limitation year—the calendar year unless the employer elects otherwise.

For limitation years beginning before 1998, an employee's elective (before-tax) deferrals under a CODA or a tax-sheltered annuity or salary reduction contributions to a flexible benefits plan lowered his or her annual additions limit. For example, if an employee with gross compensation of $50,000 deferred $5,000 to a CODA, his or her annual additions limit was calculated on $45,000. For years beginning after 1997, however, these deferrals or salary reduction contributions do not reduce an employee's compensation for purposes of determining the annual addition limit.

Annual Benefit Limit

The maximum annual benefit that can be paid to a participant under a defined benefit plan is the lesser of (1) 100 percent of the participant's high three-year average compensation and (2) $160,000 (in 2002 and subsequently adjusted for inflation). The limit for 2002 was $160,000. The following should be kept in mind when considering this limit:

- The participant's high three-year average compensation is determined over the three consecutive calendar years during which his or her compensation was the highest.

- The compensation taken into account must meet one of the acceptable definitions of compensation described in Chapter 4.

- The compensation taken into account also must be limited to $200,000 (in 2002) adjusted for inflation.

- The limits apply only to employer-provided benefits; any after-tax employee contributions, as previously noted, will be subject to the annual additions limit, even though they are made to a defined benefit plan.

- The limits are reduced if the participant retires before age 62. Retirement prior to age 62 will be considered an early retirement for purposes of these limits, even though the retirement may be at the plan's normal retirement age.

- The limits are increased if a participant retires after his or her Social Security full benefit retirement age.

- After the dollar limits have been recalculated for changes in the CPI, the resulting figure will be rounded down to the next lower multiple of $5,000, and this rounded amount will become the current limit.

- The benefits are reduced if the participant has less than 10 years of participation or service. The dollar limit is reduced if he or she has less than 10 years of participation; the percentage limit is reduced if he or she has less than 10 years of service.

- There will be no reduction in the limits if benefits are paid in the form of a qualified joint and survivor annuity to the participant's spouse. The limits will be reduced, however, for any other optional form of payment.

- Many employers maintain both a defined benefit and a defined contribution plan. A special combined plan limit applied for years through 1999. The pension simplification provisions of the Small Business Job Protection Act of 1996 repealed this combined plan limit for years after 1999.

Joint and Survivor Annuities

The two death benefits required by law are (1) in the case of a vested participant who retires under the plan, the accrued benefit must be provided in the form of a **qualified joint and survivor annuity (QJSA);** and (2) in the case of a vested participant who dies before the annuity starting date and who has a surviving spouse, a **qualified preretirement survivor annuity (QPSA)** must be provided to the surviving spouse. The plan (or the employer) is not required to absorb the cost for either benefit; this cost may be passed on to the employee, typically in the form of a reduction in the retirement benefit otherwise payable.

These joint and survivor annuity requirements apply to all defined benefit plans and to money purchase plans.[10] They also apply to other defined contribution plans unless (1) the participant's vested account balance is paid in full upon his or her death to the participant's surviving spouse; (2) the participant has not elected benefits in the form of a life annuity contract; and (3) all or any portion of the participant's account balance has not been transferred from a plan subject to the joint and survivor rules.

The law defines a QJSA as an annuity for the life of the participant with a survivor annuity for the life of the participant's spouse that is not less than 50 percent or more than 100 percent of the amount of the annuity payable to the participant. The joint and survivor annuity must be the actuarial equivalent of a single life annuity for the life of the participant.

In general, the QPSA provides a survivor annuity for the life of the spouse in an amount not less than the amount that would be payable as a survivor annuity under the QJSA. In the case of a participant who dies after attaining the earliest retirement age, it is assumed that he or she has retired with an immediate QJSA on the day before the date of death. For a participant who dies before retirement eligibility, it is assumed that he or she has separated from service on the date of death, survived to the earliest retirement age, retired with an immediate QJSA at the earliest retirement age, and died the next day.[11] The benefit, however, need not be paid until the date the participant would have attained the earliest retirement age.

In the case of a defined contribution plan, a QJSA means an annuity for the life of the surviving spouse, the actuarial equivalent of which is not less than 50 percent of the account balance of the participant on the date of death.

---

[10] If the money purchase plan is part of an employee stock ownership plan (ESOP), the joint and survivor rules will not apply if the plan otherwise meets the conditions that exempt defined contribution plans from compliance.

[11] Note that if the plan requires a service period for early retirement that is greater than the service the participant has completed at the time of death, the earliest retirement age will be the participant's normal retirement age.

A participant may elect at any time during the applicable election period to waive the QJSA form of benefit or the QPSA form of benefit, or both, and may revoke any such election at any time during the applicable election period. However, the spouse must consent to the election. This requirement is satisfied if (1) the spouse of the participant consents in writing to such election, and the spouse's consent acknowledges the effect of the election and is witnessed by a plan representative or a notary public; or (2) it is established to the satisfaction of a plan representative that this consent cannot be obtained because there is no spouse or because the spouse cannot be located. It should be noted, however, that this notice is not required where the plan fully subsidizes the cost of the benefit, provided the plan does not permit a participant or beneficiary to select a form of benefit that does not satisfy the QJSA and QPSA requirements. The law defines this as a situation under which the failure to waive the benefit by a participant will not result in a decrease in any plan benefit for the participant and will not result in increased contributions for the participant.

These annuities need not be provided if the participant and spouse have been married less than one year. In general, QJSAs and QPSAs will not be required to be provided unless the participant and spouse have been married through the one-year period ending on the earliest of the participant's annuity starting date or the date of the participant's death. However, if a participant marries within one year before the annuity starting date, and the participant and the participant's spouse have been married for at least a one-year period ending on or before the date of the participant's death, the participant and spouse must be treated as having been married throughout the one-year period ending on the participant's annuity starting date.

The law also provides detailed notification requirements for both QJSAs and QPSAs. The rules for QJSAs require that each plan provide to each participant a written explanation of:

- The terms and conditions of the QJSA.

- The participant's right to waive the QJSA and the effect of this election.

- The rights of the participant's spouse.

- The right to revoke an election and the effect of this election.

The explanation must be provided within a reasonable period of time before the annuity starting date.

The rules for QPSAs require the plan to provide to each participant a written explanation that is comparable to that required for QJSAs. This explanation must be provided within the applicable period defined as the later of:

- The period beginning with the first day of the plan year in which the participant attains age 32 and ending with the close of the plan year in which the participant attains age 35.

- A reasonable period after the individual becomes a participant.

- A reasonable period after the plan ceases to fully subsidize the cost of the benefit.

- A reasonable period after the survivor benefit requirements become applicable with respect to the participant.

- A reasonable period after separation from service in case of a participant who separates before attaining age 35.

Distribution Rules

Unless otherwise requested by the participant, benefit payments must commence within 60 days of the latest of the following three events: (1) the plan year in which the participant terminates employment; (2) the completion of 10 years of participation; or (3) attainment of age 65 or the normal retirement age specified in the plan.

Minimum distribution rules are found in Section 401(a)(9) of the IRC. There are two distinct elements to these rules. The first is that distributions, either to an employee or a beneficiary, must commence within stated periods of time. The second is that distributions must be made in minimum amounts.[12]

The basic requirement is that distributions to a participant must commence by April 1 of the year following the later of (1) the year in which the participant retires or (2) the year in which he or she attains age 70½. In addition, distributions must be made by December 31 of each year thereafter.[13] For years prior to 1996, the rule was different—distribution had to commence by April 1 of the year following the year in which the participant attained age 70½, even though the participant was still working. While this old rule no longer applies to most employees, it still applies to 5 percent owners who must commence distribution when they reach age 70½, regardless of their employment status. The payments must be made over a period not exceeding the employee's life (or life expectancy) or the joint lifetimes (or joint life expectancy) of the employee and his or her beneficiary.

If the participant dies before payments have begun, a designated beneficiary was named, and the plan so allows; the participant's interest payable to or for the benefit of the designated beneficiary must commence within one year of the employee's death, and be distrubuted over the life of such beneficiary, or over the period not extending beyond the life expectancy of such beneficiary. This is known as the life expectancy rule. If this life expectancy rule is not used, or if the proper designated beneficiary is not named, the five-year rule requires that the entire interest of the employee be distributed within five years of the employee's death regardless of who or what entity receives the distribution. An exception to these rules is that if the beneficiary is the employee's spouse, distribution can be deferred until the employee would have reached age 70½.

---

[12] Failure to make distributions in accordance with these rules may result in the imposition of a penalty tax on the recipient of 50 percent of the amount by which the distribution falls short of the required amount. See Chapter 27 for a more detailed discussion on distribution issues.

[13] If an employee, other than a 5 percent owner, continues to work after age 70½, his or her accrued benefit under a defined benefit plan must be actuarially increased to take into account the period after age 70½ during which benefits are not being paid.

Top-Heavy Plans

If a plan is considered to be **top-heavy** (as defined in the following), it must:

- Meet one of two accelerated vesting schedules.

- Provide for minimum contributions or benefits for nonkey employees.

- Apply a reduced Section 415 combined plan limit to key employees.

Top-Heavy Plans Defined

A defined contribution plan is top-heavy in a plan year if, as of the determination date (generally the last day of the preceding plan year), either (1) the sum of account balances of all key employees participating in the plan is more than 60 percent of the sum of the account balances for all covered employees or (2) the plan is part of a top-heavy group, as explained below.

A defined benefit plan is top-heavy in a plan year if, as of the determination date, either (1) the present value of the accumulated accrued benefits of all key employees participating in the plan is more than 60 percent of the present value of the accumulated accrued benefits for all covered employees or (2) the plan is part of a top-heavy group.

A top-heavy group is the combination of two or more plans and, under the law, it may be required or permissible to aggregate two or more plans to determine top-heaviness. It is required to aggregate into a group (1) all plans covering key employees and (2) any plan upon which a key-employee plan depends for qualification under the coverage and nondiscrimination requirements of the IRC. It is permissible for an employer to expand the group by aggregating other plans as long as the resulting group continues to satisfy the coverage and nondiscrimination rules.

The 60 percent test applies to the top-heavy group. If the group is top-heavy, then each plan also is deemed to be top-heavy. However, a plan included solely at the employer's election is not necessarily considered top-heavy. In applying the top-heavy group rules, all plans of all employers who are part of the same controlled group are treated as a single plan.

In determining the present value of accrued benefits and account balances, the employer may count both employer and employee contributions. Accumulated deductible employee contributions, however, must be disregarded.[14] Also, in the past the employer counted any amount distributed to or for a participant under the plan within the five-year period ending on the current determination date. Under provisions enacted with EGTRRA, the five-year rule continues to apply with respect to in-service distributions; however, for distributions due to termination of service,

---

[14] A federal income tax deduction was available for qualified voluntary employee contributions prior to 1987.

death, or disability, only distributions during the year in which the determination is being made are taken into account.

Rollover and similar transfers to a plan made after 1983 will not be part of the top-heavy plan computation, unless they are made to a plan maintained by the same, or an affiliated, employer.

Key Employees Defined

Key employees are defined as (1) all officers[15] (up to a maximum of 50) with annual compensation in excess of $130,000 (indexed for cost-of-living adjustments in $5,000 increments); (2) an employee who owns a 5 percent or greater interest in the employer; and (3) an employee who owns a 1 percent or greater interest in the employer and whose annual compensation is more than $150,000.

The following should be considered when applying this definition:

- An employee who falls into more than one category need only be counted once.

- If an employer has more officers than are required to be counted, the officers to be considered are those with the highest compensation.

- An employee is considered to be a key employee only if he or she qualifies as a key employee during the plan year containing the determination date.

- In determining stock ownership, an employee is treated as owning stock even if it is owned by other members of his or her family or certain partnerships, estates, trusts, or corporations in which the employee has an interest. The rules for establishing ownership in noncorporate entities are similar to those for determining corporate ownership.

Top-Heavy Qualification Requirements

A top-heavy plan must meet certain additional requirements if it is to be qualified under the IRC. Moreover, the Internal Revenue Service (IRS) currently requires all plans (except governmental plans and certain plans covering only employees who are members of a collective bargaining unit), even if they are not top-heavy, to include provisions that will automatically take effect if that event should occur. These additional requirements are discussed in the sections that follow.

Vesting

A top-heavy plan must meet one of two alternative "fast" vesting schedules for all accrued benefits: (1) 100 percent vesting after three years of service; or (2) graded

---

[15] If the employer has between 30 and 500 employees, the number of officers included will never have to be greater than 10 percent of all employees. Also, the regulations state that the determination of whether a person is an officer will be based on all the facts and circumstances. Thus, not all individuals with the title of officer will be deemed officers for this purpose.

vesting of at least 20 percent after two years of service, 40 percent after three, 60 percent after four, 80 percent after five, and 100 percent after six years.[16]

Minimum Benefits for Nonkey Employees

A top-heavy plan must provide a minimum benefit or contribution for all nonkey employee participants. Social Security benefits or contributions may not be applied toward these minimums.

For each year (maximum of 10) in which a defined benefit plan is top-heavy, each nonkey employee must accrue an employer-provided benefit of at least 2 percent of compensation (generally defined as the average of the five consecutive highest years of pay). For each year in which a defined contribution plan is top-heavy, an employer must contribute at least 3 percent of compensation for each nonkey participant; however, in no case does an employer have to contribute more than the percentage contributed for key employees. Reallocated forfeitures are counted as employer contributions under a defined contribution plan. When a nonkey employee participates in both a defined benefit and a defined contribution plan, the employer does not have to provide minimum benefits under both plans. Since passage of EGTRRA, employer matching contributions are now taken into account in determining whether the minimum benefit requirement is satisfied for a defined contribution plan.

EGTRRA created a safe harbor for cash or deferred arrangements (i.e., 401 [k] plans) that meet the safe harbor requirements for the actual deferral percentage (ADP) nondiscrimination test and meet the requirements for matching contributions under Internal Revenue Code Section 401 (m)(11).[17] The impact of this provision was to expand the 401(k) ADP nondiscrimination safe harbor into a top-heavy safe harbor as well. Effectively, this provision eases the top-heavy requirements allowing smaller employers using a 401(k) safe harbor plan design to avoid the complexity of the top-heavy rules.

Other Tax Law Requirements

There are many other requirements that a plan must meet if it is to achieve and maintain a qualified status. Some of the more important ones are discussed in the following.

Must Be in Writing

A qualified plan must be in writing and must set forth all the provisions necessary for qualification. This is normally accomplished by means of a trust agreement, a plan document, or both.

---

[16] Since the provisions of EGTRRA compressed the minimum vesting schedules for voluntary employee-matched contributions from five-year cliff and seven-year graded to three-year cliff and six-year graded vesting, respectively, the vesting schedules imposed on top-heavy plans are not more onerous than normal vesting requirements if the plan involves voluntary employee-matched contributions.

[17] These safe harbor requirements are explained in Chapter 11.

A trust agreement generally is required for trust fund plans and for plans using individual insurance or annuity contracts along with a conversion fund.[18] This allows the employer to make irrevocable contributions on a basis that permits the employee to defer amounts including these contributions as taxable income until they are distributed. If a group pension contract is employed, an intervening trust usually is not necessary, since the same results can be achieved through the group contract itself.

Communication to Employees

The plan also must be communicated to employees. An announcement letter or booklet is frequently used for this purpose.[19] If employees are not given a copy of the actual plan, they should be told that a copy is available for inspection at convenient locations.

U.S. Trust

If a trust is used, it must be one organized or created in the United States and maintained at all times as a domestic trust. The earnings of a trust created outside of the United States will be taxable, although if the trust otherwise qualifies, the employer will be allowed to take appropriate deductions for its contributions.

Definitely Determinable Benefits

A qualified pension plan must provide definitely determinable benefits. A money purchase pension plan meets this requirement since the employer's contribution formula is definite and, for this reason, benefits are considered actuarially determinable. Also, variable annuity plans or plans under which the benefit varies with a cost-of-living index are acceptable.

Because of the definitely determinable benefit requirement, any amounts forfeited by a terminating employee may not be used to increase benefits for the remaining participants under a defined benefit plan. Instead, these forfeitures must be used to reduce employer contributions next due. Moreover, a defined benefit plan will not be considered to provide definitely determinable benefits unless actuarial assumptions are specified in the plan whenever any benefit under the plan is to be determined using those assumptions. The assumptions must be specified in the plan in a way that precludes employer discretion. For defined contribution plans, forfeitures can be used to increase benefits or reduce employer contributions.

The definitely determinable benefit requirement does not apply to profitsharing plans. While it is not required that there be a definite formula for determining the amount to be contributed to the profitsharing plan, it is required that there be a definite formula for allocating contributions among participants and distributing funds

---

[18] A trust agreement is not necessary for plan assets held in insurance policies or nontransferable annuities, assets held by insurance companies, or funds held in custodial accounts. However, a plan instrument of some type is still required so that plan provisions can be set forth in writing.
[19] For a discussion of employee communications using electronic means, see Final Rules Relating to Use of Electronic Communication and Record Keeping Technologies by Employee Pension and Welfare Benefit Plans; Final Rule, 29 CFR Part 2520 issued on April 9, 2002.

after a fixed number of years, upon the attainment of a stated age, or upon the happening of some event such as layoff, illness, disability, retirement, death, or severance of employment.

Anti-Cutback Rules

Because of the **anti-cutback rules,** a qualified plan may not be amended to eliminate or reduce a benefit that has already accrued unless the Internal Revenue Service (IRS) approves a request to amend the plan or the elimination or reduction satisfies certain requirements. However, a plan (subject to certain notice requirements) may be amended to eliminate or reduce benefits yet to be accrued.

Mergers and Consolidations

A plan must provide that the value of an employee's accrued benefit cannot be diminished in any way by any merger or consolidation with, or transfer of assets or liabilities to or from, any other plan.

Rollovers and Transfers

A plan must provide, as a condition of qualification, that recipients of distributions eligible for rollover treatment may make direct rollovers or transfers of the amounts to an individual retirement account (IRA) or another qualified plan. While plans are required to make such rollovers or transfers for distributees, they are not required to accept them on behalf of new employees.

EGTRRA expanded the flexibility associated with rollovers by permitting an employee to roll over after-tax contributions to an employee plan, an individual retirement account (IRA), or another defined contribution plan. EGTRRA also made a direct rollover the default option for involuntary distributions that exceed $1,000 when the qualified retirement plan provides that nonforfeitable accrued benefits which do not exceed $5,000 must be distributed immediately.

Assignments/Qualified Domestic Relations Orders (QDROs)

The law requires that a plan prohibit the assignment or alienation of benefits, with three exceptions: (1) an employee may be permitted to assign up to 10 percent of any benefit payment; (2) an employee may use his or her vested interest as collateral for a loan from the plan (if such loan is not a prohibited transaction and meets certain requirements[20]); and (3) a payment may be made to an alternate payee pursuant to a **qualified domestic relations order (QDRO).**

A QDRO is a domestic relations order that satisfies all of the following requirements:

1. It must create or recognize the existence of an alternate payee's right to, or assign to an alternate payee the right to, receive all or a portion of the benefit payable with respect to a participant under the plan. An alternate payee is a spouse, former spouse,

---

[20] See the discussion of loans in Chapter 9.

child, or other dependent of a participant who is recognized by a domestic relations order as having a right to receive all, or a part of, the benefits payable under the plan.

2. It must clearly specify certain facts about the participant's benefits. The order must clearly specify the name and the last known mailing address of the participant and the name and mailing address of each alternate payee covered by the order; the amount or percentage of the participant's benefit to be paid by the plan to each such alternate payee, or the manner in which such amount or percentage is to be determined; the number of payments or periods to which such an order applies; and each plan to which such an order applies.

3. It must not alter the amount or form of benefits. The QDRO may not require the plan to provide (1) any type or form of benefit, or any option, not otherwise provided under the plan; (2) (actuarially) increased benefits; or (3) the payment of benefits to an alternate payee when such benefits are already required to be paid to another alternate payee under another order previously determined to be a QDRO.

In the case of any payment before a participant has separated from service, a QDRO may require that payment be made to an alternate payee on or after the date on which the participant attains the earliest retirement age[21] as if the participant had retired on the date on which payment is to begin under the order. In this case, the amount of the payment is determined by taking into account the present value of the benefits actually accrued, rather than the present value of an employer subsidy for early retirement. The QDRO must be limited to a form that may be paid under the plan to the participant.

ERISA-Required Provisions

In addition to some of the provisions already mentioned, ERISA requires that several other items be covered in the plan. For example, the plan must provide for named fiduciaries and must set forth a procedure for establishing and carrying out the plan's funding policy. The plan also should describe clearly any procedure for the allocation of fiduciary and administrative duties and responsibilities, and it should stipulate the basis on which payments will be made to and from the plan. The plan also should spell out the procedure for making claims and for appealing claim decisions.

Chapter Summary

- The law establishes specific requirements for the determination of an employee's service in three key areas: (1) initial eligibility to participate; (2) vesting; and (3) the right to a benefit accrual. The law does not mandate how service is to be determined for other purposes (for example, the right to retire early).

- The Internal Revenue Code (IRC) requires that the employee's rights to that portion of his or her accrued benefit attributable to his or her own contributions be fully vested

---

[21] This has been defined as the earlier of (1) the earliest date benefits are payable under the plan or (2) the later of the date the participant attains age 50 or the date on which the participant could obtain a distribution from the plan if the participant separated from service.

at all times. In any event, accrued benefits attributable to employer contributions must vest when the employee reaches normal retirement age. Otherwise, they must vest at least as rapidly as provided by one of the following standards. The first standard requires that all accrued benefits must be 100 percent vested after five years of service. The second standard permits graded vesting, with 20 percent of accrued benefits vesting after three years of service and that percentage increasing in 20 percent multiples each year until 100 percent vesting is achieved after seven years. With passage of the Economic Growth and Tax Relief Reconciliation Act of 2001 (EGTRRA), the minimum vesting schedules were shortened beginning generally in 2002 for employer matching contributions to:

- 100 percent vesting after three years of service.
- Graded vesting, with 20 percent vesting after two years of service, increasing by 20 percent multiples for each year until 100 percent vesting is achieved after six years.

These accelerated vesting schedules apply only to employer matching contributions that match voluntary before- or after-tax employee contributions (as opposed to involuntary contributions made as a condition of employment). Similarly, employer contributions made to noncontributory, employer-pay-all type plans are subject to the previously mentioned five-year cliff and seven-year graded schedules.

- To achieve a tax-qualified status, a plan must observe two statutory limits on contributions and/or benefits. The first is a limit on the amount of an employee's compensation that may be taken into account when determining the contributions or benefits made on his or her behalf. The second is a limit on the annual additions that may be made to an employee's account in the case of a defined contribution plan, or on the benefits payable to an employee in the case of a defined benefit plan. Through 1999 there was a combined limit in the case of an employee who participated in both types of plans.

- The Tax Reform Act of 1986 added Section 401(a)(17) to the IRC, limiting the amount of an employee's compensation that can be taken into account in determining contributions or benefits under a qualified plan. For 2002, the limit is $200,000.

- In the case of a defined contribution plan, the basic limit is that the amount added to an employee's account each year cannot exceed the smaller of (1) 100 percent of the employee's compensation or (2) $40,000. This $40,000 amount (in 2002) is adjusted for changes in the CPI. The adjusted amount will then be rounded down to the next lower multiple of $1,000.

- In the case of a defined benefit plan, the maximum annual benefit that can be paid to a participant is the lesser of (1) 100 percent of the participant's high three-year average compensation and (2) $160,000 (in 2002 and subsequently adjusted for inflation).

- The two death benefits required by law are (1) in the case of a vested participant who retires under the plan, the accrued benefit must be provided in the form of a qualified joint and survivor annuity (QJSA); and (2) in the case of a vested participant who dies before the annuity starting date and who has a surviving spouse, a qualified preretirement survivor annuity (QPSA) must be provided to the surviving spouse. These joint and survivor annuity requirements apply to all defined benefit plans and to money purchase plans. They also apply to other defined contribution plans unless (1) the participant's vested account balance is paid in full upon his or her death to the participant's surviving spouse; (2) the participant has not elected benefits in the form of a life annuity contract; and (3) all or any portion of the participant's account balance has not been transferred from a plan subject to the joint and survivor rules.

- Unless otherwise requested by the participant, benefit payments must commence within 60 days of the latest of the following three events: (1) the plan year in which the partici- pant terminates employment; (2) the completion of 10 years of participation; or (3) the attainment of age 65 or the normal retirement age specified in the plan.

- If a plan is considered to be top-heavy, it must:
  - Meet one of two accelerated vesting schedules for all employer contributions.
  - Provide for minimum contributions or benefits for nonkey employees.

- Cash-or-deferred arrangements (i.e., 401[k] plans) meeting the safe harbor requirements for the actual deferral percentage (ADP) nondiscrimination test effectively comply with the top-heavy rules.

Key Terms

anti-cutback rules, p. *96*
break-in-service, p. *80*
computation period, p. *80*
elapsed-time method, p. *82*
hour of service, p. *81*
key employees, p. *93*
minimum distribution
    rules, p. *91*

qualified domestic relations
    order (QDRO), p. *96*
qualified joint and survivor
    annuity (QJSA), p. *89*
qualified preretirement
    survivor annuity
    (QPSA), p. *89*

Section 401(a)(17) of the
    IRC, p. *87*
Section 415 limits, p. *87*
standard hours–counting
    method, p. *81*
top-heavy (plan), p. *92*

Questions for Review

1. The law establishes specific regulations for the determination of service in what key areas?

2. When will an employee incur a break-in-service? Why is this significant?

3. Explain (a) how hours of service are generally related to the calculation of service for plan participants; (b) the break-in-service rules for maternity or paternity absences; and (c) the compliance methods available for counting hours of service.

4. Describe the vesting requirements for accrued benefits attributable to (*a*) the employee's contributions, (*b*) the employer's nonelective contributions, (*c*) the employer's matching contributions for employee voluntary contributions.

5. Does an employer have complete flexibility in determining the minimum benefit amount that must be credited to a participant who terminates from the plan in a vested status? Explain.

6. Describe the dollar limits for defined benefit and defined contribution pension plans.

7. Describe a qualified joint and survivor annuity (QJSA).

8. Describe the payments that must be provided under a qualified preretirement survivor annuity (QPSA) if (a) a participant dies after reaching the earliest retirement age and (b) a participant dies on or before the date of attaining the earliest retirement age.

9. When must a qualified plan start distributing plan benefits?

10. How is top-heaviness determined for a qualified pension plan? What are the consequences of such a status?

11. What are the three exceptions to a qualified plan's prohibition on the assignment and alienation of benefits?

Questions for Discussion

1. What public policy objectives are served by establishing specific requirements in connection with (*a*) service and vesting; (*b*) limits on plan contributions and/or benefits; (*c*) joint and survivor annuities; and (*d*) top-heavy rules?

2. An employer maintains two plans. Plan A covers key employees, while plan B covers nonkey employees. Both plans independently satisfy the coverage and nondiscrimination requirements of the IRC. (*a*) *Must* the employer aggregate the two plans to determine top-heaviness? (*b*) *May* the employer aggregate the two plans to determine top-heaviness? (*c*) Why would an employer want to aggregate the two plans if this option were available?

Resources for Further Study

Allen, Everett T., Jr. "Retirement Plan Design." *The Handbook of Employee Benefits.* 5th ed. Jerry S. Rosenbloom, ed. New York: McGraw-Hill, 2001.

Bloss, Julie L. *QDROs: A Guide for Plan Administration.* 2nd ed. Brookfield, WI: International Foundation of Employee Benefit Plans, 1997.

CCH Editorial Staff. "2001 Tax Legislation: Law, Explanation, and Analysis." *Commerce Clearing House Pension Plan Guide* (2001).

McDonnell, Ken; Paul Fronstin; Kelly Olsen; Pamela Ostuw; Jack Van Derhei; and Paul Yakoboski. *EBRI Databook on Employee Benefits.* 4th ed. Deborah Holmes, Lynn Miller, and Maureen Richmond, eds. Washington, DC: Employee Benefit Research Institute Education and Research Fund, 1997.

Salisbury, Dallas L. "Regulatory Environment of Employee Benefit Plans." *The Handbook of Employee Benefits.* 5th ed. Jerry S. Rosenbloom, ed. New York: McGraw-Hill, 2001.

Chapter 6

Other Legal Requirements

After studying this chapter you should be able to:

- Identify disclosure items that must be automatically filed with the government under Title I of ERISA.

- Describe the information that must be included in a summary plan description (SPD).

- Explain the claim denial procedure that a plan sponsor must include in an employee benefit plan.

- Describe what is meant by fiduciary responsibility under ERISA and who qualifies as a fiduciary.

- Distinguish ERISA exemptions for nonqualified plans and explain how these plans are treated differently from qualified employee benefit plans.

- Discuss other legislative requirements that affect employee benefit plans.

While tax law is clearly the most important law affecting qualified retirement plans, employers also must be concerned about the effects of other laws. This chapter briefly reviews some of the major laws that need to be considered in this regard.

The chapter first discusses the provisions of **Title I of ERISA**—the labor law provisions dealing with reporting, disclosure, and fiduciary responsibilities. This coverage of labor law provisions also discusses the potential application of other Title I requirements to executive benefit arrangements that do not meet the tax law standards for a qualified plan.[1] The chapter next treats prohibitions against age and sex discrimination. Securities and Exchange Commission (SEC) requirements also are

---

[1] The provisions of Title IV of ERISA deal with plan termination insurance and the Pension Benefit Guaranty Corporation (PBGC). Due to their complexity and the fact that they are applicable to defined benefit plans only, these provisions are treated separately in Chapter 16.

covered in this chapter because of their relevance for plans that permit employees to invest in employer stock. The chapter also includes a limited discussion of collective bargaining issues as well as a brief discussion of military leaves and unrelated business income.

ERISA—Title I

The labor law provisions of ERISA contained in Title I of the act include many provisions which are virtually identical to the tax law provisions that were passed at the same time. Thus, for example, Title I has minimum participation, funding, and vesting requirements, as well as joint and survivor protection for the spouses of employees. For the most part, however, jurisdiction and administration of these provisions has been assigned to the Internal Revenue Service (IRS) under the tax provisions—a notable exception being that the Department of Labor (DOL) was given jurisdiction over the determination of service for eligibility, vesting, and benefit accrual.

Title I, however, contains important provisions concerning two key areas: (1) reporting and disclosure and (2) fiduciary responsibilities. Except for some restrictions on prohibited transactions, there is no counterpart for these provisions in the tax law.

The following first discusses reporting and disclosure and then provides an overview of the fiduciary provisions of the law. There is also discussion of executive benefit plans that are not tax-qualified and which could come within the purview of other Title I provisions if certain conditions are not observed.

Reporting and Disclosure

A major aspect of Title I concerns the disclosure of information—to participants and their beneficiaries and to the government. These requirements generally apply to most tax-qualified plans regardless of the number of participants involved. There are, however, a limited number of exemptions. They do not, for example, apply to **unfunded excess benefit plans,** which are maintained to provide employees with benefits they would otherwise have received but which were not provided under the qualified plan because of Section 415 limitations. It should be noted that this exemption is limited in scope and does not, for example, apply to so-called excess benefit plans that restore benefits lost because of the maximum limit on pay that can be taken into account when calculating plan benefits or contributions. Also, if an unfunded plan is maintained for the exclusive benefit of a "select group of management or highly compensated employees," the only disclosure requirement is that the DOL be notified of the existence of the plan and the number of employees that it covers.

Otherwise, the disclosure and reporting provisions require that certain items be automatically filed with the government, others automatically given to employees, and still others made reasonably available to employees upon request. The following items are important disclosure documents:

- The plan's **summary plan description (SPD)**—that is, the booklet, folder, or binder that describes the plan and is given to employees.

- Any **summary of material modifications (SMM)**—a summary of any plan amendment or change in information that is required to be included in the SPD after the initial SPD has been issued.[2]

- The plan's annual financial report (filed using **Form 5500**).

Items that must be automatically distributed to employees include:

- The plan's SPD.

- Any SMMs.

- A **summary annual report (SAR)**—a summary of the plan's annual financial report.

- A statement of benefits for all employees who terminate employment.

- A written explanation to any employee or beneficiary whose claim for benefits is denied.[3]

There are other items that must be given to employees upon request and/or made available for examination at the principal office of the plan administrator and at other locations convenient for participants. These items include:

- Supporting plan documents.

- The complete application made to the IRS for determination of the plan's tax-qualified status.

- A complete copy of the plan's annual financial report.

- A personal benefits statement (on written request only and required to be furnished only once a year).

- A plan termination report (IRS Form 5310) should the plan be terminated.

The locations at which documents must be made available include any distinct physical location where business is performed and in which at least 50 participants work. Plan materials need not be kept at each location as long as they can be provided there within 10 working days after a request for disclosure. The employer may charge for reproduction of all materials requested unless the material falls in a category where it must be automatically furnished. Any item automatically distributed by mail must be sent by a class of mail that ensures timely delivery.

[2] Although previously an employer was required to automatically submit plan SPDs and SMMs to the Department of Labor, as of August 5, 1997, with passage of the Taxpayer Relief Act of 1997, plan administrators subject to the Employee Retirement Income Security Act were no longer required to file SPDs and SMMs or updated SPDs with the Labor Department. A plan sponsor must supply these documents to the Labor Department if requested. Civil penalties of up to $100 per day (not to exceed $1,000 per request) may be assessed against administrators who fail to furnish the requested information to the department within 30 days.
[3] There are many other items that also must be automatically furnished to employees under other provisions of the law (e.g., employees must be notified of rollover opportunities and related tax treatment).

Summary Plan Description (SPD)

The SPD must be given to new employees within 90 days after they become participants and to beneficiaries within 90 days after they start receiving benefits. For new plans, the initial SPD must be given to participants within 120 days after establishment of the plan. New, complete SPDs must be filed and distributed at least every 10 years. If there have been material changes since the last SPD was issued, however, the employer must file and distribute a new SPD every five years.

The SPD must be in permanent form and must be current regarding all aspects of the plan and the information required by Title I of ERISA. It must include the following information:

- The plan name and the type of plan (e.g., profit sharing).

- The type of plan administration (e.g., trusteed).

- The name (or position title) and address of the person designated as agent for the service of legal process, as well as a statement that legal process also may be served on a plan trustee or the plan administrator.

- The name, address, and telephone number of the plan administrator.

- The name and address of the employer (or employee organization) that maintains the plan.

- The name and/or title and business address of each trustee.

- The employer's identification number assigned by the IRS and the plan number assigned by the plan sponsor.

- In the case of a collectively bargained plan maintained by at least one employer and one employee organization, or, in the case of a plan maintained by two or more employers, the name and address of the most significant employer or organization plus either of the following: (1) a statement that a complete list of sponsors may be obtained on written request and is available for review or (2) a statement that, on written request, participants may receive information about whether a particular employer or organization is a sponsor and, if so, the sponsor's address.

- If a collective bargaining agreement controls any duties, rights, or benefits under a plan, a statement that the plan is maintained in accordance with the agreement and that a copy of the agreement may be obtained on written request and is available for examination.

- Plan requirements as to eligibility for participation and benefits (e.g., age, service, retirement age, and so forth).

- A description of the provisions for nonforfeitable benefits.

- Information about vesting, forfeiture of benefits, credited service, breaks-in-service, and so forth.

- A description of any joint and survivor benefits and any action necessary to elect or reject them.

- Circumstances that may result in disqualification, ineligibility, denial, loss, forfeiture, or suspension of benefits.

- A statement of the extent to which a pension plan is insured by the Pension Benefit Guaranty Corporation (PBGC); where more information about this insurance is available (usually from the administrator); and the name and address of the PBGC. A summary of the pension benefit guaranty provisions of Title IV of ERISA is included in the SPD content regulations. An SPD incorporating this language will be in compliance. In addition, SPDs for any pension plans that are not insured (e.g., profit sharing plans) must note the reason for lack of insurance.

- The source of contributions to the plan, the method by which contributions are determined, and the identity of any organization through which the plan is funded or benefits are provided.

- A description and explanation of plan benefits.

- The date of the end of the plan year for purposes of maintaining the plan's fiscal records.

- The procedures to be followed in presenting claims for benefits under the plan and the remedies available under the plan for the redress of claims that are denied in whole or in part.

- A statement of the participants' rights under Title I of ERISA. This must appear as a consolidated statement; no information may be omitted. (The regulations contain suggested language which, if used, will ensure compliance.)

When different classes of participants are covered with different benefits under the same plan, prominent notice must appear on the first page of the text listing the various classes for whom different SPDs have been prepared.

All this information must be "written in a manner calculated to be understood by the average plan participant" and should be "sufficiently accurate and comprehensive" to inform employees and beneficiaries of their rights and obligations under the plan. The explanations provided by legal plan texts and insurance contracts ordinarily will not meet these standards. The DOL regulations recommend the use of simple sentences, clarifying examples, clear and liberal cross-references, and a table of contents in the SPD. The use of type is important; varying sizes and styles of type may not be used when they may mislead employees.

If a plan covers 500 or more people who are literate only in a language other than English, or if 10 percent or more of the participants working at a "distinct physical place of business" are literate only in a non-English language (25 percent or more where the plan covers fewer than 100 participants), the SPD must include a prominent notice in the familiar language offering assistance—which may be oral—in understanding the plan.

Retired and terminated vested participants, as well as beneficiaries receiving benefits, come under Title I's definition of participants. Thus, they must be furnished automatically with copies of SPDs and SMMs; irrelevant plan amendments, however, need not be communicated, although copies must be available upon request.

Annual Report

A plan's annual financial report is filed on Form 5500. This form must be filed with the DOL[4] within seven months after the close of each plan year. For employers who have received extensions from the IRS for income tax filings, identical extensions are automatically granted for the plan's annual financial report.

The annual report is designed to require a complete disclosure of all financial information relevant to the operation of the plan. Thus, for example, it includes items such as a statement of assets and liabilities presented by category and valued at current value; changes in assets and liabilities during the year; and a statement of receipts and disbursements. It requests details, where applicable, for transactions with parties in interest, loans and leases in default or uncollectible, and certain reportable transactions (e.g., transactions involving in excess of 3 percent of the current value of plan assets). The report also requires information on plan changes made during the reporting period and on employees included or excluded from participation.

Certain financial statements in the report have to be certified by an independent qualified public accountant. Insurance companies and banks are required, within 120 days after the end of the plan year, to furnish any information necessary for the plan administrator to complete the annual report.

Plans that are fully insured are granted limited exemptions. These plans do not have to complete the financial information sections of the form, nor need they engage an accountant for audit or include an accountant's opinion. Plans with fewer than 100 participants have less complex filing requirements for their Form 5500.

Summary Annual Report (SAR)

An SAR must be automatically distributed to plan participants within two months after the filing date for Form 5500. The SAR is a simplified summary of the full annual report and may use language prescribed in current DOL regulations.

Summary of Material Modification (SMM)

When a material modification is made to a plan, a summary description of that change, written in clear language, must be distributed automatically to all affected participants and beneficiaries. The SMM must be furnished within 210 days after the end of the plan year in which the change is adopted.

Plan Documents

Plan documents include the text of the actual plan itself and any collective bargaining agreement, trust agreement, contract, or other document under which the plan is

---

[4] Traditionally Form 5500 was filed with the Internal Revenue Service. When Form 5500 was revised for 1999 and subsequent plan-year filings, completed forms and any required attachments could be filed electronically through the "EFAST" system. The Internal Revenue Service contracts the processing for Forms 5500 to the Department of Labor. However, should a plan sponsor file for an extension of time to file Form 5500, this is done by directly filing the application for extension (Form 5558) with the Internal Revenue Service.

established or operated. Plan participants and beneficiaries are entitled to receive copies of these documents within 30 days of making a written request. The DOL may request copies of these documents at any time.

Benefit Statements for Terminating Employees

Each **terminated vested participant**—that is, a participant who terminates service with a vested right in his or her plan benefits—should receive a clear statement of these benefits and the percentage that is vested. The statement should include the nature, amount, and form of the benefit. Any participant who has had a break-in-service of one year is automatically entitled to receive a benefits statement. Statements must be given to vested participants within 210 days after the end of the plan year in which they terminate service.

A statement also should be given to employees who terminate or incur a one-year break-in-service without a vested interest, thus clearly communicating that any such individual is not entitled to receive benefits under the plan.

Personal Benefits Statement

Plan participants and beneficiaries may request in writing a statement of their own benefits, but not more often than once in any 12-month period. The statement should include the total benefits accrued and the portion, if any, that is vested or, if benefits are not vested, the earliest date on which they will become vested.

Claim Denials

Anyone denied a claim under any plan is entitled to a written statement giving the reasons for the denial, usually within 90 days. This explanation should be a clear, comprehensible statement of the specific reasons for the denial of the claim. The explanation also must include a description of any material or information necessary for the claimant to improve the claim and the reasons why this additional material is needed. Also in the explanation should be a full description of the plan's appeal procedure. The claimant must be given at least 60 days thereafter in which to appeal the claim and is entitled to a final decision in writing within 60 days of the appeal (120 days in special circumstances).

Joint and Survivor Notifications

Under defined benefit pension plans and some defined contribution plans, each participant must be informed, individually and in writing, of the right to elect or reject both pre- and postretirement survivor benefits.

Timing for **notification as to postretirement survivor benefits** is nine months before the earliest retirement date under the plan. **Notification** for **preretirement survivor benefits** must be provided between the first day of the plan year in which the participant becomes age 32 and the end of the plan year in which he or she becomes 35. If an employee is over age 32 when hired, notification must be provided within three years after that employee becomes a plan participant. If a vested participant terminates employment before age 32, notice must be provided within one year after the termination date.

The notifications must include enough information about the potential financial impact on the individual's own benefit for the participant to make an informed decision. Contents of the notification are specified by regulations.

Rollover Notifications

When a distribution from a qualified plan is eligible to be rolled over into an individual retirement account (IRA) or another employer's qualified plan, the plan administrator, within a reasonable period of time before making the distribution, must send a **rollover notification** to the participant or beneficiary explaining the rollover and direct transfer rules, the tax withholding requirements on distributions that are not directly transferred, and how taxes can be reduced or deferred (e.g., rollover). In general, the timing of the notice must meet the same requirements that apply to notifying participants of their rights as to the qualified joint and survivor annuity rules under a defined benefit plan.

The Economic Growth and Tax Relief Reconciliation Act of 2001 (EGTRRA) expanded notice requirements for eligible rollover distributions by requiring that the written explanation being provided to recipients of eligible plan rollover distributions include a discussion of the potential restrictions and tax consequences that may apply to distributions from the new plan to which the distribution is rolled over that are different from those applicable to the distributing plan.

EGTRRA also made a direct rollover the default option for involuntary distributions that exceed $1,000 when the qualified retirement plan provides that nonforfeitable accrued benefits which do not exceed $5,000 must be distributed immediately.

Enforcement

ERISA provides for a number of penalties for violation of the disclosure requirements. Among the penalties are the following:

• If a plan administrator does not fill a participant's or beneficiary's request for information to which he or she is entitled under the plan within 30 days, the plan administrator may be personally liable to the individual who made the request, for a fine of up to $110 per day.

• Willful violation of any of the reporting and disclosure provisions may incur a criminal penalty of up to a $5,000 fine and/or one year in prison for an individual, and up to a $100,000 fine for a corporation.

• Civil actions may be brought against the plan administrator by participants or beneficiaries to obtain information to which they are entitled under their plan, to enforce their rights under the plan, or to clarify their rights to future benefits under the plan.

• Civil action also may be brought by the secretary of labor, a participant, a beneficiary, or another fiduciary against an individual who breaches his or her fiduciary duty.

It is expected that random audits will be performed continually and that a team of investigators will follow up on all discrepancies found and all complaints filed by plan participants or beneficiaries. Records now are required to be kept for a period of six years after the documents are due for filing, even for those plans that are exempt from filing.

Disclosure of Plan Information Using Electronic Media[5]

On April 9, 2002 the DOL issued final regualtions on disclosing plan information using electronic media. Previously safe harbors only were provided when issuing SPDs, SMMs, and SARs. The final regualtions expaned the scope of safe harbors to all ERISA Title I disclosures. Such items as pension plan investment information, material on pension plan loans, responses to written requests from plan participants and beneficiaries, and notices relating to qualified domestic relations orders may now be conveyed in electronic form. Compliance with the regualtion meets ERISA's general requirement that disclosure be "reasonably calculated to insure actual receipt." The regulation was effective October 9, 2002, regardless of plan year.

Electronic delivery may be used if the employee has access to the employer's computer system where the employee is reasonably expected to perform his or her duties. Access to the computer system must be an integral part of the employee's duties. Providing access to electronic documents using the computer kiosk in a common area would not meet this requirement. Use of electronic media is permitted for disclosure to non-employees as long as these individuals provide an address for electronic delivery of documents and affirmatively consent to the electronic disclosure in a manner that reasonably demonstrates the individual's ability to access information in electronic form. Non-employees must give this consent after receiving a statement from the plan sponsor explaining the electronic delivery system and the hardware and software needed to use it. Additionally, all of the following conditions must be met:

- The administrator must take appropriate and necessary measures to ensure that the system for furnishing the document results in actual receipt by participants of the transmitted information and documents.

- Each participant must be provided with notice, through electronic means or in writing, apprising the participant of the document to be furnished electronically, the significance of the document, and the participant's right to request and receive a paper copy of the document.

- On request, the plan administrator must provide the document in paper form to a participant.

- The electronically furnished version of the document must be the same in all material respects as the paper version.

- The electronically furnished document must satisfy all other requirements with respect to the substance and presentation required to be in the paper version of such a document.

[5] Neal S. Schelberg, Craig A. Bitman, and Steven D. Weinstein, "Paperless Benefit Plan Administration," *Compensation & Benefits Review* (July/August 2000), pp. 59–61. Reprinted with Permission of Sage Publications, Inc. Copyright © Sage Publications, Inc., Thousand Oaks, CA.

- When a disclosure includes personal information relating to an individual's accounts or benefits, the plan administrator must take reasonable and appropriate steps to safeguard the confidentiality of the information.

The Internal Revenue Service has stated in Notice 99–1 that where the code or regulations do not specify how a particular transaction is to be conducted (e.g., in writing), then a plan may perform the transaction electronically without jeopardizing the plan's qualified status under the code. The IRS provided various examples of activities that can be performed with the assistance of electronic media. The enumerated actions include the following:

- Enrolling participants in a plan.

- Designating employee contribution rates.

- Designating beneficiaries (except where spousal consent is required).

- Designating investment allocation of future contributions and currently held assets.

- Receiving and responding to participant information requests.

- Electing direct rollovers.

With respect to those plan activities for which the IRS has detailed a specific means of execution, electronic media may not be used unless the IRS has issued specific guidance permitting such use.

According to the IRS, functions may be performed through the use of electronic media if the following conditions are satisfied:

- The electronic media must be reasonably accessible to the participant.

- The electronic form of the notice must be as understandable as the paper version.

- The participant must be advised that he or she has the right to request and receive the notice or consent forms in paper version at no charge.

- The system must be reasonably designed to preclude someone other than the appropriate party from giving consent (e.g., by using passwords).

- The system must give the participant a reasonable opportunity to review, modify, or rescind his or her consent before an election becomes effective.

- The participant must be given confirmation of his or her consent and the terms thereof either through paper or electronic media.

Fiduciary Requirements

Fiduciary provisions are set forth in Part Four of Title I of ERISA, although the definition of fiduciary is found in Part One of ERISA, Section 3(21). The following provides a brief overview of these provisions.

Definition of Fiduciary

A person (or corporation) is considered a **fiduciary** under ERISA if that person exercises any discretionary authority or control over the management of the plan;

exercises any authority or control over assets held under the plan or the disposition of plan assets; renders investment advice for direct or indirect compensation (or has any authority or responsibility to do so); or has any discretionary authority or responsibility in the administration of the plan.

Clearly, the trustee of a plan is a fiduciary. So also are officers and directors of a corporation who have responsibility for certain fiduciary functions—for example, the appointment and retention of trustees or investment managers. On the other hand, individuals whose duties are purely ministerial (e.g., applying rules of eligibility and vesting) are clearly not fiduciaries.

Fiduciary Responsibilities

A fiduciary is required to discharge all duties solely in the interest of participants and beneficiaries and for the exclusive purpose of providing plan benefits and defraying reasonable administrative expenses. In addition, a fiduciary is charged with using the care, skill, prudence, and diligence that a prudent person who is familiar with such matters would use under the circumstances then prevailing—a standard that has come to be called the **prudent expert rule.** A fiduciary also is responsible for diversifying investments so as to minimize the risk of large losses unless it is clearly prudent not to diversify.[6] Finally, the fiduciary must conform with the documents governing the plan and must invest only in assets subject to the jurisdiction of U.S. courts. This latter requirement does not preclude investing in international securities; it simply requires that the assets be held in a manner such that they are subject to the jurisdiction of U.S. courts.

Prohibited Transactions

Both labor law (Title I of ERISA) and the IRC prohibit certain transactions between the plan and "disqualified persons."[7] A disqualified person is broadly defined to include any plan fiduciary; a person providing service to the plan; any employer or employee organization whose employees or members are covered by the plan; a direct or indirect owner of 50 percent or more of the business interest of the employer; a relative of any of the above; an officer, director, and certain HCEs; or a person having 10 percent or more of the ownership interest in any of the above. Under ERISA, an employee also is considered to be a party in interest; an employee, however, is not considered to be a disqualified person.

The following transactions between the plan and a party in interest or a disqualified person are prohibited:

- The sale, exchange, or leasing of property.

- Lending money or extending credit (including funding the plan by contributing debt securities).

---

[6] Investments in employer securities in accordance with the prohibited transaction rules also are permitted under the diversity requirement; however, they must comply with the prudence and "exclusive benefit of employees" standards.

[7] The IRC refers to transactions between the plan and disqualified persons. ERISA refers to transactions between the plan and "parties in interest." For the most part, IRC and ERISA provisions are similar, although the penalties for engaging in a prohibited transaction differ.

- Furnishing goods, services, or facilities.

- A transfer or use of plan assets.

- The acquisition of qualifying employer securities and real property in excess of allowable limits.

These prohibitions apply even to "arm's length" transactions and even though the plan is fully protected.

Under ERISA, a fiduciary will be personally liable for any breach or violation of responsibilities and will be liable to restore any profits made through the use of plan assets. Under the IRC, an excise tax of a percentage of the amount involved in a prohibited transaction may be levied on the disqualified person who engages in the transaction. For prohibited transactions occurring after August 5, 1997, the initial excise tax is 15 percent of the amount involved. If the situation is not corrected within the time allowed (90 days unless extended by the IRS), a further excise tax of 100 percent of the amount involved may be imposed. However, engaging in a prohibited transaction will not cause the plan to be disqualified.

As noted above, the prohibited transaction rules limit the investment of plan assets in qualifying employer securities and real property. Qualifying employer securities include stock. Marketable obligations (e.g., bonds and notes) also are considered to be qualifying employer securities if certain requirements are met. Qualifying employer real property includes real property that is dispersed geographically, is suitable for more than one use, and has been leased to the employer.

In general, defined benefit and money purchase plans cannot invest more than 10 percent of the fair market value of plan assets in employer securities. Deferred profit sharing plans that specifically so provide may invest without limit in employer securities or real property; if the plan does not so specify, however, a 10 percent limit will apply. Of course, stock bonus plans are primarily invested in employer securities.

Even though investment in employer securities and real property is permitted under the prohibited transaction rules (and under the fiduciary requirements for diversity), investments of this type must still satisfy the overriding requirement that they be for the exclusive benefit of employees. Moreover, they also must satisfy the fiduciary requirement of prudence.

Fiduciary Liabilities

Apart from excise taxes that might be imposed because of a prohibited transaction under the tax law, a fiduciary will be personally liable for any breach or violation of responsibilities and will be liable to restore any profits made through the use of plan assets.

In addition, the DOL may impose a 20 percent penalty on any fiduciary who is found liable for a breach of fiduciary rules. The penalty is applied to the recovery amount—that is, the amount recovered from the fiduciary on behalf of the plan or its participants pursuant to either an out-of-court settlement with the DOL or a court order under a judicial proceeding instituted by the DOL. The DOL may waive or reduce the penalty in cases where the fiduciary acted reasonably and in good faith or where the fiduciary will not be able to restore all losses to the plan absent the waiver or reduction. The penalty is automatically reduced for prohibited transactions by the 15 percent excise tax imposed in those cases.

A fiduciary also may be liable for the violations of a cofiduciary if the fiduciary knowingly participates in or conceals a violation, has knowledge of a violation, or by the fiduciary's own violation enables the cofiduciary to commit a violation. If a plan uses separate trusts, however, a trustee of one trust is not responsible for the actions of the other trustees. Also, a fiduciary will not be responsible for the acts of a duly appointed investment manager (except to the extent that the fiduciary did not act prudently in selecting or continuing the use of the investment manager). A trustee also is not responsible for following the direction of named fiduciaries in making investment decisions if the plan so provides.

Delegation of Authority

Noninvestment activities can be delegated by a fiduciary if the plan so permits and the procedure for doing so is clearly spelled out; however, fiduciaries remain responsible,

Liability of Service Providers   1

In *Mertens* v. *Hewitt Associates,* 61 USLW 4510, 1993 U.S. LEXIS 3742 (June 1, 1993), the Supreme Court held that a non-fiduciary who knowingly participates in a breach of fiduciary duty is not liable under ERISA for losses that an employee benefit plan suffers as a result of such a breach. In *Mertens,* pension plan participants alleged that the plan actuary caused losses to the plan by failing to change actuarial assumptions to reflect the additional costs of early retirement prompted by Kaiser's phase-out of its steelmaking operations, which caused inadequate funding and ultimate termination of the plan. Plaintiffs filed suit under ERISA Section 502(a)(3), which authorizes civil actions to enjoin violations or "to obtain other appropriate relief." The court rejected plaintiffs' contention that "appropriate equitable relief" encompasses monetary damages.

Without congressional action, the *Mertens* decision probably forecloses actions for monetary damages against actuaries, accountants, attorneys, insurance companies, and other professional service providers. The majority opinion acknowledges in dicta that state laws addressing the liability of nonfiduciaries may be preempted under ERISA, thus leaving beneficiaries with "less protection than existed before ERISA." According to the court, however, ERISA is "an enormously complex and detailed statute that resolved innumerable disputes between powerful competing interests—not all in favor of potential plaintiffs."

Source: Reprinted with permission from *Employee Benefit Issues: The Multiemployer Perspective,* vol. 35, chap. 36, 1993, pp. 418–427, by Stuart W. Davidson and Caren Litvin. Copyright 1994 published by the International Foundation of Employee Benefit Plans, Brookfield, WI. All rights reserved. Statements or opinions expressed in this article are those of the authors and do not necessarily represent the views or positions of the International Foundation, its officers, directors, or staff.

under the prudent expert rule, for persons delegated those responsibilities. Similarly, they remain responsible for the acts of their agents in performing ministerial duties.

Earmarked Investments—Section 404(c)

The law permits a defined contribution plan to be established on a basis that allows **earmarked investments**—that is, employees are allowed to direct the investment of their own accounts. Under these plans, sponsors and other plan fiduciaries might be exempt from liability for investment returns that result from participant choices, provided that participants are given the opportunity to exercise control over the assets in their individual accounts and can choose from a broad range of categories.

The DOL has issued regulations that provide statutory relief from fiduciary liability under these plans if certain requirements are met. Failure to comply with these requirements does not necessarily mean that the fiduciaries will be liable for investment performance; it simply means that this regulatory protection is not available.

To ensure that participants have both control over their assets and the opportunity to diversify their holdings, the regulations:

- Require the plan to provide participants with reasonable opportunities to give investment instructions to the plan fiduciary, who is obligated to comply with these instructions.

- Require that a plan offer at least three "diversified categories of investment"— with materially different risk and return characteristics—that collectively allow participants to construct a portfolio with risk and return characteristics within the full range normally appropriate for a plan participant.

- Establish specific rules regarding participant transfer elections; sponsors must allow at least quarterly elections for transfers in or out of the three diversified investment options that must, as a minimum, be offered under the plan, and more frequent transfers may be required if appropriate in light of the volatility of a particular investment.

Look-through investment vehicles, such as mutual funds or bank commingled funds and guaranteed investment contracts, qualify as diversified categories of investment because the underlying assets are diversified. Employer stock, however, does not qualify as a diversified category of investment, although some liability protection is provided if the stock is publicly traded and if certain other conditions are met.

Each participant must be provided with or have the opportunity to obtain sufficient information to make informed decisions as to investment alternatives under the plan, as well as financial information concerning these alternatives. This includes, among other things:

- A general description of the investment objectives and risk and return characteristics of each investment alternative.

- An explanation of how to give investment instructions and any limitations on such instructions.

- An identification of investment managers.

- An explanation of voting, tender, and similar rights.

- A description of transaction fees and expenses that could affect the participant's account balance.

- The name, address, and phone number of the plan fiduciary.

- Where appropriate for the investment alternative, any applicable prospectus.

- A notice that the plan is intended to comply with ERISA Section 404(c) and that fiduciaries' liability is thereby limited.

Employee Investment Education

The majority of defined contribution plans let participants direct how their account balances will be invested. While employers recognize the need to encourage employees to save, they have been reluctant to provide extensive education about investing these savings. This reluctance has been due, in part, to the fiduciary provisions of ERISA, which impose both responsibility and liability on those who provide investment advice for a fee or other compensation. The concern for these employers has been to distinguish between investment education and investment advice, recognizing that some efforts to provide only education may end up being interpreted as advice.

The DOL has issued an interpretive bulletin to enable employers and providers to distinguish between education and advice. The bulletin specifies four types of investment-related information that employers can provide without fear of exposing themselves to fiduciary liability in the view of the DOL.[8]

These safe harbors are:

- *General plan provisions.* This includes information about plan features and operations, the benefits of participating in the plan, and descriptions of the plan's investment alternatives, including investment objectives, risk and return characteristics, and historical information—as long as such information does not address the appropriateness of particular investment options for a given participant or beneficiary.

- *General financial and investment information.* Information about general investment concepts may be provided—for example, risk and return, diversification, dollar-cost averaging, and the advantages of tax-favored savings. It is also acceptable to provide information as to historical differences in rates of return between different asset classifications, investment time horizons, and estimates of future retirement income needs.

- *Asset allocation models.* Participants and beneficiaries can be provided with asset allocation models illustrating the projected performance of hypothetical asset allocations using varying time horizons and risk profiles.

---

[8] The Securities and Exchange Commission (SEC) has indicated that *employers* whose educational efforts conform to these four "safe harbors" will not be subject to registration or regulation under the Investment Advisors Act of 1940 (unless, of course, they hold themselves out as investment advisors or otherwise meet the definition of advisors in the 1940 law).

• *Interactive investment material.* Acceptable material here includes items such as questionnaires, worksheets, computer software, and other materials that employees can use to estimate their retirement income needs and the potential impact of various investment strategies on their ability to meet those needs.

To qualify for safe harbor treatment, asset allocation models and interactive materials must be based on generally accepted investment theories and their underlying assumptions must be disclosed (or, in the case of interactive materials, selected by the participant). And, if allocation models or interactive materials identify a specific investment option under the plan, they should indicate that other investment alternatives having similar risk and return characteristics may be available under the plan and must identify where information on these alternatives may be obtained. Further, models and interactive materials must be accompanied by a statement explaining that participants should consider all of their other income, assets, and investments in applying the model or using the interactive tool.

The DOL's bulletin also points out that employers may be able to provide investment education that falls outside these safe harbors without automatically being viewed as providing investment advice.

American Savings Education Council (ASEC)   2

Concern about the need to educate employees as to investment issues has led to the formation of the American Savings Education Council—a partnership of employers and organizations in the investment field. The stated aims of this organization are to

• Increase the quality and volume of public and worker education on the virtues of saving and planning for retirement.

• Facilitate easy access to information on; "what to," "how to," and "where to" find information and opportunities for retirement saving.

• Disseminate best practices and examples of tools for saving education.

• Document results within employer settings, analyzing the relative success of educational initiatives.

• Highlight the many ways individuals can save for retirement through defined benefit, 401(k), 403(b), 457, and simplified employee pension plans, money purchase plans, profit sharing plans, savings bonds, and individual retirement accounts.

• Make saving and retirement planning a permanent concern in the lives of Americans.

Source: ASEC Informational Brochure or www.asec.org/pamphlet.htm, 2000. ASEC, Suite 600, 2121 K Street NW, Washington, DC, 20037-1896. 202-659-0670.

The Economic Growth and Tax Relief Reconciliation Act of 2001 (EGTRRA) provided that employer-provided qualified retirement planning services are excludable from employees' gross wages. The exclusion applies to qualified retirement planning services offered to both employees and their spouses by employers sponsoring qualified retirement plans for years beginning after December 31, 2001. In order for this exclusion to apply to highly compensated employees, it must be available on substantially the same terms to rank and file employees. The provision allows for overall retirement income planning such as how the employer's plan fits into an employee's overall retirement income plan. The provision does not allow for related services such as tax preparation, accounting, legal, or brokerage services.

Remittance of Employee Contributions

The DOL has taken the position that participant contributions become plan assets as of the date they can be segregated from the employer's general assets but no later than 90 days after withholding. However, the DOL issued final regulations in August 1996 that shorten this outside deadline to the 15th business day following the month in which the employee contribution is received or withheld. A procedure is set forth under which an employer can obtain an additional 10 business days if certain conditions are met. This rule was generally effective February 3, 1997, although for collectively bargained plans, the effective date was extended to the first day of the plan year after the latest bargaining agreement in effect on August 7, 1996, had expired.

Miscellaneous Requirements

Plan provisions that purport to relieve a fiduciary of responsibilities are void and of no effect. However, a plan, employer, union, or fiduciary may purchase insurance to cover the fiduciary's liability, but if the plan purchases this insurance, the insurer must have subrogation rights against the fiduciary. An employer or union also may agree to indemnify a fiduciary against personal liability.

If convicted of certain specified crimes, a person cannot serve as a plan administrator, fiduciary, officer, trustee, custodian, counsel, agent, employee, or consultant for five years after conviction (or the end of imprisonment, if later). This prohibition will not apply if citizenship rights have been restored or if approved by the United States Board of Parole.

All fiduciaries and persons who handle plan funds or other plan assets are to be bonded for 10 percent of the aggregate amount handled, with minimum and maximum dollar amounts specified.

A plan must be established and maintained pursuant to a written instrument that specifically provides for one or more named fiduciaries. Each plan must provide a procedure for establishing and carrying out a funding policy and method to achieve plan objectives, and it must describe any procedure for allocating operational and administrative responsibilities. There also must be a provision that sets forth the amendment procedure and identifies the persons who have authority to amend the plan. The plan also must specify the basis on which payments are made to and from the plan.

Nonqualified Plans

As noted earlier, Title I of ERISA contains a number of labor law provisions that parallel the tax law requirements for qualified plans. For the most part, these provisions do not come into play insofar as qualified plans are concerned and—with the exception of determining service for eligibility to participate, vesting, and benefit accruals—the tax law provisions are controlling.

It must be remembered, however, that ERISA defines **pension plan** in very broad terms—on a basis that encompasses any plan, fund, or program maintained by an employer to the extent that, by its express terms or as a result of surrounding circumstances, it provides retirement income to employees or results in a deferral of income for periods extending to termination of employment or beyond.

Thus, any plan of deferred compensation, to the extent that it does not meet the tax law requirements for a qualified plan, comes under the purview of Title I and, unless exempted, must comply with various requirements such as minimum participation, funding, and vesting, joint and survivor provisions, and the like. If a plan is not tax-qualified, and if it must be funded and vested, the tax consequences could be undesirable—with employees being in constructive receipt of the value of vested benefits. Thus, most employers prefer to design programs that qualify for one of the available exemptions.

One specific exemption is granted for **excess benefit plans**—plans that provide employees with contributions and/or benefits that would otherwise have been provided to them under the qualified plan were it not for the limitations of Section 415. This exemption is total for excess benefit plans that are unfunded; if funded, the exemption is partial and compliance is required only for reporting, disclosure, and fiduciary rules.[9]

Another exemption applies to plans that are "unfunded and . . . maintained by an employer primarily for the purpose of providing deferred compensation for a select group of management or highly compensated employees." However, these plans are still subject to the reporting and disclosure requirements of Title I.[10] Although ERISA has been in effect since the mid-1970s, this phrase has never been clarified by the DOL. Thus, there is some uncertainty as to how it may be applied. The concern, of course, is that if the group covered does not come within this exemption, the entire plan could become subject to all Title I provisions.

Despite this uncertainty, many employers have established supplemental executive benefit programs that rely on this exemption. Many of them are limited to **restoration plans** that simply restore benefits lost under qualified plans because of restrictions other than Section 415—for example, the limitation on pay that can be used to determine contributions and benefits or the annual limit on elective deferrals. Other plans are much broader in scope, encompassing all forms of deferred compensation and providing benefits for executives that are clearly in addition to those contemplated by broad-based programs. Executive benefit programs are covered at length in Chapter 20.

---

[9] A partial exemption from disclosure and reporting has been provided by the DOL for these plans. In essence, all that is required is that the DOL be notified of the existence of any such plan and the number of individuals it covers.

[10] The partial exemption from disclosure and reporting also applies to these plans.

Unrelated Business Income

While the investment income of a qualified trust established in conjunction with a qualified plan is generally exempt from tax, all or part of this income could be subject to tax if it is considered to be **unrelated business income.**

Unrelated business income is the gross income derived from any unrelated trade or business regularly carried on by the trust, less allowable deductions directly connected with the carrying on of such trade or business, with certain exclusions.

Only income resulting from the *direct* operation of the unrelated trade or business is subject to tax. Thus, for example, if the trust owns all of the stock of a corporation but the corporation directly operates the business, the stock dividends received by the trust will not be subject to tax.

The following income is not considered to be unrelated business income: dividends, interest, annuities, royalties, most rents from real property, and gains from the sale or exchange of noninventory property, except if such income is attributable to debt-financed property.

Age/Sex Discrimination

Discrimination on the basis of age is prohibited by the **Age Discrimination in Employment Act (ADEA),** as amended; discrimination on the basis of sex (or sex-related conditions, such as pregnancy) is prohibited by Title VII of the Civil Rights Act of 1964, as amended.

In the case of age discrimination (which protects employees age 40 and older), the major requirements for retirement-type plans are as follows:

• An employee cannot be excluded from participation because of age. Use of a minimum age of up to 21, as permitted under ERISA and the tax law, is acceptable; use of any maximum age is prohibited.

• An employee cannot be required to contribute more or at higher levels because of having attained an age that is 40 or more, nor can employer contributions and/or employer-provided benefits be increased or decreased by reason of age. It is permissible, however, for both employee and employer contributions and for employer-provided benefits to change with respect to length of service where this is clearly not age-related.[11]

• An employee cannot be made to retire upon attaining any specified age, such as the plan's normal retirement age.[12]

• As long as a participating employee remains employed, he or she must be eligible to continue full participation in the plan. In the case of a defined contribution

---

[11] In the case of a defined benefit pension plan, any increase in employer-provided benefits on account of length of service would have to comply with the benefit accrual rules that limit the extent to which a plan can be "backloaded."

[12] There is a limited exception for "bona fide" executives whose annual employer-provided benefit from all sources is $44,000 or more. For these individuals, an employer can enforce mandatory retirement at age 65.

plan, this means that the employee must continue to share in employer contributions (assuming the employee makes any mandatory contributions or elective deferrals that are required as a condition of receiving such contributions). In the case of a defined benefit plan, the employee must continue to accrue benefits for actual pay changes up to the time of retirement; the employee also must continue to accrue benefits for service until the plan maximum on service, if any, has been reached.

The prohibitions against sex discrimination are similar:

- Different employee and/or employer contributions cannot be made or required on account of the employee's sex.

- Benefits provided cannot be different by reason of the employee's sex.

- There can be no distinction in any plan eligibility requirements—for initial participation, rights to certain options or benefits, treatment of leaves of absence, and so forth—on account of sex.

- If annuity or lifetime installment benefits are offered by the plan, there can be no distinction in annuity or installment costs and/or benefits on account of sex; these costs and benefits must be based on unisex mortality tables.

Military Leaves

Although prior law required employers to give vesting and eligibility credits for periods of military service under all types of retirement plans, benefit accruals were clearly required only under defined benefit plans. Legislation passed in 1996 broadened veterans' pension rights by requiring employers to also make retroactive contributions for periods of military service to defined contribution plans upon the employees' return to work.

For a cash or deferred arrangement (CODA) or a plan permitting after-tax contributions, the returning employee must be allowed to make up missed deferrals or contributions over a period equal to three times the period of military service—up to a maximum of five years. If the employee does this, the employer must make up any missed matching contributions. Employers also are required to contribute any missed profit sharing allocations. However, employers are not required to make up earnings and forfeitures with respect to missed contributions.

Amounts credited to employees under pay-based plans must be based on the compensation rate the employee would have received had he or she not taken military leave. If the pay that would have been paid is not "reasonably certain," the credit could be based on the employee's pay for the 12-month period preceding military service.

Securities and Exchange Commission (SEC) Requirements

Various securities law requirements affect employee benefit and executive compensation plans. The following is a brief discussion of registration requirements and insider trading restrictions.

Offering Registration

In general, an offer to sell securities must either be registered with the SEC or conform to an available exemption from registration. If an offering must be registered with the SEC, a prospectus generally must be prepared for distribution to potential purchasers.

For purposes of this registration requirement, employee benefit plans can be divided into two groups: (1) those under which *employee* contributions are invested in employer stock and (2) all other plans. After-tax contributions always are considered employee contributions for this purpose. Elective deferrals, however, are treated differently, depending upon whether they are made by way of salary reduction or by foregoing a year-end profit sharing contribution or bonus. The former type of elective deferral is considered to be an employee contribution, notwithstanding the fact that for tax purposes, it is considered to be an employer contribution. The latter type is treated by the SEC, as well as by tax law, as an employer contribution.

A plan that does not involve the investment of employee contributions in employer stock does not have to be registered with the SEC (e.g., an employee stock ownership plan [ESOP] funded entirely with employer contributions). However, any employee benefit plan in which employee contributions may be invested in employer stock is considered an offering to sell securities. Thus, such a plan must be registered with the SEC (and a prospectus prepared) or it must fit within an exemption. In many cases, no exemption is available for plans of publicly traded companies and such plans must be registered. A special type of registration, using the format of Form S-8, is available.[13]

In lieu of using a prospectus, an employer can meet its disclosure requirements through a variety of documents, including SPDs; however, the typical SPD will not be sufficient, by itself, to meet the SEC disclosure requirements (e.g., that there be a three-year history of financial data on investment alternatives).

It also should be noted that a prospectus (or equivalent information) must be given to employees before they are eligible to participate in the plan.

Plans that are registered with the SEC must file annual reports with the commission, using Form 11-K; this requirement, however, does not apply (except for the initial filing) to plans with fewer than 300 participants.

Insider Trading Restrictions

Section 16(b) of the Securities Exchange Act prohibits an insider from buying and selling, or selling and buying, company stock within a six-month period. Insiders who violate this six-month trading restriction are required to return all short-swing profits made on such a transaction to the company.

These insider trading rules are not relevant to a variety of broad-based retirement and allied make-up plans covering insiders—for example, defined benefit plans. However, they must be considered for any such plans that are individual account plans and

---

[13] Plans of private companies may be exempt under Rule 701. This rule permits an employer to grant up to $5 million worth of stock annually to employees without registration. This rule also requires that employees be given a copy of the plan document and that they receive adequate disclosure of material information. Further, the SEC must be notified within 30 days after sales total $100,000 and annually thereafter.

provide for investments in actual or phantom employer stock by insiders. In this case, transactions that increase the amount of stock allocated to an insider are "purchases," and transactions that decrease the amount of stock allocated to an insider are "sales."

The SEC completely revised the insider trading rules with respect to broad-based plans in 1996. The revised rules, and their application to defined contribution and other plans, are discussed next.

Blanket Exemption

Nearly all transactions under broad-based plans are now exempt without any conditions—other than that the plan involved must satisfy one of the definitions so as to be a "qualified plan," an "excess benefit plan," or a "stock purchase plan"—or unless they constitute a discretionary transaction (described in the next section).

• To be a qualified plan, the plan must satisfy the coverage and participation requirements of Section 410 of the IRC.[14]

• An excess benefit plan is defined as one that is operated in conjunction with a qualified plan and that provides *only* the benefits or contributions that cannot be provided under the qualified plan because of the limitations of Section 401(a)(17),[15] Section 415, and any other applicable contribution or benefit limit set forth in the IRC.[16]

• A stock purchase plan is defined as a plan that meets the coverage and participation requirements of Sections 423(b)(3) or 423(b)(5), or, in the alternative, Section 410 of the IRC. The purpose of including this alternative is to make the exemption available to plans that do not satisfy Section 423 but nonetheless cover a broad base of employees. For example, a plan that is limited to nonunion employees and that does not qualify under Section 423 could still qualify for the exemption if the minimum coverage requirements of Section 410 were satisfied. Consistent with the broad exemptive relief provided to tax-conditioned plans, all purchases under a stock purchase plan are exempt and will not be matched with any other sale during the preceding or succeeding six-month period for purposes of determining any short-swing profit. However, an open market sale of stock acquired in an exempt purchase under a stock purchase plan is matchable with any nonexempt purchase (e.g., an open-market purchase during the relevant six-month periods).

Because of this **blanket exemption,** a variety of purchases and sales of stock that may occur under a qualified plan are now unconditionally exempt. For exam-

---

[14] See the discussion of these requirements in Chapter 4. Note that a plan does not have to meet all of the tax-qualification requirements—just those relating to coverage and participation.

[15] Note the SEC regulations use the term "excess benefit plan" in a broader context than does ERISA.

[16] Excess benefit plans would appear to include nonqualified plans that permit 401(k) deferrals in excess of the elective deferral limit as adjusted ($11,000 in 2002) or allow contributions to make up for limitations resulting from actual deferral percentage (ADP) or actual contribution percentage (ACP) nondiscrimination tests. However, many types of deferred compensation plans (e.g., a plan permitting an executive to defer a percentage of base pay or bonus) would not be included. Also, deferred compensation plans for outside directors could never qualify as excess plans under this definition because a company cannot sponsor a qualified plan for its outside directors.

ple, insiders can enroll, receive stock distributions, change the level of their contributions, cease contributions, or change the amount of future contributions invested in employer stock without any special restrictions. Only transactions that are defined as "discretionary transactions" must satisfy added conditions to be exempt—even under a tax-conditioned plan.

The regulations also provide a separate, unconditional exemption for purchases and sales of employer stock made pursuant to domestic relations orders (DROs), as defined under ERISA and the IRC. This exemption applies both for purposes of the short-swing profit restriction and for reporting purposes. It should be noted that DROs do not have to meet the more stringent requirements of QDROs imposed under the tax law. This means that potentially more transactions could be exempted—for example, those under nonqualified plans.

Discretionary Transactions

For qualified, excess benefit, and stock purchase plans, the only types of transactions that must satisfy an extra condition in order to be exempt are so-called discretionary transactions. These are defined as involving either:

- An intraplan transfer (i.e., a transfer of an existing account balance from one plan fund to another where one of the funds involves actual or phantom employer stock).

- A cash distribution funded by a sale of such employer stock.

These transactions are only subject to this extra condition if they are made at the election of an insider. Hence, an involuntary distribution from an employer stock fund triggered by an actual deferral percentage (ADP), actual contribution percentage (ACP), or Section 415 limit failure is not subject to this special rule. Also, transactions are exempt from the extra condition if made "in connection with" the insider's death, disability, retirement, or termination of employment or if they are required to be made available to the insider pursuant to the IRC.[17]

Even for discretionary transactions, the condition for exemption is relatively easy to satisfy and administer. All that is required is for every election of a discretionary transaction to occur at least six months after the most recent preceding election of a discretionary transaction that is the "opposite way." As long as six months have elapsed between the elections by the insider to make such transactions, they will be exempt. It should be noted that the focus is on the date of the elections, not the transactions themselves.

Reporting Requirements

Insiders generally are required to file periodic reports and annual reports (on Forms 4 and 5, respectively) with the SEC concerning their transactions in employer stock. The aforementioned regulations liberalize the scheme for reporting transactions in tax-conditioned plans. Most transactions under qualified, excess benefit, and stock purchase

---

[17] Examples within this last category of transactions include an ESOP diversification election or an age 70½ minimum required distribution.

plans—those covered by the blanket exemption—will be completely exempt from reporting. Only intraplan transactions and cash distributions would be subject to annual reporting on Form 5. An executive can choose, however, to voluntarily report discretionary transactions on an earlier Form 4 (within 10 days after the close of the calendar month in which the transaction occurs) rather than at year-end on Form 5. Discretionary transactions must be reported even though they qualify for the conditional exemption.

Collective Bargaining Requirements

It has long been recognized that employee benefits are mandatory subjects of collective bargaining under the National Labor Relations Act (NLRA). Thus, employers may not refuse to discuss providing employee benefits to employees who are represented by a collective bargaining unit, and they must negotiate in good faith concerning their demands.

In many situations, plans negotiated for union employees are unilateral plans that cover only individuals who work for the employer. Typically, the negotiation process involves design issues, such as eligibility, contribution levels, vesting provisions, and so forth, with funding of the benefits being left under employer control. On occasion, however, a union's proposal may be for coverage under a joint labor–management trust fund—a multiemployer or Taft–Hartley plan—as this is sometimes called. The law requires that these plans have equal labor and management representation on the board of trustees. For the most part, multiemployer plans have been limited to defined benefit pension plans and health and welfare programs.

Chapter Summary

- There are a number of legal requirements that plan sponsors must recognize in the administration of pension plans beyond the tax law qualification requirements. These requirements include
  - Title I of ERISA labor law provisions.
  - Title I of ERISA requirements for nonqualified executive benefit arrangements.
  - Prohibitions against age and sex discrimination.
  - Unrelated business income requirements when such income is earned within benefit plans.

- Securities and Exchange Commission (SEC) requirements apply to defined contribution plans investing in employer securities.

- Title I of ERISA contains labor law provisions dealing with the reporting, disclosure, and fiduciary responsibilities of plan sponsors. The intent of the reporting and disclosure requirements is to clearly inform plan participants and their beneficiaries regarding the benefit provisions and financial operation of their plans. Title I stipulates that certain documents must be filed with the government, certain documents must be automatically distributed to employees, and other items must be given to participants upon request and/or made available for examination.

- ERISA defines a fiduciary and requires that fiduciaries discharge all duties solely in the interest of plan participants and their beneficiaries and for the exclusive purpose of providing plan benefits and defraying reasonable administrative expenses. ERISA prohibits certain transactions between a plan and "parties in interest."

- According to the prudent expert rule, a fiduciary is charged with using the care, skill, prudence, and diligence that a prudent person who is familiar with such matters would use under the circumstances then prevailing.

- ERISA provides limited exemptions from its requirements for certain types of plans. Any plan of deferred compensation, to the extent that it does not meet the tax law requirements for a qualified plan, comes under Title I and, unless exempted, must comply with various requirements, such as the minimum participation, funding, and vesting and joint and survivor provisions. Plans qualifying for exemptions include:
  - Excess benefit plans.
  - Plans that are "unfunded and maintained by an employer primarily for the purpose of providing deferred compensation for a select group of management or highly compensated employees."

- The investment income of a qualified trust established in conjunction with a qualified plan is generally exempt from tax, although all or part of this income could be subject to tax if it is deemed to be unrelated business income.

- Various securities law requirements affect employee benefit and executive compensation plans.

Key Terms

Age Discrimination in Employment Act (ADEA), p. *119*

blanket exemption, p. *122*

earmarked investments, p. *113*

excess benefit plans, p. *118*

fiduciary, p. *110*

Form 5500, p. *103*

look-through investment vehicles, p. *114*

notification(s) as to pre- and postretirement survivor benefits, p. *107*

pension plan, p. *117*

prudent expert rule, p. *110*

restoration plans, p. *118*

rollover notification, p. *108*

Section 16(b) of the Securities Exchange Act, p. *121*

summary annual report (SAR), p. *103*

summary of material modifications (SMM), p. *103*

summary plan description (SPD), p. *102*

terminated vested participant, p. *107*

Title I of ERISA, p. *101*

unfunded excess benefit plans, p. *102*

unrelated business income, p. *118*

Questions for Review

1. List the disclosure items that must be either automatically furnished to the government or supplied to the government upon request under Title I of ERISA?

2. What information must be included in an SPD?

3. Describe the claim denial procedure that must be included in an employee benefit plan.

4. Are the directors of a corporation fiduciaries under Title I of ERISA? Why or why not?

5. Under what circumstances do the provisions of Title I of ERISA apply to nonqualified plans maintained for executives?

6. Describe the requirements of the ADEA that apply under defined benefit plans when an employee continues employment beyond his or her normal retirement date.

7. Under what circumstances do SEC requirements apply to qualified profit sharing and savings plans?

Questions for Discussion

1. An employee can become fully vested in his or her accrued benefits after three years of service and well before he or she has attained age 32. Once vested, the employee must be automatically protected by the joint and survivor provisions of the law. Nevertheless, the law does not require that the employee be notified of the joint and survivor benefits and rights until he or she has attained age 32. Explain why notification is not required before age 32 even though the employee could be entitled to the benefit.

2. Explain the rationale for the DOL's position concerning the granting of safe harbors for plans that permit earmarked investments (where employees choose the funds in which their contributions will be invested), and describe the conditions under which these safe harbors apply.

3. Do SEC requirements concerning the disclosure of information to eligible employees (when employee contributions may be used to purchase employer stock) supplant the SPD disclosure requirements of Title I of ERISA? Why or why not?

Resources for Further Study

CCH Editorial Staff. "2001 Tax Legislation: Law, Explanation, and Analysis." *Commerce Clearing House Pension Plan Guide* (2001).

Cleveland, Alan P. "Fiduciary Liability Issues under ERISA." *The Handbook of Employee Benefits.* 5th ed. Jerry S. Rosenbloom, ed. New York: McGraw-Hill, 2001.

Geller, Sheldon M. "Compliance Audits Can Protect Plan Sponsors." *Journal of Compensation and Benefits* 17, no. 2 (March/April 2001).

Mahoney, Dennis F. "Managing Employee Benefit Plans." *The Handbook of Employee Benefits.* 5th ed. Jerry S. Rosenbloom, ed. New York: McGraw-Hill, 2001.

Maniaci, Serafina. "Communicating Employee Benefits Programs." *The Handbook of Employee Benefits.* 5th ed. Jerry S. Rosenbloom, ed. New York: McGraw-Hill, 2001.

McDonnell, Ken; Paul Fronstin; Kelly Olsen; Pamela Ostuw; Jack Van Derhei; and Paul Yakoboski. *EBRI Databook on Employee Benefits.* 4th ed. Deborah Holmes, Lynn Miller, and Maureen Richmond, eds. Washington, DC: Employee Benefit Research Institute Education and Research Fund, 1997.

Munson, Arlene; and David Leach. "SEC Liberalizes Insider Trading Rules." *Journal of Compensation and Benefits* 17, no. 2 (March/April 2001).

Reish, C. Frederick; Bruce Ashton; and Gail Reich. "Revised Form 5500 and ERISA 404(c) Compliance." *Journal of Pension Benefits* 8, no. 2 (Winter 2001).

Reish, C. Frederick; Bruce L. Ashton; and Nicholas J. White. "The Employee Plans Compliance Resolution System for Qualified Plans." *The Handbook of Employee Benefits.* 5th ed. Jerry S. Rosenbloom, ed. New York: McGraw-Hill, 2001.

Vitiello, James. "Internet/Web-Based Administration of Benefits." *Employee Benefits Journal* 26, no. 3 (September 2001).

Chapter 7

Money Purchase Pension Plans

After studying this chapter you should be able to:

- Describe the characteristics of money purchase pension plans.

- Identify some basic differences between money purchase plans and other defined contribution plans.

- Explain the factors that influence the amount of retirement benefit under a money purchase or other defined contribution plan.

- Describe the actual contribution percentage (ACP) test that applies to money purchase plans requiring employee contributions.

- Explain the limitations on employers in terms of contribution levels and deductibility of contributions to money purchase plans.

- Describe how the deduction limits of a money purchase plan are affected if the employer sponsors another qualified plan.

Since the tax and legal requirements applicable in general to qualified plans have been reviewed in Chapters 4, 5, and 6, various types of retirement plans will now be examined, highlighting their unique characteristics. To briefly review the discussion in Chapter 3, pension plans are either *defined benefit* or *defined contribution* in nature. Traditionally the majority of employees in the United States were covered by defined benefit plans, reflecting the fact that most large employers and almost all union-negotiated plans had used this approach. A defined benefit plan provides a fixed amount of pension benefit. The amount of each employee's benefit usually depends on length of service and pay level—for example, a pension of 1 percent of pay for each year of service. In collectively bargained plans, however, pay often is not taken into account; the monthly pension is typically a fixed dollar amount (such as $30) for each year of service. In any event, a defined benefit plan promises a fixed level of benefit and the employer contributes whatever is necessary to provide this amount.

By contrast, the defined contribution or money purchase pension approach focuses on contribution levels. The employer's contribution is fixed as a percentage of pay or as a flat dollar amount.[1] This contribution, along with any amounts contributed by the employee, is accumulated and invested on the employee's behalf. The amount of pension an employee receives will thus vary depending on such factors as length of plan participation, the level of contributions, and investment gains and losses.

Since the passage of ERISA, there has been a growing interest in the defined contribution concept. In fact, approximately 80 percent of all new plans established since the mid-1970s use the defined contribution approach. Even though many of these defined contribution plans have been supplemental in nature—and most have been profit sharing or stock bonus programs, including so-called savings plans and cash or deferred arrangements (CODAs)[2]—some of these plans have been true pension arrangements that use defined contribution concepts. These latter plans are called *money purchase* pension plans.

This chapter begins with a review of the general characteristics of money purchase pension plans. It then considers the contribution structure of these plans. The chapter concludes with a discussion of the additional or different tax law requirements that apply to these plans.

General Characteristics

In a sense, **money purchase pension plans** are hybrids. Because they technically are pension plans, they are treated for many purposes in much the same fashion as defined benefit plans. They are, for example, subject to the minimum funding and joint and survivor requirements of the tax law that apply to defined benefit arrangements. In other areas, however, the tax law treats money purchase plans as defined contribution arrangements. Thus, individual accounts must be maintained for employees, the plans are subject to the annual addition limits of Section 415 of the Internal Revenue Code (IRC), and they are not subject to the plan termination provisions of Title IV of ERISA.

Although they are treated differently for different tax law purposes, money purchase plans are fundamentally defined contribution plans. For this reason, they have many of the same basic characteristics that are found in all defined contribution plans—particularly when contrasted with defined benefit arrangements.

---

[1] This fixed contribution requirement is a characteristic of money purchase plans that distinguishes them from other defined contribution arrangements in which the employer's contribution is a variable that is related to profits or is made on a discretionary basis.

[2] Technically, the tax law only provides for pension, profit sharing, and stock bonus plans. Savings plans are *generally* not a recognized form of plan, as such, and are usually qualified as profit sharing plans. CODAs are not plans but rather are arrangements that are attached to an underlying profit sharing or stock bonus plan. Nevertheless, common usage refers to both savings plans and CODAs as though they were separate types of plans.

One example of this concerns the allocation of employer contributions. The amount an employer contributes for each employee under a money purchase plan is usually expressed as a percentage of the employee's current pay (for the year involved), with the result that each employee, regardless of age, receives the same percentage-of-pay contribution. By contrast, the allocation of employer contributions under a final-pay defined benefit plan is such that age and prior service also are taken into account. Thus, the amount of aggregate employer contributions allocated to younger employees usually is much higher under a money purchase plan than it is under a defined benefit plan. Some employers believe that this is an equitable allocation of their contributions. Others, however, feel that it is fairer to allocate contributions in such a way that older (and usually longer service) employees receive proportionately greater amounts. Regardless of how an employer views this issue, the fact remains that this type of allocation pattern can produce higher levels of severance benefits for employees who terminate at younger ages with a vested interest and, to this extent, higher plan costs. It should be noted, however, that it is possible to design a money purchase plan so that contributions increase with age and service, provided this does not produce discriminatory results. In such a plan, the pattern of allocations will more closely resemble that of a defined benefit plan.

Another example concerns the way in which money purchase plans respond to inflation. In essence, the retirement benefits that might be provided to an employee are the result of contributions that are based on the employee's career average compensation. There will be some reflection of inflation that takes place during the employee's preretirement years, in that current and future contributions will take the accumulated effects of inflation into account. And, if the employee's account balance is invested in equity-type investments, some inflation protection may be provided by investment results.[3] Also, because of the very nature of the employer's commitment, no postretirement inflation protection is provided under a money purchase plan. By contrast, the typical final-pay defined benefit plan provides for an initial level of income that reflects inflation up to the time of retirement. Further, a great many employers provide for "ad hoc" increases for their retirees, from time to time, under defined benefit arrangements.

A related comparison concerns investment risk. Under defined contribution plans, including money purchase plans, the employee both receives the benefit of all positive investment returns and bears the risk of all unfavorable results. Under a defined benefit plan, investment risk and reward is borne by the employer.

Some of the more specific or typical characteristics of money purchase plans are as follows:

• In establishing the plan, the employer agrees to make a fixed contribution each year for each eligible employee. This contribution is usually expressed as a percentage of pay, although it may be a flat dollar amount. This constitutes a definite commitment

---

[3] Many employees, however, tend to select relatively conservative investments (fixed income or guaranteed interest funds) when choices are made available to them, with the result that significant inflation protection may not be provided from this source—at least in many situations.

on the part of the employer and the contribution must be made each year, regardless of profits, and cannot be varied except by plan amendment.

• The plan may require employees to make contributions in order to participate. If so, these contributions can be made only from after-tax income—that is, salary reductions or elective deferral contributions cannot be made under a money purchase plan. When employees do contribute:

- The contribution rate is fixed (unlike the typical savings plan, where the employee can choose from among different levels of participation).

- The employer's contribution rate is often set with reference to what employees are contributing—for example, at two times the employee contribution rate.

• Regardless of whether employees are required to make mandatory contributions in order to participate, they may be permitted to make **voluntary contributions,** that is, contributions that do not generate any type of employer contribution.

• **Forfeitures** that arise when partially vested or nonvested employees terminate employment may be used to reduce employer contributions or may be reallocated among the remaining plan participants; the customary practice in money purchase plans is to use these contributions to reduce the employer contributions due next.[4]

• Both employer and employee contributions are transferred to a trustee (or an insurance company under a group annuity type of contract), where they are invested on behalf of the employees.

• Individual accounts are established for participating employees. Each account is credited with employer and employee contributions, reallocated forfeitures (if applicable), and its proportionate share of investment gains and losses.

• As with other types of defined contribution plans, employees frequently are given a choice of several investment funds in which to invest their account balances.

• An employee's benefit, at any given time, is whatever can be provided by his or her vested account balance at that time. If the employee retires, the employee will usually have the option of receiving this account balance in a lump sum or in the form of monthly installments—over a period equal to the employee's life expectancy or the joint life expectancy of the employee and his or her spouse, if married.

• The employee's account balance (even if not otherwise vested) usually is payable in full in the event of the employee's death.

• Unlike conventional profit sharing and savings plans, a money purchase plan generally cannot make distributions until the employee has severed employment. Thus, **in-service withdrawals** are not permitted.

---

[4] Prior to the Tax Reform Act of 1986, forfeitures under money purchase plans could be used only to reduce employer contributions.

• While it is possible for a money purchase plan to provide for loans to employees, this practice is unusual. In general, money purchase plans focus on their role as retirement vehicles; permitting loans could be viewed as being inconsistent with this fundamental purpose.

Contribution Structure

As previously noted, money purchase plans do not provide a fixed benefit for employees. Instead, the employer (and any employee) contributions, together with investment income, are applied to provide as much in the way of pension benefits as possible. Since the cost of a given amount of benefit varies by entry age and retirement age, the benefits of any employee will depend on these factors as well as on contribution levels and investment results.

In the past, the employee's gender also was a factor in determining the amount of retirement benefit that could be provided under a money purchase plan. If a male and female employee were the same age and had exactly the same amount accumulated under such a plan, the male employee would receive a higher lifetime pension than the female employee. This was because the female employee was expected to live longer and, in anticipation of this, the same initial amount was expected to be paid over a longer period of time. Because of this difference in life expectancies, the actuarial value of the pension, in both cases, was considered to be the same. In 1983, however, the Supreme Court ruled (in *Arizona Governing Committee* v. *Norris*) that life annuities under an employer-sponsored defined contribution plan must be provided on a uniform basis.[5]

Defined contribution plans are often contributory. In this case, the employer's contribution is usually a match or multiple of the employee's contribution. For example, the plan could call for the employer and employee each to contribute 5 percent of the employee's compensation; or the employee's contribution could be set at 3 percent of compensation with the employer contributing 6 percent.

It should be noted that defined contribution plans have several inherent limitations when viewed from the perspective of providing retirement income. First, an employee who joins the plan at an older age will have only a short period of time to accumulate funds, with the result that the employee's benefit often will be inadequate. Table 7.1 indicates the results that could flow under a money purchase plan and the disparity in benefits that could be produced. This table assumes that the compensation shown for each employee will continue until normal retirement; that the contribution made by the employer each year is 10 percent of the employee's pay; that this contribution will accumulate at 6 percent compound interest until retirement; and that the fund accumulated at retirement will be applied under representative annuity purchase rates to provide a monthly pension benefit.

---

[5] It should be noted that employees can buy annuities from insurance companies on the open market (i.e., apart from the qualified plan). At this time, insurers are not required to offer such annuities on a unisex basis, although legislation that would require this has been proposed. Even though not required to do so, however, many insurers provide for unisex premiums.

Possible Obsolescence of Money Purchase Pension Plans
1

Prior to the passage of the Economic Growth and Tax Relief Reconciliation Act of 2001 (EGTRRA), it was common for many self-employed individuals to sponsor money purchase pension plans paired with profit sharing plans. The reason these types of plans were common in Keoghs or HR-10 plans was that the combination provided the maximum deductible contribution with the most flexibility. A profit sharing plan in the past only allowed a 15 percent of pay contribution and deduction. The advantage of the profit sharing plan was, and still is, that the annual contribution can be discretionary, and the individual need not make a contribution if cash is scarce. The money purchase pension plan, however, requires a fixed annual contribution. The combination money purchase pension plan paired with a profit sharing plan allowed a self-employed person to reach the maximum deduction of 25 percent of pay with a fixed annual contribution of 10 percent to the money purchase plan and a discretionary contribution of 15 percent of pay to the profit sharing plan. EGTRRA increased the allowable deductible contribution to a profit sharing plan from 15 percent of pay to 25 percent of pay. Therefore, it appears that a profit sharing plan alone allows both the maximum deductible contribution and the most flexibility with a discretionary contribution.

Some practitioners believe the money purchase pension plan will become obsolete. However, there are still some applications for money purchase pension plans. Because money purchase pension plans are subject to minimum funding standards, they provide plan participants with added security regarding plan contributions. This may be important in certain situations such as with collectively bargained plans or if employers are concerned with the perception that future plan contributions will not occur. Some participants will obviously prefer the money purchase pension plan over the profit sharing plan with the assurance of annual contributions. Also, target benefit plans that comply with safe harbor requirements, must be money purchase plans.*

* These examples of situations where use of a money purchase pension plan is appropriate were referenced in Amy L. Cavanaugh, "The Money Purchase Plan: R.I.P.," *Journal of Pension Benefits* 9, no. 1 (Autumn 2001), p. 48.

Table 7.1 also shows that younger employees have a much longer time to accumulate funds and thus receive a proportionately larger benefit. Moreover, the money purchase plan has an additional weakness since, because of the effect of compound interest, greater weight is given to the employee's lower compensation at the younger ages than will be given to the higher compensation the employee receives when he or she is older.

An additional comment about the potential disadvantages of money purchase plans has to do with their ability to respond to growth in an employee's earnings—particularly during periods of inflation. Table 7.1 projects benefits for employees on

TABLE 7.1   Illustration of Money Purchase Formula without Earnings Projection

Age at Entry	Normal Retirement Age	Pay	Contribution	Fund at Retirement	Monthly Benefit	Benefit as a Percentage of Pay
30	65	$12,000	$1,200	$141,745	$1,274	127%
40	65	14,000	1,400	81,419	732	63
45	65	9,500	950	37,043	333	42
53	65	30,000	3,000	53,646	482	19
55	65	12,000	1,200	16,766	151	15

TABLE 7.2   Illustration of Money Purchase Formula with and without Projection of Pay

Age at Entry	Pay at Entry	Final Pay	Fund at Retirement With Flat Pay	Fund at Retirement With Projected Pay	Monthly Benefit With Flat Pay	Monthly Benefit With Projected Pay	Benefit as Percentage of Entry Pay	Benefit as Percentage of Final Pay
30	$12,000	$45,532	$141,745	$237,864	$1,274	$2,139	127.4%	56.4%
40	14,000	35,886	81,419	120,652	732	1,085	62.7	36.3
45	9,500	20,015	37,043	51,156	333	460	42.1	27.6
53	30,000	46,184	53,646	65,375	482	588	19.3	15.3
55	12,000	17,080	16,766	19,754	151	178	15.1	12.5

the assumption that earnings will remain constant. This is not a realistic assumption since, in all probability, most employees will receive a number of pay increases over their working careers. Thus, it is important to illustrate and compare the results depicted in Table 7.1 with what would be the case if all assumptions remained the same except for future pay growth. This comparison for the same group of employees is set forth in Table 7.2, which assumes that earnings will grow at the rate of 4 percent a year. As can be seen, the potential benefit, as a percentage of final pay, is considerably lower when future earnings growth is taken into account.

Another observation about the deficiencies of a money purchase plan is that the employee's benefit under this approach can only be estimated. This lack of certainty as to benefits could prove to be an unsatisfactory employee relations feature of such a plan. Also, the variation in benefit levels for different employees makes it difficult, if not impossible, to design a contribution formula that produces benefit levels uniformly responsive to employer objectives. As a final observation, a money purchase plan is a career-pay plan; however, unlike the practice for career-pay defined benefit plans, it is relatively uncommon for an employer to update accrued benefits to take inflation into account.

Tax Law Provisions

Money purchase plans are subject to almost all of the tax law provisions applicable to qualified plans. The following is a brief discussion of the major tax law provisions that are different as they apply to money purchase plans. In some instances, the discussion is in terms of how money purchase plans are treated differently from other types of defined contribution plans.

Nondiscrimination in Contributions and Benefits

When a money purchase plan involves after-tax employee and matching employer contributions, an **actual contribution percentage (ACP) test** must be satisfied each year in accordance with the terms of **Section 401(m) of the IRC.**[6] The ACP test also applies to voluntary after-tax employee contributions even when there is no employer match. This test limits the participation of highly compensated employees (HCEs) so that their average contribution percentages cannot exceed the average contribution percentages of the nonhighly compensated employees (NHCEs) by more than a stipulated amount. In general, the ACP for HCEs cannot be more than 125 percent of the ACP for NHCEs. An **alternative limitation** permits the ACP for HCEs to be as much as two times the ACP for NHCEs, but not more than two percentage points higher. If the portion of the plan that is subject to this test meets its requirements each year, this portion will satisfy the nondiscrimination in contributions and benefits requirements of **Section 401(a)(4) of the IRC.**

If the ACP test is not applicable to employer contributions because there are no mandatory employee contributions, this portion of the plan must satisfy the nondiscrimination requirements of Section 401(a)(4) of the IRC.[7] However, the regulations prescribe two **safe harbors** that can be met in order to satisfy these requirements. The first safe harbor is for plans with a **uniform contribution formula**—where contributions equal the same percentage of pay or the same dollar amount for every covered employee—and will apply to most money purchase plans. To use this safe harbor, the same vesting schedule and definition of years of service must apply to all participants. Also, if the plan integrates with Social Security benefits by providing a higher contribution percentage for pay above a specified level than for pay below that level, the plan will be deemed to satisfy this safe harbor if the plan meets the permitted disparity requirements of Section 401(l).[8]

The second safe harbor applies to **nonintegrated "uniform points plans"** (other than employee stock ownership plans [ESOPs]) that allocate contributions based on a formula weighted for age and/or service and units of pay that do not

---

[6] The complete details of this test are discussed in Chapter 11, since the ACP test is similar to the actual deferral percentage (ADP) test applicable to elective deferrals under cash or deferred arrangements (CODAs) and, quite often, the two tests must both be made for the same plan. Also, if this plan meets certain safe harbor requirements, ACP testing will not be required for the matching employer contributions.

[7] These requirements are discussed in Chapter 4.

[8] These permitted disparity requirements are discussed in the following section of this chapter.

exceed $200. This safe harbor is available to such plans if the average of the allocation rates for HCEs does not exceed the average of the allocation rates for the NHCEs.

Integration with Social Security

Section 401(l) of the IRC permits most qualified plans to "integrate" or coordinate contributions and/or benefits with the benefits provided by Social Security. In essence, this provision of the law provides for a limited form of discrimination in that it permits plans to provide higher contributions or benefits for higher-paid employees so as to compensate for the fact that the relative value of Social Security decreases as pay goes up.

Thus, a money purchase plan can have two employer contribution levels—one level for pay up to a specified amount and another higher contribution level for pay in excess of that amount. Section 401(l) requires that the difference between these two employer contribution levels cannot exceed a certain amount—called the **permitted disparity.**

The point at which the contribution percentage changes is called the plan's **integration level.** The law permits the use of an integration level in any plan year of any amount up to the Social Security taxable wage base at the beginning of that year.

When a plan's integration level equals the Social Security taxable wage base or is set at a level at or below 20 percent of this taxable wage base, the contribution percentage for pay above this amount may exceed the contribution percentage for pay below this amount by the lesser of (1) 5.7 percent and (2) the percentage applicable to pay below the wage base. In other words, when the contribution percentage applicable to pay below the integration level is equal to or less than 5.7 percent, the contribution percentage for pay above the integration level cannot be more than twice the lower contribution percentage; if the lower percentage is greater than 5.7 percent, the higher percentage cannot be more than the lower percentage plus 5.7 percent.

Thus, for example, if the lower contribution percentage is 4 percent, the higher percentage cannot exceed 8 percent; if the lower percentage is 6 percent, the higher percentage cannot exceed 11.7 percent. Table 7.3 shows illustrative maximums for plans that are integrated at the Social Security wage base or at or below 20 percent of this amount.

TABLE 7.3   **Defined Contribution Plan Integration Limits (If Integration Level Is at Social Security Taxable Wage Base or at or below 20 Percent of This Amount)**

If Lower Contribution Percentage Is:	Upper Contribution Percentage Cannot Exceed:
1.0%	2.0%
2.0	4.0
3.0	6.0
4.0	8.0
5.0	10.0
5.7	11.4
6.0	11.7
7.0	12.7
8.0	13.7

If a plan's integration level is between 20 and 100 percent of the Social Security taxable wage base, the 5.7 percent standard in these rules is reduced. If the plan's integration level is more than 80 percent of the Social Security taxable wage base, it is reduced to 5.4 percent; if the integration level is between 20 and 80 percent of the wage base, it is reduced to 4.3 percent.

It should be noted that if a money purchase plan is part of an arrangement that involves an ESOP, this portion of the program may be integrated. Also, if a plan fails to meet the specific requirements of Section 401(l), it may still be able to qualify if it can pass the nondiscrimination tests of Section 401(a)(4) of the IRC.

Section 415 Limitations

As noted earlier, a money purchase plan is considered to be a defined contribution plan for purposes of the limitations of Section 415. Thus, the annual additions to an employee's account (employer and employee contributions plus any reallocated forfeitures) cannot exceed the lesser of (1) $40,000 indexed to increase with changes in the consumer price index (CPI) or (2) 100 percent of compensation. Further, a combined Section 415 limitation was applicable for years prior to 2000 if the employer also maintained a defined benefit plan.[9]

Joint and Survivor Requirements

The joint and survivor requirements (both pre- and postretirement) that apply to defined benefit plans apply as well to money purchase plans. It should be noted that other forms of defined contribution plans are exempted from these requirements if (1) the employee's spouse is the beneficiary for 100 percent of the employee's account balance unless the spouse consents in writing to the designation of another beneficiary; (2) if the employee does not elect an annuity distribution and (3) the plan can not have received a transfer from a pension plan. This exemption is also available to money purchase plans that are part of an employee stock ownership plan (ESOP).

Before-Tax Contributions

The CODA feature of Section 401(k) of the IRC, which permits employees to make elective deferrals and thus make before-tax contributions, is not available to money purchase plans. These elective deferral contributions can be made only in conjunction with profit sharing and stock bonus and savings plans that are qualified as profit sharing plans. If a savings plan is qualified as a money purchase pension plan, as is occasionally the case, the elective deferral option will not be available (nor will the plan be able to permit in-service withdrawals).

Forfeitures

The amounts forfeited when an employee terminates employment with less than full vesting can be applied in two ways under a money purchase plan. These amounts can be used to reduce employer contributions or they can be reallocated among the remaining employees.

---

[9] The Section 415 limitations are discussed in Chapter 5.

Employer Securities

Generally, defined benefit plans are prohibited from having more than 10 percent of their assets invested in qualifying employer securities. Profit sharing and stock bonus plans, on the other hand, are permitted to invest up to 100 percent of their assets in qualifying employer securities if the plans so provide. Money purchase plans, even though they are defined contribution plans, are subject to the same 10 percent limitation that applies to defined benefit plans.[10]

In-Service Distributions

As noted in an earlier discussion, since it is a pension plan, a money purchase plan is not permitted to make distributions to employees on an in-service basis. In general, these plans can make distributions only in the event of termination of employment (including retirement, death, and disability). They also may make distributions upon termination of the plan. In this regard, they differ significantly from other types of defined contribution arrangements that are qualified as profit sharing or stock bonus plans.

Minimum Funding Standards

Again, because a money purchase plan is a pension plan, it is subject to the minimum funding requirements of the IRC. While an **actuarial valuation** is not required, the plan must maintain a **minimum funding standard account.** The operation of this account is much simpler than is the case with a defined benefit plan since, for example, there is no amortization of liabilities or funding gains and losses. The account must be maintained and will be charged each year with the amount of the contribution that is required to be made under the plan. In effect, there is no flexibility in meeting this requirement and, in normal circumstances (absent a **funding waiver**), the required contribution must be made in full each year. As a result, the money purchase plan can be viewed as being the most rigid of all plans in terms of funding flexibility.

Deduction Limits

Prior to EGTRRA there were no specific deduction limits, as such, for money purchase plans. The general concept that the amount contributed must represent reasonable compensation applied, of course, and there was a practical limit in that Section 415 stipulated that the maximum annual addition to an employee's account could not exceed a certain amount. Also, if another plan(s) existed, there would be a maximum combined deductible limit for all plans of 25 percent of covered payroll. Under EGTRRA, there is a uniform limit of 25 percent of compensation for all defined contribution plans.

Chapter Summary

- Money purchase pension plans involve characteristics of defined benefit pension plans and defined contribution arrangements. On the defined benefit side, minimum funding and joint and survivor requirements of the tax law apply. On the defined contribution side, individual

---

[10] A limited grandfathering provision is provided for money purchase plans in existence on September 2, 1974, and provides for investing more than 10 percent of their assets in employer securities.

accounts must be maintained, plans are subject to the annual addition limits of IRC Section 415, and plans are exempt from the plan termination provisions of Title IV of ERISA.

- The employer contribution to a money purchase pension plan constitutes a definite commitment on the part of the employer, and the contribution must be made each year—regardless of profits—and cannot be varied except by plan amendment. These employer contributions may be a fixed dollar amount but are more commonly expressed as a percentage of pay.

- Since the passage of ERISA, money purchase plans requiring employee contributions can make these contributions only on an after-tax basis. A plan involving after-tax employee and matching employer contributions is subject to the actual contribution percentage (ACP) test each year.

- An employee's benefit under a money purchase pension plan is determined by the accumulation in his or her vested account balance. Employees frequently are given a choice of several investment funds where their account balances can be invested.

- Money purchase pension plans are subject to almost all of the tax law provisions that generally apply to qualified plans. Money purchase plans generally are subject to a 10 percent limitation on investments in qualifying employer securities.

- Generally, employees are prohibited from making withdrawals from a money purchase pension plan until employment has been severed. Thus, in-service withdrawals are not permitted from these plans.

Key Terms

actual contribution percentage (ACP) test, p. *134*
actuarial valuation, p. *137*
alternative limitation, p. *134*
forfeitures, p. *130*
funding waiver, p. *137*
in-service withdrawals, p. *130*
integration level, p. *135*

minimum funding standard account, p. *137*
money purchase pension plans, p. *128*
nonintegrated "uniform points plans," p. *134*
permitted disparity, p. *135*
safe harbors, p. *134*
Section 401(a)(4) of the IRC, p. *134*

Section 401(l) of the IRC, p. *135*
Section 401(m) of the IRC, p. *134*
uniform contribution formula plans, p. *134*
voluntary contributions, p. *130*

Questions for Review

1. What characteristic of a money purchase plan distinguishes it from other defined contribution plans?

2. What are the factors that ultimately influence the amount of retirement benefit an employee might receive under a money purchase pension plan?

3. Describe the ACP test that applies to a money purchase plan that requires employee contributions.

4. Describe the Section 415 limitations that apply to money purchase plans.

5. What limitations apply to the investment of plan assets in employer securities under a money purchase plan?

6. What deduction limits apply to a money purchase plan? Explain the limits when a money purchase plan is offered alone and in conjunction with another qualified plan.

7. Are money purchase plans subject to the minimum funding standards of the tax law? Why or why not?

Questions for Discussion

1. Describe the permitted disparity limitations that apply to a money purchase plan that is integrated with Social Security benefits.

2. The text states that money purchase plans are, in a sense, hybrids. Describe the ways in which money purchase plans are sometimes treated in much the same fashion as defined benefit pension plans, and the ways in which they are sometimes treated as defined contribution plans. What reasons exist for these differences in treatment?

3. Evaluate the efficiency of a money purchase plan as an employer's primary vehicle for providing retirement benefits.

Resources for Further Study

Cavanaugh, Amy L. "The Money Purchase Plan: R. I. P." *Journal of Pension Benefits* 9, no. 1 (Autumn 2001).

Donovan, Kevin J.; and Gucciardi, Joan. "Designing Plans after EGTRRA." *Journal of Pension Benefits* 9, no. 1 (Autumn 2001).

Chapter 8

Profit Sharing Plans

After studying this chapter you should be able to:

- Describe the characteristics of profit sharing plans.

- Explain the purposes of profit sharing plans and how these purposes influence elements of plan design.

- Discuss contribution requirements imposed on profit sharing plans by the Internal Revenue Code.

- Explain allowable and customary approaches to allocating employer contributions in profit sharing plans.

- Describe what happens to forfeited nonvested contributions in a profit sharing plan.

- Discuss allowable and customary approaches regarding withdrawals from profit sharing plans.

Profit sharing plans constitute an important component in the overall structure of employee benefit programs in the United States. The requirements imposed by the Employee Retirement Income Security Act (ERISA) as to minimum funding and employer liabilities for plan terminations have resulted in a growing interest in **individual-account retirement programs.** Profit sharing and thrift plans have considerable appeal in this regard since they embody the individual account concept without imposing any fixed commitment on employers to provide any specific level of benefits. Thus, one can expect to see greater use of profit sharing plans in lieu of pension plans or a greater use of basic pension plans plus a supplemental savings or profit sharing program. Particularly in today's competitive business climate, with its primary emphasis on pay-for-performance, profit sharing plans are well-suited to supply this component of total compensation on a tax-deferred basis.

Definition of Profit Sharing

Many definitions of profit sharing have been suggested. One broad concept is that profit sharing is a plan in which the company's contributions are based upon business profits, regardless of whether the benefit payments are made in cash, are deferred, or are a combination of the two. This definition suggests three basic profit sharing plan approaches, which may be defined as follows: (1) **current** (cash)—profits are paid directly to employees in cash, check, or stock as soon as profits are determined (for example, monthly, quarterly, semiannually, or annually); (2) **deferred**—profits are credited to employee accounts to be paid at retirement or upon other stated dates or circumstances (for example, disability, death, severance, or under withdrawal provisions); and (3) **combined**—part of the profit is paid out currently in cash and part is deferred. This can take place under one plan with both current and deferred features or under two separate plans—one cash and the other deferred—covering, by and large, the same employee groups.

The definition of a profit sharing plan as set forth in federal income tax regulations is as follows:

> A profit sharing plan is a plan established and maintained by an employer to provide for the participation in his profits by his employees or their beneficiaries. The plan must provide a definite predetermined formula for allocating the contributions made to the plan among the participants and for distributing the funds accumulated under the plan after a fixed number of years, the attainment of a stated age, or upon the prior occurrence of some event such as layoff, illness, disability, retirement, death, or severance of employment.[1]

The qualification of profit sharing plans for tax exemption under Section 401 of the Internal Revenue Code (IRC), then, is restricted to deferred or combination-type plans. Current or cash profit sharing plans (approach [1] above), therefore, are not treated in this chapter. Also, combination cash or deferred plans (approach [3] above), because of the unique requirements of federal tax law that apply to such plans, are treated separately in Chapter 11. Thus, this chapter relates only to tax-qualified deferred profit sharing plans (approach [2] above).

Qualification Requirements

The qualification requirements for profit sharing plans are, for the most part, identical to those for pension plans, which are described in Chapters 4 and 5. However, this chapter discusses these requirements in terms of their application to profit sharing plans. This discussion relates only to plans that are not top-heavy. The special requirements applicable to top-heavy plans are covered in Chapter 5.

---

[1] Reg. 1.401(b)(1)(ii).

Coverage Requirements

In order to qualify and thus receive favorable tax treatment under the IRC, a profit sharing plan must be for the **exclusive benefit** of employees or their beneficiaries. Therefore, a plan will not qualify if the coverage requirements result in discrimination in favor of the highly compensated employees—that is, the plan must meet the coverage requirements of Section 410(b) of the IRC. Restriction of coverage by type of employment (for example, salaried employees, hourly employees, sales representatives) is permitted, provided that such coverage requirements do not result in prohibited discrimination.

Relatively few profit sharing plans impose a minimum age requirement, but practically all profit sharing plans specify a service requirement as a condition for participation in the plan. The IRC permits the use of a minimum age of up to 21 and a service requirement of up to one year (two years if the plan provides for full and immediate vesting and is not a cash or deferred arrangement).

Contribution Requirements

The Internal Revenue Code does not require as a condition for qualification that a profit sharing plan include a **definite predetermined contribution formula.** And, for plan years beginning after December 31, 1985, it is no longer necessary that contributions be based on profits. In the absence of such a formula, however, the regulations require that **substantial and recurring contributions** be made if the requirement of plan permanency is to be met.

Contributions under a profit sharing plan may be made on a discretionary basis (for example, as determined annually by the board of directors of the company) or in accordance with a definite predetermined formula. The **discretionary contribution approach** offers the advantage of contribution flexibility. The board of directors can adjust contributions in view of the firm's current financial position and capital needs. Also, the discretionary approach precludes the possibility that contribution payments will exceed the maximum amount currently deductible for federal income tax purposes (to be discussed later in this chapter). If the amount of contribution is discretionary, the plan often imposes certain minimums and maximums. For example, the plan may provide that contributions cannot exceed 15 percent of profits but can be discretionary up to that limit; or it may stipulate that contributions cannot exceed 10 to 30 percent of profits, with the percentage to be determined by a board of directors.

There are advantages in using a definite predetermined formula. A definite formula promotes increased employee morale and feelings of security. Without a definite formula, employees may feel unsure of receiving a share of what they have helped to produce.

Whether the definite formula or discretionary contribution approach is used, management still must determine the extent to which employees are to directly or indirectly share in the firm's profits. In arriving at this decision, management must take into account factors such as the objectives of the plan, the nature of the firm's business, the pattern of profits, and the age and service composition of the employee group. Obviously, a good deal more thought must be given to this matter if a definite contribution formula is used.

The contribution commitment under definite-formula plans generally is expressed as a fixed percentage or a sliding scale of percentages of profits. The specified percentages usually are applied to profits before taxes, although a base of after-tax profits can be used. The sliding scale formula provides for higher percentage contributions for higher levels of profits. A percentage-of-compensation formula also can be used.

Whether the definite formula or discretionary contribution approach is used, the plan usually specifies some limitation on the amount of annual contribution. One reason is to give priority to a minimum rate of return on capital for stockholders. Limitations on contributions can be expressed in several different ways. For example, the plan may provide that no contribution will be made in years in which dividend payments are less than a specified amount, or unless aggregate profits exceed a stated amount, or when profits are less than a given percentage of the firm's capital funds. Many plans also impose the limitation that contributions in any one year cannot exceed the maximum amount deductible for federal income tax purposes by the employer.

Employee Contributions

It is conceptually illogical to *require* employee contributions under profit sharing plans. Furthermore, in those plans that require employee contributions, the employer's contribution usually is based on the amount of the employee's contribution. For these reasons, contributory plans generally are referred to as thrift or savings plans to distinguish them from traditional profit sharing plans. For a complete discussion of these plans, see Chapters 9 and 11.

Even though employee contributions usually are not required under profit sharing plans, it is quite common to permit them on a "voluntary" basis, with employees being given this option regardless of the level of employer contributions involved. When allowed, these voluntary contributions may be made as **elective deferrals** under Section 401(k) of the IRC or as contributions from after-tax income. If made as elective deferrals, the plan must meet the actual deferral percentage (ADP) test requirements of Section 401(k) unless the plan is designed to meet safe harbor requirements; if made as after-tax contributions, the plan must meet the actual contribution percentage (ACP) test requirements of Section 401(m).

Allocations to Employee Accounts

It was noted above that the Internal Revenue Service (IRS) does not require a plan to include a definite contribution formula as a condition for qualification. However, it is necessary that the plan include a definite **allocation formula** to become qualified. Since contributions to the plan generally are based on profits, a method or formula is needed to determine the amount to be credited to each participant's account.

The employer must decide the basis upon which the contributions to the plan are to be divided among the various participants. The allocation of contributions to the account of each participant usually is made on the basis of compensation or a combination of compensation and service. If compensation is used, then allocations are made on the basis of the proportion of each participant's compensation to the total compensation of all participants. For example, if employee A earns $10,000 a year and the total annual compensation for all participants is $200,000, employee A will be credited with 5 percent of the employer's total annual contributions because $10,000 is 5 percent of $200,000. Under a formula that reflects both compensation and service, a unit of credit might, for example, be given for each year of service and an additional unit given for each $100 of compensation. With 20 years of service, employee A would have 20 units of service and 100 units of compensation. Therefore, employee A's share of contributions is determined by the fraction of 120 over the total number of units similarly calculated for all participants. The most popular allocation formulas are those based on compensation, although many plans use a combination of compensation and years of service.

The IRS requires a definite allocation formula in qualified plans so that it may determine whether contributions are shared in a nondiscriminatory manner. The plan also must meet the nondiscrimination requirements of Section 401(a)(4) of the IRC. The typical profit sharing plan, however, generally will have no trouble in meeting these requirements since such a plan usually allocates contributions on the basis of a uniform percentage of pay. Where this is the case, and if the same vesting schedule and years of service definition apply to all participants, the plan will be considered to meet the nondiscrimination requirements. (For purposes of these requirements, a plan having an integrated allocation formula that meets the permitted disparity requirements of Section 401(l) will be considered to have a uniform percentage allocation formula.) If the allocation formula is weighted for age and/or service and for units of pay that do not exceed $200, the plan will meet the nondiscrimination requirements if the average of the allocation rates for highly compensated employees (HCEs) does not exceed the average of the allocation rates for the nonhighly compensated employees (NHCEs). Otherwise, the plan will have to meet the testing requirements of Section 401(a)(4).

The allocation formula is used to determine the employee's share of contributions for accounting or record-keeping purposes. The contribution dollars are not segregated on behalf of each participant. Contributions are received, administered, and invested by the trustee as unallocated assets. The balance in each participant's account represents the participant's share of the assets of the fund at that moment. An exception is the case where the trust permits each participant's account to be invested in "earmarked" investments. Whether the participant is currently entitled to all or a part of the money credited to his or her account depends upon the provisions of the plan.

Finally, it should be noted that the allocation of employer contributions is subject to the contribution and benefit limitations of the IRC. These limits are described in Chapter 5.

Under many profit sharing plans, there may be some forfeited amounts when employees terminate with less than full vesting. These forfeitures may be used to reduce employer contributions. More typically, in profit sharing plans, they are reallocated among remaining participants. These reallocations generally are based on the pay of each remaining participant in relation to the total pay of all remaining participants. The IRS will not permit reallocations on the basis of the account balances of the remaining participants if such a procedure would produce discrimination in favor of HCEs. However, the investment income of a profit sharing plan may be allocated on the basis of account balances. Thus, it is possible to have different allocation formulas for contributions, forfeitures, and investment income.

Integration with Social Security

As mentioned earlier, profit sharing plans seldom are integrated with Social Security benefits. While these plans *can* be integrated with Social Security benefits subject to the IRC requirements for defined contribution plans,[2] no portion of a plan that consists of a cash or deferred arrangement (CODA) may be integrated. It should be noted that the maximum deductible amount that can be allocated to each participant's account in any one year pertains to the aggregate of employer contributions and forfeitures of nonvested accumulations during the year. In nonintegrated profit sharing plans, the maximum deductible annual contribution is 25 percent of compensation. Furthermore, if the plan is not integrated, forfeitures may be reallocated among remaining participants without reducing the 25 percent maximum. Last, if an employer has integrated both its pension and profit sharing plans covering any of the same employees, the integration under both plans cannot exceed 100 percent of the integration capability of a single plan. The objective of this requirement is to avoid the discrimination in favor of HCEs that would otherwise result.

Provision for Distributions

As indicated earlier, the definition of profit sharing in the federal income tax regulations permits distributions "after a fixed number of years, the attainment of a stated age, or upon the prior occurrence of some event such as layoff, illness, disability, retirement, death, or severance of employment."

The primary objective of many deferred profit sharing plans is to permit the employee to build up an equity in the fund to enhance his or her economic security after retirement. The law requires that the accumulations credited to the employee's account vest in full at normal retirement age, regardless of the employee's length of service. Most plans also fully vest the amounts credited to the employee upon death, while a lesser but still significant number of plans provide full and immediate vesting upon the occurrence of total and permanent disability.

Whether an employee is entitled to a distribution from the fund upon voluntary termination of employment or upon being laid off depends upon the vesting provisions of the plan. Of course, if the plan is contributory, the employee is always enti-

---

[2] The IRC requirements for integrated defined contribution plans are described in Chapter 4.

tled, at a minimum, to a return of the benefit attributable to his or her contributions upon death, total and permanent disability, or severance of employment.

The value of employer-provided contributions under a deferred profit sharing plan also must vest upon severance of employment in accordance with the requirements of the IRC. Thus, the plan must satisfy one of the alternative minimum vesting schedules.[3]

Withdrawals during Active Employment

Some plans also permit participants to withdraw a portion of their vested benefits in the plan prior to separation of employment.[4] The regulations permit distributions from a qualified profit sharing plan "after a fixed number of years." The IRS has interpreted this to mean that accumulations cannot be distributed in less than two years. In other words, if contributions have been credited to an employee's account for three years, he or she can withdraw an amount equal to the first year's contribution and the investment income credited in that year (assuming that the plan permits such withdrawals). Tax law also permits the withdrawal of funds upon the happening of an event such as hardship or, as interpreted by the IRS, upon the completion of five years of plan participation. The right to withdraw may be restricted to employee contributions, or it may apply to the vested portion of accumulations attributable to employer contributions. Of course, the participant must report the withdrawn amount as taxable income in the year in which it is received (except to the extent it is considered to be a return of the employee's own contributions), and such amount will be taxable as ordinary income. Moreover, an additional tax of 10 percent of the taxable portion of the distribution could be assessed on distributions before the participant reaches age 59½. Although a withdrawal provision may be desirable in a plan, care should be exercised, since a provision that is too liberal could result in defeating the long-term savings objective of the plan. Since the withdrawals are now prevalent (and more complex) in savings plans, they are discussed at greater length in Chapter 9.

Loans

Loan provisions also are found in some deferred profit sharing plans. Under a loan provision, a participant generally is entitled to borrow up to a specified percentage (50 percent, for example) of the vested portion of his or her account (including any employee contributions). The loan provision has an advantage over a withdrawal provision in that repayment of the loan will permit achievement of the objective of a long-term program geared toward retirement. However, some employers may prefer the withdrawal provision, since such a provision might help in avoiding possible employee dissatisfaction that could result from the feeling that they must pay interest on the use of "their own money." The loan provision is also advantageous in that, if IRS requirements are met, the sums borrowed are not subject to federal income

---

[3] See Chapter 5 for a full discussion of these minimum vesting requirements.
[4] Contributions made on an elective deferral basis are subject to the withdrawal restrictions described in Chapter 11.

tax. However, the interest payments are not deductible for federal income tax purposes. The law requires that loans be available to all participants on a reasonably equivalent basis and that a loan not be made available to HCEs in a percentage greater than that made available to other employees. The law also requires that the loan bear a reasonable rate of interest, be adequately secured, and be made only by the plan (and not by a third party, such as a bank, with the employee's account balance as security). If the loan provision meets the requirements of the Department of Labor (DOL) and the IRS, the loan will be exempted from the prohibited transactions provisions of ERISA and the IRC. If a loan is made and is not exempted, this could constitute a prohibited transaction and could be in violation of the legal requirement that a plan prohibit assignments and alienations; this could result in a plan disqualification.

A loan to an employee will be treated as a taxable distribution unless certain requirements are met. These requirements involve the amount of the loan (or accumulated loans), the agreement concerning loan terms, and the time period for repayment. The maximum amounts that can be borrowed without being considered a distribution depend upon the amount of the employee's vested interest in his or her account balance. If it is (1) $10,000 or less, the entire vested interest is available; (2) between $10,000 and $20,000, $10,000 is available; (3) between $20,000 and $100,000, 50 percent of the vested interest is available; or (4) $100,000 or more, $50,000 is available. The $50,000 limitation on loans from qualified plans is reduced by the excess of the highest outstanding loan balance during the preceding one-year period over the outstanding balance on the date a new loan is made.[5]

The loan must be evidenced by a legally enforceable agreement setting forth the amount, term, and repayment schedule of the loan.

As to the time period for repayment, the loan, by its terms, must be repaid within five years; substantially level amortization of the loan is required, with payments made at least quarterly. If the loan is used to acquire a dwelling unit (which is to be used as a principal residence of the participant) and meets the amount limitation, the five-year time limit does not apply.

Investment Options

It is possible for the assets of a profit sharing plan to be invested in a single fund, with all employees sharing proportionately in the investment gains and losses of that fund. But, in fact, few plans are designed and operated in this fashion. Most plans allow employees to direct the investment of their accounts and to choose from among several different investment options. These options typically include two or more of the following: a guaranteed interest contract or arrangement; a corporate bond or fixed income fund; a government bond fund; one or more equity funds (with varying degrees of risk); and an employer stock fund. Larger employers might have

---

[5] The Department of Labor has taken the position that a loan cannot exceed 50 percent of the employee's vested account balance. Because of this conflict between the DOL and the IRS, most plans limit the loan to 50 percent of the vested account balance and ignore the $10,000 minimum.

even more funds to choose from and might include, for example, a real estate fund. Some employers make these choices available by arranging for a choice among several of the funds offered by an investment company.

A major reason for permitting these choices is to limit the employer's fiduciary responsibility. Some statutory relief from this liability can be obtained by complying with regulations issued by the DOL. In general, these regulations require that a plan offer at least three diversified categories of investment with materially different risk and return characteristics and that participants have the right to change investments at least quarterly—more often if needed because of the volatility of a particular fund. Regulatory liability protection can be afforded to employer stock if the shares are publicly traded in a recognized market and if the plan also offers the three required options; however, all purchases, sales, voting, and related share activities must be implemented confidentially through a fiduciary. It should be noted that failure to comply with the DOL regulations does not mean that fiduciaries are automatically

---

Evaluating the Costs of Plan Loans to Employees   1

Loan provisions have proven attractive to many employees who feel they are getting a "break" in the form of a no-cost loan since they are paying interest to themselves—as the loan is repaid, both principal and interest are credited to their accounts. This, of course, is not the case. Assuming that the rate of interest charged by the plan is the same as the rate the employee would pay to a commercial lender, there is no difference in the cost of the loan. In fact, making the loan from the plan could be more costly. When a loan is made from the plan, the employee's account balance, to the extent of the loan, is credited only with the interest charged by the plan. If the account would have been credited with a higher rate of return during the loan period had a loan not been made, the employee will have lost this additional investment income. This amount, compounded over the years remaining until a distribution is made, could add significantly to the real cost of the loan—over and above the interest rate charged.

This result can be avoided (or at least minimized) if the employee adjusts the investment mix of his or her account balance to treat the loan amount as part of the fixed income portion of the total account. For example, an employee with an account balance of $50,000 might be invested 80 percent in common stock ($40,000) and 20 percent in fixed income investments ($10,000). If the employee takes a loan of $10,000 and does not adjust the portfolio, the typical plan would reduce her mix so that $32,000 would be invested in stock and $8,000 would be invested in fixed income investments. The loan, however, is a fixed income investment, making a total of $18,000 in this category. She could counter this effect by directing that all of the remaining account balance ($40,000) be invested in stock, thus restoring the original mix with the expectation of not reducing overall returns.

liable—it simply means that the regulatory safe harbor for liability attributable to participants' investment choices will not be available. Also, compliance does not relieve the employer from responsibility for ensuring that the investments are prudent and properly diversified.

If employer stock is an investment and can be purchased with employee contributions, the requirements of the Securities and Exchange Commission (SEC) will have to be met. These requirements are discussed in Chapter 6.

A plan also can be written to permit employees to invest part of their account balances in life and health insurance. When this is done, and when a participant is investing funds that have accumulated for less than two years, additional IRS requirements must be met. These requirements are that such amounts, when used to purchase life or health insurance, must be incidental. The IRS has defined **incidental insurance benefits** as follows:

1. If only ordinary life insurance contracts are purchased, the aggregate premiums in the case of each participant must be less than one-half the total contributions and forfeitures allocated to his or her account.

2. If only accident and health insurance contracts are purchased, the payments for premiums may not exceed 25 percent of the funds allocated to the employee's account.

3. If both ordinary life and accident and health insurance contracts are purchased, the amount spent for the accident and health premiums plus one-half of the amount spent for the ordinary life insurance premiums may not, together, exceed 25 percent of the funds allocated to the employee's account.

In addition, the purchase of an ordinary life insurance contract will be incidental only if the plan requires the trustee to convert the entire value of the life insurance contract at or before retirement into cash; provides periodic income so that no portion of such value may be used to continue life insurance protection beyond retirement; or distributes the contract to the participant.

Other Requirements

Qualified profit sharing plans, like qualified pension plans, must meet the requirements of the IRC. Thus, they must be in writing, be permanent, be communicated to employees, and preclude diversion or recapture by the employer of contributions to the plan. A qualified profit sharing plan must treat service as required by ERISA and permit employees to buy back their benefits under stated conditions. It also must include a number of other features, such as a prohibition against assignments (with the exception of certain specified events), the protection of an employee's benefits in the event of plan merger or consolidation, and the payment of benefits by prescribed times. The plan also must comply with the top-heavy provisions of the law.

The requirement that a qualified pension plan provide definitely determinable benefits obviously does not apply in the case of qualified profit sharing plans. Also, certain other provisions of ERISA are not applicable to qualified profit sharing plans—for example, the minimum funding standards and the plan termination insurance requirements.

Limits on Deductibility of Employer Contributions

The limits on the deductibility of employer contributions to a profit sharing plan are set forth in **Section 404 of the IRC.**

For profit sharing plans, the **maximum deductible contribution** is equal to 25 percent of the compensation paid or otherwise accrued during the employer's taxable year to all covered employees for years beginning after 2001 as a result of EGTRRA. The maximum deductible contribution for profit sharing plans had previously been 15 percent of the compensation paid or otherwise accrued during the employer's taxable year to all covered employees for years prior to 2002.[6] Carryover provisions apply in profit sharing plans when the contribution in one taxable year is greater than the deductible limit for that taxable year. This type of carryover is called a **contribution carryover.** Thus, if a contribution is made in a given year in excess of the allowable deduction for that year, the employer will be allowed to take a deduction for such excess payment in a succeeding taxable year if it does not bring the deduction for the succeeding year to over 25 percent of the participating payroll for that succeeding year. However, any excess contribution is subject to a 10 percent penalty tax.

If both a pension plan (defined benefit or money purchase) and a profit sharing plan exist, with overlapping payrolls, the total amount deductible in any taxable year under both plans cannot exceed 25 percent of the compensation paid or accrued to covered employees for that year.[7] When excess payments are made in any taxable year, the excess may be carried forward to the succeeding taxable year, subject to the limitation that the total amount deducted for that succeeding taxable year (including the deduction for the current contribution) cannot exceed 25 percent of the compensation paid or accrued for that subsequent year.

The 25 percent overall limitation can be achieved by a profit sharing plan alone since a currently deductible profit sharing contribution must not exceed 25 percent of the payroll of the participating employees for years beginning after 2001.[8] The 25 percent overall limitation does not eliminate the requirement that a currently deductible pension contribution must not exceed the amount that would have been the limit had only a pension plan been in effect.

---

[6] If the contribution to the profit sharing plan was less than the allowable 15 percent, the difference between the amount actually paid in and the 15 percent limit (called a "credit carryover") could be contributed and deducted in succeeding years, but only if the carryover was accumulated before 1987. The credit carryover contribution in any later year could not exceed the allowable percent of the compensation paid or otherwise accrued during such later year. Also, there was an overall annual limitation when a credit carryover was involved. This overall limit was and is 25 percent of current covered payroll.

[7] This 25 percent limit will be increased to the extent larger contributions are required by the IRC's minimum funding standards, as described in Chapter 15.

[8] See the insight box in Chapter 7 on page 132 describing the popularity in years before 2002 of combination plans involving money purchase pension and profit sharing plans. The insight box explains how increasing the maximum deductible contribution from 15 percent to 25 percent for years beginning after 2001 will favor profit sharing plans alone in many situations.

Taxation of Distributions

The taxation of distributions from a qualified profit sharing plan is identical to the tax treatment of distributions from a qualified pension plan, discussed in detail in Chapter 27. However, the tax treatment of distributions of securities of the employer should be mentioned here because investing a portion of trust assets in the securities of the employer is a common practice under profit sharing plans. Securities of the employer include stocks, bonds, and debentures issued by the employer's parent or subsidiary corporations. If a total distribution (defined in Chapter 27) of the employee's account is made under qualifying conditions, the employee can elect to include either the market value of the employer securities or their cost basis to the trust as taxable income at the time of distribution. In other words, the employee need not be taxed on the unrealized appreciation at the time of distribution unless he or she so elects. If the employee elects to defer taxation, the unrealized appreciation, along with any subsequent increase in the value of the securities, is taxed as a capital gain when the securities are sold. If the securities are held until the employee's death prior to EGTRRA's elimination of the estate tax in 2010, the employee's heirs will have a cost basis in the securities equal to their market value at the time of death (i.e., the appreciation in value unrealized at the time of death will not be taxed as income). If the securities of the employer are included in a distribution that does not meet qualifying conditions, only the portion of the securities attributable to employee contributions can be valued on the basis of cost to the trust.

Termination of a Plan

Although a qualified profit sharing plan must be permanent, the IRS does permit inclusion of a provision giving the employer the right to amend or terminate the plan. However, if the vesting schedule is changed, any participant with at least three years of service must be given the election to remain under the preamendment vesting schedule. If the plan is terminated for reasons other than "business necessity" within a few years after its inception, this action will be considered by the IRS as evidence that the plan, from its inception, was not a bona fide program for the exclusive benefit of employees in general. If business necessity exists, the employer may terminate the plan without adverse tax consequences.

If a plan is terminated, all assets in the fund are vested immediately in plan participants. Since all plan assets are allocated to specific participants, no problem exists regarding any order of priorities in the distribution of the fund. Each participant is entitled to the balance in his or her account.

Upon termination of the plan, the trustees will determine, in accordance with plan provisions, a method of distributing the plan assets. The participants' shares may either be distributed in a lump sum; distributed in installments over a period of years; used to purchase immediate or deferred annuities (either fixed or variable); or distributed in kind.

Chapter Summary

- Profit sharing plans have considerable appeal since they embody the individual account concept without imposing any fixed commitment on employers to provide any specific level of benefits. The IRC does not require that a qualified profit sharing plan include a definite predetermined contribution formula. In the absence of such a formula, the regulations require that contributions be made on a substantial and recurring basis in order for plan permanency to be established. Though plans are not required to provide a definite contribution formula, it is necessary that such plans include a definite allocation formula to become qualified.

- A profit sharing plan must be for the exclusive benefit of employees or their beneficiaries and is generally subject to the same coverage and qualification requirements attributable to pension plans.

- Contributions under a profit sharing plan may be made on a discretionary basis or in accordance with a definite predetermined formula. Both of these approaches have relative advantages and disadvantages from both an employee and employer perspective. It is conceptually illogical to require employee contributions under profit sharing plans, although some plans provide for voluntary employee contributions. Such voluntary contributions may be made as elective deferrals on a pretax basis under Section 401(k) of the IRC or as after-tax contributions.

- Some profit sharing plans permit distributions after a fixed number of years while employees are still actively employed. The IRS has interpreted this requirement to mean that accumulations cannot be distributed in less than two years. Distributions also can be made upon the occurrence of an event such as hardship or the completion of five years of participation. Loan provisions also are allowable in qualified profit sharing plans as long as plans meet certain requirements prescribed by the IRS and DOL.

- For profit sharing plans, the maximum deductible contribution is equal to 25 percent of the compensation paid or otherwise accrued to all covered employees during the employer's taxable year, for years beginning after 2001 as a result of EGTRRA.

Key Terms

allocation formula, p. *144*
combined (approach), p. *142*
contribution carryover,
  p. *151*
current (approach), p. *142*
deferred (approach), p. *142*
definite predetermined
  contribution formula,
  p. *143*

discretionary contribution
  approach, p. *143*
elective deferrals, p. *144*
exclusive benefit, p. *143*
incidental insurance
  benefits, p. *150*
individual-account
  retirement programs,
  p. *141*

maximum deductible
  contribution, p. *151*
profit sharing plans, p. *141*
Section 404 of the IRC,
  p. *151*
substantial and recurring
  contributions, p. *143*

Questions for Review

1. What are the typical participation requirements found in a profit sharing plan? Explain.
2. What contribution requirements are imposed by the IRC on profit sharing plans?

3. What advantages can be ascribed to a definite predetermined contribution formula for a profit sharing plan?

4. Describe a common approach for allocating employer contributions that recognizes both compensation and length of service.

5. What usually happens to forfeited amounts of nonvested contributions in a profit sharing plan? Explain.

6. Is a profit sharing plan obligated to permit participants to withdraw a portion of their vested benefits prior to separation from employment? Explain.

7. Explain a typical loan provision that may be included in a profit sharing plan.

8. Can a qualified profit sharing plan be terminated? Explain.

9. What is meant by an incidental insurance benefit under a profit sharing plan?

Questions for Discussion

1. Discuss the conditions under which an employer may desire to establish a profit sharing plan.

2. Assume that an employer has had a profit sharing plan for several years and that the reaction of the employees toward the plan has been unsatisfactory. Discuss the plan design flexibility available for a profit sharing plan that may be used by the employer to improve the employees' reaction without increasing the employer's annual cost.

3. Assume that a publicly held firm decides to sponsor a profit sharing plan that will incorporate a definite predetermined contribution formula. Discuss how you would establish such a formula, keeping in mind the need to be equitable to stockholders, bondholders, and employees.

Resources for Further Study

Krass, Stephen J. *The Pension Answer Book: 2002 Edition.* New York: Panel Publishers, 2002.

Palmer, Bruce A. "Profit Sharing Plans." *The Handbook of Employee Benefits.* 5th ed. Jerry S. Rosenbloom, ed. New York: McGraw-Hill, 2001.

www.psca.org—website of the Profit Sharing/401(k) Council of America.

Chapter

9

Savings Plans

After studying this chapter you should be able to:

- Describe the characteristics of savings plans.
- Explain the primary objectives of savings plans and how savings plans may be designed to achieve those objectives.
- Describe design features in a savings plan that promote employee participation.
- Explain how vesting provisions operate in savings plans and how these provisions compare with those found in profit sharing plans.
- Discuss federal tax law restrictions on the ability of participants to obtain loans from savings plans.
- Explain how benefits are distributed from savings plans and the tax considerations when benefits payments are made.

Savings plans have become an increasingly popular form of employee benefit. Starting with the large petroleum companies, these plans spread gradually to many corporations in a number of other industries. Most of the major companies in manufacturing and service industries now have such plans for their employees. Early savings plans provided for employee contributions to be made on an after-tax basis. With the advent of Section 401(k) and cash or deferred arrangements (CODAs), almost all savings plans have shifted over to permit and/or require before-tax employee contributions. Since CODAs can attach to profit sharing plans and employee stock ownership plans (ESOPs), as well as savings plans, they are covered separately in Chapter 11. This chapter focuses on the objectives and provisions of savings plans, regardless of the manner in which employee contributions are made.

Unlike other employee benefit plans, which usually are designed with a specific purpose or objective in mind, savings plans generally meet a number of objectives and provide for the payment of benefits under several different contingencies. From an employer's viewpoint, they offer most of the advantages of profit sharing plans at a considerably lower cost. As a result, many employers have instituted savings plans to provide relatively low-cost supplemental benefits in the event of the retirement, death, or disability of an employee, as well as to provide meaningful benefits during active employment. Further, they may be used to provide employees with some protection against the erosive effects of postretirement inflation. It generally is recognized, however, that because of relatively lower contribution levels, savings plans do not have the same incentive value for employees as do profit sharing plans.

Under federal tax law, a savings plan may achieve a qualified status and, as a result, the employer and employees may obtain the favorable tax benefits associated with such a plan. For this purpose, savings plans generally are designed to meet the qualification requirements applicable to profit sharing plans.[1] Thus, with the exception of employee and employer contribution patterns, savings plans possess most of the general characteristics of deferred profit sharing plans. The significant characteristics of savings plans are as follows:

1. Employee participation in the plan is voluntary, and, to participate, an employee must agree to make contributions.

2. An employee usually has the option of determining the level of his or her contributions—that is, the employee may choose to make contributions at the minimum or maximum level set by the plan or at permitted intermediate levels.

3. **Employer matching contributions** usually match or are equal to some fraction of the contributions made by employees up to a specified level. In most savings plans, the employer contributes a fixed percentage of employee contributions, although employer contributions sometimes are made in full or in part by means of a profit sharing formula or on a discretionary basis.

4. Both employer and employee contributions generally are made to a trust fund.

5. Assets of the trust usually are invested in one or more investment funds, with the employee frequently having the option of choosing how his or her own contributions (and sometimes the employer contributions on the employee's behalf) are invested. In some plans, employer contributions are invested automatically in securities of the employer, with the employee having an investment option only for his or her own contributions.

6. An employee's account is generally paid to or on behalf of the employee in the event of retirement, death, disability, or termination of employment. Benefits on termination of employment are limited to the employee's vested interest, but savings plans usually have relatively liberal vesting provisions.

7. Most savings plans permit an employee, during active employment, to withdraw the value of employee contributions as well as all or part of the employee's vested interest in employer contributions. Such withdrawals, however, are often sub-

---

[1] A contributory money purchase pension plan also can be regarded as a savings plan, particularly if it is supplemental in nature. However, such plans are relatively uncommon since they do not permit employees to withdraw funds prior to termination of employment. The discussion in this chapter relates only to savings plans that are tax-qualified as profit sharing plans.

ject to some form of penalty (such as a period of **suspended participation**). Some plans limit withdrawals to those made for specific financial needs, such as those associated with illness, the purchase of a home, college education, and the like.[2]

The balance of this chapter discusses the various objectives that may be met by savings plans, as well as their basic features. The prevalence of certain plan provisions, as documented by the Towers Perrin Employee Benefit Information Center (EBIC), is also noted.

Savings Plan Objectives

As noted earlier, a savings plan may serve a number of different objectives. It is important, when designing such a plan, to establish those objectives that are of paramount importance to the employer. This is necessary since the design of the plan will be influenced by the objectives it is to serve. For example, if a major objective of a plan is to provide supplemental retirement income, withdrawal privileges, if permitted at all, will be restricted; otherwise, an employee could defeat the employer's basic objective by making substantial withdrawals prior to retirement.

Savings plans usually serve one or more of the following objectives:

1. To attract and retain employees.

2. To provide deferred compensation on an advantageous tax basis.

3. To encourage employee thrift and savings.

4. To provide benefits to supplement other employee benefit plans in the event of illness, disability, death, retirement, or termination of employment.

5. To accumulate funds for other purposes.

6. To foster a greater sense of company identification through the purchase of company securities.

Each of these objectives and its influence on plan design is discussed below.

Attracting and Retaining Employees

Generally speaking, most employee benefit plans serve the broad purpose of attracting and retaining employees. In that sense, then, savings plans are the same as other benefit programs. However, savings plans (and profit sharing plans) have a somewhat greater appeal to younger employees, since they offer immediate and tangible benefits during the early years of employment. For this reason, savings plans can be particularly effective in attracting new employees.

Where this is a primary objective of a savings plan, it generally would indicate that the plan should be designed with minimum eligibility requirements, a definite

---

[2] Withdrawals could be subject to an additional 10 percent tax if considered to be an early distribution, as discussed in Chapter 27.

formula for determining employer contributions, relatively generous benefits, and liberal vesting requirements.

Deferred Compensation

As noted earlier, if it meets the necessary requirements, a savings plan may be considered a qualified plan under federal tax law. Employer contributions made on behalf of the employee are not taxable until they are distributed. This is true even though the employee has a vested right to such contributions. Moreover, investment income earned on both employer and employee contributions qualifies for the same deferred tax treatment. Distributions to an employee may be taxed at a comparatively low rate, particularly when they begin after age 59½. For these reasons, a significant objective of many savings plans is to provide tax-deferred compensation.

When deferred compensation is a key objective, the plan generally is designed to permit maximum employer and employee contributions, as well as permit employee contributions to be made on a before-tax basis. As noted earlier, so-called 401(k) plans that permit before-tax employee contributions will be examined in Chapter 11.

Employee Savings

Even though they are called savings plans, the specific objective of encouraging employees to save is not always a primary consideration in the establishment of such a plan. Nevertheless, many employers believe that employees should plan on meeting at least part of their own economic security needs without relying fully on government and employer-provided benefits. A savings plan is a most efficient vehicle in meeting such an objective.

To further such an objective, a savings plan generally is designed with liberal eligibility requirements and with maximum flexibility in terms of the levels at which an employee may contribute. The plan also may permit employees to contribute additional amounts (without a matching employer contribution) up to the maximum permitted by federal tax law. Also, to overcome any reluctance on the part of an employee to tie up savings until some future event such as retirement, death, or termination of employment, the plan probably should permit loans and, possibly, withdrawals during active employment—at least with respect to the employee's own after-tax contributions.

Supplemental Benefits

The vested portion of an employee's account under a savings plan is paid to or on behalf of the employee in the event of retirement, death, disability, or termination of employment. As a result, a savings plan can provide meaningful **supplemental benefits** in addition to an employer's other benefit plans that deal with these contingencies. It is common for an employer to adopt a savings plan for the specific purpose of supplementing another benefit plan rather than making direct improvements in the plan itself. For example, an employer might feel that the level of benefits provided under its pension plan is not adequate. Rather than improving the benefit formula under its retirement plan, the employer might seek to remedy the inadequacy of the retirement plan by instituting a savings plan. The two plans together could meet the employer's objectives in terms of total retirement income and, at the same time, create the additional advantages that would accrue from the savings plan itself.

If supplementing other employee benefit plans is an important objective of a particular savings plan, this will have a material influence on the design of the plan as it relates to employer contributions. Also, this objective generally suggests that employees be given only limited, if any, withdrawal privileges during active employment, since to do otherwise could defeat a major plan objective.

Company Identification

It is quite possible, in the case of a publicly held corporation, that a major objective of instituting a savings plan might be to promote a greater sense of **company identification** by having employees become corporate shareholders. While this also may be accomplished with other plans, a savings plan under which part of the assets are invested in employer securities can assist in achieving this employer objective. On occasion, the assets of a savings plan of a privately held firm are invested in the same fashion; however, this is relatively uncommon.

If assets are to be invested in employer securities, a common plan provision is to require that all employer contributions be invested in this manner, while employees have the option of having their own contributions invested in fixed income or equity investments. Employees are sometimes given the option of having their own contributions invested in employer securities. Some plans, rather than mandating that employer contributions be invested in employer securities, give the employee complete investment freedom for both employer and employee contributions.

Basic Features

The preceding discussion touched upon the basic features of savings plans. The balance of this chapter discusses each of the following major plan provisions in greater detail: eligibility requirements, nondiscrimination requirements, employee contributions, employer contributions, allocations to employee accounts, investment of funds, vesting, withdrawals and loans, and the distribution of benefits.

Eligibility Requirements

Savings plans are subject to the same Internal Revenue Code (IRC) requirements as pension and profit sharing plans. Typically, an employee is required to meet some minimum service requirement and to have attained some minimum age before being given the opportunity to join the plan. Under tax law, the service requirement cannot exceed one year (two years if the plan provides for full and immediate vesting and is not a CODA), and the minimum age cannot be higher than 21.

While it is possible to use other eligibility requirements, such as an employment classification, such requirements are not common in savings plans.

To be considered a qualified plan under federal tax law, a savings plan must not discriminate in favor of highly compensated employees (HCEs). Thus, the eligibility requirements chosen must not result in discrimination in favor of this group, and the plan must meet the coverage requirements of Section 410(b) of the IRC.

Nondiscrimination Requirements

The same nondiscrimination tests that apply to elective deferrals under CODAs are applied to employee after-tax contributions and employer matching contributions in a savings plan. Although these tests are described in considerable detail in Chapter 11, the following description provides a brief summary of the operation of the actual deferral and contribution percentage tests in general and the specific manner in which they apply to a savings plan.

The actual deferral percentage (ADP) for HCEs for their before-tax contributions cannot exceed the greater of (1) 125 percent of the ADP for all other eligible employees or (2) the lesser of 200 percent of the ADP for all other eligible employees, or such contribution percentage plus two percentage points. The actual contribution percentage (ACP) test applies to after-tax contributions and matching employer contributions, and is the same. The contribution percentage for a group of employees is the average of the contribution ratios computed separately for each individual employee in the group. The contribution ratio for an individual is the sum of the employee contributions (and the employer matching contributions) expressed as a percentage of the employee's compensation for the year.

Employee Contributions

As noted earlier, most savings plans are contributory and an eligible employee must agree to make contributions to participate. While it is possible to have a single employee contribution rate, it is customary to permit an employee to elect to contribute at any one of several different levels. Thus, for example, the plan may permit an employee to contribute 1, 2, or 3 percent of compensation. Another common provision is to permit the employee contribution rate to be any whole percentage, from 1 to 6 percent. Employee contributions also can be established as flat dollar amounts or by the use of earnings brackets.

Many savings plans permit supplemental employee contributions to be made. Such contributions become part of the employee's account, and investment income on such contributions is not subject to federal income tax until distributed. Both basic and supplemental employee contributions are considered both for the contribution tests referred to above and as part of the maximum annual addition that may be made on an employee's behalf under federal tax law.

Permitting an employee to elect the level at which he or she wishes to participate is generally desirable, since each employee can select the level best fitted to his or her individual needs. This flexibility is continued by permitting the employee to change contribution rates from time to time after becoming a participant. Thus, for example, an employee who initially contributed at a rate of 3 percent might, after participating for a year or so and finding that personal circumstances have changed,

Compensation Base 1

Since an employee's contribution is determined as a percentage of compensation, it is necessary for a plan to define the "compensation" upon which contributions will be based. The tax law permits any definition of compensation to be used, provided that the definition does not result in prohibited discrimination. Many plans define compensation to be base pay only; others define compensation to be total W-2 earnings or some combination of base pay and other elements such as overtime.

The Towers Perrin Employee Benefit Information Center (EBIC) database contains detailed information on the provisions of 472 savings plans. The definition of compensation used by these plans breaks down as follows:

Definition of Compensation	Number of Plans Reporting
Base pay only	92
Base pay and overtime	32
Base pay and commissions	24
Base pay and bonus	25
Base pay, overtime, and commissions	41
Base pay, overtime, and bonus	41
Base pay, commissions, and bonus	9
Base pay, overtime, commissions, and bonus	178
other 30	30

reduce the contribution rate to 2 percent or increase it to 6 percent, assuming that these rates are permitted by the plan. By the same token, the employee is usually granted the privilege of suspending contributions for some period of time.

The right to change contribution rates or to suspend contributions usually may be exercised, after reasonable notice, at various times during the plan year. Some plans restrict these rights so that they may be exercised only at the beginning of each month; others are more flexible and permit a change at the beginning of any pay period following the required notice. For administrative reasons, plans often impose some form of limitation on the number of times such changes can be made. For example, the right to change or suspend contributions might be limited so that the right can be exercised only once in any 12-month period. Also, for administrative reasons, some plans require that if an employee suspends contributions, this must be done for a minimum period, such as six months or one year.

Consistent with these requirements, most savings plans do not impose any penalty on employees who do not elect to participate when first eligible. Any such employee is usually permitted to join the plan on any subsequent entry date.

Employer Contributions

Under federal tax law, savings plans generally are designed to be profit sharing plans. As a practical matter, however, most such plans contemplate that employer contributions will be made on a fixed basis related to employee contributions.[3]

The basic approach used by most savings plans is to provide for an employer contribution equal to some percentage of the employee's contribution. Typical employer contribution schedules call for an employer contribution of 25 or 50 percent of the employee's contribution.[4] One variation of this basic approach is to increase the employer's contribution as the employee's length of participation increases. For example, the plan could provide for an employer contribution rate of 50 percent during the first 10 years of the employee's participation, 75 percent during the next 10 years, and 100 percent for participation in excess of 20 years. However, this type of plan may have difficulty satisfying the nondiscrimination tests described earlier, particularly if there is a substantial correlation between service and pay level.

Another variation in determining employer contribution levels is to provide for a basic contribution related to employee contributions, such as that described, plus a supplemental contribution based on current profits. The supplemental contribution might be made in accordance with a predetermined formula, or it could be made on a discretionary basis. It is also possible to design a plan so that the entire employer contribution is determined on a current profit basis; such a provision, however, is fairly uncommon in savings plans.

As with profit sharing plans, forfeitures arising when participating employees terminate without full vesting may be reallocated among employees or may be used to reduce employer contributions. While the majority of profit sharing plans reallocate such forfeitures among employees, the common provision in savings plans is to use them to reduce employer contributions.

Allocations to Employee Accounts

An individual account is maintained for each participating employee under a savings plan. An employee's account is credited with the employee's own contributions, including any supplemental contributions, along with employer contributions made on the employee's behalf. The employee's account also is credited with its proportionate share of the investment income (or loss) of the trust fund. In this regard, the employee's account might be subdivided to reflect the different investment funds available under the plan and the different investment results that these funds might have achieved.

If the plan so provides, the employee's account also is credited with the employee's share of any forfeitures that might arise. When this is the case, forfeitures usually are allocated among employees based on the compensation of each participating employee in relation to the total compensation of all participating employees.

---

[3] The IRC does not generally recognize savings plans as a separate category of deferred compensation plans. Since savings plans possess many of the characteristics of profit sharing plans, they generally have been considered in that category.
[4] This would apply only for the employee's basic contribution. A corresponding employer contribution is not made for supplemental employee contributions.

Employer Matching Contribution Levels   2

The employer matching contribution rates in the 472 savings plans included in the Towers Perrin EBIC database are as follows:

Employer Matching Contribution Rate	Number of Plans Reporting
No company contribution	19
Match is 25%	11
Match is 50%	122
Match is more than 50% and less than 100%	35
Match is 100% or more	86
Match varies*	199

*Match varies by profits or service or uses different base and supplemental percentages.

Investment of Funds

Although individual accounts are maintained for each participating employee for record-keeping purposes, contributions and actual trust funds are not segregated on behalf of each individual participant. Such contributions are turned over to a trustee (or trustees) and/or insurance company who invests these contributions for the benefit of the participating employees.

A few savings plans are structured so that all contributions are held and invested as a single investment fund. This approach might be attractive when the size of the fund is relatively small. Under such an arrangement, the employee has no choice as to how his or her account will be invested.

Most savings plans provide for two or more investment funds and give the employee a choice of investments. For example, the plan might provide for two funds, one consisting of a guaranteed interest contract or fixed income securities and the other consisting of equity-type investments. The employee would be permitted to have all of the account values invested in either fund or to have part of such values invested in each fund.

Other investment variations are possible, of course. Some savings plans give employees the opportunity of investing in more than one equity-type fund, each having a varying degree of potential risk and return. Also, if employer securities are involved, a separate fund usually is established for this purpose.[5] A further

[5] If the employee has the option of having his or her own employee contributions invested in employer securities, it will be necessary to register the plan with the Securities and Exchange Commission (SEC); it is then necessary that requirements of the SEC be observed, with particular reference to any descriptive or enrollment material given to employees. Also, it will be necessary that employees be given a prospectus. SEC requirements are discussed in Chapter 6.

investment variation might give an employee the opportunity to invest a portion of the account in life insurance.

A number of plans give an employee additional investment opportunities as the employee approaches retirement age by permitting the employee to transfer all or part of his or her account to an account not subject to market value fluctuations. Such a provision enables an employee to exercise some degree of control over the timing of the liquidation of account values and protects the employee from being forced to accept the market conditions that might exist at the time of retirement.

One reason for permitting these investment choices is to limit the employer's fiduciary liability for poor investment performance. Some **statutory relief** from this liability can be obtained by complying with the Section 404(c) regulations issued by the Department of Labor (DOL). In general, these regulations require that a plan offer at least three diversified categories of investment with materially different risk-and-return characteristics and that participants have the right to change investments at least quarterly—more often if needed because of the volatility of a particular fund. Regulatory liability protection can be afforded to employer stock if the shares are publicly traded in a recognized market and if the plan also offers the three required options; however, all purchases, sales, voting, and related share activities must be implemented confidentially through a fiduciary. It should be noted that failure to comply with the Section 404(c) regulations does not mean that fiduciaries are automatically liable; it simply means that the regulatory safe harbor for liability attributable to participants' investment choices is not available. Also, compliance does not relieve the employer from responsibility for ensuring that the investments are prudent and properly diversified.

Regardless of the number of investment funds involved, there remains the further question of the **trustee's investment powers.** Under some plans, the trustee is granted full authority for the investment of the fund; under others, the trustee is subject to control that ranges from broad directives to the approval of each investment. In some situations, the employer might retain investment counsel to be responsible for the investment of plan assets, with the trustee acting primarily as a custodian. In making investments, the trustee might maintain an individually managed portfolio or use one or more common trust funds.[6]

If an employee is given investment options, some restrictions may be imposed upon the employee's right to make and change investment elections. For example, the plan may permit the employee to invest 100 percent of account values in either of two available funds—say, 50 percent in each fund, or 25 percent in one fund and 75 percent in the other. Another similar restriction would be that the employee can exercise investment options only in multiples of 10 percent.

An employee generally is permitted to change investment elections only as of a date that the funds are being valued. Many plans are valued monthly and some—particularly those that make use of mutual funds—are valued on a daily basis. A lesser

---

[6] The manner in which investment responsibilities are handled can have a significant effect on the fiduciary responsibilities of the parties involved. These fiduciary responsibilities are discussed in Chapter 6.

number are valued quarterly, with the result that there are only four times a year that an employee can make such a change.[7] If a plan is valued frequently, the employee's right to make changes might still be restricted to a limited number of times during the year. Any restrictions on an employee's right to change investments should not contravene the requirements of Section 404(c) if relief from fiduciary liability is desired under that section of the law.

Vesting

All savings plans stipulate that 100 percent of the value of an employee's account shall be paid to the employee (or on behalf of the employee) in the event of retirement, disability, or death. For this purpose, retirement usually is defined as retirement in accordance with the employer's retirement plan. The definition of disability is more varied, but frequently it is the same as that applicable to the employer's disability income plan.

A few savings plans also provide for 100 percent vesting in the event of severance of employment. However, most plans require that the employee complete some period of service before being entitled to full vesting of the value of employer contributions.[8] While plans vary considerably as to the degree of service or participation required for vesting, the general pattern is that full vesting is achieved after a relatively short time. Savings plans frequently develop more **liberal vesting provisions** than those found in profit sharing plans intended as the basic plan for retirement income. A typical vesting provision might provide that an employee be vested at the rate of 20 percent for each year of service (or participation), so that full vesting is achieved after five years. In any event, a savings plan must meet the requirements of federal tax law and satisfy one of the alternative vesting schedules described in Chapter 5.

Withdrawals and Loans

A most valuable aspect of a savings plan is that it can be designed to permit the distribution of benefits during active employment. Such a distribution may be made by permitting employees to make either withdrawals or loans.

Withdrawal Provisions

When a savings plan has been designed to be a profit sharing plan under federal tax law, it is possible to make distributions to employees after a fixed number of years. This provision has been interpreted by the Internal Revenue Service (IRS) to be a period of at least two years. Thus, it is possible to permit the withdrawal of monies that have been held in the fund for at least two years. Federal tax law also permits funds to be distributed from a profit sharing plan upon the happening of an event such as a hardship or, as interpreted by the IRS, upon the completion of five years

---

[7] Internal Revenue Service (IRS) regulations require that the assets of a profit sharing plan be valued at least once a year at fair market value; also, a plan with only annual valuations will not qualify for the regulatory safe harbor from fiduciary liability under Section 404(c).

[8] The value attributable to the employee's own contributions is, of course, always vested.

Vesting Provisions   3

The vesting provisions of the 472 savings plans included in the Towers Perrin EBIC database (as they relate to the vesting of employer contributions) are as follows:

Vesting Provisions*	Number of Plans Reporting
Plans with vesting that is . . .	
Immediate	184
After 1 year of service/participation	6
After 2 years of service/participation	8
After 3 years of service/participation	47
After 4 years of service/participation	18
After 5 years of service/participation	155
After 6 years of service/participation	3
After 7 years of service/participation	5
Other circumstances	46

*This data was gathered prior to the implementation of vesting schedule changes resulting from EGTRRA.

of plan participation. It should be pointed out that withdrawals are permitted on a relatively liberal basis for the value of after-tax employee contributions and employer contributions that are not subject to an actual deferral percentage (ADP) test. This is unlike the restrictions on withdrawals that apply to elective deferrals and employer contributions used for ADP testing; these latter restrictions applicable to 401(k) plans are described in Chapter 11.

Withdrawal provisions vary widely and reflect the desires and objectives of individual employers. For example, some plans permit withdrawal rights only for the value of employee contributions. Others permit withdrawal of the value of vested employer contributions, but only after the value of employee contributions has been withdrawn. Some plans limit the right of withdrawal so that only 50 or 100 percent of the value of the employee's contributions may be withdrawn and, if a right to withdraw employer contributions also is granted, a similar percentage restriction also might apply.

Another common approach to the design of withdrawal provisions is much more flexible and allows withdrawals to be made at any time after the employee has completed at least five years of plan participation. A more restrictive approach, found in some plans, is to permit withdrawals only in the event of hardship—for example, for the purchase of a new home, college education, and the like. The definitions of hardship used for this purpose in a savings plan without elective deferrals can be much more liberal than the definitions used in a CODA under Section 401(k).

Withdrawals usually are permitted only on a date the fund is otherwise being valued. Also, there usually is a requirement that the amount withdrawn be at least some minimum dollar amount, such as $500. Further, once a withdrawal has been made, the employee may not be permitted to make a second withdrawal until some period of time has elapsed. A typical provision might restrict withdrawals to not more than one or two in any 12-month period.

Some plans impose a penalty on an employee who makes a withdrawal. The penalty might suspend an employee's participation in a plan for a period of time following withdrawal. The suspension operates as a penalty, since it automatically results in the employee's forgoing some amount of future employer contributions.[9]

Loans

A common provision permits an employee to use the value of his or her account during active employment by making a loan from the plan. Under a loan provision, an employee usually is allowed to borrow up to a specified percentage (such as 50 percent) of the vested portion of the employee's account.

A loan to an employee is treated as a taxable distribution unless certain requirements are met. These requirements involve the amount of the loan (or accumulated loans), the agreement concerning loan terms, and the time period for repayment. The maximum amounts that can be borrowed without being considered a distribution depend upon the amount of the employee's vested interest in his or her account balance. If it is (1) $10,000 or less, the entire vested interest is available; (2) between $10,000 and $20,000, $10,000 is available; (3) between $20,000 and $100,000, 50 percent of the vested interest is available; or (4) $100,000 or more, $50,000 is available.[10] The $50,000 limitation on loans from qualified plans is reduced by the excess of the highest outstanding loan balance during the preceding one-year period over the outstanding balance on the date a new loan is made.

The loan must be evidenced by a legally enforceable agreement setting forth the amount, term, and repayment schedule of the loan.

The loan must be repaid within five years; substantially level amortization of the loan is required, with payments made at least quarterly. However, if the loan is used to acquire a dwelling unit (which is to be used as the principal residence of the participant) and meets the amount limitation, the five-year time limit does not apply.

The loan provision must be available to all participants on a reasonably equivalent basis and must not be made available to HCEs in a percentage greater than that made available to other employees. The law also requires that the loan bear a reasonable rate of interest, be adequately secured, and be made only by the plan (and not by a third party, such as a bank, with the employee's account balance as security). If the loan provision meets the requirements of the DOL and the IRS, the loan

---

[9] As mentioned earlier in this chapter, withdrawals may be subject to federal income tax. Moreover, a 10 percent penalty tax may apply to distributions made before the participant's death, disability, or attainment of age 59½. See Chapter 27 for a detailed discussion.

[10] The DOL has taken the position that a loan cannot exceed 50 percent of the employee's vested account balance. Because of this conflict between the DOL and the IRS, most plans limit the loan to 50 percent of the vested account balance and ignore the $10,000 minimum.

Loan Availability 4

The availability of loans in the 472 savings plans in the Towers Perrin EBIC database are as follows:

	Count	Percent
Available	450	95%
Not available	22	5%
Total	472	100%

will be exempted from the prohibited transaction provisions of ERISA and the IRC. If a loan is made and is not exempted, this could constitute a prohibited transaction and could be in violation of the legal requirement that a plan prohibit assignments and alienations; this could result in a plan disqualification.

Distribution of Benefits

Most savings plans provide that the value of an employee's account be distributed in the form of a cash payment. Usually, there is also a provision that allows an employee to elect to have a distribution in the form of installments over a period of time or to have all or part of the account applied to the purchase of an annuity contract. If the possibility exists that the benefit could be paid out in the form of a life annuity, federal tax law requirements with respect to joint and survivor annuities for married employees could apply.

When any part of the employee's account is invested in employer securities, it is customary to provide that this portion be distributed in the form of securities rather than in cash. This could produce a tax advantage for an employee who receives a distribution of such securities purchased by employer contributions upon severance of employment or after age 59½ and under circumstances when the entire value of his or her account is distributed within one year. Under such circumstances, the value of the securities is the lower of their cost to the trust or their fair market value. Thus, if the employee so elects, he or she would not be taxed, at the time of distribution, on any **unrealized appreciation** that has taken place since the time the securities were acquired by the trust. If the employee should subsequently sell the securities, the gain would then be taxable. If securities purchased by employee contributions are distributed, deferral of the tax on any unrealized appreciation is available without the requirement that the employee receive the distribution upon severance of employment or after age 59½, or that it be part of a total distribution within one year.

Chapter Summary

- The Internal Revenue Code (IRC) does not recognize savings plans as a separate category of deferred compensation plan. As a result, these plans are most often qualified as profit sharing plans, although some are qualified as money purchase plans.

- Savings plans usually are designed to provide an employer contribution that either matches or equals some fraction of the contributions made by employees up to a specified level. The employer matches generally represent relatively lower contribution levels than are found in profit sharing plans and consequently do not have the same incentive value for employees as do profit sharing plans.

- Usually savings plans permit an employee the option of determining his or her level of contribution within a range of options. Employees usually are able to select the investment fund where employee contributions are invested. Some plans permit employees to select the fund where employer matches are invested.

- Many employers have instituted savings plans to provide relatively low-cost supplemental benefits in the event of the retirement, death, or disability of an employee, as well as to provide meaningful benefits during active employment. When a savings plan has been designed to be a profit sharing plan under federal tax law, it is possible to make distributions to employees after a fixed number of years—considered by the IRS to be two years—or upon the happening of an event such as hardship or the completion of five years of plan participation.

- If the primary objective of a savings plan is to encourage employee savings, then the plan usually will have liberal eligibility requirements and maximum flexibility in terms of withdrawal privileges and the levels at which an employee may contribute. If the primary objective of a savings plan is to provide supplemental retirement income, withdrawal privileges will likely be more restrictive than in the purely savings-oriented plan.

- Employer contributions made on behalf of the employee are not taxable until they are distributed even though the employee has a vested right to such contributions. In order to receive preferential tax treatment as a qualified plan, these arrangements are subject to tax law nondiscrimination requirements and the actual deferral percentage (ADP) and actual contribution percentage (ACP) tests.

Key Terms

company identification, p. *159*
employer matching contributions, p. *156*
liberal vesting provisions, p. *165*

savings plans, p. *155*
statutory relief, p. *164*
supplemental benefits, p. *158*
suspended participation, p. *157*

trustee investment powers, p. *164*
unrealized appreciation, p. *168*

Questions for Review

1. Explain the significant characteristics of savings plans.
2. Explain the basic objectives of savings plans.
3. What eligibility requirements are typically found in savings plans? Explain.
4. How is flexibility incorporated into a savings plan with respect to employee contributions?
5. What approaches are used for determining the extent of an employer's contribution to a savings plan?
6. How are savings plan assets invested? Explain.
7. Explain vesting as it pertains to savings plans. How do the vesting requirements compare with those typically found in profit sharing plans?
8. Explain the approaches that are used in providing withdrawal benefits.
9. Does the federal tax law impose any restrictions on loan provisions in a savings plan? Explain.
10. What alternative ways may benefits be distributed in a savings plan?

Questions for Discussion

1. Discuss the conditions under which an employer may desire to establish a savings plan.
2. Assume that an employer has had a savings plan for several years and that the reaction of the employees toward the plan has been unsatisfactory. Discuss the plan design flexibility features available for a savings plan that may be used by the employer, if not currently used, to improve the employees' reaction without increasing the employer's annual cost.
3. Discuss how the nondiscrimination requirements for matching contributions and after-tax employee contributions are likely to affect plan design for savings plans.

Resources for Further Study

Krass, Stephen J. *The Pension Answer Book: 2002 Edition.* New York: Panel Publishers, 2002.

Palmer, Bruce A. "Profit Sharing Plans." *The Handbook of Employee Benefits.* 5th ed. Jerry S. Rosenbloom, ed. New York: McGraw-Hill, 2001.

www.psca.org—website of the Profit Sharing/401(k) Council of America.

Employee Stock Ownership Plans (ESOPs)

After studying this chapter you should be able to:

- Describe the characteristics of employee stock ownership plans (ESOPs).

- Explain the potential advantages an employer might realize in adopting a leveraged ESOP.

- Describe the special requirements that are imposed on an ESOP that are not imposed on other types of qualified plans.

- Explain the rationale for the special requirements that are imposed on ESOPs.

- Discuss how fiduciary requirements such as the diversification requirement apply to an ESOP.

- Distinguish how an ESOP might be used differently by a large, publicly held company and a small, privately held business.

Overview

ESOP Defined

In a broad sense, an employee stock ownership plan (ESOP) could be defined as any type of qualified employee benefit plan (including profit sharing and savings) that invests some or all of its assets in employer securities. The definition of ESOP contained in the law, however, is much narrower in scope. Specifically, the Internal Revenue Code (IRC) defines an ESOP as a qualified stock bonus plan or a combination qualified stock bonus plan and defined contribution (money purchase) plan designed to invest primarily in employer securities.[1] Internal Revenue Service (IRS) regulations, in turn, define a **stock bonus plan** as a plan established and maintained by an employer to provide benefits similar to those of a profit sharing plan except that the contributions by the employer are not necessarily dependent upon profits and the benefits are distributable in the stock of the employer company. (Cash distributions are permitted; however, the employee must have the right to demand a distribution in the form of employer securities.) The plan must formally state that it is an ESOP and that assets are to be invested primarily in employer securities.

Simple or Nonleveraged ESOP

ESOPs have existed for many years, but it was not until the 1970s that these plans began to grow in popularity. Much of the early interest in the plans was attributable to the "tax credit" ESOP where the plan was financed with an employer tax credit and, typically, where there was no additional employer contribution. The tax credit for these plans expired on January 1, 1987, however, so that no additional funding of these plans is now taking place. Nevertheless, some of these plans continue to exist in terms of their accrued benefits and many have been modified or incorporated into other qualified plan arrangements such as savings plans or cash or deferred arrangements (CODAs).

---

[1] The phrase "designed to invest primarily in employer securities" has never been defined by the government, but most practitioners believe that this requirement will be met if more than 50 percent of the plan's assets are so invested when viewed over the life of the plan.

NONLEVERAGED ESOP

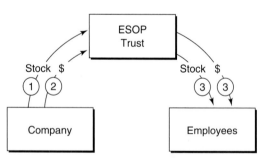

1. Each year, company gives stock to ESOP.
2. Or, each year, company gives cash to ESOP to buy stock. Employees pay nothing. ESOP holds stock for employees and periodically notifies them of how much they own and how much it is worth.
3. Employees collect stock or cash according to a vesting schedule when they retire or otherwise leave the company.

Source: Robert W. Smiley, Jr., and Ronald J. Gilbert, *Employee Stock Ownership Plans,* © 1989, pp. 1–3. Reprinted with permission from Warren, Gorham & Lamont, Park Square Building, 31 St. James Avenue, Boston, MA 02116-4112. 1-800-950-1211. All rights reserved.

Leveraged ESOP

The ongoing interest in ESOPs is largely attributable to the so-called **leveraged ESOP,** where the plan is used in conjunction with debt financing. As a result of the Tax Reform Acts of 1984 and 1986, leveraged ESOPs offer several significant tax advantages not available to other types of qualified retirement plans. In exchange for these privileges, however, they must meet a unique set of qualification rules.

LEVERAGED ESOP

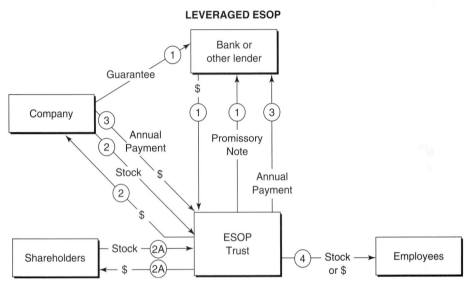

1. Bank lends money to ESOP with company guarantee.
2. ESOP buys stock from company.
2A. Or, ESOP buys stock from existing shareholders.
3. Company makes annual tax deductible contributions to ESOP, which in turn repays bank.
4. Employees collect stock or cash when they retire or leave company.

Source: Robert W. Smiley, Jr., and Ronald J. Gilbert, *Employee Stock Ownership Plans,* © 1989, pp. 1–5. Reprinted with permission from Warren, Gorham & Lamont, Park Square Building, 31 St. James Avenue, Boston, MA 02116-4112. 1-800-950-1211. All rights reserved.

To set up a leveraged employee stock ownership plan, a trust is created by the employer and the trustee acquires funds through a loan. The loan may be made directly to the trustee by the lending institution, in which case the loan is usually guaranteed by the employer because the trust cannot generate income (other than investment income) on its own. Alternatively, the employer can borrow the funds directly from the lending institution and immediately lend the same amount to the trustee in what is termed a **back-to-back arrangement.** In either case, the trustee uses the borrowed funds to purchase employer stock, usually directly from the employer.

The stock purchased by the trustee is held in an **unallocated suspense account** and is pledged as collateral for the loan. The employer then makes contributions to the plan for the benefit of employees. The plan uses these contributions to repay the loan, including interest. As the loan is repaid, shares of stock are released from the suspense account and allocated to the individual accounts of eligible employees. In most situations, the number of shares released is determined under what is termed the **fractional method.** This method reflects the ratio of the amount of the current principal and interest payment to the total current and future principal and interest payments. A second method relates only to current and future principal payments and may be used if the loan duration is less than 10 years.

This type of loan under an ESOP is exempt from the prohibited transaction provisions of the Employee Retirement Income Security Act (ERISA), provided the loan is made primarily for the benefit of participants in the plan and the interest is not in excess of a reasonable rate. In this regard, the regulations note that these loans "will be subject to special scrutiny by the Department of Labor (DOL) and the Internal Revenue Service (IRS) to ensure that they are primarily for the benefit of plan participants and beneficiaries."[2] Also, ESOPs are exempt from the diversity requirements of the fiduciary provisions of ERISA; they are not, however, exempt from the prudency requirements, nor are they exempt from the requirement that fiduciaries must act solely for the exclusive benefit of employees and their beneficiaries.

Advantages and Disadvantages of a Leveraged ESOP Significant advantages (including tax advantages) exist for ESOPs, and they can serve many useful purposes. An ESOP can be an effective employee benefit plan capable of satisfying important employer objectives. It also can be an effective device for converting a public company to a private organization, for disposing of a corporate division (the selling corporation would establish a new corporation that, in turn, would establish an ESOP for the purpose of raising capital and purchasing the division), and for providing **estate liquidity** to a major shareholder.

Many employers will find leveraged ESOPs attractive because they can put relatively large blocks of stock into presumably friendly hands. While this could be an advantage in case of a takeover attempt, a leveraged ESOP must still exist primarily for employee benefit purposes and takeover protection can only be incidental.

Using a leveraged ESOP gives the employer the advantage of avoiding some of the expenses and complexities of selling stock to the public and/or existing shareholders. Also, the plan may create a proprietary interest on the part of employees and can supplement existing compensation and benefit plans.

Advocates of the leveraged ESOP often claim that since employer contributions are tax deductible, the debt created in conjunction with the ESOP is retired with pretax dollars and, as a result, the ESOP is a tax-efficient way to raise capital (as contrasted with conventional debt and equity financing). This claim is, at best, an oversimplification. Technically, the *trust* and not the employer has incurred the debt, with the employer having contingent liability as the guarantor of the loan. The debt is retired by the trust using contributions made by the employer. The employer is entitled to a deduction only because its contributions are being made to a qualified plan for the benefit of employees. Thus, while the debt is being retired indirectly with pre-

---

[2] DOL Reg. 54.49975–7(b)(2).

tax dollars, it must be clearly understood that the way it is being done is by a charge to earnings. This could result in lower net income and lower earnings per share for the firm. There also could be a dilution in share value as well as cash flow implications. Also, it must be remembered that employer contributions (and resulting expenses) often will continue under the ESOP long after the debt has been retired. In short, careful analysis is necessary to fully evaluate the financial implications of a leveraged ESOP.

From an employer's viewpoint, there is the potential disadvantage that no portion of the stock held in the unallocated suspense account can revert to the employer if the trust is terminated prematurely. Also, there may be some risk of disqualification because of failure to meet the "exclusive benefit" requirements of the law. Another potential drawback to the employer is that an ESOP could be an inefficient compensation tool if the stock appreciates in value because the company forgoes a tax deduction for capital appreciation on shares that under a typical nonleveraged plan would have been made in future years. This same aspect, however, can produce an advantage to employees, particularly to highly compensated employees (HCEs), since this appreciation in the value of stock will not be a part of the employee's annual addition under Section 415.

An additional advantage to employees is that with an ESOP there is a greater assurance of employer contributions than with a profit sharing plan. There is a potential disadvantage to employees, however, in that their financial security may be too closely tied to the fortunes of the employer.

As will be seen in the next portion of this chapter, there are several tax advantages for both employers and employees associated with ESOPs. These advantages can be quite valuable and place ESOPs in a unique category in terms of qualified plan benefits.

Like any other employee benefit plan, careful consideration should be given to the employer's objectives and the plan's relative advantages and disadvantages before it is adopted. Even though financial aspects may be the driving force behind a plan's adoption, it must always be remembered that an ESOP is still an employee benefit plan and should thus accommodate the employer's overall human resource philosophy and objectives.

ESOP Qualification Requirements

At the outset, it should be recognized that an ESOP is a qualified plan, and as such it must meet the general requirements applicable to all qualified plans. These requirements are described in Chapters 4 and 5. In addition, ESOPs must meet a number of special requirements, and there are unique provisions of the tax law that apply only to ESOPs. The major ESOP requirements and tax law provisions are described in the following section.

Employer Securities Requirements

ESOP assets may be invested only in **qualifying employer securities.** In general, this includes both common and convertible preferred stock that are publicly tradable.

In the case of stock that is not readily tradable on an established securities market, the term means common stock having a combination of voting power and dividend rights equal to or greater than (1) that class of the employer's common stock having the greatest voting power and (2) that class of the employer's stock having the greatest dividend rights.

Voting Rights

Participants must be given the right to vote shares that have been allocated to their accounts. In the case of a closely held company, **voting rights** generally have to be given only for major issues: mergers, consolidations, recapitalization, reclassification, liquidation, and the dissolution or sale of substantially all of the firm's assets. However, if the shares of the closely held company were acquired with the proceeds of a loan where the lender was able to exclude 50 percent of interest from income, all voting rights on allocated shares must be given to participants.[3] The voting requirements for closely held companies can be satisfied by providing each participant with one vote, regardless of the number of shares actually allocated, and voting all shares held by the plan (whether or not allocated) in proportion to the vote.

Rights of First Refusal

Stock may be made subject to a **right of first refusal** in favor of the employer, the ESOP, or both. However, the stock must not be publicly traded at the time the right may be exercised. Also, the selling price and other terms under the right must not be less favorable to the seller than the greater of the value of the stock or the purchase price and other terms offered by a buyer, other than the employer or ESOP, making a good faith offer to purchase the security. The right of first refusal must lapse no later than 14 days after the stockholder gives written notice that an offer by a third party to purchase the stock has been received.

Put Options

A **put option** is not required for publicly traded stock. Otherwise, such an option is required and, under this option, the employee will have the right to require the employer to repurchase the stock. This put option must be exercisable only by the employee (or his or her donee, the employee's estate, or a distributee from the employee's estate).

The put option may not bind the plan, but it may grant the plan the option to assume the rights and obligations of the employer at the time it is exercised. The put must be exercisable for at least 60 days following the distribution of the stock and, if not exercised, for a second period of at least 60 days in the plan year following the distribution. The price must be determined under a fair valuation formula.

---

[3] The Small Business Job Protection Act of 1996 repealed the interest income exclusion for ESOP loans that allowed banks, insurance companies, regulated investment companies, and certain corporations to exclude 50 percent of the interest received on ESOP loans. Repeal of the interest income exclusion became effective with loans where a contract for the loan agreement occurred on or after June 10, 1996.

If an employer is required to repurchase employer stock that is distributed to the employee as part of a total distribution of the entire amount of the employee's account within one taxable year, the payment may be made in substantially equal periodic payments over a period not exceeding five years. The payments may not be made less frequently than annually and must begin no later than 30 days after the option is exercised. In addition, the employer must provide adequate security and pay reasonable interest on the unpaid amount. If the employer is required to repurchase the stock as part of an installment distribution, it must pay for the stock in full within 30 days after the option is exercised. A separate put option exists for each installment.

Valuation of Securities

Stocks must be valued at fair market value, which presents no difficulty if stock is regularly traded in a recognized market. If the stock is closely held or not publicly traded, an acceptable procedure must be developed for appraising and determining the fair market value of the stock. Generally, determination of fair market value must be on at least an annual basis and independently arrived at by a person who customarily makes such appraisals and who is independent of any party to a transaction involving a right of first refusal or a put option.

Nondiscrimination Testing/Integration with Social Security

An ESOP cannot be combined with other plans to satisfy the coverage and nondiscrimination requirements of the IRC, except for the purposes of the average benefits test.[4] Similarly, the portion of a plan that is an ESOP and the portion that is not must be treated as separate plans.

The contributions (and allocations) made for employees under an ESOP may *not* be integrated with Social Security benefits.

Diversification Requirement

Employees who are at least age 55 and who have completed at least 10 years of participation must be given the opportunity to diversify their investments by transferring from the employer stock fund to one or more of three other investment funds.[5] The right to diversify need be granted only for a 90-day window period following the close of the plan year in which the employee first becomes eligible to diversify and following the close of each of the next five plan years. This right is limited to shares acquired after 1986 and is further limited to 25 percent of such shares until the last window period, when up to 50 percent of such shares may be eligible for **diversification.**

Section 415

An employee's annual addition limit under Section 415 is determined on the basis of the employer's contributions to the plan and not on the value of the stock at the time it is allocated to the employee's account. Also, stock dividends, since they are

---

[4] See the discussion of these requirements in Chapter 4.
[5] Alternatively, amounts subject to the right of diversification may be distributed from the plan.

considered to be investment income, are not counted toward the annual addition limit when they are added to the employee's account.

In the case of a leveraged ESOP, if no more than one-third of the deductible employer contribution for the year is allocated to HCEs, repayments of interest on the loans and reallocated forfeitures derived from leveraged shares will not be considered part of the annual addition either.

Distribution Requirements

As noted earlier, an ESOP generally is required to make distributions to employees in the form of employer securities. Cash payments may be established in a plan as the normal form of distribution, but the participant must have the right to elect to receive stock. (This requirement does not apply to other investments into which the participant has elected to diversify his or her account balance.)

Like all qualified plans, an ESOP cannot force distribution of a participant's account (if more than $5,000) until the later of age 62 or the plan's normal retirement age, and it must observe the minimum distribution rule requirements. Unlike other qualified plans, ESOPs are required to permit accelerated distributions for stock acquired after 1986 when participants terminate employment. Unless otherwise requested by the participant, ESOPs must distribute such stock by the end of the year following the later of (1) the year in which the participant dies, retires, or becomes disabled; or (2) the fifth plan year following the year of termination for any other reason. (Longer periods are allowed if the participant's account balance exceeds $500,000 [indexed]. In 2002, the indexed amount was $800,000, and an ESOP sponsor could extend the payout period by one additional year [not to exceed five additional years] for each $160,000 [in 2002, as indexed] or a fraction there of, by which the employee's account balance exceeded $800,000.) The employer may delay distribution of stock acquired under a loan until the plan year following the plan year in which the loan has been repaid in full.

Joint and Survivor Requirements

As noted in Chapter 7, money purchase pension plans generally are subject to the qualified joint and survivor rules. A money purchase plan that is part of an ESOP, however, will be exempt from these rules to the same extent as other defined contribution plans if (1) the participant's account balance is payable in full to his or her spouse unless the spouse consents in writing to the designation of another beneficiary; (2) the participant does not elect benefits in the form of a life annuity; and (3) all or any portion of the participant's account balance has not been transferred from a plan subject to the joint and survivor rules.

Dividends

As a general rule, a corporation will not be allowed a tax deduction for dividends paid to shareholders. These dividends normally are paid out of after-tax income. If dividends are passed through or paid in cash to employees on a current basis under an ESOP, however, the employer will be able to claim a tax deduction for the dividends so paid.[6] This

---

[6] Dividends so paid to employees will be taxable; however, they will not be subject to the 10 percent early distribution tax.

Dividend Pass-Throughs 3

Employers must consider a number of issues in administering a dividend pass-through feature. Will minimums be imposed on the pass-through? Are the appropriate plan accounts clearly designated as ESOP accounts and eligible for the dividend pass-through? Will it be necessary to coordinate the pass-through with concurrent in-service withdrawals? Are dividends to be passed through for terminated participants? These questions illustrate the administrative considerations involved when including a pass-through provision in an ESOP.

particular feature has attracted the attention of many employers who are considering establishing an ESOP for a conventional employer stock fund under a CODA.

Cash dividends also are deductible if they are used to repay an ESOP loan where the shares on which the dividends are paid have been acquired with the proceeds of such a loan. If the dividends are for allocated shares, participants must receive an allocation of employer securities with a fair market value equal to or greater than the amount of such dividends.

As a result of the Economic Growth and Tax Relief Reconciliation Act of 2001 (EGTRRA), cash dividends may also be deducted by a C corporation when they are reinvested in qualified employer securities at the election of plan participants and their beneficiaries.

EGTRRA expanded the situations whereby a plan could deduct the payment of dividends. Prior to the passage of EGTRRA, dividends were only deductible (1) if paid in cash directly to plan participants or their beneficiaries, (2) if paid to the plan and subsequently disbursed in cash to plan participants and beneficiaries no later than 90 days following the close of the plan year in which the dividends were paid to the plan, or (3) when the dividends were used to make a leveraged ESOP's loan payment. This provision was added to the law as a savings incentive to encourage ESOPs to allow plan participants and beneficiaries to retain and reinvest the dividend proceeds in the plan without the firm loosing a tax deduction.

At the same time that EGTRRA expanded the deductibility of dividends, the law provided the Internal Revenue Service with greater authority to disallow deductions for dividends determined to be unreasonable. In the case of a dividend paid on common stock that is primarily and regularly traded on an established securities market, the dividend will generally be considered reasonable. For common stock not traded on an established securities market, the reasonableness of a dividend involves comparing the dividend rate on ESOP-held stock with the dividend rate for comparable corporations whose stock trades on an established market. Such characteristics as type of industry, size of corporation, earnings level, capital structure, and dividend history would be relevant.

Deductibility of Employer Contributions

In the case of a nonleveraged ESOP, the normal deduction limits apply to employer contributions. Prior to the passage of EGTRRA, 15 percent of covered compensation could be deducted in the case of a conventional stock bonus plan. Under a leveraged ESOP, in this prior era, the employer was able to contribute and deduct up to 25 percent of covered payroll on an annual basis for principal repayments on the loan. In addition, contributions made for the entire amount of loan interest also were deductible. For plan years following December 31, 2001, with the passage of EGTRRA, the amount deductible for stock bonus plans has risen from 15 percent to 25 percent of covered compensation giving it parity with the leveraged ESOP. The leveraged ESOP still holds an advantage in that the entire amount of the loan interest is still deductible.

Deferral of Gain on Stock Sales to ESOPs

A shareholder of a closely held company may be able to sell stock to the ESOP and to defer recognition of the gain on such sale if certain conditions are met. One such condition is that immediately after the sale, the ESOP must own at least 30 percent of the total value of outstanding employer securities or 30 percent of each class of outstanding stock. Also, the employer stock must have been held by the selling shareholder for more than one year and must not have been received as a distribution from a qualified plan or pursuant to stock options.

To qualify for the deferral, the selling shareholder must reinvest the entire proceeds in either debt securities or stock of another domestic corporation that does not have passive investment income in excess of 25 percent of its gross receipts for the preceding taxable year. Also, 50 percent of the new corporation's assets must be used in the active conduct of a trade or business. This reinvestment must occur within a period beginning 3 months before and ending 12 months after the sale to the ESOP.

The selling shareholder (and family members) and any other person owning more than 25 percent of any class of the employer securities will not be able to participate in the ESOP if this option is exercised.

Chapter Summary

- The Internal Revenue Code defines an ESOP as a qualified stock bonus plan or a combination qualified stock bonus plan and defined contribution (money purchase) plan designed to invest primarily in employer securities.

- IRS regulations define a stock bonus plan as a plan established and maintained by an employer to provide benefits similar to those of a profit sharing plan except that contributions by the employer are not necessarily dependent on profits and the benefits are distributable in the stock of the employer. (Cash distributions are permitted; however, the employee must have the right to demand a distribution in the form of employer securities.)

- The phrase in the IRC definition of an ESOP, "designed to invest primarily in employer securities," has never been precisely defined by the government. Most practitioners believe that this requirement will be met if more than 50 percent of the plan's assets are so invested when viewed over the life of the plan.

- An ESOP may use debt financing, thus creating the so-called leveraged ESOP. A leveraged ESOP offers special exemptions from certain prohibitions that apply to other qualified plans. For example, ESOPs are exempt from the diversity requirements of the fiduciary provisions of ERISA. However, ESOPs are *not* exempt from the prudency requirements, nor are they exempt from the requirement that fiduciaries act solely for the exclusive benefit of employees and their beneficiaries.

- There are many good reasons for the creation of an ESOP. An ESOP can be an effective employee benefit plan. An ESOP can be an effective device for converting a public company to a private organization. Similarly, an ESOP can be used to dispose of a corporate division. An ESOP also may be useful for providing estate liquidity to a major shareholder. A leveraged ESOP can put relatively large blocks of stock into presumably friendly hands, an advantage in the case of a takeover attempt.

- While enjoying special advantages, an ESOP also is subject to a number of important requirements. In addition to the general requirements applicable to qualified plans, other unique provisions apply. An ESOP cannot be combined with other plans in applying the coverage and nondiscrimination requirements of the IRC, except for the purposes of the average benefit test. Similarly, the portion of a plan that is an ESOP and the portion that is not must be treated as separate plans. Contributions made for employees under an ESOP may *not* be integrated with Social Security benefits.

- Other unique requirements attributable to ESOPs involve the stipulation that participants be given the right to vote shares that have been allocated to their accounts; the ability of a sponsoring employer to make stock subject to a right of first refusal by the employer, the ESOP, or both when the participant seeks to sell the stock; and the necessity to provide a put option to have the employer repurchase the stock if the ESOP stock is not publicly traded.

Key Terms

back-to-back arrangement, p. *173*	leveraged ESOP, p. *173*	stock bonus plan, p. *172*
diversification, p. *177*	put option, p. *176*	unallocated suspense account, p. *173*
estate liquidity, p. *174*	qualifying employer securities, p. *175*	voting rights, p. *176*
fractional method, p. *174*	right of first refusal, p. *176*	

Questions for Review

1. Describe a back-to-back loan that is sometimes entered into under a leveraged ESOP.
2. Identify the potential advantages that might accrue to an employer who adopts a leveraged ESOP.
3. Describe the potential advantages and disadvantages that might accrue to employees under a leveraged ESOP.
4. What types of securities meet the definition of qualifying employer securities in the case of a company whose stock is not readily tradeable on an established securities market?
5. What voting rights must be given to employees when the stock of an ESOP is the stock of a closely held company?

6. Under what circumstances may stock held under an ESOP be made subject to a right of first refusal?
7. Under what circumstances must stock held under an ESOP be subject to a put option?
8. Describe the diversification requirement that must be included in an ESOP.
9. Under what circumstances may an employer be allowed a tax deduction for dividends paid for stock held under an ESOP?

Questions for Discussion

1. ESOP loans are exempted from some of the fiduciary requirements of ERISA. Which fiduciary requirements continue to apply to these loans and from which requirements are they exempted? What rationale exists for granting these exemptions?
2. ESOP advocates often claim that a leveraged loan allows the employer to retire debt with pretax dollars. Explain why this is an oversimplification of the financial aspects of a leveraged ESOP.
3. Describe the special tax advantages that have been granted to leveraged ESOPs and why these plans have received more favorable tax treatment than other qualified plans.

Resources for Further Study

CCH Editorial Staff. "2001 Tax Legislation: Law, Explanation, and Analysis." *Commerce Clearing House Pension Plan Guide* (2001).

Hart, Michael A. "ESOPs in Corporate Acquisitions: What Every Buyer Should Know about the Target Company's ESOP." *Benefits Law Journal* 14, no. 1 (Spring 2001).

Kornfeld, Judith. "ESOP Repurchase Obligation Issues in S Corporations." *Journal of Pension Benefits* 8, no. 3 (Spring 2001).

Rodrick, Scott S. *ESOP Valuation.* Oakland, CA: The National Center for Employee Ownership, 2001.

Rodrick, Scott S. *Leveraged ESOPs and Employee Buyouts.* 4th ed. Oakland, CA: The National Center for Employee Ownership, 2001.

Rodrick, Scott S. *Selling to an ESOP.* 6th ed. Oakland, CA: The National Center for Employee Ownership, 2000, rev. March 2001.

Rodrick, Scott; and Corey Rosen. *Employee Stock Ownership Plans: 2000 Edition.* Orlando, FL: Harcourt, 1999.

Smiley, Robert W., Jr.; and Gregory K. Brown. "Employee Stock Ownership Plans (ESOPs)." *The Handbook of Employee Benefits.* 5th ed. Jerry S. Rosenbloom, ed. New York: McGraw-Hill, 2001.

www.nceo.org—website of the National Center for Employee Ownership.

11

Cash or Deferred Plans under Section 401(k)

After studying this chapter you should be able to:

- Describe the advantages of CODAs from both employer and employee perspectives.

- Describe the characteristics of cash or deferred arrangements (CODAs).

- Explain the applicability of the ADP and ACP tests to CODAs.

- Describe the safe harbor and simplified testing options available for CODAs.

- Describe the special nonforfeitability requirements that apply to CODAs.

- Explain the limitations on withdrawals that apply to CODAs.

- Discuss how CODA deferrals impact Social Security taxes and benefits.

Cash or deferred arrangements (CODAs) came under intense scrutiny in recent years primarily because of the collapse of the Enron Corporation and the resulting decline in the value of the company's 401(k) plan, which was very highly concentrated in employer stock. Concern for 401(k) plans in general arose because these plans had become such an important component of most employees' overall retirement security. A number of congressional reform proposals were sponsored whose intent was to attempt to protect plan participants. Among the areas targeted for reform were limits on investments in employer stock, general investment diversity requirements, changes in rules regarding "blackout periods" when employers switch between plan service providers, the tax treatment of investment advice, and employee representation regarding plan design and administration. This chapter profiles the fundamental characteristics of 401(k)s and emerging issues regarding these plans.

Advantages and Disadvantages of CODAs

The advantages of CODAs are significant, although most of these accrue to employees rather than employers. Nevertheless, the advantages to employers are important.

From an employer's viewpoint, CODAs have all the advantages normally associated with any employee benefit plan. Thus, they should be of material value in attracting and retaining employees, improving employee morale, achieving a better sense of corporate identification (when employer securities are involved), and so forth. In addition, they can serve specific corporate objectives, such as increasing the level of participation in an existing plan that has had conventional after-tax employee contributions. For some employers, converting a conventional savings plan to a CODA, and thus increasing take-home pay for participating employees, could minimize pressures for additional cash compensation.

From the viewpoint of employees, the first and foremost advantage involves taxes. If a conventional savings plan is converted to a CODA, the participating employees can realize an immediate increase in take-home pay. But of more importance is the fact that contributions are accumulating under a tax shelter. This means that an employee can receive investment income on amounts that otherwise would have been paid in taxes. Over a period of years, the cumulative effect of this can be quite substantial. Finally, when amounts are distributed and subject to tax, the actual amount of tax paid might be considerably less than would otherwise have been the case. Installment distributions could be taxed at a lower effective tax rate (due to lower levels of taxable income and indexed tax brackets).

Employees also have the flexibility of determining, on a year-to-year basis, whether to take amounts in cash or defer these amounts under the plan. Since employee needs and goals change from time to time, this element of flexibility can be quite important.

The disadvantages of CODAs also should be recognized. From the employer's viewpoint, these plans involve complex and costly administration. Also, the employer must be prepared to deal with employee relations and other problems that can occur in any year that the plan fails to satisfy the ADP and ACP tests. These plans also will involve a greater communications effort than is associated with conventional employee benefit plans.

From the viewpoint of employees, the disadvantages of CODAs are not as great. In fact, the only significant disadvantage is that elective contributions are subject to withdrawal limitations and the possible application of the early distribution tax (described in Chapter 27). This could be of major importance to some employees, particularly those at lower pay levels, and could be a barrier to their participation in the plan.

The Future

CODAs have already become an important part of the employee benefit planning process. A majority of organizations already have established CODAs or have converted existing plans to CODAs. Many others are actively moving in this same

Enron Corporation Bankruptcy and the Reform of 401(k) Plans 2

In reaction to the bankruptcy of Enron Corporation, there was widespread clamor for reform of regulations governing 401(k) plans. The reason for this call to reform involved the fact that many Enron employees nearly lost their entire retirement savings when the company collapsed. Under the Enron plan, employees received company stock as a match to their employee contributions. Most employees were unable to diversify the company stock they received as a plan match. Although employees could diversify their own contributions on which they received the company match, many employees chose not to do so since Enron stock had performed so well in prior years. Another complicating factor was that Enron Corporation was in the process of switching 401(k) plan administrators and was in the midst of a "blackout period" when the company stock began to plummet downward. Under the rules applicable at the time of the Enron collapse, employees were unable to switch out of company stock during the "blackout period" while a new vendor was taking on its role as the 401(k) administrator.

Employees could only watch in horror as they saw the value of their retirement savings dramatically disappear.

President Bush weighed in on this issue by creating a Task Force on Retirement Security. The task force was charged with developing new safeguards to protect the pensions of American workers. Following receipt of advice from the Task Force on Retirement Security, President Bush recommended the following four-point pension proposal in early 2002:

1. Provide workers greater freedom to diversify and manage their own retirement funds.

2. Ensure that senior corporate executives are held to the same restrictions as average American workers during "blackout periods" and that employers assume full fiduciary responsibility during these times.

3. Give workers quarterly information about their investments and rights to diversify them.

4. Expand workers' access to investment advice.

direction. There is every reason to believe that the growth of these plans will continue in the foreseeable future. Although it appears that there will be certain legislative changes and governmental regulations impacting the operation of CODAs both in the near term and in the more distant future, the essential characteristics of 401(k) plans likely will remain intact.

CODAs are an interesting and tax-efficient way of providing employee benefits. They are consistent with the growing concept that employee benefit plans need to be flexible and need to address the varying needs of employees at different times during their careers. There seems little doubt that they will continue to be a major factor in the employee benefit planning process of the future.

Cash or deferred arrangements (CODAs) are not an entirely new concept. They have existed since the 1950s. However, they were originally beset with legislative and regulatory doubt during the mid-1970s. The Revenue Act of 1978, along with proposed regulations issued by the IRS in 1981, opened the way for these plans, and their growth since 1981 has been significant.

The following sections review the legislative history of these plans, the technical requirements they must meet, and some special considerations that must be taken into account. General matters of plan design and tax qualification that apply equally to CODAs as well as to other tax-qualified plans are not discussed in the remainder of this chapter since they are covered elsewhere in the book. It should be noted that a 401(k), though often referred to as a type of retirement plan, is not in actuality a specific type of plan. Rather a 401(k) provision is attached to another type of plan allowing an employee a choice of receiving an employer contribution in cash or having it deferred under the plan and/or the choice of making his or her own contribution to a plan from before-tax income. This allows the employee to avoid any federal tax on these amounts until they are received in the form of a plan distribution. A 401(k) provision can be added to a conventional deferred profit sharing plan, a savings plan, a stock bonus plan, or an employee stock ownership plan.

Legislative History of CODAs

Before 1972, the IRS provided guidelines for qualifying cash option CODAs in a series of revenue rulings. In essence, more than half of the total participation in the plan had to be from the lowest paid two-thirds of all eligible employees. If this requirement was met, employees who elected to defer were not considered to be in constructive receipt of the amounts involved, even though they had the option to take cash. Salary reduction plans satisfying these requirements also were eligible for the same favorable tax treatment.

In December 1972, the IRS issued proposed regulations stating that any compensation that an employee could receive as cash would be subject to current taxation even if deferred as a contribution to the employer's qualified plan. Although primarily directed at salary reduction plans, the proposed regulations also applied to cash option profit sharing plans.

As the gestation period for ERISA was coming to an end, Congress became increasingly aware of the need to devote additional time to the study of the CODA concept. As a result, ERISA included a section providing that the existing tax status for CODAs was to be frozen until the end of 1976. Plans in existence on June 27, 1974, were permitted to retain their tax-favored status; however, contributions to CODAs established after that date were to be treated as employee contributions and, as a result, were currently taxable.

Unable to meet its self-imposed deadline, Congress extended the moratorium on CODAs twice; the second time, the deadline was extended until the end of 1979.

The Revenue Act of 1978 enacted permanent provisions governing CODAs by adding Section 401(k) to the IRC, effective for plan years beginning after December 31, 1979. In essence, CODAs are now permitted, as long as certain requirements are met.

This legislation, in itself, did not result in any significant activity in the adoption of new CODAs. It was not until 1982, after the Internal Revenue Service issued proposed regulations in late 1981, that employers began to respond to the benefit-planning opportunities created by this new legislation. By providing some interpretive guidelines for Section 401(k), and by specifically sanctioning **salary reduction plans,** the IRS opened the way for the adoption of new plans and for the conversion of existing, conventional plans. For example, many employers converted existing after-tax savings plans to CODAs to take advantage of the Section 401(k) tax shelter on employee contributions.

The Tax Reform Act of 1984 provided some subtle modifications to Section 401(k). Among other things, it made it clear that CODAs could not be integrated with Social Security. The 1984 legislation also extended cash or deferred treatment to pre-ERISA money purchase plans, although contributions were limited to the levels existing on June 27, 1974.

The changes imposed by the Tax Reform Act of 1986 were much more substantive. In addition to reducing the limit on elective deferrals, this legislation provided a new definition of highly compensated employees; restricted the actual deferral percentage (ADP) test; established a new test for after-tax and matching employer contributions; imposed an additional tax on early distributions; and reduced the employer's flexibility in designing eligibility requirements for these arrangements.

Another law affecting CODAs was the Small Business Job Protection Act of 1996. Among other things, this legislation simplified the ADP test and created safe harbor arrangements that can eliminate the need for ADP testing.

The Economic Growth and Tax Relief Reconciliation Act of 2001 (EGTRRA) had far-reaching impact on CODAs. A number of favorable provisions applicable to CODAs were included as part of the Act. Among the most notable provisions, EGTRRA increased the elective deferral limit in 2002 and scheduled further escalation through 2006 at which time its increases would be indexed in $500 increments; catch-up contributions were permitted allowing employees age 50 and older at the end of a tax year to electively defer even greater amounts; the multiple-use test applying to plans needing to conduct both the ADP and ACP tests was repealed for years beginning after 2001; the 401(k) ADP nondiscrimination safe harbor was broadened making it a top-heavy safe harbor; a "qualified Roth contribution program" could be added to 401(k) plans beginning after 2005 whereby participants electing to have all or a portion of their elective deferrals designated as after-tax "Roth contributions" would not be taxed on qualified distributions when they occur in the future; and the "same desk rule" was eliminated allowing employees continuing in the same job for a different employer following liquidation, merger, consolidation, or other corporate transaction to receive a distribution on the basis of having separated from "employment" rather than "service." Generally the changes affecting 401(k) plans enacted into law with EGTRRA were intended to allow individuals to save more for retirement, make plan administration less complex allowing the offering of such plans to be broadened, enhance the portability of retirement benefits in such plans, reduce administrative burdens for employers sponsoring 401(k)s, and bring greater parity between all types of retirement savings vehicles.

Technical Requirements

IRC **Section 401(k)** states that a qualified CODA is any arrangement that:

1. Is part of a profit sharing or stock bonus plan, a pre-ERISA money purchase plan, or a rural electric cooperative plan[1] that meets the requirements of Section 401(a) of the IRC.

2. Allows covered employees to elect to have the employer make contributions either to a trust under the plan on behalf of the employees or directly to the employees in cash.

3. Subjects amounts held by the trust to certain specified **withdrawal limitations,** when those amounts are attributable to employer contributions made pursuant to an employee's election.

4. Provides that accrued benefits derived from such contributions are **nonforfeitable.**

5. Does not require, as a condition of participation in the arrangement, that an employee complete a period of service with the employer maintaining the plan in excess of one year.

As a tax-qualified plan, a CODA must meet all of the nondiscriminatory requirements generally applicable to such plans. The special requirements for CODAs are covered in the following discussion. Before discussing these requirements, however, it is important to understand the difference between the different types of employee and employer contributions that can be made under a CODA:

• **Elective contributions** are amounts an employee authorizes the employer to contribute to a CODA on a pretax basis—either by way of salary reduction, in the case of a typical savings plan, or through an election to defer, in the case of a cash option profit sharing plan. Elective contributions are sometimes called pretax contributions or elective deferrals.

• **After-tax employee contributions** consist of money an employee is deemed to have received and taken as income.

• **Matching contributions** are employer contributions made when an employee authorizes an elective deferral or makes an after-tax employee contribution.

• **Nonelective contributions** are employer contributions made on behalf of eligible employees regardless of whether they have made elective deferrals.

• **Qualified nonelective contributions (QNECs)** are nonelective contributions to which two special rules apply: (1) the contribution must be fully vested at

---

[1] For purposes of IRC Section 401(k), the term *rural electric cooperative plan* means any pension plan that is a defined contribution plan and that is established and maintained by a rural electric cooperative or a national association of such cooperatives. For further details, see IRC Section 457(d)(9)(B).

all times, and (2) it generally may not be distributed to the employee on an in-service basis for any reason before the employee reaches age 59½.

• **Qualified matching contributions (QMACs)** are matching contributions that meet the same rules a nonelective contribution must meet to become a QNEC.

• **Safe harbor contributions** are employer contributions made to allow a plan to meet safe harbor requirements and avoid the need for ADP testing. Like QNECs, they must be fully vested and are subject to distribution restrictions.

The passage of EGTRRA in 2001 created new types of contributions that could be made to CODAs. The following types of contributions are now specifically permitted:

• **Employee catch-up contributions** are increased elective deferrals permissible for employees who are at least age 50 before the end of the tax year. At the time EGTRRA was enacted, employee catch-up contributions were scheduled to increase as follows:

Year	Allowable Catch-up
2002	$1,000 additional
2003	$2,000 additional
2004	$3,000 additional
2005	$4,000 additional
2006	$5,000 additional
Years following 2006	Additional amounts are indexed in $500 increments

Employee catch-up contributions are not subject to any other contribution limits and are not taken into account in applying other contribution limits to other contributions or benefits under a plan. An employer will not fail the Internal Revenue Code (IRC) Section 401(a)(4) nondiscrimination rules if the plan allows all eligible plan participants to make the same election regarding catch-up contributions. However, all plans maintained by related employers are treated as one plan if the employers are treated as a single employer. According to the Conference Committee report, an employer can make matching contributions with respect to catch up contributions, although these matches would be subject to all the rules typically applicable to matching contributions. It should be noted that one of the major motivations for allowing catch-up contributions was to aid women approaching retirement whose savings may have been insufficient because of career interruptions and absences from the workforce.

Designated Roth contributions are employee contributions effective for tax years beginning after 2005 whereby an employee elects to have all or a portion of his or her annual elective deferral treated as an after-tax "Roth contribution." In order to allow for such an election, an employer must incorporate a "qualified Roth contribution program" as part of the 401(k) plan. A 403(b) plan (see Chapter 12) may also offer such a program. The advantage to employees in electing to have all or a portion of their elective deferrals treated as designated Roth contributions is that, although these monies will be taxed currently when contributed into the plan, qualified distributions from a designated Roth account (both contributions and subsequent investment earnings) are not subject to taxation when disbursed.

Since these Roth contributions are treated as elective deferrals, they fully and immediately vest. Roth contributions are subject to the withdrawal restrictions that generally prohibit payment from the account prior to the participant's retirement, separation from service, death, disability, or the occurrence of another distributable event authorized by the Internal Revenue Service. The Conference Committee report indicates Congressional intent that designated Roth contributions may only be made prospectively and that employees may not make retroactive designations of prior year elective deferrals into Roth contributions. Designated Roth contributions are treated as elective deferrals for purposes of the ADP test. A 401(k) or 403(b) plan offering the option of a qualified Roth contribution program must establish, for each participating employee, a separate "designated Roth account" that will hold designated Roth contributions and earnings allocable to those contributions.

Type of Plan

As already mentioned, a CODA may be part of a profit sharing or stock bonus plan. This, of course, includes savings plans. The only qualified, defined contribution plan that cannot be established as a CODA is a post-ERISA money purchase or defined contribution pension plan.[2]

As a practical matter, most CODAs fall into one of two categories—either cash or deferred profit sharing plans or savings plans. CODAs also can be subdivided into plans that involve employer contributions only, both employer and employee contributions, and employee contributions only. Plans involving only employee contributions are not used to a great extent, largely because of the difficulty these plans experience in satisfying the special nondiscrimination tests described later in this chapter.

Individual Limitations

There is a limitation on exclusion for elective deferrals for any taxable year. This limit was initially set at a fixed dollar amount and was indexed to changes in the consumer price index. At the time of EGTRRA's passage in 2001, the limit on elective deferrals was set at $10,500. EGTRRA increased the elective deferral limit for 2002 and scheduled it to increase in subsequent years according to the following schedule:

Year	Elective Deferral Limit
2002	$11,000
2003	$12,000
2004	$13,000
2005	$14,000
2006	$15,000
Years following 2006	Additional amounts are indexed in $500 increments

---

[2] CODAs are not available to states or local governments unless they were adopted before May 6, 1986. Tax-exempt organizations were previously subject to similar limitations; however, the Small Business Job Protection Act of 1996 repealed these limitations, and tax-exempt organizations were able to adopt CODAs beginning in 1997.

It should be noted that any excess amounts are included in the employee's gross income. This limitation applies to the aggregate elective deferral made in a taxable year to all CODAs.

A second limit caps the amount of pay that can be taken into account for most qualified plan purposes, including the determination of contributions and benefits. Initially, this limit was set at $200,000 and was indexed to increase with changes in the CPI. By 1993, the limit had reached $235,840. The Omnibus Budget Reconciliation Act of 1993 (OBRA '93) reduced the limit to $150,000, effective in 1994. The limit was still indexed to changes in the CPI; however, changes took place only when accumulated changes due to movement in the CPI amounted to at least $10,000. For 2001, this limit had reached $170,000. EGTRRA increased this limit on includible compensation from $170,000 in 2001 to $200,000 in 2002 and revised the indexing so that it would increase in $5,000 increments in years after 2002.

Nondiscrimination in Coverage and Contributions

A CODA will not have a tax-qualified status unless the employees eligible to benefit under the arrangement satisfy the coverage provisions described in Chapter 4 and the contributions under the plan are deemed to be nondiscriminatory. To satisfy the nondiscrimination-in-contributions requirement, an **actual deferral percentage (ADP) test** must be met; if after-tax employee contributions and/or employer matching contributions are involved, an **actual contribution percentage (ACP) test** also must be met. These tests (except for the ACP test for after-tax employee contributions) will not have to be performed, however, if safe harbor contributions are made, as described later in the chapter.

The ADP test is a mathematical test that must be satisfied by the close of each plan year. The first step in applying this test is to determine the **actual deferral percentage** for each eligible employee. This is done by dividing the amount of contribution deferred at the employee's election (plus, at the election of the employer, any QNECs or QMACs) by the amount of the employee's compensation. This percentage is determined for all eligible employees, whether or not they are actually participating. Thus, the ADP for a nonparticipating but eligible employee is zero. For purposes of this test, the compensation used must meet one of the four acceptable definitions of compensation found in the regulations.[3]

The next step is to divide the eligible employees into two groups—the highly compensated employees (HCEs) and all other eligible nonhighly compensated employees (NHCEs). For each of these groups, the actual deferral percentages are mathematically averaged. If the average ADP for the HCEs does not exceed the average ADP for the NHCEs by more than the allowable percentage, the test is satisfied for the year. The basic test is that the ADP for HCEs cannot be more than 125 percent of the ADP for NHCEs. An *alternative* limitation can produce a higher ADP for the HCEs in many situations. This **alternative limitation** permits the ADP for

---

[3] These definitions are described in Chapter 4. It should be noted, however, that even though one of these definitions must be used for testing, the plan may use another nondiscriminatory definition of compensation for purposes of determining plan contributions.

HCEs to be as much as two times the ADP for the NHCEs, but not more than two percentage points higher. The allowable percentages are set forth in Table 11.1. Table 11.2 shows the permissible ADPs for HCEs at various levels, assuming whichever of the above tests permits the highest result.

For years prior to 1997, these steps had to be followed using compensation and deferrals for the current year—both for NHCEs and HCEs. Beginning with the 1997 plan year, employers were allowed to conduct the ADP test using actual deferral percentages of NHCEs for the prior year. Employers are not required to use prior-year percentages; however, if an employer elects to use current-year percentages, this election can be changed only in accordance with IRS regulations.

Beginning with the 1999 plan year, the ADP test could be performed excluding any NHCEs who participate before attaining age 21 and completing one year of service (the maximum statutory eligibility requirements permitted), as long as the plan separately passes the 410(b) coverage tests for all participants in that age/service group.

TABLE 11.1
Allowable ADP Percentages for HCEs

If the ADP for NHCEs Is	Then the ADP for HCEs May Not Exceed	
	Basic Test	Alternative Limit
1%	1.25%	2.0%
2	2.50	4.0
3	3.75	5.0
4	5.00	6.0
5	6.25	7.0
6	7.50	8.0
7	8.75	9.0
8	10.00	10.0
9	11.25	11.0
10	12.50	12.0
11	13.75	13.0
12	15.00	14.0

TABLE 11.2
Permissible ADPs for HCEs

If the ADP for NHCEs Is	Then the ADP for HCEs May Not Exceed
1%	2%
2	4
3	5
4	6
5	7
6	8
7	9
8	10
9	11¼
10	12½

It should be noted that the ADP test determines a maximum average deferral percentage for the HCEs. It does not necessarily indicate the maximum deferral percentage for an *individual* in this group. As long as the average deferral for the highly compensated employees is less than or equal to the maximum allowed, it will be permissible for an individual in this group to defer an amount in excess of that limitation.

If any highly compensated employee is a participant under two or more CODAs of the employer, all such CODAs will be treated as one CODA for purposes of determining the employee's actual deferral percentage.

A similar test, known as the actual contribution percentage (ACP) test, applies to any after-tax employee contributions and any employer matching contributions.

In addition to making safe harbor contributions and/or using prior year actual deferral percentages of NHCEs, there are several ways in which an employer can minimize or eliminate the possibility that a plan will not meet the ADP and ACP tests. The following lists some of the techniques that might be used for this purpose.

1. The plan can be designed so that it is in automatic compliance. For example, the employer might make an automatic 5 percent QNEC contribution for all employees. Employees may then be given the option of contributing up to 1.0 percent of pay by way of salary reduction. The plan will always satisfy the ADP test since the ADP for the HCEs will never exceed the 125 percent basic test.

2. The plan also could be designed to encourage maximum participation from the NHCEs. This could be done under a savings plan, for example, by providing for higher levels of employer contributions with respect to lower pay levels or with reference to lower rates of contribution.

3. Limits may be placed on the maximum amounts that might be deferred or contributed.

4. A mandatory minimum deferral or contribution may be required from all participating employees.

5. The plan could include a provision allowing the employer to adjust prospective deferrals or after-tax contributions (either upward or downward) if the plan is in danger of failing to meet the tests.

6. The employer may make additional QNEC or QMAC contributions at the end of the plan year to the extent necessary to satisfy the applicable test.

7. Contributions for a plan year could be determined in advance of the plan year and, once established on a basis that satisfies the test, requirements could be fixed on an irrevocable basis (except, possibly, that NHCEs could be given the option of increasing their contributions).

Safe Harbors—ADP/ACP Testing

A CODA plan sponsor no longer had to worry about nondiscrimination tests for elective contributions starting in 1999 if the employer satisfied one of two safe harbors by either (1) providing certain matching contributions to NHCEs or (2) making a contribution of 3 percent of compensation for all NHCEs, regardless of whether these employees contributed to the plan. Also, ACP testing was not required for matching contributions starting in 1999 if (1) the plan provided for a safe harbor matching contribution and (2) no match was provided on contributions in excess of 6 percent of compensation. (The ACP test still is required, however, for after-tax employee contributions.)

The safe harbor matching contribution must be at least 100 percent of the first 3 percent of pay contributed and 50 percent of the next 2 percent of pay contributed. Other formulas for matching contributions will qualify for this safe harbor treatment if the formula provides an amount of matching contribution at least as large as the safe harbor formula and the percent matched does not increase as the employee's contribution increases. In addition, the rate of match for HCEs cannot be greater than the rate of match for NHCEs.

To meet the safe harbor requirements, eligible employees must be informed of their opportunity to participate in the CODA prior to the beginning of the year and the matching contributions used to satisfy the safe harbor must be fully vested and subject to the same restrictions on distributions as QNECs or QMACs—that is, they can be distributed only on account of separation from service, death, disability, or attainment of age 59½.[4]

While these safe harbors eliminate the need and expense of annual testing, as well as the necessity of recharacterizing (described below) or refunding excess contributions, they can result in additional plan costs caused by the full-vesting and annual-notice requirements. As noted in footnote 4, according to IRS notice 2000-3 a plan sponsor now has the option to make a decision as late as 30 days before the end of the plan year whether to treat a 401(k) as a safe harbor plan. Essentially this allows the plan sponsor until 30 days before the end of the plan year to decide whether to subject the 401(k) to ADP testing and possible remedial actions, or instead, make the 3 percent nonelective contribution and avoid testing altogether.

Treatment of Excess Deferrals and Contributions

Excess deferrals may arise if the amount deferred by an employee exceeds the allowable elective deferral limit for the year in question. Excess contributions may arise as a result of a plan's failure to meet the ADP or ACP test.

Excess deferrals due to the elective deferral limit may be allocated among the plans under which the deferrals have been made by March 1 following the close of the taxable year, and the plan may distribute the allocated amount back to the employee by April 15. Although such a distribution will be included in the employee's taxable

---

[4] Initially when the concept of safe harbor plans was introduced, an employer needed to have safe harbor language in the plan before the beginning of the plan year. IRS notice 2000-3 changed this rule allowing a nonsafe harbor 401(k) plan that uses the current-year testing method to be amended into a safe harbor plan as late as 30 days before the end of the plan year. To take advantage of this option, the safe harbor contribution must be in the form of a 3 percent of pay nonelective contribution. Notice to eligible employees before the beginning of the year must advise them that the plan sponsor might choose to amend the plan into a safe harbor plan.

income for the year to which the excess deferral relates, it will not be subject to the 10 percent excise tax that might otherwise apply to distributions prior to age 59½; however, even though distributed, this amount will generally have to be taken into account by the employer when applying the ADP test for the year. Any income on the excess deferral will be treated as earned and received in the taxable year in which the excess deferral was made. Any excess deferral not distributed by this date (April 15 of the following year) will remain in the plan, subject to all regular withdrawal restrictions. Moreover, the amount will again be treated as taxable income when it is later distributed.

If excess contributions arise because of the ADP or ACP tests, there are several ways in which the problem can be addressed. The first, of course, is for the employer to make additional contributions to the extent necessary to satisfy the test requirements. Alternatively, if it is the ADP test that has been failed, the employer can **recharacterize the excess deferrals** as after-tax employee contributions; in this event, however, they will then be subject to the ACP test requirements. A third method is to refund the excess contributions using the method prescribed in the regulations.[5] For purposes of the law, an excess attributable to a failure of the ADP test is called an **excess contribution.** An excess attributable to failure of the ACP test is called an **excess aggregate contribution.**

If contributions are to be returned, there are two critical dates to keep in mind. The first such date is 2½ months after the end of the plan year in which the excess has occurred. If excess contributions or excess aggregate contributions are returned by that time, the amount generally will be considered as income on the earliest date that amounts deferred for the plan year being tested would otherwise have been received in cash. A return of after-tax contributions, of course, will not be taxable; however, other returned amounts, including investment income on both after-tax and elective deferrals, will be taxable. The amounts distributed will not attract the 10 percent excise tax that might otherwise apply to early distributions.

The second critical date that relates to the return of excess contributions is the last day of the plan year following the plan year in which the excess has occurred. If the required amounts are distributed after the first critical date and before the second critical date, the amount returned is taken into income in the year of distribution. In addition, the employer is subject to a 10 percent penalty tax on the amount of principal involved (but not on investment earnings).

If excess contributions are not returned by the second critical date, the consequences could be serious. If the excess is an excess contribution, the CODA portion of the plan could lose its qualified status for the years in question, with the result that *all* employees could be taxed on amounts they could have received in cash. If the excess is an excess aggregate contribution, the entire plan could lose its qualified status for the years in question; this could entail a loss of deductions, the taxation of plan investment income, and the taxation of all employees to the extent of their vested account balances.

---

[5] Prior to 1997, this method required the HCE or HCEs with the highest rate of deferral to be reduced first and to the extent necessary to satisfy the test. Beginning in 1997, refunds must be made starting with those HCEs who have made the highest dollar amount of contribution.

Nonforfeitability Requirements

The value of all elective and any after-tax employee contributions to a CODA must be fully vested at all times. QNECs, QMACs, and safe harbor contributions also must be fully vested at all times. The value of other employer contributions must vest in accordance with one of ERISA's prescribed vesting standards. It should be noted, however, that the vested amount of elective contributions cannot be considered for this purpose. Thus, the vesting of employer contributions must be accomplished independently.

As mentioned previously, if employer contributions are fully vested from the outset (and if they are subject to withdrawal restrictions), they may be taken into account when applying the ADP test.

Limitations on Withdrawals

A common provision in many profit sharing and savings plans is one that permits an employee to make a withdrawal of some part of the vested account balance while still actively employed. Sometimes, this withdrawal right is limited to hardship situations; more often than not, however, a withdrawal can be made for any reason and is typically subject to some period of suspension from plan participation.

In the case of a CODA, the ability to make in-service withdrawals is severely limited. The value of elective contributions may be distributable only upon death, disability, separation from service, the termination of the plan (provided no successor plan other than an employee stock ownership plan [ESOP] or a simplified employee pension [SEP] plan has been established), or certain sales of businesses by the employer. Distributions of elective contributions will be permitted after the employee has attained age 59½ or before this age in the case of a hardship. For hardship withdrawals, however, the amount available is limited to the elective contributions themselves; investment income on such contributions can be included only to the extent that it was earned prior to December 31, 1988 (for calendar year plans). Safe harbor contributions are subject to similar withdrawal restrictions. Also, it should be noted that if employer contributions (QNECs and QMACs) have been included in the ADP test, the withdrawal restrictions on these amounts are even greater; any such contributions and any investment income earned on such contributions are withdrawable for hardship only to the extent that they were made or earned before the end of the last plan year ending before July 1, 1989.

Limiting the withdrawal of elective contributions to hardship cases only can be of significance to many employers, since it could have a negative effect on the participation of lower-paid employees, thus creating problems in meeting the ADP and ACP tests. The regulations define hardship in a very narrow way. Specifically, these regulations require that the hardship be caused by "immediate and heavy financial needs" of the employee. Further, they require that the withdrawal must be necessary to satisfy the financial need.

The regulations permit each of these conditions to be met on a "facts and circumstances" basis, but they also provide for the use of safe harbors. For determining immediate and heavy financial need, the following events are acceptable:

- The incurring of certain medical expenses by the employee, the employee's spouse, or certain dependents of the employee, as defined in Section 152 of the IRC; or the need for "up-front" funds to obtain certain medical services for these individuals.

- The purchase (excluding mortgage payments) of a principal residence for the employee.

- Payment of room and board, tuition, and related educational fees for the next 12 months of postsecondary education for the employee or the employee's spouse or dependents.

- The need to prevent either the eviction of the employee from his or her principal residence or foreclosure on the mortgage of the employee's principal residence.

The regulatory safe harbor for the second requirement, that the withdrawal be necessary to satisfy the financial need, includes four conditions:

1. The distribution must not exceed the amount of the need.

2. The employee must have obtained all distributions (other than hardship distributions) and all nontaxable loans currently available under all plans maintained by the employer.

3. The plan (and other plans maintained by the employer) must provide that the employee's elective and after-tax contributions will be suspended for at least 6 months after receipt of the distribution.[6]

4. The plan and all other employer plans must limit the employee's elective contributions for the calendar year immediately following to no more than the excess, if any, of that year's elective contribution limit over the amount electively contributed in the year of the distribution.

A plan may use a facts and circumstances approach, rely on the safe harbors, or use a combination of both in designing and administering a hardship withdrawal provision.

It should be noted that some amounts might still be available for nonhardship, in-service withdrawals. As already noted, employer contributions may be withdrawn (unless they are designated to be part of the ADP test). Also, the value of any after-tax employee contributions may be withdrawn, as may the value of any contributions (employer and employee) made to a plan before it became a CODA. Finally, even elective contributions may be withdrawn on a nonhardship basis after the employee attains age 59½.

Separate Accounting

The regulations state that all amounts held by a plan that has a CODA will be subject to the CODA nonforfeitability and withdrawal requirements unless a separate

---

[6] The safe harbor suspension of elective deferrals and after-tax contributions following hardship distributions was originally set at 12 months. EGTRRA reduced this period of time to 6 months for years beginning after December 31, 2001.

account is maintained for benefits specifically subject to these requirements. Included are amounts contributed for plan years before 1980, contributions not subject to a deferral election, and contributions made for years when the CODA is not qualified.

The passage of EGTRRA provided for another separate accounting requirement for plan years beginning after 2005 if employers choose to offer a "qualified Roth contribution program" in connection with a 401(k) plan. A 401(k) or 403(b) plan offering the option of a qualified Roth contribution program must establish, for each participating employee, a separate "designated Roth account" that will hold designated Roth contributions and earnings allocable to those contributions.

Loans

Because of the restrictions on the in-service withdrawal of elective contributions, many employers have included loan provisions in their CODA programs. The legal requirements for loans are the same for CODAs as they are for profit sharing plans. Since these requirements were discussed at length in Chapter 8, they are not repeated here.

Other Considerations

The preceding discussion has dealt with the requirements of federal tax law for the qualification of CODAs and the income tax treatment of elective contributions. There are, however, other issues that must be addressed. The following section discusses the status of elective contributions for purposes of Social Security, other employer-sponsored plans, and state and local taxes. It also discusses the deduction limits for 401(k) contributions, the treatment of excess deferrals, and the effect of such contributions on deduction limits.

Social Security

Originally, elective contributions to a CODA were not considered to be wages for purposes of Social Security. Thus, they were not subject to Social Security (Federal Insurance Contributions Act [FICA]) tax, nor were they taken into account when calculating Social Security benefits.

This was changed by the 1983 Social Security amendments. Elective contributions are now considered as wages for Social Security (and federal unemployment insurance) purposes. Thus, FICA taxes are paid on such amounts under the taxable wage base, and they are taken into account when calculating an employee's Social Security benefits.

Other Employer-Sponsored Plans

A matter of some concern to employers in the past was the question of whether an employee's elective contributions should be considered as part of the compensation base for purposes of other tax-qualified plans. This uncertainty was resolved in 1983 when the Internal Revenue Service ruled that the inclusion (or exclusion) of elective contributions under a CODA as compensation in a defined benefit pension plan does not cause the pension plan to be discriminatory.

Employers also maintain other pay-related employee benefit plans. These include short- and long-term disability income plans, group term life insurance, survivor income benefits, and, in some cases, health care plans. There appear to be no legal reasons why pay, for the purpose of determining benefits under these plans, cannot be defined to include elective contributions made under a CODA. If such contributions are to be included, care should be taken to ensure that necessary plan and/or insurance contract amendments are made so that compensation is properly defined.

A CODA will not be qualified if any other benefit provided by the employer (other than the employer's matching contribution) is conditioned, either directly or indirectly, on the employee's electing to have the employer make or not make contributions under the arrangement in lieu of receiving cash.

State and Local Taxes

The treatment of elective contributions under state and local tax laws is not completely uniform. For years, many states followed principles of federal tax law in the treatment of employee benefits. This practice also was followed by many local governments that impose some form of income tax.

With the increased use of individual retirement accounts (IRAs) in recent years, and with the publicity that CODAs have received, there has been growing concern among state and local tax authorities over the potential loss of tax revenue. As a result, the question of state and local taxation of elective contributions has become an important issue.

At this time, most state and local authorities have indicated that they will follow federal tax law. However, a few have announced that elective contributions will be taxable and subject to employer withholding. It seems reasonable to expect that other state and local authorities might adopt this latter position.

Deduction Limits

Section 404 of the IRC imposes limits on the amount an employer can deduct for contributions made to qualified plans. For profit sharing plans prior to 2002, this limit was 15 percent of covered payroll. However, EGTRRA increased the allowable limit to 25 percent of covered payroll beginning in 2002. If the employer has both a defined benefit plan and a defined contribution plan, the combined limit is 25 percent of the covered payroll.

Elective contributions previously affected the maximum deduction in two ways. First, they reduced the amount of the covered payroll to which the percentage limitations applied, thus reducing the dollar amount available as a maximum deduction. Second, they were considered to be employer contributions, and thus they reduced the amount otherwise available for the employer to contribute and deduct.

EGTRRA modified the definition of compensation beginning in 2002 to allow greater employer deductible contributions. Elective deferrals to qualified cash and deferred arrangements, which were previously excluded from the definition of compensation, are now included. Also, elective deferrals to cash or deferred arrangements are no longer deemed employer contributions and they are, therefore, not subject to the employer deduction limitations.

For most employers, the effect of elective deferrals on deductible employer contributions in the past did not create problems. Employers who maintained liberal plans, however, may have found that the level of elective contributions permitted might have to be limited in order to preserve the ability to make regular, deductible employer contributions.

The problem was exacerbated by similar elective contributions made by employees for health care benefits and qualified transportation fringe benefits, and flexible spending accounts (FSAs) for health and dependent care. These contributions also reduced covered payroll for purposes of determining deductible limits and contributions to the CODA. The following example illustrates the impact of these factors both pre- and post-EGTRRA:

Payroll before Elective Contributions		$1,000,000
Elective Contributions for		
CODA	$80,000	
Health care	55,000	
FSA health care	25,000	
FSA dependent care	25,000	
Qualified transportation fringe benefits	5,000	
Total	$190,000	

	Pre-EGTRRA	Post-EGTRRA
Payroll base for computing employer deductible contribution employer contribution	$810,000	$890,000
Deductible CODA employer contribution		
Pre-EGTRRA: 15% of payroll base	$121,500	
Post-EGTRRA: 25% of payroll base		$222,500
Pre-EGTRRA reduction of employer contribution for employee elective deferrals	$80,000	0
Allowable employer contribution	$41,500	$222,500

In this example, if the employer matched elective contributions on a dollar-for-dollar basis, pre-EGTRRA the employer would not be able to contribute the full $80,000 necessary to accomplish this result. In fact, it would barely be able to make a 50 percent match.

Post-EGTRRA, however, the employer's ability to match or to provide nonelective contributions is dramatically increased. The ability to provide this much higher level of deductible contributions results from (1) the increased contribution limit available to profit sharing plans from 15 percent of pay to 25 percent of pay, (2) the exclusion of elective deferrals from the payroll base for computing employer deductible contributions, and (3) the fact that employee elective deferrals no longer are counted as employer contributions.

Chapter Summary

- Though cash or deferred arrangements (CODAs) have existed since the 1950s, their most significant growth has occurred since 1981, after the Revenue Act of 1978 amended the Internal Revenue Code by adding Section 401(k). In late 1981, proposed regulations were issued clarifying uncertainties regarding these arrangements.

- Distinctions between different types of employer and employee contributions to CODAs are important since the nature of these contributions determines the applicability of either the actual deferral percentage (ADP) test or the actual contribution percentage (ACP) test for nondiscrimination testing purposes.

- Excess contributions arising from a plan's failure to meet the ADP or ACP test can have important implications. Though certain remedial actions are permitted within specified time frames, certain defects, if not remedied, can result in plan disqualification.

- The value of all elective and any after-tax employee contributions, QNECs, QMACs, and safe harbor contributions to a CODA must be fully vested at all times. The value of other employer contributions must vest in accordance with one of ERISA's prescribed vesting standards.

- The ability to make in-service withdrawals is severely limited in the case of a CODA. The value of elective contributions is distributable only upon death, disability, separation from service, the termination of the plan (provided no successor plan other than an ESOP or a SEP has been established), or certain sales of businesses by the employer. Distributions of elective contributions will be permitted after the employee has attained age 59½ or before this age in the case of hardship. Similar withdrawal restrictions apply to QNECs, QMACs, and safe harbor contributions.

- Internal Revenue Service regulations define hardship in a narrow way and require that the hardship be caused by the immediate and heavy financial needs of the employee. Further, they require that the withdrawal be necessary to satisfy the financial need. Although the regulations permit each of these conditions to be met on a "facts and circumstances" basis, the regulations provide for the use of safe harbors for determining both "immediate and heavy financial need" and the means "necessary to satisfy the financial need."

Key Terms

actual contribution percentage (ACP) test, p. *191*

actual deferral percentage, p. *191*

actual deferral percentage (ADP) test, p. *191*

after-tax employee contributions, p. *188*

alternative limitation, p. *191*

cash or deferred arrangements (CODAs), p. *186*

designated Roth contributions, p. *189*

elective contributions, p. *188*

employee catch-up contributions, p. *189*

excess aggregate contribution, p. *195*

excess contribution, p. *195*

matching contributions, p. *188*

nonelective contributions, p. *188*

nonforfeitable, p. *188*

qualified matching contributions (QMACs), p. *189*

qualified nonelective contributions (QNECs), p. *188*

recharacterization of excess deferrals, p. *195*

safe harbor contributions, p. *189*

salary reduction plans, p. *187*

Section 401(k), p. *188*

withdrawal limitations, p. *188*

Questions for Review

1. Explain the advantages and limitations of a CODA from the viewpoint of employees.
2. Explain the disadvantages of a CODA from the viewpoint of the employer.
3. What requirements must be satisfied by a CODA for it to be qualified under the IRC?
4. Explain the steps involved in the ADP test.
5. May contributions (expressed as a percentage of compensation) for the higher-paid employees under a qualified CODA be larger than contributions for their lower-paid colleagues? Explain.
6. Describe the safe harbor contribution requirements for CODAs.
7. Explain the vesting requirements for contributions to a qualified CODA.
8. Describe the impact of CODA deferrals on Social Security taxes and benefits.
9. May elective contributions to a CODA be considered as part of the compensation base for purposes of other tax-qualified plans? Explain.
10. Describe how elective contributions to a CODA will affect the employer's deduction limits.

Questions for Discussion

1. Discuss the conditions under which an employer may wish to establish a CODA.
2. Assume that an employer has had a CODA for several years and that the reaction of the employees toward the plan has been unsatisfactory. Discuss the plan design flexibility available for a CODA that may be used by the employer to improve the employees' reaction without increasing the employer's annual cost.
3. Discuss how the dollar limit on elective contributions is likely to affect plan design for CODAs.

Resources for Further Study

Buckley, Allen. "401(k) Plan Loans and Participant Bankruptcy." *Journal of Pension Benefits* 8, no. 4 (Summer 2001).

CCH Editorial Staff. "2001 Tax Legislation: Law, Explanation, and Analysis." *Commerce Clearing House Pension Plan Guide* (2001).

Hoffman, Craig. "IRS Notice 2000-2—the New and Improved 401(k) Safe Harbor Plan." *Journal of Pension Benefits* 7, no. 3 (Spring 2000).

Palmer, Bruce A. "Profit Sharing Plans." *The Handbook of Employee Benefits.* 5th ed. Jerry S. Rosenbloom, ed. New York: McGraw-Hill 2001.

Pianko, Howard. "The 401(k) Plan Sponsor/Fiduciary: Understanding Aggregate Fees Received by Service Providers." *Journal of Pension Planning & Compliance* 27, no. 3 (Fall 2001).

Van Derhei, Jack L.; and Kelly A. Olsen. "Section 401(k) Plans (Cash or Deferred Arrangements) and Thrift Plans." *The Handbook of Employee Benefits.* 5th ed. Jerry S. Rosenbloom, ed. New York: McGraw-Hill, 2001.

Van Derhei, Jack L.; Sarah Holden; and Carol Quick. "Investment of Defined Contribution Plan Assets." *The Handbook of Employee Benefits.* 5th ed. Jerry S. Rosenbloom, ed. New York: McGraw-Hill, 2001.

Chapter 12

Section 403(b) Plans

After studying this chapter you should be able to:

- Identify the required statutory features of a Section 403(b) plan.

- Detail the eligibility requirements that qualify an organization to establish a 403(b) plan.

- Describe the various contribution limits applicable to 403(b) plans and special provisions allowing a contribution to exceed a limit.

- Specify the funding instruments permitted by IRC Sections 403(b) and 403(b)(7).

- Explain the IRC rules and tax aspects for distributions from 403(b) plans.

Introduction

A 403(b) plan is a retirement mechanism for employees of public educational institutions and certain nonprofit tax-exempt organizations that permits thousands of eligible organizations to provide their employees an opportunity to save for retirement on a tax-deferred basis.

A 403(b) plan can be structured in different ways. First, a 403(b) plan can be structured on a fully contributory and elective basis without employer contributions. Second, a plan can be structured involving employer contributions with or without employee contributions. Employer contributions come in three varieties: (1) fixed contributions without mandatory employee contributions; (2) fixed contributions on a matching basis requiring employee contributions (meaning that an employee will not receive an employer match unless the employee makes a contribution); and (3) variable contributions where an employer contributes to the 403(b) and may use it, in a sense, as a means of rewarding employees for achieving performance targets, much like a profit sharing plan is used. All three variations of employer contributions can permit voluntary, unmatched employee contributions.

Under most 403(b) plans, participating employees can elect to have their salaries reduced, pursuant to a **salary reduction agreement** with the employer, and have the amount of the reduction applied to purchase **403(b) annuities** (or mutual funds) within the limits established by law. Often referred to as a **tax-deferred annuity (TDA)** plan or supplemental retirement annuity (SRA) plan, this type of 403(b) arrangement is intended as a voluntary tax-deferred savings plan using salary reduction, and it generally does not involve employer contributions. Under this arrangement, once the employee decides how much to contribute (within permitted limits), a salary reduction agreement for that amount is entered into with the employer. The amount by which the employee's salary is reduced is then contributed by the employer to the TDA on behalf of the employee. Although the savings under a TDA are intended for retirement purposes, some or all of the accumulated funds in these programs can be made available to employees prior to retirement in the event of financial hardship, as defined by IRS regulations and under other specified circumstances.

If an employer contributes to a 403(b) plan in the form of matching contributions and/or discretionary contributions (similar to profit sharing plans) in addition to employees' tax-deferred salary reduction contributions, the arrangement sometimes makes up the **employer's basic retirement plan.**

The remainder of this chapter reviews the key features and legal requirements of Section 403(b) plans.

Requirements of a 403(b) Plan under the Internal Revenue Code (IRC)

The Present Statute

To qualify for the favorable tax treatment provided in the law, plans must comply with the statutory requirements of Section 403(b) of the IRC as amended, which provides, in relevant part, that

> If an annuity contract is purchased for an employee by an employer described in Section 501(c)(3) . . . or for an employee . . . who performs services for an educational organization described in Section 170(b)(1)(A)(ii), by an employer which is a State, a political subdivision of a State, or an agency or instrumentality of any one or more of the foregoing . . . , the employee's rights under the contract are nonforfeitable, except for failure to pay future premiums (and) except in the case of a contract purchased by a church, such contract is purchased under a plan which meets the nondiscrimination requirements . . . then amounts contributed by such employer for such annuity contract . . . shall be excluded from the gross income of the employee for the taxable year.

ERISA amended Section 403(b) of the IRC to add Section 403(b)(7), which further provides in relevant part:

> For purposes of this title, amounts paid by an employer . . . to a custodial account . . . shall be treated as amounts contributed for an annuity contract for (the) employee if the amounts are to be invested in **regulated investment company stock** (mutual fund shares) to be held in that custodial account.

The essential requirements to achieve the desired tax advantages similar to qualified retirement plans are as follows:

1. The employer must be a qualified educational or nonprofit organization or a public school system (or public college or university).

2. The participant must be a bona fide employee.

3. The participant's rights under the contract must be nonforfeitable.

4. The contributions paid in any year must not exceed the exclusion allowance for the years prior to 2002, the limits under IRC Section 415, the annual limit on salary reduction contributions, or the maximum amount permitted under the nondiscrimination requirements.

5. The plan must meet the nondiscrimination requirements applicable to plans involving employer contributions. For plans that include only voluntary employee salary reductions, IRS regulations simply require that the opportunity to make salary reduction contributions be effectively available to essentially all employees.

6. The annuity contract must be purchased by the employer, or the employer must make a deposit to a custodial account that will purchase mutual fund shares.

The next section analyzes these essential requirements of a 403(b) plan in greater detail.

Qualified Employers

If the employee is to qualify for tax-deferred treatment, his or her employer must be one of the following:

1. A nonprofit organization qualified under Section 501(c)(3) of the Internal Revenue Code (for example, a tax-exempt hospital, church, school, charitable organization, or other such organization or foundation).

2. A public school system or public college or university (for example, one operated by a state, or by a county, city, town, school district, or other political subdivision or agency of a state). As used in this chapter, the term *public school system* includes such public colleges and universities.

Only those tax-exempt organizations that meet the requirements of Section 501(c)(3) are qualified employers for purposes of a 403(b) plan. In the case of questions concerning the qualification of an organization, a ruling should be sought from the IRS.[1]

---

[1] If the activity of an organization is such that if it were not publicly operated, it could qualify under Section 501(c)(3), and if it has sufficient independence from the state, and so on, it may be able to obtain a ruling that it is a counterpart of a Section 501(c)(3) organization.

Eligible Employees

To be eligible for participation in a 403(b) plan, an individual must be a **bona fide employee** of a qualified nonprofit organization or a public school system. The individual may be the top-paid or the lowest-paid employee. He or she may be a seasonal, part-time, or full-time employee, but must be an *employee*—not an independent contractor. This point requires particular attention in connection with certain professional people (such as radiologists, pathologists, and anesthesiologists) who may or may not, in certain circumstances, be employees.[2] Clerical, administrative, supervisory, and custodial employees of public school systems as well as teachers qualify.[3]

Nonforfeitable Employee Rights

Nonforfeitability under a 403(b) plan essentially requires that the benefits under the plan belong to and be payable to the employee. Without a trust, the employee's rights under an annuity contract, whether under the employer's basic retirement plan or a supplemental tax-deferred retirement annuity plan, would appear to be nonforfeitable if ownership of the contract is vested solely in the employee. The same would appear to be true if there is some form of joint ownership of the contract, together with an agreement between the employer and the employee whereby the employee cannot be deprived of benefits provided by annuity premiums previously paid, even though the employer may exercise control over the time of receipt of those benefits.

As a practical matter, it would appear that nonforfeitability would require that ownership ordinarily be vested solely in the employee, thus leaving him or her free of any restrictions or problems that might arise as a result of insolvency or change of management of the employer. As sole owner of the contract, the employee is free to exercise any of his or her contractual rights, subject, of course, to restrictions on **transferability.** Thus, when an insurance company product is involved, the employee may be free, within the limitations of the contract, to elect a reduced paid-up annuity, to exchange the contract for a reduced annuity with an earlier maturity date, to surrender the contract in order to transfer the proceeds to another issuer, or to borrow from the insurer against its cash value.

However, group annuity contracts are also sometimes used to fund 403(b) plans. In that case, generally, the employer is the contract holder. Nevertheless, in such a

---

[2] Some professionals in the service of tax-exempt organizations may be barred by ethical or legal considerations from meeting the tests for the required employer–employee relationship. See Revenue Ruling 66–274, 1966–2 CB 446 for an outline of criteria used in determining the relationship between a physician and a hospital. Also, see *Ravel* v. *Comm'r.*, 26 TCM 885 (1967) and *Azad* v. *U.S.*, 388 F 2d 74 (1968).

[3] In addition, the regulations provide that one who is elected or appointed to certain public offices may qualify if there is a requirement that to hold the office such person must be trained or experienced in the field of education. For example, a commissioner or superintendent of education generally will be eligible, but a regent or trustee of a state university or a member of a board of education is not eligible. Reg. 1.403(b)-1(b)(5).

contract there are provisions that specify that the rights of participating employees are nonforfeitable.

Contributions

Two types of contributions can be made under 403(b) arrangements. These often are referred to as nonelective and elective contributions.

Nonelective contributions are those that the employer makes on behalf of the participant to the employer's basic retirement plan. **Elective contributions** to 403(b) plans are those voluntary contributions made by an eligible employee to a tax-deferred annuity under a salary reduction agreement made with his or her employer. Elective contributions also include those contributions an employee must make to receive employer matching contributions under the employer's basic retirement plan. Previously only one such salary reduction agreement per year was permitted by Internal Revenue Code (IRC) regulations. Once the employee elected the amount to be contributed for the year, he or she generally could not change the amount until the next taxable year. The Small Business Job Protection Act of 1996 repealed this prior prohibition on multiple salary reduction agreements for plan years beginning after December 31, 1995. Participants in 403(b) plans now may enter into salary reduction agreements more frequently than once per year. Effectively participants may enter into salary reduction agreements as frequently as the plan permits, provided the amounts are not currently available, meaning the compensation has not been paid to the employee or the compensation is not able to be received at the employee's discretion.

Both nonelective and elective contributions must be made by the employer and are excluded from the employee's gross income for the current year as long as such contributions do not exceed the limitations outlined below and discussed further in the next several sections of this chapter.[4]

Three possible limitations on the amount that can be contributed to a 403(b) arrangement are:

- An elective deferral limit on contributions made pursuant to salary reduction arrangements.

- An annual exclusion allowance limitation for years prior to 2002.

- An annual limit on total contributions (Section 415 annual limit).

Limitation on Salary Reduction Contributions

The maximum amount an individual may contribute on an annual basis to all 403(b) plans in which he or she participates (pursuant to a salary reduction agreement) is determined by Internal Revenue Code Section 402(g). At the time of EGTRRA's passage in 2001, the limit on elective deferrals was set at $10,500. EGTRRA

---

[4] In addition to certain other tax penalties that may apply, contributions to a custodial account (but not to an annuity contract) in excess of these limits generally are subject to a 6 percent excise tax under IRC Section 4973.

increased the elective deferral limit for 2002 and scheduled it to increase in subsequent years according to the following schedule:

Year	Elective Deferral Limit
2002	$11,000
2003	$12,000
2004	$13,000
2005	$14,000
2006	$15,000
Years following 2006	Additional amounts are indexed in $500 increments

It should be noted that the 402(g) limit moves in tandem with the limit for 401(k) cash or deferred arrangement (CODA) elective deferrals (see Chapter 11). The 401(k) elective deferral limit reached the 403(b) level in 1996. Since that time the 403(b) and 401(k) elective deferral limits are now at the same level and are indexed to increase together. The elective deferral limit does not apply to contributions made by an employer to a 403(b) plan. The employee's 402(g) limit, however, would be reduced by any additional elective deferrals the employee may have made as a participant in a 401(k) plan, a SIMPLE plan, or a simplified employee pension (SEP) plan. Formerly if an individual also contributed to a deferred compensation (IRC Section 457[b]) plan sponsored by the employer, the 402(g) limit was reduced to the lower 457(b) limit for the total salary deferral amounts contributed to both the TDA and the Section 457 plans.

With the passage of EGTRRA, the amount that could be contributed to a 457(b) plan was decoupled from the 402(g) elective deferral limit for 403(b) plans for years beginning after 2001. The net result of this change in the law is to permit employees eligible for both types of plans to be able to contribute twice as much money on a pretax basis using both a 403(b) and a 457(b) deferred compensation plan.

In special cases, an annual amount above the 402(g) limit may be contributed by an employee to a 403(b) plan under a salary reduction agreement. Under this **special "catch-up" election,** an employee of a qualifying organization[5] who has entered into a salary reduction agreement with the employer and has at least 15 years of service with the organization may make additional contributions above the 402(g) limit in an amount not to exceed the smallest of the following:

- $3,000.

- $15,000 decreased by the amount of additional salary reduction contributions made previously by the employee under these special rules.

- The excess of $5,000 times years of service minus prior tax-deferred employee contributions.

---

[5] A qualifying organization allowing for catch-up elections is more limited than the universe of employers that are permitted to offer 403(b) plans. Generally an employee must work for an educational organization, a hospital, a home health service agency, a health and welfare service agency, or a church or related organization to be eligible for catch-up elections.

Under this special catch-up election, an eligible employee can contribute a maximum of $15,000 of additional contributions through the employer after fulfilling the 15-year service requirement, but cannot, in any event, contribute more than an additional $3,000 in any single year.

EGTRRA also provides a type of employee catch-up contribution in years after 2001 for employees who are at least age 50 before the end of the tax year. These employee catch-up contributions allow for increased elective deferrals. At the time EGTRRA was enacted, employee catch-up contributions were scheduled to increase as follows:

Year	Allowable Catch-up
2002	$1,000 additional
2003	$2,000 additional
2004	$3,000 additional
2005	$4,000 additional
2006	$5,000 additional
Years following 2006	Additional amounts are indexed in $500 increments

Employee catch-up contributions are not subject to any other contribution limits and are not taken into account in applying other contribution limits to other contributions or benefits under a plan. An employer will not fail the Internal Revenue Code (IRC) Section 401(a)(4) nondiscrimination rules if the plan allows all eligible plan participants to make the same election regarding catch-up contributions. However, all plans maintained by related employers are treated as one plan if the employers are treated as a single employer. According to the Conference Committee report, an employer can make matching contributions with respect to catch-up contributions, although these matches would be subject to all the rules typically applicable to matching contributions. It should be noted that one of the major motivations for allowing catch-up contributions was to aid women approaching retirement whose savings may have been insufficient because of career interruptions and absences from the workforce.

Exclusion Allowance

Historically in years prior to 2002, 403(b) plan sponsors needed to be concerned with the calculation of the maximum **exclusion allowance** in order to determine the amount that could be contributed by an employee on a tax deferred basis to a 403(b) plan. This was a particularly cumbersome calculation because the plan sponsor was required to keep detailed records of prior plan contributions for each employee over the employee's entire career history with the employer. The methodology for calculation of the maximum exclusion allowance was contained in the Internal Revenue Code and even predated the passage of the Employee Retirement Income Security Act (ERISA) in 1974. When other limits subsequently were passed into law and made applicable to 403(b) plans, such as the Section 415 limits and the 402(g) limit on elective deferrals, the calculation became even more cumbersome. This resulted in complexity for 403(b) plan administrators since the calculation involved computation of all these multiple limits and a determination of which limit was the controlling limit on employee elective deferrals. The calculation was further complicated by the creation of alternative limits (alternative limits A, B, and C and other special catch-ups) when new limits came into being. The passage of the Economic Growth and Tax Relief Reconciliation Act of 2001 (EGTRRA) considerably simplified administration of 403(b) plans since it eliminated the exclusion allowance for years beginning after 2001. The alternative limits A, B, and C, which allowed some employees to make additional contributions, were also repealed.

Since the calculation of the maximum exclusion allowance was of such importance historically in administering 403(b) plans, a chapter appendix is included on page 221 illustrating the steps of the calculation. Since elimination of this calculation was part of EGTRRA and the law contained a sunset provision automatically repealing all tax law modifications after 2010, it is within the realm of remote possibility that the maximum exclusion allowance, without further tax law change, could reemerge in 2011. In the interests of pension law uniformity and ease of plan administration, it is the sincere hope of the authors that the need for computation of the maximum exclusion allowance never reemerges.

IRS Section 415 Limit

EGTRRA increased the **IRC Section 415 limits** for defined contribution plans to the lesser of $40,000 or 100 percent of compensation in 2002. In the future, the Section 415 limit will be indexed in $1,000 increments. The Section 415 limits include both employer and employee contributions as well as any forfeitures that result from nonvested terminations and the allocation of these forfeited amounts to the accounts of remaining participants.

IRS Section 401(a)(17) Limit on Includible Compensation

The limit on the maximum amount that can be taken into account when calculating retirement plan contributions or benefits, or when conducting nondiscrimination testing (see nondiscrimination testing discussion on p. 68), is determined by the IRS Section 401(a)(17) limit. EGTRRA increased this compensation limit to $200,000 in 2002 and indexed its escalation in future years in $5,000 increments instead of the $10,000 increments that existed pre-EGTRRA.

Limits on Elective Deferrals under Section 402(g)

As noted earlier in the chapter, EGTRRA changed the limit on elective deferrals for 2002 and scheduled its rise over the next few years.

EGTRRA also made provision for employees who attained age 50 by the end of the tax year to contribute additional elective deferral amounts for years beginning after 2001. Also of significance was EGTRRA's provision decoupling the limit for 403(b) and 457(b) plans for years after 2001, allowing employees eligible for both plans to effectively double their elective deferral limit. The elective deferral limit, however, generally does apply to the sum of the employee's other elective deferrals for the taxable year, including CODAs, SIMPLE plans, and salary reduction simplified employee pensions (SARSEPs). EGTRRA also allowed employee contributions effective for tax years beginning after 2005 whereby an employee can elect to have all or a portion of his or her annual elective deferral treated as an after-tax "Roth contribution." In order to allow for such an election, an employer must incorporate a "qualified Roth contribution program" as part of the 403(b) plan. A 401(k) plan (see Chapter 11) may also offer such a program. The advantage to employees in electing to have all or a portion of their elective deferrals treated as designated Roth contributions is that, although these monies will be taxed currently when contributed into the plan, qualified distributions from a designated Roth account (both contributions and subsequent investment earnings) are not subject to taxation when disbursed. Since these Roth contributions are treated as elective deferrals, they are fully and immediately vested. Roth contributions are subject to the withdrawal restrictions that generally prohibit payment from the account prior to the participant's retirement, separation from service, death, disability, or the occurrence of another distributable event authorized by the Internal Revenue Service. The Conference Committee report indicates congressional intent that designated Roth contributions may only be made prospectively and that employees may not make retroactive designations of prior-year elective deferrals into Roth contributions. Designated Roth contributions are treated as elective deferrals for purposes of the nondiscrimination testing, described on page 68. A 403(b) or 401(k) plan offering the option of a qualified Roth contribution program must establish, for each participating employee, a separate "designated Roth account" that will hold designated Roth contributions and earnings allocable to those contributions.

If the employee makes an elective deferral in excess of the dollar limit for a taxable year, the excess must be allocated by the employer among the plans under which the deferrals were made by March 1 of the following year. The excess contributed, including any investment income thereon, must then be distributed by the plans to the employee by April 15. Such distributions (and investment income) will be included in the employee's taxable income for the year in which the excess deferral was made, but it will not be subject to the 10 percent penalty tax for premature distributions.

If the distribution is *not* made by the April 15 deadline, however, the excess deferral will be included in the employee's taxable income for the year in which the excess deferral was made and will be taxed *again* in the year it is actually distributed to the employee.

Plans that failed to apply the elective deferral limit previously risked plan disqualification and loss of their tax-favored status. The Small Business Job Protection Act of 1996 clarified that the limits on elective deferrals apply to each individual 403(b) *contract* rather than the 403(b) *plan* as a whole. This distinction is important since it clarifies that excess deferrals could subject individual contracts to loss of tax-favored treatment, but that contracts where deferrals are not excessive will not be negatively affected. This clarification was applicable for plan years beginning after December 31, 1995.

Nondiscrimination Requirements

For plan years after 1988, 403(b) annuity arrangements, except for church plans, are generally subject to extensive IRC nondiscrimination rules as outlined by the Tax Reform Act of 1986 (TRA '86). TRA '86 basically enacted three nondiscrimination rules that have an impact on 403(b) annuity plans. Two of the nondiscrimination rules generally incorporate the rules designed to prevent discrimination in favor of highly compensated employees (HCEs) under qualified retirement plans. These rules apply only to contributions to 403(b) annuities made *other than* pursuant to a salary reduction agreement entered into by the employee (i.e., under the employer's basic retirement plan). The third rule applies only to salary reduction contributions.

The first nondiscrimination rule effective for plan years after 1988 generally applies the same rules and regulations governing coverage that apply to qualified retirement plans to nonsalary reduction contributions made to 403(b) plans. In addition, such contributions are subject to the IRC Section 401(a)(17) limit on compensation that can be taken into account. These rules are discussed in detail in Chapters 4 and 5.

The second nondiscrimination rule requires that employer and nonsalary reduction employee contributions meet the actual contribution percentage (ACP) test that compares contributions for highly compensated employees and nonhighly compensated employees. This test is basically the same as applied to 401(k) plans and is discussed in detail in Chapter 11.

The final nondiscrimination rule, which applies only to salary reduction contributions, as discussed above, requires that if the employer permits employees to make such contributions, this opportunity must generally be made available to all employees except for certain nonresident aliens; employees covered by a Section 457 plan, a 401(k) plan, or another 403(b) plan sponsored by the same employer; employees who normally work fewer than 20 hours per week; collectively bargained employees; students performing certain services; and employees whose maximum salary reduction contributions under the plan would not exceed $200. Unlike qualified retirement plans, 403(b) plans are not permitted to impose minimum age and service requirements before employees can make salary reduction requirements.

Annuity Contract Purchased by an Employer

In speaking of "an annuity . . . purchased . . . by an employer," the law gives no indication of what constitutes an annuity contract or a purchase by an employer. However, the IRS has stated that insurance companies or mutual funds must be used.[6] From the insurance company standpoint, it would appear to make no difference whether such a contract used for a 403(b) plan is a single-premium or annual-premium contract or whether it provides for fixed or variable annuity payments, provides for immediate or deferred payments, or includes a refund provision.

The regulations under IRC Section 403(b) provide, however, that "an individual contract issued after December 31, 1962, or a group contract which provides incidental life insurance protection may be purchased as an annuity contract." The

---

[6] Revenue Ruling 82–102.

expression *incidental life insurance protection* presumably has the same meaning as it has with respect to insurance purchased under qualified plans.[7] The IRS also has ruled that a modified endowment policy with an annuity rider providing a preretirement death benefit with an actuarial value of less than that of a typical retirement income policy meets the incidental death benefit test.[8]

Also, since December 31, 1962, the term *annuity* includes a so-called *face-amount certificate* but does not include a contract or certificate issued after that date that is transferable.[9] The regulations spell out in some detail what is meant by the term **nontransferable,** and the language of the regulations has been used as a guide by insurers in appropriately wording their contracts.

Thus, any annuity contract, individual or group, ordinarily issued by an insurance company may be used to provide a tax-deferred annuity, provided it contains an appropriate restriction respecting transferability.

Contracts that require periodic level premium payments have been developed to accommodate the needs of the market. One can now find contracts with premiums payable for only 9 or 10 consecutive months of a year, which have been designed to coincide with the payroll schedules of educational institutions. However, most annuity contracts issued today allow flexible premium payments. Therefore, they are readily adaptable to varying incomes (hence, varying elective deferrals) and variable frequency of payment.

It would appear that the payment of premiums satisfies the **purchase requirement** of the statute. Thus, a qualified employer may assume the payment of premiums on an individual annuity contract already owned by one of its employees and will be considered as having purchased a tax-deferred annuity for the employee in each year that premiums are so paid, provided that the contract contains the requisite restriction on transferability.

ERISA, as mentioned previously, by adding Section 403(b)(7), substantially expanded the range of permissible investments to include custodial accounts of regulated investment companies (mutual funds) as well as insurance company annuities or separate accounts.

Distributions and Taxation

Regular and Premature Distributions

For plan years after 1988, distributions from 403(b) arrangements of contributions made pursuant to an employee's salary reduction agreement and any investment income on such contributions are subject to basically the same restrictions as elective

---

[7] For a discussion of the meaning of incidental life insurance under qualified plans, see Chapter 8.
[8] Rev. Rul. 74–115, IRB 1974-11, 9.
[9] IRC 401(g), which reads in its entirety as follows: For purposes of this section and Sections 402, 403, and 404, the term *annuity* includes a face-amount certificate, as defined in Section 2(a)(15) of the Investment Company Act of 1940 (15 USC Sec. 80a-2); but it does not include any contract or certificate issued after December 31, 1962, which is transferable, if any person other than the trustee of a trust described in Section 401(a) which is exempt from tax under Section 501(a) is the owner of such contract or certificate.

deferral contributions made to qualified 401(k) plans (see Chapter 11).[10] Hence, distributions of salary reduction contributions on behalf of an employee and investment earnings on such contributions credited to a TSA after 1988 generally may be made from a 403(b) plan under the following circumstances:[11]

- Attainment of age 59½.

- Death or disability.

- Separation from service.

- Financial hardship.

Note, however, that in the case of a distribution on account of financial hardship, *only* salary reduction contributions made by an employee, and not any investment earnings thereon, may be distributed.

Distributions from a 403(b) plan, unless rolled over (discussed later in this chapter) to an individual retirement account (IRA) or another 403(b) plan, are taxed for federal income tax purposes as ordinary income in the year received.

In addition to the ordinary income tax due in the year a distribution is received, a premature distribution penalty tax of 10 percent of the taxable amount distributed generally applies to any distribution from a 403(b) plan before age 59½. The penalty tax would not apply, however, to premature (pre-age 59½) distributions made under the following conditions:

- To an employee who separates from service at or after age 55 and who receives the distribution upon separation from service of the employer.

- Upon the employee's death or disability.

- Upon the employee's separation from service from his or her employer, if the employee receives a distribution in substantially equal periodic payments over his or her life expectancy or over the joint life expectancies of the individual and his or her beneficiary.

- If the employee rolls the distribution over to an IRA or another tax-favored retirement plan.

- To pay medical expenses that are deductible for federal income tax purposes (currently those over 7.5 percent of the employee's adjusted gross income) under IRC Section 213.

- To someone other than the employee under a qualified domestic relations order (see Chapter 5).

---

[10] See John J. McFadden, *Retirement Plans for Employees* (Burr Ridge, IL: Richard D. Irwin), pp. 269–70.

[11] If the account is *invested* in a custodial account (mutual fund), the withdrawal limitations apply to all 403(b) contributions, and only salary reduction contributions may be distributed in the event of hardship. If the account is invested in an annuity contract, the withdrawal limitations apply only to salary reduction contributions and investment earnings thereon credited after 1988.

Hence, the 10 percent penalty tax applies to nonmedical financial hardship distributions if made prior to age 59½ (see Chapter 27).

Time When Distributions Must Commence

An employee generally must begin receiving distributions from a 403(b) annuity plan by the later of (1) the April 1 following the year in which the individual attains age 70½ or (2) the calendar year following the year in which the employee retires.[12] If sufficient records are maintained to segregate an employee's pre-1987 account balance, however, and if the 403(b) plan so provides, any amounts credited prior to January 1, 1987, need not be distributed until age 75. If a distribution is taken in periodic payments, a minimum distribution must be made based on the individual's life expectancy or the joint life expectancies of the individual and his or her beneficiary. A penalty tax of 50 percent of the difference between the minimum required distribution and the actual distribution received is imposed on the employee if the distribution is less than that required by law.

EGTRRA did not modify the minimum distribution rules, but instructed the Treasury Department to modify the life expectancy tables to more accurately reflect actual current life expectancies. On April 17, 2002, the Treasury Department issued updated regulations regarding minimum distributions. The updated life expectancy tables were included in these regulations.

Taxation of Distributions

Any lump sum distribution from a 403(b) plan is taxable to the participant at ordinary income tax rates. Neither capital gains income tax rates nor income averaging opportunities, available to qualified plan lump-sum distributions before the year 2000, were available for a 403(b) plan distribution. The only part of the distribution that may not be subject to taxation would be for any cost basis the employee may have in the distribution because of taxes previously paid by the employee on his or her plan contributions or for any incidental life insurance costs (PS 58 costs) on life insurance included and already subjected to taxation.

Installment payments under a 403(b) plan are taxed in accordance with the annuity rules applicable for qualified plans. See Chapter 27 for a complete discussion of the annuity rules.

---

[12] Previously, employees who continued to work past age 70½ were not required to receive distributions from their accounts while continuing in active employment. This was changed with the Tax Reform Act of 1986 (TRA '86). Though certain employees were excluded from having to take distributions if continuing to work, TRA '86 generally required distributions to commence by April 1 of the year following the year in which an employee attained age 70½ regardless of whether the individual continued in active employment. Employees participating in church or governmental plans remaining in active service and employees who reached age 70½ prior to 1988 were excluded from these distribution requirements. Effectively, the Small Business Job Protection Act of 1996 replaced the minimum distribution rules mandated by TRA '86 with the rules in effect prior to TRA '86. Therefore those still working are no longer required to commence distributions at age 70½ unless the individual is a 5 percent owner or the retirement plan in question is an individual retirement account. These new distribution rules became effective for years beginning after December 31, 1996. It should be noted that a participant receiving distributions under the TRA '86 rules who was continuing to work could be permitted to stop receiving minimum distributions, although the new law did not mandate that this option be offered by plan sponsors.

Distinction Between "Old Money" and "New Money" in 403(b) Minimum Distributions

1

Initially, there were no rules on withdrawals from 403(b) plans. In 1973, the IRS said that more than 50 percent of the money should be taken out during a participant's lifetime. Actuarial tables were drawn up that provided the framework for withdrawals, but there was no mandatory starting point.

In the late 1970s, IRS actuaries informally agreed that age 75 "might be a good starting point," according to Mr. Holmes, the agency spokesperson. The age was then mentioned in the letter rulings but never included in regulations or other guidelines.

Then along came the Tax Reform Act of 1986. Among other things, the act required that 403(b) plans be governed by the minimum distribution rules in effect for other pension plans, like 401(k) plans and IRAs.

But the 1986 law made a distinction for the "old money" (contributions that were in the plans before January 1, 1987), saying these dollars could be withdrawn on the basis of the "old rules," which were not further defined.

Most pension experts have concluded ever since that this was a reference to the actuarial tables issued in the 1970s, which allow money to be withdrawn at a slower rate than do the tables issued later for "new money." The experts also concluded that the 1986 law meant for age 70½ to be the mandatory start-up point for both old and new money.

The IRS now says those experts were right about the tables—and wrong about the age. Even though the letter rulings were never turned into formal regulations, age 75 is the rule, said Mr. Holmes.

Source: Mary Rowland, "Stumping the Pension Experts," *New York Times* (Nov. 29, 1992) Sec. 3, p. 15. © 1992 by the New York Times Company. Reprinted with permission.

Loans

Because of the restrictions and limitations on distributions from 403(b) plans previously described, loan provisions are very popular under such plans. Loans under 403(b) plans generally are permitted on the same basis and with the same limits as under qualified retirement plans (see Chapter 8). Basically, such loans must meet the following IRC requirements:

- Loans generally may not exceed the lesser of 50 percent of the participant's account balance or $50,000 (reduced by the amount of any principal repayments on any other loans outstanding during the prior year).

- Loans must bear a reasonable rate of interest.

- Loans must be repaid within five years except for a loan used in the purchase of the employee's principal residence.

- Loan repayments must be made at least quarterly.

- Loans must be on a level amortization basis.

Transfers, Rollovers, and Increased Portability

Transfers

Transferability generally refers to the ability to move some or all of the participant's 403(b) accumulated plan assets among different funds or providers sponsored by the employer—subject, of course, to the plan provisions. In addition, a participant may be allowed to transfer his or her 403(b) plan assets to another 403(b) plan without federal income tax consequences, again subject to possible restrictions imposed by the existing plan and the new plan.

Rollovers

Under IRC Section 403(b)(8), distributions from a 403(b) plan are not includable in an employee's gross income if they are properly rolled over. The basic requirements applicable to a valid rollover are that the employee, pursuant to the plan's usual distribution rules, receives all or a portion of his or her interest in the plan in an eligible rollover distribution; the employee rolls any portion of the distribution into another eligible plan or to an individual retirement account (IRA); and if property other than money is distributed, the employee transfers the same property he or she received. In addition, the employee must complete the rollover within 60 days of his or her receipt of the eligible rollover distribution.

For purposes of this discussion, an **eligible rollover distribution** is any distribution of all or a portion of an employee's interest in a 403(b) plan, but it does *not* include (1) any distribution required to be made under the required minimum distribution rules; (2) certain periodic distributions;[13] or (3) any distribution made on account of hardship. Unless made in the form of a direct rollover (i.e., where, pursuant to the employee's instructions, the distribution is paid by the payor plan directly to another plan or IRA and not to the employee), an eligible rollover distribution is subject to mandatory 20 percent federal income tax withholding. The payor (i.e., the insurer or custodian) must withhold the tax even if the employee intends to, and actually does, roll the distribution over upon receiving it. In that case, the employee will be taxed on the amount withheld unless he or she includes other funds equal to the withholding amount in the amount ultimately rolled over.

---

[13] Any distribution that is part of a series of substantially equal periodic payments made at least annually over the life or life expectancy of the employee (or the joint lives or life expectancies of the employee and his or her beneficiary), or for a period of at least 10 years, is not an eligible rollover distribution.

Increased Portability

Prior to 2002, 403(b) plan assets could only be rolled over to another 403(b) plan or to an IRA. Beginning in 2002 as a result of changes made by EGTRRA, rollover distributions may occur between qualified plans, 403(b), and eligible governmental 457(b) plans. Also, as was permitted previously for qualified and 403(b) plans, eligible distributions from governmental 457(b) plans may also be rolled over to IRAs. The mandatory 20 percent withholding rule is applicable to distributions from rollover-eligible governmental 457(b) plans if distributions fail to be directly rolled over. Rollovers from contributory and conduit IRAs (see Chapter 17) may also be made into 403(b) plans, qualified plans, or eligible governmental 457(b) plans. After-tax contributions from a qualified defined contribution plan (401[a], 403[a] or 401[k] plan) can be directly rolled over (but not indirectly rolled over, that is, in a rollover made within the 60-day period following a distribution) to another qualified defined contribution plan. Such after-tax amounts may be rolled over directly or indirectly to an IRA. The receiving qualified defined contribution plan must account for such after-tax amounts separately, but a receiving IRA does not. However, when EGTRRA was initially passed, it did not appear that distributions of after-tax amounts could be rolled over to 403(b) or governmental 457(b) plans or that distributions of such after-tax contributions from 403(b) and governmental 457(b) plans could be rolled over to another plan or IRA. Further regulatory clarification was needed.[14]

EGTRRA also permitted the Treasury Department to extend the 60-day rollover period where the failure to make a rollover within 60 days is attributable to casualty, disaster, or events beyond the reasonable control of the participant.[15]

Chapter Summary

- A tax-favored retirement mechanism exists for employees of public educational institutions and certain nonprofit tax-exempt organizations. To avail themselves of the favorable tax treatment, plans must comply with the statutory requirements of Section 403(b) of the IRC. ERISA amended Section 403(b) of the IRC adding Section 403(b)(7) to allow investments in regulated investment company stock (mutual funds) as well as annuity contracts.

- In order to offer 403(b) arrangements to its employees, an employer must be either a nonprofit organization qualified under Section 501(c)(3) of the IRC or a public school system or public college or university.

- Limitations apply to the amount that can be contributed to a 403(b) arrangement. These limitations are:
  - A limit on elective deferrals for contributions made pursuant to salary reduction agreements.
  - An annual exclusion allowance limitation (prior to 2002).
  - An annual limit on total contributions (Section 415 annual limit).

---

[14] TIAA-CREF. "Benefit Plan Counselor Special Report: 2002 and the Economic Growth and Tax Relief Reconciliation Act," Teachers Insurance Institute (January 2002), p. 4
[15] Ibid., p. 4

Additionally, employer contributions to a 403(b) plan cannot be calculated using compensation that exceeds the allowable limit prescribed by Section 401(a)(17).

- For plan years after 1988, Section 403(b) plans, other than church plans, generally became subject to the extensive IRC nondiscrimination rules mandated by the Tax Reform Act of 1986 (TRA '86).

- Distributions from 403(b) arrangements of contributions made pursuant to an employee's salary reduction agreement and any investment income on such contributions are subject to basically the same restrictions as elective deferral contributions made to qualified 401(k) plans.

- Any lump-sum distribution from a 403(b) plan is taxable to the participant at ordinary income tax rates.

- Rollover distributions may occur between qualified plans, 403(b) plans, eligible governmental 457(b) plans, and IRAs.

Key Terms

403(b) annuities, p. *204*
bona fide employee, p. *206*
elective contributions,
  p. *207*
eligible rollover
  distribution, p. *217*
employer's basic retirement
  plan, p. *204*
exclusion allowance, p. *209*

IRC Section 415 limit, p. *210*
nonelective contributions,
  p. *207*
nonforfeitability, p. *206*
nontransferable, p. *213*
purchase requirement,
  p. *213*
regulated investment
  company stock, p. *204*

salary reduction agreement,
  p. *203*
special "catch-up" election,
  p. *208*
tax-deferred annuity (TDA),
  p. *204*
transferability, p. *206*

Questions for Review

1. Briefly summarize the provisions of the tax code that permit one to set up a tax-deferred annuity.

2. What are the essential requirements to achieve the desired tax shelter for a 403(b) plan? Explain.

3. What does it mean when the IRC requires that the employee's rights be nonforfeitable? Explain.

4. Describe the historical significance of the exclusion allowance for an employee of a 403(b) plan.

5. Explain how the elimination of the maximum exclusion allowance in 2002 affected the administration of 403(b) plans.

6. What nondiscrimination tests apply to 403(b) plans?

7. When must distributions commence from a 403(b) plan?

Questions for Discussion

1. Discuss the conditions under which an employer may desire to establish a 403(b) plan.
2. Discuss how the elective deferral limitation has affected plan design for 403(b) annuities.
3. Discuss how the nondiscrimination requirements have affected plan design for 403(b) annuities.
4. Discuss the effects of EGTRRA on 403(b) plans.

Resources for Further Study

CCH Editorial Staff. "2001 Tax Legislation: Law, Explanation, and Analysis." *Commerce Clearing House Pension Plan Guide* (2001).

Cumming, Chris. "Tax-Exempt Entities: When Two Retirement Plans Are Better than One: Making the Most of Paired 401(k)–403(b) Plans." *Journal of Pension Benefits* 8, no. 4 (Summer 2001).

Davis, Michele F. "Section 403(b) Plans for Nonprofit Organizations." *The Handbook of Employee Benefits.* 5th ed. Jerry S. Rosenbloom, ed. New York: McGraw-Hill, 2001.

TIAA-CREF. "Benefit Plan Counselor Special Report: 2002 and the Economic Growth and Tax Relief Reconciliation Act." Teachers Insurance (January 2002).

TIAA-CREF. "Benefit Plan Counselor Special Report: Highlights of the Economic Growth and Tax Relief Reconciliation Act of 2001." Teachers Insurance (July 2001).

www.tiaa-cref.org—website of Teachers Insurance and Annuity Association.

www.tiaa-crefinstitute.org—website of the TIAA-CREF Institute

Calculation of the maximum exclusion allowance was a key component in the administration of 403(b) plans in years occuring before 2002. Since the requirement to calculate the maximum exclusion allowance was included in the original enabling legislation that created Section 403(b) of the Internal Revenue Code, the computation became increasingly more complex when additional limits were imposed with the enactment of subsequent legislation. ERISA established the Section 415 limit and the "415 catch up" provisions. The Tax Reform Act of 1986 imposed the 402(g) elective deferral limit and the "402(g) catch up." EGTRRA, which was passed into law in 2001, eliminated the maximum exclusion allowance limitation for 2002 and later years. Because the tax provisions of EGTRRA are scheduled to "sunset" or lapse in 2011 unless additional tax legislation is passed into law, it is possible that the maximum exclusion allowance could reemerge in the future. Since the calculation of the maximum exclusion allowance historically has been an important element in 403(b) plan administration and because of its possible reemergence, a detailed example of the steps of this calculation are provided in this chapter appendix.

Calculating the Maximum Exclusion Allowance before 2002

An employer's contributions to a 403(b) plan were excluded from an employee's gross income for federal income tax purposes in a particular year as long as such contributions did not exceed an employee's exclusion allowance. To determine an employee's exclusion allowance, the following three-step process generally was used:

1. Multiply the employee's includable compensation (gross compensation decreased by salary reduction contributions) for the most recent year of service by .20.

2. Multiply the result in step (1) above by the employee's total years of service with the employer.

3. Subtract the total amount previously contributed by the employer to the 403(b) plan or other retirement plan for that employee.

The foregoing process was translated into a mathematical formula as follows:

$$\text{MEA} = \frac{ST - 5C}{T + 5}$$

where

MEA = The maximum exclusion allowance for a given year

S = The gross compensation before salary reduction

T = The total number of years of past service plus the year of compution

C = The total prior years' contributions in the aggregate to the 403(b) plan and to any qualified retirement (pension) plan and/or Section 457 plan maintained by the employer, plus amounts previously contributed in excess of Section 415 limits

The following example illustrates how the three-step process worked to determine an employee's exclusion allowance.

Assume Harry's gross compensation was $40,000. Harry had worked for his employer for four years, during which time the employer had contributed a total of $20,000 to the 403(b) plan. The employer did not maintain any other retirement plan. In this situation, Harry's maximum exclusion allowance for the year would be determined as follows:

$$\text{MEA} = \frac{(40,000)(5) - 5(20,000)}{5 + 5} = \frac{200,000 - 100,000}{10} = \frac{\$100,000}{10} = \$10,000$$

Harry wanted to contribute $6,000. Since this was below the maximum exclusion allowance ($10,000), the entire $6,000 would be excluded from Harry's gross income for federal income tax purposes. Moreover, if Harry's contribution of $6,000 was less than the limitation for elective deferrals (402[g]), it also passed this latter requirement.

A common approach to determining an employee's annual maximum salary reduction contribution was to take 16⅔ percent of an employee's gross pay. This approach assumed that an employer made no other tax-favored retirement plan contributions on behalf of the employee. For example, assume that Sue's gross compensation for a given year was $50,000. Her maximum exclusion allowance and, thus, her allowable contribution would be $8,333.33 (16⅔% × $50,000). This figure was equal to 20 percent of the employee's reduced compensation ($50,000 − 8,333.33). If the amount was less than the limitation for elective deferrals (402[g]), the total amount could be contributed under a salary reduction 403(b) arrangement.

IRS Section 415 Limit

The third limitation was that annual contributions by an employer to a 403(b) plan, including any elective deferrals, generally could not exceed the IRC Section 415 limit, which was the lesser of $35,000 or 25 percent of the employee's taxable compensation for the year 2001, the final year when the exclusion allowance was applicable.

As an example, assume physician Jones had compensation for the 2001 year of $150,000 and had worked for a university hospital for six years, during which time a total of $66,000 had been contributed on Dr. Jones's behalf to the university's 403(b) plan. The university had not made any other contributions for Dr. Jones to any other qualified retirement plan. Using the approach outlined above, Dr. Jones's maximum exclusion allowance for 2001 would be as follows:

$$\text{MEA} = \frac{(\$150,000)(7) - 5(66,000)}{7 + 5} = \frac{1,050,000 - 330,000}{12} = \frac{720,000}{12} = \$60,000$$

However, since the IRC Section 415's maximum dollar limit was $35,000 in 2001, the maximum amount that the university could contribute on behalf of Dr. Jones was $35,000. It should be emphasized that the Section 415 limit applied to the total of elective deferrals and other employer contributions to the 403(b) plan; the 402(g) limit applied only to elective deferrals. In addition, such contributions were subject to the IRC Section 401(a)(17) limit on compensation that could be considered when calculating plan contributions.

Taxable compensation for these purposes was generally defined as gross compensation less any salary reduction contributions.[1] This limit applied to higher-income employees whose exclusion allowance could otherwise exceed the IRC Section 415 limit.

Special Catch-Up Elections

Special consideration was given in Section 415 to certain categories of employees (those who were employed in educational organizations, nonprofit hospitals, health and welfare service agencies, home health service agencies, and churches) covered by 403(b) plans to allow those employees who had made less than the maximum allowable contributions in their early careers to make larger catch-up contributions. The three alternatives allowed were as follows:

1. *The $30,000 maximum rule.* Under this approach, an eligible employee terminating employment could, on a one-time-only basis, make up the contributions that could have been made, but were not, during the 10-year period ending on the date of separation. (This amount was 20 percent of the employee's includable compensation multiplied by the number of years of service [not to exceed 10] for the employer minus the employer

---

[1] The Small Business Job Protection Act of 1996 modified the definition of compensation for IRC Section 415 purposes. Whereas previously the definition of compensation excluded elective deferrals to 401(k) plans and similar arrangements (including 403[b] plans), elective contributions to nonqualified deferred compensation plans of tax-exempt employers and state and local governments (457 plans), and salary reduction contributions to a cafeteria plan, the definition of compensation was modified by this act to include these items. This change in the definition of compensation became effective for years beginning after December 31, 1997.

contributions already made during the relevant period.) Although no percentage limitation applied, this one-shot catch-up contribution was limited to a maximum of $30,000.

2. *The $15,000 maximum rule.* Under this alternative, annual contributions could be made, at any time, equal to the lesser of 25 percent of includable compensation plus $4,000 or the exclusion allowance normally allowed under Internal Revenue Code Section 403(b). The maximum annual deduction allowable under this approach was $15,000.

3. *The 25 percent/$35,000 rule.* Under this approach, the maximum contribution was limited to the lesser of $35,000 or 25 percent of includable compensation. However, the 403(b) contribution had to be aggregated with other qualified plan contributions to meet this test,[2] and any employer contributions to a qualified defined benefit plan or other defined contribution plan had to be subtracted from the 403(b) contribution. Since, in a defined benefit plan, the employee does not know the amount contributed by the employer, the IRS had established procedures to estimate the value of the employer's contributions.

Any election made under one of these special rules was considered an irrevocable election. This meant an employee electing to contribute under one of the special rules had to continue to use the same rule in future years. However, the employee could always return to the general 403(b) limit.

---

[2]Regardless of whether this special catch-up election had been made, 403(b) plan contributions had to be aggregated with qualified plan contributions for IRC 415 purposes in the case of any employee who "controlled" the employer within the meaning of applicable regulations.

13

Defined Benefit Plan Features

After studying this chapter you should be able to:

- Describe what the term *normal retirement age* means.

- Explain why reduced benefits are often provided for early retirement.

- Identify the various types of defined benefit formulas used in calculating plan benefits.

- Understand the excess and the offset approaches for integrating benefits under defined benefit plans with Social Security.

- Determine when the overall permitted disparity limits are violated.

- Understand what is meant by an incidental death benefit.

An employer adopting a qualified defined benefit pension plan must make a number of decisions about the basic features to be included in the plan. The employer must, for example, determine what benefits the participants will receive upon retirement, death, or disability; how and when these benefits will be paid; and whether or not employees will contribute toward the cost of these benefits.

This chapter discusses the various factors that bear on an employer's decisions concerning the design of the more prominent features to be included in a defined benefit pension plan. While much of this material applies equally to defined contribution plans, it is oriented specifically toward qualified defined benefit pension plans. The features discussed in this chapter include retirement ages, employee contributions, retirement, death, and disability benefits. The chapter then discusses the plan design approaches used to counteract the effect of preretirement inflation and approaches used to offset postretirement inflation.

It should be emphasized at this point that the employer's objectives and circumstances covered in Chapter 2, the legal requirements concerning the qualification of a retirement plan covered in Chapters 4 and 5, and the other legal requirements covered in Chapter 6 must be taken into consideration at every phase of the plan design process. An employer must make sure a plan meets its objectives and does not discriminate in favor of highly compensated employees. Having to remedy either of these problems at a later point in time can result in considerable expense and administrative complexity for the employer. Consideration of employer objectives and nondiscriminatory requirements will be noted throughout this chapter where they are particularly relevant to the topic under discussion.

Employee Contributions

A major question the employer must resolve is whether employees will be required to make contributions toward the cost of plan benefits. Sound arguments may be presented for both contributory and noncontributory plans, although the ability of the employer or employees to pay is often the controlling factor. In any event, the trend is clearly in the direction of noncontributory plans, at least in the case of defined benefit plans.

Arguments advanced in favor of contributory plans include the following:

1. From a philosophical viewpoint, employees are responsible for meeting part of their own economic security needs.

2. If employees contribute, it will mean a smaller employer contribution to provide the same overall plan benefits.

3. If an employer does not want to use employee contributions to reduce its own contribution, then by making the plan contributory, the overall plan benefits will be larger.

4. Something for nothing is too often taken for granted, and the deductions from current earnings will continually remind employees that the employer is assuming a large share of providing the plan benefits. (It would seem that this argument could be minimized by an effective method of repeatedly publicizing the plan and its value to employees.)

5. Employees are encouraged to save. The contributory plan also provides an employee with additional funds in the event of termination of employment.

The proponents of a noncontributory plan hold that the contributory plan has the following disadvantages:

1. Employer contributions represent dollars that have not been taxed. On the other hand, dollars received by the employee as earnings that are then contributed under the plan are dollars that have been taxed to the employee.[1] Hence, dollar for dollar, employer contributions provide more than those of an employee.

---

[1] Salary reduction contributions under Section 401(k) of the IRC are not permitted for defined benefit or money purchase pension plans.

2. Deductions from earnings are a source of constant irritation to employees.

3. The employer might be forced to increase salaries to compensate for the additional deductions.

4. The number of participants required for a qualified plan might not enroll.

5. Some employees may refuse to participate, in which case the employer will still have a problem when these employees reach retirement age.

6. Additional records must be kept by the employer, thereby increasing administrative work and costs.

If the employer decides that employees should make contributions, the next decision will be the amount employees should contribute. While employee contributions may be related to the cost of benefits, generally it is much more satisfactory to relate these contributions to earnings. In this way, employees' contributions are geared to their ability to make them. Furthermore, in most plans it is impossible to predict exactly what the cost of an employee's pension will be until actual retirement. Hence, any contributions made by the employee and related to cost necessarily are estimated and do not have an exact relationship.

Contributory plans usually require that before becoming a participant an employee must sign a request for participation agreeing to make the required contributions and authorizing the employer to withhold contributions from earnings.

Retirement Ages

Normal Retirement Age

The normal retirement age in most plans is 65. The choice of this age was influenced not only by the fact that this was the age at which full Social Security benefits originally commenced but also that retiring employees before age 65 with full benefits could produce prohibitive costs. Federal law defines **normal retirement age** to be the age specified in the plan, but no later than age 65 or the fifth anniversary of the participant's date of initial plan participation, whichever is the last to occur. Occasionally, an earlier age such as 60 will be chosen as the normal retirement age, although, to a great extent, this practice has been confined to public, quasi-public, and charitable institutions. Also, where an employee's occupation is such that his or her working career is shorter than in most other occupations, and when this does not result in prohibited age discrimination, a plan may provide for a normal retirement age lower than 65.

Early Retirement Age

Most plans provide that an employee may choose **early retirement** on a reduced pension, although a few plans limit this feature to cases of total and permanent disability. If an early retirement option is included, it is customary to establish some requirements an employee must fulfill before being allowed to elect early retirement.

A typical requirement for early retirement is that the employee must have attained at least age 55 and completed at least 10 years of service or participation in the plan. Requirements such as these limit the option to situations where the employee is actually retiring as opposed to changing jobs. They also tend to create a situation in which the employee will receive a reasonable benefit.

The benefit payable at early retirement typically is lower than the normal retirement benefit for two reasons. First, the full benefit will not yet have accrued by the employee's early retirement date. Second, because it is starting several years earlier than anticipated, the benefit will be paid over a longer period of time. Thus, an actuarial reduction factor usually is applied to the value of the employee's accrued benefit to determine the amount of early retirement benefit.

Determining the value of the employee's accrued benefit is relatively simple under an allocated funding instrument.[2] In a pension plan funded entirely by individual insurance policies, for example, the value of the accrued benefit generally is the cash surrender value of the employee's insurance or annuity contract at the time of retirement. In this type of plan, the actuarial reduction is accomplished by the use of the settlement option rates contained in the contract. The employee's benefit is generally that amount that may be provided by applying the cash surrender value under the option at the employee's attained age on his or her retirement date.

In plans using an unallocated funding instrument and where the benefit formula reflects the employee's service, the benefit generally is measured in terms of the employee's accrued benefit to the date of retirement. If the plan uses another type of formula, however, the determination of the value of the employee's accrued benefit is more difficult. One often-used approach is to multiply the value of the employee's projected benefit at normal retirement date by a fraction, the numerator being the years of participation or service the employee has completed at the early retirement date and the denominator being the years of participation or service the employee would have completed at the normal retirement date.

In any event, an employee's accrued benefit at early retirement must meet the accrued benefit requirements of federal tax law that apply to vested benefits (see Chapter 5).

The reduction factor applied to the value of the employee's accrued benefit might be something as simple as a reduction of one-half of 1 percent for each month by which early retirement precedes normal retirement; or, as is sometimes the case, an actuarial reduction factor is determined from a table included in the plan.

There has been a growing interest in recent years in the possibility of retiring earlier than age 65. While some plans actually establish a normal retirement age earlier than age 65, a greater number encourage early retirement by not applying a full actuarial reduction if certain conditions are met. One approach, for example, is to provide for no actuarial reduction at all if the employee retires after attaining some age (such as 60) and after completing some period of service (such as 30 years). A similar approach would be to apply no reduction factor (or a minimum factor) if early retirement occurs when the employee's age and service total to some

---

[2] Funding instruments are classified on the basis of whether contributions are allocated to provide benefits to specific employees or whether contributions are accumulated in an unallocated fund to provide benefits collectively for all employees.

number such as 90—for example, an employee who is age 62 and who has completed 28 years of service would satisfy this requirement. Still another approach would be to apply some simple factor, such as one-fourth of 1 percent for each month by which early retirement precedes normal retirement, that is considerably less than the reduction that would otherwise be called for by full actuarial reduction factors. Approaches such as these will, of course, increase the cost of the pension plan; however, employees generally find such a provision to be attractive, and quite frequently the employer finds its overall interests are best served by a provision that encourages early retirement.

Late Retirement Age

Plans also must include a provision allowing an employee to defer retirement. This feature also could be important to the employer, since it permits a greater degree of flexibility in scheduling the actual retirement of a key employee when there is a problem in obtaining or training a replacement.

The federal age discrimination law and state laws protecting employment rights are discussed in Chapter 6. In general, these laws require employees to continue accruing benefits without regard to any maximum age limit.

Retirement Benefits

The formula selected for determining an employee's retirement benefit is a vital provision in a pension plan. The employer's financial capacity and general philosophy concerning the desired level of retirement benefits, as well as the employer's specific objectives as to the distribution of benefits among employees, all play an important role in selecting such a formula.

Many employers believe that a plan should be designed to provide a higher-paid career employee with an income after retirement that, together with primary Social Security benefits, will be about 50 to 55 percent of earnings just before retirement. For lower-paid employees, the percentage generally is set at a higher level—perhaps as much as 80 to 85 percent. For employees considered to be less than career employees (usually those employees with fewer than 25 or 30 years of service with the employer), these percentages would be proportionately smaller. From the employer's viewpoint, the benefit formula selected should in no event result in a plan that produces unacceptable costs so as to endanger the continuation of the plan if corporate earnings are decreased or if current tax advantages are reduced.

Basically, there are two types of benefit formulas for the employer to consider. The first is called a *defined contribution* or a *money purchase formula.* Under this type of formula, contribution rates are fixed, and an employee's benefit varies depending upon factors such as the amount of the contributions made, investment earnings on plan assets, and the employee's entry age and retirement age.[3]

---

[3] This chapter is concerned only with defined benefit pension plans. Defined contribution plans, such as money purchase pension plans, profit sharing plans, and thrift and savings plans, are discussed in Chapters 7 through 11.

The second type is called a *defined benefit* or an *annuity purchase formula.* Here, a definite benefit is established for each employee, and contributions are determined to be whatever is necessary to produce the desired benefit results. Defined benefit formulas may be subdivided into several different classifications.

Determination of Compensation

Since the amount of benefit under most formulas is based on an employee's compensation, it is important, before discussing specific formulas, to have a clear idea of the various considerations involved in selecting the compensation base to which the benefit formula will be applied. Items such as overtime pay, holiday pay, sick pay, bonuses, and commissions must be specifically excluded or included. The definition chosen must not discriminate in favor of highly compensated employees (HCEs) (i.e., it must satisfy the requirements detailed in Chapter 4).

The question of whether plan benefits should be based on the average of the earnings paid over the entire period of the employee's participation in the plan or on an average of the employee's earnings during some shorter period of time that is near the employee's retirement age is crucial to proper plan design. The latter type of provision, often called a **final-pay provision,** would base benefits on the employee's earnings averaged, for example, over the last three or five years of employment, or over the three or five consecutive years in the 10-year period immediately prior to retirement during which the employee's earnings are the highest.

The advantage of a final-pay plan is that it relates benefits to the employee's earnings and standard of living during a period just preceding retirement. As a result, the employee's initial benefit keeps pace with any preretirement inflationary trends. Moreover, a final-pay plan is more likely to meet employer objectives as to benefit levels than is a **career-pay plan.** This type of plan, however, is usually more expensive than one that bases benefits on career-average earnings. Many employers believe it is best to use a career-average earnings plan and to make periodic adjustments in the benefit formula when economic trends justify such an action.

While a final-pay plan has the disadvantage of committing an employer to increased costs during an extended inflationary period, it should be remembered that in many situations the employer's capacity to absorb these increases also may be increased. Moreover, a final-pay plan generally produces more favorable results for key employees than the career-average approach.

A final point to be noted concerns the requirement of federal tax law that an employee's normal retirement benefit can never be less than the highest early retirement benefit that he or she could have received. Thus, any salary reductions that occur after an employee first becomes eligible to retire early cannot have the effect of reducing the employee's normal retirement benefit.

Defined Benefit Formulas

Broadly speaking, there are four basic defined benefit formulas. They are (1) a flat amount formula, which provides a flat benefit unrelated to an employee's earnings or service; (2) a flat percentage of earnings formula, which provides a benefit related to the employee's earnings but does not reflect service; (3) a flat amount per year of service formula, which reflects an employee's service but not earnings; and (4) a percentage of earnings per year of service formula, which reflects both an employee's earnings and service. Defined benefit formulas also may be integrated with Social Security benefits.

Flat Amount Formula

As indicated above, this type of formula provides for a flat benefit that treats all employees alike, regardless of their service, age, or earnings. For example, the benefit might be $300 or $400 a month. The **flat amount formula,** since it is considered to produce inequitable results, seldom is used by itself. On occasion, this formula is used in conjunction with some other type of formula; for example, a plan may provide a flat benefit of $400 a month for a covered employee, plus a percentage of his or her earnings in excess of the current Social Security taxable wage base. Any such formula, of course, would not be acceptable for qualified plan purposes if it resulted in discriminatory benefits for HCEs.

While the employee's length of service is not reflected directly in this type of formula, service is in effect recognized since most plans require that an employee, upon attaining the normal retirement age specified by the plan, must have been employed for some period of time, such as 25 years. Plans that include such a requirement provide for a proportionately reduced benefit if the employee has accumulated fewer than the required number of years, thus creating, in effect, a formula weighted for service.

Flat Percentage of Earnings Formula

This type of formula is sometimes used today, particularly in plans that cover salaried or clerical employees. Some **flat percentage of earnings,** usually ranging from 25 to 50 percent, is selected as the measure of the pension benefit. It may be used with either career-average or final-average earnings, although it is used most frequently in final-pay plans.

This type of formula does not take an employee's service into account, except in those plans which require that the employee must have completed a minimum period of service by the normal retirement date and which provide for a proportionately reduced benefit if the employee's service is less than the required number of years.

Flat Amount per Year of Service Formula

This type of formula often is found in negotiated plans. It provides a **flat dollar amount per year of service** completed by the employee. Thus, in a plan that provides for a benefit of $20 a month for each year of service, an employee with 27 years of employment would receive a monthly pension of $540.

This type of formula frequently requires that an employee must have worked for a minimum number of hours during a plan year to receive a full benefit credit for such year. Minimums often used for this purpose are 1,600 and 1,800 hours. An employee who works fewer than the required number of hours in a given year usually receives some proportionate credit for the actual hours worked. Federal tax law requires that a proportionate credit be given if the employee is credited with at least 1,000 hours of service in the 12-month computation period used by the plan.

Some plans limit benefits to service performed after the plan became effective, although in most cases credit is given for service prior to the inception of the plan. When this is done, credit may or may not be given for service needed to meet any eligibility requirements of the plan. Also, it is not uncommon to include a provision that limits the total service that may be credited for benefit purposes to a period such as 30 years.

Percentage of Earnings per Year of Service Formula

A formula that gives specific recognition for service as well as earnings is considered by many pension practitioners to produce the most equitable results in terms of a benefit formula that provides benefits for employees in relation to their value or contributions to the firm. A formula producing this result often is called a *unit credit* or *past and future service formula.* Under such a formula, an employee receives a benefit credit equal to a **percentage of earnings per year of service** for each year that he or she is a participant under the plan. This benefit credit is called the employee's "future service" or "current service" benefit. The percentage of earnings credited varies from plan to plan, but a typical percentage would be 1 percent or 1.25 percent. It may be used with either career-average or final earnings, and it works particularly well with career-average plans.

Many plans also include a "past service" benefit for employees who enter the plan on its effective date. In a plan that bases future service benefits on career-average earnings, the past service benefit is usually expressed as a fixed percentage of the employee's earnings on the effective date of the plan multiplied by the employee's years of past service. In determining past service benefits, however, it is customary to exclude service that would have been required to join the plan had it always been in effect. It also is possible to limit the total years of past service credited. For example, past service could be limited to a given number of years (such as 10); to service completed after a certain calendar year (such as the year in which the firm was acquired by the current ownership interests); to service completed after attaining a certain age (such as 21); or to a combination of these factors. The percentage applied to earnings to determine past service benefits is usually a lower rate than is applied for future service benefits. The reason for this is that the earnings of an employee on the effective date of the plan generally are higher than the average of the employee's earnings over the period of his or her past service. Rather than determine the employee's actual average earnings during his or her past service, which is often difficult or even impossible because of the lack of records, a rough approximation is made by reducing the percentage applicable to the employee's higher earnings at the time the plan is established.

If the plan bases benefits on final earnings, a distinction usually is not made between past and future service benefits. Here, the employee's total service (subject to any limitations such as a maximum service credit provision or excluding service needed to meet eligibility requirements) is applied to the percentage of final earnings to determine the total retirement benefit.

Variable Benefit Formulas

Variable benefit plans are designed to protect against the effects of inflation on a retired employee's pension benefit. They take either of two general forms: (*a*) the benefit varies to reflect changes in the value of a specific portfolio of common stocks and similar investments, or (*b*) the benefit varies to reflect changes in a recognized cost-of-living index such as that published by the Bureau of Labor Statistics. In either case, the plan attempts to adjust benefits to keep an employee's purchasing power on a relatively level basis. These plans are discussed in detail later in this chapter.

Integration with Social Security

For most individuals, retirement income will be derived from both Social Security and private pension plans. Since the employer bears part of the cost of Social Security benefits, it is only logical for the employer to recognize this source of benefits when designing the benefit formula of its retirement plan. Moreover, Social Security favors the lower paid, providing a much higher level of income replacement for individuals at low income levels than it does for those who are highly paid. This difference in the relative value of Social Security benefits by income level is accentuated when replacement ratios are compared on an after-tax basis—Social Security benefits are not taxed at all for individuals with low income; by contrast, up to 85 percent of Social Security benefits are taxable to the highly paid.

For these reasons, most pay-related defined benefit plans are integrated in some fashion with Social Security. This approach is sanctioned by federal tax law, but stringent rules must be followed to prevent the plan from discriminating in favor of the highly paid.

There are, in general, two ways for integrating a benefit plan and Social Security benefits. The first approach—the "excess" method—provides a benefit for pay over a stipulated level (the integration level) that is higher than that provided for pay below this level. The second approach—the "offset" method—provides that the employee's gross plan benefit is reduced by some amount representing all or part of the employer-provided portion of the employee's Social Security benefit.

The following is a very brief summary of how the integration rules affect defined benefit plans. These rules are discussed in greater detail in Chapter 4.[4]

• **Excess plans.** The accrual rate for pay above the plan's integration level cannot be more than two times the accrual rate for pay below this level. In addition, the spread between these accrual rates cannot exceed a "permitted disparity"—three-quarters of 1 percent for each year of participation up to a maximum of 35 years, or a maximum spread of 26¼ percent. The integration level may be any amount up to the Social Security taxable wage base at the beginning of the plan year. The permitted disparity will be reduced, however, if the plan's integration level exceeds the

---

[4] Also, see James G. Durfee, Russell E. Hall, Christian L. Lindgren, Frances G. Sieller, and John Woyke, *A Guide to the Final Nondiscrimination Requirements* (New York: Research Institute of America, January 1994).

Social Security–covered compensation level—the average of the Social Security taxable wage bases for the preceding 35 years. The permitted disparity also is reduced for early retirement (before the Social Security full-benefit retirement age).

• **Offset plans.** The gross plan benefit cannot be reduced by more than 50 percent. Also, the offset cannot exceed three-quarters of 1 percent of final average pay up to the Social Security–covered compensation level, multiplied by years of service up to a maximum of 35 years. The three-quarters of 1 percent factor will be reduced if the offset is based on pay above the Social Security–covered compensation level and for early retirement.

A plan that does not meet these integration requirements may still be able to achieve a qualified status by demonstrating that contributions or benefits, or both, do not discriminate in favor of the highly compensated employees under the general nondiscrimination requirements of Section 401(a)(4) of the IRC.

Minimum Benefits

Closely related to the choice of an adequate benefit formula is the question of whether provision for a minimum pension should be included in the plan.

A minimum pension provision is generally a desirable feature of any pension plan. It is often possible for a benefit formula to produce a very small pension benefit as applied to certain employees. The use of a minimum pension can result in the payment of at least a minimum amount to these employees, while at the same time avoiding the embarrassment and ill will that might otherwise be generated in these situations. Apart from these considerations, if the plan is insured, the insurer may insist on the inclusion of a minimum pension provision as part of its general underwriting requirements—particularly in the case of a plan funded with individual policies.

Death Benefits

An employer-provided death benefit is an optional benefit under a pension plan; however, a great many plans include such a benefit.[5] Broadly speaking, such a death benefit may take one of two forms. The first consists of life insurance provided under some form of individual policy or group life insurance contract issued by an insurer, and the second consists of cash distributions from plan assets. Death benefits also may be classified as being payable in the event of death either before or after retirement.

Death benefits provided under individual policy plans and death benefits provided from plan assets are considered a part of the plan and, as such, are subject to the requirement of the Internal Revenue Service that the death benefit must be "incidental." In a defined benefit plan using life insurance, the incidental test is satisfied

---

[5] In the case of a married participant, a qualified retirement plan is required to provide a death benefit to the participant's surviving spouse unless an election and consent to waive such benefits has been made. However, the employer is not required to pay the cost of providing this benefit.

if the benefit does not exceed 100 times the expected monthly pension benefit or, if greater, the reserve for the pension benefit. The incidental test is not violated if the death benefit does not exceed the sum of the reserve of the life insurance policy and the amount held for the employee in the conversion fund. Also, as long as less than 50 percent of the employer's contributions for an employee have been used to purchase life insurance, the face amount of the life insurance plus the employee's share of the conversion fund may be paid as the death benefit under a defined benefit plan without violating the incidental death benefit rules.

A plan may provide both a lump-sum preretirement death benefit and the qualified preretirement survivor annuity (QPSA) required by law,[6] as long as the incidental death benefits rule is not violated. A plan under which the only preretirement death benefit is a QPSA satisfies the incidental death benefits rule. However, a QPSA is considered an integral part of a preretirement death benefit. Thus, for defined benefit plans, the QPSA must be considered with other preretirement benefits to determine whether the benefits provided are incidental. A plan that provides a lump-sum preretirement death benefit equal to 100 times the monthly annuity amount and a QPSA violates the incidental death benefits rule.[7]

According to Revenue Ruling 85–15, however, there are several amendments that would enable a plan with a lump-sum preretirement death benefit to satisfy the incidental death benefits requirement. For example, the plan could offset the (otherwise) incidental preretirement death benefit by the value of the QPSA. In this regard, if life insurance contracts are purchased by the plan to provide the lump-sum preretirement death benefit, the proceeds could be paid to the plan's trust with the trust providing the QPSA to the surviving spouse and the excess, if any, of the lump-sum preretirement death benefit over the value of the QPSA to the participant's beneficiary (who could also be the surviving spouse).

Disability Benefits

In the pension area, disability benefits, even in insured plans, generally have been provided on a self-insured basis; that is, the benefits are paid in some form directly from plan assets, and the employer's experience in this regard is reflected in the cost level of the plan.

A number of pension plans, particularly those funded with individual policies, provide for full vesting if an employee becomes totally and permanently disabled. Other plans treat such a disability as an early retirement if the employee has completed some minimum period of service or participation in the plan and has attained some minimum age. Unfortunately, the disability benefits provided under such provisions are either nonexistent or inadequate for disabilities occurring at younger ages.

[6] See Chapter 5 for a discussion of this required benefit.
[7] Rev. Rul. 85–15. Since the lump-sum preretirement death benefit already equals the maximum amount considered "incidental," the addition of a preretirement survivor annuity would cause the plan's total preretirement death benefit to violate Internal Revenue Service regulations.

Some group pension and trust fund plans, however—particularly union-negotiated plans—provide for a separate and distinct benefit in the event of total and permanent disability. The benefit provided under such plans sometimes is a specified dollar amount, a specified percentage of earnings, or an amount equal to the employee's accrued or projected pension credits (with or without actuarial reduction). Often, the disability benefit under the plan is integrated with benefits available under government plans such as worker's compensation or Social Security benefits. Sometimes, the plan provides that the disability benefit will terminate when the employee reaches normal retirement age, at which time the accrued normal pension benefit will be payable.[8]

Most plans continue to accumulate pension credits during disability and while long-term disability benefits are being paid. If the pension benefit is based on the participant's salary, additional credits often are frozen at the level of the predisability salary.

The Impact of Inflation on Pensioner Income[9]

Everyone, in one way or another, bears the burden of inflation. For many individuals, this burden can be lightened or even eliminated by improvements in pay, investment opportunities, changes in lifestyle, and the like. One segment of the population, however—pensioners who are living on a fixed income—has limited opportunity to counteract the effects of inflation and, as a result, can suffer to a greater extent than those who are still actively employed or those who have accumulated independent wealth.

The rate of inflation has slowed to a considerable extent in recent years. Even so, the general expectations that inflation will continue, at least to some extent, and that the number of years employees will spend in retirement will increase (as a result of recent trends in early retirement and increases in life expectancy), make it important to consider the needs of the retired population. It also is significant that the size of this population is increasing not only in numbers, but also as a percentage of the total population.

Inflation affects pensioners not only in the period following retirement but also during the period of active employment while their pensions are being accrued. The following discusses, first, the plan design approaches used to counteract the effect of preretirement inflation and, second, approaches used to offset postretirement inflation.

Preretirement Inflation

As noted earlier, employer commitments to provide private plan retirement benefits vary from none at all to the replacement of a substantial part of an employee's pay determined at or shortly before retirement.

---

[8] It would seem such a provision is consistent with the Age Discrimination in Employment Act, as amended in 1986. However, the Department of Labor and the Equal Employment Opportunity Commission have indicated, in their opinion, such a provision might be in violation of the law concerning disabilities occurring after age 60—where the continuation of some disability income benefit might have to be provided for some period after age 65.

[9] The material in this section is based on material prepared by Towers Perrin. All rights reserved.

If an employer's plan provides a specific amount of retirement benefit, the amount of this benefit is expressed either as a dollar amount or in relation to the employee's pay. If pay related, the benefit may be determined as a percentage of pay averaged over the employee's career or over a relatively short period such as three or five years—often the high three- or five-year average during the last 10 years of employment.

Dollar amount plans (e.g., plans that provide a benefit such as $30 per month per year of service) do not directly reflect inflation because they are not pay related. However, these plans are typically union negotiated and, in practice, the dollar amount is increased periodically via the collective bargaining process. Thus, in fact, these plans tend to provide initial retirement benefits that allow for preretirement inflationary trends. Of course, the extent to which this is so for any specific pensioner will depend upon the time of actual retirement and the dollar level then in effect for benefits under the plan.

Those plans that base benefits on final pay provide a retiring employee with an initial benefit that reflects inflation that has taken place prior to retirement. In fact, the majority of the nonnegotiated defined benefit plans in effect today use some form of final-pay base to determine benefits and thus recognize most of the inflation that takes place prior to retirement. The use of a five-year average for this purpose has been quite common. Because most of these plans are noncontributory, the cost of accommodating **preretirement inflation** is being borne primarily by employers. This cost becomes dramatically evident in inflationary periods as total pension plan costs rise, relative to payroll costs, because of pay movement in excess of that anticipated.

Some employers have chosen to develop benefit and cost commitments on the basis of career-pay plans. These plans, of course, reflect some part of the inflation that takes place prior to retirement. However, unless the rates of accrual are set unusually high, or the employer has updated the benefits that have accrued for employees, or the plan also has a minimum benefit formula based on final pay, the initial level of benefit provided for a pensioner will not fully reflect the inflation that has taken place during a working career. In many situations, employers periodically update career-pay plans by recalculating accrued benefits on the basis of then-current pay. Although the career-pay approach, with periodic updates, provides less assurance to employees than the final-pay approach concerning the adequacy of their benefits, there are definite advantages to the employer. First, the employer retains control over the timing and extent to which the cost of inflation is assumed. Second, the employer also receives credit for making periodic benefit improvements.

Postretirement Inflation

The techniques used to adjust benefits for employees who have already retired may be automatic or nonautomatic. The automatic adjustments for **postretirement inflation** provide for increases, at stated intervals, that are related to some form of index such as the consumer price index (CPI) or to rates of return on an investment fund. The nonautomatic increases are provided on an irregular basis, at the employer's discretion, with the amount of increase determined in a variety of ways. The following discusses and evaluates these different techniques.

Automatic Adjustments

Four basic forms of automatic adjustment techniques have been used for making postretirement benefit changes:

1. Equity pensions

2. Cost-of-living formulas

3. Wage-related formulas

4. Specified percentage formulas

Equity Pensions An **equity pension,** often called a variable annuity, provides retirement income that varies in dollar amounts to reflect the investment results of an underlying fund of common stocks. The equity feature (usually affecting only a portion of the retirement income amount) may operate during the years of active employment as well as during the postretirement payout period. In either case, the assumption is that stock price movement will vary with the movement of all other prices and, hence, reflect the general level of inflation. Proponents of the equity pension approach argue that active employees and pensioners have some assurance their retirement income will fluctuate with the general level of economic activity. Calculations of stock market performance have indicated that only in a few periods would the pensioner have been better off with fixed-dollar retirement income. Also, from the employer's standpoint, the cost of equity pensions can be predicted beforehand. This is because the risk of potential investment gains and losses has been shifted to plan participants. Another potential advantage to the employer is that equity pensions may eliminate or reduce the need for other pension benefit liberalizations. Finally, an equity pension plan, at least during a rising market, could prove to be popular with employees, particularly where preretirement accruals are geared to stock performance.

Despite these points, equity pensions have some disadvantages:

1. Employees and/or pensioners are required to assume the risk of investment loss as well as the reward of investment gain. It is questionable whether individuals at lower income levels should be asked to assume this risk/reward situation for an item that constitutes an important part of their economic security.

2. The downward fluctuations in pension payments, which invariably occur from time to time, may cause hardship for pensioners. Recognizing this problem, employers may limit the amount of annual downward (or upward) adjustment through the use of a securities fluctuation reserve.

3. Equity pensions are more complicated than fixed-dollar pensions and are often more difficult to explain than other methods of adjusting pensions. This could be particularly important in a situation where the employer's fund fails to perform as well as recognized equity indexes.

4. If the objective is to have an employee's retirement income vary directly with cost- or standard-of-living changes, equity pensions may not be appropriate in the

timing and magnitude of the pension fluctuations. At best, equity pensions are only an indirect means of relating retirement income to economic trends. At worst, and particularly over the short term, equity pensions may result in decreasing pension amounts during periods of rampant inflation.

5. From the employer's viewpoint, the equity pension approach may, in fact, produce additional or unnecessary costs. If the value of equities increases faster than the cost of living, benefits will be greater than may be needed to maintain the original income-replacement ratios of pensioners. At the same time, the excess investment return that causes this result will not be available to reduce employer costs. On the other hand, if the cost of living outpaces the performance of the equity market, the employer may very well feel the need to assume the additional cost of providing some form of supplemental benefit for pensioners. Thus, the employer reaps none of the gain of superior investment performance and might become involved in the cost of underwriting this performance when it falls short of cost-of-living changes.

Cost-of-Living Formulas   A direct approach to automatic pension adjustments involves linking retirement income amounts by formula to upward (and in some cases, downward) changes in a cost-of-living or price index such as the CPI. Under these plans, pension amounts increase periodically, subject to limits, if the increase in the price index equals or exceeds a predetermined level. The major advantages of this approach are that employees have advance assurance their retirement income will be adjusted periodically to help preserve their purchasing power and that the CPI, used almost exclusively in such plans, is well known and at least partially understood by most employees. Consequently, the employer has a good chance of avoiding criticism that the pension adjustment technique is faulty.

The following are possible disadvantages:

1. The employer assumes a largely undeterminable future liability tied to a government index over which it has no control. (However, the adjustment formula may be designed to provide ceilings on the amount of the increase in benefits and thus the maximum additional costs that are assumed.)

2. No allowance is made for any rising standard of living that may be experienced by active employees.

3. The CPI may, in fact, overstate rates of inflation and the presumed needs of pensioners, thus resulting in additional and unnecessary costs.

4. The tax law requires that any automatic increases be given to vested terminations—individuals for whom the employer may feel little or no continuing obligation.

5. If the pension plan provides for subsidized early retirement benefits, the cost of this subsidization very possibly will increase because the assurance of protection against inflation will most likely cause an increase in the incidence of early retirement.

6. Providing automatic cost-of-living adjustments for pensioners could create pressure to follow the same approach (i.e., automatic cost-of-living adjustments for wages) for active employees.

The cost implications of providing automatic cost-of-living increases for pensioners can be quite significant. The actual cost increases associated with such a benefit will, of course, vary from plan to plan and can range from about 8 to 20 percent for each 1 percent annual increase in benefits. Paradoxically, the greater the degree of funding achieved by a plan, the greater the percentage increase in plan costs when pensioner benefits are increased (as would be true whenever any of the benefits of such a plan are increased). Also, the greater the proportion of females covered by the plan, the greater the actual cost of pensioner increases. Assuming that a plan is approximately 50 percent funded and that the majority of pensioners are male, one rule of thumb is that pension costs will increase by about 10 percent for each 1 percent annual increase in pensioner benefits. Increases in accrued benefit liabilities would generally follow the same increase pattern. The extent of the increase in accrued benefit liabilities would be different for each plan and would be most significant where existing pensioner liabilities are small compared with total plan liabilities and where females form a substantial portion of all plan participants.

Cost-of-living formulas frequently are found in the public sector (e.g., the federal civil service and military retirement systems, and various state and municipal plans), but they are still relatively rare in the private sector.

Wage-Related Formulas This method involves the automatic fluctuation of retirement income payments in response to changes in some designated wage index. This permits pensioners to benefit from standard-of-living improvements enjoyed by active employees. The index could be one of a general nature, such as the Bureau of Labor Statistics' index of the average wage for industrial workers, or a more specialized one, such as the average wage paid by the individual employer. The former alternative normally would seem most appropriate as a measure of general standard-of-living variations, but it might have limited application to a specific employee group. The latter alternative could have a significant impact on pension plan costs if an employer maintains a liberal salary or wage increase policy. Some governmental units sponsor plans with wage-related formulas for pension adjustments; however, this type of plan is relatively uncommon, particularly in the private sector.

Specified Percentage Formulas Under this approach, a predetermined percentage formula governs the amount of annual increase in retirement income. Unlike cost-of-living or wage-related plans, the company, in a sense, estimates future economic trends and commits itself to a specific increase based on this estimation. For example, the pension may be increased automatically by 1.5 percent a year on the assumption that this increase will offset, at least partially, upward trends in prices. When compared with cost-of-living and wage-related formulas, a specified percentage formula permits a more reliable prediction of plan costs. The primary disadvantage is that no assurance exists that the retirement income increases will actually reflect shifts in the cost of living, particularly over the short run. It is only by coincidence that such a plan would respond precisely to inflation and fulfill employee needs.

Nonautomatic Adjustments

The most popular method of coping with postretirement inflation, and the one that has been adopted by a majority of large, well-known organizations, has been the nonautomatic or discretionary form of adjustment made at irregular intervals and with varying ways of determining the amount of increase provided. Reasons for adopting a discretionary rather than an automatic approach to pension increases include the following:

1. Because the rate of inflation is uncertain, an organization should not commit itself to a predetermined or formula method.

2. Discretionary adjustments have a predictable cost because they remain under the employer's control, in regard to both timing and amount.

3. Both the scope and level of Social Security benefits may eliminate or reduce substantially the need for future retirement income improvements.

4. The employer receives credit for making a plan improvement each time benefits are increased.

One obvious disadvantage of the discretionary approach is the lack of assurance for pensioners that retirement income levels will continue to meet their needs. Another possible disadvantage is that this technique offers no possibility of prefunding the cost of the increases or having employees share in this cost during their active employment.

The discretionary adjustment techniques most frequently used are either fixed-percentage, or flat-dollar formulas, or a combination of the two.

A **fixed-percentage increase** may be applied uniformly to the retirement income of all pensioners. Alternatively, graded percentages may be used with variations based on a pensioner's age group, years of service prior to retirement, or the number of years since retirement date or the last pensioner increase. In a few instances, the pension increase may be limited to a defined "subsistence" income group—that is, a percentage increase may be applied only if a pensioner's total income from the company's plan and Social Security falls below certain dollar amounts. The percentage increase may be at least indirectly contingent on changes in the CPI. Frequently, the increase is subject to a stated dollar minimum and/or maximum; for example, the minimum monthly increase might be $10, with the maximum established at $75 or $100. The usual rationale for having a maximum is that the need for additional income is not as acute for pensioners who are receiving substantial pension payments. However, the higher the level of total pension income, the greater the loss of purchasing power because of inflation. This, of course, is because of the effect of automatic Social Security increases and the significance they have for pensioners at lower income levels.

A **flat-dollar increase** may be applied uniformly or on a variable basis. The latter approach is often used for nonunion, salaried pensioners to provide them with the same level of benefit increases provided for union pensioners.

The choice of formula and the level of percentage or dollar amount chosen depend upon a number of factors, including the cost and funding implications involved; the original level of pension provided; actual CPI movement; changes in Social Security benefits; the timing and form of the last pensioner increase (if any); competitive practices; and the cost and level of other benefits (death and medical expense) being provided.

It also should be noted that nonautomatic adjustments have been negotiated for retired members of a collective bargaining unit. Although these increases are not a mandatory subject of collective bargaining, there is nothing to prevent voluntary negotiations on this issue.

These discretionary adjustments are sometimes made part of the underlying formal plan. At other times, particularly when the formula will not meet Internal Revenue Service requirements for a qualified pension plan, discretionary adjustments are provided as a separate, nonqualified benefit. Even so, such nonqualified benefits are still subject to the labor provisions of ERISA unless they qualify for the exemptions provided.

Although the nonqualified approach has the advantage of permitting flexibility in the design of the formula, it has potential funding disadvantages; for example, the liability for the increase must be funded on a current disbursement basis over the remaining lifetimes of the pensioners, and there is no ability to vary this funding level from year to year without affecting the benefits payable to pensioners. (However, the possibility of some overall funding flexibility is available if the funded position of the underlying formal plan is such that its funding level can be reduced to reflect payments being made under the nonqualified supplement.) Although the same rate of funding probably is desirable if the benefit is funded as part of the formal plan, the flexibility does exist for amortizing this additional liability over as much as a 30-year period.

Chapter Summary

- A major question the employer must resolve is whether employees will be required to make contributions toward the cost of plan benefits. Sound arguments may be presented for both contributory and noncontributory plans, although the ability of the employer or employees to pay is often the controlling factor. In any event, the trend is clearly in the direction of noncontributory plans, at least in the case of defined benefit plans.

- The normal retirement age in most plans is 65. The choice of this age was influenced not only by the fact that this was the original age at which full Social Security benefits commenced but also that retiring employees before age 65 with full benefits often produces prohibitive costs. Federal law defines normal retirement age to be the age specified in the plan, but no later than age 65 or the fifth anniversary of the participant's date of initial plan participation, whichever is the last to occur.

- The formula selected for determining an employee's retirement benefit is a vital provision in a pension plan. The employer's financial capacity and general philosophy concerning the desired level of retirement benefits, as well as the employer's specific objectives as to the distribution of benefits among employees, all play an important role in selecting such a formula.

- A plan will not be discriminatory merely because it uses a benefit formula that provides a larger percentage of benefits for earnings in excess of some amount (such as the Social Security taxable wage base) than it does for earnings under this amount. However, if the benefit formula is in any way integrated with Social Security benefits, certain requirements are imposed to prevent discrimination in favor of the highly compensated employees. The basic concept of these requirements is that the benefits from the employer's plan must be dovetailed with Social Security benefits in such a manner that employees earning over the taxable base will not receive combined benefits under the two programs that are proportionately greater than the combined benefits for employees earning under this amount.

- Death benefits provided under individual policy plans and death benefits provided from plan assets are considered a part of the plan and, as such, are subject to the requirement of the Internal Revenue Service that the death benefit be "incidental."

- Plans that base benefits on final pay provide a retiring employee with an initial benefit that reflects inflation that has taken place prior to retirement. In fact, the majority of the nonnegotiated defined benefit plans in effect today use some form of final-pay base to determine benefits and thus recognize most of the inflation that takes place prior to retirement. The use of a five-year average for this purpose has been quite common. Because most of these plans are noncontributory, the cost of accommodating preretirement inflation is being borne primarily by employers. This cost becomes dramatically evident in inflationary periods as total pension plan costs rise, relative to payroll costs, because of pay movement in excess of that anticipated.

Key Terms

career-pay plan, p. *230*
contributory plans, p. *227*
early retirement, p. *227*
equity pension, p. *238*
excess plans, p. *233*
final-pay provision,
    p. *230*
fixed percentage increase,
    p. *241*

flat amount formula, p. *231*
flat dollar amount per year
    of service formula, p. *231*
flat-dollar increase, p. *241*
flat percentage of earnings
    formula, p. *231*
normal retirement age,
    p. *227*
offset plans, p. *234*

percentage of earnings per
    year of service formula,
    p. *232*
postretirement inflation,
    p. *237*
preretirement inflation,
    p. *237*
Social Security–covered
    compensation level, p. *234*

Questions for Review

1. Describe the advantages and disadvantages of a final-pay pension plan.
2. Explain the various considerations for an employer in selecting the compensation base that will be used in pension calculations.
3. Explain the four basic defined benefit formulas.
4. Describe how defined benefit pension plans may be integrated with Social Security.
5. Describe how preretirement inflation would be treated in (*a*) dollar amount plans, and (*b*) career-pay plans.
6. From the employer's viewpoint, what advantages are offered by a career-pay approach with periodic updates?

7. Describe the potential advantages and disadvantages of an equity pension.

8. Describe how wage-related formulas may be used to treat the impact of postretirement inflation on pensioner income.

9. Describe the advantages and disadvantages associated with the use of a specified percentage formula.

10. Why might an employer adopt a discretionary rather than an automatic approach to pension increases?

Questions for Discussion

1. Summarize the general theory behind the nondiscrimination requirements for integrated pension plans.

2. Assume that you have been asked to prepare a report to determine if the current system of benefit adjustments for private pension plans could be replaced by automatic benefit increases tied to specific price indicators. What are the major points that need to be covered in such a report?

3. An employer asks you to comment on a new concept of providing pension adjustments for retirees. Under this concept, employees are provided with an option to receive benefits in the form of an increasing annuity. Describe the plan design considerations of such an approach and its relative advantages and limitations.

Resources for Further Study

CCH Editorial Staff. "2001 Tax Legislation: Law, Explanation, and Analysis." *Commerce Clearing House Pension Plan Guide* (2001).

Krass, Stephen J. *The Pension Answer Book: 2002 Edition.* New York: Panel Publishers, 2002.

Perdue, Pamela D. "Going, Going, Gone: The Continuing Decline of the Traditional Defined Benefit Plan." *Journal of Pension Planning & Compliance* 26, no. 4 (Winter 2001).

Chapter 14

Cost and Funding Considerations

After studying this chapter you should be able to:

- Explain the difference between the estimated cost and the ultimate cost of a retirement plan.

- Identify the factors determining the total benefits paid under a retirement plan.

- Describe the impact of mortality assumptions on the cost of a retirement plan.

- Describe the impact of turnover assumptions on the cost of a retirement plan.

- Explain the factors that should be considered in setting an interest rate assumption when calculating future retirement plan benefits.

- Describe the impact of interest assumptions on the cost of a retirement plan.

In its simplest form, a pension plan is a promise by an employer to pay a periodic benefit for life to employees who meet the requirements set forth in the plan. For a given pension benefit, the amount of annual benefit payments under the plan depends upon the number of retired workers. The number of retired workers, in turn, depends upon the rate at which already-retired workers die and the rate at which new employees are added to the retirement rolls. Since the average life expectancy for a 65-year-old person is about 15 years, it is quite likely that for some time after the plan is established, more new members will be added to the retired employee group than will be removed from the group as a result of death. Therefore, under a typical plan, the aggregate annual benefit payout should increase for a substantial number of years after the inception of the plan. The annual benefit payout continues to increase until a point is reached at which the size of the retired employee group tends to stabilize; that is, the point at which the number of retired workers dying is about equal to the number of new additions to the retired group.

However, when the employer prefunds the plan, the pattern of annual contributions under the plan will differ from the benefit payout pattern because, as indicated earlier, the benefit payout pattern for a given level of pension benefit is dependent upon the number of retired workers eligible for benefits during each year and will be the same regardless of the manner in which contributions are made.

The objective of this chapter is to consider some of the important implications of funding a pension plan and to acquaint the reader with the factors affecting the ultimate cost of a pension plan, apart from specific plan provisions and benefits. Particular reference is made to the various actuarial assumptions and cost methods that can be used in determining the incidence and amount of pension costs.

Estimated Cost versus Ultimate Cost

The only way to determine the true cost of a pension plan would be to wait until the last retired employee dies, add up all the benefit payments and administrative expenses that have been paid since the inception of the plan, and subtract the investment earnings. The **ultimate cost** of the plan could then be stated as the benefits paid plus administrative expenses less investment earnings over the total life of the plan.

However, no business firm would ever establish a pension plan if the cost of the plan were completely uncertain until the plan was terminated at some date in the distant future. The obvious solution is that, although the specific ultimate cost is unknown, actuaries are able to estimate the ultimate cost of the plan with reasonable accuracy and thus arrive at a level of estimated plan contributions. To do this, assumptions must be made regarding the factors that affect the plan's ultimate cost. In subsequent years, adjustments in the estimated amounts of contributions required will have to be made, based on comparisons between the actual experience under the plan and the assumed experience. Experience more favorable than expected permits a reduction in future contributions. Conversely, adverse experience under the plan requires an increase in future contributions.

The point that pension cost projections are estimates and not actual cost figures cannot be overstressed. A moment's reflection regarding the nature of a pension plan should make this point quite clear. Assume, for example, that a pension plan provides employees with a retirement benefit only after attainment of age 65 and completion of a minimum of five years of service with the employer. It is obvious that not all current employees of the firm would be entitled to a retirement benefit under the plan. Some employees may die and others may quit, be laid off, or become disabled prior to age 65. Other employees may defer their retirement beyond age 65. Also, the number of years that retired workers will live cannot be predicted with certainty. Furthermore, in the case of funded plans, the rate of investment income to be earned in the future on accumulated assets in the pension fund can only be estimated.

So how does the pension actuary make an estimate of the ultimate cost of a pension plan? The first step is to make estimates of the various components of the ultimate cost—that is, estimates of the benefits paid, the expenses, and the investment return expected. The estimate of **benefits paid** depends on three things: the benefit provisions of the pension plan; the characteristics of the participants in the plan (age, sex, salary, and length of service); and the actuarial assumptions used to predict the amount of future benefit payments. The benefit provisions and characteristics of plan participants are unique to the plan being valued, while the actuarial assumptions are determined by the pension actuary valuing the plan. Selection of the appropriate actuarial assumptions for predicting future benefit payments along with actuarial assumptions as to expenses and investment return are discussed in the next section of this chapter.

Once an estimate of the ultimate cost of the plan is determined, the next step is to determine the contributions required to pay for the estimated cost in an orderly manner. One of several actuarial cost methods may be used to allocate the costs to the various years, and these will be discussed in the next chapter.

Choice of Assumptions

Two important points should be made regarding the choice of assumptions for the calculation of estimated pension costs.

First, the flexibility available in choosing a particular set of actuarial assumptions depends in large part upon the funding instrument involved. The greatest flexibility is available under trust fund plans and under unallocated group pension contracts. If the employer has competent advice, the assumptions used will be reasonable for the type of plan and the characteristics of the employee group covered. Fully insured individual policy plans and group permanent and group deferred annuity instruments offer the employer the least choice in cost assumptions, since the insurance company effectively establishes the assumptions to be used by its premium rates.

Second, the choice of a particular set of assumptions does not normally alter the ultimate cost of the plan. The choice of assumptions will affect the cost allocated to a given year, but the ultimate cost is primarily dependent on actual experience over the life of the pension plan. Obviously, the ages at which employees retire or the rate at which they die or leave their jobs is not necessarily the same as the assumptions in these areas made by the pension actuary. The relative magnitude of actuarial gains and losses under the plan will vary, given different original assumptions, but the end result will be an approximately similar ultimate cost picture except to the extent that investment earnings are affected by the incidence of contributions produced by the funding assumptions chosen. This conclusion does not fully apply in the case of plans funded with individual policies. In the case of individual contracts, there is a certain degree of pooling of experience among the whole class of business. For example, the mortality or expense experience under a particular plan is not directly reflected in the insurance company's dividends paid to that group since the dividend scale for individual policies is determined by the experience for that class of business as a whole. There is also an element of pooling in some group plans.

Cost Assumptions

As discussed above, one approach in considering the factors affecting the cost of a pension plan is to relate these factors to the formula for determining the ultimate cost of the plan; that is, benefits paid plus administrative expenses less investment earnings.

Benefits Paid

Number of Employees Retiring

The amount of benefits paid under a plan depends upon several factors. The first factor is the number of workers who will ultimately be entitled to receive benefits under the plan. The number of employees who will be eligible for benefits will depend on four factors: (1) mortality rates among active employees; (2) rates and duration of disabilities among active employees under a plan that offers a disability benefit; (3) layoffs and voluntary terminations of employment; and (4) rates of retirement at different ages. Let us now turn to a consideration of each of these cost factors.

Mortality   The higher the rate of **mortality** among active employees, the lower will be the cost of retirement benefits under the plan. However, if a participant is entitled to a preretirement death benefit, this will increase the cost of the plan, as additional benefits are being provided.

Mortality among active employees can be an important cost-reducing factor in those plans providing little or no death benefit beyond the mandated death benefits described in Chapter 5. This is particularly true for small plans, where a few deaths can have a significant impact on the cost of the plan.

Actuaries generally use the same mortality table in projecting mortality among both active and retired employees. Several mortality tables are available for pension cost calculations.[1] Projections also have been developed to reflect the probable continuing improvements in mortality. Thus, as improvements in mortality occur, or are expected to occur, the actuary often uses a group annuity mortality table with the projection that he or she believes to be appropriate for the given case. Mortality gains or losses will develop from year to year, and the actuary can keep abreast of the experience through subsequent modifications of the mortality assumption.

Rate and Duration of Disability   If a pension plan offers a disability benefit, cost projections for that plan should include a disability assumption. The plan actuary must establish two sets of probabilities in evaluating the cost of providing a disability benefit. First, a **rate of occurrence (frequency) of disabilities** of the nature entitling the disabled employee to a benefit under the plan must be estimated. The rates of disability will vary with the plan's definition of disability, the age and sex composition of the covered employee group, the nature of the employment, and the general level of economic activity. At the inception of a plan, the disability experi-

---

[1] For plan years beginning in 1995, plans were required to determine current liability (a concept primarily associated with underfunded plans; see Chapter 16).

ence projected for a particular plan may be based on insurance company data, the actual experience of the employer, or the experience of a large company in the same or a comparable industry. Ultimately, the plan's own experience may be used as a yardstick.

Having determined the probable incidence of disability, the actuary must then project the duration of the disability. The **duration of the disability** will be affected by reemployment opportunities, which in turn will be related to the nature of the employment and general economic conditions. The duration of the benefit period also will be affected by the mortality rates among disabled workers.

It can be seen, then, that the ability to project future disability rates is a difficult task. The actuary must keep a careful check on the actual disability experience evolving under the plan.

Turnover   Employees who voluntarily quit or who are laid off represent a cost-reducing factor to a pension fund, assuming the absence of full and immediate vesting. Separate assumptions may be made regarding mortality, disability, and **turnover;** or, as is quite common, the plan actuary may use one set of termination rates covering all causes of termination of employment among nonretired workers.

The illustration in Figure 14.1 shows the effect on costs using different turnover assumptions.

The problems of developing accurate turnover rates for a specific plan are obvious. Future withdrawal rates vary among employers and industries and with changing economic conditions. The age composition of the covered group has a significant impact on turnover rates. It is generally recognized that turnover rates for younger workers are very high. Turnover rates also vary depending on the length of service of employees. Furthermore, working conditions and the personnel policies and benefit programs of a particular employer may affect turnover rates in that firm. Last, economic recessions or periods of prosperity may significantly alter turnover rates. During periods of recession, employees will be less likely to quit, while the rate of layoffs will probably increase. The opposite situation generally prevails during periods of economic prosperity.

The concept of turnover is broader for multiemployer plans than it is for single-employer pension funds. In the former, the employee's coverage is terminated only if he or she fails to be reemployed by a participating employer within a specified time period, usually one or two years. In the skilled trades, withdrawal from the industry is less likely than separation from an individual employer. One of the basic assumptions justifying the existence of a multiemployer pension arrangement is the high degree of job mobility of the covered employees. But it also is assumed that there is a tendency for employees to be reemployed within the scope of coverage of the plan.

It is not surprising, therefore, that two actuaries may recommend considerably different withdrawal rates for the same plan. The choice of turnover assumption must rest, in the final analysis, on the sound judgment of the actuary. This judgment is based on the characteristics of the employee group, the factors discussed above, and the actuary's overall experience in pension cost projections. Turnover tables developed to guide pension consultants are of assistance for initial cost calculations, and

FIGURE 14.1 Effect of Alternative Termination Rates

Source: Howard E. Winklevoss, *Pension Mathematics,* 2nd ed. (Burr Ridge, IL: Richard D. Irwin, for The Pension Research Council, 1993).

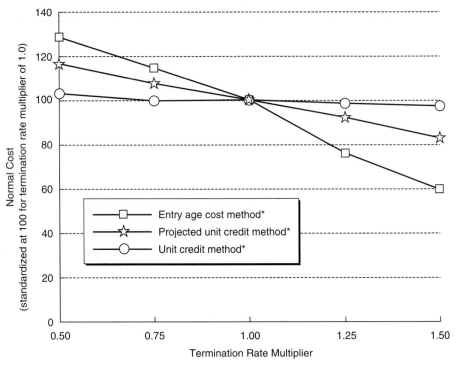

*These actuarial cost methods are described in Chapter 15.

adjustments in assumed turnover rates can be made as the actual experience under the plan evolves.

The question arises whether a turnover assumption should be used in calculating the level of annual contributions to be made under a plan using an unallocated funding instrument when the plan covers a relatively small number of employees. The arguments for and against the use of a turnover assumption in these cases are somewhat similar to the arguments regarding the advisability of a mortality assumption under these plans. Turnover is even less predictable than mortality for relatively small groups of employees. However, those pension planners who are in favor of using a turnover assumption say that there will obviously be some turnover in a plan (where there may be no mortality) and to ignore it is to be unrealistic.

Rate of Retirement In estimating the cost of pension benefits, one must make an assumption regarding the ages at which individuals will retire under the plan.

For those plans that allow retirement at ages other than the normal retirement age, it would be appropriate to make an assumption about the percentage of people retiring at each age (just as the turnover assumption varies by age). However, for practical reasons, most actuaries assume that all employees retire at one age.

The higher the retirement age, the lower will be the cost of a given amount of retirement benefit. For example, if an employee decides to work up to age 65 rather than retiring at age 62, there is an additional three-year period during which the employee may die, with the resulting possibility that the employee will never receive retirement benefits. More important, the requirement of retiring at age 65 will reduce the length of the benefit period. In most plans, offsetting these two factors is the fact that the individual will continue to accrue benefits and hence will be entitled to a larger basic pension.

An actuary generally will use a retirement age assumption lower than the normal retirement age specified in the plan when the plan provides some form of subsidized early retirement benefit (i.e., an early retirement benefit that is greater than the actuarial equivalent of the normal retirement benefit) and when it is expected that many employees will, in fact, retire early.

It is not unusual to find that some employees defer retirement beyond the normal retirement age. Thus, it may be logical to assume in cost estimates that the actual average retirement age is higher than the normal retirement age. This will tend to lower the estimated costs for the plan. However, requirements under age discrimination laws that benefits continue to accrue for service after normal retirement age will tend to offset this automatic reduction in cost. Although not typical, some plans provide actuarially equivalent (larger) benefits to persons deferring retirement beyond normal retirement age. In these plans, no discount should be reflected in the cost calculations for postponed retirements.

Length of Benefit Period

In addition to the number of employees retiring, the amount of benefit paid under the plan is affected by the length of time that retired workers receive their pension benefits (or the length of time payments will be continued under the normal form to a beneficiary of the retired worker after his or her death). The **length of the benefit period** depends upon the longevity of retired workers and the normal annuity form. Therefore, an assumption must be made regarding mortality among retired lives. As indicated earlier, the mortality table used for retired lives is generally identical to the table used for active lives, except in the case of individual policy plans.

Benefit Formula

The last factor affecting the total amount paid under the plan is the amount of pension paid to each retired worker. It goes without saying that the higher the benefit level, the greater will be the cost of the plan.

However, projecting benefit levels is more difficult under some benefit formulas than under others. The least difficult formula is one that provides a flat benefit for all retired workers—for example, a $400-a-month benefit. On the other hand, if the benefit formula calls for a pension benefit related to compensation, cost projections may include an assumption regarding expected future increases in the salaries of covered employees. For example, if a plan provides a pension benefit of 1 percent of final five-year average pay per year of covered service, future increases in salary will increase benefit levels and, therefore, the cost of the plan.

The decision regarding the size of the salary progression assumption is an extremely important one because of its dramatic impact on the level of projected costs. Other things being equal, the use of a salary progression assumption substantially increases cost estimates. The substantial impact on a cost estimate that results from use of a salary progression can be illustrated as follows: If a salary progression in the future is at the rate of 5 percent a year, the employee hired at age 20 for $10,000 a year would be receiving about $90,000 a year at age 65.

Also, in the case of negotiated plans providing a flat benefit per year of service, there is generally no advance provision for future increases in the unit benefit amount, and, in fact, current IRS regulations do not allow an assumption of future increases. It generally is recognized that benefit levels will be increased periodically due to inflationary pressures, but recognition is not given to this fact in cost projections until increases actually are negotiated.

Expenses

The expenses of administering the pension plan must be added to the benefits paid in arriving at the ultimate cost of the plan. The expense assumption used depends upon the type of administration and the funding instrument involved. Under individual policy plans and some group pension contracts, the insurance company includes a loading for expenses in the gross premiums charged for purchased benefits. The expense loading is largest under individual policy plans and decreases considerably under group pension contracts. Additionally, some administrative fees necessitated by ERISA may be charged separately from the gross insurance premium.

In the case of trust fund plans, the employer may pay the actuarial, legal, administrative, and investment expenses associated with the plan separately from the contribution payments to the plan. Nevertheless, these expenses must be added to the amount of benefit payment in arriving at the ultimate cost of the plan, even though they may not be included in the actual cost estimates.

Possible differences in the handling of expenses, then, must be recognized in comparisons of cost projections involving different funding instruments.

Investment Return

The investment income earned on the accumulated assets of a funded pension plan reduces the ultimate cost of the plan. Thus, the higher the **investment return** assumption, other things being equal, the lower will be the projected cost of the plan. The following illustration in Figure 14.2 demonstrates the difference in the amount initially needed to be invested to provide $1 at age 65 at 6 and 8 percent, respectively. For a given plan, the impact of a change in the investment return assumption on the estimated cost of the plan depends on the age distribution of participants and their relative benefit credits.

The investment return assumption used should recognize the total anticipated rate of return, including investment income, dividends, and realized and unrealized capi-

FIGURE 14.2 **Amount Initially Invested to Provide $1 at Age 65**

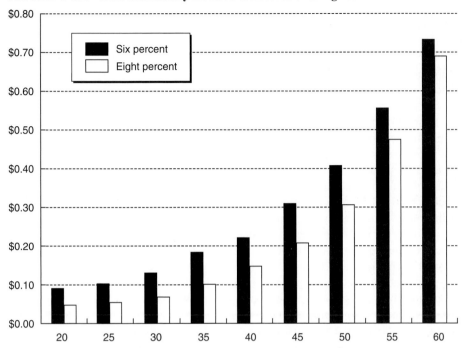

tal appreciation (or depreciation).[2] Therefore, selection of an appropriate investment return assumption should take into account the size of the fund, the anticipated investment policy of the plan trustees, current and projected long-term rates of return, and any other factors that might affect the future pattern of investment earnings of the fund. The choice of an appropriate rate of investment return is particularly difficult if a sizable portion of the assets is invested in common stocks, since these investments are subject to significant fluctuations in value. In addition to having an impact on the selection of an investment return assumption, investments in equities raise the rather difficult issue of when to recognize unrealized capital gains or losses.

For a number of reasons, current market values of securities have seldom been used in actuarial valuations. Two of the most important reasons are (1) market values generally will be relatively high in periods of high corporate earnings, thereby reducing the

[2] Similar to the constraints on mortality assumptions, underfunded plans had less flexibility in choosing interest rates for determining the current liability following passage of the Retirement Protection Act of 1994. Prior to 1995, plans were required to use an interest rate between 90 and 110 percent of the weighted average of 30-year Treasury securities during the four-year period prior to the beginning of the plan year. The Retirement Protection Act of 1994 lowered the maximum interest rate that could be used for this purpose. (The Job Creation and Worker Assistance Act of 2002 expanded the aforementioned range to between 90 and 120 percent for years after December 31, 2001, and before January 1, 2004, for plans that were adequately funded.)

apparent need for contributions (and also the tax-deductible limits) at times when the employer may be best able to make large contributions toward the pension fund (in periods of low corporate earnings the reverse will often be true, with required contributions and tax deductible limits increased at a time when the employer's capacity to contribute is at a minimum); and (2) due to market value fluctuations, measuring a plan's unfunded liabilities on any given date by the current market values of the fund's equities can produce a very irregular funding pattern—the antithesis of the orderly procedure, which is an essential characteristic of a satisfactory pension funding program.[3]

In spite of the above objections, current market values are used in some situations. In fact, the Internal Revenue Code requires that the value of a defined benefit plan's assets shall be determined by any reasonable actuarial valuation method that takes into account fair market value.[4] Generally, the IRS has taken the position that this condition is satisfied if the asset valuation method generates an asset value that is between 80 and 120 percent of fair market value.[5] Obviously, fair market value alone would be an acceptable method.

A number of approaches have been developed to overcome the drawbacks to the use of current market value noted above. For example, to minimize the effects of short-term market fluctuations, a moving average (e.g., a five-year average) of market values may be used. Another method used to minimize such fluctuations is to recognize appreciation annually, based on an expected long-range growth rate (e.g., 3 percent) applied to the cost (adjusted for appreciation previously so recognized) of common stocks. When this method is used, the total cost and recognized appreciation (or depreciation) usually are required to be within a specified percentage (e.g., 80 percent) of the market value.

In 1998 the Society of Actuaries' Committee on Retirement Systems Research began the first phase of a two-phase research initiative on asset valuation methods for defined benefit pension plans. The objective of the first phase was to conduct a survey of asset valuation methods used in Canada and the United States for valuations of defined benefit plans. The objectives of the second phase were to fine-tune the classification system presented in the study, compare and contrast key characteristics of the various asset valuation methods, and assess each asset valuation method's effectiveness in achieving particular objectives. Though the second phase of the study had not yet been completed, the first phase classified asset valuation methods into four groups and nine specific methods.

Overview

Historically, pension actuaries have used actuarial assumptions considered reasonable "in the aggregate" while each assumption might not be "individually realistic."

---

[3] William F. Marples, *Actuarial Aspects of Pension Security* (Burr Ridge, IL: Richard D. Irwin, 1965), p. 107.

[4] Money purchase plans must value assets solely on the basis of fair market value.

[5] For multiemployer plans, valuation of assets rules do not apply to bonds (or other evidences of indebtedness) if a plan administrator makes a special election to value these instruments on an amortized basis.

For example, when making cost estimates where the benefit is related to final five-year average earnings, a zero percent salary increase assumption might be used, but the corresponding understatement in costs is offset by a conservative (low) investment return assumption.

However, actuaries now are required to use actuarial assumptions that are individually realistic. As can be seen from the above discussion, the choice of actuarial assumptions has a significant impact on the estimated costs of a pension plan. It must be repeated, however, that the choice of a particular set of assumptions generally has little effect on the ultimate cost of the plan. As with the choice of an actuarial cost method (which is discussed in the next chapter), the choice of assumptions can have an impact on the incidence of plan costs. As gains or losses arise in the future, the annual contribution amount will be affected, even though the ultimate cost of the plan remains unchanged.

Chapter Summary

- The only way to determine the true cost of a pension plan would be to wait until the last retired employee dies, add up all the benefit payments and administrative expenses that have been paid since the inception of the plan, and subtract the investment earnings. The ultimate cost of the plan could then be stated as the benefits paid plus administrative expenses less investment earnings over the total life of the plan.

- The estimate of benefits paid depends on three things: (1) the benefit provisions of the pension plan; (2) the characteristics of the participants in the plan (age, sex, salary, and length of service); and (3) the actuarial assumptions used to predict the amount of future benefit payments. The benefit provisions and characteristics of plan participants are unique to the plan being valued, while the actuarial assumptions are determined by the pension actuary valuing the plan.

- The higher the rate of mortality among active employees, the lower will be the cost of retirement benefits under the plan. However, if a participant is entitled to a preretirement death benefit, this will increase the cost of the plan as additional benefits are being provided.

- In addition to the number of employees retiring, the amount of benefit paid under the plan is affected by the length of time that retired workers receive their pension benefits (or the length of time payments will be continued under the normal form to a beneficiary of the retired worker after his or her death). The length of the benefit period depends upon the longevity of retired workers and the normal annuity form. Therefore, an assumption must be made regarding mortality among retired lives. The mortality table used for retired lives is generally identical to the table used for active lives, except in the case of individual policy plans.

- The investment return assumption used should recognize the total anticipated rate of return, including investment income, dividends, and realized and unrealized capital appreciation (or depreciation). Therefore, selection of an appropriate investment return assumption should take into account the size of the fund, the anticipated investment policy of the plan trustees, current and projected long-term rates of return, and any other factors that might affect the future pattern of investment earnings of the fund. The choice of an appropriate rate of investment return is particularly difficult if a sizable portion of the assets is invested in common stocks, since these investments are subject to significant fluctuations in value. In addition to having an impact on the selection of an investment return assumption, investments in equities raise the rather difficult issue of when to recognize unrealized capital gains or losses.

- For a number of reasons, current market values of securities seldom have been used in actuarial valuations. Two of the most important reasons are (1) market values generally will be relatively high in periods of high corporate earnings, thereby reducing the apparent need for contributions (and also the tax-deductible limits) at times when the employer may be best able to make large contributions toward the pension fund (in periods of low corporate earnings the reverse will often be true, with required contributions and tax-deductible limits increased at a time when the employer's capacity to contribute is at a minimum); and (2) due to market value fluctuations, measuring a plan's unfunded liabilities on any given date by the current market values of the fund's equities could produce a very irregular funding pattern—the antithesis of the orderly procedure, which is an essential characteristic of a satisfactory pension funding program.

Key Terms

benefits paid, p. *247*
duration of the disability,
  p. *249*
investment return, p. *252*
length of the benefit period,
  p. *251*

mortality, p. *248*
rate of occurrence
  (frequency) of
  disabilities, p. *248*

turnover, p. *249*
ultimate cost, p. *246*

Questions for Review

1. What factors enter into the determination of the number of employees who will be eligible for benefits under a pension plan?
2. Describe how the type of benefit formula used may present difficulties in projecting the costs of a pension plan.
3. How does administrative expense relate to ultimate pension plan cost? What are some of the major administrative costs?
4. Does the federal law require the use of current market value in the valuation of securities used to fund pension plans? Explain.
5. Describe the approaches used to overcome the drawbacks of using current market value in the valuation of pension plan assets held in the form of securities.
6. Does the choice of actuarial assumptions affect the ultimate cost of a pension plan? Explain.
7. Explain how the investment rate assumption affects the ultimate cost of a pension plan.

Questions for Discussion

1. Assume that you are asked to set assumptions for a new defined benefit pension plan. Describe the procedure you would follow.
2. How often should the assumptions established in Question (1) be updated?

3. Comment on how you would expect each of the following to influence retirement age: (*a*) changes in Social Security; (*b*) government regulations, such as the Age Discrimination in Employment Act; (*c*) early retirement incentives; and (*d*) cost-of-living adjustments for retirees.

Resources for Further Study

Amoroso, Vincent. "Costing and Funding Retirement Benefits." *The Handbook of Employee Benefits*. 5th ed. Jerry S. Rosenbloom, ed. New York: McGraw-Hill, 2001.

CCH Editorial Staff. "2002 Tax Legislation: Law, Explanation, and Analysis. Job Creation and Worker Assistance Act of 2002." *Commerce Clearing House Pension Plan Guide* (2002).

CCH Editorial Staff. "2001 Tax Legislation: Law, Explanation, and Analysis." *Commerce Clearing House Pension Plan Guide* (2002).

Committee on Retirement Systems Research. "Survey of Asset Valuation Methods for Defined Benefit Pension Plans." Society of Actuaries, 2001.

Fife, Gene. "Plan Actuary: Factors to Consider in Choosing a Funding Interest Rate Assumption." *Journal of Pension Benefits* 8, no. 2 (Winter 2001).

Krass, Stephen J. *The Pension Answer Book: 2002 Edition.* New York: Panel Publishers, 2002.

www.soa.org—website of the Society of Actuaries.

15

Budgeting Pension Costs

After studying this chapter you should be able to:

- Distinguish among the three methods of budgeting pension costs.

- Describe the calculation used by accrued benefit actuarial cost methods.

- Describe the calculation used by projected benefit actuarial cost methods.

- Describe the operation of the funding standard account.

- Explain the basic requirements for deductibility of employer contributions.

Budgeting Pension Costs

The discussion in Chapter 14 set forth the various factors that affect the ultimate cost of a pension plan and how the choice of actuarial assumptions can significantly affect the estimated costs. What is still needed, however, is some actuarial technique to determine how the estimated costs of the plan are to be spread over future years. These techniques are referred to as **actuarial cost methods.** More specifically, an actuarial cost method is a particular technique for establishing the amounts and incidence of the normal and supplemental costs pertaining to the benefits (or benefits and expenses) of a pension plan.[1]

Two approaches have been used to finance pension plans in the past. Before describing the different actuarial cost methods, it might be helpful to review the

---

[1] The terminology pertaining to the actuarial aspects of pension planning reflects, wherever possible, the thinking of the Committee on Pension and Profit Sharing Terminology, sponsored jointly by the American Risk and Insurance Association and the Pension Research Council, University of Pennsylvania.

current disbursement approach and the terminal funding approach. Though these two approaches are basically no longer permitted by the Internal Revenue Code for qualified plans, knowledge of them should provide a better basis for understanding advance funding required by law, which follows.

Current Disbursement Approach

Under the **current disbursement approach,** the employer pays each retired worker's monthly pension as each payment becomes due. There is no accumulation of pension funds in an irrevocable trust or through a contract with an insurance company.

An illustration of the current disbursement approach would be a supplemental executive retirement plan (described in Chapter 20) under which the employer promises all employees with at least 10 years of service a lifetime pension of $1,000 a month beginning at age 65. If no employees are eligible for benefits during the first two years of the plan's existence, the employer does not make any pension plan payments during that period. The employer's pension outlay of $1,000 a month begins with the retirement of the first eligible employee; the outlay increases by that amount as each new retired worker is added to the pension rolls and decreases by $1,000 a month as each retired worker dies. These monthly pension outlays are provided out of current operating income and, in effect, are treated as a part of wage costs.

Terminal Funding

Under the **terminal funding approach,** the employer sets aside for each employee, on the date the latter retires, a lump-sum amount sufficient to provide the monthly pension benefit promised under the plan. The lump-sum amount needed to provide the promised benefit is a function of the amount of benefit assumptions as related to the expected benefit period and the rate of investment return expected to be earned on the investment of this principal sum. For example, assuming mortality rates will occur in accordance with a recent group annuity mortality table and assuming the rate of investment return will be 6 percent, the sum needed to provide $100 a month for life to a male, age 65, is $11,122.[2]

If the mortality and investment return assumptions prove to be accurate, the principal plus investment earnings will be sufficient, on the average, to provide the $100-a-month benefit.

The employer, therefore, sets aside the appropriate single-premium sum as each employee retires. Like the current disbursement approach, terminal funding does not require the employer to make any contributions on behalf of employees who are still actively at work.

---

[2] An expense assumption is ignored in the above calculation, since the authors are interested solely in illustrating the concept of terminal funding. In practice, the expenses of administering the benefit would be taken into account in the single-premium rate charged by an insurance company or in determining the amount to be set aside in a trust fund under noninsured plans, if expenses associated with the plan are paid from the trust fund. Normally, the expenses under trust fund plans are paid directly by the employer, and therefore no expense allowance is required.

The benefits can be funded through the purchase of single-premium annuities from insurance companies, or the employer can transfer the estimated single-premium sums to a trust fund.

The reader should not confuse the concept of terminal funding with the practice of split funding that is prevalent in the pension field. The term **split funding,** as it is commonly used in pension planning, refers to the use of two different funding agencies in administering the assets of a pension plan. For example, a plan may provide that contributions on behalf of active employees are to be administered by a corporate trustee. When an employee retires, the trust agreement may require the corporate trustee to withdraw from the trust fund and transfer to an insurance company the single-premium sum needed to purchase a life annuity equal to the monthly pension earned by the employee under the terms of the pension plan. This type of plan is considered to be an advance funded plan unless the employer is paying to the corporate trustee an annual sum that is exactly equal to the amount of single premiums needed to provide the benefits for workers retiring each year—a highly unlikely situation.

Advance Funding

Under **advance funding,** the employer (and the employee, under contributory plans) sets aside funds on some systematic basis prior to the employee's retirement date. Thus, periodic contributions are made on behalf of the group of active employees during their working years. This does not mean that each dollar of contributions is necessarily earmarked for specific employees. As will be noted in subsequent chapters, contributions are not allocated to specific employees under certain funding instruments (for example, trust fund and group deposit administration plans). Thus, it is true that in some plans using unallocated funding instruments, contributions in the early years may be sufficient to provide lifetime benefits only to the first group of employees retiring under the plan. However, if contributions are continued on an advance funding basis, the accumulated assets in the pension fund soon will exceed the aggregate single-premium sums needed to provide benefits to those workers who are already retired. This excess of pension assets, then, represents the advance funding of benefits that have been accrued or credited to the active (nonretired) employees.

Pension plans operating on an advance funded basis are invariably qualified with the Internal Revenue Service (IRS). An employer generally is not willing to make advance contributions to an irrevocable trust fund unless it receives the tax advantages of a qualified plan.

The relatively even distribution of annual pension outlays under advance funding produces a more equitable allocation of the firm's cash flow over the years. The pension is being provided to employees for the year of service rendered to the firm. Thus, it would seem that the funds available to the owners of the firm (e.g., stockholder dividends) should be reduced by pension contributions in an amount approximately equal to the present value of benefits accruing under the plan. It is true that credit for past service, offered at the inception of the plan, creates a problem. Since the plan was not in existence during those past service years, it is highly improbable that previous generations of owners would be willing to retroactively refund a portion of the funds they received from the firm. The next best solution seems to be to amortize past service cost in the first 20 or 25 years after the inception of the plan. The Employee Retirement Income Security Act originally required that for new plans, past service costs must be amortized over no more than 30 years. The amortization period was reduced substantially as a result of the Omnibus Budget Reconciliation Act of 1987 and modified by the Retirement Protection Act of 1994.

The accumulation of assets in a pension fund resulting from the advance funding of benefits serves as a buffer during periods of financial stress. During a period of low earnings or operating losses, an employer may find it advisable to reduce or eliminate pension contributions for a year or for an even longer period. This can be done in those cases where the pension fund is of sufficient size that a temporary reduction of contributions does not violate the minimum funding requirements imposed by ERISA. It should be noted that this financing flexibility does not necessitate any reduction or termination of pension benefits.

Under advance funding, then, the plan actuary uses a set of assumptions and an actuarial cost method in estimating the annual cost of a plan. Annual contribution payments usually are based on these estimated annual costs. However, it should be noted that actual annual contribution payments need not be identical to the estimated annual costs generated by a given actuarial cost method, nor is it necessary that they be identical to the accounting expenses described in Chapter 26.[3] As will be noted in later chapters, the employer has some flexibility in the timing of contribution payments under unallocated funding instruments.

There are several different actuarial cost methods, each producing different patterns of annual costs under the plan. Having different actuarial cost methods to calculate annual pension costs is analogous to having different methods for determining the annual amount of depreciation of plant and equipment to charge against operations. The depreciation methods that can be used may produce different annual charges, but the total value of the building and equipment to be depreciated is constant regardless of the depreciation formula used. Similarly, the various actuarial cost methods will produce different levels of annual cost, but the choice of a particular actuarial cost method will not affect the ultimate cost of the plan. One important exception to the latter conclusion is the fact that if an actuarial cost method is chosen that produces higher initial contributions than other methods, then the asset accumulation will be greater (assuming a positive rate of return) in the early years of the plan, thereby producing greater investment income. An increase in investment income will decrease the ultimate cost of the plan.[4]

If the choice of actuarial cost method usually has little effect on the ultimate cost of a pension plan (after taking into consideration interest, and so on), what factors determine which method will be used in calculating the amount and incidence of

---

[3] Moreover, the valuation of liabilities described in this chapter will most likely differ from those in Chapter 26 and those used for plan termination insurance purposes (Chapter 16).

[4] More precisely, the timing of contribution payments has additional cost implications if federal income tax rates change, alternative uses of capital vary over time, or investment return rates vary over the life of the plan.

pension contributions? The answer to this question will become more apparent after the following discussion of the specific cost methods. However, the reader may find it helpful to keep in mind that the choice of a specific actuarial cost method is significantly influenced by the degree of flexibility desired by the employer in annual contribution payments and the amount of flexibility available under the particular funding instrument used.

Actuarial Cost Methods

Actuarial cost methods can be broadly classified into (1) accrued benefit and (2) projected benefit cost methods.[5]

As further explained below, the class into which a particular cost method falls depends upon whether, for cost determination purposes, an employee's benefits under the pension plan are deemed to "accrue" in direct relation to years of service or are viewed as a single "projected" total.

Most actuarial cost methods break down the total actuarial cost into the **normal cost** and the **supplemental cost** of the plan. The normal cost of the plan is the amount of annual cost, determined in accordance with a particular actuarial cost method, attributable to the given year of the plan's operation.

Most plans provide credit for service rendered prior to the inception date of the plan. If the normal cost under the particular cost method is calculated on the assumption that annual costs have been paid or accrued from the earliest date of credited service (when in fact they have not), the plan starts out with a supplemental liability. At the inception of the plan, the supplemental liability (also known as the actuarial accrued liability, the accrued liability, or the past service liability) arises from the fact that credit for past service is granted, or part of the total benefit is imputed, to years prior to the inception of this plan. The annual contribution normally will be equal to the normal cost of the plan plus at least enough of a contribution to **amortize the supplemental liability** over a specified period of time.[6] If it is desired to fund this supplemental liability in a more rapid manner (10 years is generally the minimum period over which it can be funded on a deductible basis), larger annual contributions will be required. The portion of the annual cost applied toward the reduction of the supplemental liability is referred to as the plan's supplemental cost. As the plan continues in operation, the size of the supplemental liability normally will change. In addition to normal changes in the supplemental liability that may occur as a result of the actuarial method being used, these changes in the size of the supplemental liability

---

[5] Parts of the material in this section were drawn from Joseph J. Melone, "Actuarial Cost Methods—New Pension Terminology," *Journal of Insurance* 30, no. 3 (September 1963), pp. 456–64.
[6] The minimum amortization amount will depend upon when the supplemental liability was created and may also depend upon the funding status of the plan. See the Minimum Funding Standards section of this chapter for a detailed explanation.

may result from variations in benefit formulas, deviations of actual from expected experience, and changes in the actuarial assumptions or in the actuarial cost method used in subsequent normal cost calculations. Offsetting any increase in the supplemental liability will be any unanticipated increase in the size of pension fund assets. The unfunded supplemental liability, then, is the difference between the supplemental liability and any assets that may have accumulated under the plan as a result of prior contributions.

Accrued Benefit Cost Method

An **accrued benefit cost method** is one under which the actuarial costs are based directly upon benefits accrued to the date of cost determination, such benefits being determined either by the terms of the plan or by some assumed allocation of total prospective benefits to years of service. To determine the actuarial cost of the plan for a given year, the method assumes that a precisely determinable unit of benefit is associated with that year of a participant's credited service.

This method of calculating the actuarial costs of pension plans is sometimes referred to as the single-premium, unit credit, unit cost, or step-rate method.

The accrued benefit method is limited to those plans that provide a unit benefit type of formula based on career average compensation (for example, a percentage of each year's compensation) or a specified dollar amount for each year of credited service.[7] Under these benefit formulas, a precisely determinable unit of benefit is associated with each year of a participant's credited service.

Although best adapted to those plans that use a unit benefit type of formula, the accrued benefit cost method also can be used when the plan provides a composite benefit based on the participant's total period of credited service. For example, the plan may provide a $1,000 monthly pension benefit at age 65 after 25 years of service, or the plan may use a benefit formula based on final average compensation. In these instances, the accrued benefit method requires that a portion of the prospective benefit be imputed to each year of credited service. This requires some arbitrary basis of allocating total prospective benefits to particular years of service. When used for plans of this type, it is usually referred to as the projected unit credit method.[8]

The first step in the calculation of the normal cost under the accrued benefit cost method is to determine the present value of each participant's benefit credited during the year for which costs are being calculated. The cost per dollar of benefit is a function of the participant's age and of the mortality, interest, and other assumptions used. Thus, the normal cost per dollar of benefit under the accrued benefit cost method increases with the age of the participant, assuming that all other assumptions are held constant. For example, using a recent group annuity mortality table, a 6 per-

---

[7] Because of sharply increasing costs, regulations do not permit use of the accrued benefit cost method for minimum funding requirements for final average plans.

[8] As explained in Chapter 26, the projected unit credit method is required by Financial Accounting Standards Board Statement 87 for calculating service cost.

cent interest assumption, and a 5 percent loading factor, the normal cost per $1 of monthly benefit beginning at age 65 for a male employee at various ages would be as follows:

Age	Normal Cost
25	$ 9.24
30	12.41
35	16.69
40	22.48
45	30.39
50	41.45
55	57.31
60	80.70

If the benefit formula is related to salary, increases in compensation also would increase the normal cost for a given participant.

The normal cost of the plan as a whole is simply the sum of the separate normal costs for the benefits credited for each participant during that particular year. Although the normal cost for a given participant increases over time under the accrued benefit cost method, the normal cost for the plan as a whole generally does not increase as rapidly, or may even remain fairly constant or decrease. The reason for this is that some older employees will die or terminate, and they probably will be replaced by much younger workers. If the distribution of current service benefit credits by age and sex remains constant, the total normal cost of the plan will remain constant.

At the inception of the plan, the supplemental liability under the accrued benefit cost method arises from the fact that either past service credits have been granted or a portion of the benefits of the plan have been imputed to past service. The supplemental liability at the inception of the plan under the accrued benefit cost method is simply the present value of the accrued past service benefits credited as of that date. Using the single-premium rates indicated above, the supplemental liability for a male employee, age 40, at the inception date of the plan would be $22.48 per $1 a month of past-service benefit payable beginning at age 65. If the benefit formula provides a $10-a-month benefit per year of service and the employee has 10 years of credited past service, the supplemental liability for that individual would be $2,248.00 ($22.48 × $100 past-service benefit). The supplemental liability for the plan as a whole at the inception would be the sum of the supplemental liabilities for each of the covered employees.

It now should be clear why the accrued benefit method is readily adaptable to unit benefit formula plans. Also, this method generally is used under group deferred annuity plans, since a unit of benefit usually is purchased for each year of credited future service under these contracts. The employer has some flexibility in funding the supplemental liability.

Projected Benefit Cost Methods

Rather than costing the benefits credited during a specific period, one can project the total benefits that will be credited by retirement date and spread the costs for these benefits evenly over some future period. These costing techniques are referred to as **projected benefit cost methods.** More specifically, a projected benefit cost method is one under which the actuarial costs are based upon total prospective benefits, whether or not they are attributed to any specific periods of service. The actuarial cost determination assumes regular future accruals of normal cost, generally a level amount or percentage of earnings, whose actuarial present value is equal to the present value of prospective benefits less the value of plan assets and unfunded supplemental liabilities. From the preceding definition one can see that projected benefit cost methods differ from accrued benefit cost methods in two important respects. First, the normal cost accrual under a projected benefit cost method is related to the total prospective benefit, rather than the benefit for a particular year. The projected benefit methods generally are used when the plan provides a composite benefit based upon the participant's total period of credited service, such as $100 per month or 30 percent of average earnings for the last five years of service. These latter formulas do not allocate benefits to any particular year. However, it may be necessary, in the case of early retirement or termination of service with vested rights, to allocate the total potential benefit to actual years of service or to define the accrued benefit in terms of the amount purchasable by the accrued level annual cost. A projected benefit cost method can be, and is, used with benefit formulas that allocate units of benefit to particular years of service. When so used, the normal cost accruals are still calculated on the basis of total projected benefits rather than annual units of benefit. For example, if a plan provides a retirement benefit of $10 a month per year of service, the normal cost computation is based on a projected monthly retirement benefit of $10 times the expected number of years of credited service as of normal retirement age. If the employee is age 35 upon entry into the plan and the normal retirement age is 65, then the total projected benefit is $300 a month.

A second distinguishing characteristic of projected benefit cost methods is that these techniques generally are applied with the objective of generating a normal cost that is a level amount or percentage of earnings for either the individual participants or the participants as a group. Therefore, these methods can be characterized as level cost methods. A cost method is characterized as level if it is based on an actuarial formula designed to produce a constant year-to-year accrual of normal cost (either in amount or as a percentage of payroll or other index) and if (1) the experience conforms with the actuarial assumptions; (2) there are no changes in the plan; and (3) certain characteristics of the employee group remain unchanged.

However, the actual experience of the plan seldom conforms precisely with the actuarial assumptions used, and it is likely that there will be changes in the composition of the group for which cost accruals are assumed. Nevertheless, these methods are characterized as level cost methods, since the theoretical objective of most of these methods is to produce a level normal cost. By contrast, the accrued benefit cost method theoretically should produce increasing annual costs until the plan matures. However, as noted earlier, changes in the composition of the group may, in practice, result in fairly level normal costs under the accrued benefit cost method.

Projected benefit cost methods may be subdivided into (1) individual level cost methods and (2) aggregate level cost methods.

Individual Level Cost Methods

This individual subcategory of projected benefit cost methods is characterized by the assumed allocation of the actuarial cost for each individual employee, generally as a level amount or percentage of earnings, over all or a part of the employee's period of service or period of coverage under the plan, or some other appropriate period uniformly applied. Under **individual level cost methods,** the total actuarial cost is generally separable as to the various participants; that is, costs are calculated individually for each employee or are calculated by group methods in such a way as to produce essentially the same total result as though individually calculated.[9]

The individual level cost methods may be further subdivided as to whether or not a supplemental liability is created.

Without Supplemental Liability   As indicated above, projected benefit cost methods have as their objective the spreading of the costs of total projected benefits evenly over some future period. One logical period over which costs can be spread is the period from the attained age of the employee at the time he or she entered the plan to normal retirement age under the plan.

The normal cost accruals are determined by distributing the present value of an individual's total projected benefits as a level amount or percentage of earnings over his or her assumed future period of coverage under the plan. Total projected benefits include past-service benefits, if any, as well as future-service benefits to be credited by retirement age. Thus, no unfunded supplemental liability is created under this cost method at the inception of the plan since the present value of future benefits is exactly equal to the present value of future normal cost accruals. Thereafter, there is still no supplemental liability if contribution payments made have been equal to the normal costs that have accrued in prior years. It must be reemphasized that a supplemental liability may be created for other reasons. The point to be made here is that this actuarial cost method, other things being equal, does not of itself generate a supplemental liability.

---

[9] It should be noted, however, that this does not mean that it is possible, at any given time, to identify a participant's "share" in the plan assets. For example, a turnover assumption reduces the normal cost attributable to each participant. However, this normal cost figure is too low for the participant who does not terminate and eventually retires under the plan. Likewise, this normal cost figure is excessive for those participants who subsequently terminate with no vested benefits. For the plan as a whole, however, this normal cost figure may be entirely appropriate. This point should be kept clearly in mind, particularly in those sections of the chapter illustrating the calculations of normal costs under the various actuarial cost methods in terms of an individual participant. The authors recognize the weakness of this approach but feel that the basic nature of each method is illustrated more clearly through use of individual participant examples.

This actuarial cost method requires, then, a projection of total benefits distributed by age at inception of coverage and a calculation of the normal cost based on a set of level premium-deferred annuity rates.[10]

The latter may be determined by dividing the present value of an annuity at normal retirement age by the present value of a temporary annuity running to normal retirement age. For example, assume that the total projected benefit for a participant age 35 at the inception date of the plan is $200 a month beginning at age 65. The normal cost for this participant's benefit would be equal to the present value at age 35 of an annuity of $200 a month beginning at age 65, divided by the present value of a temporary annuity due of $1 for 30 years.

If there is no change in the projected benefits of any employee and the covered group remains constant, the normal cost under the plan will remain constant (subject to adjustment to the extent that actual experience deviates from the assumptions employed). Obviously, this will not prove to be the case in most plans. For example, if the benefit formula is related to compensation, employees will be entitled to larger projected benefits as they receive salary increases. Where salary scales have not been used in the original cost calculations, the increase in projected benefits due to salary increases is spread evenly over the period from the year in which compensation is increased to the year in which the employee reaches normal retirement age. This, of course, results in an increase in annual contributions for the plan as a whole. Also, new employees will become eligible for participation in the plan, and some currently covered workers will terminate their participation under the plan. Since the age distribution and the benefit levels of new employees are not likely to be identical to those of terminated participants, there are bound to be variations in the annual contributions for the plan as a whole.

The reader will recognize that the individual level cost method without supplemental liability is, in effect, the actuarial cost method used under fully insured individual policy and group permanent plans. Indeed, this cost method is analogous to the level premium concept used in individual life insurance premium calculations. For this reason, this actuarial cost method is sometimes referred to as the **individual level premium method** or the **attained age level contribution method.**

With Supplemental Liability   This cost method is similar to the previous method except that the assumption is made, for the initial group of participants, that the period over which costs are spread begins with the first year they could have joined the plan had it always been in effect. For an employee who enters after the inception

---

[10] Regardless of which actuarial cost method is used, there is the question of whether to include in the cost calculations employees who have not yet met the plan participation requirements. One view is that a certain percentage of the currently noneligible employees eventually will qualify for participation in the plan, and therefore the cost calculations should recognize this fact. Some actuaries, however, project costs only for those employees who are actually eligible for participation in the plan. The latter approach generally produces lower cost estimates. Either approach can be justified, but the reader should recognize that differences in cost projections may be due, at least in part, to the approach used.

date of the plan, the normal cost under this method is the same as would be generated by the previous method.[11]

This follows since that employee's entry year coincides with the year in which participation began. In the case of the initial group of participants, a supplemental liability is automatically created because of the assumption that normal cost payments have been made prior to the inception date of the plan.

Using the example cited above, assume that an employee is entitled to a total projected benefit at age 65 of $200 a month. The employee is age 35 at the inception of the plan, but would have been eligible at age 30 had the plan been in effect. Under the individual level cost method with supplemental liability, the normal cost for this participant's benefit would be equal to the present value at age 30 (rather than age 35, as is the case under the previous cost method) of an annuity of $200 a month beginning at age 65, divided by the present value of a temporary annuity due of $1 for 35 years (rather than 30 years). In the above example, the numerator is smaller and the denominator larger than the corresponding values calculated under the individual cost method without a supplemental liability. The result, of course, is that the normal costs are lower under the individual cost method with a supplemental liability. However, since the normal costs have not been paid for the prior years, there is a supplemental liability on behalf of this employee. Unlike the accrued benefit cost method, the initial supplemental liability under the individual cost method does not bear a precise relationship to past-service benefits.

The difference between the two individual level cost methods can be made clear by reference to a situation in the individual life insurance field. Let us assume that an individual, age 25, purchased a 10-year convertible term life insurance contract. At age 30, the insured decides to convert the policy to an ordinary life insurance policy. If the conversion is made as of issue age (25), the ordinary life premium for age 25 can be viewed conceptually as the annual normal cost under the individual level cost method with supplemental liability. The sum of the annual premiums from issue date (age 25) to conversion date (age 30), improved at the assumed rate of interest and adjusted to reflect the insurance cost, would be analogous to the supplemental liability under this method. If the conversion were made as of attained age, the annual premium for age 30—adjusted to reflect the insurance cost—would be analogous to the annual cost required under the individual cost method without supplemental liability.

In valuations after the first year of the plan, the normal cost and supplemental liability would be calculated in the same manner as at the plan's inception. However, the annual contribution would be a payment of the normal cost and some payment toward the unfunded supplemental liability (the supplemental liability less any assets that have accumulated). The normal cost calculation would be affected by any changes in assumptions or plan provisions, while the calculation of the unfunded supplemental liability would be affected not only by changes in assumptions or plan provisions, but also by any actuarial gains or losses since the plan actually started.

---

[11] This statement assumes that the normal cost is calculated in a consistent manner for both the original group and subsequent entrants.

The individual level cost method with a supplemental liability also is referred to as the **entry age normal method.**

Aggregate Level Cost Methods

The distinguishing characteristic of aggregate level cost methods is that the normal cost accruals are calculated for the plan as a whole without identifying any part of such cost accruals with the projected benefits of specific individuals. The cost accruals are expressed as a percentage of compensation or as a specified dollar amount.

The normal cost accrual rate under an aggregate method can be determined by dividing the present value of future benefits for all participants by the present value of the estimated future compensation for the group of participants. This accrual rate is then multiplied by the total annual earnings to determine the initial normal cost of the plan. If the normal cost accrual rate is to be expressed in terms of a dollar amount, then the present value of $1 per employee for each year of future service must be computed. Since there is no assumption that any normal costs have been accrued prior to the inception date of the plan, the above method does not create a supplemental liability.

In the determination of cost accruals after the inception of the plan under the above method, recognition must be given to the plan assets that presumably have been accumulated to offset prior normal cost accruals. Thus, for those years subsequent to the establishment of the plan, the accrual rate is determined by dividing the present value of aggregate future benefits, less any plan assets, by the present value of future compensation.

The normal cost accrual can be calculated under an aggregate method to produce a supplemental liability. This can be done in many ways, but the most clearly understood approach to creating a supplemental liability under the aggregate method is to exclude past-service benefits in the projection of aggregate future benefits. This decreases the numerator of the fraction, thereby producing a smaller normal cost accrual rate. Or the actuary may simply use a supplemental liability generated by one of the individual cost methods. However the supplemental liability is calculated, the unfunded supplemental liability must be subtracted (along with plan assets) from the present value of aggregate future benefits in the calculation of subsequent accrual rates.

The aggregate level cost method without supplemental liability also is referred to as *the percentage of payroll, the aggregate,* or *the remaining cost method.* When there is a supplemental liability in connection with this method, it is sometimes referred to as *the attained age normal* or *entry age normal method* with initial supplemental liability.

Amortization of Supplemental Liability

The actuarial cost methods that create a supplemental liability offer the employer greater flexibility in annual contribution payments than is available under the cost methods without supplemental liability. Under the former cost methods, the employer has the alternative of funding the initial supplemental liability at a pace consistent with its financial objectives and, of course, applicable law in addition to the annual normal costs under the plan. In most cases, the employer makes some contribution toward the amortization of the supplemental liability. The length of the period over which the supplemental liability should be funded varies with the circumstances surrounding each plan and is heavily influenced by the minimum funding standards and the full funding limitation described later in this chapter.

Defined Contribution Plans

The discussion thus far in this chapter has been concerned primarily with the role of actuarial assumptions and actuarial cost methods in calculating the annual cost of a plan. The question arises as to the degree to which this discussion is pertinent in the case of defined contribution (money purchase) plans. In these plans, the employer's contribution commitment is fixed and usually is expressed as a specified percentage of the compensation of covered employees. Thus, it would seem that there is little need for actuarial assumptions and cost methods to determine annual costs under these plans. To allow the employer to estimate future costs or benefits under the plan, projections are required based on appropriate actuarial assumptions and a specific actuarial cost method. In estimating ultimate costs under a defined contribution plan, the actuary could use either the accrued benefit method or a projected benefit cost method, depending on how benefits are defined. Also, under traditional defined contribution plans, the annual contribution on behalf of each employee is viewed as a single-premium payment for a unit of deferred annuity to begin upon attainment of normal retirement age. Indeed, some of the defined contribution plans are funded through group deferred annuity contracts. Thus, the age of the employee and mortality and interest assumptions determine the amount of benefit being credited each year. The amount of benefit credited each year for a given employee will vary with the size of the contribution payment and the number of years to retirement age.

A variation of the traditional defined contribution plan is found in some negotiated plans that have both a fixed contribution and a fixed benefit. Negotiated multiemployer plans are established on this basis. The union negotiates a fixed pension contribution rate with all participating employers, and the rate usually is expressed in terms of cents per hour worked or unit of production, or as a percentage of the compensation of covered employees. The contributions are paid into a single trust fund, and a uniform benefit schedule applicable to all covered employees is established. Actuarial assumptions and an actuarial cost method are needed to determine the level of benefits that can be supported by the fixed contribution commitment. In these plans, an additional assumption must be made in actuarial computations that was not mentioned earlier in the chapter; that is, the expected level of future contributions. Since the contribution commitment usually is related to compensation or hours worked, changes in levels of economic activity affect the contribution income of the plan. The actuary, therefore, must project the future flow of contribution income to determine an appropriate benefit formula for the plan.

The cost method normally used in actuarial computations for fixed contribution–fixed benefit plans is the projected benefit cost method with a supplemental liability. One reason is that this method tends to produce annual normal costs that may be expected to remain fairly stable as a percentage of payroll or in terms of cents per hour if the actuarial assumptions are in fact realized; moreover, this is consistent with the contribution commitment under these plans, which is normally expressed as a percentage of payroll or in cents per hour of work. Another reason is the existence of a supplemental liability, which permits some flexibility in annual contribution income. As indicated above, changes in levels of employment will result in fluctuations in the annual aggregate contribution income of the plan, which may not match fluctuations in the amount of benefits credited. During periods of prosperity, the excess of actual over expected contribution income can be applied toward amortizing the supplemental liability at a rate faster than anticipated; likewise, periods of recession result in extensions of the period over which the supplemental liability is to be amortized. Of course, in both cases, the amortization periods must be in line with the minimums and maximums permitted under federal law.

Minimum Funding Standards

The basic minimum funding standard required by the Internal Revenue Code (IRC) is that a pension plan having supplemental liabilities must amortize such liabilities over a specified period of time in addition to the funding of normal cost.

The requirement for amortizing supplemental liability applies only to defined benefit plans, since a defined contribution plan cannot technically have a supplemental liability. For defined contribution plans, the minimum contribution is the amount indicated by the plan formula. The requirements also apply to negotiated plans that have both a fixed contribution rate and a fixed benefit. Such plans may use the "short-fall" method described later in this chapter.

In meeting the **minimum funding standards,** the liabilities of a pension plan must be calculated on the basis of actuarial assumptions and actuarial cost methods that are reasonable and that offer the actuary's best estimate of anticipated experience under the plan. Each individual assumption must be reasonable or must, in the aggregate, result in a total contribution equal to that which would be determined if each of the assumptions were reasonable.

For plans in existence on January 1, 1974, the maximum amortization period for supplemental liability is 40 years; for single-employer plans established after January 1, 1974, the maximum amortization period is 30 years. Moreover, experience gains and losses for single-employer plans must be amortized over a five-year period. The shorter amortization period for gains and losses was designed to stimulate the use of realistic actuarial assumptions. Changes in supplemental liabilities associated with changes in actuarial assumptions must be amortized over a period not longer than 10 years.

An amortization period may be extended by the IRS for up to 10 years if the employer shows the extension would provide adequate protection for participants and their beneficiaries. Such potential extensions are advantageous in those cases where a substantial risk exists that, unless such an extension were granted, a pension plan would be terminated or greatly reduced employee benefit levels or reduced employee compensation would result.

The Treasury Department also can allow some flexibility in employers' meeting the minimum funding standards of the IRC. In those circumstances where an employer would incur temporary substantial business hardships and if strict enforcement of the minimum funding standards would adversely affect plan participants, the Secretary of the Treasury may waive for a particular year payment of all or a part of a plan's normal cost and the additional liabilities to be funded during that year. The law provides that no more than three waivers may be granted a plan within a consecutive 15-year period; the amount waived, plus interest, must be amortized not less rapidly than ratably over 5 years.

There are certain exemptions from the mandated minimum funding standards. Generally, the minimum funding standards apply to pension plans (as opposed to profit sharing and stock bonus plans) of private employers in interstate commerce; plans of employee organizations with members in interstate commerce; and plans that seek a qualified status under the tax laws. Exempt plans include government plans and church plans, unless they elect to comply with the requirements of the IRC. Fully insured pension plans (funded exclusively through individual or group permanent insurance contracts) are exempt from the minimum funding rules as long as all premiums are paid when due and no policy loans are allowed. Plans that are also exempt include arrangements designed to provide deferred compensation to highly compensated employees; plans that provide supplemental benefits on an unfunded, nonqualified basis; and those plans to which the employer does not contribute.

Funding Standard Account

All pension plans subject to the minimum funding requirements must establish a **funding standard account** that provides a comparison between actual contributions and contributions required under the minimum funding requirements. The basic purpose of the funding standard account is to provide some flexibility in funding by allowing contributions greater than the required minimum, accumulated with interest, to reduce the minimum contributions required in future years. A determination of experience gains and losses and a valuation of a plan's liability must be made at least once every year.[12] The Economic Growth and Tax Relief Reconciliation Act of 2001 (EGTRRA) modified this rule. EGTRRA maintained the general rule that plan assets must be valued annually and indicated the valuation date must be within the plan year relating to the valuation date or within one month prior to the start of the plan year. However, EGTRRA allowed an exception whereby plan assets can be valued on any date within the plan year prior to the plan year to which the valuation refers. In order to qualify for this alternate valuation treatment, the value of plan assets cannot be less than 100 percent of the plan's current liability, (125 percent when a plan changes its

---

[12] Under certain circumstances, the IRS may require an actuarial valuation more frequently. See IRC Section 412(c)(9).

funding-method), as of that prior plan year's date. When prior year valuations are used, information determined as of the prior year valuation date must be actuarially adjusted to reflect significant differences between participants in accordance with Treasury Department regulations. Essentially this rule change allows well-funded plans the ability to conduct annual pension valuations up to a year in advance of the plan year, thus facilitating an early determination of contribution requirements.

Operation of the Account

For each plan year, the funding standard account is charged with the normal cost for the year and with the following: the minimum amortization payment required for initial supplemental liabilities, increases in plan liabilities, experience losses, the net loss resulting from changes in actuarial assumptions, waived contributions for each year, and adjustments for interest in the preceding items to the end of the plan year.[13] The account is credited in each plan year for employer contributions made for that year, with amortized portions of decreases in plan liabilities, experience gains, the net gain resulting from changes in actuarial assumptions, amounts of any waived contributions, and adjustments for interest in the preceding items to the end of the plan year.[14] If the contributions to the plan, adjusted as indicated above, meet the minimum funding standards, the funding standard account will show a zero balance. If the funding standard account has a positive balance at the end of the year, such balance will be credited with interest in future years (at the rate used to determine plan costs). Therefore, the need for future contributions to meet the minimum funding standards will be reduced to the extent of the positive balance plus the interest credited.

If, however, the funding standard account shows a deficit balance, called the accumulated funding deficiency (minimum contributions in essence have not been made), the account will be charged with interest at the rate used to determine plan costs. Moreover, the plan will be subject to an excise tax of 10 percent of the accumulated funding deficiency (100 percent if not corrected or paid off within 90 days after notice of a deficiency by the Secretary of the Treasury). All members of the employer's controlled group are liable for payment of the minimum contribution and excise tax, with a lien on the employer's assets imposed for a deficiency in excess of $1 million. In addition to the excise tax, the employer may be subject to civil action in the courts for failure to meet the minimum funding standards.

Minimum funding contributions must be made on a quarterly basis with the final payment due 8½ months after the close of the plan year.[15] The Retirement Protection Act of 1994 repealed the requirement for quarterly contributions for plans that are at least 100 percent funded for current liability for the preceding plan year.[16] Inter-

---

[13] Plan sponsors are able to change their funding methods with the (sometimes automatic) approval of the IRS. See Revenue Proceeding 85–29 and IRS Notice 90–63.

[14] In certain situations, the account also will be credited with a full funding limitation credit. See Prop. Reg. Sec. 1.412(c)(6)-1(g).

[15] This deadline does not extend the time limit for making a contribution for tax-*deduction* purposes. That time limit is described later in this chapter.

[16] This provision was effective for plan years beginning after December 8, 1994.

est on unpaid quarterly installments is charged in the funding standard account at a rate equal to the larger of 175 percent of the federal midterm rate or the rate of interest used to determine costs by the plan.

Additional Contributions for Underfunded Plans

The Omnibus Budget Reconciliation Act of 1987 (OBRA '87) established **additional minimum funding requirements** for plans that (1) covered more than 100 participants and (2) were not at least 100 percent funded for current liabilities.[17] EGTRRA extended this special rule allowing a deduction for amounts contributed of up to 100 percent of a plan's unfunded current liability to all defined benefit pension plans. The rule now includes plans with 100 or fewer participants and multiemployer plans, both of which were previously excluded from the special rule. In the case of a plan with 100 or fewer participants, however, the unfunded current liability does not include the liability attributable to benefit increases for highly compensated employees that occur from plan amendments that are made, or become effective, whichever is later, within the last two years. The rationale for generally applying this special rule to all defined benefit plans was to give all such plan sponsors added incentive to adequately fund their pension plan. In general, the current liability was the plan's liability determined on a plan termination basis. Specifically, it was the present value of accrued benefits projected to the end of the current plan year, but excluding the value of unpredictable contingent events that had not occurred. The present value of this liability was calculated using the plan's valuation interest rate, provided that it was between 90 and 110 percent of the weighted average of rates of interest on 30-year Treasury securities during the four-year period ending on the last day of the prior plan year.[18] Furthermore, the interest rate was constrained to be consistent with current insurance company annuity rates. Also, the unfunded liability was calculated by subtracting the actuarial value of assets; any credit balance in the funding standard account must first be subtracted from the actuarial value of assets.

When a plan had an unfunded current liability, the charges to the funding standard account were increased by the excess, if any, of the deficit reduction contribution over the net total of the following funding standard account amortization charges and credits:

- Charge for the initial unfunded accrued liability.

- Charges for plan changes.

- Credits for plan changes.

---

[17] The additional contributions were phased in for plans with between 100 and 150 participants. All defined benefit plans had to be aggregated to determine the number of participants in applying this exception.

[18] The Job Creation and Worker Assistance Act of 2002 expanded the interest rate range for years beginning after December 31, 2001, and before January 1, 2004. The permissible range in these years was 90 percent to 120 percent. This change occurred because the Treasury Department suspended issuance of 30-year Treasury bonds. This action caused a chain reaction where 30-year bond rates declined, triggering increased plan funding requirements, higher insurance premiums to the Pension Benefit Guaranty Corporation, and larger lump-sum payments to terminating employees.

This increase was limited by the amount necessary to increase the actuarial value of assets, net of the credit balances, to the current liability.

The deficit reduction contribution was equal to the sum of the unfunded old liability amount and the unfunded new liability amount. The unfunded old liability amount equaled an 18-year amortization, beginning in 1989, of the unfunded current liability, if any, at the beginning of the 1988 plan year (called the unfunded old liability) based on the plan provisions in effect on October 16, 1987.

The unfunded new liability amount equaled a specific percentage of the unfunded new liability. The unfunded new liability equaled the excess, if any, of the unfunded current liability over the unamortized portion of the unfunded old liability, without regard to the liability for unpredictable contingent events. The percentage of the unfunded new liability recognized depended on the funded current liability percentage, defined as the ratio of the plan's actuarial value of assets, net of the credit balance, to its current liability. If this ratio was 35 percent or less, the percentage of the unfunded new liability recognized was 30 percent. For every percentage point by which the funded current liability percentage exceeded 35 percent, the percentage of unfunded new liability recognized declined by .25 percent.

OBRA '87 was designed to have underfunded plans increase minimum funding requirements; however, the changes did not significantly improve the funding condition of many plans. As a result, the Retirement Protection Act of 1994 imposed tougher funding requirements on underfunded plans and prescribed more closely the interest rates and mortality tables that must be used in calculations. The complexity of these calculations are beyond the scope of this text; however, Table 15.1 on page 277 provides a summary of the modifications involved in calculating the minimum contribution.

Moreover, the Retirement Protection Act of 1994 imposed a liquidity requirement that ensures that the plan will have enough liquid assets to cover approximately three years of benefit payments. If the sponsor misses a liquidity contribution, there are restrictions on paying lump-sum distributions or any other distributions that use assets more rapidly than regular annuities.

Alternative Minimum Funding Standard

A pension plan using a funding method that requires contributions in all years not less than those required under the entry age normal funding method can elect compliance under the **alternative minimum funding standard.** Under this standard, the minimum annual contribution to the pension plan would be the lesser of the normal cost determined for the plan or the normal cost determined under the accrued benefit cost method plus the excess, if any, of the actuarial value of the accrued benefits over the fair market value of the assets. All assets, under this standard, are valued at their actual market value on the date of valuation without benefit of averaging or amortization, while the actuarial value of accrued benefits is calculated based on assumptions appropriate for a terminating plan; for example, rates published by the Pension Benefit Guaranty Corporation. Adherence to this standard would ensure that the pension plan would have assets, valued at market, at least equal to the actuarial value of all accrued benefits, whether vested or not. The rationale for this alternative approach is that a pension plan should not be required to hold assets in excess of those needed to meet accrued benefits.

TABLE 15.1 Illustration of Calculating the Minimum Required Contribution under the Omnibus Budget Reconciliation Act of 1987 and the Retirement Protection Act of 1994

Source: William M. Mercer, Inc., *New Rules for Underfunded Pension Plans: The Retirement Protection Act of 1994* (New York, 1994).

Omnibus Budget Reconciliation Act of 1987[†]	
Regular Minimum Contribution	
Normal cost for current plan year	Calculated according to plan's funding method
+ Unfunded liability pre-ERISA or at plan inception	Amortized over 30 or 40 years
+ Effect of plan changes	Amortized over 30 years
+ Funding waivers	Amortized over 5 years*
+ Actuarial losses	Amortized over 5 years*
+ Effect of changes in actuarial assumptions	Amortized over 10 years*
Plus Deficit Reduction Contribution, If Required	
The plan's old liability (unfunded liability on first day of 1988 plan year)	Amortized over 18 years, starting in 1989
+ A certain percentage of unfunded new liability	13.75% to 30%, depending on funded percentage
Minus Offset (but Offset Can Never Bring Deficit Reduction Contribution below Zero)	
+ Unfunded liability pre-ERISA or at plan inception	Amortized over 30 or 40 years
+ Effect of plan changes	Amortized over 30 years
+ Funding waivers	Amortized over 5 years*

Retirement Protection Act of 1994[‡]	
(If additional funding requirement applies, pay the larger of the deficit reduction contribution or regular minimum contribution)	
Deficit Reduction Contribution	
Normal cost for the current plan year	Calculated according to new law current liability method
+ Unfunded liability on first day of 1988 plan year	Amortized over 12 remaining years
+ Any increase in liability on first day of 1995 plan year because of new assumptions	Amortized over 12 remaining years
+ Remaining unfunded liabilities incurred 1988–1994	Employer's option, either (1) amortized over 12 remaining years or (2) 18 to 30% depending on funded percentage
+ A certain percentage of unfunded liabilities incurred after 1995, using new assumptions	18 to 30% depending on funded percentage

*Pre-OBRA '87 amount may be grandfathered into longer amortization schedules.
[†]Any liability for unpredictable contingent event benefits is funded for a period up to seven years.
[‡]Any liability for unpredictable contingent event benefits is funded for a period up to seven years. Use amortization for contingent benefits under old law or amortization for 1995 + liabilities under new law, whichever is faster.

A pension plan using this approach must set up an alternative minimum funding standard account. Such an account is charged each year with the lesser of the normal cost of the plan or the normal cost determined under the accrued benefit cost method plus the excess of the actuarial value of accrued benefits over plan assets (not less than zero) and will be credited with contributions. All entries are adjusted for interest to the end of a plan year. There is no carryover of contributions over the required minimum from one year to the next, since any excess contributions simply become a part of the plan assets for the following year's comparison of assets and liabilities. Conversely, as with the regular funding standard account, any deficiency of contributions is carried over from year to year, with interest, and the excise tax described earlier is payable on the cumulative funding deficiency.

A pension plan electing the alternative funding standard must maintain both an alternate funding standard account and the basic funding standard account. The basic funding standard account is charged and credited under the normal rules, but an excise tax will not be levied on any deficiency in that account if there is no deficiency in the alternate account. A pension plan making this choice is required to maintain both accounts, since the minimum required contribution in a particular plan year is the lesser of the contributions called for by the basic and alternate standards. If a plan switches from the alternate standard back to the basic standard, the excess of the deficiency in the standard account over the deficiency in the alternate standard account must be amortized over five years.

Shortfall Method

A negotiated plan that has both a defined contribution rate and a defined benefit may elect to determine entries to the funding standard account under the **shortfall method.** Under the shortfall method, the net charge to the funding standard account for a year is based on the fixed contribution rate for the year times the actual number of units of service or production during the year (e.g., hours worked or tons of coal mined). The difference between the net charge so computed and the amount that otherwise would have been computed under the funding standard account is the shortfall gain or loss that must be amortized over future years. In general, the shortfall gain or loss is amortized over the 15 years following the year in which it arose. For plans maintained by more than one employer, the start of the amortization period may be deferred up to five years after the shortfall gain or loss arose, but the amortization period still ends 15 years after the gain or loss arose. If the shortfall method is adopted after 1980 (or if the employer decides to abandon use of the shortfall method after it is once used) it requires prior approval from the Secretary of the Treasury.

Deductibility of Employer Contributions

Basic Requirements

Apart from the specific provisions of the Internal Revenue Code dealing with the deductibility of employer contributions to a qualified plan, it is first required that if such a contribution is to be deductible, it must otherwise satisfy the conditions of an ordinary and necessary business expense under IRC Sections 162 (relating to trade or business expenses) or 212 (relating to expenses for the production of income). Also, a deduction will not be allowed for any portion of the contribution for any employee that, together with other deductions allowed for compensation for such employee, exceeds a reasonable allowance for services the employee actually has rendered.

The employer's contributions to a qualified plan generally are deductible under Section 404(a) of the IRC. Expenses such as actuarial and trustee fees that are not provided for by contributions under the plan are deductible under Sections 162 or 212 to the extent they are ordinary and necessary expenses.

Employer contributions generally are deductible only in the year in which they are paid. However, an employer will be deemed to have made a contribution during a taxable year if it is in fact paid by the time prescribed for filing the employer's return for such taxable year (including extensions) and if the employer claims the contribution as a deduction for such year. It is important, however, that the plan be in existence by the close of the employer's taxable year in the case of deductions claimed for the first plan year that begins in such taxable year.

Limits on Tax-Deductible Contributions to a Defined Benefit Plan

Basically, two provisions determine the maximum amount an employer can contribute to a qualified pension plan and take as a deduction in any one taxable year. The first of these rules permits a deduction for a contribution that will provide, for all employees participating in the plan, the unfunded cost of their past and current service credits distributed as a level amount or as a level percentage of compensation over the remaining future service of each such employee. If this rule is followed, and if the remaining unfunded cost for any three individuals is more than 50 percent of the total unfunded cost, the unfunded cost attributable to such individuals must be distributed over a period of at least five taxable years. Contributions under individual policy pension plans typically are claimed under this rule.

The second rule, while occasionally used with individual policy plans, is used primarily in group pension and trust fund plans. This rule permits the employer to deduct the normal cost of the plan plus the amount necessary to amortize any past service or other supplementary pension or annuity credits in equal annual installments over a 20-year period.

The maximum tax deductible limit will never be less than the amount necessary to satisfy the IRC's minimum funding standards. By the same token, the maximum tax-deductible limit cannot exceed the amount needed to bring the plan to its full funding limit. At one time, the full funding limit for defined benefit plans was 100 percent of the projected plan liability. The Omnibus Budget Reconciliation Act of 1987 (OBRA '87) reduced the full funding limits for defined benefit plans from this 100 percent of projected plan liability to the lesser of that value or 150 percent of benefits accrued at the time of each valuation. At the time when the funding limit was based solely on the projected plan liability, plan sponsors were able to consider expected pay increases that workers would receive between the time of the annual plan valuation and their future retirement dates. However, once OBRA '87 changed the full funding limit linking it to benefits that already had been accrued, anticipated pay increases could no longer be considered. The net effect of this change was to reduce the level of funding for defined benefit plans. Following passage of OBRA

'87 the **full funding limit** was defined as the lesser of 100 percent of the plan's actuarial accrued liability (including normal cost) or 150 percent of the plan's current liability, reduced by the lesser of the market value of plan assets or their actuarial value. For the 1999 and 2000 plan years, the limit was changed by the Retirement Protection Act of 1994 to 155 percent of current liability, 160 percent for 2001 and 2002, 165 percent for 2003 and 2004, and 170 percent for 2005 and later years. EGTRRA increased full funding to 165 percent of the plan's current liability in 2002 and to 170 percent of the plan's current liability in 2003. Following 2003, EGTRRA repeals the provision regarding a plan's current liability so that the full funding limit will be the excess, if any, of the accrued liability under the plan, including normal cost, over the value of the plan's assets.

If amounts contributed in any taxable year are in excess of the amounts allowed as a deduction for that year, the excess may be carried forward and deducted in succeeding taxable years, in order of their occurrence, to the extent that the amount carried forward to any such succeeding taxable year does not exceed the deductible limit for such succeeding taxable year. However, a 10 percent excise tax was generally imposed on nondeductible contributions by an employer to a qualified plan. For purposes of the excise tax, nondeductible contributions were defined as the sum of the amount of the employer's contribution that exceeds the amount deductible under Section 404 and any excess amount contributed in the preceding tax year that was not returned to the employer or applied as a deductible contribution in the current year.

Because Congress wanted to encourage plan sponsors to adequately fund their defined benefit plans, an exception to this excise tax for defined benefit plans was enacted into law as part of EGTRRA. Under this exception, an employer can avoid the 10 percent excise tax on employer contributions that do not exceed the accrued liability full funding limit. To avail itself of this exception, an employer can elect not to take into account in determining nondeductible contributions any contributions to a defined benefit pension plan to the extent that they exceed the accrued liability full funding limit. The effect of this election is that any contributions exceeding the current liability full funding limit (in years before 2004) are not subject to the excise tax on nondeductible contributions. Plans eligible to avail themselves of this limit include both plans that are terminated and those being operated on an ongoing basis.

Overstatement of Pension Liabilities

An excise tax will be imposed on an underpayment of taxes that results from an overstatement of pension liabilities. A 20 percent penalty tax is imposed on the underpayment of tax if the actuarial determination of pension liabilities is between 200 and 399 percent of the amount determined to be correct. If the actuarial determination is 400 percent or more of the correct amount, the penalty tax is increased to 40 percent. If the tax benefit is $1,000 or less, no excise tax will be imposed.

Special Limits for Combined Plans

If both a defined benefit pension plan and a defined contribution plan exist, with overlapping payrolls, the total amount deductible in any taxable year under both plans cannot exceed 25 percent of the compensation paid or accrued to covered employees for that year.[19] When excess payments are made in any taxable year, the excess may be carried forward to succeeding taxable years, subject to the limitation that the total amount deducted for such succeeding taxable year (including the deduction for the current contribution) cannot exceed 25 percent of the compensation paid or accrued for such subsequent year.

The 25 percent limitation does not eliminate the requirement that a currently deductible pension contribution must not exceed the amount that would have been the limit had only a pension plan been in effect.

Nondeductibility of Contributions to Provide Certain Benefits

No deduction is allowed for the portion of a contribution to a defined benefit plan to fund a benefit for any participant in excess of either the Section 415 annual benefit limitation for the year or the Section 401(a)(17) allowable limit on includable compensation (see Chapter 5 for details). In calculating the contribution to a defined benefit plan, anticipated cost-of-living increases in the allowable annual retirement benefit *cannot* be taken into account before the year in which the increase becomes effective.

Chapter Summary

- Under advance funding, the employer (and the employee, under contributory plans) sets aside funds on some systematic basis prior to the employee's retirement date. If contributions are continued on an advance funding basis, the accumulated assets in the pension fund will soon exceed the aggregate single-premium sums needed to provide benefits to those workers who already are retired. This excess of pension assets, then, represents the advance funding of benefits that have been accrued or credited to the active (nonretired) employees.

- The normal cost of the plan is the amount of annual cost, determined in accordance with a particular actuarial cost method, attributable to the given year of the plan's operation.

- Most plans provide credit for service rendered prior to the inception date of the plan. If the normal cost under the particular cost method is calculated on the assumption that annual costs have been paid or accrued from the earliest date of credited service (when in fact they have not), the plan starts out with a supplemental liability. At the inception of the plan, the supplemental liability (also known as the actuarial accrued liability, the accrued liability, or the past service liability) arises from the fact that credit for past service is granted, or part of the total benefit is imputed, to years prior to the inception of the plan. The annual contribution normally will be equal to the normal cost of the plan plus at least enough of a contribution to amortize the supplemental liability over a specified period of time.

- An accrued benefit cost method is one under which the actuarial ~~~~ directly upon benefits accrued to the date of cost determination, such be either by the terms of the plan or by some assumed allocation of t

---

[19] This 25 percent limit will be increased to the extent that larger contri~ the IRC's minimum funding standards for the defined benefit plan.

to years of service. To determine the actuarial cost of the plan for a given year, the method assumes that a precisely determinable unit of benefit is associated with that year of a participant's credited service.

- Rather than costing the benefits credited during a specific period, one can project the total benefits that will be credited by retirement date and spread the costs for these benefits evenly over some future period. These costing techniques are referred to as projected benefit cost methods.

- All pension plans subject to the minimum funding requirements must establish a funding standard account that provides a comparison between actual contributions and those required under the minimum funding requirements. A determination of experience gains and losses and a valuation of a plan's liability must be made at least once every year. The basic purpose of the funding standard account is to provide some flexibility in funding by allowing contributions greater than the required minimum, accumulated with interest, to reduce the minimum contributions required in future years.

Key Terms

accrued benefit cost
  method, p. *264*
actuarial cost methods,
  p. *259*
additional minimum
  funding requirements,
  p. *275*
advance funding, p. *261*
alternative minimum
  funding standard, p. *276*
amortization of
  supplemental liability,
  p. *263*

attained age level
  contribution method,
  p. *268*
current disbursement
  approach, p. *260*
entry age normal method,
  p. *270*
full funding limit, p. *280*
funding standard account,
  p. *273*
individual level cost
  methods, p. *267*

individual level premium
  method, p. *268*
minimum funding
  standards, p. *272*
normal plan cost, p. *263*
projected benefit cost
  methods, p. *266*
shortfall method, p. *278*
split funding, p. *261*
supplemental plan costs,
  p. *263*
terminal funding approach,
  p. *260*

Questions for Review

1. Define the following terms: *(a) normal cost; (b) supplemental cost;* and *(c) past-service liability.*

2. Explain the steps in the calculation of *(a)* the normal cost and *(b)* the supplemental liability at plan inception under the accrued benefit cost method.

3. How does a projected benefit cost method differ from an accrued benefit cost method?

4. Distinguish between the individual level and aggregate level cost methods.

5. How does an employer amortize a supplemental liability? Over what time period can this be done, according to ERISA?

6. What are the amortization periods for unfunded supplemental liabilities for single-employer plans? In what situations will variance from the standards be permitted?

7. What are the exemptions from the mandated minimum funding standards?

8. What are the annual charges and credits in the funding standard account?

9. What is the impact of *(a)* a positive balance and *(b)* a negative balance for the funding standard account at the end of the year?

10. What alternate minimum funding standard exists for plans that use the entry age normal method?

Questions for Discussion

1. Discuss why an employer might prefer to use an accrued benefit cost method instead of a projected benefit cost method, and vice versa.

2. Discuss why an employer might prefer to use an aggregate level cost method instead of an individual level cost method.

3. Discuss the factors that might influence an employer's choice of an amortization period for the supplemental liability.

Resources for Further Study

Aitken, William H. *Pension Funding and Valuation.* Winsted, CT: ACTEX Publications, 1996.

Anderson, Arthur W. *Pension Mathematics for Actuaries.* Winsted, CT: ACTEX Publications, 1992.

CCH Editorial Staff. "2002 Tax Legislation: Law, Explanation, and Analysis: Job Creation and Worker Assistance Act of 2002." *Commerce Clearing House Pension Plan Guide* (2002).

CCH Editorial Staff. "2001 Tax Legislation: Law, Explanation, and Analysis." *Commerce Clearing House Pension Plan Guide* (2001).

Parks, John P. "Technical Difficulties: Correcting Pension Provisions in EGTRRA." *Enrolled Actuaries Report* 26, no. 4 (Winter 2001).

Society of Actuaries Research Project. "30-Year Treasury Rates and Defined Benefit Pension Plans." Society of Actuaries, 2002.

www.actuary.org—website of the American Academy of Actuaries.

www.soa.org—website of the Society of Actuaries.

16

Plan Termination Insurance for Single-Employer Pension Plans

After studying this chapter you should be able to:

- Identify the different types of voluntary plan terminations.

- Describe the relevance of an involuntary plan termination.

- Explain the importance of reportable events.

- Analyze the types of benefits guaranteed by the PBGC.

- Describe what happens to residual assets after a plan termination.

- Explain the premium system currently in place to finance the PBGC.

The **Pension Benefit Guaranty Corporation (PBGC)** is a federal government agency created under Title IV of ERISA. In general, the purposes of the PBGC are to encourage the continuation and maintenance of voluntary private pension plans for the benefit of their participants, provide for the timely and uninterrupted payment of pension benefits to the participants and beneficiaries under all insured plans, and maintain premiums at the lowest level consistent with carrying out the PBGC's statutory obligations. The PBGC administers two insurance programs: one for single-employer pension plans and one for multiemployer pension plans. This chapter deals exclusively with single-employer plans.[1]

In 1974, ERISA established a plan termination insurance program for the majority of defined benefit pension plans in the United States to ensure that pensioner benefit rights would be protected (up to a maximum amount per month) in the event of a pension plan's terminating with unfunded liabilities. In 1986, one of the major defects associated with the original design was corrected when the Single Employer Pension Plan Amendments Act (SEPPAA) changed the insured event from that of, in essence, any plan termination to a termination accompanied by a specified event for the plan sponsor.

This change effectively limited the insurable event to an insufficient termination due to bankruptcy by the sponsor, thereby virtually eliminating the opportunity for an ongoing sponsor to exchange the unfunded vested liabilities of the plan for 30 percent of its net worth (an option existing under the original provisions of ERISA). However, it did nothing to change the premium structure from a flat dollar amount per participant. Congress redressed this shortcoming in part by enacting a variable rate premium structure in 1987 that relates the sponsor's annual premium to the plan's underfunding (as measured on a termination basis). Although this change factors the plan's potential severity into the determination of the annual premium, it falls short of a risk-related premium structure that would characterize the insurance if it were written in the private sector. Such a structure would base annual premiums not only on the potential severity but also on the probability of an insured event's taking place (that is, bankruptcy of a sponsor with an underfunded plan). The new premium system also differs from a free market approach in that it specifies a maximum charge per participant.

Another perceived problem with the change in the premium structure in 1987 was that it provided a maximum per-participant cap on the level of the premium. The Retirement Protection Act of 1994 increased premiums for plans with the largest exposure by phasing out the per-participant cap over three years. The 1994 legislation also included provisions designed to strengthen and accelerate funding for underfunded pension plans as well as improve information for workers and retirees in underfunded plans.

Plans Covered

The PBGC's single-employer plan termination insurance provisions apply to virtually all defined benefit pension plans. The following material examines the specific plans covered and then describes the type of pension benefits protected by the PBGC's insurance program.

---

[1] ERISA, and more significantly the Multiemployer Pension Plan Amendments Act (MEPPAA) of 1980, had a major effect upon the PBGC's jurisdiction over multiemployer plans, employer liabilities, and the administrative practices of trustees. The MEPPAA has many implications for almost all aspects of multiemployer plans, especially concerning plan termination insurance and employer liabilities.

Subject to specific exceptions, ERISA Section 4021(a) requires mandatory coverage of employee pension benefit plans that either affect interstate commerce (and in the case of nonqualified plans, have for five years met the standards for qualified plans) or are qualified under the Internal Revenue Code (IRC). The following plans are specifically excluded from coverage:

1. Individual account plans (for example, money purchase pension plans, profit sharing plans, thrift and savings plans, and stock bonus plans).

2. Government plans.

3. Certain church plans other than those that have voluntarily opted for coverage.

4. Certain plans established by fraternal societies to which no employer contributions are made.

5. Plans that do not provide for employer contributions after September 2, 1974.

6. Nonqualified deferred compensation plans established for select groups of management or highly compensated employees.

7. Plans established outside of the United States for nonresident aliens.

8. So-called excess benefit plans established and maintained primarily to pay benefits or accrue contributions for a limited group of highly paid employees in excess of the Section 415 limits.

9. Plans established and maintained exclusively for "substantial owners," meaning proprietors, partners with a greater than 10 percent interest in the capital profits of a partnership, or shareholders of a corporation owning—directly or indirectly—more than 10 percent in value of either the voting stock or all the stock of the corporation.

10. Plans of international organizations exempt from tax under the International Organization Immunities Act.

11. Plans maintained only to comply with workers' compensation, unemployment compensation, or disability insurance laws.

12. Plans established and maintained by labor organizations as described in Section 501(c)(5) of the IRC that do not provide for employer contributions after September 2, 1974.

13. Plans that are defined benefit plans to the extent that they are treated as individual account plans.[2]

14. Any plan established and maintained by professional service employers, provided that there are not, at any time after September 2, 1974, more than 25 active participants in the plan.

---

[2] However, if the assets under a terminating cash balance plan (see Chapter 19) are insufficient to meet the benefit obligation under the plan, the PBGC will assume the unfunded benefits on the same terms as those applicable to traditional defined benefit plans.

For purposes of the last category, a professional service employer means any proprietorship, partnership, corporation, or other association or organization owned or controlled by professional individuals or by executors or administrators of professional individuals, the principal business of which is the performance of professional services.

Plan Termination Defined

The termination of a pension plan should be a clearly identifiable event. Otherwise, it may be difficult to assess if a termination has occurred and, if so, when. Establishing the exact date of termination is important to all parties concerned—the plan sponsor, the plan participants, their beneficiaries, and the PBGC. A plan termination can be voluntary or involuntary. However, the PBGC will not proceed with the voluntary termination of a plan if it violates the terms and conditions of an existing collective bargaining agreement.[3]

During the first 10 years of PBGC coverage, the insured event for single-employer plan termination insurance was simply the termination of the defined benefit pension plan. Because this event is generally within the control of the sponsor, coupled with the fact that the sponsor's liability to the PBGC was at that time limited to 30 percent of its net worth, several underfunded plans were terminated even though the sponsors continued in existence and in some cases even attempted to establish new pension plans immediately after the original plans were terminated. As the financial condition of the PBGC continued to deteriorate in the first half of the 1980s, several attempts were made to legislatively amend the definition of the insured event. The SEPPAA radically changed these provisions in an attempt to preserve the financial integrity of the system. The following section describes the new circumstances under which the single-employer **plan termination insurance** applies.

Voluntary Plan Termination

A single-employer plan may be terminated voluntarily only in a standard termination or a distress termination. Disclosure of the appropriate information is provided through a series of PBGC forms known as the Standard Termination Filing and Distress Termination Filing forms.

Standard Termination

A single-employer plan may terminate under a standard termination if, among other things, the plan is sufficiently funded for benefit liabilities[4] (determined as of the termination date) when the final distribution of assets occurs.

---

[3] It should be noted that this does not limit the PBGC's authority to proceed with an involuntary termination as described later in this chapter.

[4] Benefit liabilities are equal to the benefits of employees and their beneficiaries under the plan (within the meaning of Section 401(a)(2) of the Internal Revenue Code of 1986).

Provided the PBGC has not issued a notice of noncompliance and the plan's assets are sufficient for benefit liabilities when the final distribution occurs, the plan administrator must distribute the plan's assets in accordance with the requirements for allocation of assets under ERISA Section 4044 (described below).

Distress Termination

After receiving the appropriate information, the PBGC must determine whether the necessary distress criteria have been satisfied. Basically, these criteria are met if each person who is a contributing sponsor or a member of the sponsor's controlled group meets the requirements of any of the following:

1. Liquidation in bankruptcy or insolvency proceedings.

2. Reorganization in bankruptcy or insolvency proceedings.[5]

3. Termination required to enable payment of debts while staying in business or to avoid unreasonably burdensome pension costs caused by a declining workforce.

If the PBGC determines that the requirements for a distress termination are met, it will either determine that (1) the plan is sufficient for guaranteed benefits (or that such a determination cannot be made on the basis of the available information); or (2) the plan is sufficient for benefit liabilities (or that such a determination cannot be made on the basis of the available information). The plan administrator will be notified of the decision, and one of the following types of terminations will then be carried out:[6]

1. In any case in which the PBGC determines that the plan is sufficient for benefit liabilities, the plan administrator must distribute the plan's assets in the same manner as described for a standard termination.

2. In any case in which the PBGC determines that the plan is sufficient for guaranteed benefits but is unable to determine that the plan is sufficient for benefit liabilities, the plan administrator must distribute the plan's assets in the same manner as described for a standard termination.

3. In any case in which the PBGC determines that it is unable to determine that the plan is sufficient for guaranteed benefits, the PBGC will commence proceedings as though an involuntary termination (described below) were taking place.

The plan administrator must meet certain requirements during the interim period from the time the PBGC is notified to the time a sufficiency determination is made. Essentially, the administrator must:

1. Refrain from distributing assets or taking any other actions to carry out the proposed termination.

---

[5] For this requirement to be met, a bankruptcy court must determine that, unless the plan is terminated, the sponsor will be unable to pay all its debts pursuant to a plan of reorganization and will be unable to continue in business outside the Chapter 11 reorganization process.
[6] ERISA Section 4041(c)(3).

2. Pay benefits attributable to employer contributions, other than death benefits, only in the form of an annuity.

3. Not use plan assets to purchase from an insurer irrevocable commitments to provide benefits.

4. Continue to pay all benefit liabilities under the plan but, commencing on the proposed termination date, limit the payment of benefits under the plan to those benefits guaranteed by the PBGC or required to be allocated under ERISA Section 4044 (described below).

When two organizations merge, the resulting single plan does not result in a termination if the new, merged organization assumes responsibility for the plan. Also, under ERISA, a pension plan may not be merged or consolidated with another pension plan or have its assets transferred to another plan unless each participant in the prior plan is credited in the successor plan with a benefit at least as great as that which he or she would have received had the old plan been terminated.[7]

Involuntary Plan Termination

The PBGC may institute termination proceedings in a U.S. district court in the jurisdiction where the employer does business if it finds that (1) the plan does not comply with the minimum funding standards of the IRC; (2) the plan is unable to pay benefits when due; (3) within the preceding 24 months, and for a reason other than death, a distribution of $10,000 or more has been made to a participant who is the substantial owner of the sponsoring firm and following the distribution there are unfunded liabilities; or (4) the eventual loss to the PBGC for the plan may be expected to increase unreasonably if the plan is not terminated. Moreover, the PBGC is required to institute proceedings to terminate a single-employer plan whenever it determines that the plan does not have assets available to pay benefits currently due under the terms of the plan. The PBGC may decide not to seek **involuntary plan termination,** even if one of the conditions for such action has occurred, if it deems that it would be in the best interests of those involved not to force termination of the plan.

Reportable Events

Within 30 days after the plan administrator or the contributing sponsor knows or has reason to know that a **reportable event** (described below) has occurred, he shall notify the PBGC that such event has occurred. The PBGC is authorized to waive the requirement with respect to any or all reportable events with respect to any plan and to require the notification to be made by including the event in the annual report made by the plan.

The requirements shall be applicable to a contributing sponsor[8] if, as of the close of the preceding plan year, the aggregate unfunded vested benefits of plans subject

---

[7] IRC Section 401(a)(12).

[8] This will not apply to an event if the contributing sponsor, or the member of the contributing sponsor's controlled group to which the event relates, is *(a)* a person subject to the reporting requirements of Section 13 or 15(d) of the Securities Exchange Act of 1934 or *(b)* a subsidiary (as defined for purposes of such act) of a person subject to such reporting requirements.

to this title that are maintained by such sponsor and members of such sponsor's controlled groups exceed $50 million, and the funded vested benefit percentage[9] for such plans is less than 90 percent.[10]

A reportable event is said to occur under any of the following conditions:

1. When the Secretary of the Treasury issues notice that a plan has ceased to be a plan described in Section 4021(a)(2), or when the Secretary of Labor determines the plan is not in compliance with Title I of ERISA.

2. When an amendment of the plan is adopted whereby, under the amendment, the benefit payable from employer contributions with respect to any participant may be decreased.

3. When the number of active participants is less than 80 percent of the number of such participants at the beginning of the plan year, or is less than 75 percent of the number of such participants at the beginning of the previous plan year. This reduction is tested on a plan-by-plan basis.

4. When the Secretary of the Treasury determines that there has been a termination or partial termination of the plan within the meaning of Section 411(d)(3) of the Internal Revenue Code of 1986 but the occurrence of such a termination or partial termination does not, by itself, constitute or require a termination of a plan under this Title.

5. When the plan fails to meet the minimum funding standards or applies for a minimum funding waiver under Section 412 of the IRC (without regard to whether the plan is a plan described in Section 4021(a)(2) of ERISA) or under Section 302 of ERISA.

6. When the plan is unable or projects an inability to pay benefits thereunder when due. A projected inability to pay benefits exists when as of the last day of any quarter of the plan year the plan's liquid assets are less than twice its disbursements for any quarterly period.

7. When there is a distribution under the plan to a participant who is a substantial owner as defined in Section 4022(b)(6) if *(a)* the total of all distrubutions made to the substantial owner within the one-year period ending with the date of such distribution exceeds $10,000; *(b)* such distribution is not made by reason of the death of the participant; and *(c)* immediately after the distribution, the plan has nonforfeitable benefits that are not funded.

8. When a plan merges, consolidates, or transfers its assets under Section 208 of ERISA or Section 414(1) of the Code.

9. When, as a result of an event, any person(s) ceases to be a member of the plan's controlled group.

10. When a contributing sponsor or a member of a contributing sponsor's controlled group liquidates, institutes a proceeding to be dissolved, or liquidates in a case under Bankruptcy Code or under any similar law.

---

[9] The funded vested benefit percentage refers to the percentage that the aggregate value of the assets of such plans bears to the aggregate vested benefits of such plans (determined in accordance with Section 4006(a)(3)(E)(iii)).

[10] ERISA Section 4043.

11. When a contributing sponsor or a member of a contributing sponsor's controlled group declares a dividend or redeems its own stock, if the resulting distribution is an aggregate amount of stock that exceeds the shareholder's adjusted net income for the preceeding fiscal year in the case of cash distribution or 10 percent of the company's assets in the case of noncash distributions.

12. When, in any 12-month period, an aggregate of 3 percent or more of the benefits liabilities of a plan covered by this Title and maintained by a contributing sponsor or a member of its controlled group are transferred to a person who is not a member of the controlled group or to a plan or plans maintained by a person or persons that are not such a contributing sponsor or a member of its controlled group.

13. When a member of a plan's controlled group defaults on a loan of $10 million or more.

14. When there is the commencement of a bankruptcy case or any other type of insolvency proceeding by any member of a controlled group.

15. When any other event occurs that may be indicative of a need to terminate the plan and that is prescribed by the Corporation in its regulations.

In some situations certain contributing sponsors must notify the PBGC no later than 30 days before the effective date of a reportable event. A contributing sponsor is subject to this advance notice requirement if both of the following conditions apply:

- Neither the contributing sponsor nor any member of the controlled group to which the reportable event relates is a public company.

- The contributing sponsor's controlled group has one or more plans that, when combined have unfunded vested benefits of more than $50 million, and have a funded vested benefit percentage of less than 90 percent. (Unfunded vested benefits for this purpose entail participant and beneficiary vested benefits in excess of the actuarial value of plan assets.)

Provided the aforementioned conditions are met, the following type of events are subject to advance reporting:

1. Controlled group change.

2. Liquidation.

3. Extraordinary dividend or stock redemption.

4. Transfer of benefit liabilities.

5. Application for a minimum funding waiver.

6. Loan defaults.

7. Bankruptcy or similar settlement.

In terms of the method of notification to the PBGC for reportable events, the final regulations on reportable events provide detailed information on prescribed notification methods. If a commercial delivery service—such as Federal Express—is used, the PBGC considers the filing date to be the date it is deposited with the delivery service, provided it is received by the PBGC within two business days. Notices submitted by fax or electronic mail are considered timely if certain minimal information is submitted electronically by the due date and the remaining information is received by the PBGC within a day after the due date for advance notices and within two days after the due date for postevent notices.

Failure to provide a required notice or other required information may result in the PBGC assessing a penalty of up to $1,000 per day against each person required to provide the notice.[11]

Date of Termination

For purposes of Title IV of ERISA, the **termination date** of a single-employer plan is one of the following:

1. In the case of a plan terminated in a standard termination, the termination date proposed in the notice of intent to terminate.

2. In the case of a plan terminated in a distress termination, the date established by the plan administrator and agreed to by the PBGC.

3. In the case of an involuntary termination, the date established by the PBGC and agreed to by the plan administrator.

4. In the case of distress or involuntary termination in any case in which no agreement is reached between the plan administrator and the PBGC, the date established by the court.

In the latter three cases mentioned above, the date on which the termination of a plan becomes effective is significant for a number of reasons. It not only establishes the date the PBGC assumes legal obligation for the plan's benefits, but it also establishes the date for the determination of the employer's possible contingent liability for unfunded benefits (described below). The effective termination date also is important to the participant. It fixes the date on which benefit accruals cease, the vesting schedule position is determined, and the phase-in of insurance coverage stops.

Restoration of Plan

If it appears that the pension plan could be continued even though plan termination proceedings have begun, the PBGC may halt the proceedings and take whatever action is necessary to restore the plan.[12]

Benefits Guaranteed

Even though a plan is covered by the PBGC's single-employer plan termination insurance, there is no assurance that all a participant's accrued pension benefit will

---

[11] Andrew D. Eisner, "PBGC Issues Final Regulations on Reportable Events," *Journal of Compensation & Benefits* (May/June 1997), pp. 13–14.
[12] ERISA Section 4047.

be paid after the plan's termination. The individual participant (or beneficiary) must first meet three prerequisites before the benefit is guaranteed by the PBGC, and, even if the prerequisites are met, the individual still may be subject to specific limitations on the amount of the benefit covered.

Prerequisites for PBGC Guarantees

Subject to the various limits described below, the PBGC guarantees the payment of all nonforfeitable benefits that qualify as a pension benefit other than those accelerated by plan termination. A benefit that becomes nonforfeitable solely because of plan termination is not subject to ERISA benefit guarantees; however, a benefit won't fail to satisfy the PBGC requirement merely because a participant is required to submit a written application, retire, or complete a mandatory waiting period as a condition for receiving pension payments.

There are two additional exceptions to the general rule on forfeitability. First, guaranteed benefits paid to survivor beneficiaries are not deemed to be forfeitable for purposes of the PBGC guarantee merely because the plan provides for termination of benefit payments should the beneficiary remarry or attain a specific age. Second, disability benefits are not deemed forfeitable solely because they end on a participant's recovery.

For a payment to qualify as a pension benefit, it must be payable as an annuity or as one or more payments related to an annuity. Further, the benefit must be payable either to a participant who permanently leaves—or has left covered employment—or to a surviving beneficiary. It also is necessary that the pension benefit payment provide a substantially level income to the recipient, although the leveling could be accomplished in conjunction with Social Security payments. Under certain circumstances, the PBGC also guarantees annuities payable for total disability[13] and benefits payable in a single installment.[14]

The final requirement for protection under the PBGC guarantee is that the participant or beneficiary be entitled to the benefit. This prerequisite is met if any one of the following is satisfied:

1. The benefit was in pay status on the date of plan termination.

2. The benefit payable at normal retirement age is an optional benefit under the plan, and the participant elected the optional form of payment before the plan termination date.

3. The participant actually is eligible to receive benefits and could have received them before the plan terminated.

4. The benefit would be payable on the participant's retirement absent a contrary election.

---

[13] PBGC Regulation Section 2613.7.

[14] The benefit will not be paid in a single installment, but the PBGC will guarantee the alternative benefit, if any, in the plan that provides for the payment of equal periodic installments for the life of the recipient. PBGC Regulation Section 2613.8.

5. The PBGC determines the participant is entitled to the benefit based on the particular circumstances.

Limitation on Amount of Monthly Benefits

There is a limit on the amount of monthly guaranteed benefits insured by the PBGC. The amount is adjusted annually to reflect changes in the Social Security taxable wage base. The original limit was $750 per month, but for plans terminated in 2002 the limit increased to $3,579.55 per month. The limit is in terms of a single-life annuity commencing at age 65 and without a refund feature. If the benefit is payable at a lower age, it is reduced by actuarial factors denoted by the PBGC. The benefit is not actuarially increased when the participant retires at an age later than 65. Table 16.1 provides PBGC maximum monthly guarantees at various ages.

The guaranteed monthly benefit of a participant cannot be greater than his or her average gross monthly income during the five consecutive years of highest earnings (or, if the period is shorter, the time during which he or she was an active participant in the plan).

New or Amended Plans and Benefits

To prevent possible abuses, the insurance covers guaranteed benefits provided those benefits have been in effect under the provisions of the plan for 60 months or longer at the time of plan termination.[15] If benefits are attributable to a plan amendment or to a newly adopted plan, the benefits attributable to that amendment or new plan are guaranteed only to the extent of the greater of 20 percent of the amount of such increase or new benefit multiplied by the number of years (up to five) that the plan

[15] ERISA Section 4022(b)(8).

TABLE 16.1   Illustration of PBGC Single-Life Annuity Maximum
Monthly Guarantees

Year Plan Terminated	Monthly Guarantee Limit at Age 65	Monthly Guarantee Limit at Age 62	Monthly Guarantee Limit at Age 60	Monthly Guarantee Limit at Age 55
2002	$3,579.55	$2,827.84	$2,326.71	$1,610.80
2001	3,392.05	2,679.72	2,204.83	1,526.42
2000	3,221.59	2,545.06	2,094.03	1,449.72
1999	3,051.14	2,410.40	1,983.24	1,373.01
1998	2,880.68	2,275.74	1,872.44	1,296.31
1997	2,761.36	2,181.47	1,794.88	1,242.61
1996	2,642.05	2,087.22	1,717.33	1,188.92
1995	2,573.86	2,033.35	1,673.01	1,158.24
1994	2,556.82	2,019.89	1,661.93	1,150.57

or amendment has been in effect, or $20 per month multiplied by the number of years (up to five) that the plan or amendment has been in effect.

Payments in Excess of Unfunded Guaranteed Benefits

Participants, beneficiaries, and alternate payees under qualified domestic relations orders (QDROs) under a single-employer plan will be paid a percentage of the plan's unfunded benefit liabilities in excess of PBGC-guaranteed benefits equal to a percentage recovered by the PBGC on the total claim.[16] Amounts will be allocated to participants in accordance with the ERISA Section 4044 asset allocation rules. Generally, the recovery percentage will be determined from past PBGC experience. In the case of large amounts (that is, unfunded benefit liabilities in excess of guaranteed benefits of at least $20 million), data from the particular termination will be used in determining the recovery percentage.

Specifically, the amount is determined by multiplying (1) the "outstanding amount of benefit liabilities" by (2) the applicable "recovery ratio." The outstanding amount of benefit liabilities is the value of the benefit liabilities under the plan less the value of the benefit liabilities that would be so determined by only taking into account benefits that are guaranteed or to which assets of the plan are allocated under ERISA Section 4044.1.[17]

In the case of a terminated plan in which the outstanding amount of benefit liabilities is less than $20 million, the recovery ratio is the average ratio, with respect to prior plan terminations under the plan sponsor liability rules, of the following:[18]

$$\frac{\text{The value of the recovery of the PBGC under the plan}}{\text{sponsor liability rules for the prior plan terminations}}$$
$$\frac{}{\text{The amount of unfunded benefit liabilities under the plan}}{\text{as of the termination date of the prior plan terminations}}$$

In the case of a terminated plan for which the outstanding benefit liabilities exceed $20 million, the recovery ratio is:

$$\frac{\text{The value of the recovery of the PBGC under the}}{\text{plan sponsor liability rules for the terminated plan}}$$
$$\frac{}{\text{The amount of unfunded benefit liabilities under}}{\text{the plan as of the termination date}}$$

For purposes of the above ratios, the amount of unfunded benefit liabilities is (1) the value of benefit liabilities under the plan less (2) the current value of the assets of the plan.

---

[16] ERISA Section 4022(c).

[17] It should be noted that this does not limit the PBGC's authority to proceed with an involuntary termination as described later in this chapter.

[18] A prior plan termination is a termination of which (1) the PBGC has determined the value of recoveries under the plan sponsor liability rules; and (2) notices of intent to terminate were provided after December 31, 1987, and within the five fiscal years of the federal government ending before the year in which the date of the notice of intent to terminate the plan of which the recovery ratio is being determined was provided.

Determinations under these rules are to be made by the PBGC. A determination will be binding unless shown by clear and convincing evidence to be unreasonable.

Allocation of Assets on Plan Termination

Priority Categories

Plan assets must be allocated to the benefit categories applicable on plan termination under ERISA Section 4044. This prevents employers from establishing new benefit levels, terminating plans, and allocating existing plan assets to such benefits resulting in the subordination of insured to uninsured benefits. On termination, the assets of a plan must be allocated in the following order of priority:[19]

1. Employees' voluntary contributions.

2. Employees' mandatory contributions.

3. Annuity payments in pay status at least three years before the termination of the plan (including annuity payments that would have been in pay status for at least three years if the employee had retired then) based on the provisions of the plan in effect during the five years before termination of the plan under which the benefit would be the least.

4. All other insured benefits (this includes benefits that would be insured except for the special limitation with respect to a substantial owner; also, the aggregate benefit limitation for individuals does not apply).

5. All other vested, but uninsured, benefits.

6. All other benefits under the plan.

An allocation within a **priority category** that cannot be covered in full is settled on a pro rata basis, except that subpriorities within a priority category may be provided for by the plan. If there are any assets remaining after satisfaction of all liabilities for accrued benefits, they may be paid to the employer if provided for by the plan provisions.

Reversion of Residual Assets to the Employer

In general, the funds in a qualified pension plan may not be used for purposes other than the exclusive benefit of employees or their beneficiaries prior to the termination of the plan and the satisfaction of all liabilities. However, with the exception of pension plan assets attributable to employee contributions, employers may recapture any residual assets of a terminated single-employer defined benefit pension plan if the following conditions are satisfied:

1. All liabilities of the plan to participants and their beneficiaries have been satisfied.

2. The distribution does not contravene any provision of law.

3. The plan provides for such a distribution in these circumstances.

---

[19] ERISA Section 4044.

Chevron and Gulf Oil Plan Merger   1

Chevron and Gulf Oil announced a merger in 1984, and the merger was completed two years later. In July 1986, Gulf Oil's main pension plan and several subordinate plans, as well as a smaller Chevron plan, were merged into the Chevron Retirement Plan. The merger involved the transfer of approximately $700 million that had accumulated in the plans since their establishment. Chevron used the plans' assets for various corporate purposes.

In November 1986, a class action suit was filed on behalf of 40,000 former participants in the Gulf Oil plans, contending that the transfer of assets violated ERISA Section 208. That section requires that each participant in a plan must receive a benefit immediately after a merger or transfer of assets that is equal to or greater than the benefit the participant would have been entitled to receive immediately before the merger or transfer. The former participants further argued that the Gulf Oil plans had undergone a partial termination.

In 1991, the U.S. District Court ruled ERISA Section 208 affords protection only to *accrued* benefits, that an entitlement to an actuarial surplus is not an accrued benefit, and thus that the participants in the

class action suit were not entitled to the $550 million in excess assets under the main Gulf Oil plan.

The court went on to find that the Gulf Oil plans had undergone a partial termination and ordered that all participants in the plans who were employed by Chevron on the date of the merger be vested in benefits accrued under those plans as of that date.

The former participants appealed. Although the appellate court agreed that the Gulf Oil plans had undergone a partial termination, it rejected the participants' argument that they were entitled to a pro rata share of the plans' excess assets.

According to the court, if the participants had any such right, it had to be found in the plans' language (and) . . . since the plans did not discuss what happened after plan liabilities were fully satisfied, the plan language created at least an implied right to reversion in Gulf Oil.

Source: "Chevron to Retain Excess Assets from Gulf Oil Merger," *Employee Benefit Plan Review,* February 1995, pp. 46–47. Reprinted with permission of the *Employee Benefit Plan Review* magazine, Charles D. Spencer & Associates, Inc., publishers, Chicago, IL.

Residual assets are equal to the plan funds remaining after satisfaction of all liabilities.[20]

The PBGC, Treasury Department, and Department of Labor have issued the following joint implementation guidelines on asset reversions:

1. An employer may not recover any surplus assets until it has fully vested all participants' benefits and has purchased and distributed annuity contracts.

---

[20] Restrictions on reversions from recently amended plans are specified in ERISA Section 4044(d)(2). The allocation of residual assets attributable to employee contributions is described in ERISA Section 4044(d)(3).

2. If employees are offered lump-sum payments in lieu of future pensions, the amount of the lump-sum distribution must fairly reflect the value of the pension to the individual.

3. An employer that terminates a sufficiently funded defined benefit pension plan may establish a new defined benefit plan covering the same group of employees, granting past-service credit for the period during which an employee was covered by the terminated plan. This is known as a termination/reestablishment, and the successor plan is exempt from the five year phase-in of benefit guarantees that applies to newly established plans.

4. Spinoff/terminations[21] will not be recognized, and any attempt to recover surplus assets will be treated as a diversion of assets for a purpose other than the exclusive benefit of employees and beneficiaries unless the employees receive timely notice of the event and the following conditions are satisfied:

    a. The benefits of all employees must be fully vested and nonforfeitable as of the date of the termination. This also applies to the benefits covered by the ongoing plan.

    b. All accrued benefits must be provided for by the purchase of annuity contracts.

5. In the case of a spinoff/termination and a termination/reestablishment, attempts to recover surplus assets will be treated as a diversion of assets for a purpose other than the exclusive benefit of employees and beneficiaries unless the funding method for the ongoing plans is to be changed by modifying the amortization basis.[22]

6. An employer may not engage in either a termination/reestablishment or spinoff/termination transaction involving reversion of assets any earlier than 15 years following any such transaction.

Amounts recovered under a reversion are subject to a 50 percent excise tax.[23] This penalty is reduced to 20 percent if (1) 25 percent of the otherwise recoverable reversion is transferred to another qualified retirement plan that covers at least 95 percent of the active participants of the terminated plan; (2) 20 percent of the otherwise recoverable reversion is used to provide pro rata increases in the benefits accrued by participants under the terminated plan; or (3) the employer is in Chapter 7 bankruptcy liquidation.

---

[21] Under a spinoff/termination, the active participants (and their liabilities) are spun off from the original defined benefit plan. Assets are then transferred from the original plan to the new plan in an amount at least equal to the active participants' liabilities. The original plan, which at this point covers only retired and terminated employees, is then terminated, and annuities are used to satisfy the plan's obligations.

[22] The modification must be in accordance with IRC Section 412(b)(4). Details of the modification are provided in PBGC News Release 84–23.

[23] Prior to the Omnibus Budget Reconciliation Act of 1990, the tax rate had been 15 percent. In addition to the increased penalty, this legislation allowed employers to use surplus pension assets to prefund retiree health plans through 401(h) accounts.

If the employer adopts a plan amendment increasing terminated defined benefit plan benefits, the 25 percent cushion is reduced dollar for dollar by the present value of the increase. These benefit increases must satisfy the generally applicable qualification requirements, such as the nondiscrimination rules described in Chapter 4.

Compliance with the 20 percent pro rata increase option requires that increased benefits must be provided to all qualified participants. This includes active participants, participants and beneficiaries receiving benefits on the termination date, and other participants who retain rights under the plan and who terminate employment (or plan eligibility) during a period starting three years before the termination date and ending on the final asset distribution date.[24] Beneficiaries of this last group also are eligible if they have a vested plan benefit. Employees who stop working before the plan termination date and receive a lump-sum distribution are not entitled to benefit increases.

Liabilities on Plan Termination

Distributee Liability-Recapture

When a plan terminates, the termination trustee is authorized to recover for the benefit of the pension plan certain payments received by a participant within the three-year period prior to plan termination. The recoverable amount is the sum of all payments made to the participant in excess of $10,000 made during any consecutive 12-month period within three years before termination or, if less, the amount he or she would have received as a monthly benefit under a single-life annuity commencing at age 65.[25] Payments to a disabled participant and payments made after or on account of the death of a participant are not subject to recovery. The PBGC can totally or partially waive any amount otherwise entitled to be recaptured whenever recapture would result in substantial economic hardship to a participant or his or her beneficiaries.

Employer Liability

During the legislative process leading up to the enactment of ERISA, concern was expressed that in the absence of appropriate safeguards under an insurance system, an employer might establish or amend a plan to provide substantial benefits with the realization that its funding might be inadequate to pay the benefits called for. Such an employer might, it was argued, rely on the insurance as a backup, enabling it to be more generous in promised pension benefits to meet labor demands than would be the case if it knew that the benefit would have to be paid for entirely out of the assets of the employer. On the other hand, it was clear that the imposition of heavy obligations on employers would discourage provisions for adequate pension plans.

To deal with these competing considerations, the decision was made to impose on the employer a limited liability to reimburse the insurance system for a portion of the payment that must be made by the PBGC in satisfaction of its obligation if the

---

[24] The assets allocated to increase the benefit of nonactive participants cannot exceed 40 percent of the total.
[25] ERISA Section 4045.

employer plan fails. Unfortunately, the limited liability was much smaller than the amount of unfunded benefit for many sponsors, and several plans in this category were terminated to take advantage of this "pension put."

The SEPPAA substantially modified the computation of the sponsor's liability on termination, and the Omnibus Budget Reconciliation Act of 1987 made further modifications the following year. Currently, in any case in which a single-employer plan is terminated in a distress termination or an involuntary termination is instituted by the PBGC, any person who is, on the termination date, a contributing sponsor of the plan or a member of such a contributing sponsor's controlled group will incur a liability under Section 4062 of ERISA. This liability consists of two components:

1. The liability to the PBGC.

2. The liability to the Section 4042 trustee (described below).

Although special rules pertain to a case in which it is discovered that the plan is unable to pay guaranteed benefits after the authorized commencement of termina-tion,[26] the following section defines the rules generally applying to the two compo-nents of the sponsor's liability and the required means of payment.

Liability to the PBGC

The liability to the PBGC consists of the total amount of the unfunded benefit lia-bilities[27] (as of the termination date) to all participants and beneficiaries under the plan, together with interest (at a reasonable rate) calculated from the termination date in accordance with regulations prescribed by the PBGC.

The total amount of the liability is paid to the PBGC, which, as described earlier in this chapter, pays out a portion of unfunded benefit liabilities in excess of the unfunded guaranteed benefits based on the total value of the PBGC's recovery with respect to the total liability of the employer. Amounts paid to participants are allo-cated in accordance with Section 4044 as described earlier in this chapter.

The liability to the PBGC is generally due as of the termination date. The PBGC and any person liable for payment also may agree to alternative arrangements for the satisfaction of the liability.

Liability to the Section 4042 Trustee

The liability to a Section 4042 trustee for the sponsoring employer and each mem-ber of its controlled group consists of the outstanding balance (accumulated with interest from the termination date) of the following:

1. The accumulated funding deficiency of the plan, modified to include the amount of any increase that would result if all pending applications for waivers of the minimum funding standard and for extensions of the amortization period were denied and if no additional contributions were made.

---

[26] ERISA Section 4062(b)(1)(B).
[27] Benefit liabilities are defined in the Standard Termination section of this chapter.

2. The amount of waived funding deficiencies.

3. The amount of decreases in the minimum funding standard account.

Determination of Net Worth

In general, the collective net worth for purposes of determining the liability to the PBGC consists of the sum of the individual net worths of all persons who have individual net worths greater than zero and who are contributing sponsors of the terminated plan or members of their controlled groups. The net worth of a person is determined on whatever basis best reflects, in the determination of the PBGC, the current status of the person's operations and prospects at the time chosen for determining the net worth of the person. The net worth is increased by the amount of any transfers of assets made by the pension that are determined by the PBGC to be improper under the circumstances. Determinations of net worth are made as of a day chosen by the PBGC during the 120-day period ending with the termination date. Net worth is computed without regard to termination liabilities.

Liability of Substantial and Multiple Employers

A liability applies to all employers, other than multiemployer plans terminating after April 29, 1980, who maintain a plan under which more than one employer makes contributions. The liability also attaches to all employers who, at any time within the five plan years preceding the date of plan termination, made contributions under the plan. The liability is allocated among the employers in the ratio of their required contributions for the last five years prior to termination.

   If the withdrawing employer prefers, a bond may be furnished to the PBGC in an amount not exceeding 150 percent of its liability. The bond must be issued by a corporate surety acceptable on federal bonds under the authority granted by the Secretary of the Treasury.

PBGC Lien for Employer Liability

To the extent an employer liability is not satisfied and the amount does not exceed 30 percent of the collective net worth of the sponsor and its controlled group, the amount of the liability (including interest) is a lien in favor of the PBGC upon all property and rights to property, whether real or personal, belonging to the employer.

Premiums

Although Congress corrected several of the major design flaws in the single-employer plan termination insurance system with the passage of SEPPAA, there were still lingering doubts concerning the equity of a premium structure based solely on a flat-rate premium per participant. Therefore, Congress mandated that the PBGC prepare a study on several issues relating to the premium structure. On the basis of its findings, the PBGC proposed a variable-rate **premium structure** that added an additional premium charge based on the difference between the plan liabilities and the plan assets. This basic concept was incorporated into the Omnibus Budget Reconciliation Act of 1987 and later modified by the Omnibus Budget Reconciliation Act of 1990.

For plan years beginning after 1990, the single-employer flat-rate premium per participant is $19. An additional premium of $9 per $1,000 of unfunded vested benefits also is required of underfunded plans.[28] The contributing sponsor or plan administrator must pay the premiums imposed by the PBGC. If the contributing sponsor of any plan is a member of a controlled group, each member is jointly and severally liable for any premiums.

The Retirement Protection Act of 1994 required changes in several of the assumptions and methods for purposes of determining the value of vested benefits. As of 1995 the sponsor was allowed to use the mortality table used for funding in determining the unfunded vested benefits. For plan years beginning on or after January 1, 1996, sponsors were to adopt the GAM-83 mortality table; eventually, they adopted a new mortality table issued by the Treasury Department. The interest rate was equal to 80 percent of the yield per annum on 30-year Treasury securities for the month preceding the month in which the plan year began. The Retirement Protection Act of 1994 increased the interest rate to 85 percent of the Treasury spot rate for 30-year securities, effective for plan years beginning on or after July 1, 1997, and to 100 percent of the Treasury spot rate when the Treasury's new mortality table was prescribed. The Job Creation and Worker Assistance Act of 2002 increased the interest rate used for computing unfunded vested benefits for variable rate premiums for plan years beginning after December 31, 2001, and before January 1, 2004. The increase was to 100 percent of the interest rate on 30-year Treasury securities[29] for the month preceding the month in which the plan year begins. Sponsors were allowed to adopt the asset valuation method used for funding purposes in their computation of PBGC premiums under the Retirement Protection Act of 1994. As explained in Chapter 15, this allowed for the use of smoothing methods that dampen the volatility of the time series of market value changes. However, sponsors had to switch to a fair market value when the Treasury's new mortality table was prescribed.

Security Rules for Underfunded Plans

If a single-employer defined benefit plan adopts an amendment that increases current liability under the plan, and if the funded current liability percentage of the plan

---

[28] Since its inception, a cap existed on the maximum additional premium per participant. However, the Retirement Protection Act of 1994 gradually eliminated this cap. Technically, for plan years beginning on or after July 1, 1994, 20 percent of the variable rate premium over $53 had to be paid. The rate increased to 60 percent in the following year and for plan years beginning on or after July 1, 1996, the cap was eliminated.

[29] Following the discontinuation of the 30-year Treasury bond, the IRS was to determine and publish an average yield to be used in the interim period until the enactment of permanent legislation addressing this issue.

in the year in which the amendment takes effect is less than 60 percent (including the amount of the unfunded current liability[30] under the plan attributable to the plan amendment), the contributing sponsor and members of the controlled group must provide security (e.g., a bond) to the plan. The amount of the security required is the excess over $10 million or the lesser of:

1. The amount of additional plan assets that would be necessary to increase the funded current liability percentage under the plan to 60 percent, including the amount of the unfunded current liability under the plan attributable to the plan amendment.

2. The amount of the increase in current liability under the plan attributable to the plan amendment.

Chapter Summary

- A single-employer plan may be terminated voluntarily only in a standard termination or a distress termination. A single-employer plan may terminate under a standard termination if, among other things, the plan is sufficiently funded for benefit liabilities (determined as of the termination date) when the final distribution of assets occurs.

- The PBGC must determine whether the necessary distress criteria have been satisfied. Basically, these criteria are met if each person who is a contributing sponsor or a member of the sponsor's controlled group meets the requirements of any of the following:
  1. Liquidation in bankruptcy or insolvency proceedings.
  2. Reorganization in bankruptcy or insolvency proceedings.
  3. Termination required to enable payment of debts while staying in business or to avoid unreasonably burdensome pension costs caused by a declining workforce.

- Subject to various limits, the PBGC guarantees the payment of all nonforfeitable benefits that qualify as a pension benefit other than those accelerated by plan termination. A benefit that becomes nonforfeitable solely because of plan termination is not subject to ERISA benefit guarantees; however, a benefit won't fail to satisfy the PBGC requirement merely because a participant is required to submit a written application, retire, or complete a mandatory waiting period as a condition for receiving pension payments.

- There is a limit on the amount of monthly guaranteed benefits insured by the PBGC. The amount is adjusted annually to reflect changes in the Social Security taxable wage base. The original limit was $750 per month, but for plans terminated in 2002 the limit increased to $3,579.55 per month. The limit is in terms of a single-life annuity commencing at age 65 and without a refund feature. If the benefit is payable at a lower age, it is reduced by actuarial factors denoted by the PBGC. The benefit is not actuarially increased when the participant retires at an age later than 65.

- Plan assets must be allocated to the benefit categories applicable on plan termination under ERISA Section 4044. This prevents employers from establishing new benefit lev-

---

[30] In computing unfunded current liability, the unamortized portion of the unfunded old liability amount as of the close of the plan year is not taken into account.

els, terminating plans, and allocating existing plan assets to such benefits resulting in the subordination of insured to uninsured benefits. On termination, the assets of a plan must be allocated in the following order of priorities:

1. Employees' voluntary contributions.
2. Employees' mandatory contributions.
3. Annuity payments in pay status at least three years before the termination of the plan (including annuity payments that would have been in pay status for at least three years if the employee had retired then), based on the provisions of the plan in effect during the five years before termination of the plan under which the benefit would be the least.
4. All other insured benefits (this includes benefits that would be insured except for the special limitation with respect to a "substantial owner"; also, the aggregate benefit limitation for individuals does not apply).
5. All other vested, but uninsured, benefits.
6. All other benefits under the plan.

- In general, the funds in a qualified pension plan may not be used for purposes other than the exclusive benefit of employees or their beneficiaries prior to the termination of the plan and the satisfaction of all liabilities. However, with the exception of pension plan assets attributable to employee contributions, employers may recapture any residual assets of a terminated single-employer defined benefit pension plan if the following conditions are satisfied:
  1. All liabilities of the plan to participants and their beneficiaries have been satisfied.
  2. The distribution does not contravene any provision of law.
  3. The plan provides for such a distribution in these circumstances.

- For plan years beginning after 1990, the single-employer flat-rate premium per participant is $19. An additional premium of $9 per $1,000 of unfunded vested benefits also is required of underfunded plans. The contributing sponsor or plan administrator must pay the premiums imposed by the PBGC. If the contributing sponsor of any plan is a member of a controlled group, each member is jointly and severally liable for any premiums.

Key Terms

involuntary plan
  termination, p. *290*
Pension Benefit Guaranty
  Corporation (PBGC),
  p. *285*

plan termination insurance,
  p. *288*
premium structure, p. *303*
priority category, p. *297*

reportable event, p. *290*
termination date, p. *293*

Questions for Review

1. In general, what types of pension plans are covered by plan termination insurance?
2. What classes of pension plans are specifically excluded from plan termination insurance coverage?
3. How is the PBGC kept apprised of events affecting plan solvency or operations that may justify an involuntary termination?
4. Explain the significance of the date of termination for a pension plan.
5. Explain the definition of a basic benefit with respect to *(a)* early retirement incentives and *(b)* death and disability benefits.

6. Explain how insurance coverage is phased in for benefits that have been in effect for less than five years.

7. Why is it necessary to establish priority classes for pension benefits at the time of termination?

8. Is the trustee authorized to recapture benefit payments already made prior to the occurrence of the plan termination? Explain.

9. Must the sponsor of a terminated plan reimburse the PBGC for any loss that it incurs in meeting the benefit obligations of the terminated plan?

10. What condition must be satisfied before a plan sponsor is able to recapture excess assets from a pension plan?

Questions for Discussion

1. Discuss the public policy issues involved in the termination of overfunded defined benefit pension plans.

2. In 1987, the PBGC adopted a new variable rate premium structure that included a premium component based on the amount of a defined benefit pension plan's unfunded vested benefits. Discuss the relative merits of this approach.

3. Many people have suggested that the PBGC should switch to a risk-related premium structure in which the premium a sponsor pays for plan termination insurance is based on *(a)* the relative likelihood that the plan will terminate and *(b)* the potential magnitude of the claim. Discuss the relative merits of this approach.

Resources for Further Study

Buckley, Allen; and George Prothro. "Accrued Benefits of Missing Participants in Nonterminating Retirement Plans." *Journal of Pension Benefits* 8, no. 3 (Spring 2001).

CCH Editorial Staff. "2002 Tax Legislation: Law, Explanation, and Analysis: Job Creation and Worker Assistance Act of 2002." *Commerce Clearing House Pension Plan Guide* (2002).

Eisner, Andrew D. "PBGC Issues Final Regulations on Reportable Events." *Journal of Compensation & Benefits* 12, no. 6 (May/June 1997).

www.pbgc.gov—website of the Pension Benefit Guaranty Corporation.

Chapter # 17

Individual Retirement Arrangements

After studying this chapter you should be able to:

- Explain the characteristics and features of individual retirement accounts (IRAs).

- Distinguish between the various types of IRAs.

- Describe the eligibility requirements for the various types of IRAs.

- Discuss the contribution limits applicable to various types of IRAs.

- Explain the tax issues related to IRA distributions.

- Discuss prohibited transactions and other prohibitions related to IRAs.

Despite the rapid growth of the private pension system, more than 40 million American workers were not covered by qualified pension or profit sharing plans at the beginning of 1974. Congress, in recognition of this fact, included provisions in the Employee Retirement Income Security Act (ERISA) that would enable such individuals to establish their own retirement plans on a tax-deferred basis beginning in 1975. **Individual retirement arrangements** (IRAs) are defined contribution-type plans. An eligible individual could make tax-deductible contributions (up to prescribed limits) under such a plan, and the investment income earned on the contributions generally would be currently sheltered from income tax. Such contributions and investment income would be taxed as ordinary income as they were received or made available.

Over the years, Congress has made numerous changes regarding the workings of IRAs. As a result of these changes, there now are different types of IRAs with varying characteristics, various features, and differing tax treatments. This chapter will describe the various types of IRAs available under current tax law and explain the distinct attributes of each type. IRAs remain a popular way for individuals to manage their own retirement assets. Often through the use of rollover contribution IRAs (conduit IRAs), individuals bridge the gap between a qualified plan distribution on separation from service and drawing down retirement income. Funds transferred into a conduit IRA in such a transaction continue to compound on a tax-deferred basis without being subject to current taxation.

IRAs also are used as funding vehicles by some employers (both incorporated and unincorporated) that sponsor simplified employee pension (SEP) plans and savings incentive match plans for employees (SIMPLE plans), discussed in Chapter 18. In lieu of using the more traditional qualified plans, employers use these more simplified retirement planning vehicles because, under present law, the requirements that must be met by a qualified pension plan are considerably more complex than the requirements applicable to SEPs and SIMPLE plans.

The Small Business Job Protection Act of 1996 eliminated the creation of salary reduction simplified employee pension (SARSEP) plans after December 31, 1996. Employers who created SARSEPs before January 1, 1997, can continue their use, including offering these arrangements to employees hired after January 1, 1997. The curtailment of SARSEPs resulted from the creation of SIMPLE plans, discussed in the next chapter. SIMPLE plans can be configured using either IRAs or 401(k) plans. A thorough understanding of IRAs is necessary to fully understand these simpler retirement structures that use IRAs as a basis on which the employer plan is built.

The Taxpayer Relief Act of 1997 created Roth IRAs, named after Senator William V. Roth, Jr., a sponsor of the 1997 act. Roth IRAs have unique tax advantages distinguishing them from the classic, or traditional IRAs. These unique tax advantages and differing requirements necessitate that Roth IRAs be separately presented.

In this chapter we will look at traditional deductible IRAs, nondeductible IRAs, conduit IRAs (used in receiving rollover contributions from other retirement plans), employer-sponsored IRAs, deemed IRAs[1] under employer plans, and Roth IRAs. As stated previously, IRAs can serve as the underlying plan structure for other plans such as SEPs, SARSEPs, and SIMPLEs. A detailed discussion of these IRA uses within the context of plans for the self-employed is reserved until these plans are discussed in Chapter 18.

General Eligibility and Contribution Limits

The material in this section of the chapter discusses eligibility to establish an individual retirement arrangement and the various contribution limits. Also discussed are requirements relative to distributions and rollover provisions.

Eligibility to Establish IRAs

To be eligible to establish an individual retirement arrangement (IRA), an individual must have **earned income** from personal services—investment income does not

---

[1] These are traditional or Roth IRAs allowed by EGTRRA starting in plan years beginning after 2002 to be implemented by employers without impacting on the employer's other retirement plan offerings. Essentially these deemed IRAs will permit employees to save for retirement conveniently through payroll withholdings.

qualify for such a plan.[2] If both an individual and spouse have compensation or self-employment income during a taxable year, each spouse may establish his or her own IRA. Community property laws do not apply to IRAs. If an individual is married and otherwise eligible to make IRA contributions and has a nonworking spouse, an IRA for the nonworking spouse also may be established, subject to certain limitations discussed below. IRAs also may be established by rollover contributions. For example, individuals who receive distributions from qualified plans, governmental 457(b) plans, or 403(b) arrangements[3] may roll over the funds received into an IRA. Also, funds invested in an IRA may be rolled over to another IRA. A spousal death beneficiary of a qualified plan participant, a governmental 457(b) plan participant, a 403(b) arrangement owner, or an IRA owner also can establish an IRA by rolling over the death benefit. A spouse receiving amounts from a qualified plan, governmental 457(b) plan, 403(b) arrangement, or an IRA in certain divorce-related circumstances also may roll over such amounts received into IRAs. The Economic Growth and Tax Relief Reconciliation Act of 2001 (EGTRRA) expanded the situations under which a plan distribution could be rolled over into an IRA. An expanded discussion of situations allowing for eligible rollovers is contained later in the chapter.

No restrictions exist on the number of individual retirement arrangements an individual may establish; however, the aggregate contributions made to all plans in a given year must not exceed the allowable contribution limits. As a practical matter, the combination of the maximum permissible contribution under law and the minimum contribution requirements of the financial institutions offering such plans effectively limits the number of plans that can be operated at the same time. (See the section, Selection of Funding Arrangement, p. 315.)

Contribution Limits

There is no dollar limit applied to **rollover contributions to IRAs.** Accordingly, the material in this portion of the chapter applies only to nonrollover contributions (referred to as "regular annual" IRA contributions).

Regular annual IRA contributions were limited to $2,000 or 100 percent of earned income for the taxable year, whichever was less prior to 2002. With the passage of EGTRRA in 2001, the annual contribution limit for IRAs was increased to $3,000 beginning in 2002. Additionally, beginning in 2002 EGTRRA allowed for IRA catch-up contributions for any taxpayers that were age 50 or older. When EGTRRA was passed, regular annual IRA contributions and IRA catch-up contributions were scheduled to increase in future years as noted in Table 17.1 on page 310.

In any event, an individual ceases to be eligible to make regular annual contributions to either a traditional deductible or nondeductible IRA beginning with the taxable year in which the individual attains age 70½. Roth IRAs (discussed later in the chapter) permit regular annual contributions beyond age 70½ provided the individual has income from personal services as mentioned previously.

---

[2] All alimony and separate maintenance paid under a divorce or separation instrument and includable in gross income is a compensation substitute for IRA purposes.

[3] See Chapter 12 for a discussion of 403(b) plans.

TABLE 17.1   Regular Annual and Catch-up Contributions for Traditional and Roth IRAs as Enacted by EGTRRA

Year	Regular Contribution Limit	Annual Contribution Limit for Individuals 50 and Over
2001	$2,000	$2,000 (No catch-up permitted by law)
2002–2004	$3,000	$3,500 (Including a $500 catch-up)
2005	$4,000	$4,500 (Including a $500 catch-up)
2006–2007	$4,000	$5,000 (Including a $1,000 catch-up)
2008 and later	$5,000 (Indexed in future years in $500 increments.)	$6,000 (Including a $1,000 catch-up) (Indexed in future years in $500 increments.)

If both an individual and spouse have compensation, then each spouse is eligible to contribute to his or her separate IRA up to the lesser of 100 percent of earned income or the allowable annual dollar limit, whichever is less, as shown in Table 17.1.

An otherwise eligible individual also may set up and contribute to one or more IRAs for a nonworking spouse or a spouse who elects to be treated as having no compensation for the year. Under a spousal IRA plan of this type, the spouses must file a joint income tax return. Originally, if one spouse had no compensation, a married couple was restricted to a combined maximum annual IRA contribution of $2,250 when IRAs were limited to a $2,000 annual contribution. The Small Business Job Protection Act of 1996 (SBJPA) created new spousal IRA rules effective for tax years beginning after December 31, 1996. Under the new rules, nonworking spouses were able to contribute up to the full $2,000 limit existing at the time of the SBJPA's enactment. A combined maximum contribution of $4,000 was allowable— $2,000 for each spouse. Deductibility of this $4,000 was limited if the working spouse earned over $40,000 and participated in an employer-sponsored retirement program as discussed in the next section. With the passage of EGTRRA, each spouse now can contribute up to the applicable annual limit for any given year as shown in Table 17.1. There is also the additional benefit that each spouse can make a catch-up contribution if the spouses individually meet the age 50 threshold by the end of the tax year.

Regular IRA contributions to the IRA of the nonworking spouse can no longer be made beginning within the calendar year the nonworking spouse reaches age 70½. If the employee-spouse is younger, he or she can continue to make annual IRA contributions to his or her own IRA until the year he or she reaches age 70½.

Distinguishing IRAs: Contribution Deductibility and Taxation of Distributions

Deductibility of IRA Contributions

Individuals may deduct the full amount of their regular annual contributions to IRAs if they do not actively participate in a qualified plan.

If either the taxpayer or his or her spouse is an active participant[4] in an employer-maintained plan for any part of a plan year ending with or within the taxable year, the maximum[5] IRA contribution deduction is reduced (but not below zero) based on adjusted gross income (AGI), calculated without regard to any IRA contributions.[6] The phase-out thresholds that apply to the deduction on contributions to a traditional IRA by individuals who are active participants in an employer-sponsored retirement plan are unchanged by EGTRRA, but the thresholds continue to increase as a result of the previously enacted provisions of the Taxpayer Relief Act of 1997. The table below illustrates the income ranges subject to phase out of deductible contributions in a traditional IRA.

In order to compute the amount of the deductible contribution to a single or married taxpayer filing a joint return, the following calculation is made:

$$\text{Applicable annual contribution limit from Table 17.1} \times \frac{\text{Modified AGI} - \text{Lower limit of phase out from Table 17.2}}{\$10,000 \text{ or (Other difference in the phase out range from Table 17.2 if not equal to } \$10,000)}$$

In the case of contributions to an employed individual's IRA and a nonworking spousal IRA, the maximum tax deduction for the married couple (after application of the AGI test, as noted in Table 17.2) is limited to the lesser of 100 percent of earned income or twice the allowable annual dollar limit shown in Table 17.1.

---

[4] The determination of whether an individual is an active participant is made without regard to whether the individual's rights under the plan are nonforfeitable.

[5] This figure could be doubled if a nonworking spouse contributed the full amount to an individual retirement account as allowed for tax years following December 31, 1996, by the Small Business Job Protection Act of 1996. Beginning in 1998 a taxpayer was not precluded from making a contribution to a deductible IRA solely because the spouse was a participant in a qualified employer-sponsored retirement plan, but the maximum contribution was phased out for incomes above a certain level. (See Table 17.2 for a detailed description of the phase-out limits in various years.)

[6] No dollar limitation will be reduced below $200 until the limitation is completely phased out.

TABLE 17.2   Annual Phase-out Limits on Taxpayer Deductions of Regular Annual Contributions to Traditional IRAs

	Single Taxpayers			Married Taxpayers Filing Jointly	
Year	Where Phase out Starts	Where Deduction is Completely Eliminated	Year	Where Phase out Starts	Where Deduction is Completely Eliminated
2001	$33,000	$43,000	2001	$53,000	$63,000
2002	$34,000	$44,000	2002	$54,000	$64,000
2003	$40,000	$50,000	2003	$60,000	$70,000
2004	$45,000	$55,000	2004	$65,000	$75,000
2005 and later	$50,000	$60,000	2005	$70,000	$80,000
			2006	$75,000	$85,000
			2007 and later	$80,000	$100,000

Nondeductible IRA contributions also may be made if they are designated as such on the taxpayer's return. Although these contributions will be made from after-tax income, they will benefit from the compounding of tax-sheltered investment income during the time they remain in the IRA. Because the annual limit on regular contributions to any working individual's IRA is limited to the applicable dollar amount shown in Table 17.1 (or the earned income for the year, if under the allowable dollar amount) nondeductible contributions cannot exceed the same allowable dollar amount or earned income limit. Taxpayers may elect to treat contributions as nondeductible even though they are eligible to make deductible contributions. If taxpayers make any deductible contributions, nondeductible contributions may be made against the remaining limit.

Because the IRA contribution deduction is against gross income, it may be taken even though the individual does not itemize deductions. If the individual's employer makes the contribution other than as a SEP or SIMPLE employer plan contribution directly to the IRA on behalf of the individual,[7] the amount still must be reported as earnings and then taken as a deduction against gross income. This contribution will be subject to FICA (Federal Insurance Contributions Act) or Social Security tax and FUTA (Federal Unemployment Tax Act) tax but not to withholding taxes.

Individual IRA contributions must be made before the due date for the individual's filing of the federal income tax return for the taxable year for which the deduction is claimed (disregarding any filing extensions).

Any **excess contribution** is subject to a nondeductible 6 percent excise tax in addition to current income taxation. The excise tax continues to be applied each year until the excess contribution is withdrawn from the IRA. For example, if an individual makes an excess contribution of $100 to an IRA in 20X1, an excise tax of $6 is imposed for 20X1 and for each year thereafter until the excess contribution is withdrawn.

Because of the restrictions on distributions from an IRA (discussed in a later section of this chapter), the question arises whether the withdrawal of an excess contribution is itself a taxable event. If the excess contribution is withdrawn before the tax return filing date for the year for which the contribution was made, the withdrawn excess amount is not included in taxable income, and the 10 percent premature distribution tax is not applied. However, earnings must be withdrawn and are taxable and potentially subject to penalty.

Any excess contributions not taken as a distribution may be eliminated in later years by contributing less than the maximum allowable deduction in such years. For example, if an individual contributed an excess of $100 over the allowable limit in one year (as depicted in Table 17.1), the situation can be remedied by contributing $100 less than the allowable limit in the following year. If excess contributions are not eliminated through these steps, the excess amounts will be subject to a cumulative 6 percent excise tax each year until they are eliminated.

Roth IRAs

History and Distinguishing Characteristics from Traditional IRAs

As previously mentioned, the Taxpayer Relief Act of 1997 introduced another type of nondeductible IRA, the **Roth IRA,** that could be used beginning in 1998. Like tra-

---

[7] See a discussion of SEPs and SIMPLE plans in Chapter 18.

ditional IRAs, Roth IRAs permit the same regular annual contribution limit as does a traditional IRA. (The annual contribution limits are noted in Table 17.1.) If a taxpayer makes regular annual contributions to any other IRAs, for instance, to either a traditional deductible or nondeductible IRA, the maximum annual contribution limit to the Roth IRA is reduced by those contributions. The rules permitting a regular annual contribution to a Roth IRA are unique to this particular retirement savings vehicle. Unlike a traditional IRA, regular annual contributions can be made to a Roth IRA at any age (even beyond age 70½), provided the contributions do not exceed earned income for that particular year. The income phaseout on the ability to make regular annual contributions to a Roth IRA applies even if an individual is not an active participant in an employer-sponsored retirement plan. A single taxpayer must have adjusted gross income (AGI) of less than $95,000 in order to make a full annual contribution to a Roth IRA (a partial contribution can be made if AGI is between $95,000 and $110,000). A married taxpayer must have adjusted gross income (AGI) of less than $150,000 in order to make a full annual contribution to a Roth IRA (a partial contribution can be made if AGI is between $150,000 and $160,000). If a married taxpayer files his or her income tax return as married filing separately, he or she is ineligible to make a regular annual Roth contribution once AGI exceeds $10,000; a phased contribution is permissible if income is $10,000 or lower.

Contributions to Roth IRAs are not tax deductible when made, but earnings accumulate tax deferred. Like deductible and nondeductible traditional IRAs, a Roth IRA contribution must be made by the due date for the filing of the taxpayer's income tax return, not including extensions. Withdrawals of regular annual Roth contributions are tax free at any time since taxes have already been paid on these amounts. Withdrawals of earnings from Roth IRAs are tax free (rather than tax deferred) if the distribution is considered to be a qualified distribution. A qualified distribution is a distribution that is made at least five years from the first of the year in which the Roth account was established and meets at least one of the following other requirements:

1. The taxpayer has attained age 59½.

2. The taxpayer is disabled.

3. The taxpayer has died and payment is made to a beneficiary or to the individual's estate.

4. The distribution is made to pay first-time home buyer expenses and does not exceed $10,000.

Generally under other circumstances, withdrawals of earnings are taxable and would be subject to the additional early distribution federal tax of 10 percent. However, if a withdrawal of earnings meets one of the conditions to be excepted from the early withdrawal penalty tax, this 10 percent additional federal tax would not apply. Later in the chapter, the exceptions to the 10 percent early withdrawal tax are explained.

Conversion of a Traditional IRA into a Roth IRA

The owner of a traditional IRA may convert it into a Roth IRA if his or her modified adjusted gross income (AGI) does not exceed $100,000 as either a single person or as a married person filing a joint return in the year that the **conversion** occurs. Modified AGI excludes income attributable to the conversion itself and also excludes any minimum required distributions from traditional IRAs in the year of conversion.[8] The full amount of a traditional IRA or a partial lesser amount can be converted. A taxpayer making such a conversion will be subject to taxation in the year of conversion for any proceeds of the account which have been converted that would be subject to taxation upon distribution. A conversion that is subject to taxation is also subject to income tax withholding unless the account owner makes an election in writing not to have withholding occur. Though a traditional IRA that is converted into a Roth IRA is subject to regular federal income taxation, it is not subject to the 10 percent penalty tax on premature distributions.

IRA Administrative Issues

Funding

An individual may establish an individual retirement savings plan (either traditional or Roth) by making contributions to one or more of the following:

1. An individual retirement account.

2. An individual retirement annuity.

3. A U.S. retirement bond (permitted prior to May 1, 1982, and therefore not applicable to Roth IRAs because these funding mechanisms predated the introduction of Roth IRAs).

IRA contributions must be made in cash. Thus, the contribution of existing property (e.g., existing mutual fund shares) is not permitted.

The following material discusses each of these approaches in greater detail, as well as the restrictions of the Internal Revenue Code for prohibited transactions and unrelated business income.

Individual Retirement Account (IRA)

This type of plan entails the establishment of a trust or a custodial account. The trustee or custodian may be a bank or another person or organization that demonstrates to the satisfaction of the Internal Revenue Service that the IRA account will be administered in accordance with the law.

There are some restrictions on investments in such an IRA. The assets cannot be invested in life insurance contracts. (There is a limited exception for endowment contracts with incidental life insurance features that were issued before 1979.) Also, IRA investments in collectibles, such as antiques, works of art, stamps, coins, and the like, are not permitted. Most IRA accounts are invested in assets such as bank-pooled funds, savings accounts, certificates of deposit, savings and loan association accounts, mutual fund shares, face-amount certificates, and insured credit union

---

[8] This can be an important exclusion in computing modified AGI, especially for an older person attempting to make a conversion.

accounts. A **self-directed IRA** arrangement also can be established. Under this approach a corporate trustee is selected (which generally charges fees for the services provided). The individual is free to make the investment decisions, within the constraints outlined below, for his or her IRA.

The key requirements of an individual retirement account are as follows:

1. The regular annual contribution must be made in cash and must not exceed the allowable amount permitted by law in a given year as previously shown in Table 17.1.

2. The entire value of the account must be nonforfeitable.

3. No part of the funds may be invested in life insurance contracts or collectibles, other than legal tender gold and silver coins minted by the United States.

4. The assets in the account must not be commingled with any other property (except the assets of other qualified trusts).

5. Distributions must be made in accordance with the restrictions imposed by the law.

IRAs may be set up by adopting either IRS Form 5305 for Individual Retirement Trust Accounts or IRS Form 5305A for Individual Retirement Custodial Accounts. Alternatively, if the trustee or custodian wishes to use its own agreement, it may do this and submit the agreement to the IRS for approval on Form 5306. An individual who uses such approved plans does not need to submit his or her individual plan for IRS approval.

Individual Retirement Annuity

Under this type of plan, the individual's contribution is invested through the purchase of a **flexible premium annuity IRA** from a legally licensed life insurance company.

The annuity contract must involve flexible premiums and may be participating or nonparticipating. Also, the annuity may be fixed or variable. The key requirements of a flexible premium annuity IRA are as follows:

1. The annual premium must not be fixed and must not exceed the allowable amount permitted by law in a given year as previously shown in Table 17.1.

2. The contract must be nontransferable.

3. The individual's interest in the contract must be nonforfeitable.

4. Dividends must be used before the end of the next year to purchase additional benefits or to reduce future premiums.

5. Distributions must be made in accordance with the restrictions imposed by law.

Selection of Funding Arrangement

Selection of the appropriate funding arrangement involves many of the same considerations taken into account in the selection of a funding instrument for a qualified pension plan. Thus, the individual must give consideration to potential investment return as well as investment risk. The expenses associated with the particular funding arrangement also must be taken into account as must benefit security and services provided.

Prohibited Transactions

Individual retirement savings plans are subject to the prohibited transactions provisions of ERISA. If the individual engages in a prohibited transaction, the plan will be disqualified as of the first day of the taxable year in which the transaction occurred. The individual must then include the fair market value of the assets of the plan (determined as of the first day of such year) in ordinary income where applicable. In addition, if the individual has not attained age 59½ (or is not disabled), an additional 10 percent tax will be levied where applicable since this is treated as a premature distribution. Generally speaking, fiduciaries and parties in interest are prohibited from engaging in the following:

1. Selling, exchanging, or leasing property.

2. Lending money or extending credit.

3. Furnishing goods, services, or facilities.

4. Transferring to or using plan assets.

There are, of course, exceptions to the prohibited transaction rules. One of the more significant exceptions permits a financial institution to provide ancillary services where this is done without interference with the interests of the participants and beneficiaries, where not more than reasonable compensation is charged, and where adequate internal safeguards exist to prevent provision of services in an excessive or unreasonable manner.

Except for the individual (and his or her beneficiary), a party in interest who engages in a prohibited transaction will be subject to an excise tax of 10 percent of the amount involved. If the situation is not corrected within the time allowed (90 days unless extended by the IRS), a further excise tax of 100 percent of the amount involved will be levied.

If an individual has an individual retirement annuity and borrows any money under or by use of that annuity contract, the annuity will lose its tax-exempt status as of the first day of the taxable year in which the transaction occurred. The fair market value of such annuity when applicable (as of the first day of such taxable year) will have to be included in the individual's gross income for such year. If the individual has not attained age 59½ or is not disabled at such time, this also will be considered to be a premature distribution and the additional tax of 10 percent of the amount involved where applicable will be levied.

If an individual has an individual retirement account and uses all or any portion of the account as security for a loan, the portion so used will be treated and taxed as a distribution. Again, if the individual has not attained age 59½ or is not disabled, the 10 percent additional tax also will be levied where applicable.

Unrelated Business Income

An individual retirement arrangement is subject to federal income tax on any **unrelated business income** that arises from the conduct of any trade or business that is not substantially related to the exempt purpose of the plan. If a plan develops such unrelated business income, the plan will not be disqualified; however, such income will be subject to tax.

Distributions

The law contains very specific provisions that relate to distributions from traditional IRAs. In general, these provisions are designed to support the basic purpose of such plans—that they should provide retirement income. Thus, premature distributions are discouraged. On the other hand, the individual is expected to begin receiving payments by age 70½ and is encouraged to draw down benefits over his or her remaining lifetime (or the joint lifetimes of the individual and his or her beneficiary). As indicated previously, Roth IRAs are exempt from the minimum distribution rules. Therefore, the owner of a Roth IRA can hold assets in the account until death without being subject to any penalty taxes. Upon the death of the Roth IRA owner, a designated beneficiary of the account would be required to commence distributions.

The following material discusses payment requirements, the taxation of distributions, and the treatment of premature distributions and rollovers.

Required Distributions

Distribution from a traditional IRA must commence no later than April 1 of the calendar year after the calendar year in which the individual attains age 70½. Although the Small Business Job Protection Act of 1996 no longer requires participants in qualified plans to begin receiving distributions after attaining age 70½ if they are still employed, 5 percent owners and traditional IRA holders are exempted from these modified distribution rules. Accordingly, the holder of a traditional IRA must still commence distributions following attainment of age 70½. Distribution may be in the form of a lump sum, a life annuity or joint life annuity, or in periodic payments not to exceed the life expectancy of the individual or the joint life expectancy of the individual and a designated beneficiary. If the owner of the traditional IRA dies before the entire interest is distributed, the required distribution to the beneficiary depends upon whether distributions to the traditional IRA owner had already been required to start by the date he or she died. If they have, the remaining portion of the interest is distributed at least as rapidly as under the method of distribution being used at the date of death. If they have not, the entire interest of the traditional IRA owner must be distributed to a designated beneficiary commencing in the year following the year in which the employee's death occurred and the distribution must occur over the life of such beneficiary, or over a period not extending beyond the life expectancy of such beneficiary. If a designated beneficiary is not named, the entire interest of the account must be distributed within five years of the account owner's death regardless of who or what entity receives the distribution.[9] Also, under the minimum distribution rules that were amended in 2001 and further revised in 2002 by the Internal Revenue

---

[9] It should be noted that although this particular discussion began by detailing distribution requirements for a traditional IRA, once the IRA owner is deceased the rules related to minimum distributions for a beneficiary would also be applicable for beneficiaries of Roth IRAs.

Service, the determination of a designated beneficiary is not made until September 30 of the year following the IRA owner's death, allowing for postmortem estate planning.[10] If the designated beneficiary is the surviving spouse of the traditional IRA owner, additional flexibility exists. In this case, distributions do not have to begin prior to the time the traditional IRA owner would have attained age 70½. The spouse also may be able to roll over the death benefit to his or her traditional IRA or treat the deceased owner's traditional IRA as his or her own. Additionally, the spouse may then consider conversion of a traditional IRA to a Roth IRA.

If traditional IRA assets are not distributed at least as rapidly as described above, an excise tax will be levied. This excise tax will be 50 percent of the **excess accumulation.** The excess accumulation is the difference between the amount that was distributed during the year and the amount that should have been distributed under the rules described above.[11]

Taxation of Distributions

Traditional IRA distributions (to an individual or his or her beneficiary) are taxable under IRC Section 72. Generally traditional IRA distributions are fully includable as ordinary income if they have been made on a deductible basis, but if nondeductible contributions have been made, a portion of each distribution is treated on a tax-free basis. Individuals making nondeductible contributions must keep records that will enable them to establish the amount excludable from income. Lump-sum distributions do not qualify for long-term capital gains treatment, nor did they qualify for the special five-year averaging treatment made available to qualified plans before the year 2000. Federal and some state income tax withholding may be required from any traditional IRA distributions.

Premature Distributions

If a traditional IRA owner takes a distribution from a traditional IRA before attaining age 59½, it is considered to be a **premature distribution.** The taxable amount of the premature distribution is included in the individual's gross income in the year of receipt, and an additional nondeductible tax penalty of 10 percent of the taxable amount of the premature distribution also applies.

As described previously, this would not be an issue for a Roth IRA if it involved contributions to the plan, because tax would have already been paid on the contributions and contributions may be withdrawn at any time. However, the 10 percent penalty tax is applicable to earnings withdrawn from a Roth account prematurely that are not considered qualified distributions. If the withdrawal of Roth IRA earnings occurs either within the five-year period commencing from the first of the year in which the Roth account was established, or if the withdrawal occurs after this five-year period, but does not involve at least one of the relevant conditions permitting

---

[10] A detailed discussion of tax issues and distribution planning is contained in Chapter 27.
[11] An excess accumulation tax can apply to withdrawals that are not taken from a Roth IRA when the IRA owner has died and a designated beneficiary needs to receive distributions.

for a distribution, the distribution would not be considered a qualified distribution. The relevant conditions permitting a qualified distribution include:

1. The taxpayer has attained age 59½.

2. The taxpayer is disabled.

3. The taxpayer has died and payment is made to a beneficiary or to the individual's estate.

4. The distribution is made to pay first-time home buyer expenses and does not exceed $10,000.

However, certain conditions allow premature distributions from traditional IRAs and nonqualified distributions from Roth IRAs to be exempted from the 10 percent early distribution tax.

Conditions Exempting IRA Distributions from Penalty Taxes

The 10 percent penalty does not apply to distributions made on account of the IRA owner's death or disability. For purposes of the law, an individual is considered to be disabled "if he or she is unable to engage in any substantial gainful activity by reason of any medically determinable physical or mental impairment which can be expected to result in death or to be of long-continued and indefinite character."

There is also an exception for **substantially equal periodic payments** made at least annually over the life or life expectancy period of the individual or joint lives or life expectancies of the individual and a beneficiary. This payment pattern cannot be stopped or changed before the later of the IRA owner's reaching age 59½ or five years from the date of the first payment, or the penalty may be retroactively applied.

The 10 percent penalty tax does not apply if a withdrawal is made on account of an Internal Revenue Service levy on the account to collect taxes. Likewise, a payment made as a timely corrective distribution from an IRA would be exempted from penalty tax. In the case of a payment made to an alternate payee pursuant to a qualified domestic relations order (QDRO), a penalty tax is waived. Although the QDRO rules apply to retirement plans and do not apply to IRAs, the transfer of an individual's interest in an IRA to the individual's spouse or former spouse under a divorce or separation agreement is not considered to be a taxable transfer. As such, this distribution would be similarly exempted because the penalty tax applies only to amounts includible in income.

The Health Insurance Portability and Accountability Act of 1996 instituted certain exceptions that would allow early distribution from an IRA free of the 10 percent penalty tax. For distributions occurring after December 31, 1996, the penalty tax does not apply to distributions from an IRA that are used to pay medical expenses in excess of 7.5 percent of adjusted gross income. Similarly, the penalty tax does not apply to distributions from an IRA used to pay health insurance premiums after separation from employment. In order to be excused from the 10 percent penalty tax, the individual must have received unemployment compensation for at least 12 consecutive weeks under a federal or state program and the IRA withdrawal must occur during any tax year in which the unemployment compensation is received or in the following tax year. Self-employed individuals are treated as qualifying for this exception if they meet all the requirements for receiving unemployment compensation except for the fact that they are self-employed.[12]

The Taxpayer Relief Act of 1997 exempted a withdrawal from the 10 percent penalty tax in 1998 and later years if the withdrawal was for qualified education expenses of the taxpayer, spouse, child, or grandchild; or if the withdrawal is for the purchase of a first home (limited to $10,000).

Rollovers

Under certain conditions, the law permitted amounts to be rolled over on a tax-deferred basis from one plan to another. Such rollovers could be made to an IRA from a qualified plan, a 403(b) arrangement, or another IRA. Rollovers could be made from one IRA to another IRA and, in some circumstances, from an IRA to a qualified plan or 403(b) arrangement.

EGTRRA further expanded the portability of retirement plans beginning in 2002. Beginning at this time, the rollover of distributions was allowed between qualified plans, 403(b) arrangements, and eligible governmental 457(b) plans. The law also allowed eligible rollover distributions from eligible governmental 457(b) plans to be rolled into IRAs. Rollovers of contributory or **conduit IRAs** (those IRAs having received rollover contributions from other plans) into qualified plans, 403(b) plans, or eligible governmental 457(b) plans also was allowed. The law also made provision so that after-tax contributions from a qualified defined contribution plan could be directly rolled over (but not indirectly rolled over within a 60-day period following distribution by way of a regular rollover which is defined below) to another qualified plan. These after-tax contributions from a qualified defined contribution plan could be either rolled over directly or indirectly via a regular rollover into an IRA. In order for a qualified defined contribution plan to receive after-tax amounts, it was required to separately account for such amounts in its record keeping. An IRA receiving rolled-over after-tax contributions was not required to separately account for these amounts.[13]

Rollover contributions to an IRA must be **eligible rollover distributions.** That is, rollover contributions may include any distribution except a required minimum distribution (see Chapters 27 and 12 for discussion of minimum distributions from a qualified plan or 403(b) arrangement, respectively), or any distribution that is part of a series of substantially equal periodic payments over the IRA owner's life, life expectancy, or a period of at least 10 years. If an individual rolls over to an IRA a distribution that is not eligible to be rolled over, a 6 percent excise tax may be imposed on the amount rolled over until it is removed.

---

[12] CCH Editorial Staff, "1996 Tax Legislation: Law and Explanation," *Commerce Clearing House Pension Plan Guide,* no. 1123, August 1996, p. 107.

[13] At the time of publication, it did not appear that after-tax amounts from qualified defined contribution plans could be rolled over either to 403(b) or governmental 457(b) plans under EGTRRA. Nor did it appear that after-tax contributions from 403(b) and governmental 457(b) plans could be rolled over to another plan or to an IRA.

There are two methods of making rollover contributions to an IRA—a direct rollover and a regular or indirect rollover. In a **direct rollover,** the individual instructs the plan trustee or contract issuer to transfer funds directly to the IRA. In a **regular rollover,** the individual receives a check for the eligible rollover distribution from the plan trustee or the contract issuer (net of the required 20 percent federal income tax withholding) and within 60 days of receipt contributes up to the amount of the eligible rollover distribution as a rollover contribution to an IRA. The benefit of using the direct IRA rollover method is that there is no 20 percent federal income tax withholding. An individual using the regular rollover method can contribute the 20 percent withholding amount to the IRA from his or her own funds to retain the tax-deferred rollover of the entire amount of the eligible rollover distribution.

A distribution from an IRA that is reinvested in another IRA within 60 days of receipt also is not taxable to the individual. Rollover contributions are not eligible for the regular IRA contribution deduction. Also, IRA distributions that are required to be distributed at or after age 70½ may not be rolled over. It does not matter whether all or only a portion of the transferor IRA is rolled over into one or more recipient IRAs.

IRA-to-IRA rollovers are limited to one in any 12-month period beginning on the date amounts are received. This limit is applied by tracing the funds rolled over, as illustrated in the following example.

If an IRA owner has two IRAs, IRA-1 and IRA-2, and he or she rolls over the assets of IRA-1 into a new IRA-3, the owner also may make a rollover from IRA-2 into IRA-3 or into any other IRA within one year after the rollover distribution from IRA-1. These are both rollovers because the IRA owner did not receive more than one distribution from either IRA within one year. However, the IRA owner cannot, within the one-year period, again roll over the assets he or she rolled over into IRA-3 into any other IRA. Any distributions from IRA-3 made within the particular one-year period will not qualify as rollovers. They are taxable distributions and may be subject to the 10 percent tax on premature distributions.

Because of the peculiar limits on IRA-to-IRA rollovers, a number of IRA owners prefer to conduct direct transfers from one IRA to another directly.

Estate Tax

For federal estate tax purposes, the entire value of an IRA is included in the decedent's gross estate, though the decedent's estate can avail itself of the marital deduction. EGTRRA repealed the federal estate tax for years beginning after 2009. However, since EGTRRA's provisions are repealed in years after 2010 unless further legislation is passed, the federal estate tax could potentially reemerge in 2011.

Employer-Sponsored IRAs

Although the IRA is viewed primarily as a device for facilitating individual retirement savings, an employer—including a self-employed person—may sponsor an IRA for some or all employees. Sponsoring an IRA or facilitating IRA contributions through payroll deductions is not the same as establishing a SEP plan. A labor union also may sponsor an IRA plan for its members. No requirement exists that an

employer-sponsored IRA be available to all employees or be nondiscriminatory in benefits. The contributions to the IRA may be made as additional compensation or by payroll deduction. Any amount contributed by an employer to an IRA is taxable to the employee as additional compensation income. The employee is then eligible for the IRA tax deduction up to the allowable annual dollar limitation for a given year, unless the "active participation in a qualified plan" rules apply,[14] in which case the contributions may be nondeductible in whole or in part. The amounts contributed are additional compensation and subject to FICA (or Social Security) and FUTA taxes. No federal income tax withholding is required if the employer believes the employee will be entitled to the offsetting IRA tax deduction.

An employer-sponsored IRA may use separate IRA trusts or annuity plans for each employee, or a single account may be used. However, the single account must provide a separate accounting for each participant's interest. Either a commingled trust fund or a nontrusteed group annuity contract with individual certificates may be used. In an employer-sponsored IRA, the prohibited transaction rules apply to transactions between the employer or other disqualified person and the IRA itself. Such prohibited transactions are subject to the ERISA penalties. The entire IRA plan or trust will not be disqualified as a result of a prohibited transaction involving an individual participant. If the individual participant engages in a prohibited transaction with the employer-sponsored IRA, only his or her individual portion of the IRA becomes disqualified, much as if he or she maintained the IRA separately.

An employer sponsoring an IRA may request a determination letter from the IRS. Furthermore, the same reporting, disclosure, and fiduciary requirements applicable to qualified plans under ERISA may apply to an employer sponsoring an IRA plan if the employer endorses the IRA.[15] However, the participation, funding, and vesting rules of ERISA do not apply. Each participant always is 100 percent vested in his or her IRA. If an employer makes no actual contribution to employee IRAs, but merely provides certain facilities, such as payroll deductions or checkoffs, or allows the actual sponsor (e.g., an insurer or labor union) to publicize the program among employees, the reporting and disclosure requirements will not apply to the employer.

Deemed IRAs

EGTRRA created a new form of IRA beginning in 2003. Under this arrangement an employer sponsoring a qualified plan, 403(b) arrangement, or governmental 457(b) plan could add an IRA feature to their plan. Such a feature would allow employees to make voluntary employee contributions to either traditional or Roth IRAs established as separate "add-on" accounts. These add-on accounts or annuities are deemed to be either a traditional or Roth IRA, and are not subject to the normal rules applicable to the particular retirement plan to which they are attached. The **deemed IRAs** are subject to the reporting and other requirements generally applicable to IRAs under the Internal Revenue Code.

---

[14] For a Roth IRA, the active participation rules do not apply. Only income limitations govern ability to contribute to a Roth IRA.

[15] The criteria for an employer endorsement are found in Department of Labor Regulation Section 2510.3-2.

Reporting and Disclosure

An individual having an IRA is not subject to any reporting and disclosure requirements except in years in which a rollover has occurred, nondeductible contributions have been made, or one of the penalty taxes is payable. The issuer, trustee, or custodian of an IRA must provide annual reports of the value of the IRA as of the close of the calendar year, as well as reporting any distributions from the IRA. Distributions may be reported as fully taxable even though they are not because nondeductible contributions have been made. In such a case, the individual must provide documentation of the amount included.

Nonrefundable Tax Credits for Certain Retirement Savers

In an effort to encourage lower- and middle-income workers to save for their retirement, EGTRRA provided nonrefundable tax credits to individuals who are 18 years of age or over, unless they are full-time students or claimed as dependents on another taxpayer's tax return beginning in 2002. The credit may be claimed for tax years beginning in 2002 and ending in 2006. The credit is claimed on the taxpayer's tax return and applies to the first $2,000 in retirement plan contributions. Those retirement plan contributions eligible for the credit would include contributions to traditional and Roth IRAs as well as elective contributions made to SEPs, SIMPLEs, 401(k)s, 403(b)s, and eligible governmental 457(b) plans.

The amount of the nonrefundable credit depends on the individual's adjusted gross income (AGI) with a 50 percent credit available up to a full $1,000 for a single filer with AGI up to $15,000; for a head of household filer with AGI up to $22,500; and for a joint filer with AGI up to $30,000.

A 20 percent credit is available up to $400 for a single filer with AGI between $15,001 and $16,250; for a head of household filer with AGI between $22,501 and $24,375; and for a joint filer with AGI between $30,001 and $32,500.

A 10 percent credit is available up to $200 for a single filer with AGI between $16,251 and $25,000; for a head of household filer with AGI between $24,376 and $37,500; and for a joint filer with AGI between $32,501 and $50,000.

Chapter Summary

- In recognition of the fact that a significant number of American workers were not covered by the private pension system, Congress enabled individuals to establish their own retirement plans on a tax-deferred basis using individual retirement arrangements beginning in 1975. Provisions allowing for individual retirement arrangements were enacted into law as part of the Employee Retirement Income Security Act (ERISA) which was passed into law in 1974.

- Over time, there have been many modifications to the original enabling legislation that created individual retirement arrangements. As a result, there are various types of individual retirement arrangements with their own distinct features and tax implications. These various IRAs include traditional deductible IRAs, traditional nondeductible IRAs, conduit IRAs, employer-sponsored IRAs, deemed IRAs "added on" to employer plans, and Roth IRAs.

- To be eligible to establish an individual retirement arrangement (IRA), an individual must have earned income from personal services—investment income does not qualify for such a plan. However, alimony and separate maintenance paid under a divorce or separation instrument is treated as a compensation substitute and can serve as the basis for an IRA contribution.

- Individual retirement arrangements must be defined contribution–type plans. Regular annual contributions are limited to a fixed dollar amount set for any given year by law or 100 percent of earned income for the taxable year, whichever is less. An individual with a nonworking spouse can contribute a combined amount which is double what a single taxpayer could contribute with a spousal IRA, although no more than the applicable dollar amount for a single individual can be contributed to the IRA of either spouse. The deductibility of IRA contributions depends upon participation in a qualified plan and family income level.

- The Taxpayer Relief Act of 1997 introduced another type of nondeductible IRA—the Roth IRA—that could be used beginning in 1998. Roth IRAs are subject to the same regular annual contribution limits as traditional IRAs. Eligibility to make a Roth IRA regular annual contribution or to convert a traditional IRA to a Roth IRA is related to income limits and does not depend on participation in an employer-sponsored retirement plan. Roth IRAs make available the possibility that "qualified distributions," including earnings which have accumulated tax deferred while in the account, will be distributed tax free if certain conditions are met.

- Distributions must commence from a traditional IRA no later than April 1 of the calendar year after the calendar year in which the account owner attains age 70½. However, a Roth IRA does not require minimum distributions on the part of the original account owner while living, though a designated beneficiary receiving the proceeds of a Roth account is subject to taking minimum distributions. If assets are not distributed from IRAs as needed to meet the required minimum distribution requirements, they are subject to an excise tax of 50 percent on any excess accumulation that should have been distributed from the account. Some distributions from individual retirement accounts also can be subjected to a 10 percent early distribution tax if taken either before the account owner attains age 59½ or qualifies for another exemption from this penalty tax.

- An individual having an IRA is not subject to any reporting and disclosure requirements except in years in which a rollover has occurred, nondeductible contributions have been made, or one of the penalty taxes is payable. The issuer, trustee, or custodian of an IRA must provide annual reports of the value of the IRA as of the close of the calendar year, as well as reporting any distributions from the IRA. Distributions may be reported as fully taxable even though they are not because nondeductible contributions have been made. In such a case, the individual must provide documentation of the amount included.

Key Terms

conduit IRA, p. *320*
conversion, p. *314*
deemed IRAs, p. *322*
direct rollover, p. *321*
earned income, p. *308*

eligible rollover
   distributions, p. *320*
employer-sponsored IRA,
   p. *322*
excess accumulation, p. *318*

excess contribution, p. *312*
flexible premium annuity
   IRA, p. *315*
individual retirement arrangements (IRAs), p. *307*

nondeductible IRA
contributions, p. *312*
premature distribution,
p. *318*
regular annual IRA
contributions, p. *309*

regular rollover, p. *321*
rollover contributions to
IRAs, p. *309*
Roth IRAs, p. *312*
self-directed IRA, p. *314*

substantially equal periodic
payments, p. *319*
unrelated business income,
p. *316*

Questions for Review

1. Describe the reason why Congress first made individual retirement arrangements available.

2. Summarize the various types of IRAs that have developed over time.

3. What conditions must be met for an individual to be eligible to establish an IRA?

4. Can an individual be covered by a corporate qualified pension plan and also by an IRA? Explain the consequences with respect to the deductibility of the IRA contribution.

5. What is a prohibited transaction under ERISA? Explain when this concept can be relevant for IRAs.

6. Are there any restrictions on the period of time over which distributions from a traditional IRA can be made? How would your answer differ for a Roth IRA? Explain.

7. Describe a premature distribution from an IRA and explain the tax penalties that could result from a premature distribution. Explain how the tax implications are different for traditional IRAs and Roth IRAs.

8. What conditions must be met for distributions from a Roth IRA to be considered "qualified distributions" that can be received tax free?

9. Is it possible for a person to receive a lump-sum distribution from a qualified pension or profit sharing plan and transfer the funds tax free to an individual retirement savings plan? If so, what are the federal income tax results?

10. How has EGTRRA resulted in increased portability of retirement plans and what role do IRAs play in pension portability? Explain.

Questions for Discussion

1. Discuss the evolution of IRAs over time and the possible governmental policy concerns that have resulted in this evolution.

2. The IRA deduction limitation will undoubtedly decrease the participation of employees in this arrangement. Discuss how this is likely to affect plan design for qualified plans.

3. Discuss the various approaches to funding IRA plans.

4. Evaluate the relative advantages and disadvantages of traditional IRAs and Roth IRAs. If you were serving as a financial adviser, when would you recommend the use of each?

Resources for Further Study

Altieri, Mark P.; and Richard A. Naegele. "Creditors' Rights, Tax-Qualified Plans, and IRAs." *Journal of Pension Planning & Compliance* 26, no. 4 (Winter 2001).

CCH Editorial Staff. "1996 Tax Legislation: Law and Explanation." *Commerce Clearing House Pension Plan Guide* 1188, no. 1123 (August 1996).

CCH Editorial Staff. "2001 Tax Legislation: Law, Explanation, and Analysis." *Commerce Clearing House Pension Plan Guide* (2001).

Department of the Treasury, Internal Revenue Service, 26 CFR Parts 1, 54, and 602, "Required Distributions from Retirement Plans; Final Rule." (April 17, 2002).

Hansen, Kenneth A. "IRS Makes Qualified Plan and IRA Required Minimum Distributions Smaller and More Uniform." *Journal of Retirement Planning* 4, no. 3 (May/June 2001).

Martin, Ernest L.; and William H. Rabel. "Individual Retirement Arrangements (IRAs), Simplified Employee Pensions (SEPs), SIMPLE Plans, and HR-10 (Keogh) Plans." *The Handbook of Employee Benefits.* 5th ed. Jerry S. Rosenbloom, ed. New York: McGraw-Hill, 2001.

18

Keogh Plans, SEPs, and SIMPLE Plans

After studying this chapter you should be able to:

- Describe various types of tax-favored retirement plans for self-employed individuals and other simplified retirement savings vehicles.

- Note distinctions between self-employed individuals and owner-employees.

- Detail the distinct plan features applicable to Keoghs, simplified employee pension (SEP) plans, and savings incentive match plans for employees (SIMPLE plans).

- Understand the tax effects of transferring assets between various types of plans.

Previous chapters in this book covered retirement plans for employees of incorporated businesses, and Chapter 17 described individual retirement arrangements (IRAs). The focus in this chapter is on two additional groups of workers: (1) self-employed individuals and (2) the employees of self-employed individuals. Tax-favored retirement plans have been provided in the law for these groups in the form of Keogh (HR-10) plans for the self-employed and their employees. As noted in Chapter 17, individual retirement arrangements (IRAs) are available for other individuals planning for their own retirement. In addition, simplified employee pension (SEP) plans may be used by all employers to provide retirement plans for their employees using IRAs as funding vehicles.

Retirement planning for the self-employed and other individuals planning for their own retirement was impacted by the pension simplification provisions of the Small Business Job Protection Act of 1996, a predominant theme of which was to make retirement savings vehicles less complex administratively and more accessible to small businesses. In recognition of the fact that pension plan coverage is far less prevalent among small employers than among medium- and larger-sized firms, Congress was interested in permitting a retirement plan that would not be subject to the same rigors as tax-qualified plans. Although this is true of the aforementioned SEPs, overall participation rates in these arrangements have been somewhat disappointing and have not resulted in a broader level of pension coverage among small employers. Accordingly, the savings incentive match plans for employees (SIMPLE plans) were introduced. SIMPLE plans were first made available in 1997. SIMPLE plans can be designed as either individual retirement accounts (IRAs) or 401(k)-type plans. This chapter describes the historical evolution of these various retirement plan structures, their tax requirements, and their usefulness and appropriateness for accumulating retirement resources.

Plans for the Self-Employed

For many years, corporate employees enjoyed the tax benefits of qualified pension and profit sharing plans, while self-employed individuals (such as partners and sole proprietors) were denied these tax benefits even though they were permitted to establish tax-favored plans for their employees. For approximately 11 years, Congress considered a number of different bills in an effort to remove this tax inequity; the culmination of these efforts occurred in 1962 with the passage of the Self-Employed Individuals Tax Retirement Act, more popularly known as Keogh or HR-10.

This law permitted a self-employed individual to establish a qualified pension or profit sharing plan in which self-employed individuals may participate, but it entailed many restrictions and limitations when compared with the choices available to corporate employees. Because of the restrictions and limitations in **Keogh (HR-10) plans,** many unincorporated businesses incorporated primarily for the tax savings possible under corporate retirement plans. Over the years since 1962, several pieces of legislation liberalized some of the limitations of Keogh plans, and in 1982, the Tax Equity and Fiscal Responsibility Act of 1982 (TEFRA) essentially allowed retirement plans for the self-employed to include many provisions that parallel those of corporate plans. The provisions that apply only to Keogh plans following the passage of TEFRA in 1982 were:

- Employer contributions allocable to the purchase of life, accident, health, or other insurance protection on behalf of a self-employed person were not deductible.

- Loans to owner-employees were prohibited.

A few other special provisions discussed in the remainder of this chapter also applied to Keoghs. However, the passage of the Economic Growth and Tax Relief Reconciliation Act of 2001 (EGTRRA) brought further parity by removing this prohibition on loans for owner-employees. Effective for plan years beginning after December 31, 2001, the prohibited transaction exemption that applies to participant loans under qualified plans is expanded to cover owner-employees.

Plan Provisions

Eligibility

Only a sole proprietor or a partnership may establish a Keogh plan; a common-law employee or an individual partner cannot. This does not preclude, however, a proprietor or partnership from setting up a retirement plan with only the common-law employees participating.

If an owner-employee wishes to establish and participate in a Keogh plan, he or she must cover all employees who are at least 21 years of age and have one year of service with the employer. A two-year waiting period can be used if the plan provides 100 percent vesting after the two-year period. Keogh plans must meet the same nondiscrimination coverage and participation requirements as other qualified plans. These rules (discussed in detail in Chapters 4 and 5) can be especially important for owner-employees under Keogh plans.

Contribution and Benefit

Keogh plans can be established either on a defined benefit or a defined contribution basis. If a defined benefit Keogh plan is used, the same limit applies as for a defined benefit corporate pension plan; that is, the limit is the lesser of 100 percent of the average of the participant's highest three consecutive calendar years of earnings or $160,000 in 2002 (as indexed for inflation in $5,000 increments under Internal Revenue Code formulas).

For defined contribution Keogh plans, the maximum annual contribution is the lesser of 100 percent of the participant's compensation or $40,000 in 2002 (as indexed for inflation in $1,000 increments under Internal Revenue Code formulas). For the self-employed person, defined contribution plan "compensation" is the self-employed person's "earned income from self-employment" less one-half the self-employment tax (not to exceed $200,000 in 2002).

For example, assume in 2002 George Jones was a sole proprietor with two employees each earning $20,000 per year. Mr. Jones's gross revenue for the year was $230,000, and all business expenses before Keogh contributions were $50,000. The Keogh contribution rate is 10 percent. Therefore, the Keogh contribution for each employee was $2,000. George Jones's Keogh contribution would be determined as follows:

Gross revenue	$230,000
Minus business expenses	−50,000
Net income	$180,000
Minus contributions for two employees	−4,000
Net profit	$176,000

George Jones had no other income. Based on his earned income, his total self-employment tax was $12,228. George Jones's contribution would be determined as follows:

$$\text{Contribution for George Jones} = \frac{\text{Keogh contribution rate} \times (\text{Earned income} - \tfrac{1}{2} \text{ Self-employment taxes})}{1 + \text{Keogh contribution rate}}$$

Therefore,

$$\text{Total contribution for George Jones} = .10 \, (\$176,000 - \$6,114) \div 1.10$$

$$= \$16,988.60 \div 1.10$$

$$= \$15,444.18$$

However, the $15,444.18 contribution may not exceed the lesser of 100 percent of earned income less one-half the self-employment tax (which in this example is

$176,000 - $6,114 - $15,444.18) up to $200,000 (in 2002), or $40,000 (in 2002). Because ($176,000 - $6,114 - $15,444.18) was less than $200,000 and is also less than 100 percent of earned income from self-employment and $40,000, the contribution of $15,444.18 is appropriate.

Deductions for Contributions

Contributions made before the due date of the self-employed individual's tax return for the prior year (including extensions) are treated as made for the prior year as long as the plan was established by the end of the prior year, the contributions are designated as applying to the prior year, and the contributions are deducted on the prior year's tax return. The owner's deductions for contributions made on behalf of nonowner employees to a Keogh plan are calculated no differently from those of a corporate employer for its employees under a qualified plan. The owner's deduction for contributions for himself or herself is based on the owner's earned income from self-employment, which takes into account the deduction for one-half the self-employment tax and the deduction for contributions to the plan on the owner's own behalf. In a profit sharing plan, for example, the maximum deductible contribution for the self-employed individual is 20.0000 percent of earned income, less one-half the self-employment tax, before subtracting the amount of the contribution.[1]

Taxation of Distributions

Distributions are taxable in exactly the same fashion as distributions made from a qualified plan established by a corporate employer. Distributions in the form of periodic payments generally had been taxable as ordinary income in accordance with the annuity rules of Section 72 of the Internal Revenue Code. However, the Small Business Job Protection Act of 1996 introduced a simplified method for determining the investment in contract when a distribution occurs from a qualified retirement plan, qualified annuity, or tax-sheltered annuity. Under the simplified method, the employee's nontaxable component of each year's distribution generally equals the nontaxable investment in contract as of the annuity start date, divided by the number of anticipated payments to be received as indicated in the following table:

Primary Annuitant's Age When Annuity Commences	Number of Anticipated Annuity Payments*
55 or younger	360
56 to 60	310
61 to 65	260
66 to 70	210
71 or older	160

*If the annuity contract itself specifies the number of payments to be received, the contractual number of payments would be divided into the investment in contract. This simplified method for determining the nontaxable portion of each annuity distribution took effect 90 days after the signing of the Small Business Job Protection Act, which occurred in August of 1996.

[1] Section 401(c)(2) defines compensation for defined contribution plans as net earnings subject to self-employment tax less one-half the self-employment tax less the pension deduction under Section 404. If this is calculated algebraically disregarding the self-employment tax, 25 percent becomes 0.25/1.25 or 20.0000 percent.

The self-employed individual's cost basis for this purpose generally will be the sum of contributions that he or she was not able to deduct.

For years where income averaging was still available, lump sum distributions to or on behalf of self-employed individuals on account of death, disability, or after attainment of age 59 ½ were the same for regular or common-law employees; this was not applicable to other separations. The Small Business Job Protection Act of 1996 abolished five-year income averaging for lump sum distributions occurring in tax years after December 31, 1999. It should be noted that individuals who became age 50 before January 1, 1986, still may avail themselves of 10-year averaging and capital gains provisions under prior law.

Death Benefits

If a life insurance benefit is provided by the plan, the beneficiary of a plan partici-pant may consider the pure insurance portion of the benefit (i.e., the excess of the face amount over the cash value of the contract) as income tax-free life insurance pro-ceeds. The cash value of the contract, however, as well as any other form of cash distribution under the plan, is considered taxable income to the beneficiary. The ben-eficiary's cost basis is the same as the plan participant's cost basis at the time of his or her death. However, the term costs of insurance protection that were not deducted by the proprietorship would not be a cost basis to the beneficiary. The tax treatment of the distribution is the same as that described for distributions to the plan participant.

Loans

Loans from Keogh plans generally are permitted on the same basis as for qualified retirement plans. As indicated in the beginning of the chapter, plan loans were not per-mitted to self-employed individuals who were owner-employees prior to 2002. Owner-employees are sole proprietors and partners owning more than 10 percent of either the capital or profit interest in a partnership. This prohibition on loans to owner-employees was changed by EGTRRA. Effective for plan years beginning after December 31, 2001, the prohibited transaction exemption that applies to participant loans under qualified plans was expanded to cover owner-employees. This change in the law will now allow owner-employees to take loans. Owner-employees include owners of sole proprietorships, partnerships, or S corporations. Some tax practition-ers have indicated that the ability to access plan loans may provide an incentive for some owner-employees to form Keoghs rather than to use a SEP or a SIMPLE IRA as a retirement plan. Both the SEP and the SIMPLE IRA which use IRAs as funding sources for participant accounts are prohibited from making loans, as are all IRAs.

Whereas all owner-employees are self-employed individuals, not all self-employed individuals are owner-employees. The distinction is in the amount of pro-prietary interest held by the individual. An **owner-employee** is a self-employed individual who owns the entire interest in an unincorporated business (a sole pro-prietor) or a partner who owns more than 10 percent of the capital or profit interest of the partnership. Thus, a partner owning 10 percent or less of the capital or profit interest of a partnership is not an owner-employee, even though he or she is a self-employed individual. This distinction was very important regarding plan loans prior to 2002 because the provisions of the law were more restrictive for self-employed individuals who also were owner-employees.

Within the definition of owner-employee is any stockholder employee in a Subchapter S corporation.

Rollovers

Tax-free rollovers from a Keogh plan to another Keogh plan, to an employer-sponsored retirement plan, a 403(b) plan, a governmental 457(b) plan, or to an individual retirement account are permitted.

Simplified Employee Pension Plans

Congress, in an attempt to encourage the adoption of private pension plans, created the concept of **simplified employee pension (SEP) plans.** In effect, SEPs are individual retirement accounts with higher contribution limits than those normally applicable to these arrangements. Further, they allow an employer to adopt a retirement program with a minimum of paperwork and regulatory compliance. Over the years, Congress has made changes in contribution limits and plan requirements.

This part of the chapter provides a brief overview of the tax law provisions applicable to SEPs. It also includes a discussion of the eligibility requirements applicable to these plans, the deductibility of contributions, and the use of salary reduction arrangements. Because SEPs are IRAs, unless otherwise noted the IRA rules discussed in Chapter 17 generally apply.

General Tax Law Requirements

The general authority for SEPs is found in Sections 408(j) and (k) of the IRC, which provide for an increase in the normal IRA limit if certain requirements are met. Thus, a SEP is treated, under law, as an IRA with higher limits.

The employer establishing a SEP can be an incorporated entity or a self-employed individual. For the employer, a SEP is a plan that uses individual retirement accounts or annuities to provide retirement benefits for employees. The employer must notify the employees of the plan. A SEP program is a defined contribution plan; the defined benefit approach is not permitted for these plans. The SEP must be a formally adopted program having the following characteristics:

• It must be in writing and must specify the requirements for employee participation. Further, it must specify when the employee makes contributions and how each eligible employee's contribution will be computed.

• The employer must make contributions to the SEP for any employee who is at least 21 years of age, has worked for the employer during at least three of the last five years, and has received at least $450 in 2002, indexed for cost-of-living increases, in compensation from the employer for the year.

• Employer contributions may not discriminate in favor of any highly compensated employee (see Chapter 4).

• Employer contributions may be discretionary from year to year. However, the plan document must specify a definite allocation formula.

• Each employee must be fully vested in his or her account balance at all times.

• The program may not restrict the employee's rights to withdraw funds contributed to his or her SEP at any time (i.e., the program must give unrestricted withdrawal rights to the employees).

• The employer may not require that an employee leave some or all of the contributions in the SEP as a condition for receiving future employer contributions.

• In 2001, contributions for an individual in a SEP were limited to the lesser of 15 percent of compensation or $35,000. The amount of includible compensation on which SEP contributions could be based was $170,000 in 2001. EGTRRA increased the percentage of compensation allowance for SEPs from 15 percent of compensation to 25 percent of compensation beginning in 2002. The Section 415 limit was changed by EGTRRA to the lesser of 100 percent of compensation or $40,000 for 2002. The limit on includible compensation was increased to $200,000 in 2002. Also, the amount allocated or contributed in total by the employer for the employee under a SEP and other qualified pension or profit sharing plans may not exceed the Section 415 limits. In addition, an employee may make a regular contribution to an IRA, and this is not aggregated with the SEP contributions for purposes of the 25 percent or Section 415 limits.[2]

• The top-heavy provisions of the law apply to SEP programs; however, a special provision allows employers to elect to measure aggregate employer contributions, instead of aggregate account balances, to test if the SEP has exceeded the 60 percent limit discussed in Chapter 5.

• Because they are IRAs, SEPs cannot permit employees to make loans.

Eligibility

For an IRA funded by employer contributions to be treated as a SEP, the employer must contribute to the SEP of each eligible employee. As long as the employee satisfies the eligibility criteria mentioned above, the employer must make contributions on the employee's behalf. The employer does not have to make a contribution, however, for (1) members of a collective bargaining unit if retirement benefits were the subject of good-faith bargaining and (2) certain nonresident aliens with no United States income source.

Controlled group rules apply to SEPs, and if the employer is a member of a controlled group, SEP contributions must be made for all eligible employees of each one of the businesses that make up the group.

---

[2] Although the allowable contribution limit for SEPs was raised from 15 percent of compensation to 25 percent of compensation at the time of EGTRRA's passage, another section of the Internal Revenue Code dealing with the maximum amount an employer could deduct for a SEP was not changed from 15 percent by EGTRRA. However, the Job Creation and Worker Assistance Act of 2002 increased the percentage for computing the deduction limit from 15 percent to 25 percent. Now the deduction limit and contribution limit are the same.

Contributions

Employer contributions to a SEP must bear a uniform relationship to total compensation not in excess of $200,000, indexed to the consumer price index. However, employer contributions under a SEP may be integrated with Social Security benefits under the same "permitted disparity" rules that apply to defined contribution plans (described in Chapter 4).

The maximum contribution limit to a SEP is 25 percent of income up to $40,000. If the employer contribution to the SEP in any year is less than the normal IRA limit applicable for that year as noted in Chapter 17, the employee may contribute the difference up to the allowable applicable annual limit. The employee contribution may be made either to the SEP or to one or more IRAs of the employee's choice.

Contributions made up to the date of the return for the employer's taxable year (including extensions) are treated as being made on account of that year. For example, the XYZ Company has a SEP that provides for a contribution of 25 percent of an employee's compensation during each calendar year. In 2002, employee A earns $20,000 and the maximum permissible contribution under the tax law is $5,000 (.25 × $20,000). The XYZ Company makes a $2,500 contribution for employee A on December 31, 2002, and contributes the remaining $2,500 on March 15, 2003. The entire $5,000 contribution is treated as being made on account of the taxable year 2002.

It also should be noted that in the case of self-employed individuals (proprietors and partners), the 25 percent contribution limitation will be on the basis of **earned income** as that term is defined in the law. This means that the contribution will be determined with reference to earned income after having subtracted the amount of the contribution and half the self-employment tax. The result is that the 25 percent contribution limit, as it is applied to these individuals, is 20.00 percent of net income before subtracting the amount of the contribution but after subtracting half the self-employment tax.

A SEP may specify a maximum contribution limit that is lower than required by law. Although this could cause contributions to be discriminatory, they will not discriminate in favor of highly compensated employees because contributions for this group represent a smaller percentage of their earnings.

Deductions

The employer's deduction for a SEP contribution may not exceed the actual contribution made to the SEP to the extent that the contributions for each employee do not exceed the 25 percent and/or Section 415 limits. Although the allowable contribution limit for SEPs was raised from 15 percent of compensation to 25 percent of compensation at the time of EGTRRA's passage, another section of the Internal Revenue Code dealing with the maximum amount an employer could deduct for a SEP was not changed from 15 percent. However, the Job Creation and Worker Assistance Act of 2002 increased this amount to 25 percent as well. If the employer contributes more than the amount deductible, the employer can carry over the excess deduction to succeeding taxable years. A 10 percent excise tax is applied on nondeductible contributions (as discussed in Chapter 8).

Salary Reduction Agreements

In the case of a SEP maintained by an employer with 25 or fewer employees through-out the entire preceding year, an employee may elect (provided the plan allows it) to have the employer make payments as elective contributions to the SEP on behalf of the employee through salary reduction. These plans are known as salary reduction simplified employee pension (SARSEP) plans. In order that the plan may be able to receive an elective contribution, at least 50 percent of the employees must elect a salary reduction. The Small Business Job Protection Act of 1996 prohibited the cre-ation of new SARSEP plans after December 31, 1996. These plans were prohibited when SIMPLE plans (described next) were established. Employers who created SARSEPs before January 1, 1997, were permitted to retain these programs and may continue to enroll new hires in the plans according to the pre-1997 rules that govern these plans.

The elective contribution for any employee under a SARSEP may not exceed the allowable elective deferral limits (as set by EGTRRA and indexed for inflation) and the average deferral percentage for *each* highly compensated employee may not exceed 125 percent of the average deferral percentage for all non–highly compen-sated employees. In any event, elective contributions together with any other employer contributions may not exceed the 25 percent/$40,000 limit or the Section 415 limits. At the time of EGTRRA's passage in 2001, the limit on elective deferrals was set at $10,500. EGTRRA increased the elective deferral limit for 2002 and scheduled it to increase in subsequent years according to the following schedule:

Year	Elective Deferral Limit
2002	$11,000
2003	$12,000
2004	$13,000
2005	$14,000
2006	$15,000
Years following 2006	Additional amounts are indexed in $500 increments

EGTRRA also provided a type of employee catch-up contribution in years after 2001 for employees who are at least age 50 before the end of the tax year. These employee catch-up contributions allow for increased elective deferrals. At the time EGTRRA was enacted, employee catch-up contributions were scheduled to increase as follows:

Year	Allowable Catch-up
2002	$1,000 additional
2003	$2,000 additional
2004	$3,000 additional
2005	$4,000 additional
2006	$5,000 additional
Years following 2006	Additional amounts are indexed in $500 increments

Employee catch-up contributions are not subject to any other contribution limits and are not taken into account in applying other contribution limits to other contributions or benefits under a plan. An employer will not fail the Internal Revenue Code (IRC) Section 401(a)(4) nondiscrimination rules if the plan allows all eligible plan participants to make the same election regarding catch-up contributions. However, all plans maintained by related employers are treated as one plan if the employers are treated as a single employer. According to the Conference Committee Report, an employer can make matching contributions with respect to catch-up contributions, although these matches would be subject to all the rules typically applicable to matching contributions.

The definition of excess contributions and the rules for their distribution are similar to those described in Chapter 11 for cash or deferred arrangements.

Savings Incentive Match Plans for Employees (SIMPLE Plans)

General Tax Law Requirements

The Small Business Job Protection Act of 1996 instituted **savings incentive match plans for employees (SIMPLE plans)** for years beginning after December 31, 1996. The legislative intent of these plans was to create a retirement savings vehicle for small employers that was not subject to the complex rules associated with qualified plans, such as the nondiscrimination requirements and top-heavy rules. Accordingly, employers with 100 or fewer employees who received at least $5,000 in compensation from the employer in the preceding year could adopt these plans. A SIMPLE plan allows employees to make elective contributions of up to $7,000 per year in 2002 and requires employers to make matching contributions. EGTRRA increased the maximum annual deferral limits for SIMPLE plans according to the following schedule:

Year	Elective Deferral Limit
2002	$7,000
2003	$8,000
2004	$9,000
2005	$10,000
Years following 2005	Additional amounts are indexed in $500 increments

Also, as a result of EGTRRA, employees age 50 and older are permitted to make catch-up contributions in the following amounts:

Year	Allowable Catch-up
2002	$500 additional
2003	$1,000 additional
2004	$1,500 additional
2005	$2,000 additional
2006	$2,500 additional
Years following 2006	Additional amounts are indexed in $500 increments

A SIMPLE plan may be established either as an individual retirement account or as a 401(k) plan. The required employer matching contribution is either made on a dollar-for-dollar basis (up to 3 percent of an employee's compensation for the year[3]), or the employer can elect to match at a rate lower than 3 percent but not lower than 1 percent (this option to match below 3 percent is available to SIMPLE IRAs but not to SIMPLE 401[k]s). To apply the lower matching percentage, employers must notify employees of their intent to apply the lower match within a reasonable time before the 60-day election period in which employees determine whether they will participate in the plan. Instead of making a matching contribution, an employer can opt to make a nonelective contribution of 2 percent of compensation for each eligible employee who earns at least $5,000 during the year. If opting to make nonelective contributions, the employer is again required to advise eligible employees of its intention within a reasonable time before the 60-day election period during which employees decide whether to participate in the plan. Nonelective contributions are subject to the $200,000 compensation cap in 2002 (indexed) prescribed by Section 401(a)(17) of the IRC, whereas matching contributions are not subject to this limitation.

An employer electing to create a SIMPLE plan may not maintain another qualified plan in which contributions are made or benefits accrued for service in the period beginning with the year the SIMPLE plan is created. All contributions to a SIMPLE account are fully vested and nonforfeitable. In order to participate in a SIMPLE plan, an employee must have received at least $5,000 in compensation in any two prior years from the employer, and the employee must be reasonably expected to receive $5,000 in compensation from the employer during the year. There is no stipulation that a certain number of employees participate in a SIMPLE plan in order for an employer to offer such a plan. If an employer ceases to be eligible to offer such a plan because its number of employees earning over $5,000 grows to exceed 100, it may continue to maintain the plan for two years following the last year in which the employer was eligible. Employers eligible to offer SIMPLE plans are determined on a controlled-group basis, taking businesses under common control and affiliated service groups into consideration. Self-employed individuals may participate in a SIMPLE plan. Certain nonresident aliens and employees covered under a collective bargaining agreement may be excluded from participation.

Employee Contributions

Employees elect to participate in a SIMPLE plan within a 60-day period before the beginning of the year. Employees may modify previous years' elections during the 60-day period. Plans also may allow employees to reduce or change their salary reduction agreements during the year. An employee may terminate participation in the plan at any time during the year, but a plan sponsor can prohibit resumed participation until

---

[3] Although employers making a match to a SIMPLE plan are required to match dollar for dollar up to 3 percent of compensation, employers are able to match dollar for dollar up to the full limit permitted in a given year for an employee. SIMPLE IRAs have no limit applicable to employer deductions whereas SIMPLE 401(k)s are limited to an employer deduction of 25 percent of aggregate gross compensation plus elective deferrals.

the beginning of the following year. Employee elective contributions are wages for purposes of employment taxes.

Employer Contributions

Employer contributions are deductible for the employer. Nonelective contributions are deductible in the year made, and matching contributions are deductible for the employer's tax year if contributed by the due date—including extensions—for the employer's tax return.

Distribution Issues

Distributions from either a SIMPLE IRA plan or a SIMPLE 401(k) plan generally are taxed according to the rules applicable to these arrangements. Withdrawal limitations restricting early distribution from either type of plan generally apply to SIMPLE accounts. Participants in a SIMPLE IRA who take a distribution before age 59½ are subject to the 10 percent penalty tax for early withdrawals. Employees withdrawing contributions during the two-year period beginning on the date of initial participation are subject to a 25 percent penalty tax.

Plan participants may make rollovers to another SIMPLE account on a tax-free basis. A distribution from a SIMPLE account may be rolled into an IRA without penalty if the individual has participated in the SIMPLE account for two years. After the elapse of the required two-year period, SIMPLE account distributions may be rolled over into another SIMPLE plan, a traditional IRA, a qualified plan, a 403(b) plan, or a governmental 457(b) plan.

Employer Administrative Issues

Employers are required to advise employees of their right to make salary reduction contributions under the plan and of the contribution alternative if elected by the employer. Notification to employees must include a copy of the summary plan description prepared by the plan trustee for the employer. The summary plan description must be provided to the employees before the period in which employees make a plan election. Failure to furnish this information to employees can subject the employer to a penalty of $50 a day until the information is provided. Employers must contribute employee elective deferrals no later than 30 days after the last day of the month for which the contributions have been made. Employer matching contributions are due for deposit by the date that the employer's tax return is due, including extensions. An employer makes contributions on behalf of employees to a designated trustee or issuer. Plan participants must be notified that SIMPLE plan account balances may be transferred to another individual account or annuity.

Employers are not required to file annual reports. A SIMPLE 401(k) plan is not subject to the nondiscrimination and top-heavy rules generally applicable to regular 401(k) plans. This exempts them from the actual deferral percentage (ADP) test and the actual contribution percentage (ACP) test where employer matching contributions are involved. Employers also are relieved of fiduciary liability under the Employee Retirement Income Security Act, once a participant or beneficiary exercises control over account assets. Exercise of control over account assets is deemed to have taken place once an account has been established for a year or earlier if an affirmative election has been made regarding initial investment of contributions or a rollover contribution has been made to another SIMPLE account or IRA.

Trustee Administrative Issues

The SIMPLE plan trustee bears certain administrative responsibilities. Annually, the trustee must provide the employer maintaining the plan with a summary description that contains certain required information. Each individual participant must be supplied with an account statement, detailing account activity and an account balance, within 30 days following the end of the calendar year. Trustees also must file a report with the Secretary of the Treasury. Failure to file any of these documents can result in a $50-a-day penalty until the reporting failure is remedied.

Incentives for Small Employers to Offer Plans

When EGTRRA was passed, certain incentives were instituted to encourage small employers to offer retirement plans to their employees. Under these provisions of EGTRRA, small employers with no more than 100 employees will receive a tax credit for costs associated with establishing new retirement plans, effective for costs paid or incurred in tax years beginning after December 31, 2001. The credit equals 50 percent of the costs in connection with creation or maintenance of a new plan. The credit is limited to $500 annually and may be claimed for qualified plan costs incurred in each of the three years beginning with the tax year in which the plan first becomes effective. Eligible plans include defined benefit plans, defined contribution plans, SIMPLE plans, and SEPs. In order to qualify for the credit, the plan must cover at least one employee who is not a highly compensated employee. To preclude employers from receiving both a tax credit and a deduction for plan expenses, expenses used for the credit may not be double-counted as a deductible expense. Additionally to encourage the introduction of small employer plans, EGTRRA enacted provisions that exempt a small employer from paying a user fee. The law exempts the small employer from fees for any determination letter request to the Internal Revenue Service with respect to the qualified status of a pension benefit plan that the employer maintains if the request is made before the later of the fifth year that the plan is in existence, or the end of any remedial amendment period beginning within the first five years of the plan. However, sponsors of prototype plans must pay user fees in connection with any requests for letters since the prototype plan does not require a user fee for a determination letter request in order to establish a plan.

Nonrefundable Tax Credits for Certain Retirement Savers

In an effort to encourage lower- and middle-income workers to save for their retirement, EGTRRA provided nonrefundable tax credits to individuals who are 18 years of age or over, unless they are full-time students or claimed as dependents on another taxpayer's tax return beginning in 2002. The credit may be claimed for tax years beginning in 2002 and ending in 2006. The credit is claimed on the taxpayer's tax return and applies to the first $2,000 in retirement plan contributions. Those retirement plan contributions eligible for the credit would include elective contributions to SEPs, SIMPLEs, 401(k)s, 403(b)s, and eligible governmental 457(b) plans, as well as contributions made to traditional and Roth IRAs.

The amount of the nonrefundable credit depends on the individual's adjusted gross income (AGI) with a 50 percent credit available up to a full $1,000 for a single filer with AGI up to $15,000; for a head of household filer with AGI up to $22,500; and for a joint filer with AGI up to $30,000.

A 20 percent credit is available up to $400 for a single filer with AGI between $15,001 and $16,250; for a head of household filer with AGI between $22,501 and $24,375; and for a joint filer with AGI between $30,001 and $32,500.

A 10 percent credit is available up to $200 for a single filer with AGI between $16,251 and $25,000; for a head of household filer with AGI between $24,376 and $37,500; and for a joint filer with AGI between $32,501 and $50,000.

Chapter Summary

- Self-employed individuals may use a Keogh (HR-10) plan to save for retirement. Additionally, simplified employee pension (SEP) plans may be used by all employers to provide retirement plans for their employees using IRAs as funding vehicles.

- Whereas all owner-employees are self-employed individuals, not all self-employed individuals are owner-employees. The distinction is in the amount of proprietary interest held by the individual:
  - An owner-employee is a self-employed individual who owns the entire interest in an unincorporated business (a sole proprietor) or a partner who owns more than 10 percent of the capital or profit interest of the partnership.
  - A partner owning 10 percent or less of the capital or profit interest of a partnership is not an owner-employee, even though he or she is a self-employed individual.

- Keogh plans can be established either on a defined benefit or a defined contribution basis. If a defined benefit Keogh plan is used, the same limit applies as for a defined benefit corporate pension plan; that is, the amount necessary to fund a benefit is the lesser of 100 percent of the average of the participant's highest three consecutive calendar years of earnings or $160,000 in 2002 (as indexed for inflation under IRC formulas). For defined contribution Keogh plans, the maximum annual contribution is the lesser of 100 percent of the participant's compensation or $40,000 (as indexed for inflation in $1,000 increments).

- Sponsoring an individual retirement arrangement or facilitating IRA contributions through payroll deduction is not the same as establishing a simplified employee pension (SEP) plan. A SEP must be a formally adopted program.

- Simplified employee pension (SEP) plans allow an employer to adopt a retirement program with a minimum of paperwork and regulatory compliance. Using individual retirement arrangements as funding vehicles, these plans permit higher contribution limits than those normally associated with IRAs. Contributions for an individual in a SEP are limited to the lesser of 25 percent of compensation or $40,000 in 2002.

- A SIMPLE plan is available to employers with 100 or fewer employees. SIMPLE plans may be structured either as IRAs or 401(k)-type plans. These plans afford employees the opportunity to make elective contributions of up to $7,000 per year in 2002 and indexed by EGTRRA in future years (after increasing according to the EGTRRA schedule, these amounts are indexed for inflation) and require employers to make matching contributions under various prescribed formulas. Generally an employer match will take the form of a dollar-for-dollar match up to 3 percent of an employee's compensation, although an employer also can opt for either a match that is lower than 3 percent but not lower than 1 percent (if the plan is an IRA) or alternatively a nonelective contribution of 2 percent of pay.

Key Terms

earned income, p. *334*
Keogh (HR-10) plans, p. *328*
owner-employee, p. *331*

savings incentive match plans for employees (SIMPLE plans), p. *336*

simplified employee pension (SEP) plans, p. *332*

Questions for Review

1. Describe the types of tax-favored retirement plans available to self-employed individuals.
2. Distinguish between a self-employed individual and an owner-employee.
3. Describe the contribution deduction limits available for defined benefit and defined contribution Keogh plans.
4. What annual limitations apply to the maximum amount that may be contributed by or on behalf of an employee under a SEP?
5. For whom must employers make contributions under a SEP?
6. Explain how the limitation on compensation that may be taken into account under a SEP can also affect the percentage of pay that must be contributed for non–highly compensated employees.
7. What is the deduction limit for employer contributions made to a SEP?
8. Under what circumstances may a SIMPLE plan be offered by an employer?
9. What are the different types of employer contributions that can be made to SIMPLE plans?
10. Distinguish between employer and trustee administrative responsibilities in operating a SIMPLE plan.

Questions for Discussion

1. Discuss how retirement plans for the self-employed compare with qualified corporate retirement plans.
2. Discuss the decision factors in the selection of an appropriate retirement plan for a small employer.
3. Evaluate the relative advantages and disadvantages of a conventional deferred profit sharing plan and a SEP in terms of their application to a self-employed individual as a means of establishing a formal program for accumulating retirement funds.
4. SEPs are, under law, treated as IRAs with higher limits. Likewise, SIMPLE plans established as IRAs allow for higher limits than standard IRAs. What justification exists for permitting higher-limit IRAs for some individuals and not for others?

Resources for Further Study

CCH Editorial Staff. "1996 Tax Legislation: Law and Explanation." *Commerce Clearing House Pension Plan Guide* 1188, no. 1123 (August 1996).

CCH Editorial Staff. "2001 Tax Legislation: Law, Explanation, and Analysis." *Commerce Clearing House Pension Plan Guide* (2001).

Damato, Karen. "The One-Man Band Gets a Gift from 401(k) Rules." *Wall Street Journal,* August 17, 2001.

Kaster, Nicholas. *A Guide to SIMPLE Plans.* Chicago: CCH Incorporated, 1997.

Martin, Ernest L.; and William H. Rabel. "Individual Retirement Arrangements (IRAs), Simplified Employee Pensions (SEPs), SIMPLE Plans, and HR-10 (Keogh) Plans." In *The Handbook of Employee Benefits.* 5th ed. Jerry S. Rosenbloom, ed. New York: McGraw-Hill, 2001.

19

Hybrid Retirement Plans[1]

After studying this chapter you should be able to:

- Identify the various types of hybrid benefit plans.

- Note similarities between various hybrid plans and the primary differences that distinguish each of these plans.

- Explain the advantages and disadvantages associated with hybrid plan designs.

- Describe employer characteristics and business conditions that warrant the use of hybrid plan designs.

- Explain the nondiscrimination testing considerations that are important with certain hybrid plan designs.

- Suggest approaches for introducing hybrid plans and explain the challenges that may be encountered in migrating to these newer plan designs from traditional defined benefit or defined contribution plans.

What Is a Hybrid Plan?

Traditional defined benefit and defined contribution plans all have a set of advantages and disadvantages that may or may not meet the needs of employers and workforces.

[1] The authors wish to express their appreciation to the International Foundation of Employee Benefit Plans (IFEBP) for permission to use this material. "What's on the Menu Today? Hybrid Retirement Plans" by Peter J. Alles is reprinted with permission from the *Employee Benefits Practices*, 1st Quarter 2000, published by the International Foundation of Employee Benefit Plans, Brookfield, WI. All rights reserved. Statements or opinions expressed in this article are those of the author and do not necessarily represent the views or positions of the International Foundation, its officers, directors, or staff.

Some plan sponsors, finding it difficult to tweak the design of traditional defined benefit and defined contribution plans to meet the unique needs of their business or employees, have responded by offering two separate plans, one a defined benefit and the other a defined contribution plan. Others have begun turning to hybrid retirement plans.

The concept of a hybrid plan is not entirely new. Floor-offset hybrid plans were fairly common before an Internal Revenue Service (IRS) revenue ruling disallowed them in 1969, but have again been allowed since an IRS revenue ruling in 1976.[2] Form 5500 filing data indicates there were 6,778 target benefit hybrid plans in existence in 1996, and 1,009 had effective dates prior to 1980.[3] Cash balance hybrid plans made their debut in the mid-1980s,[4] although momentum among employers to adopt cash balance plans did not appear to build significantly until more recent years. In contrast, pension equity plans came of age in the early 1990s, as did age-weighted profit sharing and new comparability plans, which were given a boost by Internal Revenue Code Section 404(a)(4) nondiscrimination regulations released in 1993.[5]

Hybrid retirement plans blend attributes of traditional defined benefit pension plans and defined contribution plans in an effort to meet objectives plan sponsors find difficult to achieve with traditional defined benefit or defined contribution plans, alone or in pairs. While hybrid plans come in several types and plan designs, each is considered either a defined benefit or a defined contribution plan for the purposes of tax qualification.[6] Within these two categories the design and purpose of the plans vary significantly. Some defined benefit hybrids are designed to appeal to younger and more mobile workers by providing a portable lump sum benefit option, while maintaining some of the security of a defined benefit structure for older workers. Others use age-weighted formulas that appeal more to older workers. Defined contribution hybrids, on the other hand, are sometimes designed to provide more assurance that income replacement goals will be met while retaining defined contribution flexibility. Others are used to provide a larger allocation of contributions to specific types of workers.

While hybrid plans are often touted as offering flexible options for employers to meet the needs of diverse and changing workforces, the advantages and disadvantages are as varied as the plans and plan designs. In addition, features advantageous to one plan sponsor or participant may not be advantageous to others. As a result, plan sponsors need to review the current benefit package and any possible changes

---

[2] Pati Robinson and William Small, "The Floor Offset Retirement Plan: Versatile and Tested, It Merits More Attention," Compensation & Benefits Review, May/June 1993, 32, 33.

[3] The Form 5500 data is from Pension/Benefits DataMaster, Summer 1998 Release, Version 5.2 by Larkspur Data Resources, Inc. Larkspur combines 5500 filings from several years, conducts edit checks and eliminates duplicates to establish a set of plans existing in a particular calendar year, in this case, 1996.

[4] Raymond J. Lee and William P. Bishop, "Trends in Pensions—Hybrid Pension Plans," The Pension Actuary, March–April 1999, 4.

[5] See Michael E. Lloyd and Mark K. Dunbar, "Benefits Testing: The Dawn of a New Day for Defined Contribution Planning," Journal of Pension Planning & Compliance, Fall 1993, 49.

[6] An exception is a floor-offset plan, which is really two plans working together. The defined benefit plan funds the difference between the benefit accumulated by a defined contribution plan and a minimum benefit level, or floor benefit.

in light of various factors including, but not limited to, workforce demographics and mobility, employee attitudes toward current retirement benefits, relative levels of benefits and rates of benefit accrual, and cost constraints for the plan sponsor. Finally, some hybrid plan types and their sponsors have been criticized for negative effects on the benefit accruals or values of certain groups of plan participants. These criticisms and concerns make awareness of the legal, regulatory, and public relations environment of hybrid plans particularly important for plan sponsors considering a hybrid.

Defined Benefit Hybrid Plans

As with traditional defined benefit plans, sponsors of defined benefit hybrid plans promise a specific benefit level and direct investment of plan assets through commingled funds, bear investment risk, and reap investment reward. The plans are relatively easy to integrate with Social Security and establish income replacement targets. Although defined benefit plans must offer distributions in the form of annuities, hybrids also offer lump sums as an option. Defined benefit hybrids are also subject to Employee Retirement Income Security Act (ERISA) requirements for defined benefit plans, including minimum standards for eligibility, vesting, and funding. Chapter 5 provides a detailed discussion of eligibility, vesting, and funding requirements. Annual valuations are required, as is payment of Pension Benefit Guaranty Corporation (PBGC) premiums for plan termination insurance. As hybrid plans, however, they have some of the attributes normally associated with defined contribution plans, such as portable benefits and benefits expressed in terms of lump sum values instead of annuities.

Cash Balance Plans

A cash balance plan is considered a defined benefit plan because the sponsor makes contributions based on a specified formula that provides an annual contribution credit and applies a fixed interest rate credit, making the eventual benefit definitely determinable.[7] **Cash balance plans** take on the appearance of defined contribution plans to participants who receive periodic benefit statements based on hypothetical accounts showing accrued benefit balances. The hypothetical statements are only a communication tool, however, because plan assets are commingled and directed by the plan sponsor. There are no individual accounts, and the amount of benefit shown on the account statement bears no relationship to actual assets held by the plan.

Cash balance plans are career average plans because the contributions credited to participants are typically based on a formula that considers their pay in each year of

---

[7] Some hybrid designs similar to cash balance plans link benefits to an equities index rather than a fixed rate of return. Other cash balance plan sponsors reduce costs by offering a lower level of guaranteed benefits with a cash balance plan, but introduce profit sharing elements that increase contributions in periods of good business performance. See Patricia Rotello and Thomas Osmond, "Part Cash, Part Balancing Act: Why Cash Balance Plans Get So Much Attention," *Journal of Compensation and Benefits,* May/June 1999, 14.

employment.[8] The portable lump sums and relatively early accrual of benefits under cash balance plans are attractive to employees terminating at younger ages and after fewer years of service, while workers with more years of service are likely to receive more benefits from the traditional defined benefit formula. See Figure 19.1 for a comparison of accrual patterns under traditional defined benefit, cash balance, and pension equity plans.

Plan sponsors also may benefit from conversion to a cash balance plan because, as career average plans, they are likely to be less expensive than a final pay defined benefit plan. In addition, the plan sponsor may guarantee an interest rate below what the sponsor expects it can generate on investments, and the higher rate of return reduces the future plan costs for the sponsor.[9]

A disadvantage of cash balance plans is that older participants and those with more years of service have less protection from pre- and post-retirement inflation. Their benefits have less direct relation to income replacement needs than under a plan linking benefits to final average pay. Nonetheless, plan sponsors may use flexible formulas that include age or service weights, integration with Social Security, or the ability to use part of plan benefits to pay health insurance premiums after retirement.[10]

---

[8] Everett T. Allen et al., *Pension Planning: Pension, Profit Sharing, and Other Deferred Compensation Plans,* 8th ed. (New York: The McGraw-Hill Companies, Inc., 1997), 328.

[9] Dennis R. Coleman, "Cash Balance Pension Plans and Other Evolving Hybrid Pension Plans," in *The Handbook of Employee Benefits: Design, Funding and Administration,* ed. Jerry S. Rosenbloom, 4th ed. (Chicago: Irwin Professional Publishing, 1996), 766.

[10] Rotello and Osmond, 14. Concerning Integration with Social Security, see Gerald E. Cole, "An Explanation of Pension Plans," *Employee Benefits Journal,* June 1999, 8, 9.

FIGURE 19.1   Comparison of Accrual Patterns: Traditional Defined Benefit, Cash Balance, and Pension Equity Plans

Source: Gerald E. Cole, Milliman & Robertson, Inc.

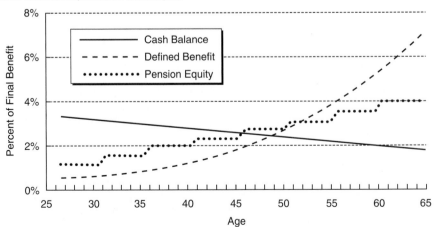

Pension Equity Plans

Pension equity plans are based on final average pay and the percentage credits participants receive each year. Upon termination of employment or retirement, the sum of percentage credits is applied to final average pay to determine the lump sum benefit, which is portable.[11] The percentages upon which credits are based can be relatively flat, but often increase in steps with age or length of service. The age- or service-weighted credits and final average pay formula make pension equity plans appealing to older workers and persons hired in midcareer who have fewer years to accrue benefits. See Example 19.1 for details on how credits often increase by age and/or service in a pension equity plan.

EXAMPLE 19.1   Pension Equity Plan

The year is 2020. Joe Cubicle began working for Company X in 1999, at age 34. His pay has averaged $74,000 for the past five years. He is deciding whether to retire now, at age 55, or work until age 67. His credited percentages in the pension equity plan are as follows.

Age	Annual Percentage Credited	Number of Years	Total Percentage	Factor Applied to Final Average Pay
34–35	3.0%	2	6.0%	
36–40	4.0	5	20.0	
41–45	5.0	5	25.0	51% at age 45
46–50	6.5	5	32.5	
51–55	8.5	5	42.5	126% at age 55
56–60	10.5	5	52.5	
61–67	13.5	7	94.5	273% at age 67
Total			273.0	

What will Joe's lump-sum benefit be?

If he retires at 55, then: $74,000 final average pay × 1.26 = $93,240 lump sum benefit.

If Joe decides to wait until age 67 and assumes steady 2.5% annual pay Increases, then: $104,200 final average pay × 2.73 = $284,466 lump sum benefit.

If Joe assumes he is moving onto the fast track and will receive steady 5.0% annual pay increases, then $139,000 final average pay × 273 = $379,470 lump sum benefit.

Alternatively, if Joe leaves to take another job at age 45 with a final average pay of $65,700, then: $65,700 final average pay × 0.51 = $33,507 lump sum benefit.

Source: Age brackets and percentage credits are from Everett T. Allen et al., *Pension Planning: Pension, Profit Sharing, and Other Deferred Compensation Plans,* 8th ed., 1997, 339.

---

[11] Although expressed in a lump sum, participants must have an option to take pension equity benefits as an annuity. Allen et al., 337.

There is not always a strong distinction drawn among pension equity, life cycle, and cash balance plans.[12] The most widely mentioned pension equity plan was adopted by RJR Nabisco when the company determined its cash balance plan did not adequately meet the needs of its workforce.[13] RJR Nabisco determined a pension equity plan would more equitably meet the needs of an emerging two-tiered workforce, in which a large number of baby boomers are aging and becoming less mobile while a shrinking number of younger and more mobile workers are joining the workforce each year.[14]

Life Cycle Pension Plans

Similar to pension equity plans, and sometimes considered a pension equity variation, is the **life cycle pension plan.** Life cycle plans make use of hypothetical account balances to communicate benefits to participants.

In addition, **retirement bonus** or mobility bonus **plans** are names sometimes used interchangeably with life cycle plans and are sometimes considered variations of the pension equity plan. Participants in these plans receive, upon retirement, a lump sum based on an accumulation of annual credits multiplied by final average salary.[15] However, adding to the possible confusion, the term *retirement bonus* also appears to be used for some defined contribution plans that allocate contributions on the basis of performance-related pay.[16] See Table 19.1 for a summary of key features of defined benefit hybrid plans.

Benefit Accrual

The relative rates of benefit accrual and methods with which benefits are allocated are central to understanding the purpose of defined benefit hybrid retirement plans and their effect on plan sponsors and participants. Compared with the traditional defined benefit plans they often replace, more benefit accrual typically takes place in earlier years of service for participants of cash balance plans. Expressed in terms of a chart (see the Figure 19.1 on page 346), benefit accrual for cash balance plans is flat and steady. Traditional defined benefit plans have rates of accrual that remain relatively low, but jump considerably in later years.

Combining earlier benefit accrual with portability makes the cash balance plan more favorable to younger, mobile workers. Conversion to a cash balance plan from a traditional defined benefit plan can negatively affect the benefits, however, of midcareer or older workers who had begun to accrue sizable benefits in a traditional

---

[12] Michael Karlin, "The Life Cycle Pension Plan: A Step Ahead," *Pension World,* May 1992. See also David M. Traverso, "New DB Plan Designs," *The Pension Actuary,* December 1992.

[13] Jeff Barge, "Designing Equitable Pensions," *Crain's New York Business,* 17 June 1996, 33.

[14] Gerald Angowitz and Eric Lofgren, "A Pension Plan for Today," *Financial Executive,* January/February 1993, 24.

[15] Allen et al., 338. See also Traverso, 5. Traverso refers to a multivalue pension plan and describes it as a combination of cash balance and traditional defined benefit plan in which a benefit is calculated using both the cash balance and traditional defined benefit formulas, and the participant receives the greater of the two.

[16] See Kevin Fliege's article, "The Qualified Retirement Bonus Plan," *Journal of Pension Benefits,* Fall 1996.

TABLE 19.1   Key Features of Defined Benefit Hybrid Plans

	Traditional Defined Benefit	Cash Balance	Pension Equity
Benefit Determination	Can be based on career average or final average pay.	Based on career average pay. May include age or service weights.	Based on final average pay, typically with age or service weights.
Benefit Accrual	Most accrual in later years, favoring employees with long service records.	Age-natural accrual favors younger employees and midcareer hires.	Age-weighted accrual favors older employees and fast-track employees.
Distribution	Traditionally an annuity with no portability. Alternate designs may offer lump sums.	Annuity or lump sum. Vested lump sums are portable upon termination.	Annuity or lump sum. Vested lump sums are portable upon termination.
Hypothetical Accounts/ Balances	Not used.	Used to communicate lump-sum benefit.	Not generally used, but possible with life cycle plan.

defined benefit plan (although there are additional provisions plan sponsors can use to hold older workers harmless).

In the case of pension equity plans, benefits build steadily, but in steps, as credit percentages increase as participants move from one age bracket to the next. (Again see Figure 19.1 on page 346.) The age-weighted brackets often used by pension equity plans increase the rate of accrual with age. In contrast to cash balance plans, pension equity plans are more favorable to older workers and persons hired at mid-career who have fewer years to accrue benefits. Yet, the effect of age-weighting is not likely to tilt benefit accrual toward later years as significantly as a traditional defined benefit plan.

Earlier benefit accruals and portability features, in either the cash balance or pension equity plans, may increase plan costs in the short run as mobile employees terminate and take benefits with them.[17] As a result, knowledge of employee turnover rates and the expected effects of plan design on turnover rates may affect a plan sponsor's choice of plans or plan designs. On the other hand, a cash balance plan sponsor reflects only the expense of current pay on financial statements, whereas the sponsor of a final average pay plan must recognize future salary increases.[18]

[17] Elayne Robertson Demby, "Cash Balance Converts," *Plan Sponsor,* June 1999, 24.
[18] Ibid., 30.

Benefit Portability and Lump Sums

A key feature of cash balance and pension equity plans is how they combine a defined benefit plan structure with the participant option to roll over a lump sum into another plan or an individual retirement account upon separation. Portability has been recognized as a way to attract younger and more mobile employees who would not normally expect to receive a significant benefit from traditional defined benefit plans. Portability can be advantageous to some midcareer employees who may otherwise feel bound to stay with a company in anticipation of traditional defined benefits. (Some refer to this condition as pension jail because these participants have enough service to have retirement security within sight if they stay, but they are likely to have very limited benefits from the plan if they leave. The result is that separating participants need to start rebuilding their retirement benefits, but with fewer working years left.) With a cash balance or pension equity plan, midcareer employees can take their account balances and move their careers in a new direction. At the same time, portability serves as a release valve for some companies because employees who are unhappy are able to leave.

There are several possible disadvantages of portability. First, some plan sponsors may find the portable account balances make it too easy for employees to leave for other employment too quickly. Second, the meaningfulness of portability is driven, in part, by rates of benefit accrual. If benefits do not accrue quickly enough, younger and more mobile participants may not view the portable benefit as sufficient and may not perceive the plan as attractive. For example, benefit portability would not be as meaningful with the accrual rates of a traditional defined benefit plan as with the accrual rates in cash balance plans because the lump sums are likely to be very small comparatively until the very later years of a career. Midcareer workers seeking a new employer will view the pension equity accrual rates more favorably than under a cash balance plan because benefits accrue more rapidly in higher age categories under the age-weighted approach. (Cash balance plan sponsors may also add age weights to the benefit plan formula.)

Third, if the overriding purpose of the plan sponsor is to provide retirement benefits, then the option to take a lump sum distribution upon retirement or termination may defeat this purpose. Participants may choose not to roll over their distributions to new plans or to individual retirement accounts, jeopardizing their retirement security. One survey indicates a much higher percentage of 401(k) plan participants with smaller account balances take their lump sums in cash and do not roll over balances to other plans or individual retirement accounts.[19] Although the survey shows a higher percentage of participants with larger account balances roll over their lump sum payments to other plans or individual retirement accounts, the concern remains that the smaller account balances taken as cash are accounts that could have grown to help build retirement security in later years. The small accounts could also represent the bulk of retirement funds for some low–wage earners who are likely to find it more difficult to "catch up" with retirement saving as they age.

---

[19] Survey results by Hewitt Associates LLC as reported in "DC Plan Participants Aren't Rolling Over," *Pensions & Investments,* 4 October 1999, 28.

In addition to the portability of funds, proponents of some hybrid plans assert that benefits expressed in terms of lump sums, such as the hypothetical account balances in cash balance plans, are more easily understood by participants and more appreciated. Whether this is true may be a point of debate and may depend on individual participants and their circumstances. A portable lump sum dollar amount is easily understood and appreciated in present terms for participants deciding whether to depart for other employment. On the other hand, it is possible for sponsors of traditional defined benefit plans to provide participants with summaries of projected and accrued benefits.[20] In addition, hypothetical account balances can cause some confusion. For example, if the interest credits of a cash balance plan are indexed rather than fixed, the amount of benefit shown by the hypothetical account balance may be different from the actual payout because the balance changes with interest fluctuations. When interest credits increase, it may actually appear to the participants that benefits have been cut.[21]

Investment Risk and Reward

Traditional defined benefit plans and defined benefit hybrid plans place investment decisions and the resulting risk and reward in the hands of plan sponsors, who guarantee a defined benefit. But the entire allocation of risk and reward does not always have to fall upon plan sponsors. Defined benefit hybrid plans can include design features that shift investment risk and reward opportunities to participants in whole or in part. In some instances, some shared risk and reward may be appreciated by plan participants, some of whom are familiar with investing. They may want some of the opportunities, and may be willing to bear some of the risks associated with investing in equities.

Some varieties of cash balance and other defined benefit hybrids are creative in how they assign risk and reward. For example, a **minimum balance pension plan** is a cash balance variant that offers participants the greater benefit of either a traditional defined benefit pension plan (often final average pay) or the benefit accumulated by the cash balance method.[22] Other cash balance variations give employees the option of linking the growth rate of their accounts with an equities index, introducing the prospect of both higher returns and more risk to participants.[23]

Outside of plan design variations, plan sponsors may be able to help with preretirement inflation and the possibility of lagging income replacement needs on an ad hoc basis. Several multiemployer funds with cash balance plans have made it a practice to periodically share positive investment experience in excess of the guaranteed interest rate by making adjustments to accrued benefits that are reflected in the account balance statements participants receive.[24] Not only do participants see a very

[20] Thomas O'Conner and William F. Noyes, "Ten Issues to Consider with a Cash Balance Retirement Plan," *Benefits & Compensation Solutions,* September 1999, 59.
[21] Ibid.
[22] Allen et al., 333 and 334.
[23] Ibid.
[24] Joseph Moynihan, "Introduction to Cash Balance Plans," presentation at the 44th Annual Employee Benefits Conference of the International Foundation of Employee Benefit Plans, Las Vegas, 13 and 14 October 1998, cassette. For information on how to order this cassette or other cassettes, contact IFEBP Audiovisual Department at (888) 33-IFEBP, option 6.

direct additional benefit and some protection against preretirement inflation (which can be troublesome for cash balance plans because they are based on career average pay), but the plan sponsor gets direct credit for the increase. Regardless, the opportunity to grant ad hoc benefit adjustments to share good investment experience is not unique to cash balance plans and has been used with traditional defined benefit retirement plans.

The Transition to Defined Benefit Hybrid Plans

Many defined benefit hybrid plans begin with conversion from a traditional defined benefit plan. Plan conversions can be a sensitive issue regardless of the types of plans involved. Since different plans have different rates of accrual or allocation methods, some plan participants will fare better than in the previous plan and others will see a less favorable situation with the new plan. Furthermore, regardless of how individuals or groups of participants actually fare in the new plan compared with the old (which they may not be able to determine without help from the plan sponsor), attitudes toward change and feelings about employer motives are important to consider. Some plan participants may be wary of any type of change. And, in some cases, employers have been criticized for using plan conversions as a way to recoup large amounts of surplus pension plan assets. Other possible reasons for differing levels of acceptance among participants in some plans include the relative levels of interest or indifference to benefit changes, differences in the amount of participant knowledge of the changes and their effects, and the relative success of some participants in publicizing views concerning changes.

Much of the negative attention concerning conversions has been focused on cash balance plans. The conversion of a traditional defined benefit plan to a cash balance plan often causes a condition some call "**pension wear away**" for participants with longer service records because of the difference in benefit accrual patterns between plans. Employees who have reached or are nearing the final stage of a traditional defined benefit plan, generally the later years of a career when the benefit accrual rate increases rapidly, will experience a sudden decrease in accrual rates and expected benefit under a cash balance plan with less of the overall benefit accrual taking place in later years.[25]

Another concern is that some companies convert from traditional defined benefit plans to cash balance plans to take advantage of the reduced rates of accrual. Reduced rates of accrual may result in a larger surplus for the new plan, and a larger surplus can translate into lesser future costs for the plan sponsor.[26] In addition, plan sponsors can report surplus assets on their income statements and pension income can constitute as much as 3 percent of annual corporate operating income for large companies.[27] Regardless, a strong motivation for conversion can be plan design changes,

---

[25] Rotello and Osmond, 19, suggest the effect on older workers' benefits may be an advantage to some plan sponsors because it will help the sponsor retain older workers.

[26] In the case of a sufficiently large surplus, plan sponsors may make their future contributions from surplus assets rather than from the operating income of the company. Plan sponsors then have more operating income available to meet other goals and objectives.

[27] Mike Barry, "Who Gets the Surplus: No One," *Pensions & Investments,* 4 October 1999, 16.

and some conversions appear to have been positively received by employers and employees alike. Reasons for the more favorable reception toward some conversions can be attributed in some cases to provisions to hold employees harmless. Methods for holding employees harmless from adverse effects of a conversion include:

- Allowing all employees to choose between the old plan and the new plan

- Allowing employees whose benefits are adversely affected by the conversion the choice to remain in the old plan

- Making an adjustment to initial account balances of the new plan for adversely affected employees

- Making additional contributions to other plans sponsored by the employer and within which the adversely affected employees are participating.

Plan sponsors need to carefully consider the cost of these types of **"grandfather" provisions** and adjustments. For example, when one company recently announced the addition of a pension equity formula to its defined benefit plan, the company also enhanced the match on its 401(k) plan. The company is also creating retirement planning software and holding workshops to assist plan participants in understanding the combined impact of the pension equity formula and the new 401(k) plan options.[28] Other companies have enhanced or started stock option programs.[29]

Although a number of companies have already converted traditional defined benefit plans to cash balance plans, uncertainty surrounding future conversions of traditional defined benefit plans to cash balance plans has been a political and regulatory issue for hybrid plans. In light of the conversion controversy, the IRS stopped issuing letters of determination for new cash balance plans. In addition, the federal Equal Employment Opportunity Commission (EEOC) established a "National Cash-Balance Pension Team" to investigate the effects of plan conversions to determine whether they unlawfully discriminated against older plan participants covered by the Age Discrimination in Employment Act (ADEA).[30]

Defined Contribution Hybrid Plans

Defined contribution hybrid plans combine a defined contribution plan structure with attributes of a defined benefit plan, such as the ability to allocate benefits in favor of specific participant groups or plan sponsor contributions that are determined actuarially and are fixed obligations. Defined contribution hybrid plans include target benefit plans, age-weighted profit sharing plans, and new comparability plans. Table 19.2 compares key features of defined contribution hybrid plans.

---

[28] Arleen Jacobius, "Motorola Adds PEP to Its Defined Benefit Plan," *Pensions & Investments,* 12 July 1999, 3.
[29] Robertson Demby, 27.
[30] U.S. Equal Employment Opportunity Commission, "EEOC Creates National Cash-Balance Pension Team," Press Release, http://www.eeoc.gov/press/9–20–99.html.

TABLE 19.2 Key Features of Defined Contribution Hybrid Plans

	Target Benefit Plans	Age-Weighted Profit Sharing Plans	New Comparability Plans
Contribution Flexibility	Contributions are a fixed annual obligation of plan sponsor.	Contributions are discretionary.	Contributions are discretionary.
Contribution Determination/ Allocation	Contributions are determined actuarially to meet targeted income replacement.	Contributions are allocated on an age-weighted basis favoring older, highly compensated participants.	Contributions are allocated among separate and distinct allocation groups keyed to criteria such as ownership or position. This plan favors specific employees.
Contribution Targets	Specific income replacement levels are targeted for all participants, but not guaranteed.	Contributions are skewed toward older, highly compensated participants.	Contributions are skewed toward a narrow, select group of participants.
Investment Direction	Most often participant directed.	Most often participant directed.	Most often participant directed.
Accounts and Accumulation	Individual account balances reflect contributions, investment gains and losses. Participants bear risk and receive rewards.	Individual account balances reflect contributions, investment gains and losses. Participants bear risk and receive rewards.	Individual account balances reflect contributions, investment gains and losses. Participants bear risk and receive rewards.

Target Benefit Plans

Although **target benefit plans** are considered defined contribution plans, the plan sponsor's required contributions are determined actuarially in order to meet income replacement targets established in the plan and expressed in terms of a percentage of salary near the time of retirement. Once an initial contribution formula is established, subsequent adjustments to actuarial assumptions are not made.[31] Despite using actuarially determined contributions, target benefit plans are defined contribution plans because the targets are not guaranteed, individual participant account

---

[31] Michael J. Canan, *Qualified Retirement and Other Employee Benefit Plans,* 1998 Practitioner Edition, vol. 1 (St. Paul: West Publishing Co., 1997), 190.

values reflect the gains and losses from investments, and the investments of most target benefit plans are participant directed.[32] While the exact benefit to be received is less certain than in a defined benefit plan, employer contributions are more certain than in a typical profit sharing plan. Contributions in target benefit plans tend to be heavily weighted by age to favor older participants.[33]

Age-weighted profit sharing (age-weighted) and new comparability plans take a different approach. Both are considered vehicles through which the owners of a company and select individuals, or a relatively narrow select group, can receive a disproportionate share of annual contributions to a profit sharing plan. In addition, the plans maximize contribution flexibility to the owner.

Age-Weighted Profit Sharing Plans

Age-weighted plans are very similar to traditional profit sharing plans except they apply age factors to allocate contributions more heavily to older participants, much like traditional defined benefit plan benefits favor workers with more years of service (who are typically older participants).[34] Age-weighted plans tend to appeal to smaller employers with older executive staff and younger rank and file employees. Plan sponsors with a goal of allocating as much benefit as possible to higher level employees (who tend to be older) may see some unintended effects if some higher level employees are relatively young and receive less benefit than some lower level employees who are at an advanced age. Furthermore, two participants with the same years of service and pay levels may receive different annual allocations because they fall within different age categories, creating potential for dissatisfaction and misunderstanding among some participants.

New Comparability Plans

New comparability is a term used for a set of plan types that are similar to the age-weighted plans, but take a further step in directing allocations by dividing participants into separate **allocation groups** (or rate groups) to provide larger percentage contributions to select participants. Plan sponsors have wide latitude in the criteria used to establish allocation groups, such as job descriptions, ownership interest, age, and length of service.[35]

Just as there are multiple options for categorizing participants for the purpose of allocation, new comparability plan sponsors also have flexibility in determining how the allocation process will work. "Super-integrated [new comparability] plans use formulas similar to normal safe harbor integrated formulas, but ignore the limitations to the formulas since the plans are being generally tested. These plans may use

---

[32] Sharyn Campbell, "Hybrid Retirement Plans: The Retirement Income System Continues to Evolve," EBRI Special Report SR-32/Issue Brief Number 171, March 1996, 22.

[33] Norman Gerber, "Age Weighted Profit Sharing vs. Target Benefit Plans," *The Tax Adviser,* August 1991, 510.

[34] It is possible to have age-weighted money purchase plans or stock bonus plans; however, profit sharing plans are much more common. Lloyd and Dunbar, 57.

[35] Campbell, 21.

a contribution formula such as 3% of pay plus 50% of pay in excess of $100,000."[36] Allocations are often arranged in several stages. For example, the first-stage allocation may consist of 3 percent of pay allocated to all employees, followed by second- and third-stage allocations based on formulas designed to favor a select few. Alternatively, a first-stage allocation can be the maximum contribution allowed for one key employee ($40,000 in 2002), followed by minimum top-heavy contributions for all non–highly compensated employees, and possibly followed by another round of contributions with remaining funds to highly compensated employees who have not yet received the maximum contribution.[37]

Nondiscrimination Requirements

In contrast to the defined benefit hybrids, which directly alter rates of accrual, the age-weighted and new comparability plans use their defined contribution features to provide larger contribution allocation to certain types or specific groups of workers. Both age-weighted and new comparability plans must satisfy the requirements of IRC Section 401(a)(4) that benefits not discriminate in favor of highly compensated employees. They satisfy the nondiscrimination requirements using a process called **cross-testing** (also referred to as benefits testing because nondiscrimination is tested on the basis of projected benefits rather than current contributions). Under one method of cross-testing, the annual profit sharing contribution for a participant is projected with interest to age 65, then converted to an annuity. The annuity is expressed as a percent of each participant's pay and then the percentages for highly compensated employees are compared with percentages for non–highly compensated employees. The testing approach makes it possible to allocate more to highly compensated and older participants because, when compound interest assumptions are used to project benefits, lesser amounts of annual contribution are needed to provide younger and lower-paid participants with a projected benefit that is a substantial percentage of pay.[38] In addition, the age-weighted and new comparability plans can be integrated with Social Security.

Floor-Offset Plans: Two Plans Working as One

The **floor-offset plan** differs from other hybrids because it is actually two separate plans, a defined benefit plan and a defined contribution plan, working to complement one another. The structure coincides with the floor-offset plan's somewhat unique purpose of protecting participants from potential negative effects of market risk or unfortunate investment decisions, while allowing them to direct their own investments in some plans. The defined benefit plan establishes a minimum level

---

[36] Fliege, 21.

[37] See Lloyd and Dunbar, 60–67, for examples. See also Jeffrey D. Poland, "New Comparability—A New Concept in Profit Sharing Plan Design," *Journal of Compensation and Benefits,* July/August 1996, 55.

[38]Poland, 55.

(floor) of benefit participants will receive if the defined contribution benefit does not exceed the minimum (floor) benefit. Upon retirement, the benefit of a given participant is the amount accumulated in the defined contribution plan, if that amount meets or exceeds the minimum (floor) benefit. If the benefit accumulated in the defined contribution plan is less than the minimum (floor) benefit, the difference between the defined contribution account balance and the minimum (floor) is paid by the defined benefit floor plan.[39] Floor-offset plans are most useful for employers seeking to balance the goals of providing meaningful benefit accumulation and portability for younger and shorter-term workers, and providing income and security for older and longer-term employees.[40]

Although floor-offset plans offer flexibility of plan design, plan sponsors are responsible for administering two separate plans. In terms of administrative work and cost, the existence of the defined benefit plan means the plan sponsor must pay termination insurance premiums to the PBGC, file two separate 5500 forms, and include Schedule B as an attachment for the defined benefit plan. However, there are some efficiencies because much 5500 information is the same for both plans.[41] Plan sponsors must also comply with Section 404 deduction limits and the Section 416 top-heavy test for both plans combined. They are also responsible for all the usual administrative duties of a defined contribution plan, including record-keeping functions, selection and monitoring of investment options, and providing participants with adequate information and opportunities to make investment decisions (if participant direction is allowed). Explaining the interaction of the defined contribution plan with the defined benefit plan and their effects on benefits can be difficult. Nonetheless, during times of low investment returns or losses, reminding participants of the floor plan guarantee can calm nerves and enhance appreciation. Establishing a reasonable floor benefit level, however, is a balancing act. If the floor benefit guaranteed by the defined benefit plan is not too high, it may encourage excessively risky investment behavior by participants. On the other hand, a reasonable floor may help encourage some risk averse participant investors to accept more of the risk required to generate the returns necessary for retirement security.

Conclusion

Variety in retirement plan design is nothing new. The relatively recent development and growing popularity of some additional hybrid plan designs, however, offer more choices for plan sponsors seeking to achieve an optimal balance between providing adequately for participant retirement needs and working within financial and administrative business constraints. The introduction of more choices does not necessarily make choices any easier for sponsors. Sponsors need to be aware of the effects of, and

[39]The defined benefit formula is usually offset by 100 percent of the defined contribution plan balance, but it may be offset by only a specified part of the balance. See Allen et al., 340, endnote 9.
[40]Robinson and Small, 29.
[41]Ibid., 32.

likely reaction to, various plan and design options on various participant groups and individuals in today's workforce and the workforce of tomorrow. They also need to keep an ear to the ground to listen for changes in the sometimes dynamic regulatory and legislative landscape in which hybrid plans exist. At the same time, some plan sponsors may be able to accomplish the same allocation, accrual, and portability goals for various segments of the workforce by offering separate defined contribution and defined benefit plans in tandem.

Chapter Summary

- Hybrid retirement plans combine attributes of both traditional defined benefit and defined contribution plans. Although there are various types and plan designs associated with hybrids, for the purposes of tax qualification, a hybrid is either considered to be a defined benefit or a defined contribution plan.

- Sponsors of defined benefit hybrid plans promise a specific benefit level, direct the investment of plan assets through commingled funds, bear investment risk, and reap investment reward. Defined benefit hybrids are subject to ERISA requirements for defined benefit plans, including minimum standards for eligibility, vesting, and funding. Annual actuarial valuations are needed, and plan termination insurance premiums must be paid to the PBGC.

- Cash balance plans are career average defined benefit hybrids. Although qualified as a defined benefit plan, these hybrids take on the appearance of defined contribution plans to participants. Typically contributions are credited to participants based on a formula that considers pay in each year of employment. Portable lump sums and earlier accrual of benefits appeal to employees terminating at younger ages with fewer years of service. Workers with more years of service are likely to receive more benefits from a traditional defined benefit plan.

- Pension equity plans are final average defined benefit hybrids. When employees terminate employment or retire, the sum of percentage credits which have accrued is applied to final average pay to determine a lump sum benefit which is portable. Age- or service-weighted credits and a final average pay formula make pension equity plans appealing to older workers and persons hired in midcareer who have fewer years to accrue benefits.

- Life cycle pension plans, sometimes considered a pension equity plan variation, use hypothetical account balances to communicate plan benefits to participants. These plans provide a lump sum based on an accumulation of annual credits multiplied by final average salary. Life cycle plans are also referred to using such terms as retirement bonus plans or mobility bonus plans.

- A minimum balance pension plan is a cash balance plan variant offering plan participants the greater benefit of either a traditional defined benefit pension plan (often based on final average pay) or the benefit accumulated on a career average basis through the cash balance method.

- Defined contribution hybrid plans combine a defined contribution plan structure with certain attributes of a defined benefit plan. Defined contribution hybrid plans include target benefit plans, age-weighted profit sharing plans, and new comparability plans.

- Target benefit plans are a defined contribution hybrid where the plan sponsor's required contributions are determined actuarially to meet income replacement targets expressed in terms of a percentage of salary near the time of retirement. However, these targets are not guaranteed once initially set and the ultimate pension benefits depend on account values reflecting the actual gains and losses from plan investments. Typically target benefit plans permit participant-directed investments, and contributions tend to be heavily weighted by age to favor older participants.

- Age-weighted profit sharing plans are similar to traditional profit sharing plans except they apply age factors to allocate contributions more heavily to older participants. These plans tend to appeal to smaller employers with older executive staff and younger rank and file employees.

- New comparability plans are similar to age-weighted plans but have plan contributions provided to separate allocation groups in order to provide larger percentage contributions to select plan participants. Allocation groups are determined using certain business criteria, such as job descriptions, ownership interest, age, and length of service.

- A floor-offset plan is a hybrid plan involving two separate plans, a defined benefit and a defined contribution plan. The defined benefit plan establishes a minimum level (floor) of benefit participants will receive if the defined contribution benefit does not exceed the minimum (floor) benefit.

Key Terms

age-weighted (profit sharing) plans, p. *355*
allocation groups, p. *355*
cash balance plan, p. *345*
cross-testing, p. *356*
floor-offset plan, p. *356*
"grandfather" provisions, p. *353*

hybrid retirement plans, p. *344*
life cycle pension plan, p. *348*
minimum balance pension plan, p. *351*
new comparability (plans), p. *355*

pension equity plans, p. *347*
pension wear away, p. *352*
retirement bonus plans, p. *348*
target benefit plans, p. *354*

Questions for Review

1. What is a hybrid retirement plan?
2. What are the features of a defined benefit hybrid plan?
3. Describe the characteristics of a cash balance plan.
4. What is a pension equity plan?
5. Note the similarities between cash balance plans and pension equity plans and the key characteristic differentiating these two plan types.
6. Compare and contrast pension equity and retirement bonus plans.
7. What is a life cycle pension plan?
8. Explain the operation of a minimum balance pension plan.
9. List various types of defined contribution hybrid retirement plans.
10. Describe the characteristics of a target benefit plan.

11. What is an age-weighted profit sharing plan?

12. Describe the use of "allocation groups" and "rate groups" in connection with a new comparability plan.

13. Describe the employer conditions under which the new comparability plan may have the most appeal.

14. When are floor-offset plans most useful?

15. What are some of the disadvantages of a floor-offset plan?

Questions for Discussion

1. Discuss the issues an employer would face in migrating from a more traditional retirement plan design to one of the hybrid plans described in the chapter. Describe employer characteristics, business conditions, and specific hybrid designs that would allow such a change.

2. Select a specific hybrid plan design and discuss its advantages over a more traditional retirement plan. Discuss how these advantages could be communicated to a large employer's workforce, particularly one where there is a diversity of educational backgrounds, age demographics, and geographical work locations.

3. An employer is looking at a merger with a company with an equivalent workforce size. The employer offers a traditional defined benefit plan, but the merger candidate has recently converted from a defined benefit plan to a cash balance plan. Describe the considerations involved in offering a recommendation whether to retain both pension forms or consolidate into one unified program.

Resources for Further Study

Bureau of National Affairs, Inc. "IRS Issues Guidance on Qualification Requirements for Cash Balance Plans." *Daily Tax Report,* January 19, 1996, pp. G-5, L-2, L-6.

Charles D. Spencer & Associates, Inc. "Company Continues Target Benefit Plan after Growing from 200 to 4,000 Employees." *Spencer's Research Reports on Employee Benefits.* Chicago, IL: Charles D. Spencer & Associates, 1993.

Charles D. Spencer & Associates, Inc. "Pension Equity Plans: Comparison of Plan Features Reveals Ability to Satisfy Mid-Career Hires." *Spencer's Research Reports on Employee Benefits.* Chicago, IL: Charles D. Spencer & Associates, Inc., July 8, 1994.

Coleman, Dennis R.; and Lawrence J. Sher. "Cash Balance Pension Plans and Other Evolving Hybrid Pension Plans." *The Handbook of Employee Benefits.* 5th ed. Jerry S. Rosenbloom, ed. New York: McGraw-Hill, 2001.

Edwards, J. Robert. "An Overview of Age-Based Profit Sharing Plans." *BookeMarks.* Winston-Salem, NC: Booke & Company, February 1992.

McKeon, David. "New Opportunities with Age-Weighted Profit Sharing Plans." *Pension World,* October 1993.

Robinson, Pati; and William S. Small. "The Floor-Offset Retirement Plan: Versatile and Tested, It Merits More Attention." *Compensation & Benefits Review,* May/June 1993.

20

Executive Retirement Arrangements[1]

After studying this chapter you should be able to:

- Explain the various circumstances under which an executive retirement plan may be appropriate in furthering an employer's business objectives.

- Identify two types of executive retirement plans that receive special treatment under ERISA and Department of Labor regulations.

- Explain the factors an employer should consider in determining eligibility conditions for executive retirement arrangements.

- Discuss how various design features of executive retirement arrangements will differ depending upon the employer objectives in establishing the plan.

- Describe various benefit security techniques that attempt to give an executive some assurance that unfunded benefits will be paid in the future.

- Note the differences in nature and intent between supplemental executive retirement arrangements and deferred compensation agreements.

Up to this point, the discussion in this text has been confined, for the most part, to tax-sheltered qualified retirement plans. Under the Internal Revenue Code, such plans must be nondiscriminatory in order to maintain their tax-favored status; that is, they must not discriminate in favor of highly compensated employees. Several situations exist when an employer may *wish to* discriminate in favor of a specific executive or group of executives. For these situations, executive retirement arrangements

---

[1] The authors wish to express their thanks to Towers Perrin for its permission to use material and text appearing in *The Handbook of Executive Benefits* (Burr Ridge, IL: Irwin Professional Publishing, 1995). The reader is referred to that handbook for a thorough discussion of all types of executive benefit plans.

can be used. Generally the limits on qualified plans have resulted in interest in executive retirement arrangements from both employer and employee perspectives.

ERISA Requirements

ERISA contains a panoply of rules governing employer-sponsored benefit plans. Many executive retirement arrangements are exempt from, or can be designed to avoid the impact of, some or all of these rules. ERISA requirements, as they apply to executive benefits, were discussed briefly in Chapter 6. The following provides a more detailed discussion of these requirements.

Pension Plans

ERISA defines the term *pension plan* broadly to include any plan, fund, or program that provides retirement income or results in the deferral of income until termination of employment or beyond. This definition does not necessarily encompass every plan that defers receipt of compensation or provides retirement income, however. Certain of these plans receive special treatment under the statute and Department of Labor (DOL) regulations.

Two types of executive retirement plans are (1) excess benefit plans and (2) top hat plans.

• **Excess benefit plans** provide benefits that cannot be provided through qualified plans solely because of IRC Section 415 limits on benefits and contributions. If it is unfunded, an excess benefit plan is completely exempt from Title I of ERISA. If it is funded, it is subject to Title I's reporting and disclosure, fiduciary responsibility, and enforcement provisions. A supplemental plan providing benefits that a qualified plan cannot provide for reasons other than Section 415 limits—including the limit on compensation under Section 401(a)(17) and the dollar limit on elective deferrals—would not fall within the excess benefit plan exemption. But such a plan might be considered a top hat plan, as discussed below and would, provided it is unfunded, be exempt from most ERISA requirements.

• **Top hat plans** are plans that are "unfunded and maintained by an employer primarily for the purpose of providing deferred compensation for a select group of management or highly compensated employees." Although they are ERISA Title I pension plans, they are *not* subject to the participation, vesting, funding, or fiduciary responsibility provisions of Title I. However, the enforcement and reporting and disclosure requirements do apply to these top hat plans.[2] Under the enforcement provisions, a top hat plan must comply with ERISA's claims review procedures and provide participants with access to federal courts to pursue a claim for benefits. The reporting and disclosure requirements that apply are simplified; the employer need only file a letter with the DOL setting forth its name, address, and taxpayer identification number; the number of top hat plans it maintains; and the number of employees in each.

---

[2] Note that "top hat plan" is an informal designation; the term does not appear in ERISA or in any regulations.

Early DOL letters were fairly liberal in interpreting the **"select group" require-ment.** Since issuance of ERISA Proc. 76-1, the DOL has declined to rule on whether a plan is a top hat plan. Despite its failure to issue regulations or a defini-tive advisory opinion, the DOL clearly has not adopted the IRC definition of highly compensated employees. In a statement on the subject, the DOL expressed the view that the top hat exemption would be available only for those employees who "by virtue of their position or compensation level, have the ability to affect their deferred compensation plan, taking into consideration any risks attendant thereto, and, [who] therefore, would not need the substantive rights and protection of Title I."[3] The DOL also said that the term *primarily,* as used in the phrase "primarily for the purpose of providing deferred compensation for a select group of management or highly com-pensated employees," refers to the purpose of the plan (i.e., the benefits provided) and not the participant composition of the plan. Thus, if a plan extended coverage beyond a select group, the DOL would not consider it to be a top hat plan.

In addition to limiting participation to a select group, a top hat plan also must be unfunded. The DOL has expressed the view that any determination concerning the funded or unfunded status of a plan must be based on surrounding facts and cir-cumstances, including the status of the arrangement under relevant non-ERISA law. In this regard, the DOL has indicated that, in the absence of pertinent legislative his-tory defining the term *unfunded* for purposes of Title I of ERISA, a significant weight will be accorded to positions adopted by the Internal Revenue Service.

Nonexempt Plans

A plan's ERISA status has important implications for both employers and executives. Proceeding under one of the exemptions to Title I could result in a significant level of unsecured benefits—benefit promises that are not backed with irrevocably com-mitted assets. Further, compliance with the "select group" provision would obviously require that the plan be limited in terms of its coverage. Electing to comply with Title I provisions would provide some level of benefit security, but it also could produce undesirable income tax results (at least for deferred compensation plans) and limit plan design choices. An exemption from Title I requirements gives the employer con-siderable flexibility in plan design in areas such as participation requirements, vest-ing, and the forfeiture of otherwise vested benefits under certain conditions.

If a plan comes within the purview of Title I (for example, if it is funded or if it extends beyond a select group of executives), the following provisions of Title I apply:

• *Reporting and disclosure.* Full compliance with all disclosure requirements— summary plan descriptions, annual financial reporting, and so forth—is required.

• *Participation requirements.* The use of minimum age and service requirements must be limited to age 21 and one year of service (unless full and immediate vest-ing are provided).

• *Vesting.* Use of vesting schedules prescribed by ERISA is required (see Chap-ter 5 for a description of allowable vesting schedules). In addition, the vesting rules

---

[3] DOL Opinion Letter 90-14A.

also place restrictions on mandatory distributions and cash-outs and forbid non-compete clauses that call for forfeitures.

• *Joint and survivor requirements.* Spousal protection, through the joint and survivor requirements, is applicable.

• *Funding.* Minimum funding requirements must be met.

• *Fiduciary responsibility.* The fiduciary provisions apply in full to nonexempt plans. This includes the requirement that assets of the plan be held in trust for the exclusive benefit of participants.

• *Accrual rules.* Nonexempt plans must meet accrual rules identical to those applicable to qualified plans.

Objectives of Executive Retirement Arrangements

Because the design of an executive retirement arrangement must be responsive to the basic objectives of the plan, it is necessary to establish these objectives before any questions of design, costing, and funding can be considered. The objectives most frequently set forth for implementing a **supplemental executive retirement plan (SERP)** are discussed in the following sections.

Restoring Base Plan Benefits

Most major employers have adopted excess benefit plans to replace retirement benefits that would have been payable under broad-based qualified plans were it not for the Section 415 limits. Many employers also have acted to restore qualified plan benefits lost by reason of other tax law provisions, such as the limit on pay that can be taken into account for qualified plan contributions and benefits under IRC Section 401(a)(17), and the elective deferral limit for 401(k) plans.

Providing More Benefits

Perhaps the simplest and most direct objective of an executive benefit program is to provide a higher level of benefits than that generated by the company's broad-based plans. The relationship between Social Security and employer-sponsored plans is a case in point. Social Security will replace a relatively high percentage of pay—as much as 35 to 40 percent—for lower-paid employees but will replace only 5 to 10 percent of pay, and sometimes even less, for the highly paid. Because of tax law provisions governing the integration of Social Security benefits with broad-based plans, a qualified plan designed to provide reasonable total benefits for the rank-and-file employees probably will provide inadequate benefits for the highly paid. If the broad-based plan is structured to provide what the employer believes to be an adequate pension for the highly paid, combined pension and Social Security benefits for the lower paid could be excessive. One solution to this problem is to design the broad-based plan to meet the needs of the majority of employees and to provide the highly paid with a supplemental plan.

Midcareer Recruiting

An executive who changes jobs in mid- to late career could suffer a significant loss in expected pension benefits because the pension from his or her former employer, although vested, will be frozen at the executive's pay level at the time of change. Even though pension benefits from the new employer will accrue at future pay levels, the total benefit from the two sources could fall substantially short of the benefit that might have been payable had the executive been employed by only one employer for his or her entire career.

While many factors influence an executive's decision to change jobs, the prospect of losing pension benefits can be a major concern. One way for employers to address this problem is to establish a supplemental retirement plan that provides additional benefits to an executive hired in midcareer—by recognizing service with the former employer as though it were service with the current employer, for example, or by granting relatively generous accruals for the first few years of new employment.

Recognizing Incentive Pay

Many broad-based plans provide benefits related to base pay only; other forms of compensation, such as overtime, shift differentials, and bonuses, are not included in the plan's definition of earnings.

Incentive pay normally constitutes a significant part of total compensation for executives, however, and many employers believe that at least some incentive pay should be treated as an element of pay for benefit purposes—in part because an executive's standard of living is based on total compensation, and in part because they believe an executive whose pay is at risk should also reap commensurate rewards.

While employers can base benefits for all employees on total compensation, this approach could generate excessive benefits for some employees and an overall level of higher plan costs. Many companies are more comfortable establishing supplemental plans for executives for the express purpose of providing benefits related to incentive pay.

Executive Transfers

If an organization's benefit programs are not uniform from one operation or location to another, differing to reflect factors such as industry practice, profit margins, local competitive practice, and the like, executives could gain or lose benefits every time they transfer jobs within the organization. A disruption in benefits could present significant problems in individual situations. One solution is a supplemental **umbrella plan** that makes up any difference between the specified umbrella level of benefits and the benefits actually provided at the locations where the executive has been employed.

Other Objectives

Other executive benefit program objectives include the following.

Recognizing Deferred Compensation

It is relatively common for employers to permit executives to defer some part or all of their base salary and/or incentive pay. Some employers may even require that some part of compensation be deferred. Because deferred compensation cannot be considered as pay for determining qualified plan benefits or contributions, employers often establish supplemental arrangements to provide benefits related to deferred amounts.

Golden Handcuffs

Unfunded executive retirement plans need not comply with the vesting rules that apply to broad-based plans. Thus, they can be written so that they include **golden handcuffs.** In these arrangements, a terminating executive will forfeit accrued benefits unless termination occurs under circumstances where the employer is willing to provide these amounts—for example, termination after age 62. Pension benefits accrued under one of these arrangements can be substantial, and the prospect of losing them may deter an executive who is otherwise thinking of leaving the organization. Thus, a supplemental plan with rigorous vesting standards can help retain key executives.

Noncompete Provisions

Broad-based plan benefits cannot be forfeited once they are vested; such is not the case for unfunded supplemental executive benefits, which can be forfeited even after they are in payment status. Making benefits subject to forfeiture if an executive goes to work for a competitor after retirement could be a way of providing some protection in this event.

Golden Handshakes

A number of factors, including human resource needs and deteriorating performance, may make it desirable to encourage certain executives to retire before their normal retirement ages. If benefits available under broad-based plans are not sufficient to meet the financial needs of these executives, supplemental benefits (referred to as **golden handshakes**) can be used to provide incentives to retire early.

Uniform Treatment

Organizations often enter into different deferred compensation and supplemental benefit arrangements with individual executives, usually as a result of negotiated employment agreements or corporate acquisitions. Supplemental executive benefit plans can be used to standardize these arrangements, thus establishing a uniform policy and avoiding the need for special contracts and disclosure.

General Design Considerations

Many factors can influence the structure of an executive benefit program—beginning with the employer's objectives. Before designing or modifying a plan, an employer should articulate those objectives and, if necessary, rank them in order of importance to ensure that they are supported by actual plan provisions.

If the employer wants to facilitate midcareer recruiting, for example, it should probably impose relatively short service requirements for eligibility to participate in its plan and liberal vesting requirements. In addition, it probably will make sense to use a benefit formula that either recognizes service with the prior employer or provides for relatively generous accrual rates during the first few years of the executive's employment. As another example, employers that are interested in golden handcuff retention devices may want to impose stringent vesting requirements.

The employer's basic views on executive compensation and benefits, as well as the environment in which the company operates, also will influence plan design, as will the factors summarized below.

Internal Equity

Many plans provide the same (or close to the same) level of benefits for all executives, while imposing relatively short service requirements. Long-service executives might consider such plans inequitable, since their benefits will not be proportionately greater than those of their shorter-service colleagues. Concern over this issue often prompts employers to include additional service-related benefits—perhaps additional pension accruals at a lower rate for service in excess of some stipulated period such as 20 or 25 years.

Cost and Accounting Considerations

As with any employee benefit plan, the ultimate cost of an executive retirement plan will equal the sum of the benefits paid plus any expenses associated with plan administration. Benefit amounts will, in turn, reflect eligibility requirements, the pay base, service requirements, and other plan design elements. If the benefits are not prefunded, as is typically the case, there is no investment income on plan reserves to offset these costs.

Although employers can and should consider plan costs from a cash flow perspective, they also should consider charges to the company's financial statements (both profit and loss and balance sheet) made in accordance with relevant accounting requirements. Supplemental executive retirement benefits generally fall within the scope of Financial Accounting Standard 87 (FAS 87) and its subsequent refinement with Financial Accounting Standard 132 (FAS 132).

Employers also should take care in selecting the actuarial assumptions used to estimate costs—assumptions that will not necessarily parallel those used in estimating costs under broad-based plans. Assumptions as to future salary growth, turnover, and retirement ages for an executive group might very well differ from those used for rank-and-file employees.

Tax Considerations

Tax results, including the deductibility of employer contributions and the taxation of contributions and benefits, also will differ for broad-based and executive benefit plans. In an unfunded retirement plan, for example, the employer generally is entitled to a deduction only when benefits are paid or become taxable to the executive; by contrast, the employer's contribution to a tax-qualified plan generally is deductible when made.

Also, the employer cost of providing a given amount of supplemental executive retirement benefit could be higher than the cost of providing the benefit under a broad-based plan because investment income under a tax-qualified plan accumulates tax free.

Another important point is that retirement benefits for executives will be treated as ordinary income, with no special treatment for lump-sum distributions. But these benefits will not be subject to penalty taxes for early withdrawals or failures to meet minimum distribution requirements as will be qualified plan payments.

From an executive's standpoint, the employer must make sure that neither the tax doctrine of economic benefit nor the tax doctrine of constructive receipt applies. Under these two doctrines, an employee can be taxed currently on deferred benefits or compensation. The **doctrine of economic benefit** states that if a taxpayer is receiving a current benefit, he or she should be taxed currently on the value of that benefit; the **doctrine of constructive receipt** states that if a taxpayer could receive income at any time but elects to receive it later, he or she is still taxed currently because of having the nonforfeitable right to the income. Revenue Ruling 60-31 states that deferred compensation is not taxed before actual receipt whether it is forfeitable or nonforfeitable, provided the deferral is agreed to before the compensation is earned; the deferral amount is not unconditionally placed in trust or in escrow for the benefit of the employee; and the promise to pay the deferred compensation is merely a contractual obligation not evidenced by notes or secured in any other manner. Thus, while certain assets may be earmarked and informally set aside to give some assurance that benefits will be paid, there must be no formal funding instrument and the executive must not have current access to the benefits if current taxation is to be avoided.

Defined Contribution Versus Defined Benefit Plans

While the relative merits of defined benefit and defined contribution plans receive considerable attention when it comes to rank-and-file employees, the differences between these two approaches are less significant in the executive arena. Potential coverage under the plan termination provisions of ERISA often deters a company from establishing a broad-based defined benefit plan, for example, but defined benefit executive plans are not subject to these rules. Similarly, a defined contribution executive benefit plan can be structured to avoid one of the key characteristics of a broad-based plan—the transfer of investment and inflation risks to employees.

Most executive benefit plans have been established on a defined benefit basis, particularly in cases where the plan builds on an underlying broad-based defined benefit plan—for example, by applying the base plan benefit formula to short-term incentive pay.

The defined benefit approach works well when the plan is unfunded because it can accommodate most employer objectives and serves to coordinate benefits from all sources. It also is easy to explain and administer.

With a funded defined benefit executive plan, difficulties may arise when executives have to include the value of their accrued and vested benefits in taxable income, since these values will be based on assumptions as to future pay growth, inflation rates, investment returns, mortality, and the like. If the assumptions prove to be too conservative, the plan may have created more value than is necessary. Because executives will already have been taxed on this value, it cannot be taken away (except on a prospective basis to the extent future accruals and/or compensation can be adjusted). The use of more-aggressive assumptions or less-than-full funding to provide a margin can avoid or minimize such problems.

As an alternative, employers can adopt a defined contribution approach to establishing benefit levels and, as a result, funding levels. The defined contribution approach is attractive for a number of reasons, whether or not the plan is funded. For example,

• Executives are accustomed to dealing with the idea of capital accumulation and might feel more comfortable with this approach than with conventional income replacement concepts.

• The defined contribution approach more readily coordinates with the use of company stock and the role of stock in overall executive compensation.

• Any imputed rates of return (where benefits are not funded and otherwise invested) can be tied to company performance measurements such as growth in profits, company stock prices, dividend growth, or return on assets.

• Several design issues are easier to deal with, such as offsets for vested benefits from prior employment, making additional contributions sufficient to attract executives in midcareer, and so forth.

Hybrid approaches also warrant consideration. Under a target benefit plan, for example, the employer uses a defined benefit formula to establish a projected retirement benefit, converts the benefit to a lump sum value, and establishes the annual contribution or credit necessary to fund this value at some assumed interest rate. Once the contribution level has been established, the plan operates like a defined contribution plan.

The cash balance approach is another alternative. A cash balance plan is a defined benefit plan that looks like a defined contribution plan. A participant's account is credited with a specified percentage of pay each year, and the account earns interest at a specified rate; the participant's ultimate benefit equals contributions plus earnings. Annual contributions also may be weighted to reflect age and service. See Chapter 19 for details on hybrid plan designs.

An employer establishing a new executive retirement plan should evaluate the advantages and disadvantages of defined benefit, defined contribution, and hybrid arrangements in light of its specific plan objectives.

Coordination With Broad-Based Plans

By design, an executive benefit plan will have many provisions that differ significantly from corresponding provisions in the employer's broad-based plan—the definitions of pay and service, for example, and benefit accrual rates and early retirement provisions. In other areas, there is little need for different treatment, and consistency is, in fact, desirable.

One such area is the form and manner in which benefits are distributed. The law requires a broad-based plan to provide a joint and survivor benefit as the normal form of distribution for a married employee. The benefit payable to the employee typically will be reduced to reflect the value of the survivor benefit, although this is not always the case. In any event, the executive plan should specify the form in which its payments will be made and whether any offset for base plan benefits will be made before or after any reduction called for by the joint and survivor provision.

Other optional forms of payment also should parallel the broad-based plan, although the executive plan should be structured to avoid constructive receipt by the executive of the entire value of his or her supplemental benefit.

Other provisions where some coordination with base plan provisions might be desirable include the right to make and change beneficiary designations; facility of payment authority (if the payee is mentally or physically incapable of accepting payment); procedures to be followed if a beneficiary cannot be located and which state law will govern plan interpretation; and the right to amend or terminate the plan.

Along these same lines, it may be advisable to coordinate executive and base plan administration and communication, although confidentiality considerations may dictate that the plans be handled separately.

General Plan Features

Eligibility for Participation

Eligibility for participation normally is limited to members of top management who make significant contributions to the organization's success. This definition is subject to wide interpretation, however, and care should be taken to restrict eligibility to those executives for whom the plan is really intended. Eligibility requirements that are too broad or that are established so that they automatically expand the group covered (for example, a minimum salary requirement that could be eroded by inflationary pressure) can lead to substantial cost increases for an employer.

The most frequently used criterion to establish eligibility for participation is position. For the reason noted above, a minimum salary requirement generally is not desirable unless it is tied to some sort of price or wage index. Some organizations determine eligibility by whether the executive is eligible for the company's incentive compensation program.

Some plans avoid the use of specific eligibility requirements and require the executive to be designated for consideration by a group such as the compensation committee of the board of directors of the corporation. Even when specific eligibility requirements are used, it might be desirable to have the flexibility of permitting the designation of individual executives who might not otherwise be eligible but to whom, for unusual reasons, coverage should be extended.

No constraints are imposed by the IRC or ERISA on the selection of eligibility criteria; however, if the group covered is so large that it extends beyond "a select group of management or highly compensated employees," the plan could become a retirement plan as defined under Title I of ERISA and become subject to all of its requirements.[4]

Definition of Compensation

Two factors must be considered in defining the compensation on which benefits will be based: (1) the elements of pay that will be included and (2) the period of time (if any) over which compensation will be averaged.

Elements of Compensation

Base salary and short-term incentives typically are included as compensation elements in executive retirement plans. In fact, providing benefits relating to short-term incentive pay is frequently a key plan objective.

The definition of pay also may include compensation that the executive has deferred for payment at some future time since these amounts cannot be used to determine benefits under a broad-based plan.

While it is possible to include the value of long-term incentive compensation in the pay base, this practice is relatively uncommon. Long-term incentive plans are basically capital accumulation programs that are not considered part of regular, year-to-year compensation and thus need not be replaced when the executive is no longer working. Further, it is extremely difficult to value these plans and arrive at an amount to replace.

Other elements of executive pay, such as perquisites and other forms of imputed income, are typically disregarded in establishing the pay base for executive benefits.

Compensation Averaging Period

Because bonus amounts can vary substantially from year to year, plans that include bonuses in the definition of compensation often use averaging. An executive's year 1 plan compensation might be the sum of his or her year 1 base pay plus an average of bonuses paid during the preceding three years, for example. Longer averaging periods may be appropriate where bonus payments vary significantly over the years.

Current compensation also is appropriate for determining the contributions credited to the executive's account each year under defined contribution or capital accumulation programs. In a conventional defined benefit plan, benefits typically are averaged over a three- or five-year averaging period. Bonuses may be averaged over the same or an even longer period.

Although many executive defined benefit plans use the same averaging period as that used in the broad-based plan, some use a shorter period to produce a relatively higher level of income replacement for the executive group. In fact, some executive plans base pension benefits on the final year's pay without averaging (with the possible exception of bonuses).

---

[4] In the *Extebank* case, a district court provided support that under the right circumstances potentially 15 percent of the total workforce could be eligible to participate in a top hat plan.

Service

An executive's service is relevant for determining initial eligibility to participate, vesting rights, benefit accruals, and eligibility for benefit payments.

In most situations, an executive's service will be defined as the period of employment with the employer, measured from date of hire to date of termination. Like broad-based plans, executive benefit plans should specify whether time on leave (paid or unpaid and/or on account of disability) will be counted as service and whether broken periods of service will be aggregated for various purposes. In the case of plans designed to facilitate midcareer recruiting, service might be defined to include service with the prior employer.

Although it is not common practice, a plan may limit service to the period of time an individual is employed as an executive. It also is possible, though unusual, to limit service to the period of time that the executive participates in the plan.

Retirement Ages

Retirement age is not critical for defined contribution or capital accumulation plans; an executive's benefit equals the account balance at termination—whether for normal, early, or deferred retirement; death; disability; or any other reason. Thus, such a plan can be designed without any specific reference to retirement age. As a practical matter, however, most defined contribution plans do specify normal, early, and deferred retirement ages. One reason for defining normal retirement age is to make it clear when the employer expects executives to retire. Another is to tie the definition to other plans and be consistent in matters such as postretirement health care eligibility.

Normal Retirement Age

Most broad-based plans establish age 65 (or the completion of five years of service, if later) as normal retirement age. Many executive plans do the same, though some employers prefer that executives retire earlier and thus specify an age such as 60 or 62 as normal retirement age under the executive plan.

With one exception, Equal Employment Opportunity Commission (EEOC) requirements prohibit the use of a mandatory retirement age. The exception relates to individuals who have been employed for at least two years as bona fide executives or executives in "high policy-making positions" and whose nonforfeitable employer-provided retirement benefits from all sources are at least $44,000. An employer can force any such individual to retire at or after age 65. Employers need to consider whether they want to take advantage of this limited exception and mandate retirement at age 65 to the extent allowed.

Early Retirement Age

Many executive plans define early retirement eligibility in exactly the same way that it is defined in the underlying broad-based plan—typically, the attainment of age 55 and the completion of at least 10 years of service. Some executive plans are more liberal, particularly when encouraging early retirement as a plan objective. In any case, it is customary for the early retirement service requirement to at least equal the service required for full vesting.

Employers who want to create golden handcuffs may want to be more restrictive, perhaps requiring that executives attain age 62 to be eligible for executive benefits even though the base plan is more liberal. Another approach is to permit early retirement under the executive plan only with employer consent.

Benefits available at early retirement can be designed in a conventional manner—that is, with benefits actuarially reduced if they begin before normal retirement age. Employers also can subsidize the executive plan's early retirement benefits in line with base plan subsidies or to an even greater extent.

Deferred Retirement

Deferred retirement refers to an executive's right to remain employed after his or her normal retirement date. With the exception noted above, EEOC regulations apply to executive plans and, as a result, exert significant influence on this plan provision. Thus, individuals who are not bona fide executives or who are not in high policy-making positions must not be discriminated against on account of age. Even those individuals who come within the scope of the exemption must not be discriminated against on account of age if the employer does not use the exemption.

Compliance with EEOC regulations means there can be no mandatory retirement prior to age 65 for bona fide executives and no mandatory retirement at any age for protected executives. Further, benefit accruals must continue until an executive actually retires.

Because defined benefit executive plan accrual rates often are generous, many employers cap recognized service to control benefit levels and costs for employment beyond stipulated periods of time. Such a cap, which is permissible under the law, also can encourage executives to retire early—or at least by the plan's normal retirement age—if that is an employer objective.

Benefit Structure

The benefit structure of an executive retirement plan will vary depending on whether a defined contribution or defined benefit approach is used.

Defined Contribution Plans

The benefit structure of a defined contribution or capital accumulation plan is relatively straightforward. The employer establishes a contribution or credit amount, accumulates the contribution or credit with actual or imputed investment income, and pays out the accumulated amount at some future time—usually upon retirement, death, disability, or other termination of employment. The plan may be unfunded (as is typically the case) or funded. Some employers earmark or conditionally contribute amounts in the executive's name, but these arrangements are usually not considered to be funded as contemplated by ERISA and the tax law, and they do not involve irrevocably committed assets.

Many defined contribution executive plans exist solely to restore benefits lost under broad-based plans due to IRC limitations. In these plans, the amount of employer contribution or credit simply reflects the provisions of the base plan and the tax law.

Other plans go further, providing more substantial employer credits or contributions, sometimes as an alternative to conventional defined benefit arrangements. Employers have several options for establishing contributions, including the target benefit approach. Contributions may be incentive-oriented, reflecting employer profits, or they may represent a fixed percentage of pay. If assistance in midcareer recruiting is a plan objective, additional contributions may be made in the early years of participation to compensate for the potential loss of benefits under a prior employer's plan.

Determining the rate of return on credits or contributions made under a defined contribution executive plan is a key design consideration. If the plan is funded, this rate of return obviously will reflect actual investment results. If the plan is unfunded, the employer must establish some method of imputing investment return. Some companies determine this rate with reference to one or more prime rates; others tie the rate to their own return on capital or their own cost of borrowing. Still others use an external base such as Moody's Bond Index.

Special issues arise if the plan is a restoration plan, because the underlying plan typically will permit several investment choices. Will the rate of return on amounts credited under the executive plan mirror the investment results of the choices the executive made under the base plan, the composite result of all funds under the base plan, the rate of return under a designated fund of the base plan, or something else?

Some observers have suggested that the IRS might consider participants in a nonqualified, unfunded plan to be in constructive receipt of income if participants are given investment authority. Discussions with an IRS official indicate that this does not accurately depict the IRS's attitude in this regard and it appears that a participant may be permitted to direct the investment of his or her account balance in an unfunded plan without being in constructive receipt of the account balance for tax purposes. It may be prudent to include an express provision in the plan stating that the employer is under no obligation to make any investments or to segregate any of its assets in any way in response to a participant's "investment elections" in order to ensure that the plan maintains its status as unfunded for both tax and ERISA purposes. While an employer might actually make investments to match the participant's elections, it should be under no legal obligation to do so.

Defined Benefit Plans

The benefit formula in a defined benefit plan should reflect the employer's income replacement objectives. Key factors include:

- The percentage of pay to be continued in retirement and whether this percentage will vary by income level.

- The definition of what constitutes pay.

- The length of service required for full (or optimal) benefits under the plan.

- The retirement age at which full (or optimal) benefits are provided.

- Sources of income recognized in determining whether income replacement objectives have been met.

The typical broad-based plan replaces a relatively high percentage of preretirement income for lower-paid employees, dropping that percentage as income levels increase. Such a plan typically seeks to replace about 80 to 85 percent of pay for employees at low pay levels, grading down to perhaps 55 to 60 percent for the higher paid.

If the executive plan is strictly a restoration plan, then by definition, it has the same income replacement objectives as the broad-based plan. If the executive plan is to provide benefits over and above those of the broad-based plan, the employer must decide what income replacement percentages to use and whether to use the same percentage for executives at all pay levels. The income replacement target for executives is often 55 to 60 percent of pay, regardless of income level. Higher percentages could provoke shareholder criticism and even raise questions as to reasonableness of compensation from the standpoint of the deductibility of plan costs.

In designing the plan to meet income replacement objectives, the employer must consider how to structure and combine the five components that help design the plan benefit formula: (1) accrual rate, (2) pay base, (3) recognized service, (4) normal retirement age, and (5) any offsets.

1. *Accrual rate.* The rate at which to accrue benefits in the executive plan may be identical to the base plan rate; this would be the case in a restoration plan or in a plan that simply applies the base plan formula to incentive pay. An employer may choose to use a different accrual rate or to front- or backload the formula, depending on its objectives. To facilitate midcareer recruiting, for example, the accrual rate in early years could be quite a bit higher than the rate applied to the later years. Backloaded formulas might be used where an employer objective is to reward long service.

2. *Pay base.* As noted earlier, there are two elements the employer must consider when defining pay: (1) the elements of pay to be included and (2) the period (if any) over which pay is to be averaged. This definition may or may not be the same as that used in the broad-based plan. The most common differences are to include short-term incentive pay in the executive plan and to use a shorter averaging period (for example, three years or even the executive's pay in his or her final year of employment).

3. *Length of service.* The accrual rate chosen in a broad-based plan usually reflects what the employer believes to be an appropriate period over which to accrue full or optimum plan benefits. Typically, this benefit accrues over a 25- or 30-year period. Often, however, employers want executive benefits to accrue over a shorter period—say 10 or 15 years. Some employers may want the executive benefit to accrue only over the period of service during which the individual is considered to be an executive. Whatever the decision, the plan should specify the service required before an executive is entitled to full benefits. This, in turn, will help determine the plan's accrual rate.

4. *Normal retirement age.* Broad-based plans typically define normal retirement age as 65. Executive plans, however, often use a younger normal retirement age, such as 62.

5. *Income sources.* Once an employer has established its overall income replacement objectives, it needs to decide which sources of income it will take into account to determine whether those objectives have been met. Obvious sources are the executive plan itself, the underlying broad-based plan, and Social Security. The employer also may want to take the annuity value of any broad-based or supplemental defined contribution plan into account. Another potential offset is the value of any vested benefits the executive might have from prior employment; this type of offset sometimes is found in plans that are designed to facilitate midcareer recruiting and where the executive receives relatively high early year accruals or where service with the prior employer is recognized as service with the current employer.

Vesting

A funded executive plan that is subject to Title I of ERISA must comply with minimum vesting standards similar to those that apply to tax-qualified plans.

No vesting requirements apply to unfunded executive plans. Thus, an employer's options in this regard range from full and immediate vesting to no vesting at all until retirement. Even at retirement, the executive's benefit can be made forfeitable under certain conditions—for example, if he or she goes to work for a competitor.

Vesting in executive benefit plans often parallels the vesting provisions of the underlying broad-based plan. In some cases—for example, in plans designed for midcareer recruiting or to encourage executives to retire early—vesting provisions may be more liberal than those of the broad-based plan. If the executive plan is designed to create golden handcuffs, however, vesting may be restricted and may occur only when the executive qualifies for retirement.

An unfunded plan can provide for forfeiture of benefits that might otherwise have been vested. For example, an executive's benefits might be forfeited if his or her employment is terminated for acts of dishonesty such as fraud or embezzlement. As noted above, forfeiture also might occur (even after retirement) if the executive goes to work for a competitor or reveals trade secrets. Such provisions are sometimes difficult to enforce, but many employers believe they provide reasonable and necessary protection.

Disability

Many executive plans treat disability in much the same way it is treated under broad-based plans. A typical provision might continue to accrue service during the period of disability and while disability benefits are being paid to the executive under the firm's long-term disability program.

In some cases, particularly with older individuals, the executive plan may treat disability as early retirement without reducing the benefit for early commencement of payments. The plan might even credit the disabled executive with additional service for the period remaining until normal retirement age—in effect treating him or her as a normal retiree with full service.

Death

Most executive benefit plans provide for some type of death benefit when an executive dies before retirement. In the case of defined contribution plans, the benefit is usually the executive's account balance. A defined benefit plan often provides a lifetime benefit to the spouse equal to part or all of the executive's accrued benefit. This type of benefit also might be payable to dependent children (or parents) in the absence of a spouse. A few defined benefit plans provide for lump sum benefits; however, employers who prefer a lump sum benefit generally find it more effective to provide it through additional amounts of life insurance.

Postretirement death benefits are less common than preretirement benefits, largely because the cost of such benefits is significant.

The design of death benefit provisions in a defined benefit plan requires answers to many of the questions that arise in designing a broad-based plan. Should the plan require a minimum period of marriage (for example, one year) before the spouse becomes eligible, for example? If the executive dies before eligibility for early retirement, will the spouse be entitled to immediate payment, or will payments commence only when the executive would have reached early retirement eligibility? Will amounts payable to a joint annuitant be adjusted if he or she is more than a certain number of years younger than the executive? These are among the issues that employers must address in designing executive death benefit provisions.

Benefit Security Arrangements

Since executive benefits are typically unfunded, an executive's retirement income under the plan is dependent on the solvency of the company and its willingness to pay promised benefits. An additional complicating factor is the length of time over which the benefits accrue and the ultimate payout date. The period could be 25 to 30 years in the future. Consequently, strong interest exists in methods that attempt to give an executive some assurance that these benefits will be paid. Several techniques are now in use to accomplish this purpose.

Probably the most common method is the use of the so-called **rabbi trust.** Under this approach, the company creates an irrevocable trust for the benefit of an executive or a group of participating executives. The terms of the trust limit the use of the assets to providing benefits for the participating executives. Thus, the trust assets cannot be used by current or future management but remain subject to the claims of creditors in the event of the firm's insolvency.

Corporate-owned life insurance (COLI) is another commonly used technique for benefit security. The basic concept under this approach is that the employer is the owner and beneficiary of a life insurance contract designed to accumulate sufficient cash values to pay the benefits promised the executive. The life insurance policy must be carried as a corporate asset and therefore provides only very limited benefit security for the executive since cash values and death benefits are within the employer's control. So-called split dollar life insurance is another mechanism often used in an effort to achieve some level of benefit security.

Other techniques sometimes used to attempt to provide benefit security for executive benefits include employee-owned annuities and irrevocable trusts—sometimes called **secular trusts**—where employer contributions are made on an irrevocable basis for the benefit of participating executives. These are funded plans and are subject to Title I of ERISA, with executives being considered in constructive receipt of the value of their benefits when vested.[5]

Deferred Compensation Agreements

While the main purpose of supplemental executive retirement plans (SERPs) is to provide the executive with an additional layer of retirement benefits over and above those provided by the employer's basic plan, **deferred compensation agreements** deal primarily with earnings deferral, usually to gain tax advantages, with retirement income as a secondary consideration. Postponing the receipt of current income not only reduces executives' current taxable income but puts them in receipt of the funds after retirement, when they may be in a lower tax bracket. However, any deferral of income to a future date must take into consideration the potential effects of increased interest and inflation rates as well as current tax considerations.

Reasons for deferring current income from both the executive's and the employer's viewpoints are (1) extending the executive's income beyond normal working years into retirement; (2) spreading bonuses over a wider span of years; (3) tying the executive to the employer by stipulating conditions on the receipt of deferred amounts; and (4) adding to the executive's retirement income.

The factors to be considered in drawing up the agreement are much the same as those that were discussed for supplemental executive retirement plans. For example, the employer must determine how much compensation will be deferred, whether and how much investment growth will be added to such amounts, whether there will be conditions on receiving the funds, and what the various benefit options will be.

To avoid the possibility of the executives' being judged to be in constructive receipt of the deferred funds, three rules contained in Revenue Ruling 60–31 must be followed in drawing up a deferred compensation agreement. They are that the deferral must be (1) irrevocable; (2) agreed to before the compensation is earned; and (3) for a specified length of time. The agreement also must serve a business purpose.

Overview

Because of their nonqualified status, executive retirement arrangements permit a degree of flexibility unavailable in the more restricted qualified plans. When properly designed and administered, they can serve a number of needs that exist in the relationship between an employer and the executive that do not apply to the rest of

---

[5] G. Victor Hallman and Jerry S. Rosenbloom, *Personal Financial Planning,* 8th ed. (New York: McGraw-Hill, 2000), p. 385.

The Employer "Cost" of Deferred Compensation

1

The employer cost of an unfunded deferred compensation arrangement will be sensitive to the before-tax rate of return credited to deferred amounts relative to the gross rate of return the employer can achieve with respect to these amounts. This is illustrated in the following table, which shows the after-tax cost of deferring a $10,000 payment for 10 and 20 years, respectively, and crediting this amount annually with a 10 percent before-tax return. The table assumes the company has a 35 percent tax rate and that it could earn—before tax—either 10, 15, or 20 percent per year.

| | | Cost to Corporation | | |
| | | Corporate Rate of Return | | |
Deferral Period	Amount Payable to Executive	10%	15%	20%
10 yrs.	$25,937	$ 4,658	$ 379	($ 5,205)
20 yrs.	67,271	20,825	1,945	(31,171)

The higher the corporate rate of return and the longer the period of deferral, the more favorable the results for the corporation. In fact, at very high rates of corporate return, the cost to the corporation is negative.

the workforce. From the employer's point of view, such arrangements can help attract and keep qualified executives, reward such executives for productivity and loyalty, and encourage the early retirement of certain executives. The executive, on the other hand, may look forward to retirement income higher than that provided by the employer's regular plan, or at least to full pension benefits in the case of a short-service executive; certain tax advantages; additional death benefit coverage; early retirement with full benefits; and the extension of income into retirement.

Chapter Summary

- Executive retirement arrangements are established for a variety of reasons. The most common reasons include (1) to replace retirement benefits lost by reason of other tax law provisions; (2) to provide a higher level of benefits than would be generated by a company's broad-based plan; (3) to facilitate midcareer recruiting; (4) to recognize incentive pay excluded from recognition in the company's broad-based plan; and (5) to avoid executives' turning down transfers because of benefit disparities when programs are not uniform throughout an organization. The design features of the executive benefit plan should reflect the objectives for establishing the plan.

- An excess benefit plan provides benefits that cannot be provided through a qualified plan solely because of IRC Section 415 limits on benefits and contributions. If it is unfunded, an excess benefit plan is completely exempt from Title I of ERISA. If it is funded, it is subject to Title I's reporting and disclosure, fiduciary responsibility, and enforcement provisions.

- A plan that is "unfunded and is maintained by an employer primarily for the purpose of providing deferred compensation for a select group of management or highly compensated employees" is an ERISA Title I pension plan but is *not* subject to the participation, vesting, funding, or fiduciary responsibility provisions of Title I. However, the enforcement and reporting and disclosure requirements do apply to these top hat plans.

- The differences between defined benefit and defined contribution approaches are less significant with executive retirement plans than they are with broad-based plans. Coverage issues under the plan termination provisions of ERISA, which often deter a company from establishing a broad-based defined benefit plan, do not apply to defined benefit executive plans. In a similar way, a defined contribution executive benefit plan can be designed to avoid the transfer of investment and inflation risks to employees.

- Most executive benefit plans have been established on a defined benefit basis. This is especially true where the plan is structured to build upon an underlying broad-based defined benefit program. Certain characteristics of executive benefit plans should differ from the employer's broad-based plan, while the coordination of other features provides consistency that is desirable.

- While the main purpose of SERPs is to provide the executive with an additional layer of retirement benefits over and above those provided by the employer's basic plan, deferred compensation agreements deal primarily with earnings deferral, usually to gain tax advantages, with retirement income as a secondary consideration. In order to avoid the possibility of the executives' being judged to be in constructive receipt of the deferred funds, three rules must be followed in drawing up a deferred compensation agreement. They are that the deferral must be (1) irrevocable; (2) agreed to before the compensation is earned; and (3) for a specified length of time. The agreement also must serve a business purpose.

Key Terms

corporate-owned life
   insurance (COLI), p. *377*
deferred compensation
   agreements, p. *378*
doctrine of constructive
   receipt, p. *368*
doctrine of economic
   benefit, p. *368*

excess benefit plans, p. *362*
golden handcuffs, p. *366*
golden handshakes, p. *366*
rabbi trust, p. *377*
secular trust, p. *378*
"select group" requirement,
   p. *363*

supplemental executive
   retirement plan (SERP),
   p. *364*
top hat plans, p. *362*
umbrella plan, p. *365*

Questions for Review

1. What are the typical objectives of an employer in establishing an executive retirement arrangement? Explain.
2. What is the ultimate cost of an executive retirement plan for an employer? Explain.

3. Describe the eligibility requirements typically used under an executive retirement arrangement.

4. Identify the considerations typically used to establish the level of retirement benefits and the income objectives available under an executive defined benefit retirement plan.

5. Describe how the compensation base applicable to benefits under an executive retirement arrangement usually is established.

6. Explain the reasons for including service requirements in executive retirement arrangements and the types of service requirements used.

7. How can an executive retirement arrangement be used to encourage early retirement? Explain.

8. Are lump sum options normally made available under executive retirement arrangements? Explain.

9. Why are executive retirement arrangements typically not prefunded? Explain.

10. Describe the advantages of deferred compensation arrangements.

Questions for Discussion

1. Discuss the conditions under which an employer may desire to establish an executive retirement arrangement.

2. Compare the similarities and differences in plan design issues between qualified retirement plans and executive retirement arrangements.

Resources for Further Study

Ellerman, Brian G. "The Importance of Nonqualified Benefits during Times of Economic Slowdown." *Compensation & Benefits Management* 17, no. 4 (Autumn 2001).

Goldstein, Michael G.; William A. Drennan; and Christopher E. Erblich. "The Expanding Top Hat: Greater Opportunities with Nonqualified Deferred Compensation." *Journal of Financial Service Professionals* 55, no. 4 (July 2001).

Kirk, Kenneth A.; and William J. Bowden. "Finding and Fixing 'Broken' Nonqualified Plans." *Employee Benefits Journal* 26, no. 4 (December 2001).

Chapter 21

Employee Stock Compensation Plans[1]

After studying this chapter you should be able to:

- Explain the tax advantages of statutory employee stock plans.

- Discuss the general tax principles that provide advantages to nonstatutory employee stock plans.

- Describe the characteristics and tax treatment of incentive stock options (ISOs).

- Explain the attributes and tax treatment of nonqualified stock options (NQSOs).

- Detail other alternate forms of employee stock compensation and describe the merits of each as a form of executive compensation.

- Discuss important issues regarding stock option plans such as common plan provisions and methods of valuation.

Use of employer stock in compensating employees has grown tremendously in recent years. As a result, many employees have a substantial part of their investment portfolios in employer stock, stock options, and other stock-based compensation.

General Considerations

Employee stock options and other stock plans have been used for many years, and the tax law has had various provisions concerning them.[2] But for most of this time,

---

[1] This chapter is reprinted from G. Victor Hallman and Jerry S. Rosenbloom, *Personal Financial Planning*, 6th ed. Minor editorial adaptation has occurred, for example, to refer readers to other chapters in the book.

[2] At various times, tax-favored stock options were called *restricted stock options* and *qualified stock options*. These particular plans have been discontinued. The present tax-favored stock option is called an *incentive stock option* (ISO).

stock options were granted only, or mainly, to senior executives. However, in recent years a significant percentage of corporations have begun adopting more broadly based plans covering more levels of management or even most of their full-time employees. Having said this, however, it must be recognized that employee stock options and many other stock plans still are often viewed as primarily for higher-paid, selected, managerial employees. Of course, many companies also have employee stock purchase plans that are designed to cover virtually all employees.

Types of Plans

In the classification that follows, we have divided employer stock plans into **statutory plans** and **nonstatutory plans.** Statutory plans are those to which the tax law accords special tax advantages but which also must meet certain requirements to be eligible for the advantages. On the other hand, nonstatutory plans are not based on any special tax provisions but rather are governed by general tax principles.

Statutory Plans

Incentive Stock Options

Incentive Stock Options were created by the Economic Recovery Tax Act of 1981 (ERTA) in Section 422 of the IRC. They can be made available at the employer's discretion to only some employees, normally certain highly compensated executives, and hence can be discriminatory in nature.

Requirements for ISOs A number of requirements must be met before a plan can qualify as an ISO plan. For example, the term (duration) of an option cannot exceed 10 years; the option price must equal or exceed the value of the stock when the option was granted; no disposition can be made of the stock by the person within two years from granting the option or within one year of the transfer of the stock to him or her (i.e., after exercise of the option); the option must be nontransferable (except by will or inheritance at death); and the maximum value of stock for which an employee can exercise ISOs for the first time in a calendar year generally cannot exceed $100,000 (valued as of the date of the grant).

Tax Treatment to Employees The main tax advantage of ISOs is that there is no regular income tax levied at the **grant** or at the **exercise** of the option by the employee. However, the bargain element upon *exercise* of an ISO (i.e., the difference between the fair market value of the stock at exercise and the option price) is an adjustment item for individual AMT purposes. Aside from this AMT issue, the employee is taxed only when he or she sells the stock purchased under the option plan, and then any gain realized is taxed as a capital gain. The capital gain would be the difference between the option price (the income tax basis of the stock) and the stock's fair market value on the date of sale.

As an example, assume that in 1998 Laura Johnson was granted an ISO to purchase 1,000 shares of her employer's (Acme Corporation's) common stock at an option price *(strike price)* of $20 per share, which was its fair market value at the time. The ISO's term was 10 years. Laura had no gross income for federal income tax purposes at the *grant* of this option. Assume further that in 2001 Laura *exercised* the option with cash and purchased 1000 shares of Acme common from her employer for $20,000 (1,000 shares × $20 per share = $20,000). At that time (2001), the stock's fair market value was $50 per share, and the bargain element was $30,000 ($50 − $20 = $30 × 1000 shares = $30,000). Laura had no regular gross income at exercise of the ISO, but she did have an AMT adjustment item of $30,000. Laura's regular income tax basis for the 1000 shares is her cost (purchase price) of $20,000, or $20 per share.

Now assume that in 2003 Laura sells the 1,000 shares for $80 per share. At this point Laura realizes and recognizes long-term capital gain of $60 per share, or $60,000 ($80 − $20 = $60 per share × 1,000 shares = $60,000).[3] Further, if Laura does not sell during her lifetime but holds the Acme stock until her death, it currently would get a stepped-up income tax basis and the gain to that point would never be taxed.

Tax Treatment for the Employer   The general principle is that an employer gets a corporate income tax deduction for compensation expense at the same time and in the same amount as the employee realizes gross compensation income from the stock plan. In the case of an ISO, an employee never realizes compensation income and so the employer never gets a corporate tax deduction.

Employee Stock Purchase Plans

Basic Characteristics   **Employee Stock Purchase Plans** are option arrangements under which all full-time employees meeting certain eligibility requirements are allowed to buy stock in their employer corporation, usually at a discount. The option price cannot be less than the lower of (1) 85 percent of the stock's fair market value when the option was granted or (2) 85 percent of the stock's fair market value when the option was exercised. Many employers use these maximum discounts as the option (strike) prices under their plans. Employees who participate agree to have an estimated amount withheld from their pay to provide the funds with which to exercise their options at the end of an option period. If an employee decides not to exercise an option, the plan will return the amounts withheld to the employee, usually with interest.

Employee stock purchase plans are nondiscriminatory in that they cannot favor the highly paid executives of a corporation. In fact, no employee who owns 5 percent or more of the stock of a corporation can be granted such an option, and the maximum annual value of stock subject to these plans (determined as of the grant of the option) is $25,000.

---

[3] Note that in this example the holding requirements for an ISO have been met (i.e., two years from grant and one year from exercise). However, if the requirements for an ISO had been violated, the option would be treated as a nonqualified stock option (NQSO) described later in this chapter.

Tax Treatment to Employees If the requirements of Section 423 of the IRC are met, there is no gross income for participating employees at the grant or exercise of options under employee stock purchase plans. However, to get this favorable tax treatment no disposition can be made of the stock by the employee within two years from grant of the option and within one year from its exercise. If such a disqualifying disposition were to occur, the employee would be taxed as having ordinary compensation income in the year of disposition on the difference between the fair market value of the stock and the option strike price when the option was exercised.

For dispositions (sales) of the stock after the two-year and one-year holding periods (or upon death whenever occurring), when the option price was between 85 percent and 100 percent of the stock's fair market value at grant, the employee (or his or her estate) will be taxed as ordinary compensation income on the lesser of (1) the difference between the fair market value of the stock and the option price at the time of disposition or death, or (2) the difference between the fair market value of the stock and the option price as of the time the option was granted. The remainder of any gain at sale during the employee's lifetime would be capital gain. At the employee's death, his or her estate or heirs would get a stepped-up basis for the remainder of any gain, and it would never be taxed.

Many corporations have adopted employee stock purchase plans. While a company's plan may not necessarily be as liberal as permitted by the tax law, a great many are. Therefore, it would seem that eligible employees normally would be well advised to participate in these plans if they are at all financially able to do so. If an employee really does not want to hold the stock, he or she can simply sell it at a profit (assuming the stock price was such that the employee should have exercised the option in the first place).

Tax Treatment for the Employer The employer does not get a corporate income tax deduction at grant or exercise of options under employee stock purchase plans.

Qualified Retirement Plans Invested in Employer Securities

These plans were discussed in Chapters 8, 9, and 10. Stock bonus plans permit investment in employer stock and allow distribution of that stock to participants. Employee stock ownership plans (ESOPs) must invest primarily in employer stock. Qualified savings plans with Section 401(k) options often allow significant portions of employee account balances to be invested in employer stock. These plans were explained in Chapter 11. The planning issue of possible lump sum distributions of employer securities was explored in Chapter 8.

Nonstatutory Plans

General Tax Law Principles Governing Stock Compensation Plans

General Provisions Since there are no special provisions governing these plans, they are interpreted under provisions of the code related to income—Section 61 in general and Section 83 in particular. Section 61 is simply the all-inclusive definition of gross income for federal income tax purposes. The more significant provision is Section 83, which deals with taxation of property transferred in connection with the performance of services.

Section 83 in essence provides that the fair market value of property (less any amount paid for the property) transferred to a person for the performance of services shall be included in that person's gross income in the first taxable year in which the person's rights in the property become transferable or are not subject to a substantial risk of forfeiture, whichever is applicable. A substantial risk of forfeiture might exist, for example, if an employee has to remain with the employer for a certain number of years to receive unfettered ownership or rights to the property. In effect, the property (less any amount paid for it) is taxable to the person rendering the services as soon as all substantial conditions on his or her having it are removed.

Section 83(b) Election However, an important subsection, **IRC Section 83(b)**, provides that a person performing services (e.g., an employee) may elect within 30 days of a transfer to include the fair market value of the transferred property (less any amount paid for the property) in his or her gross income, even though the property then was subject to a substantial risk of forfeiture or was not transferable and hence under Section 83 normally would not have been taxable at that point. This is called a *Section 83(b) election.* It can be an important planning tool.

However, if one makes a Section 83(b) election and the value of transferred property is included in the person's gross income, and the property subsequently is forfeited (because, say, the employee did not remain with the employer for the required period), no tax deduction is allowed for the forfeiture. The election also cannot be revoked without the consent of the Secretary of the Treasury. On the other hand, when the substantial risk of forfeiture expires, there is no tax then.

Normally, of course, one does not want to pay taxes any sooner than necessary. On the other hand, a person receiving property for the performance of services (e.g., an executive receiving restricted employer stock) might want to make a Section 83(b) election and be taxed on the current value of the stock, if the current value is relatively low, the person expects it to rise significantly in the future, and he or she expects to remain with the employer at least through the forfeiture period. These, of course, may be big "ifs." Much depends on the circumstances. But if the stock price currently is low and is expected to do well in the future (as in some start-up situations, for example), the only real risk the person would seem to be taking is the possible loss of his or her current tax payment.

If an employee makes a Section 83(b) election and is currently taxed, the employer gets a corporate income tax deduction for compensation paid in the amount taxable to the employee. The effects of a Section 83(b) election will be illustrated later in connection with the discussion of restricted stock.

Current Stock Bonus

Some employers pay part of employees' current compensation in unrestricted stock. In this case, the employees receive current compensation equal to the fair market value of the stock. On the other hand, employers often pay part of a current bonus in cash and part in restricted stock (i.e., subject to the condition that the employee stay with the employer for a minimum period). In this case the rules for restricted stock apply.

Nonqualified Stock Options (NQSOs)

Basic Characteristics **Nonqualified Stock Options (NQSOs)** are stock options that do not meet the requirements for ISOs and so are taxed on the basis of the general principles just discussed. Correspondingly, NQSOs can have terms decided upon by the parties and are not limited in the amount of stock subject to such options exercisable by an employee in any one year (as are ISOs). Hence, NQSOs can be considerably more flexible for employers and employees. Like ISOs, they can be granted only to certain employees and hence may be discriminatory. NQSOs generally have become more popular than ISOs as a compensation technique. While there are no statutory requirements to do so, NQSOs are often granted with an option price equal to 100 percent of the fair market value of the stock on the date of grant and for option terms of around 10 years.

Tax Treatment to Employees There normally is no taxable event (gross income) at grant because the tax regulations view their value then as not being readily ascertainable.[4] On the other hand, upon exercise of an option (and transfer of the stock to the employee), the employee will receive ordinary compensation income for regular federal income tax purposes equal to the difference between the fair market value of the stock at exercise and the option price (the bargain element). The employee's income tax basis in the stock is its fair market value at exercise. This is because the employee paid the option price to the employer (a cost basis) and included the remainder of the stock's value (bargain element) in his or her gross income as compensation (basis under the tax benefit principle). Thus, an immediate sale of the stock by the employee (there are no two-year and one-year holding periods for NQSOs) will produce zero capital gain or loss since the amount realized would equal the adjusted basis for the stock.

Let us illustrate these principles by returning to our example involving Laura Johnson. If we assume the same facts except that Laura was granted an NQSO in 1998 instead of an ISO, the tax results would be as follows. Laura would have no gross income at grant of the option. However, when Laura exercised her NQSO in 2001, she would have had ordinary compensation income of $30,000 in that year.[5] Laura's income tax basis for the 1000 shares is $50,000, or $50 per share ($20 per share of cost basis and $30 per share of basis due to that amount having been taxed).

Now when Laura sells her 1000 shares of Acme common in 2003 at a price of $80 per share, she will realize and recognize long-term capital gain of $30 per share, or $30,000 ($80 − $50 = $30 per share × 1000 shares = $30,000). Thus, for the NQSO the total gain on the option stock would still be $60,000, except that $30,000 would be ordinary compensation income and $30,000 long-term capital gain taxable at a maximum 20 percent rate.

---

[4] Employee stock options, of course, are not traded on organized or over-the-counter markets, may not be transferable, and normally are not vested at grant.

[5] Note that the AMT is not involved here because the $30,000 bargain element is taxable for *regular* income tax purposes.

Tax Treatment for the Employer The employer gets a corporate income tax deduction for the amount of compensation income the employee realizes at exercise of the option.

Restricted Stock

Basic Characteristics **Restricted stock plans** are arrangements whereby a corporation grants stock (or stock options) to an employee (or someone rendering services to the corporation), but where ownership of the stock is subject to a substantial risk of forfeiture (such as the employee's remaining with the employer for a certain number of years or the corporation's meeting certain profit goals). Such stock may be provided to employees in a variety of circumstances. It can be part of a general compensation package, perhaps to entice the person to go with the employer. It can be part of a bonus plan as noted earlier. And in some cases, stock issued on exercise of an NQSO can be restricted stock in order to further postpone taxation.

Tax Treatment to Employees and the Section 83(b) Election As explained earlier, an employee receives ordinary compensation income in the year the employee's rights to the stock are first not subject to the substantial risk of forfeiture or are transferable. The gross income is measured by the fair market value of the stock at that time less any cost to the employee. However, depending on the circumstances, a Section 83(b) election (described earlier) may be considered. A person receiving restricted stock must make a planning decision regarding this election.

Again to illustrate these principles, let us assume that John Venturesome is a young information executive with a large corporation. Recently a former college classmate invited him to join a newer start-up company (XYZ.com) that has some exciting new products in information technology. The offer is for less salary, but XYZ.com, which recently went public, will give John a compensation package that includes NQSOs and 10,000 shares of restricted stock (which is conditioned on John's staying with the company for at least three years). John does not have to pay anything for the 10,000 shares. XYZ.com common stock currently is selling at $2 per share.

John accepts the offer in 2002 and makes no Section 83(b) election. First, John has no gross income from receipt of the 10,000 shares of restricted stock since it is subject to a substantial risk of forfeiture. Let us further assume that at the end of three years (in 2005) John is still with XYZ.com and that its stock has done very well. Its price in 2005 is $20 per share. When the substantial risk of forfeiture ends (in 2005), John will have ordinary compensation income of $200,000 (10,000 shares × $20 per share = $200,000). His income tax basis in the 10,000 shares also will be $200,000, or $20 per share.

Now let us change our facts and assume John made the Section 83(b) election in 2002 within 30 days of when the 10,000 shares were transferred to him. He then would be taxed on $20,000 in year 2002 ($2 per share × 10,000 shares = $20,000) as ordinary compensation income, and his basis in the 10,000 shares also would be $20,000, or $2 per share. If John is still with XYZ.com at the end of the three years (in 2005), the substantial risk of forfeiture would end, and he would have unrestricted right to the stock. He would incur no further gross income then. On the other hand, if John should leave XYZ.com after, say, two years, he would forfeit the 10,000 shares and could take no tax deduction for that. In effect, he would lose the tax he paid in 2002 on the $20,000 of ordinary income.

Let us now assume that John stayed with XYZ.com until 2005 and that two years later (in 2007) John sells the 10,000 shares for $30 per share. If he had not made the Section 83(b) election in the year 2002, he would have $100,000 of long-term capital gain ($300,000 amount realized − $200,000 adjusted basis = $100,000 gain realized and recognized). In effect, he would have had $300,000 of total gain on the 10,000 shares of restricted stock ($200,000 of ordinary compensation income and $100,000 of long-term capital gain). On the other hand, if John had made the Section 83(b) election in the year 2002, he would have $280,000 of long-term capital gain ($300,000 amount realized − $20,000 adjusted basis = $280,000 gain realized and recognized). In this situation, he also would have had $300,000 of total gain on the 10,000 shares of restricted stock, but now it is divided as $20,000 of ordinary compensation income and $280,000 of long-term capital gain. Further, if John does not sell the 10,000 shares (or all of them) during his lifetime, he can consider other techniques for possibly avoiding capital gains taxation. Finally, if he does not sell or otherwise dispose of his stock, it currently will get a stepped-up basis at death. But if the market price of the stock falls or it becomes worthless, John would have been better off not making the Section 83(b) election.

Tax Treatment for the Employer   Again, the employer gets a corporate income tax deduction when the employee receives gross compensation income. This is either when the substantial risk of forfeiture ends or the Section 83(b) election is made.

Other Stock-Based Plans

This is a complex field and only a brief description of some of these plans will be given here.

Stock Appreciation Rights (SARs)   These are accounts maintained for selected employees that reflect the appreciation in the employer's stock over a certain period. When an executive's rights to an SAR become final, it normally is paid out to him or her in cash and is taxable then.

Phantom Stock   These also are accounts maintained for selected employees, but they normally reflect the full value of a certain amount of employer stock. The account value varies with the stock's value and normally is paid to the executive in cash at some point. However, there is no actual stock in the account.

Performance Shares or Performance-Based Stock Options   In this case, selected employees are granted stock or stock options whose vesting is contingent on certain corporate or other performance measures being met.

Provisions of Stock Option Plans

Vesting of Options

This is the period of continuous employment that must elapse after an option is granted and before the employee can exercise the option. There generally are vesting requirements in stock option plans. The periods required for vesting vary but often range from two to four years.

Transferability of Options

Traditionally, employee stock options have not been transferable by the employees receiving the options other than at death. They could not be sold or given away. One of the requirements to be an ISO is that the option by its terms must not be transferable (other than by will or intestate distribution) and must be exercisable during the employee's lifetime only by him or her.

There is no corresponding prohibition for NQSOs. But in the past, corporations in practice have not allowed their NQSOs to be transferable. Recently, however, this has changed. Some corporations have amended their stock option plans to allow NQSOs to be transferred by the holder to members of his or her family, trusts for such members, or possibly family limited partnerships with such members as partners, with the consent of the corporation. Thus, in these cases there might be gifts of NQSOs to family members or entities for them.

Effect of Certain Contingencies on Options

Stock option plans normally have certain forfeiture provisions in the event of termination of employment for various reasons. The option holder (or his or her estate or heirs) usually has a limited period of time to exercise the option after he or she retires (such as three to five years), becomes disabled on a long-term basis (such as three to five years), dies (such as one or two years), voluntarily terminates employment (such as three months), or for other reasons. The option holder should be careful to observe any such time limits lest valuable option rights be lost. Some plans also provide that options will be automatically forfeited if the holder becomes employed by or associated with a competitor of his or her former employer. In such a case, if an option holder is planning to change jobs and go with a competing firm, he or she should exercise favorable (i.e., "in the money") vested options before terminating employment.

Exercise of Options

Stock options generally can be exercised in several ways.

Cash Exercise   An option holder can make a **cash exercise** by paying the option price to the employer and having the stock transferred to him or her. In the case of an NQSO, the employer also will require withholding of federal, state, local, and FICA taxes on the taxable amount. The option holder must lay out the option price (and any withholding) in cash.

Stock-for-Stock Exercise   A plan may allow payment of the exercise price by delivering previously owned shares of stock of the employer that are equal in value to the option price to the employer and having the option stock transferred to the option holder. This may be referred to as a **stock-for-stock exercise.**

As an example, suppose that Ahmed Bastor exercises an NQSO to buy 1,000 shares of ABC Corporation common stock at an option price of $20 per share at a time when the fair market value of the stock is $50 per share. Ahmed already owns ABC common through previous stock option exercises. In a stock-for-stock exercise, Ahmed could deliver 400 shares of his previously owned ABC common to the corporation in payment of the $20,000 exercise price (1,000 shares × $20 per share = $20,000 exercise price ÷ $50 per share = 400 shares of stock to deliver). Assume the 400 shares of previously owned stock had an income tax basis to Ahmed of $10 per share. There is no gain recognized on the exchange of the 400 previously owned shares for 400 of the new option shares, and the new shares will have the same holding period for capital gain purposes as the previously owned shares. This is because this is a tax-free exchange of common stock in a corporation for common stock in the same corporation as provided in Section 1036 of the IRC.

The income tax basis of the exchanged shares ($10 per share) will be carried over to 400 of the new option shares. The remainder of the new option shares will be as if it were a cash exercise. The difference between the fair market value of the stock received (600 shares × $50 per share = $30,000) less any cash paid for the stock (0 in this example) would be ordinary compensation income to Ahmed, and his income tax basis in these 600 shares would be $50 per share (or $30,000), which is the amount taken into his gross income for them. The corporation may require cash withholding or allow withholding in the form of stock otherwise issuable to the option holder. It can be seen that in this case the option holder is paying for some of the new option stock with existing stock in the same corporation. This reduces the option holder's overall stock position in the company as compared with a cash exercise and is the reason reload options (discussed below) may be granted in this situation.

Cashless Exercise   This type of exercise was first made possible by the Federal Reserve Board in 1988. It involves working through a stockbroker who can buy the option stock from the corporation at the exercise price, sell enough stock in the open market to cover the purchase price plus broker's commissions and a small amount of margin interest, and then deliver the remaining stock to the option holder. If the exercise is a taxable event, the broker also may sell enough stock to cover tax withholding, which the broker will remit to the employer. If the option holder wants to receive cash from the transaction rather than stock, the broker may sell all the option stock and credit the net cash to the option holder.

Reload Options   These are additional options that may be granted to employees when they pay the exercise price for stock with previously owned stock of the corporation (a stock-for-stock exercise). The **reload option** normally is for the same number of shares used to pay the exercise price (plus perhaps shares used for federal, state, local, and FICA withholding tax purposes) and is for the remainder of the option period of the underlying option that was exercised.

A stock-for-stock exercise of an underlying option when there is a reload option can be attractive for an option holder. Using our previous example of Ahmed Bastor, assume that ABC's plan provides for reload options. In this case, if the underlying option Ahmed exercised originally had a term of 10 years and Ahmed engaged in the stock-for-stock exercise described previously four years after the grant date, he might be granted a reload option for 400 shares (ignoring, for the sake of simplicity, any stock used for tax withholding purposes) at an option price of $50 per share (the current fair market value of the stock) for a term of six years (the remaining term of the exercised underlying option).

Compared with a cash exercise and a stock-for-stock exercise with no reload option, Ahmed now is in a better position. Under a cash exercise, he would have an exposure to ABC Corporation stock of 1400 directly owned shares (400 previously owned and 1000 option shares), but he would have had to come up with the $20,000 needed to exercise the underlying option. Under a stock-for-stock exercise with no reload feature, Ahmed's exposure to ABC stock would be reduced to 1000 directly owned shares (the option shares). However, under the stock-for-stock exercise with a reload feature, his exposure to ABC stock remains at 1400 shares (1000 directly owned option shares and 400 reload option shares), but he would not have needed to disturb his other assets or cash reserves to exercise the underlying option. This occurs because Ahmed has been given a new option (the reload option) which itself has value.

Valuation of Stock Options

This is a very complex subject. It is made even more so by the fact that employee stock options are different in many ways from publicly traded stock and other options. In essence, however, employee stock options are really call options for the employees on employer stock.

People may be concerned about the **valuation of** employee **stock options** for many reasons. Employees want to know what they are really worth, since options have become an important part of many compensation arrangements. They also need to be valued for purposes of an employee's asset allocation planning. In some cases, employees may give up cash compensation in exchange for stock options and so they want to have an idea of what the options are worth to evaluate the exchange. Finally, employee stock options may need to be valued for estate planning purposes.

Traded Options

The market prices of publicly traded options are readily available in the financial press and from other sources. Employee stock options, of course, are not publicly traded and have no readily ascertainable market value.

Most traded options are for relatively short durations, such as a few months. However, just to get an idea of how the market values longer-term options relative to the prices of the underlying stocks, it may be instructive to note the market premiums (prices) for leaps. **Leaps** are longer-term publicly traded options. For example, as of this writing, the price of a 30-month call option on one major company's stock with a strike price of $115 when the underlying stock's current market price was $94 1/16 (i.e., this call option was out of the money) was $40 per share, or about 42.5 percent of the underlying stock's market price.

Naturally, the prices of such publicly traded long-term options will vary considerably with the characteristics of the underlying stocks and with market conditions. The only point we are making here is that the market itself sets a considerable value on longer-term options (30 months in this example), even when they have no intrinsic value (described next). Clearly then, the market value (as well as the economic or true value) of long-term options can be substantial.

Intrinsic Value

The intrinsic value of a stock option is the difference between the underlying stock's current market price and the option's strike price. For example, if an employee is granted a 10-year NQSO with an option price of $25 per share when the underlying stock's market price also is $25 per share, the intrinsic value of the option is $0 at grant. As we have just seen for traded options, the intrinsic value does not reflect the fair value or economic worth of an option. In fact, as will be shown in the next section, the economic worth of a long-term option such as that previously cited can be quite substantial.

Option Pricing Models

A number of models (mathematical systems of analysis) have been developed to compute the fair value or economic worth of options. Probably the best known is the Black-Scholes option pricing model. This model is based on the following six factors to determine the economic value of an option.[6] (Let us say for the following illustration of these factors that we are valuing an employee stock option.)

- Option exercise price (strike price).

- Current market price of the underlying stock.

- Risk-free interest rate during the expected term of the option.

- Expected dividend yield on the stock.

- Expected life of the option. The expected life is the time period the employee is actually expected to hold the option before exercising it. It may be shorter than the maximum option period in the plan.

---

[6] The concept behind these option pricing models is that the fair value of an option (which, in general, is an instrument that allows, but does not require, a person to buy or sell an asset at a prearranged price during a set time period) consists of two elements: (1) the intrinsic value and (2) a time value, arising because the option holder may benefit from favorable future price movements (volatility) in the asset without having the downside risk of actual ownership of the asset.

- Expected volatility of the underlying stock's market price. This normally is the most important factor in the model. The greater the expected volatility, the more likely there will be time value gains (see note 6) and the greater the option value will be. Volatility can be estimated from the historical standard deviation of the stock's price changes over past time periods.

To illustrate the *fair value* of an option, let us continue our fact pattern for the NQSO noted earlier with respect to intrinsic value. Using the factors just listed, we assume that this NQSO has an option exercise price of $25 per share, the current market price of the underlying stock also of $25 per share, the assumed risk-free interest rate is 5%, an expected dividend yield of 0, an assumed expected life of the option of 10 years, and an expected volatility of the underlying stock's price of 20 percent per month. Under these assumptions, the Black-Scholes model would produce a fair value of $19.75 per option. This equals 79 percent of the underlying stock's current price. Of course, if the assumed expected life of the option were reduced, the fair value would decline. For example, if the expected life were one year, the fair value would be $7.24 per option. Most employee stock options have an expected life of considerably more than one year. Software is available for calculating the fair value of options under option pricing models.

It is clear from this discussion that the *economic value (fair value)* of stock options granted to employees can be substantial. However, it must also be recognized that the *actual value* of such options may never reach the fair value at grant (from an option pricing model) and may even be zero if the actual market price of the underlying stock should decline (or fail to rise) from the option price.

Sometimes when a stock's price falls and many executive stock options are "under water" (i.e., the stock's market price is below the option price and the option is out of the money), the employer will *reprice the options* to be equal to the stock's current market price (i.e., cancel the old out-of-the-money options and issue new ones at the stock's current market value). However, this is a controversial tactic.

Some Caveats concerning Stock Options and Other Plans

While employee stock options and other stock compensation plans have been a boon for many employees and a bonanza for some, some caveats concerning them are still in order.

What Goes Up Can Still Come Down!

It seems almost trite to say that while employee stock plans can be very attractive when the price of a company's stock is rising, the reverse will be true when the price is falling. However, some employees may not truly understand this. They can overcommit themselves financially on the basis of paper gains in their stock options and other plans.

Some Employees May Not Realize the True Economic Worth of Options

The other side of the coin is that some employees may not truly understand, or may have difficulty in analyzing, the economic value of options or other stock rights granted to them.

Risk of Excessive Concentration in Employer Stock

While employees usually are well advised to take advantage of these plans when they are attractive to them, they also should attempt to deal with any overconcentration issue, assuming they want a reasonably diversified investment portfolio.

Planning Issues regarding Stock Options and Other Stock Plans

Some of these issues may be summarized as follows:

- Whether to participate in employee stock purchase plan offerings. This depends on the terms of the plan and the employer stock, but in general, these plans are advantageous for employees and are flexible as to whether participating employees will take the stock.

- When to exercise stock options. This can be a complicated issue. If an employee simply holds a vested, unexercised option for as long as possible, given the plan's option period, before exercising it, he or she can benefit from the underlying stock's possible increase in price over the exercise price without actually committing any investment funds until exercise. This is attractive if the stock's price does increase during the remaining option period. But if the concern is that the stock's price may fall and not really recover during the remaining option period, then it is better to exercise the option now and sell the stock as soon as possible. Also, if overconcentration in employer stock is an issue, as it often is, exercise of NQSOs and immediate sale of the stock can be a tax-efficient remedy.

- Whether to change an ISO into an NQSO by breaking an ISO requirement. This may be done to avoid an AMT problem without the funds with which to pay the tax or if the stock's price is expected to fall dramatically.

- How to exercise options (including the possible availability of reload options), as described previously.

- Whether to make a Section 83(b) election with regard to restricted stock or other plans, as described previously.

- Whether to take option stock as restricted stock if available. This is done, when available, to further delay recognition of income on exercise of NQSOs.

- Whether to take bonuses or other compensation in the form of stock options if available.

- How to maintain investment diversification in light of likely favorable terms for acquiring more and more employer stock.

- Any estate planning actions with regard to stock plans if possible. This might include making gifts of NQSOs if allowed by the plan. However, such gifts should be analyzed carefully. It also may include the exercise of any in-the-money unexercised NQSOs before death (e.g. a "death bed exercise") for estate tax reasons.

Chapter Summary

- Statutory employer stock plans are those plans to which the tax law accords special tax advantages in recognition of their being subject to certain requirements. Nonstatutory employer stock plans are not subject to these requirements, do not receive special tax advantages, but are governed by general tax principles. Among the most common statutory employer stock plans would be incentive stock options (ISOs), employee stock purchase plans governed by Section 423 of the Internal Revenue Code, and qualified retirement plans invested in employer securities. Among the most common forms of nonstatutory employer stock plans would be current compensation paid as a bonus in unrestricted stock, nonqualified stock options (NQSOs), restricted stock plans, stock appreciation rights (SARs), phantom stock, and performance shares or performance-based stock options.

- Incentive stock options require:
  - The term of the option cannot exceed 10 years.
  - The option price must equal or exceed the value of the stock when the option was granted.
  - No disposition can be made of the stock by the person granted the ISO within two years from the granting of the option or within one year of the transfer of the stock to him or her following stock option exercise.
  - The option must be nontransferable except by will or inheritance at death.
  - The maximum value of stock for which an employee can exercise ISOs in any year generally cannot exceed $100,000.

    The main tax advantage of ISOs to employees is that there is no regular income tax levied at the grant or at the exercise of the option by the employee. Since the employer receives a corporate income tax deduction for compensation expense when the employee realizes gross compensation income from a stock plan, in the case of an ISO, the employer never gets a corporate tax deduction.

- Section 423 employee stock purchase plans are structured so that:
  - All full-time employees meeting certain eligibility requirements be permitted to buy stock in their employer corporation.
  - The option price cannot be less than the lower of:
    (1) 85 percent of the stock's fair market value when the option was granted, or
    (2) 85 percent of the stock's fair market value when the option was exercised.
  - If an employee does not exercise an option, the plan returns amounts withheld from the employee's pay, usually with interest.
  - No employee who owns 5 percent or more of the corporation's stock can be granted such an option.
  - The maximum annual value of stock subject to these plans determined as of the grant of the option is $25,000.

    The main tax advantage of a Section 423 plan is that no gross income is attributable to participating employees at either the grant or exercise of the options, provided no disposition of the stock occurs by the employee within two years from grant of the option and within one year from the option's exercise. When dispositions of the stock occur after the requisite holding period, the employee is taxed as having received ordinary compensation income on the lesser of:

(1) The difference between the fair market value of the stock and the option price at the time of disposition or death, or

(2) The difference between the fair market value of the stock and the option price as of the time the option was granted.

The employer does not get a corporate income tax deduction at grant or exercise of options under employee stock purchase plans.

- Nonqualified stock options are stock options that do not meet the tax requirements for ISOs and are taxed on the basis of general tax principles. There normally is no taxable event when the option is granted to the employee. When the option is exercised and stock is transferred to the employee, the employee receives ordinary compensation income equaling the difference between the fair market value of the stock at exercise and the option price of the stock. The basis of the stock at exercise is the stock's fair market value because the employee paid the option price for the stock and reported the difference between fair market value and option price as reportable income. The employer receives a corporate income tax deduction for the amount of compensation income the employee realizes at exercise of the option.

- Internal Revenue Code (IRC) Section 83 provides that the fair market value of property that is transferred to a person as compensation for the performance of services, less any amount the person pays for the property, is included in the person's gross income in the first taxable year in which the person's rights in the property become transferable or are not subject to a substantial risk of forfeiture. However, subsection (b) of Section 83 allows a person performing services to elect within 30 days of grant to include the fair market value of transferred property, less any amount paid for the property, in his or her gross income immediately. This inclusion occurs even though the property is still subject to a substantial risk of forfeiture or is not transferable and subject to taxation according to Section 83. When the substantial risk of forfeiture subsequently expires, a tax would not be levied on the person at that time because the person already included the fair market value of the property in his or her income with the Subsection 83(b) election. Appreciation in the property would be taxed as a capital gain upon subsequent disposition of the property. An employer takes a corporate income tax deduction when the employee receives gross compensation income—either when the substantial risk of forfeiture expires, or when the Subsection 83(b) election is made.

- Stock options can be exercised in the following ways:
  - *Cash exercise* The option holder pays the option price to the employer, and the stock is transferred to the option holder.
  - *Stock-for-stock exercise* The option holder delivers previously owned shares of employer stock to the employer that are equal in value to the option price required for the employer stock under the terms of the option. This transaction is a tax-free exchange as provided in Section 1036 of the IRC.
  - *Cashless exercise* A stockbroker buys the option stock from the corporation at the exercise price, sells enough stock in the open market to cover the purchase price plus broker's commissions and a small amount of margin interest, and delivers the remaining stock to the option holder. If the option holder wishes to receive cash rather than stock, the option stock is sold and the cash proceeds are remitted to the option holder.
  - *Reload options* Additional options are granted to employees when they pay the exercise price for stock with previously owned stock of the corporation. A stock-for-stock exercise with a reload feature allows the option holder to exercise without disturbing other assets or cash reserves and continue to hold an increased option and stock position with upside potential because of the new option which was granted.

Key Terms

cash exercise, p. *391*

exercise, p. *384*

grant, p. *384*

incentive stock options
(ISOs), p. *384*

IRC Section 83(b), p. *387*

leaps, p. *394*

nonqualified stock options
(NQSOs), p. *388*

nonstatutory plans, p. *384*

performance shares, p. *390*

phantom stock, p. *390*

reload options, p. *392*

restricted stock plans,
p. *389*

statutory plans, p. *384*

stock appreciation rights
(SARs), p. *390*

stock-for-stock exercise,
p. *392*

valuation of stock options,
p. *393*

Questions for Review

1. Distinguish what is meant by both statutory and nonstatutory employer stock plans.
2. Identify common forms of statutory employer stock plans.
3. Identify common forms of nonstatutory employer stock plans.
4. Explain the specific requirements for incentive stock options (ISOs) to receive special tax treatment by employees, and detail what this special tax treatment is.
5. What are the requirements and tax advantages of employee stock purchase plans under Section 423 of the IRC?
6. Discuss the general tax law provisions that govern stock compensation plans.
7. Describe the workings of a Section 83(b) election, its tax ramifications, and its usefulness in the context of tax planning for resticted stock options.
8. Summarize the common provisions needed to be included in stock option plans.
9. Identify and explain the ways in which stock options can be exercised.
10. How are stock options commonly valued?
11. What factors are used to determine the value of an option using the Black-Scholes option pricing model?
12. What caveats or concerns should be recognized by employees eligible for employer stock option plans?
13. List common planning issues for employees eligible for stock options and other employer stock plans.

Questions for Discussion

1. Discuss the advantages and risks involved for an employee who can either accept an employment opportunity with a relatively higher direct compensation package with little or nothing in employer stock plans or, alternatively, a relatively lower direct compensation package with greater exposure to employer stock plan participation.
2. Discuss what personal factors may influence the exposure one might be willing to accept for high concentrations of employer stock beneficially received through employer stock plans.

3. Discuss various financial planning strategies to increase asset diversification when employer stock results in a heavy concentration of employee wealth.

Resources for Further Study

Banham, Russ. "Sunk by Options." *Journal of Accountancy* 192, no. 4 (October 2001).

Ferracone, Robin A.; and John P. Borneman. "Putting Pay for Performance Back into Incentive Programs." *Compensation & Benefits Management* 17, no. 4 (Autumn 2001).

Lowry, Susan. "Granting Options below the Executive Level." *Journal of Compensation & Benefits* 16, no. 1 (January/February 2000).

Ramagnano, Thomas W.; and David M. Sugar. "Executive Compensation Plans." In *The Handbook of Employee Benefits*. 5th ed. Jerry S. Rosenbloom, ed. New York: McGraw-Hill, 2001.

Sweeney, Paul. "Stock Option Pitfalls and Strategies du Jour." *Journal of Accountancy* 192, no. 4 (October 2001).

www.nceo.org—web site of the National Center for Employee Ownership.

Chapter 22

Investment Issues for Defined Benefit Plans

After studying this chapter you should be able to:

- Determine how the characteristics of various investments impact their suitability for use in a defined benefit pension plan.
- Understand the importance of a guideline statement for investment managers.
- Illustrate how risk-adjusted performance may be calculated.
- Identify the major classes of assets for defined benefit plans.
- Explain the process used to select an investment manager.
- Explain the relative advantages and limitations of passive and active investing.

Although the investment of pension plan assets is important in individual account plans (i.e., money purchase, profit sharing, thrift and savings, and cash or deferred arrangements, or CODAs), a fundamental difference exists between these plans and defined benefit pension plans. Namely, the investment risk is borne directly by the employees covered by individual account plans. As a result of this difference, sponsors of individual account plans typically provide participants with a choice of investment vehicles. Alternative funds provided under individual account plans generally include company stock, diversified funds, equity funds, fixed-income funds, guaranteed investment contracts (GICs), and a money market fund. These plans are discussed in some detail in Chapter 23.

By contrast, the investment risk under a defined benefit pension plan is borne almost entirely by the plan sponsor. It should be noted that active and retired employees may have at least an indirect interest in the performance of the plan assets, however. Many defined benefit pension plans grant ad hoc increases every few years to counter the effects of inflation. To the extent that these increases depend upon a particular "cushion" of plan assets, the sponsor's investment perform-ance may indeed have an impact on the participants. The participants also may have a stake in the adequacy of plan assets if a plan is terminated with unfunded liabilities.

This chapter provides a broad overview of basic investment issues. These funda-mental principles of investing are relevant to both defined benefit and defined con-tribution plans. The chapter also explores those investment issues that are of partic-ular importance to defined benefit plans.

Investment Policy

An investment policy prescribes an acceptable course of action to the fund's invest-ment managers. It communicates a risk policy in that it states the degree of invest-ment risk that the sponsor is willing to assume.

Determining Investment Objectives

In contrast to an investment policy, an investment objective is a desired result of the investment process. Before such objectives can be established, the various risk-return characteristics of the alternative investments must be recognized.

Types of Risk

Modern portfolio theory (described later in this chapter) defines *risk* in terms of the volatility of an investment (or portfolio of investments) in relation to the market. How-ever, it is useful to consider the individual components of this aggregate concept:[1]

1. Purchasing power risk.

2. Business risk.

3. Interest rate risk.

4. Market risk.

5. Specific risk.

Purchasing power risk reflects the relationship between the nominal rate of return on an investment and the increase in the rate of inflation. **Business risk** involves the prospect that the corporation issuing the security may suffer a decline in earnings power that would adversely affect its ability to pay interest, principal, or dividends. **Interest rate risk** comprises the well-known inverse relationship between interest rates and (long-term) bond prices; that is, when interest rates increase, the value of long-term bonds falls.

The final two types of risk are usually used exclusively to explain stock price behavior. **Market risk** can be thought of as an individual stock's reaction to a change in the market. In general, most stock prices will increase if the stock market

---

[1] Jerome B. Cohen, Edward D. Zinbarg, and Arthur Zeikel, *Investment Analysis and Portfolio Management,* 5th ed. (Burr Ridge, IL: Richard D. Irwin, 1987), pp. 6–11.

increases appreciably and decrease if the market decreases appreciably; however, the price of one stock may change half as fast as the market, on average, while another may change twice as fast. This relationship is quantified later in the chapter by a measure known as *beta.*

Obviously, market risk cannot account for the entire fluctuation of a stock's price. For example, if a biotechnology firm suddenly patents an unexpected cure for cancer, there would most likely be a rapid increase in its stock price in expectation of the future profit stream. In contrast, if the product developed by this firm later resulted in a massive product liability award for which the firm was not adequately insured, the stock price would most likely fall. These factors, intrinsic to the firm, are known as **specific risks.**

Characteristics of Investments

There are four primary characteristics of pension plan investments that need to be considered:

1. Tax advantages.

2. Liquidity.

3. Stability in value.

4. Ability to preserve purchasing power.

The tax aspect of the investment is important due to the tax-exempt status of the pension fund. Because the investment income of qualified pension plans is tax-exempt, certain types of investments may not be as attractive to pension funds as they would be for other types of funds. For example, the price of municipal bonds is likely to be bid up by individual investors in the highest marginal tax rates until they reach a point where their before-tax rates of return are below those that can be realized on corporate bonds or U.S. government bonds of a similar maturity.

Liquidity refers to the ability to convert an investment to cash within a short time period with little, if any, loss in principal. This may be an important attribute for at least a portion of the pension plan assets in case the plan has to weather a short period of time when the plan sponsor is unable to make contributions (or contributions are less than the amount of the benefit payments for the year) and at the same time the securities markets are depressed. If the plan does not possess an adequate degree of liquidity, the sponsor might have to sell securities at an inopportune time, perhaps resulting in the realization of capital losses.

Stability in value is closely akin to liquidity in that it emphasizes investments with minimal fluctuations in value. Achieving maximum stability in value is not particularly difficult—one need only limit investments to U.S. Treasury bills and money market instruments. However, the opportunity cost of foregone higher investment returns in riskier assets may be prohibitive. Instead, the objective of the sponsor should be to construct a portfolio that will maximize investment income for the desired level of risk.

The ability to preserve purchasing power is important because many defined benefit pension plans attempt to provide at least a partial offset against inflation for their retirees.

Historical Returns Achieved by the Various Classes of Investments

Although there have been several empirical studies of the historical risk-return trade-off exhibited by the major classes of investments, the seminal work is that of Ibbotson and Sinquefield.[2] More recently, Ibbotson Associates, Inc., has statistically analyzed a 75-year time series of the major classes of investments and found, as expected, that the riskiest investments also generated the highest yields.[3] Common stocks provided the highest annual return with small-company stocks having a compound annual growth rate of 12.4 percent and large-company stocks having a compound annual growth rate of 11.0 percent.[4] However, investors purchasing common stocks paid a price in terms of the volatility of their investment. Over the past several decades, the large-company stocks experienced one-year losses of as high as 29.72 percent (in 1974). Long-term bonds issued by the government had a significantly lower return (5.3 percent). U.S. Treasury bills were obviously the safest investment in terms of annual volatility; however, they generated a return of only 3.8 percent.

These figures cannot be viewed in isolation, and it is important to consider how they fared after the effects of inflation had been removed. During this period, the compound inflation rate was 3.1 percent, an amount that should be subtracted from the nominal rate of return to find the real rate of return produced by an investment. For example, the real rate of return of large company stocks during this period was 7.9 percent, while U.S. Treasury bills generated a real rate of return of only 0.7 percent.

Guidelines for Investment Managers

After the investment objectives have been developed, they need to be expressed in a manner that is useful to the investment manager. Often, this expression takes the form of a guideline statement. The guideline statement should cover questions such as:[5]

1. How much risk is the plan sponsor prepared to take to achieve a specific benchmark rate of return?

2. What is the time period for measurement of performance relative to objectives?

3. What is the sponsor's preference in terms of asset mix, especially as it relates to stocks?

---

[2] Roger G. Ibbotson and Rex A. Sinquefield, *Stocks, Bonds, Bills and Inflation: Historical Returns 1926–1978* (Charlottesville, VA: The Financial Analysts Research Foundation, 1979).

[3] Ibbotson & Associates, Inc., *Stocks, Bonds, Bills, and Inflation 2001 Yearbook,* pp. 25–29 and 39.

[4] Technically, the returns reported in this chapter are geometric average returns (sometimes referred to as compound annual returns). The figure can be obtained by multiplying (1 + rate of return) for each of the *n* years in the time series and then taking the *n*th root of the product. It should be noted that this is not the same as computing an arithmetic average, which is obtained by simply adding the rates of return for each of the *n* years in the time series and then dividing by *n*. Unless the rate of return is constant over the *n*-year time series, the geometric average will be less than the arithmetic average.

[5] Martin D. Sass, "How (Not) to Manage Your Pension Fund Manager," *FE Manual,* August 1985, pp. 38–39.

4. What is the liability outlook for the plan and what should the fund's investment strategy be in light of this outlook?

5. What are the sponsor's cash flow or liquidity requirements?

6. How much discretion is the manager permitted regarding foreign investment, private placements, options, financial futures, and so on?

Another matter that needs to be discussed at an early stage is exactly what constitutes an acceptable level of turnover. If the sponsor has decided that extensive turnover activity does not add value to the portfolio performance, guidelines to limit this activity should be established. If the sponsor has come to the conclusion that turnover expenses should be virtually eliminated, a tactic known as passive investment should be considered.[6]

Performance Measurement

The primary purpose of **performance measurement** is to "obtain information on which to base decisions in regard to investment objectives, portfolio strategy, and manager selection. In addition, performance measurement should improve communications with managers by creating a standard format for discussion."[7]

Effective performance measurement requires four steps:[8]

1. *Definition.*   The establishment of investment objectives and, to the extent practical, a clearly formulated portfolio strategy.

2. *Input.*   The availability of reliable and timely data. Incorrect and tardy data will render the most sophisticated system ineffective.

3. *Processing.*   The use of appropriate statistical methods to produce relevant measurements. The complex interaction of objectives, strategies, and managers' tactics cannot be understood if inappropriate statistical methods are used. A meaningful summary will make possible analysis of the investment process at the necessary depth.

4. *Output.*   The analysis of the process and results presented in a useful format. Presentation should relate realized performance to objectives and pre-established standards. Enough material should be available to understand and analyze the process. Exhibits should be designed to highlight weaknesses in the investment process and to suggest possible improvements.

Four important caveats must be kept in mind in choosing a performance measurement system:[9]

1. There is a danger that a hastily chosen system, poorly related to real needs, can rapidly degenerate into a mechanistic, pointless exercise.

---

[6] See the latter part of this chapter for a more-detailed discussion of this topic.
[7] Sidney Cottle, "Pension Asset Management—Measuring Performance," *Financial Executive,* September 1981, p. 24.
[8] Ibid, p. 25.
[9] Ibid.

2. The system should fit the investment objectives and not the reverse.

3. Measuring the process may alter it.

4. To save time and cost, it is important that overmeasurement be avoided.

Performance Measurement Methodology

Before any performance is measured, it is necessary to agree upon the correct definition for the return that is being measured. Two alternative definitions, internal rate of return and time-weighted rate of return, have been used in the investment community for over 30 years. It is quite likely that the two rates of return will vary considerably. Therefore, it is critical that the sponsor understand the differences.

The **internal rate of return** (or dollar-weighted rate of return) is the rate that accumulates all of the cash flows of a portfolio, including all outlays, to exactly the market value of the ending balance.

The internal rate of return is valuable in that it allows the sponsor to determine whether the investment is achieving the rate of return assumed for actuarial calculations; however, it is largely ineffective as a means of evaluating investment managers because it is contaminated by the effects of the timing of investments and withdrawals—a factor over which the investment manager presumably has no control. In response to this limitation of the internal rate of return approach, the Bank Administration Institute published a study in 1968 suggesting a different performance measurement technique known as the **time-weighted rate of return**. This value is computed by

> . . . dividing the interval under study into subintervals whose boundaries are the dates of cash flows into and out of the fund and by computing the internal rate of return for each subinterval. The time-weighted rate of return is the [geometric] average for the rates for these subintervals, with each rate having a weight proportional to the length of time in its corresponding subinterval.[10]

Assessing Risk

Having correctly measured the time-weighted returns, it is necessary to evaluate the risk-adjusted performance of investment managers. Although some investment managers still report their performance by comparing their equity portfolio return with a common stock index (such as the Standard & Poor's 500 Stock Average) and their bond portfolio results with a bond index (such as the Lehman Brothers aggregate bond index) without any adjustment for their portfolio's risk, there is a growing realization that return cannot be meaningfully evaluated without simultaneously considering the risk of the investment. Portfolio risks are commonly measured in one or more of the following three ways:[11]

1. Total variability in absolute terms.

---

[10] *Measuring the Investment Performance of Pension Funds for the Purpose of Inter-Fund Comparison* (Park Ridge, IL: Bank Administration Institute, 1968).
[11] Cottle, "Pension Asset Management," p. 28.

2. Total variability in relative terms.

3. Market-related variability.

Absolute risk can be measured in one of two ways. The most common is to compute the standard deviation of the periodic returns. Another method is to rank the returns in order over a particular period and to divide the distribution into percentiles. The range from the 25th to the 75th percentile, referred to as the semi-interquartile range in several measurement systems, is then used as a measure of the portfolio's absolute risk.

Relative risk measurements start with one of the two absolute risk measurements for the portfolio in question and then divide it by a similar measure for the market during the same time period. For example, if the absolute risk measure for an equity portfolio was its standard deviation based on quarterly returns for the last five years, the denominator for the relative risk measure might be the standard deviation of the S&P 500 based on quarterly returns for the last five years.

Standards for Comparing Investment Manager Results   1

For investment managers trying to secure new clientele in the lucrative pension industry, "putting your best foot forward" was a saying that took on a new meaning. Providers in the industry recognized there was a need for a level playing field where plan sponsors could compare apples to apples without fear of any hidden bruises. Instrumental in bringing about these changes was the Association of Investment Management and Research (AIMR), which formed a committee in 1987 to investigate and suggest methods for standardizing the presentation of data by investment managers. Its Performance Presentation Standards, which describe the minimum guidelines managers must follow when presenting performance to existing and potential clients, finally were implemented officially in 1992. . . .

Although AIMR task force members could not make compliance with the standards mandatory, they nonetheless felt the marketplace would force investment managers to do so. To a large extent, this has happened.

According to Greenwich Associates research, more money managers are presenting their performance results according to AIMR standards. More important, an increasing number of plan sponsors are insisting that they do so. . .

An ancillary benefit of AIMR's standards is that other groups have adopted their own performance-reporting standards. In particular, the Investment Management Consultants Association (IMCA) has implemented its own set of performance measurement standards based on AIMR's procedures.

Source: Steve Bergsman, "Comparing Apples to Apples." Reprinted with permission, from the December 1994 issue of *Pension Management* magazine, pp. 12–13. © Intertec Publishing Corp.

Although relative risk measurement is an improvement over absolute risk measurement in that it factors in the activity of the market over the measurement period, at present the state of the art for adjusting returns for risk is to use the **capital asset pricing model (CAPM).**[12] The CAPM uses standard statistical techniques (simple linear regression) to analyze the relationship between the periodic returns of the portfolio and those of the market (e.g., the S&P 500). Although several modifications of the basic regression analysis exist, most applications will begin by subtracting out a risk-free rate of return (e.g., the Treasury bill rate) from both the portfolio and market returns.

For those not familiar with regression analysis, this technique can be thought of as simply plotting the periodic returns of the portfolio (on the vertical axis) against the periodic returns of the market (on the horizontal axis). A minimum number of data points are required for the statistical procedure to operate with the desired degree of confidence. The number of observations plotted depends upon the type of returns measured—five years of data are typically used in the case of quarterly returns, while three years of data are typically considered to be sufficient if monthly information is used. The straight line that provides the "best fit" for the observations is drawn on the graph, and two features of this line are noted. The first is the point at which the line crosses the vertical axis and zero on the horizontal axis. This is referred to as the portfolio's **alpha value** and can be thought of as the amount of return produced by the portfolio, on average, independent of the return on the market. The second feature is the slope of the line measured as the change in vertical movement per unit of change in the horizontal movement. This is referred to as the portfolio's **beta value** and represents the average return on the portfolio per 1 percent return on the market. For example, if the portfolio's beta is 1.25, then a 2 percent increase (decrease) in the market would be expected to be associated with a 2.5 percent (1.25×2) increase (decrease) in the portfolio, on average.

Assessing Performance

Once the portfolio's beta has been computed, it is possible to use the CAPM to provide a risk-adjusted measure of the portfolio's performance. The CAPM asserts that the predicted **risk-adjusted rate of return** for the portfolio (R_p) will be equal to the risk-free rate (R_f) plus a risk premium that is equal to the amount of risk, beta (β), times a market risk premium that is equal to the difference between the market rate of return (R_m) and the risk-free rate:

$$R_p = R_f + (R_m - R_f) \times \beta$$

To illustrate this concept, assume that an investment manager's portfolio has a beta of 1.25, the risk-free rate of return is 6 percent, and the market rate of return is

[12] It should be noted that this theory is based on a number of very restrictive assumptions: investors are risk-averse individuals who maximize the expected utility of their end-of-period wealth; investors make their investment decisions based on a single-period horizon; transaction costs are low enough to ignore; taxes do not affect the choice of buying one asset versus another; all individuals can borrow and lend unlimited amounts of money at a single-period riskless rate of interest; and all individuals agree on the nature of the return and risk associated with each investment. However, extensions of the CAPM have solved many of these problems.

10 percent. If the portfolio yielded a rate of return of 11.5 percent, what would be the risk-adjusted rate of return? The answer is found by first finding the predicted risk-adjusted rate of return for the portfolio. This is accomplished by simply substituting the values in the equation above:

$$R_p = .06 + (.1 - .06) \times 1.25 = .11$$

This predicted value is then subtracted from the portfolio's actual value to produce a risk-adjusted rate of return of a positive 0.5 percent (11.5 − 11). The risk-adjusted rate of return can be used to measure risk-adjusted performance and to compare portfolios with different risk levels developed by actual portfolio decisions.

Allocation of Fund Assets

The asset allocation decision is a process that determines the best portfolio composition among the various major types of assets (stocks, bonds, etc.). This decision takes into account the sponsor's investment objective and, as a result, reflects the level of risk desired by the sponsor.

Major Factors to Be Considered

In addition to the type of plan (i.e., defined benefit versus individual account), there are three considerations that must be assessed in setting investment objectives:

1. Characteristics of the sponsor and its industry.

2. Demographics of the workforce and maturity of the plan.

3. Possibility of plan termination.

Characteristics of the sponsor and its industry must be considered in determining policy. For example, a sponsor with thin profit margins and high labor costs in a highly cyclical industry has less tolerance for variability in pension costs than does a company with relatively large profit margins, low labor costs, and a less-cyclical earnings pattern. Whether the industry as a whole is growing, stagnant, or declining also will affect the degree of conservatism built into the investment strategy.

Demographics also are important because a rapidly growing company with a young workforce has less concern for cash flow and investment liquidity than does a company with a more mature workforce and many pensioners. A sponsor in the first category would be more likely to be able to withstand several years of capital losses on the pension plan portfolio without impeding benefit payments.[13]

---

[13] This statement only considers the cash flow aspects of the plan. As described in Chapter 15, many of the actuarial cost methods used to determine the minimum funding standard for a defined benefit pension plan will amortize investment gains and losses over a maximum of five years. Therefore, if the sponsor desires to control volatility of the contribution stream from year to year, it is important that pension plan investments do not experience a large decline in value. Moreover, with the advent of Financial Accounting Standards Board (FASB) '87, there are now several accounting consequences of pension plan asset allocation that must take into consideration the goals of the plan.

The possibility of plan termination is important for companies with some risk of plant shutdown, merger, acquisition, or other corporate reorganization because the investment policy must take into account the possibility that the PBGC will take over the plan and value the plan assets at the time of termination at the current market value. If a plan termination occurs during a business recession and the PBGC steps in, the claim against the sponsoring company will be larger.

Classes of Assets

Retirement plan assets are estimated to be more than $4.8 trillion for the 1,000 largest U.S. plans. The largest 1,000 defined benefit and defined contribution funds held the following assets in their portfolios in 2001:[14]

Asset Category	Defined Benefit	Defined Contribution
Stocks	60.7%	61.7%
Fixed income	31.8	8.6
Cash	1.9	7.2
Real estate equity	3.9	n/a
GICs/BICs	n/a	15.0
Mortgages	0.9	n/a
Other	0.8	7.5

Annuities are discussed in Chapter 25. The other major classes, as well as mutual funds and financial futures, are discussed below.

Money Market Instruments

As discussed earlier, pension plans typically will have a need to retain at least a portion of their assets in vehicles that will be readily convertible to cash. The exact portion will depend upon the specifics of the plan design (e.g., loan features and employees' ability to select lump sum distributions) and the demographics of the plan participants. This portion of the portfolio should be invested in assets that have a low default risk, have a short maturity, and are readily marketable. There are five major categories of this type of investment alternative: U.S. Treasury bills and notes, federal agency issues, certificates of deposit, commercial paper, and money market mutual funds.

U.S. Treasury Bills and Notes

Treasury bills have maturities at issue ranging from 91 to 360 days, while Treasury notes have initial maturities ranging from one to five years. There is almost no default risk on these investments. In other words, the probability that either interest or principal payments will be skipped is nearly zero.

---

[14] "The P&I 1000," *Pensions & Investments,* January 21, 2002, pp. 1, 11, 38.

Federal Agency Issues

The Treasury is not the only federal agency to issue marketable obligations. Other agencies issue short-term obligations that range in maturity from one month to over ten years. These instruments typically will yield slightly more than Treasury obligations with a similar maturity.

Certificates of Deposit

These certificates are issued by commercial banks and have a fixed maturity, generally in the range of 90 days to one year. The ability to sell a certificate of deposit prior to maturity usually depends upon its denomination. If it is over $100,000, it usually can be sold in a secondary market; if it is under that amount, banks usually will assess a penalty if they buy it back early. The default risk for these certificates depends upon the issuing bank, but it is usually quite small. Therefore, their yield is generally only slightly higher than similar maturities in the previous two categories.

Commercial Paper

This is typically an unsecured short-term note of a large corporation. This investment offers maturities that range up to 270 days, but the marketability is somewhat limited if an early sale is required. The default risk depends upon the credit standing of the issuer, but commensurately higher yield is available.

Money Market Mutual Funds

These funds invest in the money market instruments described above. As a result, investors achieve a yield almost as high as that paid by the direct investments themselves and at the same time benefit from the diversification of any default risk over a much larger population of investments. In addition, these funds allow the pension plan to maintain complete liquidity with respect to this portion of its portfolio.

Bonds

The use of bonds in pension plan portfolios typically can be attributed to one of two reasons. First, if the sponsor realizes that (to a large extent) the pension plan's obligations are fixed-dollar obligations that will be paid out several years in the future, there may be a desire to purchase assets that will generate a cash flow similar to the benefit payments. This technique is referred to as dedication or immunization and is described in detail later in this chapter. Second, the investment manager may be willing to purchase assets with a longer maturity than the money market instruments described above. This assumption of interest rate risk is presumably compensated for by a higher yield than that available from shorter maturities.

Bonds are simply long-term debt claims entitling the holder to periodic interest and full repayment of principal by the issuer. For purposes of this discussion, the universe of bonds will be dichotomized into corporate bonds and government bonds.

Corporate Bonds

There are several characteristics of corporate bonds that are important to pension plan investment managers. For example, there are different degrees by which the promises of future cash flow are secured. Under a **mortgage bond,** a corporation pledges certain real assets as security for the bond. In contrast, a **debenture** is a long-term bond that is not secured by a pledge of any specific property. However, it is secured by any property not otherwise pledged.

The ability of the issuing corporation to call in the bond for redemption prior to the stated maturity date is known as a **call provision.** Although the issuer typically must pay some type of penalty (known as a *call premium*) for exercising this right, the holder of a bond with a call provision must be cognizant of the fact that the amount received (call premium plus principal) may be less than the value of the bond if the call had not been exercised. This typically will be the case in times of declining interest rates.

The marketability of corporate bonds usually is not an issue. However, if the investment manager sells them prior to the maturity date, the price received will be subject to both the business risk and interest rate risk described earlier. Investment managers also must be concerned with business risk, even if there is an intention to hold the bonds until maturity.

Government Bonds

Pension plans will limit their investments in government bonds to those that generate taxable investment income. Hence, municipal bonds are not candidates for inclusion in a pension plan portfolio. Federal government bonds are possible candidates and they are evaluated in a manner similar to corporate bonds. The major exception is that the default risk is nearly nonexistent and, as a result, the yield would be expected to be lower than that available on corporate bonds of similar maturities.

The field of government bonds has expanded to include mortgage-related securities. Government National Mortgage Association (GNMA) pass-through certificates have an interest in a pool of single-family residential mortgages that are insured by the Federal Housing Authority or the Veteran's Administration. The timely payment of principal and interest on these securities is guaranteed by the U.S. government. The Federal Home Loan Mortgage Corporation (FHLMC) issues another mortgage-backed security, known as Freddie Mac. Although this instrument is not guaranteed by the U.S. government, it is unconditionally guaranteed by the FHLMC.

Common Stocks

Although there is no definitive manner of categorizing common stocks, it is customary to speak of them in the following terms:[15]

1. *Blue chip stocks.* These are stocks issued by major companies with long and unbroken records of earnings and dividend payments. They should appeal primarily to pension plans seeking safety and stability.

---

[15] Jerome B. Cohen, Edward D. Zinbarg, and Arthur Zeikel, *Investment Analysis and Portfolio Management,* 5th ed. (Burr Ridge, IL: Richard D. Irwin, 1987), pp. 21–29.

2. *Growth stocks.*   These are stocks issued by companies whose sales, earnings, and share of the market are expanding faster than either the general economy or the industry average. They represent a higher risk, but the prospects for capital appreciation should produce a correspondingly higher total return. Because they pay relatively small dividends, they may not be attractive to pension plans with cash flow problems.

3. *Income stocks.*   These are stocks that pay higher-than-average dividend returns. They have been attractive to pension plans that purchase stock for current income.

4. *Cyclical stocks.*   These are stocks issued by companies whose earnings fluctuate with and are accentuated by the business cycle.

5. *Defensive stocks.*   These are stocks issued by recession-resistant companies. This may be an important consideration for pension plans that cannot afford major capital losses.

6. *Interest-sensitive stocks.*   These are stocks whose prices tend to drop when interest rates rise, and vice versa.

Mutual Funds

For plans with assets too small to be handled by an investment manager, mutual funds may be the only choice, other than a common trust fund. Larger plans also may choose mutual funds as a relatively inexpensive way of diversifying their portfolios.[16]

Pension plans choose mutual funds to invest in for the following reasons:[17]

1. Greater liquidity through ease of entry and exit.

2. Greater degree of diversification.

3. Easier means of portfolio specialization.

4. Daily update of holdings through newspaper listings.

5. Ease of meeting asset allocation or market timing goals.

6. Ease of checking past performance through published studies and indexes.

Real Estate

The enormous number of real estate investments available in today's market makes a comprehensive treatment of this topic beyond the scope of this book.[18] However, certain basic characteristics of this market provide insight as to its overall place in a pension plan portfolio. First, real estate investments (particularly ownership

---

[16] See the Passive versus Active Management section later in this chapter for more detail.

[17] Jay M. Dade, "Mutual Funds Today: Strength through Diversity," *Pension World,* December 1986, pp. 34–36.

[18] For an excellent discussion of this topic, see *Investment Policy Guidebook for Corporate Pension Plan Trustees,* Appendix A (Brookfield, WI: International Foundation of Employee Benefit Plans, 1984).

interests) appear to offer an adequate inflation hedge under most scenarios. Second, real estate investing does not operate in the same efficient market as stocks and bonds. Instead of having several thousand individuals bidding on the price of a homogeneous asset each day, a real estate property may be on the market for months before any offer is made. A third point, closely related to the second, is the relative lack of marketability for many real estate investments. This feature alone would prevent most pension plans from investing the preponderance of their assets in real estate. A final point deals with the volatility of real estate investments. Although it is difficult to develop reliable estimates in the absence of an active market, the consensus opinion appears to be that the volatility of real estate investments has been significantly below that of common stocks.

Futures

A futures contract is an agreement to make or take delivery of a specified commodity (e.g., the S&P 500 index) at a specified date at an agreed-upon price. No money changes hands until the delivery date; however, a deposit is required that may be invested in Treasury securities in the interim. The account is settled each day. This means that if a pension plan made a contract to sell the S&P 500 in the future and the index declined that day, money would be deposited into the pension plan's account; however, money would be withdrawn from the account if the index had increased.

Although this may appear to be a highly speculative investment when viewed in isolation, many pension plans have used this technique in conjunction with an existing portfolio of equities. This may serve as a useful hedge against losses in the equity portfolio.

Selecting an Investment Manager

The process of selecting an investment manager obviously differs from sponsor to sponsor; however, the following five steps are typical of the procedure employed by many sponsors.[19]

Review Investment Firms

The first step in selecting an investment manager is to initiate a search to screen initial candidates. This procedure generally is conducted by an individual within the plan sponsor's firm, perhaps with the aid of outside consultants. Plan sponsors can obtain outside consulting services from a number of sources, including brokerage firms, actuarial and accounting organizations, and pension consulting firms.

Although many sponsors may be inclined to perform the investment firm review solely on an in-house basis, there are several potential advantages to using a consultant that should be considered. First, since the consultants have continuing exposure to the investment firms, they probably will have a better understanding of which

[19] Ibid., pp. 103–6.

investment firms could best serve the sponsor's objectives. Second, consultants have much more experience in the evaluation process. They are more likely to ask the investment firms pertinent investment questions, and they are less inclined to have their decisions swayed by the marketing aspects of client presentations. On a more positive side, they can pinpoint the specific information needed from investment management candidates, frame the questionnaire, and help organize the subsequent interviews. Third, consultants can help construct the initial list, so that firms may be screened efficiently without the search team having to waste time and effort.

Regardless of whether the plan sponsor is being aided by a consultant, there is an obvious need to obtain information on investment firms at this stage. Fortunately, several sources exist for this purpose. Included among these are top management and members of the board of directors, counterparts at other companies, pension fund actuaries, accountants and attorneys, specialized magazines, and senior officers of brokerage companies.

Send Detailed Questionnaires

After the original list has been reduced to a manageable size (perhaps with the aid of a consultant), a detailed questionnaire should be sent to the remaining investment firms. The questionnaire should be carefully designed to elicit specific information on several topics, including:

1. Portfolio strategies and tactics.
2. Ownership as well as employee compensation.
3. Decision-making procedures.
4. List of current clients and specific people to contact for references.
5. Names of accounts lost as well as those gained in recent years.
6. Historic performance of each class of assets managed.
7. Explanation of exactly how the firm's performance statistics have been computed.

Conduct Interviews

After the questionnaires have been reviewed and the references have been thoroughly checked, interviews should be conducted (in the presence of the sponsor's consultant, if one is used). Whether it is better to hold the initial interview at the sponsor's location or to visit the offices of candidates is debatable; however, it is argued that the latter produces a more realistic impression of the investment firm.

It is important that specific guidelines for the presentations be formulated in advance. For example, the "canned presentations" should be limited within some specific time frame. Moreover, questions should be designed to elicit specific information on:

• Research procedures.
• Decision-making routine.

- Strategies and tactics employed.

- Control disciplines.

- Transaction guidelines.

- Levels of salaries and other incentives for employees.

- Key personnel.

- Investment performance statistics and the degree of performance variation among accounts.

Final Evaluation

Before an attempt is made to analyze the information obtained from the interviews, it may be useful to review sample portfolios of the investment firms to assess whether a firm actually uses the methods described by its literature and representatives. At this time, the written questionnaires often are reviewed to check for inconsistencies with oral statements made during the interviews. Using the assembled information, the list of investment firms is condensed to a small group of finalists (i.e., less than five) and the information is given to the sponsor's top management.

The management of the sponsor will then meet with senior officers and relevant portfolio personnel of the finalist firms, and the decision regarding which firm(s) shall be retained to manage the pension assets will be made.

Postselection Activity

A substantial amount of activity remains after the decision has been made. For example, legal agreements should be reviewed, all fees and other costs should be determined, and the initiation date for performance measurement should be established.

The selection of the investment firm is not the final step in this process. Indeed, it is just the first iteration of a continuing operation. Portfolio review and evaluation using the performance measurement techniques described earlier must be performed periodically. This will be facilitated by having the mechanics of fund and reporting systems worked out as soon as possible.

Passive versus Active Management

A passive investment strategy is characterized by a broadly diversified buy-and-hold portfolio aimed at replicating the return on some broad market index at minimum cost. The costs of highly trained professionals can be minimized and the transaction costs kept relatively low due to the reduced amount of trading. In contrast, active investment strategies attempt to outperform the market either by selecting assets whose returns, on average, exceed those of the market, or by timing the movement of funds into and out of the market in an attempt to capitalize on swings in the prices of the assets.

Proponents of the passive strategy argue that as the stock market becomes increasingly efficient, it is more difficult for investment managers to consistently outperform the market. If actively managed funds do indeed encounter difficulties producing a gross rate of return superior to that of the market, it will obviously be even more difficult to produce a superior return on a net basis (after the effects of fees and transaction costs have been accounted for).

There are various degrees to which passive investing may be implemented. The two most popular forms—index funds and dedication and immunization techniques—are described below.

Index Funds

Index funds represent the ultimate form of passive investing. An equity index fund replicates a particular index such as the S&P 500 and is designed to generate a beta of 1.0 (i.e., the rate of return on the fund is expected to be equal to that of the S&P 500). These funds are based on the efficient market hypothesis (EMH), which states that the securities markets are efficient in the processing of information. In other words, the prices of securities observed at any time are based on a correct evaluation of all information available at the time.

If this hypothesis were true, the value of an investment manager's services would be far less than the current level of compensation enjoyed by these professionals. However, a number of published studies have reported contrary evidence indicating at least a lack of complete efficiency in the market. Anomalous results have been found in the so-called weekend, small-firm, and January effects.[20]

Some sponsors will use index funds as an investment for the core of their portfolio and allow active management of the remaining amount of the assets. This tactic possesses the advantage of freeing the investment managers from having to deal with the core portfolio and, instead, allowing them to focus their time on their specialty areas. Moreover, given a relative sense of security for the core investment, investment managers are able to pursue a higher-risk strategy on their subset of the plan's assets in hopes of above-average returns.

Dedication and Immunization Techniques

Another form of passive investment of pension plan assets makes use of the bond market and has been variously referred to as dedication, immunization, and contingent immunization.[21] This technique attempts to construct a bond portfolio such that its cash flow can be used to fund specific plan liabilities—for example, to pay benefits to a group of retirees.

The typical **dedication program** will start by modeling the expected schedule of liabilities under a particular subset of the plan. The benefits related to the retired population often are chosen due to the fact that the benefits are already determined (i.e., there is no uncertainty regarding career- or final-average salary) and the time horizon will be shorter than the liabilities associated with the active employee population. The

---

[20] Jeremy J. Siegel, *Stocks for the Long Run* (New York, NY: McGraw-Hill, 1998), pp. 253–259, 260–266.

[21] Martin L. Leibowitz, "The Dedicated Bond Portfolio in Pension Funds—Part I: Motivations and Basics," *Financial Analysts Journal,* January–February 1986, pp. 68–75.

model will produce a monotonically decreasing payout schedule over time, most likely reaching a negligible amount by the end of 30 years (the maximum maturity for most types of bonds). A computer program will then search for an optimal combination of acceptable bonds that will produce a cash flow over this period to meet the liability payout schedule.

Perhaps the easiest way to visualize this is to assume that all payouts will be met through principal payments (when the bonds mature) or coupon payments. This would certainly minimize the administrative complexity of the program since, if principal and coupon payments are exactly equal to the payouts each year, there would be no need to reinvest the proceeds. However, this may not produce the optimal combination of bonds in that another combination of maturities (one that assumes some proceeds need to be reinvested for a period of time before they are used to satisfy plan liabilities) may produce a lower total cost to the sponsor. It should be realized that this is a riskier undertaking, however, since the eventual cost to the sponsor may increase if the assumed rates at which these proceeds may be reinvested prove to be too optimistic.[22]

In contrast to the cash-matching nature of dedication, an **immunization program** attempts to construct a portfolio of bonds whose market value equals the present value of the selected subset of liabilities and whose value, even if the interest rate changes, will always be at least as great as the value of the liabilities.[23] Although the feasibility of this approach may not be intuitively obvious, it depends upon the capital gains on the assets offsetting the decrease in reinvestment income when interest rates fall. This balancing is accomplished through a concept known as "duration," which provides a measure of the portfolio's sensitivity to interest rate changes.[24]

As opposed to the relatively simple administrative requirements involved in a dedicated portfolio, an immunized portfolio will require subsequent rebalancing. Moreover, although immunization provides more flexibility in constructing the bond portfolio (and should therefore result in a lower cost to the sponsor), it is possible for the assumptions used in the immunization model to be violated and, as a result, the sponsor may experience a shortfall from this approach.

Largely in response to the limitations of the immunization approach, a hybrid technique known as **horizon matching** has been introduced. In essence, this approach splits the liabilities into two portions. The first portion consists of all lia-

---

[22]Other risks that may exist in either type of dedication include call vulnerability, quality, type of issue, and diversification across type and individual issues. See Leibowitz, "The Dedicated Bond Portfolio in Pension Funds—Part I," *Financial Analysts Journal,* January–February 1986, pp. 73–74.

[23]Martin L. Leibowitz, "The Dedicated Bond Portfolio in Pension Funds—Part II: Immunization, Horizon Matching and Contingent Procedures," *Financial Analysts Journal,* March–April 1986, pp. 47–57.

[24]The duration measure can be thought of as the average life of the liabilities when weighted by the present value of their respective cash flows. Technically, the duration match of assets and liabilities is not a sufficient condition for an "immunized" portfolio. In addition, certain second-order conditions must be satisfied. See Michael R. Granito, *Bond Portfolio Immunization* (Lexington, MA: Lexington Books, 1984) for more detail.

bilities that occur up to a certain horizon (three to five years) and is handled through a dedicated portfolio. The second portion consists of liabilities beyond the horizon and is treated through immunization. Although this tactic will give up some of the cost savings of a full immunization approach, the restructuring will mitigate the effects of failing to satisfy the assumptions of the immunization approach.[25]

A major disadvantage of the immunization approaches is that the sponsor gives up the opportunity to produce additional income through active management of the bond portfolio. This is overcome, to a certain extent, through a device known as **contingent immunization.** Basically, this approach assumes the sponsor is willing to accept a minimum rate of return on the bond portfolio a percentage point or two below the current market rate. This differential provides a safety margin for the investment manager to adopt an active management strategy. If the safety margin is exhausted through market losses, the portfolio will be in a position such that it can be immunized at the minimum rate of return.

Chapter Summary

- An investment policy prescribes an acceptable course of action to the fund's investment managers. It communicates a risk policy in that it states the degree of investment risk that the sponsor is willing to assume.

- The primary purpose of performance measurement is to "obtain information on which to base decisions in regard to investment objectives, portfolio strategy, and manager selection. In addition, performance measurement should improve communications with managers by creating a standard format for discussion."

- The asset allocation decision is a process that determines the best portfolio composition among the various major types of assets (stocks, bonds, etc.). This decision takes into account the sponsor's investment objectives and, as a result, reflects the level of risk desired by the sponsor.

- A passive investment strategy is characterized by a broadly diversified buy-and-hold portfolio aimed at replicating the return on some broad market index at minimum cost. The costs of highly trained professionals can be minimized and the transaction costs kept relatively low due to the reduced amount of trading. In contrast, active investment strategies attempt to outperform the market either by selecting assets whose returns, on average, exceed those of the market, or by timing the movement of funds into and out of the market in an attempt to capitalize on swings in the prices of the assets.

- Another form of passive investment of pension plan assets makes use of the bond market and has been variously referred to as dedication, immunization, and contingent immunization. This technique attempts to construct a bond portfolio such that its cash flow can be used to fund specific plan liabilities—for example, to pay benefits to a group of retirees.

[25]Specifically, this is designed to dampen the effect of yield curve reshaping.

Key Terms

alpha value, p. *408*
beta value, p. *408*
business risk, p. *402*
call provision, p. *412*
capital asset pricing model
(CAPM), p. *408*
contingent immunization,
p. *419*
debenture, p. *412*
dedication program, p. *417*

horizon matching, p. *418*
immunization program,
p. *418*
index funds, p. *417*
interest rate risk, p. *402*
internal rate of return,
p. *406*
market risk, p. *402*
mortgage bond, p. *412*

performance measurement,
p. *405*
purchasing power risk,
p. *402*
risk-adjusted rate of return,
p. *408*
specific risks, p. *403*
time-weighted rate of
return, p. *406*

Questions for Review

1. Describe the major types of investment risk.
2. Describe why an investment's relative liquidity may be important to a pension plan's investment manager.
3. What have historical studies demonstrated with respect to the risk-return characteristics of the major classes of investments?
4. What types of questions should the investment manager's guideline statement cover?
5. Describe the steps involved in effective performance measurement.
6. Explain how the internal rate of return and the time-weighted rate of return are calculated.
7. Which of the two rates of return mentioned in the previous question should be used for performance measurement? Explain.
8. Explain the importance of the alpha and beta values produced by the capital asset pricing model (CAPM).
9. Explain the importance of the risk-adjusted rate of return.
10. Explain the factors that should be considered in the allocation of pension fund assets.
11. Describe the various forms of money market instruments.
12. Explain why a pension plan investment manager might invest pension assets in bonds instead of money market instruments. What are the additional risks associated with this decision?
13. What type of information should be elicited in questionnaires sent to prospective investment managers?
14. Explain why a passive investment strategy may be attractive to a pension plan sponsor.
15. Describe the basic objectives behind the use of dedication or immunization techniques for pension plan portfolios.

Questions for Discussion

1. If common stocks are assumed to produce a higher long-term rate of return than bonds, discuss why many defined benefit pension plan portfolios contain a significant percentage of bonds.

2. Discuss how the beta value produced by the capital asset pricing model could be used to construct an investment portfolio suited to the employer's objectives.

3. Discuss why performance measurement based exclusively on rate of return may lead to nonoptimal investment strategies.

4. Discuss how an employer might decide between active and passive investment strategies.

Resources for Further Study

Birley, Cindy S.; and Rebecca L. Hudson. "New Trends in Public Sector Plans." *Trusts & Estates,* September 2001.

Bodie, Zvi; P. Brett Hammond; and Olivia S. Mitchell. "New Approaches to Analyzing and Managing Retirement Risks." *Benefits Quarterly* 17, no. 4 (Fourth Quarter 2001).

Burroughs, Eugene B. "Funding Retirement Plans—Investment Objectives." In *The Handbook of Employee Benefits.* 5th ed. Jerry S. Rosenbloom, ed. New York: McGraw-Hill, 2001.

Pension & Investments Editorial Staff. "The P & I 1000." *Pension & Investments,* January 21, 2002.

23

Investment of Defined Contribution Plan Assets[1]

After studying this chapter you should be able to:

- Identify employer responsibilities in administering a defined contribution plan.

- Specify employee responsibilities as stakeholders in a defined contribution plan.

- Analyze the workplace and market trends that have contributed to the popularity of defined contribution plans.

- Explain the fiduciary duties of an employer sponsoring a defined contribution plan.

- Discuss the legal and communications considerations of a plan sponsor developing an investment education program for defined contribution plan participants.

- Describe the ongoing nature of employer responsibilities in the design, implementation, and monitoring of a defined contribution plan.

The previous chapter examined many investment concepts applicable to both defined benefit and defined contribution plans. This chapter examines the particular investment issues relevant to defined contribution plans, where employees bear the risk associated with plan asset investment choices. Both employers and employees have a vital stake in the plan investment provisions of a defined contribution plan. The employer is responsible for structuring appropriate investment programs,

[1]The authors wish to express their appreciation to Towers Perrin for permission to use this material—much of which is contained in *The Handbook of 401(k) Plan Management* (Burr Ridge, IL: Irwin Professional Publishing, 1996).

selecting suitable investment managers, monitoring investment performance, and communicating critical investment provisions to employees. In the typical plan, employees are responsible for deciding how to invest their account balances, and they assume all of the risks associated with investment performance. Both employers and employees must have a sound understanding of basic investment principles if they are to succeed in fulfilling their respective responsibilities.

For the employer, the benefits of a successful investment program include low cost fees, ease of administration, flexibility to make needed changes in investment arrangements, and improved recognition of the company as a source of valuable benefits. For employees, a well-executed investment program maximizes capital accumulation through increased participation, improved returns, and lower costs.

Although written in the context of defined benefit plans, most of the material in Chapter 22 regarding matters such as asset classes, asset allocation strategies, types of investment risk, investment objectives, and investment manager selection is equally applicable to defined contribution plans. For this reason, the following discussion relates primarily to fiduciary responsibilities and design features that are unique to defined contribution plans.

Historical Development

The initial era of defined contribution investing was driven, to a large extent, by expediency. Ease of administration—particularly participant record keeping—often dictated the number and types of investment choices that were made available. Some plans provided no choice at all, simply investing plan assets in a single fund. Others offered two investment funds: one a fixed income fund such as a guaranteed investment contract (GIC), in which all employee contributions were invested, and the other an employer stock fund in which all employer contributions were invested. Still others allowed a relatively limited choice, such as a choice between a fixed-income and an equity fund.

Another factor that tended to limit investment options was employer concern about potential legal liability for giving employees any kind of financial advice. Restricting investment choice obviously limited the need for such counsel.

Most important, however, was the fact that few employers had articulated specific investment objectives for their defined contribution plans. In many situations, this reflected the fact that investment results in these plans do not affect the employer's financial statements; thus, pressure from this source to improve financial results does not exist. Most employers designed their defined benefit plans to replace specified levels of preretirement income and viewed their defined contribution plans as simply providing supplemental benefits. Thus, little thought was given to defined contribution plan investment choices or investment performance. For example, while the need to diversify is a staple of modern investment theory, many plans gave employees little or no opportunity to diversify, either among or within various investment classes. Further, employers tended to do little in the way of providing useful investment information to their employees—either about the options available to them or about basic principles of investing. In short, the early age of defined contribution plan asset management was characterized by limited employee choice and a lack of well-defined plan and investment objectives.

The last 20 years have seen a definite shift—at least in terms of the investment opportunities made available to employees. Many factors have contributed to this change, including a growing public awareness of the role of defined contribution plans in providing economic security and the importance of saving and investing wisely; an increased recognition on the part of employers of the need to provide flexibility of choice and investment education; improved and more-efficient administrative capabilities; and the aggressive marketing efforts of the leading mutual funds.

Table 23.1 shows the current prevalence of investment options in a 472-plan database maintained by Towers Perrin. Of these plans, 99 percent (467) provide employees with a choice of three or more funds for investing their own contributions. Approximately 95 percent (449) provide a choice of five or more funds for this purpose. The options for investing employer contributions are not as great, reflecting the fact that many plans automatically invest these amounts in employer stock. Nevertheless, about 76 percent (361) provide a choice of three or more funds for employer contributions.

Table 23.2 depicts the actual investment choices offered by plans in another Towers Perrin database. Clearly, most of these plans provide a wide variety of investment funds for their participants, and the number of choices available in these plans underscores the need for educating employees to become better investors. The fact that employees have more investment choices does not mean they are making the most of what their plans have to offer. Overall, billions of dollars in defined contribution plan assets are still being invested very conservatively and with little diversification. While this reflects the fact that employees need to know more about investments and financial planning, it also reflects the fact that many employers still have not focused on managing their plans as effectively as possible.

TABLE 23.1   **Number of Funds Available for Investment**

Number of Funds	Employee Contributions	Employer Contributions*
1	3	107
2	2	4
3	9	6
4	9	7
5	10	6
6	20	14
7	38	25
8	47	30
9	64	47
10 or more	246	208
Other	24	18
	472	472

*18 plans do not provide for employer contributions.

TABLE 23.2 Types of Investment Funds Available

Fund	Employee Contributions	Employer Contributions
Employer stock	353	375
Domestic balanced	404	241
Fixed income	314	183
Growth equity	264	160
Diversified equity	233	146
Equity index	267	147
GIC/BIC	244	154
Money market	257	148
International equity	169	104
Small cap equity	131	72
Equity income	101	60
U.S. government obligations	92	55
Short-term fixed income	80	38
Global balanced	25	11
Fixed-income indexed	26	14
Other	34	26
No choice	1	45

The situation is changing, however. Employers are beginning to look more closely at plan objectives and plan performance and are recognizing that more effective plan management can improve plan values with no additional company contributions to the plan. The components of effective plan management—including the design of investment structures and overall investment operations—are discussed in the following sections.

Plan Design Considerations

The investment provisions of a defined contribution plan should be compatible with the plan sponsor's objectives. Three major areas to be considered are (1) fiduciary responsibilities; (2) the role employer stock will play; and (3) administrative issues.

Fiduciary Considerations

As noted in Chapter 6, a fiduciary must discharge its duties solely in the interests of plan participants and their beneficiaries and for the exclusive purpose of providing plan benefits and meeting administrative expenses. Further, a fiduciary is held to a prudent expert standard in the discharge of its duties.[2]

---

[2]It should be noted that fiduciary responsibilities, in the context of an ERISA plan, apply the concept of portfolio diversification to the total portfolio and not on an asset-by-asset basis.

How Long Must a Plan Sponsor Contract with an Investment Advisor?

1

Securities and Exchange Commission (SEC) "no-action" letters and Department of Labor (DOL) regulations prohibit advisory contracts from binding plans for unreasonable lengths of time (e.g., one year or more) or from imposing a penalty upon a plan's termination. Both of these practices are deemed to violate the advisor's fiduciary duties.

Reasonable cancelation provisions could be included, for example, setting forth a certain number of days or months that advance written notice must be given to the advisor and, if appropriate, the reimbursement by the advisor of any reasonable expenses caused by such cancelation.

Source: Robert B. Van Grover, "Advisory Agreements: A Guide to Advisors and Trustees of Benefit Plans." Reprinted with permission, from the August 1993 issue of *Pension Management* magazine, p. 36. © Intertec Publishing Corp.

It is not uncommon for plans to be structured so that trustees and external investment managers, rather than the employer, are responsible for the investment of plan assets. In these plans, the plan sponsor has delegated specific investment authority to outside professionals, thus limiting its own fiduciary liabilities. It is important to emphasize, however, that delegating responsibilities to outside professionals does not relieve the employer of all fiduciary responsibilities; the employer is still responsible, as a fiduciary, for the proper selection and retention of these external fiduciaries.

A plan sponsor can further limit its fiduciary liability by permitting employees to make their own allocations among the various investment options, provided a certain minimum number of options spanning a range of investment classes are offered and employees are permitted to make changes to their allocations no less frequently than quarterly. The employer also must provide employees with information sufficient for them to make an informed choice among the various options available. These requirements are covered in more detail in Chapter 6 and are commonly referred to as the Section 404(c) safe harbor provisions. In general, these safe harbor provisions require that a plan offer at least three diversified categories of investment with materially different risk and return characteristics. Compliance with these guidelines does not relieve the employer of the responsibility of ensuring that the investment options offered under the plan are prudent and properly diversified and does not relieve the employer of fiduciary responsibility for investments over which the employee has no control, such as employer contributions that are automatically directed to one of the investment options.

Employer Stock as an Investment Option

The Section 404(c) safe harbor provisions permit a company to offer employer stock as one of the investment options, provided the plan also offers the three required options and the employer's shares are publicly traded in a recognized market. In addition, all purchases, sales, voting, and related share activities must be implemented on a confidential basis. If the employer stock option meets these criteria, the fiduciary liability protection afforded plan sponsors under Section 404(c) is extended to the employer stock option.

Employer stock is a common investment option in many defined contribution plans. Some employers believe that stock ownership strengthens the link between employee and corporate interests. Others seek to create or expand a friendly group of shareholders as a barrier to hostile takeover attempts.

However, there are several potential disadvantages to the use of employer stock as an investment option:

• Employer stock is a completely undiversified investment option and may be inappropriate from a financial perspective.

• Employer contributions invested in company stock at the employer's direction are not eligible for the Section 404(c) safe harbor provisions.

• Plan sponsors who permit employee contributions to be invested in company stock must comply with Securities and Exchange Commission (SEC) registration and reporting requirements.[3]

• Employee relations problems may surface if the value of the employer stock declines.

• If significant balances are built up in the company stock fund, employees have not only their livelihood but also a sizable block of their savings tied to the well-being of the company.

• Any investment in employer stock, while not subject to the requirement for a diversified investment alternative, must be shown to satisfy the requirement that plan assets be "expended for the exclusive benefit of employees" and must satisfy the **fiduciary requirement for prudence.**

If employer stock is offered as one of the investment options, the employer also must consider what opportunities an employee will be offered to diversify out of the employer stock as he or she approaches retirement.[4]

If the plan is an employee stock ownership plan (ESOP) or if the employer stock fund has been designed as an ESOP, yet another issue to be considered is whether dividends will be passed through to employees and, if so, how frequently (e.g., quarterly or annually). Paying such dividends might be attractive to some employers since the dividends paid will be tax deductible; however, paying them in cash might be viewed as being inconsistent with a major plan objective—that of accumulating assets for the purpose of providing an additional measure of retirement security. Employers whose stock is not publicly traded also must deal with issues such as the inclusion of rights of first refusal and put options.

---

[3]See Chapter 6.
[4]Such a diversification right is required if the plan is an employee stock ownership plan (ESOP). See the discussion of this issue in Chapter 10.

Administrative Issues

There are several administrative issues that need to be addressed in structuring the investment provisions of a defined contribution plan.

Frequency of Valuation

How often will plan assets and account balances be valued for purposes of processing loans, distributions, withdrawals, and investment election changes? If monthly or daily valuations are preferred to quarterly valuations, what will be the additional expense? How long will it take to process a requested transaction subsequent to the valuation date? How does the choice of valuation frequency affect other plan provisions such as the availability and repayment of loans?

Frequency of Change

How often will employees be permitted to change their investment elections? The **Section 404(c) safe harbor provisions** require that employees must be permitted to make changes at least quarterly, and more often for more-volatile investment options. (An employer, of course, may choose not to comply with these safe harbor provisions.) Plans generally permit employees to make changes to the investment elections on either a quarterly, monthly, or daily basis. Some plans differentiate between changes intended to accommodate new contributions and those that affect existing plan balances. Others place limits on the total number of changes an employee may make in any one year; however, this provision may inadvertently violate the Section 404(c) safe harbor provisions if the employee has used up all of his change options by the third quarter of the year.

   Allowing employees to change their investment elections frequently—for example, on a daily basis—may send them mixed signals. The primary focus in educating employees to save wisely for their futures requires an emphasis on setting and achieving long-term goals. Permitting frequent changes to investment elections may appear to be inconsistent and may potentially thwart the long-term focus of defined contribution plan investing.

Default Provisions

Employers must provide some sort of **default option** in the event an employee fails to make an investment election for contributions. The employer may opt for the most conservative option—an investment in GICs, for example—or may choose to have contributions invested in proportion to the employee's existing account balances. In setting this provision, the employer must consider the trade-offs between fiduciary liability and investment responsibility.

Negative Elections

Instead of following the usual method of requiring an employee to elect to participate in a defined contribution plan such as a 401(k), some employers redesigned their plans to automatically enroll eligible employees. Under this enrollment method, employees are deemed to have elected to defer a certain percentage, say 1 percent or 2 percent, of their eligible compensation unless they affirmatively elect not to participate in the plan, or elect a different deferral amount. These assumed automatic plan enrollments are referred to as **negative elections.** When employers first started implementing negative elections in their retirement plans, there was some concern specifically regarding 401(k) plan contributions. Because participants had not made an affirmative election between receiving cash and having compensation deferred as a plan contribution, it was thought that these contributions may not be considered elective deferrals under Regs. Sec. 1.401(k)-1(g)(3). However, the Internal Revenue Service clarified this issue with Revenue Ruling 98–30 in which it concluded that if employees have the opportunity to elect out of a plan's automatic deferral provisions, contributions made under a negative election will not fail to be considered elective deferrals.

There are several advantages that make negative elections attractive to both plan sponsors and employees. First, negative elections encourage employees to start saving for retirement sooner. More employees are brought into the plan and the plan enjoys greater overall participation. Also, negative elections often help a plan to pass the actual deferral percentage (ADP) test by assuring this higher participation in the plan. Greater plan participation from a broad cross section of employees with a certain predetermined level of contribution may also be beneficial to highly compensated employees already participating in the plan. Participation by non–highly compensated employees at a certain level of contribution may permit highly compensated employees to increase their plan contributions, thus enhancing the retirement security of the higher-paid employees.

Employee Communications

Employee communication is a critical link in the long-term success of defined contribution plans. The Department of Labor (DOL) now requires that the employer offer participants sufficient information to enable them to make an intelligent choice among the investment options available to them. Among other things, this information should encompass investment basics such as the importance of diversification, the relationship between risk and reward, and the influence of the investment time horizon on the potential outcome of plan investments. With the additional guidance furnished by the DOL in terms of distinguishing between investment education and investment advice, many employers are expected to go beyond these minimum requirements in providing employees with investment education.

The Economic Growth and Tax Relief Reconciliation Act of 2001 (EGTRRA) contained a provision that excludes employer-provided qualified retirement planning services from employees' gross wages. The exclusion not only applies to such services offered to employees, but also to services offered to spouses of employees. According to the law, qualified retirement planning services involve any retirement planning advice or information provided to an employee and his or her spouse by an employer maintaining a qualified employer plan. Reference to a qualified employer plan, as it is used here, is not in the usual restrictive sense. Such services can be provided by an employer offering a qualified plan under IRC 401(a), governmental plans, 403(b) plans, annuity plans, simplified employee pensions (SEPs), SIMPLE plans, and certain employee-only trusts established prior to June 25, 1959. The exclusion extends to services provided to highly compensated employees only if the qualified retirement planning services are available on substantially the same terms to all employees who normally receive education and information regarding the plan. Qualified retirement planning services do not include such items as accounting services, tax preparation, legal services, or brokerage services.

Special Rights

In plans that provide for the automatic investment of contributions in certain funds (e.g., employer contributions in employer stock), employers need to consider whether employees should be given **special rights of diversification** as they approach retirement age. The issue also arises in ESOPs, where a diversification right is mandatory under certain circumstances.[5] Employers who decide to include special rights will have to establish eligibility requirements; these requirements typically will be tied to early retirement eligibility requirements (e.g., the attainment of age 55 and, possibly, the completion of 10 years of service).

Design, Implementation, and Monitoring of Plan Investments

There are three continuing stages in the development of plan investment provisions: design, implementation, and monitoring.

Design

In the design phase, the employer must make a series of decisions about plan assets. The first is to consider what asset classes will be offered. This decision will be influenced by administrative costs, risk and return characteristics, plan objectives, and participant needs. The range of asset classes to be considered includes cash equivalents, guaranteed investment contracts (GICs), bank investment contracts (BICs), bonds, large-capitalization stocks, small-capitalization stocks, international stocks and bonds, emerging markets, and employer stock. Some employers also may wish to consider the use of real estate, energy, and private equity (venture capital) investments. However, these asset classes are somewhat more cumbersome to include given the private nature of the markets in which they exist and the liquidity constraints this imposes.

The next issue in the design phase is whether to offer these asset classes as distinct investment options from which the employees will choose their own mix, or to combine them into predetermined sets of diversified portfolios reflecting different risk and return characteristics. This issue will be discussed in more detail in the next section.

Each asset class in and of itself also can be diversified, combining different management styles such as growth and value in the equity portfolio, long-term and short-term fixed-income strategies, and a stable of GIC providers in a GIC portfolio.

[5]See Chapter 10 for further discussion of this issue.

Employers who offer company stock as an investment option may want to consider an alternative equity option specifically designed to complement the company stock. For example, an energy company, whose economic fortune is closely tied to the rise and fall of the energy markets, may want to ensure that at least one plan equity option involves less market exposure to energy stocks.

Combining Asset Classes into Predetermined Portfolios

Different employees will have different degrees of risk tolerance, depending not only on their investment horizon but also on their own psychological preferences. It is quite difficult for a professional investor to gauge the relative risk and return trade-offs of the various potential combinations of assets, even with the benefit of years of education and experience. If plan participants are to make an intelligent allocation of their investment dollars, then substantial guidance is required from the plan sponsor.

One approach is to combine the asset classes in varying degrees into a series of portfolios lying across the efficient frontier, in order to express successively higher risk/reward expectations. One company, for example, combined the five basic asset classes (money market, bonds, large-company domestic stocks, intermediate- and small-company domestic stocks, and international stocks) into six different portfolios, five of which are as illustrated in Table 23.3.

Mix A is the most conservative, but still diversified, portfolio option available to participants. Moving from left to right, the portfolios become progressively more aggressive, with Mix D having the minimum allocation to fixed income, at 20 percent, and Mix E being the most aggressive, invested 100 percent in stocks. Each of the portfolios is regularly rebalanced to the original allocation in order to retain the same risk/reward characteristics that were established at the outset. For those employees who believe themselves more conservative or more aggressive than any of the predetermined mixes, a sixth choice (Mix F) is offered, in which the employee is free to allocate his or her contributions among any of the five asset classes in any proportion. Mix F is also beneficial to employees who are attempting to coordinate their defined contribution plan investments with other savings programs, whether their own or a spouse's.

This company's experience with the introduction of these preselected mixes was quite striking. Prior to the rollout of the new investment program, approximately

TABLE 23.3 **Illustration of Preselected Mixes**

Asset Class	A	B	C	D	E
Money market	50%	30%	10%	0%	0%
Bonds	30	30	30	20	0
Large-company domestic stocks	12	24	36	48	60
Intermediate- and small-company domestic stocks	4	8	12	16	20
International stocks	4	8	12	16	20

60 percent of all employee dollars in the plan were invested in the fixed-income asset class. Active employees had 48 percent of their assets in fixed income, while retirees had 77 percent of their assets held in this fashion. After the new investment options were introduced, total employee dollars in fixed-income investments dropped to 45 percent, with the corresponding numbers for active employees and retirees dropping to 35 percent and 64 percent, respectively. Fully 75 percent of active employees invested in one of the predetermined mixes.

Implementation

Once the asset classes or portfolios to be offered have been determined, appropriate investment objectives for each asset class must be established. This is essential in order to ascertain that the right investment managers are selected. The objectives should clearly articulate the employer's expectations as to risk and return, any investment style preferences, and the time horizon over which the assets will be managed. For example, an employer may wish to introduce an equity option intended to replicate the broad market averages without taking undue amounts of risk. Alternatively, another equity option may be offered with the objective of substantially outperforming the market averages but with a higher degree of risk.

The relevant time horizon also is critical for guidance in selecting the appropriate manager. In a balanced fund targeted toward employees within five years of retirement, aggressive equity options are probably inappropriate. Where corporate circumstances are such that it is known that the plan will terminate within a certain time frame—for example, upon an anticipated merger or divestiture—it is equally inappropriate to offer investment options whose success is dependent on long-term investment horizons.

Within each asset class, the employer also must decide whether to pursue an **active** or **passive investment management style.** Passive styles are designed to replicate their respective markets. They have the advantage of being easy to communicate to employees and tend to be significantly less expensive than active investment management options. If, however, the employer believes it can be successful in choosing active managers who will outperform the markets in the long run, then the range of options broadens considerably. It may be appropriate to combine both active and passive management styles, either within or across asset classes.

The next major task in the implementation process is the selection of investment managers. Some employers have chosen the route of selecting a single provider of investment and administrative services (e.g., a mutual fund) in an attempt to simplify administration and communication responsibilities. However, this results in considerably less flexibility in structuring investment options and the potential of suboptimal performance for one or more of the funds made available, and it may not necessarily result in lower fees. In addition, use of a single, brand-name provider may have the unintended result of identifying that provider, rather than the employer, as the source of benefits.

Selecting appropriate investment managers requires consideration of a number of factors, including the goals and objectives of the portfolio and the employer, past performance, and fees. In general, it is essential to develop an understanding of the

Structuring Compensation of Investment Advisors   2

Performance fees, fees based on capital appreciation of plan assets, generally are prohibited under the Investment Advisors Act of 1940 (the '40 Act) and the Employee Retirement Income Security Act (ERISA), although fees may be based on a percentage of assets under management. Certain exceptions to this prohibition have been permitted by regulation under the '40 Act and by the Department of Labor (DOL) opinions under ERISA, but parties must be careful to structure such arrangements in conformity with such approved standards or be prepared to request interpretive advice from the DOL (and possibly the Securities and Exchange Commission if guidance is needed for '40 Act compliance).

Source: Robert B. Van Grover, "Advisory Agreements: A Guide to Advisors and Trustees of Benefit Plans." Reprinted with permission, from the August 1993 issue of *Pension Management* magazine, p. 36. © Intertec Publishing Corp.

factors that have led to the manager's historical investment performance and gain some level of assurance that those same factors will be brought to bear on future investments.[6]

The bottom line for any investment manager is how well it has performed in the asset class for which it is being considered. **Performance evaluation** is more than a simple comparison of the past one, three, or five years against a market index, however. Both long-term and short-term performance and trends in performance over these time frames and over market cycles need to be evaluated against a universe of other money managers with similar investment objectives as well as against appropriate market benchmarks. It is commonly recognized that certain investment styles go in and out of favor on an unpredictable basis. Thus, to compare a growth manager against the broad market indexes over a period when growth has been out of favor does little to inform the observer as to how well the growth manager fulfilled its assignment. Instead, it is more appropriate to compare the manager's performance against both a passive portfolio of growth stocks (such as the Russell 1000-Growth if it is a large-capitalization growth manager) and a universe of managers with comparable investment styles and objectives. In addition to evaluating the return characteristics of the firm, it also is important to understand the risks that the manager assumed in generating the historical performance record. It is the **risk-adjusted return** that truly distinguishes good management.

---

[6] The process of selecting investment managers is discussed at length in Chapter 22. Although that chapter relates primarily to defined benefit plan investing, the comments there concerning manager selection are equally applicable to defined contribution plans.

Monitoring Performance

Both the structure of plan investments and the performance of the investment manager must be monitored on an ongoing basis. Performance must be monitored in the context of the objectives that were established at the outset. Key matters to be covered in the review process include the following:

- Returns for the last quarter and the last one- and two-year periods.

- A comparison of these returns with agreed-upon benchmarks and objectives.

- A comparison of these returns with the results of other managers with similar objectives.

- An analysis of whether these returns are meeting expectations over the long run.

- An analysis of any trends of consistent underperformance that have emerged.

- A determination of whether the manager's investment policy is still sound in light of any changing capital market conditions.

- A review of whether there have been any substantive changes in the manager's investment policies, procedures, or personnel.

Replacement of investment managers can be expected, from time to time, either because of changes in the plan itself or because of unsatisfactory investment performance. Questions to be asked periodically in evaluating the overall structure of plan investments include:

- Have the original goals and objectives changed?

- Are the number and type of investment options offered sufficient?

- Is employee usage of the available options appropriate given their demographics?

- Are investment and administrative expenses at an acceptable level?

An Investment Management Checklist

The following checklist summarizes some of the key questions that employers should address in structuring and managing their defined contribution investment programs.

Design

- Do the investment choices span the appropriate spectrum of risk and reward choices given plan objectives and participant demographics?

- Are employer contributions and undirected employee contributions invested in appropriate asset classes?

- Is the ability to change investment mix decisions appropriate given the choices available, plan objectives, and participant demographics?

- Is the plan designed to take advantage of the Section 404(c) safe harbor provisions?

- Is each investment option prudently diversified?

- How frequently will plan assets be valued?

- How often and when will participants be able to change their investment choices?

- Is useful investment information communicated to participants for each investment option, including accurate, meaningful descriptions; qualified risk and return expectations; investment objectives; and frequent, consistent, and understandable investment reports?

- Are participants provided with sufficient information to enable them to make informed allocations among the investment options offered?

- Will employees be provided with educational materials (brochures, seminars, interactive software, etc.) to make them more proficient investors?

Implementation

- Has an explicit active/passive investment decision been made for each investment alternative?

- Has a prudent manager selection process been documented and applied to each manager selected?

- Is there a written statement of investment policies and objectives for each investment manager?

Monitoring

- Is a review of manager performance undertaken quarterly, with a more formal, in-depth review conducted at least annually?

- Have clear criteria been established for use in determining whether to retain and/or replace an investment manager?

- Are plan investment policies, procedures, and objectives formally reviewed and verified at least annually?

- Are the investment options offered evaluated at least annually?

Chapter Summary

- Both employers and employees have a vital stake in the plan investment provisions of a defined contribution plan. The employer is responsible for structuring appropriate investment programs, selecting suitable investment managers, monitoring investment performance, and communicating critical investment provisions to employees. In the typical plan, employees are responsible for deciding how to invest their account balances and they assume all of the risks associated with investment performance. Both employers and employees must have a sound understanding of basic investment principles if they are to succeed in fulfilling their respective responsibilities.

- The benefits of a successful investment program include, for the employer, low cost fees; ease of administration; flexibility to make needed changes in investment arrangements; and improved recognition of the company as a source of valuable benefits. For employees, a well-executed investment program maximizes capital accumulation through increased participation, improved returns, and lower costs.

- Historically, most employers designed their defined benefit plans to replace specified levels of preretirement income and viewed their defined contribution plans as simply providing supplemental benefits. This perspective of defined contribution plans as supplemental savings vehicles may partially account for the little attention some employers have paid to managing their plans as effectively as possible.

- The last 20 years has seen a movement toward increased investment opportunities being made available to employees. Many factors have contributed to this change, including a growing public awareness of the role of defined contribution plans in providing economic security and the importance of saving and investing wisely; an increased recognition on the part of employers of the need to provide flexibility of choice and investment education; improved and more-efficient administrative capabilities; and the aggressive marketing efforts of the leading mutual funds.

- The investment provisions of a defined contribution plan should be compatible with the plan sponsor's objectives. Three major areas to be considered are (1) fiduciary responsibilities; (2) the role employer stock will play; and (3) administrative issues.

- There are several administrative issues that need to be addressed in structuring the investment provisions of a defined contribution plan. These include frequency of valuation, frequency of change in investment elections, default provisions, employee communications (including investment education), and special rights regarding diversification when employer securities are involved.

- There are three continuing stages in the development of plan investment provisions: design, implementation, and monitoring. Design issues require the employer to make a series of decisions about plan assets, including what asset classes to offer and whether these asset classes will be offered as distinct investment options or combined into predetermined sets of diversified portfolios. Implementation involves explicitly deciding on how these assets will be managed. Decisions must be made regarding active or passive investment styles and manager selection must occur. Likewise, a drafting of investment policies and objectives should occur. Monitoring involves the ongoing review of manager performance; the development of a predetermined schedule for performance review; and the establishment of criteria for use in determining whether to retain and/or replace an investment manager.

Key Terms

active versus passive
   investment management
   styles, p. *433*
default option, p. *429*
fiduciary requirement for
   prudence, p. *428*

negative elections, p. *430*
performance evaluation,
   p. *434*
risk-adjusted return, p. *434*

Section 404(c) safe harbor
   provisions, p. *429*
special rights of
   diversification, p. *431*

Questions for Review

1. Explain the reasons for limited investment options in early defined contribution plans.

2. Describe the factors in the last 20 years that have contributed to an expansion in employee investment options in defined contribution plans.

3. Discuss employer motivations to look more closely at plan objectives and plan performance.

4. Identify three major areas where plan investment provisions should be compatible with plan sponsor objectives.

5. How can a plan sponsor limit its fiduciary liability regarding the investment of plan assets?

6. What are the Section 404(c) safe harbor provisions?

7. What are the disadvantages to using employer stock as an investment option in a defined contribution plan?

8. What administrative issues need to be addressed in structuring the investment provisions of a defined contribution plan?

9. What does Section 404(c) require regarding the frequency of change of investment elections?

10. What are the three continuing stages in the development of plan investment provisions?

11. What decisions must be made in the design phase of developing plan investment provisions?

12. What types of questions should the plan sponsor ask during the design, implementation, and monitoring phases of the development of plan investment provisions?

13. Describe the difference between active and passive investment management styles.

14. Identify key matters to be addressed in the review process of investment management performance.

15. What is meant by risk-adjusted return?

Questions for Discussion

1. Discuss the merits of various default options for investment elections and the disadvantages of these same default options.

2. Discuss alternative approaches to investment education and what techniques may be particularly effective in instructing employee participants on retirement planning issues.

3. Discuss employer situations where the selection of predetermined sets of diversified portfolios may be preferred to distinct investment options in certain asset classes.

4. Discuss the criteria that you would use to make a change in plan investment managers.

Resources for Further Study

Arsenault, Stephen J. "The Risks and Rewards of Sec. 401(k) Plan Negative Elections." *The Tax Adviser,* April 1999.

CCH Editorial Staff. "2001 Tax Legislation: Law, Explanation, and Analysis." *Commerce Clearing House Pension Plan Guide* (2001).

Siegel, Jeremy J. *Stocks for the Long Run.* New York: McGraw-Hill, 1998.

Towers Perrin. *The Handbook of 401(k) Plan Management.* Burr Ridge, IL: Irwin Professional Publishing, 1996.

Van Derhei, Jack; Sarah Holden; and Carol Quick. "Investment of Defined Contribution Plan Assets." In *The Handbook of Employee Benefits.* 5th ed. Jerry S. Rosenbloom, ed. New York: McGraw-Hill, 2001.

Chapter 24

Trust Fund Plans

After studying this chapter you should be able to:

- Identify various types of funding instruments used to hold and accumulate qualified plan assets.

- Explain the functions, responsibilities, and duties of a trustee under a trust fund plan.

- Discuss the administrative functions commonly carried out by plan trustees for multiemployer and single-employer plans.

- Detail the advantages provided to plan sponsors by using a collective investment fund.

- Explain how particular aspects of benefit design are affected by the particular funding instrument used.

- Address the merits of using more than one type of funding instrument to hold and accumulate plan assets.

A qualified plan must use a **funding instrument** (trusts, custodial accounts, or insurance company contracts) to hold and accumulate plan assets. This chapter deals with trust fund plans. The trust fund arrangement was the first of the existing funding instruments to be used to fund private pension benefits. In addition to using the oldest of the funding instruments, trust fund plans currently account for the bulk of the employees covered and the assets held by private plans. The trust fund approach is used extensively by multiemployer plans and large single-employer plans, although the increased flexibility now available under group pension contracts has resulted in greater life insurance company competition for multiemployer and large single-employer plan business.

This chapter is concerned with those plans in which all or a substantial portion of the plan assets are accumulated and invested by the trustee in a trust fund arrangement.

General Characteristics

A **trust fund plan** is an arrangement under which employer and employee contributions, if any, are deposited with a **trustee.** The trustee is responsible for the administration and investment of these monies and the income earned on accumulated assets of the fund and normally is responsible for the direct payment of benefits to eligible participants under the plan.

Increasingly, trustees are no longer responsible for making decisions regarding the investment of a plan's assets. The responsibility for allocating plan assets among investment options is assumed by asset managers hired by the employers who sponsor the pension plans.

Mutual funds also have become a preferred investment custodian used with trust fund plans. Particularly when participant-directed investing is provided, mutual fund families provide a convenient means of supplying a variety of investment choices to plan participants. The mutual fund company selects and monitors the performance of asset managers. The mutual fund company also provides or contracts for the administrative services required for its funds. Therefore a mutual fund company supplies administrative services, invests plan assets, and serves as the trust's trustee.

If the trust fund arrangement is used in combination with an insured funding instrument, benefit payments to participants generally are made by the insurance company, with transfers from the trust fund made as required. The trustee usually is a corporate trustee (trust company). Individuals also can serve as trustees of the plan, although this practice has become less frequent, except in small single-employer plans, because of the fiduciary requirements of ERISA.

Trust Agreement

The duties and responsibilities of the trustee are set forth in a **trust agreement** executed by the employer and the trustee.

In the case of a negotiated multiemployer plan, the trust agreement is executed by individuals representing the unions and individuals representing the employers, and these persons often compose the board of trustees responsible for the administration of the plan. The board of trustees may retain the task of investing plan assets, or it may delegate this duty to an asset management company or a corporate trustee. In the latter case, a trust agreement setting forth the duties and responsibilities of the corporate trustee is executed by the board of trustees and the corporate trustee.

A typical trust agreement between an employer and a corporate trustee contains provisions regarding the irrevocability and nondiversion of trust assets; the investment powers of the trustee, if any; the allocation of fiduciary responsibilities; the payment of legal, trustee, and other fees relative to the plan; periodic reports to the employer to be prepared by the trustee; the records and accounts to be maintained by the trustee; the conditions for removal or resignation of the trustee and the appointment of a new trustee; the payment of benefits under the plan; and the rights and duties of the trustee in case of amendment or termination of the plan.

The trust agreement, then, is concerned primarily with the receipt, investment, and disbursement of funds under a pension plan. The plan provisions may be incorporated in the trust agreement or they can be set forth in a separate plan document. The use of two separate documents is prevalent in trust fund plans and is almost always the approach used in multiemployer plans. The advantage of a separate plan document is that amendments to the plan can be made without the need to involve the trustee in frequent amendments to the trust agreement.

Administrative Duties of a Trustee

The bulk of the record keeping associated with a pension plan normally is performed by the employer under single-employer trust fund plans. If the plan is contributory, the employer generally retains responsibility for maintaining a record of employee contributions. In this case, total contributions are paid to the trustee without reference to any division of employer and employee contributions. The employer normally also assumes responsibility for the maintenance of records of earnings and credited service for each participant. In some cases, the record-keeping function is performed by the consulting actuary for the plan or a third-party administrator.

Most corporate trustees are able to relieve the employer of the burden of maintaining the necessary records associated with the plans. Corporate trustees sometimes maintain records in the case of profit sharing plans or defined contribution pension plans and, to a more limited extent, for multiemployer plans. If the trustee performs any record-keeping function, a service charge, in addition to the trustee's investment fee, is levied on an account basis. The advantages of specialization and economies of scale permit corporate trustees who handle a substantial volume of pension business to perform these services for a reasonable fee. The employer must decide whether it is more economical in its case to maintain these records itself or to have this service provided by the trustee or by a consulting actuary or service organization.

In the case of a negotiated multiemployer plan, the board of trustees, rather than the individual employers, generally is responsible for the maintenance of plan records. The record-keeping function usually is performed by a pension fund office created by the board of trustees. If a corporate trustee is retained to manage the assets of the fund, the plan trustees may delegate the task of record keeping to the corporate trustee. In recent years, there has been a significant increase in the number of professional plan administrators. The function of a professional administrator is to keep all the specific records of service and earnings for individual members of the plan and to handle all routine administrative transactions.

Whether or not the corporate trustee performs the record-keeping function, it never makes any benefit distributions from the fund without authorization from the employer or retirement committee. In the case of a single-employer trust fund plan, the employer generally appoints a plan or retirement committee, usually composed of officers of the company. It is the responsibility of this committee to determine a participant's eligibility for benefits under the plan, generally based on the recommendations or guidance of a third-party administrator. Under multiemployer plans, authorization of benefit payments is the responsibility of the board of trustees or a committee of its members appointed by the board; however, in some cases, this function is delegated to a professional administrator.

Apart from the administrative aspects of trust fund plans, a corporate trustee is always responsible for maintaining accurate and detailed records of all investments, receipts, disbursements, and other transactions involving the trust assets. In addition, the trustee is required to submit an annual statement regarding these trust transactions to the plan or retirement committee, usually within 90 days of the close of the plan's fiscal year. The trust agreement may require that statements be rendered to the committee more frequently than annually; for example, quarterly or monthly. Also, in some cases, the trustee assumes responsibility for the filing of forms for the trust as required by tax regulations.

Additionally, the trustee must make annual reports under the provisions of ERISA and the basic information must be made available in summary form to all participants and beneficiaries.[1]

Investment Powers of a Trustee

For very large pension plans, it is common to use investment advisors or multiple investment managers with the corporate trustee serving as custodian. For other pension plans, the primary function of a trustee is the investment management of trust assets, although for most relatively small single-employer plans, much of the so-called investment management duties of the trustees are reduced to serving as conduit or to carrying out the investment decisions of the employers. The trustee invests the trust assets (including contributions and investment income) in accordance with the provisions of the trust agreement, the investment policy desired by the employer or retirement committee, and the fiduciary standards imposed by ERISA and by general trust laws. The investment power granted to a trustee by the trust agreement varies among plans; it may range from approval by the investment committee of every action affecting the fund's assets to full discretion in investment affairs. Furthermore, the corporate trustee does maintain personal contact with the employer, and therefore the latter may influence, directly or indirectly, investment decisions. If the trust agreement fails to specify the investment powers of the trustee, the trustee is restricted to investments that are legal for trust funds in the state in which the trust is established and the federal statute governing fiduciary investments.

Before the enactment of ERISA, the trustee could invest all trust assets in the securities of the employer. Essentially, ERISA restricts investment of pension plan assets in an employer's securities to 10 percent of the fund value. The limit does not apply to profit sharing or thrift plans that explicitly permit larger investments in employer securities. Nor does it apply to stock bonus plans or employee stock ownership plans that are invested primarily in employer securities.

The trustee is required to maintain a separate accounting and an actual segregation of the assets of each trust. In other words, the assets of a trust generally cannot be commingled with the assets of other trusts or with the general assets of the

---

[1] See Chapter 6 for a description of ERISA-mandated reporting requirements.

trustee. Thus, under these circumstances, there is no pooling of the investment experience of a number of trusts. If the investment experience has been exceptionally favorable for a particular trust, the full benefit of that experience is credited to the trust account. On the other hand, the trust must bear the full impact of adverse investment income and capital loss experience. Therefore, a relatively small trust fund plan would be subject to the danger of inadequate diversification of its investment portfolio. To meet this problem, corporate trustees have established collective investment funds. A **collective investment fund** permits the commingling of assets of all participating trusts. Although originally established to meet the needs of smaller trusts, corporate trustees have obtained permission to allow pension trusts of any size to participate in collective investment funds established specifically for qualified pension plans. A trust participating in a commingled fund for investment purposes buys units or shares of the fund.[2] Dividends are paid on each unit, each dividend being a proportionate share of the total income earned by the commingled fund. These units fluctuate in value as the value of the assets of the commingled fund fluctuates.

The principal advantage of a collective investment fund is that it permits any trust to enjoy the investment advantages normally available to only the very large funds. These potential advantages have been described as follows.[3]

1. *Higher rate of return on fixed-income investments.* Commingled investment permits purchases in amounts large enough to take advantage of private placements and special offerings of securities, which generally carry higher yields than regular market offerings, and in mortgages, leaseback arrangements, or other interests in real property.

2. *Increased growth potential through selective stock holding.* Commingled investment permits such funds to achieve a degree of selective diversification in equities that would be impossible to attain through individual investment, except in sizable funds.

3. *Maximum liquidity of funds for cash requirements.* Commingled investment permits redemption of units at the end of any month at the current market value of units, so that money required for payouts is made available through use of current cash flow rather than having to sell investments, as might have to be done in a separate fund.

4. *Dollar averaging on investment purchases.* Current cash flow from incoming contributions, spaced as they are at intervals throughout a given year, has the effect of dollar averaging on investment purchases, which generally works to the advantage of all participating trusts.

5. *Lower investment brokerage fees.* A collective investment fund can purchase stocks in round lots and in amounts that entail lower brokerage commissions.[4]

---

[2] Bank of New York, *Trusteed Employee Benefit Plans* (New York: Bank of New York, 1966), p. 10.
[3] Ibid., pp. 10–11.
[4] A small trust fund plan also can obtain the advantages of commingling through investments in mutual fund shares.

Most corporate trustees believe collective investment funds offer significant advantages to the larger plans as well as to smaller plans. In one large urban bank, approximately 55 percent of all its pension trust accounts participate in the bank's commingled pension trust. However, there is an element of inflexibility in the use of a collective investment fund that should be noted: the inability to transfer specific fund assets to another funding agency. Units can be liquidated, but during a period of depressed security prices, the employer may prefer to transfer trust assets in kind, with the expectation that market prices will be higher at some future date.

Participation in a commingled pension trust is restricted to qualified plans. Participation by a nonqualified trust could result in loss of the qualified tax status of the entire collective investment fund.

Some corporate trustees have established many collective investment funds, with each fund designed to provide an investment medium having certain principal characteristics and objectives. For example, one fund may emphasize investments in bonds, notes, debentures, and other fixed-income obligations. A second fund may be invested principally in private placements, mortgages, or other interests in real property. A third fund may be invested in a selection of quality common stocks with the objective of growth of principal and income over the long term. In addition, a special equity fund may be available for those trusts interested in pursuing a more aggressive investment policy. The multiple collective investment funds offer the employer considerable flexibility in the proportion of trust assets to be invested in each of the classes of investments.

Investment flexibility has been an attractive feature of the trust arrangement for many employers. During the past several decades, many employers have expressed a preference for investment of a relatively large proportion of pension assets in common stocks. Insured plans were not able to offer this investment flexibility until the development of separate account funding.

Benefit Structure

Retirement Benefits

The trust fund arrangement offers maximum flexibility in the design of a retirement benefit formula. Since funds are not allocated, even for retired employees, any type of benefit formula can be used under a trust fund plan. As is true in the case of several of the insurance products described in the next chapter (deposit administration and immediate participation guarantee plans), retirement benefits based on final earnings can be provided without difficulty under trust fund plans. Likewise, benefit formulas that provide for the integration of Social Security benefits can be accommodated readily under the trust fund arrangement.

It is true that the more complex the benefit formula, the more difficult is the task of the actuary in projecting costs and calculating contribution payments under the plan. The fact remains, however, that the trust fund instrument does not in itself present any obstacles to the use of the most complex of benefit formulas. For example, even those few plans that have a provision for adjustments of retired employees' benefits in accordance with a designated cost-of-living index can be provided under this funding instrument. The actuary can include in the cost calculations an assumption regarding future price level changes, although these are not readily predictable with a great degree of accuracy. However, actuarial gains and losses because of variations of actual from expected price levels can be reflected in subsequent valuations and determinations of contribution payments. Trust fund plans also can provide a retirement benefit that varies with the market value of the assets supporting the pension benefits of retired workers (variable annuities).

Money purchase defined contribution designs also can be used in trust fund pension plans. A money purchase pension plan generally provides a lifetime annuity benefit to retired employees. The law requires the plan to provide a joint and one-half survivor annuity for an employee and his or her spouse unless there is an election to the contrary. Therefore, under a money purchase pension plan, at some point in time the accumulations on behalf of each participant must be expressed in terms of a lifetime monthly benefit. The monthly benefit may be calculated as each annual contribution is received, or annual contributions may be accumulated to the retirement date and the determination of the level of monthly benefits made at that time.

In the case of some negotiated plans, particularly multiemployer plans, the employer's financial commitment is expressed as some specified cents-per-hour worked or as a fixed percentage of compensation. However, these plans generally are not traditional defined contribution plans in that they also provide a defined benefit. The trust fund instrument can accommodate these plans without any difficulty.

Early retirement benefits can be, and frequently are, provided under trust fund plans. The amount of early retirement benefit may be the actuarial equivalent of the participant's accrued normal retirement benefit, or, if the employer desires, a more liberal early retirement benefit may be provided. The additional cost under the latter alternative can be anticipated in computations of contribution payments required under the plan.

Death Benefits

An increasing proportion of the money purchase trust fund plans provide preretirement death benefits. The law requires all qualified plans to include an option providing at least a 50 percent joint and survivor annuity. As described in Chapter 5, if a participant dies before the annuity starting date and has a surviving spouse, the automatic benefit must be in the form of a qualified preretirement survivor annuity (QPSA) to the surviving spouse.

The availability of postretirement death benefits depends on the normal annuity form under the plan. A pure life annuity has been the typical normal annuity form under trust fund plans, while a modified refund annuity has been the typical normal annuity form in the case of contributory plans. Once again, however, the law provides that the joint and one-half survivor annuity be the normal annuity form for a participant and his or her spouse unless an election is made to the contrary. The level of benefits under a joint and one-half survivor annuity can be greater than the actuarial equivalent of the previous normal annuity form. If the cost of this increase in benefit is not passed on to the participants and is assumed by the employer, it can be projected in the actuary's calculations of the periodic contributions required under the plan. These benefits can be provided without difficulty under trust fund plans.

Disability Benefits

Some trust fund plans provide disability benefits. Responsibility for determining whether a participant is eligible for disability benefits usually rests with a retirement committee appointed by the employer. In the case of a multiemployer plan, this function is assumed by the board of trustees or a committee composed of board members. The trustee begins payment of disability benefits on receipt of certification by the retirement committee of a participant's eligibility for benefits. The retirement committee also assumes responsibility for reviewing approved disability claims to determine whether continuance of disability exists.

Several reasons exist for the prevalence of disability benefits under trust fund plans. First, union leaders strongly favor provision of disability benefits under pension plans, and a substantial proportion of negotiated plans use the trust fund approach. Second, disability benefits provide employers with a desirable personnel management tool if control over the determination of disability rests with the employer. Third, the historic reluctance of insurance companies to insure long-term disability benefits has encouraged the self-insuring of these benefits under trust fund plans.[5] However, in recent years, the use of insured group long-term disability plans has increased.

Vested Benefits

The rights of trust fund plan participants to benefits derived from employer contributions, as is true under other funding instruments, depend upon the vesting provisions of the plan. The vesting provisions in the plan must be at least as generous as those required under the law. If the actuarial value of the employee's vested benefit is less than $5,000, the employer may cash out the benefit. This reduces the administrative expense of keeping records of terminated employees. Additionally, if the terminating employee agrees, a vested benefit in excess of $5,000 may be cashed out under certain conditions. The value of the vested benefit may be transferred to an individual retirement account (IRA) or to the qualified plan of the employee's next employer if the new employer consents. Of course, terminating employees always are entitled to the benefit attributable to their own contributions. The availability of vested benefits may be deferred until the terminating employee reaches the later of age 62 or normal retirement age.

Since contributions to a trust fund are not allocated to specific participants under the plan (with the exception of a traditional defined contribution plan), vesting always is expressed in terms of benefits rather than contributions. A terminating

---

[5] It should be noted that under deposit administration and immediate participation guarantee plans, disability benefits, when provided, generally are self-insured by the employer in that these benefits are paid directly by the employer or charged directly to the unallocated account.

employee's vested benefits represent a deferred claim against the assets of the trust fund. This claim is conditioned on (1) the terminating employee's living to retirement age (except for his or her own contributions); (2) the employee's applying for the benefit in accordance with plan provisions; and (3) the adequacy of the trust fund to provide the vested benefit and the protection afforded by the PBGC for defined benefit plans. In case of termination of the plan, the priority, if any, of vested benefits is dependent on plan provisions subject to the requirements of the law.

Contributions

The annual contribution payments under a defined benefit trust fund plan are determined by periodic actuarial valuations by the plan actuary who must be an enrolled actuary under the law. The plan actuary calculates the amount of contributions to be made to the trust fund on the basis of (1) actuarial assumptions; (2) a particular actuarial cost method; and (3) the census data for the group of employees covered under the plan. It is the task of the actuary, as strongly reinforced by the law, to choose actuarial assumptions and techniques that, based on his or her judgment and experience, appear to be reasonable for the particular plan. This obligation is imposed on all enrolled actuaries who provide actuarial services for plans covered under the law, whether such actuaries are acting in a consulting capacity or working for insurance companies. Generally, the actuary will choose assumptions that are more conservative than the experience actually expected under the plan to provide a margin for contingencies. It is also the responsibility of the actuary to choose an appropriate actuarial cost method to be used in calculations of contribution payments. Since the choice of an actuarial cost method has a significant impact on the incidence of contribution payments, it is important that the employer have a clear understanding of the factors involved in the final selection of a cost method.

Under defined benefit trust fund plans, the employer has some input in decisions regarding the choice of actuarial assumptions and the cost method to be used in calculations of contribution payments. Thus, the employer has maximum flexibility under a trust fund plan in directing the timing of contribution payments as long as such contributions meet the minimum funding standards of the law.

Of course, this does not mean the ultimate cost of the plan is necessarily lower under trust fund plans. The actuarial gains from turnover and mortality under allocated funding instruments eventually are recognized in the form of employer credits against premiums due in future years. Also, lower levels of contributions in the initial years of the plan must be offset by higher contribution levels in subsequent years. Actuarial assumptions and cost methods do not affect the ultimate cost of the plan, except to the extent that they influence levels of funding and, therefore, the amount of investment income earned on plan assets. The fact remains that the employer has greater control over the incidence of contribution payments under trust fund plans because of the way in which actuarial assumptions and methods are established and the unallocated nature of the funding instrument. This flexibility also is available, to almost the same degree, under most group pension contracts.

In addition to the contribution payments necessary to provide the benefits to participants of the plan, the employer must make some provision for the expenses associated with trust fund plans. The major expenses under trust fund plans are trustee, consulting actuary, and legal fees, as well as record-keeping and other administrative expenses. Investment fees of corporate trustees usually are expressed as a percentage of the trust corpus—the percentage being graded downward with the size of the fund.

The trustee imposes additional charges if it maintains plan records, makes pension payments to retired employees, or holds insurance and annuity contracts. Because of the additional reporting and other administrative requirements of ERISA, additional fees for the additional services probably are necessary. Mutual funds sometimes provide administrative services at no additional fee, covering these costs under their overall management fee. If the employer performs the administrative functions associated with the plan, the cost of performing these duties should be recognized in determining the true cost of a trust fund plan.

With reference to legal and actuarial fees, it is virtually impossible to quote any figures that can be viewed as typical charges under trust fund plans since fees for these services vary so widely among plans. The legal services required for the plan normally are performed by the attorney who handles all other legal work for the employer and therefore usually are incorporated into the overall legal retainer paid by the employer. A consulting actuary's fee varies with the type and amount of service rendered. The actuary may perform preliminary cost studies or special projects on a fixed-fee basis, but most of his or her services to the plan are billed on an hourly or daily rate basis. The fees for legal and actuarial services can be paid by the trustee out of trust assets, or they can be paid directly by the employer.

No guarantees are available under trust fund plans.[6] The trustee cannot guarantee a minimum rate of investment income, nor can it guarantee plan assets against capital losses. Likewise, the mortality risk cannot be transferred to the trustee. The absence of guarantees is consistent with the legal nature of trust arrangements. A trustee's obligation is limited to the management of trust assets in a reasonable and prudent manner and in accordance with the duties set forth in the trust agreement and state and federal law. The adequacy of the fund to provide the benefits promised under the plan is the responsibility of the employer. The high degree of responsibility imposed on the employer under a trust fund plan is consistent with the maximum degree of flexibility available to the employer under this funding instrument. Guarantees must be minimized or eliminated if an employer desires maximum contribution flexibility and complete and immediate reflection of plan experience. Therefore, in choosing a funding instrument, the employer should consider the extent to which guarantees and flexibility are desired.

---

[6] In order to compete with the guaranteed investment contracts (GICs) offered by insurance companies, many sophisticated techniques are being used to try to match maturities of investments with the time that specific amounts are needed to pay benefits. These include approaches such as immunization and dedicated portfolio techniques, which are discussed in Chapter 22.

Many large employers have chosen funding instruments that offer a high degree of flexibility and immediate reflection of plan experience. In the case of a trust fund plan, the actual experience of the plan is reflected immediately in the status of the fund. For example, if investment experience has been favorable, the fund receives the full benefit of the favorable experience. Likewise, the full impact of adverse investment experience is borne by the individual trust. However, the investment risk can be spread to some extent through the use of a commingled investment fund. The use of a collective investment fund reduces a plan's investment risk as a result of the greater investment diversification available; but it still does not offer a guarantee of principal or a minimum rate of return. The employer cannot shift the mortality risk under trust fund plans. If the plan covers a large number of employees, the employer may be willing to assume the mortality risk. The mortality risk becomes a more significant consideration as the size of the group covered decreases. Deviations of actual from expected experience for other factors (for example, turnover, disability rates, and actual retirement ages) also are immediately reflected in the status of the trust fund.

Under trust fund plans, actuarial valuations are performed annually to determine the adequacy of the fund. If the actual experience evolving under the plan indicates the current level of funding is inadequate, actuarial assumptions can be revised to produce higher levels of contributions in future years.

Termination of Plan

In the event of termination of a trust fund plan, the disposition of plan assets is determined in accordance with the provisions of the law.

Situations sometimes arise in which an employer desires to switch funding agencies without any intention of terminating the plan. A **transfer of assets** to another trustee or to an insurance company can be effected without difficulty under trust fund plans. The trust agreement contains no prohibitions against transfer of plan assets (assuming that such transfers are made in accordance with the requirements of the Internal Revenue Service). The trustee may impose a minor charge for the administrative duties associated with a termination of the trust. Of course, losses may be sustained if assets must be liquidated over a relatively short period of time. In some cases, transfers of securities and other assets may be permitted rather than requiring liquidation of investments unless the assets are held in a commingled trust, in which case transfers of securities generally are not permitted. The freedom to transfer plan assets and the flexibility it offers in the case of mergers or other circumstances is viewed by some employers as an important advantage of trust fund plans.

Split Funding

The trust fund arrangement can be used in conjunction with individual insurance and annuity contracts as one approach in funding pension benefits. This approach generally is referred to as a **combination plan.** Group pension contracts also can be used in combination with the trust fund arrangement. These latter arrangements usually are referred to as **split-funded plans** (although the term *combination plan* can be applied to describe any plan using two or more funding instruments).

Split-funded plans generally use group deposit administration or immediate participation guarantee or modified immediate participation guarantee contracts. The decision of the employer to split-fund its pension plan usually is motivated by a desire to obtain, at least in part, the advantages of an insurer's guarantees and a possibly favorable investment opportunity. For example, the trust agreement may provide that the trustee administer all assets held on behalf of active employees and that an immediate annuity be purchased as each employee retires. Likewise, an insurer may enjoy relatively high yields on direct placement and mortgage investments, and therefore the employer may decide to invest a portion of plan assets in a deposit administration contract, an immediate participation guarantee contract, or a guaranteed investment contract.

Chapter Summary

- A qualified plan must use a funding instrument such as a trust, custodial account, or insurance company contract to hold and accumulate plan assets.

- The trust fund arrangement, the oldest funding instrument used, currently accounts for the majority of employees covered and assets held by private pension plans. This popularity is largely attributable to the flexibility that this funding instrument affords a plan sponsor. The trust fund plan offers maximum flexibility in the design of a retirement benefit formula, largely because funds are not allocated to the individual accounts of either active or retired employees.

- ERISA restricts investment of pension plan assets in an employer's securities to 10 percent of the fund value. The limit does not apply to profit sharing or thrift plans that explicitly permit larger investments in employer securities. Nor does it apply to stock bonus plans or employee stock ownership plans that are typically invested primarily in employer securities.

- The assets of a trust generally cannot be commingled with the assets of other trusts or with the general assets of the trustee. As a result, no pooling of the investment experience of a number of trusts occurs. If the investment experience has been favorable for a particular trust, that trust fully benefits. Conversely, the trust bears the full impact of adverse investment results. To deal with the issue of inadequate diversification, particularly for smaller trusts, collective investment funds provide a remedy.

- A collective investment fund permits the commingling of assets of all participating trusts. Although collective investment funds were originally developed to benefit smaller trusts, pension trusts of any size can participate in collective investment funds established for qualified plans. Participation in a commingled pension trust is restricted to qualified plans. Participation by a nonqualified trust could result in the loss of the qualified tax status for the entire collective investment fund.

- Under defined benefit trust fund plans, the employer has some input into decisions regarding the choice of actuarial assumptions and the cost method to be used in calculations of contribution payments. Thus, the employer has maximum flexibility under a trust fund plan in directing the timing of contribution payments, as long as such contributions meet the minimum funding standards of the law.

• No guarantees are available under trust fund plans. The trustee cannot guarantee a minimum rate of investment income, nor can it guarantee plan assets against capital losses. Mortality risk cannot be assumed by the trustee. The absence of guarantees is consistent with the legal nature of trust arrangements. A trustee's obligation is limited to the management of trust assets in a reasonable and prudent fashion according to the duties set forth in the trust agreement and specified by state and federal law. The employer is responsible for funding the trust at an adequate level to ensure benefits delineated in the plan can be paid. The high level of employer flexibility available under a trust fund also imposes a high level of responsibility on the employer.

Key Terms

collective investment fund, p. *445*	funding instrument, p. *441*	trust agreement, p. *442*
combination plan, p. *451*	split-funded plans, p. *452*	trust fund plan, p. *442*
	transfer of assets, p. *451*	trustee, p. *442*

Questions for Review

1. What is a trust fund plan?
2. Describe the provisions that generally are found in a trust agreement.
3. Describe the typical administrative duties and investment powers of a trustee.
4. How does the federal law restrict the trustee's investment powers?
5. What is a collective investment fund?
6. What advantages does a collective investment fund have over an individually managed fund?
7. It has been said that any benefit formula can be used in conjunction with trust fund plans. Explain.
8. What are the major expenses of a trust fund plan in addition to the contributions needed to pay plan benefits?

Questions for Discussion

1. Discuss how the investment risks assumed under a trust fund plan should be treated by the employer.
2. Discuss how the mortality risks assumed under a trust fund plan should be treated by the employer.

Resource for Further Study

Amoroso, Vincent. "Costing and Funding Retirement Benefits." In *The Handbook of Employee Benefits.* 5th ed. Jerry S. Rosenbloom, ed. New York: McGraw-Hill, 2001.

Chapter 25

Insured Funding Instruments

After studying this chapter you should be able to:

- Describe the different funding instruments, their unique characteristics, and the reasons why they have been developed for use with qualified plans.

- Explain the importance of the advent of separate accounts to insurers' ability to compete with trust fund plans in providing flexibility to plan sponsors.

- Identify the specific guarantees that insurers customarily have provided to plan sponsors under various insured funding instruments.

- Discuss the relationship between funding instruments and plan design features and why certain funding instruments are not conducive to certain plan designs.

- Specify alternative ways of handling plan administration and the relative advantages and disadvantages of the different approaches.

- Describe the considerations involved in choosing either a single administrative provider or a combination of providers to supply plan administrative services.

Introduction

Originally, the majority of pension plan assets were placed with insurance companies and were protected by strong guarantees as to investment and mortality experience. Beginning with group deferred annuity contracts in the early 1920s, insurance products were designed specifically for use in pension plans. These contracts provided that a single premium would be paid to purchase an annuity for each employee promising to pay (at normal retirement age) the equivalent of his or her accrued benefit for that year. Although all investment and mortality risks were transferred from the employer to the insurance company once the annuities were purchased, it was difficult to provide a substantial degree of flexibility in plan design features, such as past-service benefits and supplemental benefits, since the price of funding a dollar's worth of monthly retirement income increases substantially as the employee approaches normal retirement age.

The limited flexibility of this contract eventually led the insurance industry to develop unallocated forms of funding vehicles, such as deposit administration and immediate participation guarantee contracts, which are described in this chapter. Funding instruments generally are classified on the basis of whether contributions are **allocated** to provide benefits to specific employees prior to retirement or whether contributions are accumulated in an **unallocated fund** to provide benefits for employees when they retire.

In time, some sponsors began to question the need for locking up funds for annuity purchases, as is generally the case under deposit administration and immediate participation guarantee contracts, and many were disenchanted with the restrictions or implicit penalties imposed on the withdrawal of funds from such contracts. Many employers used trust fund plans to provide a more flexible funding instrument.[1] The insurance industry responded to the competition from trust fund plans by offering features and products that provided greater flexibility. The introduction of separate accounts permitted sponsors a broader array of investment vehicles, not commonly permitted in the general accounts of insurers. Sponsors also sought investments that had a fixed maturity and did not require an ongoing relationship with the insurer. The insurance industry again responded to this demand by offering guaranteed investment contracts, which offer a unique type of investment guarantee and are described in this chapter.

The major development in the group pension field in the last 15 years has been the substantial increase in flexibility under insurance contracts. Insurers now are in a position to tailor the contract to the specific needs of the employer. Employer demands for greater flexibility in investment policy and the timing of contribution payments have led to a strong preference for the unallocated type of contract in the group pension market. This demand for greater flexibility has extended to the small-employer market, and insurers have accommodated this demand by making unallocated contracts available to relatively small firms. While there are some deposit administration and immediate participation guarantee contracts still active at most insurers, many policyholders have opted to convert their funds into more modern funding vehicles.

Funding Instruments—General History

The **group deferred annuity contract,** unlike individual insurance and group permanent contracts, was devised specifically to meet the funding needs of pension plans, the first such contract being issued in 1921. The volume of these contracts

---

[1] Trust fund arrangements are discussed in Chapter 24.

grew very rapidly in the following two decades, and they constituted by far the most prevalent group-insured funding instrument prior to the growth of deposit administration plans in the 1950s. However, they are rarely used today. Group deferred annuity contracts provide for the funding of benefits through the purchase of units of single-premium deferred annuities for each participant.

The **deposit administration contract,** which first appeared in the 1920s, evolved from the basic group deferred annuity contract. The deposit administration contract was developed to overcome certain of the inflexibilities associated with the group deferred annuity contract. Because of the other more flexible funding instruments currently available and discussed later in this chapter, group deposit administration contracts are no longer issued as new contracts.

The distinguishing characteristic of deposit administration contracts, as contrasted with group deferred annuity contracts, is that employer contributions are not allocated to specific employees until retirement date. Stated differently, the actual purchase of annuities (which includes a charge for expenses) does not take place until an employee retires.

Contributions are credited to an unallocated fund that, under a conventional deposit administration contract, is variously referred to as the deposit fund, active life fund, deposit account, or purchase payment fund. Contributions credited to the deposit account are invested in the insurer's general investment portfolio or the insurer's separate accounts. **General account investments** principally are fixed-income securities. **Separate accounts** offer a broader choice of investments between fixed-dollar and equity securities. The type of separate account available under the deposit administration contract is primarily one that is invested in common stocks. *Fixed-dollar account* and *equity account* are terms that are used when discussing the features of deposit administration contracts from the policyholder's viewpoint.

The contributions credited to the fixed-dollar account become part of the general assets of the insurance company for investment purposes. The account is credited with the rate of interest guaranteed in the contract. Also, dividends due under the contract are credited to the fixed-dollar account. As pensions become payable to retiring employees, annuities may be provided by allocations from either the fixed-dollar or the equity account, although generally annuities are provided by allocations from the fixed-dollar account. When an annuity is established, a certificate is issued to the retired employee describing the benefits.

The contributions credited to the policyholder's equity account are invested in one or more of the insurer's separate accounts provided under the contract. While accounting procedures for the equity account differ among insurance companies, the following approach is illustrative of the general concepts involved in separate account funding. Each policyholder's share of the separate account is determined on a participation unit (or variable unit) basis. The policyholder's equity account provides a cumulative record of the number of participation units credited to the account and the number of units allocated or withdrawn from the account. The balance of participation units credited to the account multiplied by the current participation unit value equals the amount of equity account assets held on behalf of the policyholder at any given point in time. The participation unit value is adjusted periodically, usually each business day, to reflect investment results under the separate account. The insurer offers no guarantee as to principal or interest on monies credited to the equity account.

The policyholder generally has some flexibility in transferring funds between the fixed-dollar account and the equity account. Generally, advance written notice to the insurer (e.g., 15 business days) is required. The advance notice requirement serves to minimize the potential problem of an undue amount of switching activity that might arise from attempts to play the market. Also, the insurer generally reserves the right to limit the amount or the percentage permitted to be transferred from the fixed-dollar account to the equity account either on a per-policyholder basis or on a book-of-business approach. For example, the total of the amounts transferred in any month may not exceed $1 million for all policyholders, or each policyholder may transfer up to 20 percent of the fixed-dollar account in any one year. The objective of this provision is to minimize potential financial antiselection and liquidity problems arising from such transfers. Likewise, the insurer has the right—which it might exercise under some conditions, as when the stock markets are unstable—to limit transfers in a given month from the equity account according to the restrictions described above.

If the policyholder decides to place future contributions with a new funding agency, such as another insurance company or a bank, the policyholder may either (1) permit the fixed-dollar and equity accounts to be used to purchase annuities until exhausted or (2) elect a transfer date for the transfer of funds credited to the fixed-dollar and equity accounts. If the policyholder has elected to transfer the funds in its accounts, the purchase of annuities will cease as of a specified date, such as the 15th business day after the insurer receives such request. Transfer payments begin on the transfer date and usually are made on a monthly basis. The minimum amount that can be transferred monthly from the fixed-income account is specified in the contract; for example, 1 percent of the amount of the account on the date annuity purchases cease, with insurer permission required to transfer amounts in excess of the minimum monthly amount. Thus, the insurer reserves the right to spread transfer payments over a period of time. In other words, if the contract provides that monthly transfer payments will not be less than 1 percent of the amount of the account on the date purchases cease, the insurer has the right to stretch transfer payments over a 15- or 20-year period or more, depending on the interest rate being credited to the account.

In practice, the agreed-upon transfer schedules generally are considerably shorter than the maximum permissible contractual period. The insurer generally permits lump sum transfers, on a market value basis, although, for very large accounts, the insurer may reserve the right to spread payments over a period of time. With reference to the equity account, the contract generally provides that the sum transferable is the contract fund balance valued on a market value basis. Also, the maximum payout period generally is shorter than the period applicable to the fixed-dollar account. For example, the contract might provide that monthly transfer payments from the equity account will not be less than (1) the greater of $1 million worth of participation units or 5 percent of the amount of the account on the date annuity purchases cease; or (2) the balance of the account, if less. In this latter case, the maximum period over which insurer transfer payments can be made is 20 months. The difference in treatment of transfers from each account is due to the differences in liquidity and marketability between fixed-dollar and equity securities.

In the case of transfers to another funding agency, the insurer usually reserves the right to withhold some amount of the fund (usually up to 5 percent, the specific percentage to be determined by the insurer) to cover expenses not yet recovered and to offset possible financial antiselection (although transfers on a market-value basis minimize the latter problem).

An administration charge normally is levied when annual premiums are less than a specified amount. The contract administration charge generally is allocated from the fixed-dollar account.

In the intervening decades since their introduction, group annuity contracts following the basic deposit administration concept have been offered in considerable variety, including immediate participation guarantee (IPG) and guaranteed investment contracts (GICs), varying from product to product in both the degree of insurer guarantee and the degree of contract-holder discretion as to contributions, investment, and the mobility of funds. Some such contracts were, in fact, group annuity contracts in name only, functioning solely as investment vehicles, with the purchase of annuities a seldom-used contract-holder's option. Most GICs and many separate account contracts are, in practice, investment-only contracts. A major variant of the deposit administration theme, the group immediate participation guarantee contract, is described next.

Major Insurance Product Developments

Group Immediate Participation Guarantee Contracts

The deposit administration contract went a long way toward providing employers with the desired degree of flexibility not available under the traditional group annuity contract. In addition, the deposit administration contract offers certain interest and annuity rate guarantees. However, the insurance company is able to provide these guarantees only because it accumulates a contingency reserve and because it has control, through dividend computations, over the rate at which actuarial gains pertaining to guaranteed items are credited to the employer. In reaction to employer requests for an immediate reflection of the actual experience under their contracts and their willingness to give up the guarantees of the deposit administration contract to get it, insurance companies developed the **immediate participation guarantee (IPG) contract,** the first contract of this type being issued in 1950. Under an IPG contract, the employer's account is credited with the contributions received during the contract period plus its share of actual investment income for the year according to the investment year method. The account is charged with all the expenses associated with the particular contract. As issued by many insurance companies, these contracts provide that all benefits, including annuity payments, are charged directly against the account as they are paid. In other words, annuities are not actually purchased for participants at retirement date, as is the practice under deposit administration contracts. Some insurance companies do segregate from the account the gross premium for the annuities of retired workers in order to provide annuity guarantees. However, in these latter cases, the premium amount remains in the policyholder's contract funds. The result is similar to that achieved by insurers that charge to the account only the annuity payments actually made. There is no charge to the account for an allocation directed toward building up a contingency reserve. Also, since no dividend as such is paid, all the record keeping pertaining to a particular contract can be maintained in one account. Thus, the employer can be quickly apprised of the experience to date under the contract.

The IPG contract also specifies a schedule of guaranteed annuity gross premium rates. However, since annuities are not actually purchased at retirement date, these guaranteed annuity rates are only of significance if the plan or contract is terminated. IPG contracts as initially developed typically did not provide for a guarantee of principal or a minimum rate of interest.

As IPG contracts developed and grew in popularity, the use of separate accounts, and the types of separate accounts available, grew, enabling insurers to offer group clients a wide range of investment choices. The assets held in separate accounts are not commingled with the general assets of the insurer and are exempt from state statutory investment restrictions normally applied to life insurance companies.

Separate Account Funding

Historically, life insurance companies have invested the bulk of their assets in fixed-dollar investments. The laws in most states restrict the investments of life insurance companies' general account assets in common stocks to some specified percentage (e.g., 5 percent) of the total assets of the company. This restriction is imposed because of the fixed-dollar obligations and contractual guarantees provided in traditional life insurance and annuity contracts and, also, because of the relatively small surplus maintained by life insurance companies.

However, with the advent of separate accounts in 1962, insurers could offer group clients a wide range of investment choices. The assets held in separate accounts are not commingled with the general assets of the insurer and are exempt from state statutory investment restrictions normally applied to life insurance companies.

There is much variety in the manner in which separate accounts are operated by the various insurance companies. Some insurers offer accounts only on a commingled basis; others also offer accounts maintained solely for a single customer. Initially, separate accounts were invested primarily in common stocks, but other forms are now available; further major developments in the nature and form of the separate accounts available can be expected as the types of underlying investments in these accounts are broadened. For example, some insurers have established separate accounts invested primarily in mortgages, including equity participations; others have established commingled separate accounts invested primarily in the ownership of income-producing real property; and other accounts are invested in publicly

John Hancock Mutual Life Insurance Company v. Harris Trust & Savings Bank

1

In 1993, the U.S. Supreme Court issued its ruling in *John Hancock Mutual Life Insurance Co. v. Harris Trust & Savings Bank.* The Court held that "free funds" held in John Hancock's general account under an IPG contract issued to Harris Trust as trustee of the Sperry Rand Corporation (now Unisys Corporation) pension plan were "plan assets" under the Employee Retirement Income Security Act (ERISA) and, thus, Hancock was a fiduciary of those assets and subject to all the restrictions and rules of ERISA fiduciaries. The Court held that the contract in question was not a "guaranteed benefit policy," as defined in ERISA. Assets backing guaranteed benefit policies will not be deemed to be "plan assets."

In examining whether the Sperry contract met the requirements for treatment as a guaranteed benefit policy, the Court said that the proper approach to resolving this issue is to divide the contract into its component parts and examine the risk allocation between the parties for each component of the contract. ERISA's guaranteed benefit policy exclusion applies to a contract component only if the contract component allocates investment risk to the insurer, the Court stated, and such an allocation is present only when the insurer provides a genuine guarantee of an aggregate amount of benefits payable to retirement plan participants and their beneficiaries. As applied to the "free funds" portion of a contract—which was

defined by the Court as those "funds in excess of those that have been converted into guaranteed benefits"—the following were found to be indicative of a genuine guarantee: (1) the insurer's guarantee of a reasonable rate of return on those funds and (2) the provision of a mechanism to convert the funds into guaranteed benefits at rates set by the contract.

Insurers issuing group pension annuity contracts have had to determine what portion, if any, of their general accounts consist of assets subject to ERISA and what steps to take to reduce their exposure to liability for breaches of ERISA's fiduciary rules in the operation of their business. The restrictions on fiduciaries in ERISA differ from the normal principles of risk pooling and spreading that characterize an insurance business. Functions such as the allocation of income, expenses, and surplus among its lines of business, could be said to violate ERISA rules if pension plan assets are imbedded in the insurer's general account.

The Small Business Job Protection Act of 1996 included a provision giving the Department of Labor (DOL) authority to clarify the status of plan assets held in insurance company general accounts. The DOL was given the authority to grant protections to insurance companies for past practices and develop clarifying regulations. Policies issued after December 31, 1998, are subject to the fiduciary obligations under ERISA.

traded bonds, short-term securities, direct placements, and, most recently, foreign securities. One or more separate accounts may be used under the same group pension contract.

Separate accounts were developed for two reasons: (1) to compete with trust fund plans in making equity investments available to employers for funding fixed-dollar plans and (2) to fund variable annuity plans. In the first case, many employers believe the long-term rate of return on equities will be greater than the return on fixed-income investments and the increased return will serve to reduce their cost of providing the fixed benefits promised under the plan. In the second case, equity-based variable annuities by definition generally require that the assets supporting these annuities be fully invested in equity securities.

The insurer does not guarantee principal or interest for plan assets held in a separate account. The income and gains or losses, realized or unrealized, on separate account investments are credited to or charged against the separate account without regard to the other income, gains, or losses of the insurance company.

Separate accounts are subject to regulation by the Securities and Exchange Commission (SEC). However, exemptions from certain provisions of the acts administered by the SEC have been accorded to qualified retirement plans over the years.[2]

Annuity Separate Account Contract

In the late 1980s, the annuity separate account contract was developed. This contract provides for the establishment of fixed-dollar annuity guarantees for which underlying reserves are invested, not in the insurer's general account, but in one or more of the insurer's market-valued separate accounts. Annuity separate account contracts have been written primarily on the deposit administration pattern, with unallocated funds and annuities at retirement, but they also have been used for single-premium annuities with both immediate and deferred annuities. Although the participation aspect of an annuity separate account contract is highly comparable to the IPG, with regard to mortality experience, and to separate account unit valuation, with regard to investment results, it is unique in combining the two in a way that allows plan sponsors to direct the investment of assets supporting their already annuitized pensions.

---

[2] First, exemptions under the Securities Act of 1933 and the Investment Company Act of 1940 were provided by Rule 156 and Rule 3(c)3 for noncontributory, qualified plans covering at least 25 lives at the time the contract was issued. Later, Rule 6(e)1 extended the exemption to contributory plans, provided that certain conditions were satisfied regarding employee contributions allocated to separate accounts. Last, the Investment Company Amendments Act of 1970 exempts from the 1940 act separate accounts used exclusively to fund qualified plans, and from most provisions of the 1933 act and the Securities Exchange Act of 1934 separate account interests issued in connection with qualified plans (except for HR-10 and individual retirement account plans). Separate accounts also are subject to state regulatory requirements. A 1980 change to the Securities Acts extended the exceptions to plans of governmental units even though not qualified. SEC Rule 180 (December 1981) provides an exception to the registration requirements of the 1933 act for certain financially sophisticated HR-10 plans.

Single Premium Group Annuity Contracts

Single-premium group annuity contracts were designed to provide annuities for participants in an uninsured pension or profit sharing plan that has been terminated.[3] The high level of interest rates in the 1980s, increasing government regulations impacting defined benefit pension plans, and financial accounting standards contributed to the decline in use of defined benefit pension plans in favor of defined contribution plans. Also in the 1980s, the pace of corporate mergers and takeovers led to considerable interest in single-premium group annuity arrangements. This apparently was due at least in part to the concern among the officers of the corporations being absorbed that pension assets would be used by the new management for subsequent acquisitions or that the rate of funding would be reduced to a point at which the security of their pension benefits would be impaired, although this should not have been much of a problem since the enactment of ERISA. If annuities were purchased, the funds would be unavailable to the new management and the purchased annuity benefits would be guaranteed by the insurance company.

During the late 1980s in particular, before the enactment of stronger federal constraints on plan asset reversions to employers, single-premium group annuity contracts were used as a vehicle for meeting federal prerequisites. An employer terminating a pension plan in order to recover excess funding was required to purchase annuity guarantees for all the given plan's accrued-but-uninsured benefits as a precondition of such reversion.

Under a single-premium group annuity contract, immediate annuities are provided for present pensioners and deferred annuities are provided for those who are below retirement age. This type of contract usually is nonparticipating. It also may be used by plans that have not terminated but wish to purchase annuities for a block of retired persons to take advantage of favorable rate guarantees and possibly favorable corporate balance sheet effects.

As defined contribution plans have grown, becoming more popular than defined benefit plans through the 1980s and into the new millennium, funding vehicles intended primarily for defined contribution plans also have grown. The later sections of this chapter describe these funding vehicles.

Growth of Defined Contribution Plans

Marketplace Trend to Defined Contribution Plan Creation

Chapter 3 discusses the legislative factors that have had an impact on defined benefit plans and enhanced the attractiveness of defined contribution plans. Since 1980, the growth rate of defined contribution plan assets has been greater than that of defined benefit plan assets. In 1979, approximately 29 percent of total plan assets

---

[3] For a detailed discussion of what happens when a pension plan terminates, see Chapter 16.

were held in defined contribution plans; by 1998, this percentage had grown to 52 percent. Specifically,[4]

	1979		1998	
	Number of Plans	Assets ($ Millions)	Number of Plans	Assets ($ Millions)
Total plans	470,921	$445,430	730,031	$4,021,849
Defined benefit	139,489	319,595	56,405	1,936,600
Defined contribution	331,432	125,835	673,626	2,085,250

Insurance Group Products Related to Defined Contribution Plan Growth

Contributions to defined contribution plans have increased each year since 1975, while contributions to defined benefit plans generally have declined in a number of those years. However, defined benefit plans continue to be an important feature of employers' benefit programs.

Guaranteed Investment Contracts (GICs)

As defined contribution plans have grown in popularity, funding vehicles intended primarily for such plans have developed. A major vehicle is the **guaranteed investment contract (GIC).**

GICs were first introduced in the 1970s. The basic concept in the early GICs was to offer an "open window," as long as 10 years, during which contributions could be placed in the GIC and credited with interest at a guaranteed rate. By the 1980s, in order to reduce investment risk and cash flow risk of the insurance company, the contribution window was shortened considerably, typically to a period of 3 to 12 months. Many GICs now provide for a one-day "window," whereby a single contribution is made, as opposed to a series of contributions over several months.

Under the typical GIC, the contribution window is followed by a "holding period," during which interest is credited at a rate guaranteed not to change during the life of the contract and during which withdrawals may be made at book value to provide plan benefits. Payment of the accumulated amounts may be made in a single sum at the end of the holding period or in a series of installments over a stated period of months or years. The terms of the GIC are agreed upon between the insurance company and the plan sponsor as part of the negotiation process before the GIC is issued. These terms include the entire length of the contract, the contribution window, the amount of the contribution (or the minimum and maximum amount, if a series of contributions will be made), the payment terms, and the guaranteed interest rate.

---

[4] Data from "Abstract of 1998 Form 5500 Annual Reports," *Private Pension Plan Bulletin* 11 (Washington, DC: Department of Labor Pension and Welfare Benefits Administration, Office of Research and Economic Analysis), Spring 2002.

GICs also are used as a funding vehicle for defined benefit plans, although to a lesser extent than for defined contribution plans. Under a GIC issued for a defined benefit plan, a single contribution typically is made and held until the scheduled payment date, accumulated with interest at the specified guaranteed rate. It is usually a "nonbenefit responsive" GIC, in that it is not intended that withdrawals will be made from the GIC to meet plan benefit requirements.

The "guarantees" provided by GICs are only guarantees to the extent that the issuing insurance company is able to fulfill the contractual terms that it has "guaranteed" for the purchaser of the investment contract. In the 1980s, this aspect of GICs became problematic to many plan sponsors when certain insurance companies were unable to fulfill their contractual obligations. Accordingly, some plan sponsors have diminished their reliance on GICs for other fixed-income alternatives, while some plan sponsors have sought greater security to ensure guarantees from insurers. The traditional type of GIC described above is part of the insurance company's general account assets. In the late 1980s, insurance companies also began to offer GICs funded in a separate account. By contract, contributions deposited and held in the separate account may be insulated from the other assets and liabilities of the insurer; separate account assets cannot be subject to claim from general creditors or other contract holders. Amounts are invested by the insurance company according to investment guidelines that have been agreed upon between the insurance company and the plan sponsor. A minimum guaranteed interest rate may apply; actual investment returns are credited according to terms specified in the contract.

In the mid-1980s, banks began issuing GICs in competition with the insurance companies. GICs issued by banks commonly are referred to as "BICs." A BIC represents a means of diversification for a plan that has a significant amount of assets held in insurance company vehicles. Another form of diversification is provided by the synthetic GIC, developed in the late 1980s.

Synthetic GICs

A **synthetic GIC** consists of a portfolio of fixed-income securities, "wrapped" with a guarantee (typically by the insurance company or bank) to provide benefit payments according to the plan at book value. The wrap provider guarantees such payments by making up any difference between the book value and the market value of the securities in the portfolio. The synthetic GIC resembles the separate account GIC, except that ownership of the portfolio assets remains with the plan (as opposed to the insurance company separate account) and custody of the assets is with a third party (which manages the investment of the assets). Since the plan owns the assets, if the issuer defaults, the assets will continue to be held by the plan. Investment returns belong to the plan sponsor who holds the contract; the issuer receives only a fee for services in making benefit payments and providing the wrap.

Table 25.1 summarizes the historical introduction of various funding instruments and reviews their primary characteristics. This comparison indicates whether investment risk and mortality risk are transferred to the insurance company. The comparison further examines whether an allocated instrument is used and whether investments are held in an insurer's general account or in separate accounts.

TABLE 25.1 Funding Instrument Characteristics and Their Development[a]

Product Name ⇒	Group Deferred Annuity Contracts	Deposit Administration Contracts (DA)	Immediate Participation Guarantee Contracts (IPGs)		Guaranteed Investment Contracts (GICs)		Trust Fund Plans: Repository for various types of investments, including GICs.
First Introduced ⇒	Early 1920s	1920s	1950s		1970s		Predates Insured Products
Use & Prevalence ⇒	Rapid growth until 1950s when deposit administration contracts introduced. Rarely used today.	Growth in popularity in the early 1950s due to competition from trust fund plans. Not popular today because of more flexible alternatives.	Primary growth occurs in the 1960s. Competition from banks offering diversified forms of investments for pensions, requires a move to a more competitive investment alternative.[b]		During the mid-1970s aggressive competition from banks and mutual funds along with stellar performance of the equity markets forced the insurance industry to revise its investment products.... The perpetual relationship.... with the DA and IPG disappeared. The GIC had a known maturity date and constant rate for contract period (akin to a CD).[c]		Though trust fund plans are the oldest and currently the predominant funding instrument used in pension funding, their use has increased over time, eroding market share for insured products that largely were used as the pension marketplace developed.
			Original IPGs	Modified IPGs	Original GICs	"Synthetic" GICs	
Investment Risk —Preretirement —Postretirement	Transferred Transferred	Transferred* Transferred	Not transferred*/† Not transferred†	Not transferred* Transferred	Transferred Transferred	Transferred Transferred	Not transferred Not transferred
Mortality Risk —Preretirement —Postretirement	Transferred Transferred	Not transferred Transferred	Not transferred† Not transferred†	Not transferred Transferred	Not transferred Not transferred	Not transferred Not transferred	Not transferred Not transferred
Allocated Instrument —Preretirement —Postretirement	Yes Yes	No Yes	No No (Annuities not actually purchased)	No Yes	No No	No No	No No
Insurer Holding Investments in —General account (A/C), or —Separate accounts (A/Cs)	General A/C	Originally general A/C; separate accounts introduced in 1962	Originally general A/C; separate accounts introduced in 1962	Originally general A/Cs; separate accounts introduced in 1962	Predominantly through general A/C, though possible with separate A/C.	Backed by pool of securities placed in separate account controlled by plan sponsor.	Noninsurer arrangement: Assets held as corpus in trust.
Later Developments and Other Modifications			In the late 70s and early 80s, many insurers began offering one-year investment guarantees based on expectations of earnings for new monies.		Bullet-type receives a single deposit. Extended-guarantee type accepts payments over several-year period.		

*Only if in general account.

†Annuity guarantees still provided. Since annuities are not actually purchased at retirement date, guarantees only of significance if plan or contract terminated.

[a]Source: © Dennis F. Mahoney, 1996. *Funding Instrument Characteristics and Their Development*, All rights reserved.

[b]Kenneth L. Walker, *Guaranteed Investment Contracts* (Burr Ridge, IL: Richard D. Irwin, 1989), p. 5.

[c]Ibid., p. 8.

Stable Value Pooled Funds

During the 1990s, GIC pooled funds grew. As these funds include several types of fixed-income investments, they are more generally referred to as **stable value pooled funds.** The investments typically are GICs, BICs, synthetic GICs, money market instruments, and cash. Each participating plan in essence has a pro rata share of each investment. The rate of return for the fund is a blended rate of the actual returns from the fund investments.

The stable value pooled fund provides diversification that plan sponsors, especially those involving plans with smaller asset amounts, might otherwise not be able to obtain directly with issuers of the fund investments. In addition to diversification provided through the types of investments in the fund, diversification is provided by spreading assets among a number of issuers; investment guidelines with respect to a pooled fund typically include a maximum percentage (such as 15 percent) of fund assets that may be placed with any single issuer.

Another feature of a stable value pooled fund is the credit quality required by the terms of the fund. The investment guidelines require that each issuer meet specific credit quality standards by major credit rating agencies (such as Standard & Poor's, Moody's Investors Service, and A.M. Best). Thus, a plan sponsor will know the average quality rating that the fund is intended to meet. An example of an average quality rating is "AA" by Standard & Poor's (or the equivalent from another rating agency), which is the "excellent" category with respect to the claims payment ability of the issuer.

Changes in the Stable Value Marketplace   2

The stable value marketplace has undergone significant changes during the last several years. Traditional guaranteed investment contracts (GICs) and separate account investments have been under pressure by the newer synthetic GICs and are losing market share. Further pressure can be expected as a result of two rulings issued in August by the New York Insurance Department. The department's Circular Letter 12 rescinds last year's ban on synthetic GICs, clearing the way for companies licensed in the state to sell those products. Circular Letter 13 expands the ability of monoline financial guaranty issuers (bond insurers) to operate in the stable value market. These actions may expand the number of issuers in the stable value marketplace and encourage providers to develop a variety of new stable value products. Since New York is considered a leader in insurance regulation, the impact of the actions is expected to be felt across the country. . . .

"The regulatory changes, and the advent of third-party credit enhancement by triple-A rated financial guaranty companies like ourselves, open up many more possibilities for insurance companies that may be less than triple-A rated to provide a fully competitive product," says Charlie Williams, managing director of CapMAC.

Source: Anthony G. Balestrieri, "New GIC Products—and How to Judge Quality." Reprinted with permission, from the October 1995 issue of *Pension Management* magazine, pp. 28–30. © Intertec Publishing Corp.

A stable value pooled fund also provides benefit responsiveness. Withdrawals may be made at book value in order to provide the benefits payable to plan participants.

The plan sponsor participating in a stable value pooled fund need deal only with the investment manager of the fund. It is the manager who is responsible for obtaining the investments according to the fund guidelines, reviewing the credit quality of the fund and of each issuer, processing deposits and withdrawals, and reporting returns and fund balances to the plan sponsor.

Individual Contracts/Policies Used with Defined Contribution Plans

Individual (Deferred) Annuity Contracts

For small defined contribution plans, tax-deferred annuity (TDA) plans (403(b) plans—see Chapter 12), or individual retirement accounts (IRAs), (see Chapter 17) including simplified employee pension (SEP) plans, salary reduction simplified employee pension (SARSEP) plans, and savings incentive match plans for employees (SIMPLE plans) (see Chapter 18), the preferred funding vehicles offered by insurance companies are individual contracts. Separate individual annuity contracts are purchased for each participant. Generally, such contracts are issued to a trusteed plan with the trustee as owner and/or custodian. For a plan that does not have a trust (e.g., TDAs), the individual annuity contract is issued directly to the participant as annuitant and owner.

Individual annuity contracts usually have many of the same features as group annuity contracts—for example, a variety of investment options, including a guaranteed interest account and separate accounts, charges, restrictions, guaranteed annuity settlement rates, and so forth. Moreover, premium payments are flexible, both as to amount and frequency. Some differences, however, may exist in the amounts or types of charges. Group annuities usually have an advantage in terms of possible lower charges or expenses due to the relatively larger size of investments that may have an effect directly or indirectly on the investment results of the plan's assets.

On the other hand, individual annuity contracts are more portable. This is an important feature particularly to participants of 403(b) plans and IRAs including SEPs. Such individual annuity contracts may be retained as funding vehicles by an employee who transfers from one employer to another and from one plan to the next (provided that the succeeding plan does not prohibit their use). In the case of defined contribution plans, the plan may distribute the individual annuity contract to a terminating or retiring participant. As an annuity contract with a nontransferable provision (required by the Internal Revenue Service) other than to the plan participant, the participant does not incur a taxable distribution and is able to continue the benefit of retaining his funds in the investment options offered by the contract.

Some small defined benefit plans are funded exclusively through the purchase of individual life insurance policies or individual annuity contracts (also referred to as Internal Revenue Code 412[i] plans). Under these plans, the individual annuity contract purchased for a plan participant guarantees a specific monthly pension equal to the amount stated in the plan for such participant but requires a periodic, level premium payment.

Single-Premium Deferred Annuity Contracts

While most individual (deferred) annuity contracts permit recurring premium or deposit payments, there are contracts that are referred to as **single-premium deferred annuity (SPDA) contracts.** The basic characteristic of SPDA contracts is that only one premium or deposit payment may be made. Also, these contracts generally have higher minimum premium requirements than recurring premium annuities. Early generations of SPDAs provided yearly guaranteed cash values and periodic income payments to the annuitant on such cash values. Some of those contracts simply provided guaranteed periodic income payments to the annuitants at maturity dates without commuted surrender values prior to the maturity dates.

SPDAs may offer a variety of investment options; however, most SPDAs are designed to offer only a guaranteed interest investment option. Usually, the interest rate credited under an SPDA is guaranteed for a longer period than in recurring premium annuity contracts (e.g., 3, 5, 7, or 10 years); because of such relatively longer guarantee periods (compared with the guarantees in recurring premium annuity contracts), withdrawals from or surrenders of SPDAs generally are not allowed without substantial penalties prior to the expiration of the guarantee period. An SPDA with a bail-out provision, on the other hand, allows its owner to surrender the contract for its total value prior to the expiration of the guarantee period, without penalties, but usually only if the interest rate guaranteed to new contracts issued subsequently is higher (by a specified percentage) than the interest rate guaranteed under such SPDA contract.

Insured Plans

For plans that wish to provide life insurance protection to participants prior to retirement, a separate life insurance policy may be purchased for each insurable participant. This type of funding usually is done for trusteed plans with the trustee as owner of the policies. One of the advantages of using life insurance as a funding vehicle under a plan is the ability of the employer to provide not only retirement benefits, but also a substantial death benefit (over and above the required qualified preretirement survivor annuity) to the beneficiaries of the participants in the event of death before retirement. In addition, if permanent types of individual life insurance policies are purchased, plan participants may be given the option to continue the life insurance coverage after ceasing participation in the plan due to termination of employment, disability, or retirement by making the policy part of the benefit distribution. However, individual life insurance policies generally are priced to reflect higher individual marketing costs. Accordingly, the use of individual life insurance policies under qualified plans is advisable only for small plans and not for group plans where marketing is done on a "mass" basis.

Under a fully insured pension plan, a retirement income type of life insurance policy is purchased by the plan for each plan participant. The retirement income policy is designed specifically by insurance companies to provide the proper ratio of insurance to income and to generate the cash values needed to provide a specified monthly income as of a given retirement age.[5]

---

[5] In order to conform to the Internal Revenue Service (IRS) incidental benefit rule for life insurance provided under a qualified plan, the face amount of the policy must never be greater than 100 times the monthly income generated under the policy when the policy's guaranteed annuity settlement rates are applied to the cash values.

Combination Plans

The term *combination plan* can be used to describe any funding arrangement that employs two or more different funding instruments. However, the term generally is used to describe those plans that use a combination of individual life insurance policies and other funds (usually referred to as "auxiliary funds" or "side funds"). The objective of the combination plan is to retain, in part, the guarantees and death benefits associated with individual life insurance policies, while at the same time obtaining a degree of flexibility and potentially better investment returns through the auxiliary fund. Combination plans generally allow the investment of auxiliary funds in any funding vehicle available to noninsured plans, such as group annuities, mutual funds, bank accounts, and so forth.

The mechanics of the plan involve the purchase of a life insurance policy on the life of an insurable participant. If the plan is a trustee- or employer-directed plan, then a life insurance policy is purchased for every insurable participant. In the case, however, of employee-directed plans, life insurance policies are purchased only for insurable participants who elect to be insured.[6]

If a plan participant is not insurable, then either an individual annuity contract is purchased or no individual contract is purchased at all. In the latter case, all of the benefits of such participant are funded through the auxiliary or side fund.

Under a fully insured or combination plan, each year that the life insurance policy is in effect, the insured participant is required to report for tax purposes the economic value of the life insurance protection as taxable income.[7]

At retirement, if annuitization is desired by an insured participant, the cash value of the life insurance policies and the funds in the auxiliary fund attributable to the retiring participant are withdrawn by the plan trustee(s) to be used either to purchase an immediate annuity contract or to be applied under the settlement options available in the life insurance policies.

Guaranteed Income Annuities

Guaranteed income annuities may be purchased with a lump sum amount for the benefit of a plan participant who is entitled to receive a distribution in the form of periodic payments either for the life of an annuitant or the joint life expectancies of the annuitant and a designated surviving annuitant or a designated (temporary) period of time.

---

[6] In order not to violate the IRS incidental benefit rule for life insurance provided under a qualified retirement plan, the amount of life insurance protection that may be purchased is limited. The face amount of the policy must either be no greater than 100 times the monthly expected pension benefits (as in the case of defined benefit plans), or the total premium payment to the participant's life insurance policy must be less than 50 percent of the total contribution to the plan for such participant if the life insurance policy is of a whole life type. If the life insurance is other than a whole life insurance policy (e.g., universal life, term, etc.), the total premium payment may not exceed 25 percent of the total contribution to the plan for the insured participant.

[7] This reportable income is the product of the face amount of the policy less the policy cash values, if any, and a one-year term rate per $1,000 of protection—often referred to as PS 58 cost. The term rate may be based on the insurer's one-year term rate applicable to its term insurance policy, if any, or based on a government table. The reported term cost, in the aggregate, becomes the cost basis for tax purposes to the insured participant for those distributions made under the life insurance policy.

For some contracts, the periodic payments are a fixed level amount that can never vary after such payments commence, except in the case of a participating contract—that is, they are subject to increase depending upon excess interest or dividends that an insurance company (usually a mutual insurance company) may declare in a given year. Fixed-income payments under an annuity contract generally are invested in the general account of the issuing insurance company.

Alternatively, there are guaranteed income annuities whose periodic payments may be variable. Some contracts may offer to vary the payments with changes in the cost of living. Others may offer participants the ability to invest the lump sum premium in a variety of separate accounts and, as the market value of the separate accounts changes, the periodic payments also will change.

Whether benefit payments are fixed or variable, they may be paid for life or only for a designated period of time.

Immediate Annuities

An immediate annuity generally is an individual annuity contract that provides payments for life at periodic intervals (e.g., monthly, quarterly, semiannually, or annually) to an annuitant or the joint life expectancies of the annuitant and a designated surviving annuitant.[8]

In any event, whether an immediate annuity contract is for a single life only or for joint lives, the income payments may be for as long as the annuitants are alive; for life but in no event less than a period certain (e.g., 5 years, 10 years, etc.); for life with refund certain (i.e., if death occurs before the aggregate of all periodic payments have exceeded the lump sum amount paid into the contract, the balance will be paid to the beneficiary of the annuitant); and so on.

Annuity Certain

For participants who wish to receive their benefits in installments or periodic payments but not for life, an *annuity certain contract* is available. Under this contract, the purchaser, depending upon the option available under the contract, may, for instance, choose a monthly payment that will last for only five years. This contract usually is suitable for individuals who wish to receive benefit payments for only a short period of time until other income payments from other sources commence.

Alternative Accumulation Instruments

There are basically no limits on the types of investments that a qualified pension or profit sharing plan can make. Accordingly, plans may invest in real properties (e.g., lands, buildings, and the like), stocks, bonds, mutual funds, insurance company contracts, gold, artwork, and so forth. However, under ERISA, only a portion of a plan's

---

[8] Except for some profit sharing plans that do not provide the payment of benefits in the form of life annuities, the law requires that the qualified joint and survivor annuity be the normal form for a married participant and his or her spouse unless an election is made to the contrary. For a single individual, the law requires that a life annuity be the normal form of payment.

assets may be invested in qualifying employer securities or qualifying employer real property. Moreover, in the choice of an investment, ERISA's fiduciary standards must be observed.

Qualifying Employer Real Property or Securities

Unless a plan is an eligible individual account plan (i.e., a profit sharing, stock bonus, thrift or savings, employee stock ownership, or certain money purchase plans grandfathered by ERISA), the plan generally may not hold qualifying employer securities or qualifying employer real property if the total market value of such assets exceeds 10 percent of the value of all the assets of the plan. Employer real property may be land, a building, a right to land such as a lease, and so on. Employer securities, on the other hand, generally are stocks or other marketable obligations issued by the employer or an affiliate of the employer.

Pooled Investment Trusts

Pooled investment trusts of a bank may be likened to separate accounts of an insurance company. These pooled investment funds that are offered by banks generally consist of a fixed-income or equity security fund in which the assets of many qualified retirement plans may be invested. To participate in such funds, the employer sponsoring the pension or profit sharing plan usually must adopt the trust established by the bank as part of the plan's own trust and must authorize investments in the bank's trust.

Mutual Funds

Mutual funds are publicly owned investment companies invested in diversified portfolios of securities. Shareholders are issued certificates as evidence of their ownership and participate proportionately in the earnings of the fund. Mutual funds may invest in a variety of portfolios, each of which is managed by a professional investment manager and has its own investment goals or objectives (similar to separate accounts issued by insurance companies).

Some insurance companies that prefer to invest and manage the assets of their separate accounts directly may purchase shares of mutual funds that become the underlying assets of their separate accounts.

Ancillary Services Provided with Investment Products

Shortly after the enactment of ERISA, many financial institutions, including insurance companies, that offered products as investment vehicles for pension and profit sharing plans felt the need to also offer plan administrative services. At that time, except for large consulting firms, there were few professional third-party record keepers or administrators who were ready to provide the services needed by pension and profit sharing plans. In addition, the most prevalent type of plan then in existence was the defined benefit plan. Over time, however, insurance companies providing such services encountered problems in terms of logistics and communications with the plan sponsors and/or trustees of the various plans being serviced. In addition, it became apparent that such services were too expensive for insurers to provide, resulting in increases in expenses and consequently decreases in profits to the insurance companies. Moreover, with the growth of efficient and affordable computers and software developed specifically for this industry, more and more third-party record-keepers and plan administrators became available to various plan sponsors. As a result, most insurance companies decided to stop providing record-keeping and plan administrative services to qualified pension and profit sharing plans.

When 401(k) plans started to become popular, the financial services industry was once again caught unprepared to provide adequate record-keeping services. Most third-party record keepers believed that the administrative and record-keeping services required by 401(k) plans were similar to the services being rendered to the traditional defined contribution plans. The 401(k) plan participants started to demand more up-to-date valuations of their account balances and the ability to make frequent changes to their investments or transfer funds from one investment option to another. As a result, financial institutions soon realized the need to offer allocated investment products with services designed specifically to meet the needs of individual plan participants. Ahead in this endeavor were the mutual fund companies plus a few insurance companies who had concentrated on offering their products and ancillary services to individual investors outside of retirement plans or as part of tax-sheltered investments, such as TDAs and IRAs. Thus, demand again increased for financial institutions, including insurance companies, to provide expanded plan record-keeping and administrative services.

Actuarial Services

Defined Benefit Plans

While the determination of contributions to a defined benefit plan always has required knowledge of some pension actuarial calculations, the actual processes involved were straightforward, if not relatively simple. Of course, this is no longer the case. Since 1974, when ERISA was first enacted, several laws and many IRS regulations, revenue rulings, and notices have been promulgated, in addition to regulations and guidelines issued by the PBGC and the DOL—all of which have added to the complexity of the present processes of valuing defined benefit plans. Complexity also has been greatly influenced by subsequent legislation that has been enacted since the passage of ERISA.

The plan actuary calculates the amount of contributions to be made to the trust using a set of actuarial assumptions and a specific actuarial cost method. While the law requires that the actuarial assumptions and methods chosen by any actuary should be based on his or her best estimate and judgment of the investment experience and future expectations of the plan, the IRS, based on recent changes in the law, requires certain additional processes to be performed, often resulting in lower tax-deductible contributions.

Based on the guidelines provided by the IRS as to what may be deemed both reasonable and acceptable, the plan's actuary chooses the actuarial assumptions to use, such as interest rates, mortality table, employee turnover, disability, salary scales, expenses, inflation, and/or cost-of-living increases. Projections of emerging liabilities (i.e., benefits to be paid out in the future) also are done. These projections enable the employer to foresee to a certain extent the cash flow (or contribution) needs of the plan for the current year, as well as the future.

Defined Contribution Plans

Calculating the amount of contributions to a defined contribution plan, on the other hand, is much simpler. With the marketplace trend toward defined contribution plans, the necessity for plan actuarial services becomes less important to many plan sponsors. Generally these services are not needed in the course of normal plan administration for a defined contribution plan such as a 401(k), 403(b), money purchase, or profit sharing plan. Although actuarial services may be necessary to test compliance with nondiscrimination requirements, particularly if the organization also sponsors a defined benefit plan, these services are much more likely to be contracted for with a benefit consulting firm rather than provided by the financial service provider.

Insurance Product Characteristics

With the growth of defined contribution plans and new product innovations, insurance companies began to offer investment vehicles that have become popular not only to relatively large plans but also to small plans. These products can be offered with considerable variation in contract terms and product characteristics. This variability permits products to be tailored to the individual needs of plan sponsors and allows the insurers to meet the needs of both larger and smaller clients.

Group Annuities

Guaranteed Interest

In the preceding section, the GIC, popular with many plan sponsors, was described. Also described were the stable value pooled funds, which enable the use of GICs and similar products by sponsors of smaller plans. In this section we describe the *guaranteed interest option,* available as an investment choice within a group annuity contract for sponsors of small, medium, and larger plans.

The popular accumulation product that continues to be offered by most medium-to-large insurance companies is the group annuity contract. Except for the fact that this type of contract provides guaranteed annuity settlement rates, it is primarily used as an investment vehicle to accumulate employer and employee contributions prior to distribution, similar to mutual funds and pooled investment funds discussed earlier in this chapter. The initial version of the group annuity contract consisted of only one type of investment option. In the past, many group annuity contracts offered only a guaranteed interest investment option in which the insurance company guaranteed principal plus interest. Investments made under such contracts usually become part of the general account of the insurance company. Most group annuity contracts guarantee a lifetime minimum interest rate (usually 3 to 4 percent) plus a more aggressive current interest rate that may be guaranteed for shorter periods (i.e., a month, quarter, year, etc.). This type of guaranteed interest investment option continues to be offered and remains popular even today. However, there are now many variations on this type of investment option.

Some guaranteed interest investment options have different types of guarantees depending upon when contributions are made to the contract. For instance, some group annuity contracts may declare an interest rate based on a portfolio method (i.e., based on the average interest rate earned on the total portfolio of investments in the insurance company's general account or on a specific segment of the general account designated for this type of contract). Other contracts may use the new money (or investment year) method (i.e., the interest rate credited by the insurance company is based on the differences in earned interest rates depending upon the year in which the investment is made). Thus, under the new money method of crediting interest, one interest rate may be guaranteed for deposits or investments made in a current period, such as a quarter or a calendar year, and other interest rates may be credited on funds attributable to investments made in prior periods or years. Still other contracts may combine both the new money and portfolio methods of declaring interest rates.

Expense Charges

Group annuity contracts impose front-end expense charges, administrative charges, and/or surrender charges, which are deducted from the investment funds of respective plans. Alternatively, there may be contracts that do not explicitly deduct any charges. Under this latter type of contract, expense and/or profit margins generally are factored into the interest rate declared by the insurance company. Most contracts have both explicit and implicit charges.

There are some contracts in which administrative charges are negotiable.[9] Generally, the administrative charges may vary to a certain extent depending upon the services that are required of the insurance company and/or the insurance agent or broker. In some situations, agents specify to their clients the types of services for which such clients will be charged a given service fee. The insurance company charges the agreed-upon fee. In turn, the agent receives a portion of the administrative fee collected by the insurance company as additional commission or compensation.

Market Value Adjustments

Instead of surrender charges, some contracts impose **market value adjustments** on withdrawals made from the contract. The method of arriving at the market value

---

[9] Very few contracts offered today have *front-end charges* (i.e., charges that are deducted immediately from the deposits remitted to the insurance company before they are invested). Administrative charges and *surrender charges,* however, are still fairly common. An administrative charge may be a flat percentage of assets or a set of percentages that declines as the size of the investment grows. Surrender charges may be imposed on all or only some types of withdrawals. Some surrender charges may be a flat percentage that is imposed over a given period of time (e.g., for the first 5 years, 10 years, etc.). Other surrender charges are based on a *class year method* (e.g., funds are grouped on the basis of when their initial investments were made, and different sets of surrender charge schedules and/or rates may be attributed to each group).

adjustment varies among different contracts. Some are based on the market values of certain bonds that are widely available in the market. Others are based on the behavior of interest rates, such as prime rates. The resulting market value adjustment may result in either a negative (a reduction) adjustment or a positive (an increase) adjustment to the value of the account. Most contracts, however, do not provide for increased or positive market value adjustments. There are also contracts that have both surrender charges and market value adjustments.

Installment Payout

In lieu of or in addition to surrender charges and market value adjustments there are group annuity contracts, which, upon their complete discontinuance, do not pay their surrender values immediately in one lump sum. Instead, if the contract is discontinued or surrendered by the contract holder, its value is paid out in installments over a period of time.

Separate Account Contract Characteristics

By far, the greatest innovation in group annuity contracts is the addition of other investment options consisting of separate accounts, as described earlier. Some group annuity contracts offer a guaranteed interest investment option and one or several separate accounts. Others may offer only separate accounts.

Each separate account consists of a portfolio or a group of securities that are actively managed by an investment manager based on a given specific objective. For instance, a separate account (generally referred to as a "common stock" account) may consist of common stocks whose primary objective is long-term growth of capital and increased income. Another may be a bond account that invests in debt securities issued by the U.S. government and/or other fixed-income securities and whose primary objective is high current income consistent with preservation or stability of capital. The assets allocated to a separate account are owned by the insurer. The contract holder has a contractual right to its proportionate share of this income or losses experienced by the separate account portfolio.

Number and Value of Separate Account Units

Each plan that invests in a separate account is assigned a number of units corresponding to the amount of investments made on a given date and the market value of a unit based on the performance of the separate account for that same date. Thus, the value of the total investments made by a plan in a separate account for any given day is equal to the number of units assigned to it times the unit value of the separate account for that day.

Investment Charges

Insurance companies also impose certain charges and expenses against the plan assets invested in separate accounts. These charges may be in the form of a direct reduction to the value of the funds invested or may be reflected in the unit value of the separate account. In addition, investment charges may consist of a single flat percentage applied to the fund or a set of percentages that declines as the size of the investment fund increases.

Investment Restrictions

In a group annuity contract that offers a guaranteed interest account plus a number of separate accounts, including fixed-income–type separate accounts (e.g., bond funds), there usually is a provision that limits the amount or frequency of transfers between the guaranteed interest account and the fixed-income–type separate accounts that have been determined to be competing funds. Generally, these limitations or restrictions are designed to protect the insurance company from losses due to adverse or antiselection (i.e., the tendency of the contract holder to take advantage of favorable but competing options). Because of this, it is not uncommon for group annuity contracts to restrict the amount of investments that can be made to or withdrawn from a guaranteed interest account.

Allocated and Unallocated

Prior to the advent of 401(k) plans and the resurgence of other types of defined contribution plans, group annuity contracts generally were unallocated. This was because most plans investing in such contracts were defined benefit plans whose assets were unallocated (i.e., not allocated among the plan participants). Under this type of funding arrangement, the employer, the plan trustee, or the plan's investment committee determines how the contributions to the plan should be invested. Such a plan also is referred to as an employer- or trustee-directed plan.

Today, many group annuity contracts are still offered on an unallocated basis. However, defined contribution plans have become the preferred type of plan among many employers and employees. Moreover, most employees prefer to direct the investments of their accounts. In addition, a growing number of employers prefer to minimize their fiduciary responsibilities under the plans. As a result, the preferred group annuity contract for such plans is one that is both allocated and employee- or participant-directed.

Annuitization

While the primary use of a group annuity contract is for investment of plan assets during the accumulation period (i.e., prior to the plan participants' retirement), it is nonetheless an annuity contract. As such, it not only provides investments, but it also can provide periodic payments, pensions to retired or terminated participants, and/or death benefits. Usually, the contract will provide a given set of guaranteed annuity settlement rates for the various types of benefit payments that may be offered (e.g., a period certain installment payment, single life annuity with or without period certain, a joint and survivor annuity with or without period certain, etc.).

Note that, unlike group deferred annuity contracts, which are seldom offered today, specific retirement benefits are not guaranteed during the accumulation period for any plan participant. Generally, the only guarantee under most group annuity contracts offered currently is the annuity settlement or purchase rate that may be applied to the account balance of a given participant at retirement.

Chapter Summary

- Funding instruments commonly are classified on the basis of whether contributions are allocated to provide benefits to specific employees prior to retirement or whether contributions are accumulated in an unallocated fund to provide benefits for employees when they retire.

- The major development in the group pension market in the last 15 years is the substantial increase in flexibility under insurance contracts. Insurers can design a contract to meet the particular needs of the employer. Employers seeking flexibility in investment policy and the timing of contribution payments prefer the unallocated type of contract in the group pension market. This demand for greater flexibility has been evident in the small-employer market as well, and insurers have accommodated this demand by making unallocated contracts available to relatively small firms.

- In the intervening decades since their introduction, group annuity contracts following the basic deposit administration concept have been offered in considerable variety, including immediate participation guarantee (IPG) and guaranteed investment contracts (GICs). These vary from product to product in both the degree of insurer guarantee and the degree of contract-holder discretion as to contributions, investment, and the mobility of funds. Some such contracts are, in fact, group annuity contracts in name only, functioning solely as investment vehicles, with the purchase of annuities a seldom-used contract holder's option. Most GICs and many separate account contracts are, in practice, investment-only contracts.

- The laws in most states restrict the investment of life insurance companies' general account assets in common stocks to a rather limited percentage—for instance, 5 percent of total company assets. This restriction has been historically common because of the fixed-dollar obligations and contractual guarantees provided in traditional life insurance and annuity products and, also, because of the relatively small surplus maintained by life insurance companies. With the advent of separate accounts, insurers now offer group clients a wide range of investment choices.

- Separate accounts were developed for two reasons: (1) to compete with trust fund plans in making equity investments available to employers for funding fixed-dollar plans and (2) to fund variable annuity plans. In the first case, many employers believe the long-term rate of return on equities will be greater than the return on fixed-income investments and the increased return will serve to reduce their cost of providing the fixed benefits promised under the plan. In the second case, equity-based variable annuities by definition generally require that the assets supporting these annuities be fully invested in equity securities.

- The deposit administration contract went a long way toward providing employers with the desired degree of flexibility not available under the traditional group annuity contract. In addition, the deposit administration contract offers certain interest and annuity rate guarantees. However, the insurance company is able to provide these guarantees only because it accumulates a contingency reserve and because it has control, through dividend computations, over the rate at which actuarial gains pertaining to guaranteed items are credited to the employer.

- In reaction to employer requests for an immediate reflection of actual experience under their contracts and their willingness to give up the guarantees of the deposit administration contract in return, insurance companies developed the immediate participation guarantee (IPG) contract. Under an IPG contract, the employer's account is credited with the contributions received during the contract period plus its share of actual investment income for the year. The account is charged with all the expenses associated with the particular contract. As issued by many insurance companies, these contracts provide that all benefits, including annuity payments, are charged directly against the account as they are paid. In other words, annuities are not actually purchased for participants at retirement date, as is the practice under deposit administration contracts.

• In 1993, the U.S. Supreme Court issued its ruling in *John Hancock Mutual Life Insurance Co. v. Harris Trust & Savings Bank.* The court held that "free funds" held in John Hancock's general account under an IPG contract issued to Harris Trust as trustee of the Sperry Rand Corporation (now Unisys Corporation) pension plan were "plan assets" under ERISA and, thus, Hancock was a fiduciary of those assets and subject to all the restrictions and rules of ERISA fiduciaries. The court held that the contract in question was not a "guaranteed benefit policy," as defined in ERISA. Assets backing guaranteed benefit policies will not be deemed to be "plan assets."

Key Terms

allocated (fund), p. *456*
deposit administration
   contract, p. *457*
general account
   investments, p. *457*
group deferred annuity
   contract, p. *456*
guaranteed investment
   contract (GIC), p. *464*

immediate participation
   guarantee (IPG) contract,
   p. *459*
market value adjustments,
   p. *476*
separate accounts, p. *457*
single-premium deferred
   annuity (SPDA)
   contracts, p. *470*

single-premium group
   annuity contracts, p. *463*
stable value pooled funds,
   p. *468*
synthetic GIC, p. *465*
unallocated fund, p. *456*

Questions for Review

1. Explain what guarantees insurers generally provided when insurance products were first used as pension funding instruments.
2. Distinguish between allocated and unallocated funding instruments.
3. What are the advantages of using a combination plan?
4. Why was the advent of separate accounts important to insurers?
5. Describe the marketplace forces and the time periods when particular funding instruments have been preferred.
6. Compare deposit administration contracts with group deferred annuity contracts with respect to the allocation of employer contributions.
7. What flexibility does an employer have with respect to annual contributions under a deposit administration plan?
8. Contrast the deposit administration contract with a group immediate participation guarantee (IPG) contract with respect to insurance company guarantees.
9. How does a guaranteed investment contract (GIC) differ from a synthetic GIC?

Questions for Discussion

1. Discuss how an employer would decide between an insured funding arrangement and a self-insured, or trust fund, arrangement.

2. Discuss how an employer would decide among the various alternative insured funding arrangements.

3. Discuss how an insurance company would price the various guarantees it offers employers through its contracts.

Resources for Further Study

Amoroso, Vincent. "Costing and Funding Retirement Benefits." In *The Handbook of Employee Benefits.* 5th ed. Jerry S. Rosenbloom, ed. New York: McGraw-Hill, 2001.

Balestrieri, Anthony G. "New GIC Products—and How to Judge Quality." *Pension Management,* October 1995, pp. 28–30.

Walker, Kenneth L. *Guaranteed Investment Contracts.* Burr Ridge, IL: Irwin Professional Publishing, 1989.

Chapter 26

Employers' Accounting for Pensions

After studying this chapter you should be able to:

- Chronicle the rationale for the development of pension accounting standards by the accounting profession.

- Contrast differences between actuarial funding methods and pension accounting standards.

- Describe the calculation of net periodic pension cost under FASB 87.

- Explain the required disclosures that an employer sponsoring a defined benefit pension plan must make as amended by FASB 132.

- Discuss limitations on interest rate assumptions used in calculating both the assumed rates at which the pension benefit obligations may be settled and the assumed rates for the return on plan assets.

- Summarize the major provisions of both FASB 87 and FASB 88 as amended by FASB 132.

Accounting procedures for pension plans consist of various components, each of which is controlled by a separate Financial Accounting Standards Board (FASB) statement. FASB Statement No. 35, *Accounting and Reporting by Defined Benefit Pension Plans* (FASB 35), establishes standards for financial accounting and reporting for the annual financial statement of a defined benefit pension plan. FASB Statement No. 87, *Employers' Accounting for Pensions* (FASB 87), establishes standards for financial reporting and accounting for an employer that offers pension benefits to its employees.[1] Closely

---

[1] In FASB parlance, pension benefits are defined as periodic (usually monthly) payments made pursuant to the terms of the pension plan to a person who has retired from employment or to that person's beneficiary.

related to FASB 87, FASB Statement No. 88, *Employers' Accounting for Settlements and Curtailment of Defined Benefit Pension Plans and for Termination Benefits* (FASB 88), establishes standards for an employer's accounting for settlement of defined benefit pension obligations, for curtailment of a defined benefit pension plan, and for termination benefits.

In February of 1998, the FASB issued Statement No. 132, *Employers' Disclosures about Pensions and Other Postretirement Benefits* (FASB 132). FASB 132 supersedes the disclosure requirements in FASB Nos. 87, 88, and 106 (mentioned on p. 486) for fiscal years beginning after December 15, 1997. FASB 132 deals only with disclosure requirements for pensions and other postretirement benefits, but does not alter measurement and recognition procedures outlined in the earlier FASBs. FASB 132 requires organizations to disclose additional information previously not required and eliminates some disclosure requirements no longer considered to be useful.

This chapter focuses primarily on the consequences of sponsoring a single-employer pension plan on the employer's financial statements. Therefore, the major emphasis is on FASB 87[2] and 88 (as updated by FASB 132). A brief discussion of the evolution of pension accounting standards is presented first, and then the FASB statements are described in detail and their impact on pension plan sponsors is analyzed.

The Evolution of Pension Accounting Standards

Although various accounting conventions were applied to pension plans prior to 1966,[3] this was an era in which the accounting profession exercised little control over pension accounting while the government exercised considerable control over pension funding. As a result, pension accounting during this time has been characterized as essentially a discretionary system that typically resulted in the amount of pension expense recorded for a year being equal to the employer's pension contribution.

Since 1966, employer pension accounting has been governed by Accounting Principles Board Opinion No. 8, *Accounting for the Cost of Pension Plans* (APB 8). This pronouncement eliminated the previous discretionary method of accounting for pension costs and replaced it with a methodology that established a range of minimum and maximum annual costs based on a number of approved actuarial cost methods. For a variety of reasons, however, the appropriateness of this standard has been questioned since the passage of the Employee Retirement Income Security Act in 1974. In that year, the FASB added two pension projects to its agenda: one to cover accounting principles for the pension plan itself and another to cover accounting by employers for pensions.

---

[2] Although they are beyond the scope of this chapter, FASB 87 also contains provisions treating multiemployer plans, non–U.S. pension plans, and business combinations.

[3] For an interesting historical analysis of the evolving relationship between the employer contributions and the charge for pension expense, see E. L. Hicks and C. L. Trowbridge, *Employer Accounting for Pensions: An Analysis of the Financial Accounting Standards Board's Preliminary Views and Exposure Draft* (Burr Ridge, IL: Richard D. Irwin for the Pension Research Council, 1985), pp. 16–18.

As a result of these projects, FASB 35 and FASB Statement No. 36, *Disclosure of Pension Information* (FASB 36), were issued in 1980. FASB 35 established rules governing the measurement and reporting of plan assets and plan obligations by the plan itself. Under this pronouncement, plan assets typically must be measured at market value, while plan liabilities (both vested and nonvested) must be measured on a basis that ignores future salary progression. FASB 36, which established rules governing how the employing firm must disclose plan assets and liabilities on its financial statements, required a measurement procedure compatible with FASB 35. Although FASB 36 was heralded by some financial analysts as a significant improvement in disclosure, it was intended to serve only as a stopgap measure until the more contentious issues raised in response to the perceived limitations for APB 8 could be resolved.

FASB 87

Even with the modifications imposed by FASB 36, the APB 8 approach to pension accounting was criticized for the following reasons:

1. Pension costs were not comparable from one company to another.

2. Pension costs were not consistent from period to period for the same company.

3. Significant pension obligations and assets were not recognized in the body of the financial statements (although FASB 36 did require footnote disclosure in the balance sheet).

The board had four basic objectives in the preparation of FASB 87. The first objective was to provide a measure of pension cost that better reflects the terms of the plan and recognizes the cost of the employee's pension over his or her service with the employer. As shown in Chapter 15, many of the actuarial cost methods chosen for funding purposes allocate pension contributions as a percentage of payroll. Of the actuarial cost methods acceptable for minimum funding purposes, only the accrued benefit cost method determines an amount that is based directly upon benefits accrued to the valuation date. Second, the board wanted to provide a more comparable measure of pension cost. Not only were pension plan sponsors able to choose from a number of acceptable actuarial cost methods, but, prior to 1987, they were also given a degree of flexibility in choosing the amortization period for supplemental liabilities (in essence, anywhere from 10 to 30 years). Third, it desired to have disclosures that would allow users to understand the effect of the employer's undertaking. Previous pension accounting standards allowed the sponsor to record one net amount for the pension expense. It was believed that disclosure of the individual components of this amount would significantly assist users in understanding the economic events that occurred. In theory, those disclosures also would make it easier to understand why the reported amount changed from period to period, especially when a large cost was offset by a large revenue to produce a relatively small net reported amount. Finally, as mentioned above, there was a desire to improve reporting of financial position. This relates primarily to the inclusion of underfunded pension liabilities on the balance sheet of the sponsor.

The new accounting requirements mandated by FASB 87 were phased in with a two-step process. The income statement (expense) provisions were applied for years beginning after December 15, 1986, while the balance sheet (liability) provisions were applied for years beginning after December 15, 1988.

Scope

FASB 87 definitely excludes postretirement health care and life insurance benefits. Although these benefits were originally part of the board's project on accounting for pension benefits, it has since been spun off into a separate endeavor and is currently controlled by FASB Statement No. 106, *Employers' Accounting for Postretirement Benefits Other than Pensions.*

Use of Reasonable Approximations

FASB 87 is intended to specify accounting objectives and results, rather than specific computational means of obtaining those results. Pension plan sponsors are allowed to use shortcuts if they will not result in material differences from the results of a detailed application.

Single-Employer Defined Benefit Pension Plans

The most significant elements of FASB 87 involve an employer's accounting for a single-employer defined benefit pension plan. After describing the basic elements of pension accounting, this section explains the recognition procedures for the net periodic pension cost and the pension liabilities and assets. Certain details concerning measurement procedures are demonstrated, and the new disclosure requirements are discussed. Finally, certain miscellaneous provisions are presented.

Basic Elements of Pension Accounting

It is important to note that FASB 87 does not apply to the government constraints on minimum or maximum (deductible) funding. Although the accrued benefit cost method (or projected unit credit method in FASB parlance) mandated for use in computing the net periodic pension cost is one of the acceptable actuarial cost methods under Internal Revenue Code Section 412, it is highly likely that the FASB 87 net periodic pension cost will differ substantially from the ERISA minimum funding amount. Furthermore, it is important to understand that FASB 87 incorporates two different definitions of the sponsor's pension liability. The **projected benefit obligation** is the amount used to measure pension cost and is defined as the actuarial present value of all benefits attributed by the plan's benefit formula to employee service rendered prior to that date, assuming future salary levels if the formula is based on future compensation.[4] In contrast, the **accumulated benefit obligation** is used for balance sheet recognition. It is determined in the same manner as the projected benefit obligation but without salary assumptions. Therefore,

---

[4] Turnover and mortality also are assumed.

for those plans with nonpay-related pension benefit formulas, the projected benefit obligation and the accumulated benefit obligation are the same.

FASB 132 eliminated the prior disclosure requirement that there be separate identification of the accumulated and vested benefit obligation components of the projected benefit obligation. FASB 132 also eliminated the prior requirement that portions of the accumulated benefit obligation attributable to retirees, other fully eligible participants, and other active plan participants be separately identified.

Recognition of Net Periodic Pension Cost

Under FASB 87, the net periodic pension cost is made up of six components:

1. Service cost.

2. Interest cost.

3. Actual return on plan assets, if any.

4. Amortization of unrecognized prior service cost, if any.

5. Gain or loss to the extent recognized.

6. Amortization of the unrecognized net asset or obligation existing at the date of the initial application of FASB 87.

Service cost is the actuarial present value of benefits attributed by the pension benefit formula to employee service during that period.[5] **Interest cost** is the increase in the projected benefit obligation due to the passage of time. This can be thought of as simply the accrual of interest on a present value or discounted amount. The actual return on plan assets is based on the fair value of plan assets at the beginning and the end of the period, adjusted for contributions and benefit payments.[6]

The prior service cost component for accounting purposes is conceptually similar to the amortization of supplemental liability described in Chapter 15; however, the allocation procedure does not result in a level dollar amount assigned to each year in the amortization period. Under FASB 87, the cost of retroactive benefits is the increase in the projected benefit obligation at the date of the amendment. This cost is then amortized by assigning an equal amount to each future period of service for each employee active at the date of the amendment who is expected to receive benefits under the plan. Once determined, the amortization period does not change for that amendment.

The basic notion represented by this new amortization procedure can be illustrated by the following simple example. Assume that a defined benefit pension plan is amended on January 1, 2001, generating an unrecognized prior service

---

[5] There are obvious similarities between this component of net periodic pension cost under FASB 87 and the normal cost under the accrued benefit cost method described in Chapter 15.

[6] While the return is titled "actual" for disclosure purposes, FASB 87 states that the difference between the actual and expected return on plan assets must be accounted for as a part of the gain or loss component of pension expense. The net result of this treatment is that the expected return on plan assets is used to calculate pension cost for the period.

cost of $100,000. At that time, the employer has three employees who are expected to receive benefits under the plan. Employee A is expected to leave after one year, employee B after two years, and employee C after three years. The expected years of service from this employee population in 2001 would be equal to three (one year from all three employees); in 2002 there would be only two expected years of service (since employee A would already have left); and in 2003 there would be only one expected year of service. Summing these figures gives an aggregate expected years of future service of six (three from 2001, plus two from 2002, plus one from 2003).

The amortization rate for each year is determined by taking the ratio of expected years of service for that year and dividing it by the aggregate expected years of service (six). The amortization rate for the year is then multiplied by the increase in the projected benefit obligation resulting from the plan amendment to determine the amortization for the year. In this example, the 2001 amortization amount would be $100,000 \times (3 \div 6) = \$50,000$. The amount in 2002 would be $100,000 \times (2 \div 6) = \$33,333$; in 2003, the amount would be $100,000 \times (1 \div 6) = \$16,667$.

In certain cases, the amortization of prior service cost must be accelerated. A history of regular plan amendments may indicate that the period during which the employer expects to realize benefits (through employee goodwill, etc.) for an amendment is shorter than the remaining service period. This is likely to transpire in collective bargaining agreements with flat dollar plans in which the dollar amount is renegotiated upward every several years.[7]

The fifth component of net periodic pension cost (gain or loss) results from changes in either the projected benefit obligation or the plan assets. These changes result either from experience different from that assumed or from changes in assumptions. Gains and losses include both realized and unrealized gains and losses. Asset gains and losses are equal to the difference between the actual return on assets during a period and the expected return on assets for that period. The expected return on plan assets is determined from the expected long-term rate of return on plan assets and the market-related value of plan assets.[8] Amortization of unrecognized net gain or loss is included as a component of net pension cost if, at the beginning of the year, the unrecognized net gain or loss (excluding asset gains and losses not yet reflected in market-related value) exceeds a so-called corridor amount. This corridor was designed to minimize the volatility in pension expense that otherwise would result from application of the new accounting convention and is defined as 10 percent of the greater of the projected benefit obligation or the market-related value of plan assets. The amortization for the year will be equal to the amount of unrecognized gain or loss in excess of the corridor divided by the average remaining service period of active employees expected to receive benefits under the plan.

---

[7] It also is possible for a plan amendment to decrease the projected benefit obligation. In that case, the reduction must be used to reduce any existing unrecognized prior service cost, and the excess, if any, must be amortized on the same basis as the cost of benefit increases.

[8] The market-related value of assets must be either fair value or a calculated value that recognizes change in fair value in a systematic and rational manner over not more than five years.

In addition to the amortization of the unrecognized net gain or loss from previous periods, the overall gain or loss component of net periodic pension cost also consists of the difference between the actual return on plan assets and the expected return on plan assets.

The final component of net periodic pension cost is the amortization of the unrecognized net asset or obligation existing at the date of initial application of FASB 87. At the time the plan sponsor first applies FASB 87, the projected benefit obligation and the fair market value of plan assets must be determined.[9] The difference between these two amounts is then amortized on a straight-line basis over the average remaining service period of employees expected to receive benefits under the plan. There are two exceptions to this general rule, though. First, if the average remaining service period is less than 15 years, the employer may elect to use a 15-year period. Second, if all, or almost all, of a plan's participants are inactive, the employer must use the inactive participant's average remaining life expectancy period instead.

Recognition of Liabilities and Assets

Under FASB 87, a balance sheet entry is made if there is a discrepancy between net periodic pension cost and employer contributions. Specifically, a liability (unfunded accrued pension cost) is recognized if net periodic pension cost exceeds employer contributions, and an asset (prepaid pension cost) is recognized if net periodic pension cost is less than employer contributions. Moreover, a balance sheet entry is made if the firm sponsors an "underfunded" plan. If the accumulated benefit obligation is greater than plan assets, employers must recognize a liability (including unfunded accrued pension cost) equal to the unfunded accumulated benefit obligation. It should be noted, however, that the treatment is not symmetrical: FASB 87 does not permit recognition of a net asset if plan assets are greater than the accumulated benefit obligation.

If an additional liability is recognized, an equal amount is recognized on the balance sheet as an intangible asset, provided that the asset recognized does not exceed the amount of unrecognized prior service cost. In the case where the additional liability is greater than the unrecognized prior service cost, the excess is reported as a reduction of equity, net of any tax benefits.

Measurement of Cost and Obligations

FASB 87 provides much more guidance than its predecessors with respect to the interest rate assumptions chosen by the plan sponsor. In essence, the interest rate assumption used for funding calculations actually has two separate elements in the pension accounting context. The first is the assumed discount rate, which must reflect the rates at which the pension benefit could be settled effectively. FASB 87 states that it is appropriate to consider rates used to price annuity contracts

---

[9] Technically, this amount will be increased by any previously recognized unfunded accrued pension cost and reduced by any previously recognized prepaid pension cost. These terms are defined in the next paragraph.

in settling the pension obligation (including the rates used by the Pension Benefit Guaranty Corporation to value the liabilities of terminating pension plans). Rates of return on high-quality, fixed-income investments currently available and expected to be available during the period to maturity of the pension benefits also may be considered.

The second assumption deals with the expected long-term rate of return on plan assets and is not necessarily equal to the discount rate assumption. FASB 87 states that this assumption must reflect the average rate of earnings expected on the funds invested or to be invested to provide for the benefits included in the projected benefit obligation. This will necessitate an assumption as to the rate of return available both for reinvestment and for the current assets.

Disclosures

An employer sponsoring a defined benefit pension plan must disclose the following:[10]

1. A reporting of the beginning of period and ending of period balances for the benefit obligation. This reporting must detail service cost, interest cost, actuarial gains and losses, participant contributions, benefits paid, plan amendments, and effects of special items such as the effects of business combinations and divestitures, foreign currency exchange rate fluctuations, and any settlements, curtailments, or special termination benefits.

2. The amount of net periodic pension cost for the period, showing separately prior service cost, recognized gains and losses, any unrecognized transition obligation, and any gain or loss because of a settlement or curtailment.

3. A schedule reconciling the beginning of period and ending of period balances for the fair value of plan assets. This reporting must detail employer contributions, participant contributions, benefits paid, actual return on plan assets, effects of business combinations and divestitures, effects of foreign currency exchange rate fluctuations, and settlements.

4. A schedule reconciling the funded status of the plan with financial statement reporting. This schedule must detail any unamortized prior service cost, any unrecognized gain or loss, any unamortized net obligation or net asset existing at the initial adoption of FASB 87, the net pension prepaid asset or accrued liability, and any intangible asset and the amount of accumulated other comprehensive income.

5. The weighted-average assumed discount rate and rate of compensation increase (if applicable) used to measure the projected benefit obligation and the weighted-average expected long-term rate of return on plan assets.

6. The amount included in other comprehensive income resulting from a change in the minimum pension liability.

---

[10] Requirements as amended by FASB 132.

7. Amounts resulting from any significant transactions between the plan, the employer, and any related parties. If applicable, the amounts and types of securities of the employer and related parties included in plan assets and the approximate amount of annual benefits for employees and retirees covered by annuity contracts issued by the employer and related parties. Also, if applicable, the alternative amortization methods used to amortize prior service cost and gains or losses and the existence and nature of commitment beyond the written terms of the plan.

8. A past practice or history of regular benefit increases.

9. Amounts resulting from termination benefits.

An explanation of any changes in the benefit obligation or plan assets that is not made evident by any of the other disclosures required by FASB 87 as amended by FASB 132.

Employers with Two or More Plans

If an employer sponsored more than one defined benefit pension plan, all provisions of FASB 87 applied to each plan separately. Moreover, unless an employer had a right to use the assets of one plan to pay the benefits of another plan, the excess assets of an overfunded plan could not offset the additional liability for unfunded accumulated benefit obligations of another plan sponsored by the same company.

FASB 132 revised disclosure requirements and permitted combined disclosures for plans with assets in excess of the accumulated benefit obligation and those with accumulated benefit obligations in excess of plan assets. However, separate disclosure must be made of the benefit obligations and fair value of plan assets for plans with benefit obligations in excess of plan assets. Also, foreign plans may not be combined with U.S. plans when the benefit obligations of the foreign plans are significant relative to the total benefit obligation and those plans use significantly different plan assumptions. Also, prepaid benefit costs and accrued benefit obligations must be separately disclosed in the balance sheet.

Contracts with Insurance Companies

Benefits covered by annuity contracts are excluded from the projected benefit obligation and the accumulated benefit obligation. If the benefits are covered by nonparticipating annuity contracts, the cost of the contract determines the service cost component of net periodic pension cost for that period. If participating annuity contracts are used, the excess premium (over that available from a nonparticipating annuity contract) must be recognized as an asset and amortized systematically over the expected dividend period under the contract.

Defined Contribution Plans

Under FASB 87, the net periodic pension cost for the typical defined contribution plan is the contribution called for in that period. However, if a plan calls for contributions for periods after an individual retires or terminates, the estimated costs must be accrued during the employee's service period. An employer that sponsors one or more defined contribution plans must disclose the following separately from its defined benefit plan disclosures:

1. The nature and effect of significant matters affecting comparability of information for all periods presented. (FASB 132 amended this requirement for the description of the nature and effect of any significant changes during the period affecting comparability, noting such items as a change in the rate of employer contributions, a business combination, or a divestiture.)

2. The amount of cost recognized during the period.

FASB 88

FASB 88 defines one event (a settlement) that requires immediate recognition of previously unrecognized gains and losses and another event (a curtailment) that requires immediate recognition of previously unrecognized prior service cost. It also changes the method of computing gains or losses recognized on asset reversions and specifies special transition rules for companies that have undergone previous asset reversions. Companies were required to adopt FASB 87 and 88 simultaneously.

Definitions

Before discussing the mechanics behind these accounting procedures, it is important to note the board's interpretation of the following terms.

Settlement

A **settlement** is defined as a transaction that is an irrevocable action, relieves the employer of primary responsibility for a projected benefit obligation, and eliminates significant risks related to the obligation and the assets used to effect the settlement. Examples of settlements include making lump sum cash payments to plan participants in exchange for their rights to receive specified pension benefits and purchasing non-participating annuity contracts to cover vested benefits. For an example of a transaction that would *not* qualify as a settlement, assume that a sponsor invests in a portfolio of high-quality, fixed-income securities with principal and interest payment dates similar to the estimated payment dates of benefits. Note that in this case, the decision can be reversed, and such a strategy does not relieve the employer of primary responsibility for an obligation, nor does it eliminate significant risks related to the obligation.

Annuity Contract

If the substance of a participating annuity contract is such that the employer remains subject to most of the risks and rewards associated with the obligation covered or the assets transferred to the insurance company, the purchase of the contract does not constitute a settlement.

Curtailment

A **curtailment** is an event that significantly reduces the expected years of future service of present employees or eliminates for a significant number of employees the accrual of defined benefits for some or all of their future services. Examples of a curtailment include the termination of employees' services earlier than expected (e.g., closing a facility) and termination or suspension of a plan so that employees do not earn additional defined benefits for future services.

Accounting for Settlement of the Pension Obligation

The maximum gain or loss in this case is the unrecognized net gain or loss plus any remaining unrecognized net asset existing at the date of initial application of FASB 87.[11] The entire maximum amount is recognized in earnings only if the entire projected benefit obligation is settled. However, if only part of the projected benefit obligation is settled, the employer will recognize in earnings a pro rata portion of the maximum amount equal to the percentage reduction in the projected benefit obligation.

If a participating annuity contract is purchased, the maximum gain is reduced by the cost of the participation right. Also, a provision is included to allow flexibility for employers who annually purchase annuities as a funding vehicle. If the cost of all settlements in a year is less than or equal to the sum of the service cost and interest cost components of the net periodic pension cost for the plan for the year, gain or loss recognition is permitted but not required for those settlements. However, the accounting policy adopted must be applied consistently from year to year.

Accounting for a Plan Curtailment

Under FASB 88, the unrecognized prior service cost associated with years of service no longer expected to be rendered as the result of a curtailment is treated as a loss. This includes the cost of retroactive plan amendments and any remaining unrecognized net obligation existing at the date of initial application of FASB 87.

It should be noted that the projected benefit obligation may be decreased or increased by a curtailment. To the extent that such a gain exceeds any unrecognized net loss (or the entire gain, if an unrecognized net gain exists), it is a curtailment gain. To the extent that such a loss exceeds any unrecognized net gain (or the entire loss, if any unrecognized net loss exists), it is a curtailment loss. Any remaining unrecognized net asset existing at the date of initial application of FASB 87 is treated as an unrecognized net gain and is combined with the unrecognized net gain or loss arising subsequent to transition to FASB 87.

Special Transition Rules for a Reversion

Employers that entered into a reversion before the effective date of FASB 88 must recognize a gain as the cumulative effect of a change in accounting principle at the time of initial application of FASB 87. The amount of gain recognized is the lesser of:

1. The unamortized amount related to the asset reversion.

2. Any unrecognized net asset for the plan (or the successor plan) existing at the time of transition.

---

[11] This will include any net gain or loss first measured at the time of settlement. This may happen if the insurance company uses an interest rate assumption for determining the annuity purchase price that differs from the discount rate assumed by the employer.

Chapter Summary

- Accounting procedures for pension plans consist of various components, each of which is controlled by a separate Financial Accounting Standards Board (FASB) statement. FASB Statement No. 35, *Accounting and Reporting by Defined Benefit Pension Plans* (FASB 35), establishes standards for financial accounting and reporting for the annual financial statement of a defined benefit pension plan. FASB Statement No. 87, *Employers' Accounting for Pensions* (FASB 87), establishes standards for financial reporting and accounting for an employer that offers pension benefits to its employees. Closely related to FASB 87, FASB Statement No. 88, *Employers' Accounting for Settlements and Curtailment of Defined Benefit Pension Plans and for Termination Benefits* (FASB 88), establishes standards for an employer's accounting for settlement of defined benefit pension obligations, for curtailment of a defined benefit pension plan, and for termination benefits.

- In February of 1998, the FASB issued Statement No. 132, *Employers' Disclosures about Pensions and Other Postretirement Benefits* (FASB 132). FASB 132 supersedes the disclosure requirements in FASB Nos. 87, 88, and 106 for fiscal years beginning after December 15, 1997. FASB 132 deals only with disclosure requirements for pensions and other postretirement benefits, but does not alter measurement and recognition procedures outlined in the earlier FASBs. FASB 132 requires organizations to disclose additional information previously not required and eliminates some disclosure requirements no longer considered to be useful.

- The standards board had four basic objectives in the preparation of FASB 87. The first objective was to provide a measure of pension cost that better reflects the terms of the plan and recognizes the cost of the employee's pension over his or her service with the employer. Second, the board wanted to provide a more comparable measure of pension cost. Third, it desired to have disclosures that would allow users to understand the effect of the employer's undertaking. This resulted in the disclosure of the individual component parts of net periodic pension cost. Finally, as mentioned above, there was a desire to improve reporting of financial position. This relates primarily to the inclusion of underfunded pension liabilities on the balance sheet of the sponsor.

- It is important to note that FASB 87 does not apply to the government constraints on minimum or maximum (deductible) funding. Although the accrued benefit cost method (or projected unit credit method in FASB parlance) mandated for use in computing the net periodic pension cost is one of the acceptable actuarial cost methods under IRC Section 412, it is highly likely that the FASB 87 net periodic pension cost will differ substantially from the ERISA minimum funding amount.

- It is important to understand that FASB 87 incorporates two different definitions of the sponsor's pension liability. The projected benefit obligation is the amount used to measure pension cost and is defined as the actuarial present value of all benefits attributed by the plan's benefit formula to employee service rendered prior to that date, assuming future salary levels if the formula is based on future compensation. In contrast, the accumulated benefit obligation is used for balance sheet recognition. It is determined in the same manner as the projected benefit obligation but without salary assumptions. Therefore, for those plans with nonpay-related pension benefit formulas, the projected benefit obligation and the accumulated benefit obligation are the same.

- Under FASB 87, the net periodic pension cost is made up of six components: (1) service cost; (2) interest cost; (3) actual return on plan assets, if any; (4) amortization of unrecognized prior service cost, if any; (5) gain or loss to the extent recognized; and (6) amortization of the unrecognized net asset or obligation existing at the date of the initial application of FASB 87.

- Service cost is the actuarial present value of benefits attributed by the pension benefit formula to employee service during that period.

- Interest cost is the increase in the projected benefit obligation due to the passage of time. This can be thought of as simply the accrual of interest on a present value or discounted amount. The actual return on plan assets is based on the fair value of plan assets at the beginning and the end of the period, adjusted for contributions and benefit payments.

- The prior service cost component for accounting purposes is conceptually similar to the amortization of supplemental liability described in Chapter 15; however, the allocation procedure does not result in a level dollar amount assigned to each year in the amortization period. Under FASB 87, the cost of retroactive benefits is the increase in the projected benefit obligation at the date of the amendment. This cost is then amortized by assigning an equal amount to each future period of service for each employee active at the date of the amendment who is expected to receive benefits under the plan. Once determined, the amortization period does not change for that amendment.

- The fifth component of net periodic pension cost (gain or loss) results from changes in either the projected benefit obligation or plan assets. These changes result either from experience different from that assumed or from changes in assumptions. Gains and losses include both realized and unrealized gains and losses. Asset gains and losses are equal to the difference between the actual return on assets during a period and the expected return on assets for that period. The expected return on plan assets is determined from the expected long-term rate of return on plan assets and the market-related value of plan assets.

- FASB 87 provides much more guidance than its predecessors with respect to the interest rate assumptions chosen by the plan sponsor. In essence, the interest rate assumption used for funding calculations actually has two separate elements in the pension accounting context. The first is the assumed discount rate, which must reflect the rates at which the pension benefit could be settled effectively. FASB 87 states that it is appropriate to consider rates used to price annuity contracts to settle the pension obligation (including the rates used by the PBGC to value the liabilities of terminating pension plans). Rates of return on high-quality, fixed-income investments currently available and expected to be available during the period to maturity of the pension benefits also may be considered. The second assumption deals with the expected long-term rate of return on plan assets and is not necessarily equal to the discount rate assumption. FASB 87 states that this assumption must reflect the average rate of earnings expected on the funds invested or to be invested to provide for the benefits included in the projected benefit obligation. This will necessitate an assumption as to the rate of return available both for reinvestment and for the current assets.

Key Terms

accumulated benefit obligation, p. *486*	interest cost, p. *487*	service cost, p. *487*
curtailment, p. *492*	projected benefit obligation, p. *486*	settlement, p. *492*

Questions for Review

1. Describe the accounting conventions used for pension plans prior to FASB 87.
2. What were the limitations of the pre–FASB 87 accounting conventions for pension plans?
3. Explain the scope of FASB 87 as subsequently amended by FASB 132.
4. Explain the difference between accumulated benefit obligation and projected benefit obligation.
5. Identify the six components of pension expense under FASB 87.
6. Under what circumstances must a pension plan sponsor recognize a pension liability on its balance sheet?
7. What types of interest rate assumptions are required under FASB 87?
8. Describe how contracts with insurance companies are handled under FASB 87.
9. Describe the FASB 88 accounting treatment for settlement of pension obligations.
10. Describe the FASB 88 accounting treatment for plan curtailments.

Questions for Discussion

1. Discuss the likely impact of FASB 87 on funding levels for defined benefit pension plans.
2. Discuss the likely impact of FASB 87 on asset allocation decisions for defined benefit pension plans.
3. Assume an employer has an overfunded defined benefit pension plan and is currently considering the merits of terminating the plan and replacing it with a defined contribution pension plan. Discuss how FASB 88 might influence the employer's decision.

Resources for Further Study

Decker, William E.; and Kenneth E. Dakdduk. "Employers' Accounting for Pension Costs." In *The Handbook of Employee Benefits.* 5th ed. Jerry S. Rosenbloom, ed. New York: McGraw-Hill, 2001.

Doran, Donald A.; and JulieAnn Verrekia. "Employee Benefit Plan Accounting and Reporting." In *The Handbook of Employee Benefits.* 5th ed. Jerry S. Rosenbloom, ed. New York: McGraw-Hill, 2001.

Luecke, Randall W.; and Chet Andrzejewski. "FASB 132: What Companies Must Disclose." *Journal of Accountancy* 86, no. 3 (September 1998).

http://accounting.rutgers.edu/raw/fasb—website of the Financial Accounting Standards Board (FASB).

www.aicpa.org—website of the American Institute of Certified Public Accountants.

Chapter 27

Taxation of Distributions

After studying this chapter you should be able to:

- Determine the taxes imposed on a distribution from a qualified plan.

- Explain the various situations under which distributions can occur from a qualified plan and the impact these varying circumstances will have on tax issues.

- Understand the concept of investment in contract.

- Identify the conditions for a qualifying lump sum distribution.

- Describe how beneficiaries and alternate payees will be taxed on plan distributions.

- Describe the special tax provisions that apply to early distributions and late distributions.

Unquestionably, a major advantage of a qualified pension or profit sharing plan is that an employer's contributions, although currently deductible, will not be considered as taxable income to an employee until they are distributed. Moreover, when a distribution does represent taxable income to the employee or a beneficiary, it may be received under favorable tax circumstances.

Broadly speaking, distributions from a qualified plan are taxable in accordance with the annuity rules of Section 72 of the Internal Revenue Code. Lump sum distributions made before the year 2000 and lump sum distributions made to individuals born before January 1, 1936, may qualify for special income-averaging treatment if certain conditions are met. Although these general principles apply regardless of the contingency that gives rise to the distribution, this chapter discusses the tax aspects of a distribution in terms of the contingency that has brought it about. Thus, this chapter briefly explores the tax situation of an employee during employment (including in-service distributions of the employee's account), as well as the tax situation when distributions are made because of the employee's retirement, death, severance of employment, or disability.

With a view toward achieving some degree of simplicity, the discussion has been confined to the federal taxation of typical forms of distribution under plans that have a qualified status when the distributions are made. In certain instances, penalty taxes are imposed in addition to federal income taxes on distributions that

- Commence too early.

- Commence too late.

The last three sections of this chapter provide a discussion of these penalty taxes.

For a complete treatment of the taxation of distributions from a qualified retirement plan, the discussion of tax-free rollovers to an individual retirement account (IRA) or another qualified retirement plan, Chapter 17 should be consulted. In addition, Chapter 8 discusses the requirements that must be met to prevent a loan from a qualified pension plan from being treated as a taxable distribution.

Taxation During Employment

Even though employer contributions may be vested fully in an employee under a qualified plan, the employee will not have to report these contributions as taxable income until such time as they are distributed. Thus, employer contributions made on behalf of an employee generally will not be considered as taxable income to the employee during the period of employment.

If the plan includes a life insurance benefit for employees, however, the employee is considered to have received a distribution each year equal to the portion of the employer's contribution (or the portion of the trust earnings) that has been applied during such year to provide the pure insurance in force on the employee's life.[1] The pure insurance is considered to be the excess, if any, of the face amount of the employee's life insurance contract over its cash value. The amount that the employee must include as taxable income for each year is the one-year term insurance rate for the employee's attained age multiplied by the amount of pure insurance involved. This insurance cost often is called the **PS 58 cost** because the original Treasury Department ruling on the subject was so numbered.

Since the term insurance rate increases each year with the employee's increasing age, this factor tends to increase the amount the employee has to include as taxable income each year. An offsetting factor, however, is the increasing cash value of the contract, which reduces the amount of pure insurance in effect each year. For plans that employ some form of whole life insurance or its equivalent, the insurance cost generally will tend to rise each year, the reduction in the amount of pure insurance

---

[1]Note that the amount applied during any year to provide life insurance often covers a period extending into the following year. The employee, however, is not permitted to apportion this insurance cost between the two years and is required to include this amount as taxable income in the year in which it is applied, even though the period of protection extends into the subsequent year.

being insufficient to offset the increase in the term insurance rate caused by the employee's advancing age. If the plan is funded with retirement income contracts, the yearly increase in cash value is more substantial and, ultimately, the cash value will exceed the face amount of the contract. Under this type of contract, the insurance cost (after the first few years) tends to decrease and ultimately disappears.

Normally, the term insurance rates employed to determine the cost of the employee's insurance coverage are the rates contained in PS 58 (reissued as Revenue Ruling 55-747, as amplified by Revenue Ruling 66-1105). However, the insurer's own rates may be used if they are lower than the rates set forth in these rulings. If an employee is insurable only on an extra-premium basis and the employer contributes the extra premium necessary to obtain full coverage (and follows the same practice for all employees in similar circumstances), the employee's insurance cost will be determined on the basis of the standard rates, and the extra premium paid because of the rating need not be taken into account.[2]

If employees are making contributions, the plan may provide that an employee's contribution will first be applied toward the cost of insurance coverage. This provision makes it possible to reduce or eliminate having any portion of the employer's contribution considered as taxable income to the employee during employment.

If the death benefit is being provided outside the qualified plan by a nondiscriminatory group term life insurance contract issued to the employer rather than to the trustee of the pension trust, the employee is not required to consider any part of the premium paid by the employer as taxable income, except to the extent that the employee's coverage exceeds $50,000. However, if the trustee of a qualified trust purchases the group term life insurance instead of the employer, the value of the insurance attributable to employer contributions will be considered as taxable income to the covered employees, regardless of the amounts of coverage involved.

Determination of Cost Basis

Before discussing the taxation of benefits, it is important to have a clear idea of the elements that constitute an employee's cost basis (or **investment in contract**), if any, since the employee's cost basis is an important factor in the taxation of distributions under the plan.

Briefly, **Section 72 of the IRC** provides that an employee's cost basis includes the following:

1. The aggregate of any amounts the employee contributed on an after-tax basis while employed.

2. The aggregate of the prior insurance costs the employee has reported as taxable income, but only for distributions made under that policy. (If the employee has

---

[2] If the contract is issued on a graded or graduated death benefit basis—that is, a standard premium is paid but there is a reduction in the amount of insurance due to the extra mortality risk involved—the employee's insurance cost will be lower since less insurance protection is being provided.

made contributions and the plan provides that employee contributions will first be used to pay any cost of insurance, the employee's reportable income for any year is the excess, if any, of the insurance cost of protection over the amount of the employee's contribution for the year, and not the full cost of insurance protection.)

3. Other contributions made by the employer that already have been taxed to the employee. An example could be where the employer has maintained a nonqualified plan that later was qualified.

4. Loans from the qualified retirement plan to the participant that were treated as taxable distributions.

There also is provision for the inclusion of other items in an employee's cost basis, such as contributions made by the employer after 1950 but before 1963 while the employee was a resident of a foreign country. For the most part, however, the items listed above will constitute an employee's cost basis in the typical situation.

Taxation of In-Service Distributions

When an employee receives an in-service cash distribution of the entire value of his or her account, the amount of the distribution that exceeds the employee's cost basis will be taxable in the year of distribution as ordinary income. In addition, it may be subject to the early distribution tax discussed later in this chapter. A distribution that occurs after age 59½ may be eligible for special averaging treatment if it meets the requirements for a qualifying lump sum distribution, as discussed in the next section, and if made prior to the year 2000 or if made to an individual born before January 1, 1936.

If the in-service distribution represents only a part of the employee's account, it still will be taxed as ordinary income, with a pro rata tax-free recovery of the employee's cost basis. The amount of the distribution that is considered a recovery of cost basis is determined by multiplying the distribution amount by a fraction. The numerator is the employee's total cost basis; the denominator is the present value of the employee's vested account balance. For example, if the value of the employee's total vested account balance is $100,000 and the corresponding cost basis is $30,000, the fraction is 3/10. If the employee's partial distribution is $10,000, 3/10 of this amount, or $3,000, would be considered as a tax-free recovery of cost basis and $7,000 would be taxed as ordinary income. It should be noted that this result occurs no matter how the plan describes the withdrawal. Thus, even though the plan permits only a withdrawal of after-tax employee contributions and an employee perceives that only his own money is being returned, the distribution will be taxed in this manner.

The Tax Reform Act of 1986 (TRA '86) mandated the pro rata recovery of an employee's cost basis. The basis recovery rules of prior law treated all distributions as a return of cost basis until that basis was fully recovered; all distributions thereafter were taxable. In plans that permitted in-service withdrawals on May 5, 1986, and had separate accounting for employee contributions, pre-1987 employee contributions can be withdrawn under the old rules until exhausted; thereafter, the new rules will apply.

TRA '86 also provided some relief for defined contribution plans (and some defined benefit plans[3]) by permitting them to categorize the portion of the employee's account balance attributable to after-tax contributions as a separate account for purposes of the basis recovery rules.[4] In effect, this permits employers to make distributions only from the account or separate contract that consists solely of after-tax employee contributions plus earnings. Thus, while the pro rata distribution rule still applies, calculations are based on the ratio of after-tax employee contributions to the value of the separate contract that consists of these contributions and earnings thereon. To use this approach, the plan must maintain adequate separate accounts by keeping separate records of after-tax contributions and earnings and by allocating earnings, gains, losses, and other credits between the separate account and other portions of the plan on a reasonable and consistent basis.

As a result, plan sponsors have three general options for establishing contracts in a plan:

1. *One contract.* There is no separate contract for employee contributions; the plan consists of only a single contract in which all contributions and associated earnings are held.

2. *Two contracts.* Pre-1987 and post-1986 employee after-tax contributions and associated earnings are held in a separate contract; all other plan contributions and earnings are held in the other contract.

3. *Two contracts.* There is a separate contract only for post-1986 after-tax employee contributions and earnings; the other contract contains all other plan contributions and earnings, including pre-1987 employee contributions and earnings. This option often has been called the "fresh start" approach.[5]

Taxation of Retirement Benefits

This section examines the taxation of retirement benefits received in the form of lump sum distributions as well as distributions in the form of periodic payments.

---

[3] A defined benefit plan is to be treated as a defined contribution plan for this purpose to the extent that a separate account is maintained for employee contributions to which is credited actual earnings and losses. Crediting employee contributions with a specified rate of earnings will not be sufficient to create a separate account. Notice 87-13, Q&A-14, except for plans permitting unmatched voluntary contributions allocated to a separate account, it is unlikely that most contributory defined benefit plans will satisfy this requirement.

[4] Internal Revenue Code Section 72(d).

[5] For examples of these options and how they differ in results, see Towers Perrin, *The Handbook of 401(k) Plan Management* (Burr Ridge, IL: Irwin Professional Publishing, 1996), pp. 166–68.

Qualifying Lump Sum Distributions

A **qualifying lump sum distribution** is a distribution from a qualified retirement plan of the balance to the credit of an employee after age 59½ and within one taxable year of the recipient. The distribution must be made on account of the employee's death, attainment of age 59½, or separation from service.[6] It should be noted that a distribution to the employee in the form of annuity payments after retirement will not prevent the employee's beneficiary from receiving a qualifying lump sum distribution.

Distributions to a Retired Employee

If an employee's benefit is paid from a qualified plan in the form of a qualifying lump sum benefit at retirement, the employee's cost basis will be recovered free of income tax. The excess of the qualifying distribution over the employee's cost basis will qualify for favorable tax treatment if made before the year 2000 or if paid to an individual born before January 1, 1936.

It should be noted, however, that even though a provision exists for the favorable taxation of some lump sum distributions, a qualified retirement plan may not make distributions to an employee prior to his or her severance of employment.[7]

A special transition rule exists for individuals born before January 1, 1936. Qualifying lump sum distributions made to these individuals, regardless of when made, can continue to use the capital gains provisions in effect prior to the Tax Reform Act of 1986 and have the pre-1974 portion of the lump sum distribution taxed as a long-term capital gain with a maximum rate of 20 percent. An eligible individual also may elect to choose 10-year (as opposed to five-year) averaging for all or the remaining portion of the distribution. If 10-year averaging is chosen, however, the individual must use the tax rates in effect for the 1986 tax year. In addition, five-year averaging can be used for all or the remaining portion of the lump sum distributions made before the year 2000. Not more than one election may be made under these transition provisions with respect to an employee, and five-year averaging is lost for any other distribution.

For purposes of determining whether there has been a qualifying lump sum distribution, all plans of the same type (e.g., defined benefit or defined contribution) and all plans within a given category (pension, profit sharing, or stock bonus) are

---

[6] The separation of service provision is not available for self-employed individuals. They are able to qualify on the basis of disability, however.

[7] For distributions prior to the year 2000, an employee who had been a participant for at least five years could elect to treat such a lump sum distribution under a five-year averaging rule; however, this election could be made only once by the participant. Under this rule, one first determined the total taxable amount, which was the amount of the distribution that was includable in income. The tax on the total taxable amount was determined by taking one-fifth of the distribution and calculating the ordinary income tax on this portion using single-taxpayer rates and assuming no other income, exemptions, or deductions. The actual tax then was determined by multiplying this amount by five. There was a minimum distribution allowance equal to the lesser of $10,000 or 50 percent of the total taxable amount, reduced by 20 percent of the amount by which the total taxable amount exceeded $20,000. If available, the minimum distribution allowance was subtracted from the total taxable distribution before calculating the tax.

No Fees for QDRO Determination   1

In Advisory Opinion 94-32A, the Department of Labor's Pension and Welfare Benefits Administration (PWBA) states that pension plans may not charge fees to individual plan participants or alternate payees in connection with the plans' determination as to whether a domestic relations order issued by a court is a qualified domestic relations order (QDRO).

According to the advisory opinion,

imposing a separate fee or cost on a participant or alternate payee (either directly or as a charge against a plan account) in connection with a determination of the status of a domestic relations order or administration of a QDRO would constitute an impermissible

encumbrance on the exercise of the right of an alternate payee to receive benefits under a QDRO. Additionally, because Title I of ERISA [the Employee Retirement Income Security Act] imposes specific statutory duties on plan administrators regarding QDRO determinations and the administration of QDROs, reasonable administrative expenses thus incurred by the plan may not appropriately be allocated to the individual participants and beneficiaries affected by the QDRO.

Source: "No Fees for QDRO Determination." Reprinted with permission, from the December 1994 issue of the *Employee Benefit Plan Review* magazine, p. 49. Charles D. Spencer & Associates, Inc., Publishers, Chicago, IL.

aggregated and treated as a single plan. Because only similar types of plans are required to be aggregated for this purpose, it is possible to have a distribution from a profit sharing plan qualify as a lump sum distribution even though the employee has an interest in a pension plan sponsored by the employer.

If a distribution includes an annuity contract and/or employer securities, some part of the distribution may not be currently taxable. The value of the annuity will not be taxed when distributed, and the employee will be taxed only on annuity payments when actually received. Similarly, any unrealized appreciation on employer securities will not be taxable in the year of distribution unless the employee so elects.[8]

Distributions to an Alternate Payee

Any **alternate payee** who is the spouse or former spouse of the participant is treated as the distributee of any distribution or payment made to him or her under a qualified domestic relations order (QDRO). For purposes of computing the tax on lump sum distributions, the balance to the credit of an employee does not include any amount payable under a QDRO.

[8] The fact that some part of the distribution was not currently taxable in either of these situations would not preclude five-year averaging in years occurring before the year 2000. This treatment would still be available for the balance of the distribution if it otherwise qualified; however, values not currently taxable were taken into account in determining the marginal tax rate on the amount being taxed.

Distributions in the Form of Periodic Payments

Distributions to a Retired Employee

If a retiring employee receives the distribution in the form of **periodic payments,** these payments will be taxed to the employee as ordinary income in accordance with the annuity rules of Section 72 of the Internal Revenue Code.

If the employee has no cost basis, all payments will be taxable as ordinary income when received. If the employee has a cost basis, part of each distribution will be considered a tax-free recovery of that cost basis. If payments are being made on a non-lifetime basis, each payment will be multiplied by an exclusion ratio or fraction to determine the amount that is tax free and the amount that is taxable. The numerator of the fraction is the total cost basis; the denominator is the employee's expected return under the payment arrangement. Thus, for example, if the employee is to receive payments of $12,000 for 10 years, his or her expected return is $120,000 (10 × $12,000). If the employee's cost basis is $10,000, his tax-free recovery each year will be $1,000, or 1/12th ($10,000/$120,000) of $12,000.

This concept of determining an exclusion ratio also was applicable to life income arrangements with an annuity starting date before November 19, 1996. For life income arrangements with an annuity starting date of November 19, 1996, or later, a simplified method is used to determine the portion of each payment that is a tax-free return of cost basis. The nontaxable portion received each month will be the employee's cost basis, divided by the following number of anticipated payments:

Age on Annuity Starting Date	Number of Payments
Up to 55	360
Over 55, up to 60	310
Over 60, up to 65	260
Over 65, up to 70	210
Over 70	160

If payments are made to the employee for a period certain or with a refund feature, the cost basis will be adjusted, when determining the employee's exclusion ratio, to reflect the value of the refund or period-certain feature.

Distributions to an Alternate Payee

Any alternate payee who is the spouse or former spouse of the participant is treated as the distributee of any distribution or payment made under a QDRO.[9] The investment in the contract must be allocated on a pro rata basis between the present value of such distribution or payment and the present value of all other benefits payable with respect to the participant to which the QDRO relates.

---

[9] For payments prior to October 22, 1986, this treatment also applies to alternate payees other than a spouse or former spouse.

Taxation of Death Benefits

Lump Sum Distributions

A lump sum distribution to the employee's beneficiary from a qualified plan made on account of the employee's death after age 59½ (either before or after severance of employment) will entitle the beneficiary to the favorable tax treatment previously described. The favorable tax treatment is granted if the distribution represents the full amount then credited to the employee's account and if it is received within one taxable year of the beneficiary. This applies, however, only to distributions before the year 2000 or distributions made with respect to individuals born before January 1, 1936.

In determining the net amount of gain subject to tax, the beneficiary's cost basis will be the same as the employee's (i.e., the aggregate of the employee's contributions and any amounts, such as insurance costs, on which the employee previously has been taxed).[10]

If any portion of the distribution consists of life insurance proceeds and the employee either paid the insurance cost or reported this cost as taxable income, the pure insurance—that is, the difference between the face amount of the contract and its cash value—will pass to the beneficiary free of income tax under Section 101(a) of the Internal Revenue Code. The beneficiary will have to treat only the cash value of the contract, plus any other cash distributions from the plan, as income subject to tax.

The following example illustrates how the death benefit under a typical retirement income contract would be taxed if the employee died before retirement and the face amount of the contract was paid to the beneficiary in a lump sum.

Face amount of contract	$25,000
Cash value of contract	−11,000
Amount of pure insurance excludable under Section 101(a)	$14,000
Cash value of contract	$11,000
Amount subject to income tax	$11,000
Beneficiary's cost basis (aggregate of prior insurance costs that employee reported as taxable income)	−940
Balance taxable to beneficiary	$10,060

The beneficiary would, therefore, receive $14,940 of the total distribution free of income tax, and only $10,060 would be considered as being taxable.

---

[10] For deaths occurring before August 21, 1996, the employee death benefit exclusion provided according to Section 101(b) of the Internal Revenue Code up to a maximum of $5,000. It should be noted that, in the case of a lump sum distribution that otherwise qualified for the favorable tax treatment, this exclusion under Section 101(b) applied regardless of whether the employee's rights were forfeitable or nonforfeitable. Briefly, Section 101(b) permitted a beneficiary to exclude from gross income any payments made by the employer of a deceased employee up to a maximum of $5,000. Except as noted, this exclusion was available only to the extent the employee's rights to the amounts were forfeitable immediately prior to death. The $5,000 death benefit exclusion was repealed for deaths occurring after August 20, 1996.

The regulations provide that if the employee has not paid the insurance cost of his or her contract or has not reported the cost of insurance as taxable income, the portion of the insurance proceeds consisting of pure insurance will be considered as taxable income to the beneficiary.

When an employee dies after retirement and after having received periodic payments, a lump sum death payment to the employee's beneficiary, if it meets the requirements previously noted, could qualify for the favorable tax treatment described. The beneficiary's cost basis, however, will be reduced by any amount that the employee had recovered free from income tax.

Distribution in the Form of Periodic Payments

Death before Retirement

If death occurs before retirement and the plan provides for the distribution of the employee's death benefit over a period of years (including payments based upon the life expectancy of the beneficiary), these payments will be taxed in accordance with the annuity rules of Section 72 of the Internal Revenue Code.

The beneficiary's cost basis will consist of the amount that would have been the employee's cost basis had the employee lived and received the payments.

If any part of the periodic payments arises from pure life insurance, the proceeds are divided into two parts:

1. The cash value of the contract immediately before death.

2. The pure insurance (the excess of the face amount of the contract over its cash value).

That portion of each periodic payment attributable to the cash value of the contract will be taxed to the beneficiary under the annuity rules. The balance of each payment that is attributable to the pure insurance element will be treated as insurance proceeds under Section 101(d) of the Internal Revenue Code.

To illustrate, if the face amount of the employee's contract were $25,000 and the proceeds were paid to the beneficiary in 10 annual payments of $3,000 each, the following would be the manner in which the payments would be taxed to the beneficiary, assuming that the contract had a cash value at death of $11,000 and that the aggregate of the insurance costs that the employee previously reported as taxable income was $940.

The portion of each annual payment of $3,000 attributable to the cash value is $1,320 (11/25 of $3,000). The beneficiary's cost basis for this portion would be $940. The expected return under this portion would be $13,200 (the annual payment of $1,320 multiplied by the 10 years of payments). An exclusion ratio would be determined by dividing the cost basis ($940) by the expected return ($13,200). This produces an exclusion ratio of 7 percent, which would be applied to the portion of each annual payment attributable to the cash value of the contract. As a result, $92 (7 percent of $1,320) would be excluded from income each year, and the balance of $1,228 would be taxed to the beneficiary as ordinary income.

The portion of each annual payment of $3,000 attributable to the pure insurance is $1,680 (14/25 of $3,000). Of this amount, $1,400 (1/10 of $14,000) is excludable from gross income as Section 101 proceeds, and only the balance of $280 is taxable as ordinary income to the beneficiary. A beneficiary of the employee would include $1,508 ($280 plus $1,228) as ordinary income each year, and $1,492 of each annual payment would be received free of income tax.

Death after Retirement

The taxation of payments to the beneficiary of an employee who dies after retirement and after periodic payments have begun depends upon whether the employee had a cost basis (and if so, whether it had been recovered by the employee) as well as upon the method of payment involved. If the employee had no cost basis, each payment would be considered as taxable income to the beneficiary as received. However, where the payments are being continued under a joint and survivor annuity form, the exclusion ratio established when the annuity became effective shall apply until the unrecovered investment in the contract is eliminated.

Taxation of Severance-of-Employment Benefits

For the most part, the discussion in this chapter on the taxation of distributions at retirement is equally applicable to the taxation of distributions on severance of employment. If the distribution is in the form of periodic payments, the taxation of payments to the employee will be governed by the annuity rules after taking the employee's cost basis, if any, into account. However, a penalty tax on early distributions may apply as explained later in this chapter.

If the distribution is in the form of a life insurance contract, its cash value less the employee's cost basis, if any, will be considered as taxable income in the year in which the employee receives the contract, even though the contract is not then surrendered for its cash value. The distribution may qualify for favorable tax treatment if all necessary conditions are met. On the other hand, the employee may avoid any current tax liability by transferring this amount, within 60 days, to a qualified individual retirement savings plan (described in Chapter 17) or to another employer's qualified plan. The employee also may avoid any current tax liability by making an irrevocable election, within 60 days of the distribution, to convert the contract to a nontransferable annuity that contains no element of life insurance.[11] If the employee would otherwise receive a cash distribution but has the option under the plan of electing, within 60 days, to receive a nontransferable annuity in lieu of the cash payment, he or she also may avoid current tax liability by making a timely exercise of

---

[11] The regulations spell out what is meant by nontransferable, and the language of the regulations has been used as a guide by many insurers in endorsing their contracts. Such an endorsement might read approximately as follows:

> This contract is not transferable except to the ABC Insurance Company. It may not be sold, assigned, discounted, or pledged as collateral for a loan or as security for the performance of an obligation or for any other purposes to any person other than this Company.
> However, notwithstanding the foregoing, the owner may designate a beneficiary to receive the proceeds payable upon death and may elect a joint and survivor annuity.

this option. It should be noted that if the employee receives a direct payment from the plan and then rolls over or transfers the gross amount to an individual retirement savings plan or another employer's plan, automatic withholding of 20 percent will be made on the distribution—even though it is rendered not currently taxable by the rollover or transfer. Any excess withholding that results can then be recaptured when the employee files his or her tax return for the year in question. Alternatively, the employee may direct the plan to transfer the amount involved directly to the individual retirement savings plan or another employer's qualified plan. In this event, the automatic 20 percent withholding will be avoided.

If current tax liability is avoided by such an election, the employee will not pay any tax until payments are made from the annuity contract. At that time, the payments will be considered ordinary income under the annuity rules.

If the distribution is in the form of an annuity contract, the tax situation is governed by the date of issue of the contract. If issued after December 31, 1962, the distribution will be treated exactly the same as the distribution of a life insurance contract unless the annuity is endorsed or rewritten on a nontransferable basis within the 60 days allowed. If issued before January 1, 1963, the employee will not have to include any amount as taxable income until payments are actually received. At that time, payments will be considered ordinary income under the annuity rules.

Taxation of Disability Benefits

Many qualified pension plans provide for a monthly benefit if an employee becomes totally and permanently disabled. Typically, the benefit is payable for life (subject to the continuance of the disability), but this is true only for a disability that occurs after the employee has attained some minimum age, such as 50 or 55, or has completed some minimum period of service, such as 10 years. The benefit may or may not be related to the employee's accrued or projected pension. Frequently, the amount of the benefit will be adjusted if disability continues until the employee attains the normal retirement age specified in the plan.

Generally speaking, disability benefits of this type will be taxed to the employee in accordance with the annuity rules of Section 72 of the Internal Revenue Code.

Tax on Early Distributions

TRA '86 added an additional 10 percent tax on any taxable amounts received before age 59½ from a qualified retirement plan. This additional tax on **early distributions** does not apply in the case of death, disability, or termination of employment after age 55. Exceptions also are granted for:

1. Distributions that are part of a series of substantially equal periodic payments made for the life (or life expectancy) of the employee or the joint lives (or joint life expectancies) of the employee and his or her beneficiary.

2. Distributions used to pay medical expenses to the extent the expenses exceed 7.5 percent of adjusted gross income. Also, distributions used to pay health insurance premiums after separation from employment.

3. Certain dividend distributions made from an employee stock ownership plan (ESOP).

4. Payments to alternate payees pursuant to a qualified domestic relations order (QDRO).

5. Distributions used to pay qualified education expenses of the tax payor or his or her spouse, child, or grandchild.

6. Distributions for the purchase of a first home (limited to $10,000).

7. Certain other distributions, such as those to pay an IRS tax levy or a timely corrective distribution from the plan.

Tax on Late Distributions

Chapter 5 described the requirement that participants must commence benefit payments by April 1 of the calendar year following the calendar year in which they reach age 70½ after terminating employment.

If the participant's benefit is determined from an individual account, the minimum amount that must be paid each year is determined by dividing the account balance[12] by the applicable life expectancy. The applicable life expectancy is the life expectancy of the employee or the joint life expectancies of the employee and the employee's designated beneficiary, if any.

If the participant's benefit is determined by the annuity distribution from a defined benefit plan, the annuity must be paid for in one of the following durations:

- The life of the participant.

- The lives of the participant and the participant's designated beneficiary.

- A period certain not extending beyond the life expectancy of the participant or the joint life expectancies of the participant and the participant's designated beneficiary.

The penalty for failure to make a required distribution of (at least) the correct amount is a nondeductible excise tax of 50 percent of the difference between the minimum required amount and the actual distribution. This tax is imposed on the payee.

Chapter Summary

- Distributions from a qualified plan generally are taxable in accordance with the annuity rules of Section 72 of the Internal Revenue Code.

---

[12] Technically this is the account balance as of the plan's last valuation date in the calendar year immediately preceding the calendar year for which the distribution is made.

- Even though employer contributions may be vested fully in an employee under a qualified plan, the employee will not have to report these contributions as taxable income until such time as they are distributed. Employer contributions made on behalf of an employee generally will not be considered as taxable income to the employee during the period of employment.

- When an employee receives an in-service cash distribution of the entire value of his or her account, the amount of the distribution that exceeds the employee's cost basis will be taxable in the year of distribution as ordinary income. In addition, it may be subject to the early distribution tax. A distribution that occurs after age 59½ may be eligible for special averaging treatment if it meets the requirements for a qualifying lump sum distribution. If the in-service distribution represents only a part of the employee's account, it still will be taxed as ordinary income, with a pro rata tax-free recovery of the employee's cost basis.

- A qualifying lump sum distribution is a distribution from a qualified retirement plan of the balance to the credit of an employee made after age 59½ and within one taxable year of the recipient. The distribution must be made on account of the employee's death, attainment of age 59½, or separation from service.

- The Tax Reform Act of 1986 imposed various tax provisions related to distributions from qualified plans. TRA '86 added an additional 10 percent tax on any taxable amounts received before age 59½ from a qualified retirement plan. The additional tax does not apply in the case of death, disability, or termination of employment after age 55. Exceptions also are granted for:
  — Distributions that are part of a series of substantially equal periodic payments made for the life (or life expectancy) of the employee or the joint lives (or joint life expectancies) of the employee and his or her beneficiary.
  — Distributions used to pay medical expenses to the extent the expenses exceed 7.5 percent of adjusted gross income. Also, distributions used to pay health insurance premiums after separation from employment.
  — Certain dividend distributions made from an employee stock ownership plan (ESOP).
  — Payments to alternate payees pursuant to a qualified domestic relations order (QDRO).
  — Distributions used to pay qualified education expenses of the tax payor or his or her spouse, child, or grandchild.
  — Distributions for the purchase of a first home (limited to $10,000).
  — Certain other distributions, such as those to pay an IRS tax levy or a timely corrective distribution from the plan.

- Participants must commence benefit payments by April 1 of the calendar year following the calendar year in which they reach age 70½ after terminating employment and over a stipulated period of time. The penalty for failure to make a required distribution of (at least) the correct amount is a nondeductible excise tax of 50 percent of the difference between the minimum required amount and the actual distribution.

Key Terms

alternate payee, p. *503*
early distributions, p. *508*
investment in contract,
  p. *499*

periodic payments, p. *504*
PS 58 cost, p. *498*
qualifying lump sum
  distribution, p. *502*

Section 72 of the IRC,
  p. *499*

Questions for Review

1. What factors are included in determining an employee's cost basis in a pension plan?
2. Under what conditions will a lump sum distribution qualify for favorable tax treatment?
3. What was the five-year averaging rule?
4. How are the pension distributions in the form of periodic payments taxed when the employee has no cost basis in the plan?
5. How will the answer to the previous question change if the employee has a cost basis in the plan?
6. How are death benefits taxed for income tax purposes when paid in the form of a lump sum distribution?
7. How are death benefits payable in the form of periodic payments taxed for income tax purposes if death takes place before retirement?
8. How will the answer to the previous question change if death takes place after retirement?
9. How are severance-of-employment benefits taxed?
10. Explain the taxation of disability benefits.

Questions for Discussion

1. Discuss how the Tax Reform Act of 1986 may have influenced employees' choices between receiving retirement distributions as lump sums versus periodic payments.
2. Discuss the likely effect of the early distribution penalty tax on plan design.

Resources for Further Study

Bloss, Julie L. *QDROs: A Guide for Plan Administration.* 2nd ed. Brookfield, WI: International Foundation of Employee Benefit Plans, 1997.

Krass, Stephen J. *The Pension Answer Book.* 12th ed. New York: Panel Publishers, 2002.

Towers Perrin. *The Handbook of 401(k) Plan Management.* Burr Ridge, IL: Irwin Professional Publishing, 1996.

Appendix

Social Security and Medicare

Robert J. Myers[1]

Economic security for retired workers, disabled workers, and survivors of deceased workers in the United States is, in the vast majority of cases, provided through the multiple means of Social Security, private pensions, and individual savings. This is sometimes referred to as a *three-legged stool* or the *three pillars of economic-security protection*. It can also be seen as a layered arrangement, with Social Security providing the floor of protection, private-sector activities building on top of it, and public assistance programs, such as Supplemental Security Income (SSI), providing a net of protection for those whose total retirement income does not attain certain levels or meet minimum subsistence needs.

Although some people may view the Social Security program as one that should provide complete protection, over the years it generally has been agreed that it should only be the foundation of protection.

Private pension plans have, to a significant extent, been developed to supplement Social Security. This is done in a number of ways, both directly and indirectly. The net result, however, is a broad network of retirement protection.

This appendix discusses in detail the retirement, disability, and survivor provisions of the Social Security program, not only their historical development and present structure but also a summary of the financial crises of the late 1970s and early 1980s (and what was done to solve them) and possible future changes. Following

[1] Robert J. Myers is Professor Emeritus, Temple University, and an international consultant on Social Security. This appendix is based on "Social Security and Medicare," in *The Handbook on Employee Benefits,* 5th ed., Jerry S. Rosenbloom, ed. Used with permission of the publisher. (Burr Ridge, IL: Irwin Professional Publishing, 2001).

this, the Medicare program is described. Also, descriptions of the two public assistance programs (Supplemental Security Income and Medicaid) that supplement Old-Age, Survivors, and Disability Insurance (OASDI) and Medicare are given.

The term *Social Security* is used here with the meaning generally accepted in the United States, namely, the cash benefits provisions of the OASDI program. International usage of the term *social security* is much broader than this and includes all other types of governmental programs protecting individuals against the economic risks of a modern industrial system, such as unemployment, short-term sickness, work-connected accidents and diseases, and medical care costs.

Old-Age, Survivors, and Disability Insurance Program

Persons Covered under OASDI

OASDI coverage—for both taxes and earnings credits toward benefit rights—currently applies to somewhat more than 90 percent of the total workforce of the United States. About half of those not covered have protection through a special government employee retirement system, while the remaining half are either very low paid intermittent workers or unpaid family workers.

The vast majority of persons covered under OASDI are so affected on a mandatory or compulsory basis. Several categories, however, have optional or semi-optional coverage. It is important to note that OASDI coverage applies not only to employees, both salaried and wage earner, but also to self-employed persons. Some individuals who are essentially employees are nonetheless classified as self-employed for the sake of convenience in applying coverage.

Compulsory coverage is applicable to all employees in commerce and industry (interpreting these classifications very broadly) except railroad workers, who are covered under a separate program, the Railroad Retirement system. However, financial and other coordinating provisions exist between these two programs, so that, in reality, railroad workers are covered under OASDI. Members of the armed forces are covered compulsorily, as are federal civilian employees hired after 1983. Compulsory coverage also applies to lay employees of churches (with certain minor exceptions), to employees of nonprofit charitable and educational institutions, to employees of state and local governments that do not have retirement systems (first effective after July 1, 1991; before then, coverage was elective, on a group basis, by the employing entity), and to American residents who work abroad for American corporations. Self-employed persons of all types (except ministers) also are covered compulsorily unless their earnings are minimal (i.e., less than $400 a year); beginning in 1990, covered self-employment is taken as 92.35 percent of the self-employment net income (such figure being 100 percent minus the OASDI-Hospital Insurance tax rate applicable to employees).

From a geographical standpoint, OASDI applies not only in the 50 states and the District of Columbia but also in all outlying areas (American Samoa, Guam, the Northern Mariana Islands, Puerto Rico, and the Virgin Islands).

Elective coverage applies to a number of categories. Employees of state and local governments who are under a retirement system can have coverage at the option of the employing entity and only when the current employees vote in favor of coverage. Similar provisions are available for American employees of foreign subsidiaries of American corporations, the latter having the right to opt for coverage. Once that coverage has been elected by a state or local government, it cannot be terminated. Approximately 70 percent of state and local government employees are now covered as a result of this election basis and the compulsory coverage applicable when the entity does not have a retirement plan.

Because of the principle of separation of church and state, ministers are covered on the self-employed basis, regardless of their actual status. Furthermore, they have the right to opt out of the system within a limited time after ordination on grounds of religious principles or conscience. Americans employed in the United States by a foreign government or by an international organization are covered compulsorily on the self-employed basis.

Historical Development of Retirement Provisions

When what is now the OASDI program was developed in 1934–35, it was confined entirely to retirement benefits plus lump sum refund payments to represent the difference, if any, between employee taxes paid, plus an allowance for interest, and retirement benefits received. It was not until the 1939 act that auxiliary (or dependents) and survivors benefits were added, and not until the 1956 act that disability benefits were made available. The likely reason that only retirement benefits were instituted initially is that such type of protection was the most familiar to the general public, especially in light of the relatively few private pension plans then in existence.

The "normal retirement age" (NRA), also called the "full retirement age," was originally established at 65. This figure was selected in a purely empirical manner; it was a middle figure between two perceived extremes. Age 70 seemed too high, because of the common belief that relatively so few people reached that age, while 60 seemed too low, because of the large costs that would be involved if that age had been selected. Many of the existing private pension plans at that time had a retirement age of 65, although some in the railroad industry used age 70. Furthermore, labor force participation data showed that a relatively high proportion of workers continued in employment after age 60. A widely cited, but erroneous, explanation of why age 65 was selected is that Bismarck chose this age when he established the German national pension program in the 1880s; the age used originally in Germany actually was 70 (actually, the plan was primarily a disability benefits one). The 1983 act provided for the NRA to increase from age 65 to age 67 in a deferred, gradual manner. Specifically, the NRA is 65 for those attaining this age before 2003 and first becomes 67 for those attaining this age in 2027.

The original program applied only to workers in commerce and industry. It was not until the 1950s that coverage was extended to additional categories of workers. Now, almost all are covered, including the self-employed.

The initial legislation passed by the House of Representatives did not require eligible persons to retire at age 65 or over in order to receive benefits, although it was recognized that inclusion of a retirement requirement would be essential in the final legislation. The Senate inserted a requirement of a general nature that benefits would be payable only upon retirement, and this was included in the final legislation. Over the years, this retirement earnings test, or work clause, has been the subject of much controversy, and it has been considerably liberalized and made more flexible over the years.

Beginning in the 1950s, pressure developed to provide early-retirement benefits, first for spouses and then for insured workers. The minimum early-retirement age was set at 62, again a pragmatic political compromise, rather than a number based on any completely logical reason. The three-year differential, however, did represent the approximate average difference in age between men and their wives; but, of course, as with any averages, the difference actually is larger in many cases. The benefit amounts are reduced when claimed before the NRA is reached and are increased when retirement is delayed beyond the NRA. As the NRA increases beyond age 65, the reduction for claiming benefits at age 62 becomes larger.

Eligibility Conditions for Retirement Benefits

To be eligible for OASDI retirement benefits, individuals must have a certain amount of covered employment. In general, these conditions were designed to be relatively easy to meet in the early years of operation, thus bringing the program into effectiveness quickly. Eligibility for retirement benefits—termed *fully insured status*—depends on having a certain number of "quarters of coverage" (QCs), sometimes referred to as "credits," varying with the year of birth or, expressed in another manner, depending on the year of an individual's attainment of age 62.

Before 1978, a QC was defined simply as a calendar quarter during which the individual was paid $50 or more in wages from covered employment; the self-employed ordinarily received four QCs for each year of coverage at $400 or more of earnings. Beginning in 1978, the number of QCs acquired for each year depends on the total earnings in the year. For 1978, each full unit of $250 of earnings produced a QC, up to a maximum of four QCs for the year. In subsequent years the requirement has increased, and it will continue to increase in the future, in accordance with changes in the general wage level; for 2002, it is $870.

The number of QCs required for fully insured status is determined from the number of years in the period beginning in 1951, or with the year of attainment of age 22, if later, and the year before the year of attainment of age 62, with a minimum requirement of six QCs. As a result, an individual who attained age 62 before 1958 needed only six QCs to be fully insured. A person attaining age 62 in 1990 has a requirement of 39 QCs, while a person attaining age 65 in 1990 needs 36 QCs. The maximum number of QCs that will ever be required for fully insured status is 40, applicable to persons attaining age 62 after 1990. It is important to note that, although the requirement for the number of QCs is determined from 1951, or from year of attainment of age 22, and before attainment of age 62, the QCs to meet the requirement can be obtained at any time (e.g., before 1951, before age 22, and after age 61).

Beneficiary Categories for Retirement Benefits

Insured workers can receive unreduced retirement benefits in the amount of the Primary Insurance Amount (or PIA), the derivation of which will be discussed next, beginning at the NRA, or actuarially reduced benefits beginning at earlier ages, down to age 62. For retirement at age 62 before 2000, the benefit was 80 percent of the PIA, while for retirement at age 62 in 2000, it was 79⅙ percent. As the NRA increases beyond 65, the reduction will become larger (eventually being 30 percent).

Retired workers also can receive supplementary payments for spouses and eligible children. The spouse receives a benefit at the rate of 50 percent of the PIA if claim is first made at the NRA or over, and at a reduced rate if claimed at ages down to 62 (before 2000, a 25 percent reduction at age 62—(i.e., to 37.5 percent of the PIA); as the NRA increases beyond 65, the reduction for age 62 will be larger, eventually being 35 percent, 25⅚ percent in 2000). However, if a child under age 16 (or a child age 16 or over who was disabled before age 22) is present, the spouse receives benefits regardless of age, in an unreduced amount. Divorced spouses, when the marriage had lasted at least 10 years, are eligible for benefits under the same conditions as undivorced spouses.

Children under age 18 (and children age 18 or over and disabled before age 22, plus children attending elementary or high school full time at age 18) also are eligible for benefits, at a rate of 50 percent of the PIA; prior to legislation in 1981, post-secondary-school students ages 18–21 were eligible for benefits, and spouses with children in their care could receive benefits as long as a child under age 18 was present. Grandchildren and great-grandchildren can qualify as "children" if they are dependent on the grandparent and if both parents of the child are disabled or deceased.

An overall maximum on total family benefits is applicable, as is discussed later. If a person is eligible for more than one type of benefit (e.g., both as a worker and as a spouse), in essence only the largest benefit is payable.

Computation Procedures for Retirement Benefits

As indicated in the previous section, OASDI benefits are based on the PIA. The method of computing the PIA is quite complicated, especially because several different methods are available. The only method dealt with here in any detail is the one generally applicable to people who reach age 65 after 1981.

Persons who attained age 65 before 1982 use a method based on the average monthly wage (AMW). This is based essentially on a career average, involving the consideration of all earnings back through 1951. To take into account the general inflation in earnings that occurred in the past, automatic-adjustment procedures were involved in the benefit computations. However, these turned out to be faulty, because they did not—and would not in the future—produce stable benefit results (as to the relationships of initial benefits to final earnings). Accordingly, in the 1977 amendments, a new procedure applicable to those attaining age 62 after 1978 was adopted, but the old procedure was retained for earlier attainments of age 62. The result has been to give unusually and inequitably large benefits to those who attained age 62 before 1979 who worked well beyond age 62, as against similar people who attained age 62 after 1978, thus creating a "notch" situation.

Persons who attain age 62 in 1979–83 can use an alternative method somewhat similar to the AMW method (but with certain restrictions) if this produces a larger PIA than the new, permanent method. In actual practice, however, this modified-AMW method generally produces more favorable results only for persons attaining age 62 in 1979–81 and not continuing in employment after that age.

Still another method is available for all individuals who have earnings before 1951. In the vast majority of such cases, however, the new-start methods based on earnings after 1950 produce more favorable results.

The first step in the ongoing permanent method of computing the PIA applicable to persons attaining age 65 in 1982 or after is to calculate the Average Indexed Monthly Earnings (AIME). The AIME is on a career-average earnings basis. For persons who attain age 67 in 1991 or after, the AIME is based on the highest 35 years of indexed earnings after 1950. Actual earnings are indexed (i.e., increased) to reflect nationwide wage inflation from the particular year up to the year of attaining age 60. Details on the computation of the AIME are given in Appendix 1A.

Now, having obtained the AIME, the PIA is computed from a benefit formula. A different formula applies for each annual cohort of persons attaining age 62. For example, for those who reached age 62 in 1979, the formula was 90 percent of the first $180 of AIME, plus 32 percent of the next $905 of AIME, plus 15 percent of the AIME in excess of $1,085. For the 2002 cohort, the corresponding dollar bands are $592, $2,975, and $3,567. These bands are adjusted automatically annually, according to changes in nationwide average wages.

A different (and less favorable) method of computing the PIA for retirement benefits (and also for disability benefits, but not for survivor benefits) is applicable for certain persons who receive pensions based in whole or in part on earnings from employment not covered by OASDI or Railroad Retirement (in the past or in the future, and in other countries as well as in the United States). This is done to eliminate the windfall benefits (due to the weighted nature of the benefit formula) that would otherwise arise. Appendix 1A gives details on the application of the Windfall Elimination provision.

Prior to legislation in 1981, if the PIA benefit formula produced an amount smaller than $122 in the initial benefit computation, then this amount was nonetheless payable. However, for persons first becoming eligible after 1981, no such minimum is applicable.

A special minimum applies to the PIA for individuals who have a long period of covered work, but with low earnings. As of December 2002, this minimum is approximately $31.50 times the "years of coverage" (see Appendix 1A for definition) in excess of 10, but not in excess of 30; thus, for 30 or more years of coverage, the minimum benefit is $630.00. In practice, this procedure rarely applies for current retirees.

The resulting PIAs then are increased for any automatic adjustments applicable, because of annual increases in the consumer price index (CPI-W) that occur in or after the year of attaining age 62, even though actual retirement is much later. These automatic adjustments are made for benefits for each December. Such CPI increases were as high as 14.3 percent for 1980 and 11.2 percent for 1981, but have been much lower in recent years (2.6 percent in 2002).

The resulting PIA then is reduced, in the manner described previously, for those who first claim benefits before the NRA. Conversely, retired workers who do not receive benefits for any months after they attain the NRA, essentially because they elect not to receive them (usually because they have high earnings and do not need them currently), receive increases that are termed delayed-retirement credits (DRCs). Such credits for those who attained age 65 in 1982–89 are at the rate of 3 percent per year of delay (actually 0.25 percent per month) for the period between ages 65 and 70. For those who attained age 65 before 1982, the DRC is at a rate of only 1 percent per year. For those who attain the NRA after 1989, such credit is gradually increased from 3.5 percent for the 1990–91 cases to 4 percent for the 1992–93 cases, 4.5 percent for the 1994–95 cases, 5.0 percent for the 1996–97 cases, 5.5 percent for the 1998–99 cases, 6.0 percent for the 2000–01 cases, and 6.5 percent for the 2002–03 cases, until it is 8 percent for those attaining the NRA (then 66) in 2009. The DRC applies only to the worker's benefit and not to that for spouses or children (but it does apply to any subsequent widow(er)'s benefits).

A Maximum Family Benefit (MFB) is applicable when there are more than two beneficiaries receiving benefits on the same earnings record (i.e., the retired worker and two or more auxiliary beneficiaries). Not considered within the limit established by the MFB are the additional benefits arising from delayed-retirement credits and the benefits payable to divorced spouses. The MFB is determined prior to any reductions made because of claiming benefits before the NRA, but after the effect of the earnings test as it applies to any auxiliary beneficiary (e.g., if the spouse has high earnings, any potential benefit payable to her or him would not be considered for purposes of the MFB of the other spouse).

The MFB is determined from the PIA by a complex formula. This formula varies for each annual cohort of persons attaining age 62. The resulting MFB is adjusted for increases in the CPI in the future (in the same manner as is the PIA). For the 2002 cohort, the MFB formula is 150 percent of the first $756 of PIA, plus 272 percent of the next $336 of PIA, plus 134 percent of the next $332 of PIA, plus 175 percent of PIA in excess of $1,424. For future cohorts, the dollar figures are changed according to changes in nationwide average wages. The result of this formula is to produce MFBs that are 150 percent of the PIA for the lowest PIAs, with this proportion rising to a peak of 188 percent for middle-range PIAs, and then falling off to 175 percent—and leveling there—for higher PIAs.

Earnings Test and Other Restrictions on Retirement Benefits

From the inception of the OASDI program, there has been some form of restriction on the payment of benefits to persons who have substantial earnings from employment. This provision is referred to as the retirement earnings test. It does not apply to nonearned income, such as from investments or pensions. The general underlying principle of this test is that retirement benefits should be paid only to persons who are substantially retired.

The basic feature of the earnings test is that an annual exempt amount applies, so full benefits are paid if earnings, including those from both covered and noncovered employment, are not in excess thereof. Then, for persons under the NRA (which is age

65 until 2003), for each $2 of excess earnings, $1 in benefits is withheld; the reduction was on a "$1 for $3" basis for those at and above the NRA in 1990–99. Legislation in 2000 eliminated the test for the month of attaining the NRA and later months; the test still applies for earlier months in the year of attaining the NRA, but applicable only to earnings in such months. For persons ages 65–69 (at any time in the year), the annual exempt amount is $17,000 for 2000, $25,000 for 2001, and $30,000 for 2002, with the amounts for subsequent years being automatically determined by the increases in nationwide wages. Beginning with the month of attainment of age 65, the test no longer applies (this limiting age was 70 before 2000). For persons under age 65, the exempt amount is $11,280 in 2002, with automatic adjustment thereafter.

An alternative test applies for the initial year of retirement, or claim, if it results in more benefits being payable. Under this, full benefits are payable for all months in which the individual did not have substantial services in self-employment and had wages of ½ of the annual exempt amount or less. This provision properly takes care of the situation where an individual fully retires during a year, but had sizable earnings in the first part of the year, and thus would have most or all of the benefits withheld if only the annual test had been applicable.

Earnings of the "retired" worker, under the earnings test, affect the total family benefits payable. However, if an auxiliary beneficiary (spouse or child) has earnings, and these are sizable enough to affect the earnings test, any reduction in benefits is applicable only to such individual's benefits.

If an individual receives a pension from service under a government-employee pension plan under which the members were not covered under OASDI on the last day of her or his employment, the OASDI spouse benefit is reduced by two-thirds of the amount of such pension. This provision, however, is not applicable to women— or to men who are dependent on their wives—who become eligible for such a pension before December 1982, while for December 1982 through June 1983 the provision applies only to those (both men and women) who cannot prove dependency on their spouse. This general provision results in roughly the same treatment as occurs when both spouses have OASDI benefits based on their own earnings records; and then each receives such benefit, plus the excess, if any, of the spouse's benefit arising from the other spouse's earnings over the benefit based on their own earnings, rather than the full amount of the spouse's benefit.

Benefits are not payable to prisoners convicted of crimes involving confinement that lasts for at least 30 days, except for prisoners who are in an approved rehabilitation program (although payable to auxiliary beneficiaries of such prisoners). This also applies to disability and survivor benefits.

Historical Development of Disability Provisions

It was not until the 1956 act that monthly disability benefits were added to the OASDI program, although the "disability freeze" provision (in essence, a waiver-of-premium provision), described later, was added in the 1952 act.[2] It may well be said that long-term disability is merely premature old-age retirement.

---

[2] Actually, it was so written in the 1952 legislation as to be inoperative, but then was reenacted in 1954 to be on a permanent, ongoing basis.

The monthly disability benefits initially were available only at age 50 and over—that is, deferred to that age for those disabled earlier, with no auxiliary benefits for the spouse and dependent children. These limitations were quickly removed by the 1958 and 1960 acts.

Eligibility Conditions for Disability Benefits

To be eligible for disability benefits, individuals must be both fully insured and disability insured.[3] Disability insured status requires 20 QCs earned in the 40-quarter period ending with the quarter of disability, except that persons disabled before age 31 also can qualify if they have QCs in half of the quarters after age 21.[4] The definition of disability is relatively strict. The disability must be so severe that the individual is unable to engage in any substantial gainful activity, and the impairment must be a medically determinable physical or mental condition that is expected to continue for at least 12 months or to result in prior death. Benefits are first payable after completion of six full calendar months of disability. For persons with alcoholism or drug abuse, disability benefits are not payable unless they have another severe disabling condition which, by itself, would be qualifying.

Beneficiary Categories for Disability Benefits

In addition to the disabled worker, dependents in the same categories that apply to old-age retirement benefits can receive monthly benefits.

Benefit Computation Procedures for Disability Benefits

In all cases, the benefits are based on the (PIA), computed in the same manner as for retirement benefits, except that fewer dropout years than five are allowed in the computation of the (AIME) for persons disabled before age 47.[5] The disabled worker receives a benefit equal to 100 percent of the PIA, and the auxiliary beneficiaries each receive 50 percent of the PIA, subject to the Maximum Family Benefit.

An overall maximum on total family benefits is applicable, which is lower than that for survivor and retirement benefits—namely, no more than the smaller of 150 percent of the PIA, or 85 percent of AIME (but not less than the PIA).

Eligibility Test for Disability Benefits and Other Restrictions on Benefits

The earnings or retirement test applies to the auxiliary beneficiaries of disabled workers, but not to the disabled worker beneficiary. However, the earnings of one beneficiary (e.g., the spouse of the disabled worker) do not affect the benefits of the other beneficiaries in the family (e.g., the disabled worker or the children). The test does not apply to disabled worker beneficiaries, because any earnings are considered in connection with whether recovery has occurred, except those during

---

[3] Blind persons need be only fully insured.
[4] For those disabled before age 24, the requirement is six QCs in the last 12 quarters.
[5] Specifically four such quarters for ages 42–46, grading down to none for ages 26 and under.

trial work periods (which earnings may possibly lead to removal from the benefit roll later).

OASDI disability benefits are coordinated with disability benefits payable under other governmental programs (including programs of state and local governments), except for needs-tested ones, benefits payable by the Department of Veterans Affairs, and government employee plans coordinated with OASDI. The most important of such coordinations is with Workers' Compensation (WC) programs, whose benefits are taken into account in determining the amount of the OASDI disability benefit (except in a few states that provide for their WC benefits to be reduced when OASDI disability benefits are payable—possible only for states that did this before February 19, 1981). The total of the OASDI disability benefit (including any auxiliary benefits payable) and the other disability benefit recognized cannot exceed 80 percent of "average current earnings" (generally based on the highest year of earnings in covered employment in the last six years, but indexed for changes in wage levels following the worker's disablement).

Disability Freeze

In the event that a disability beneficiary recovers, the so-called disability-freeze provision applies. Under this, the period of disability is "blanked out" in the computation of insured status and benefit amounts for subsequent retirement, disability, and survivor benefits.

Historical Development of Survivor Provisions

When what is now the OASDI program was developed in 1934–35, it was confined entirely to retirement benefits (plus lump sum refund payments to represent the difference, if any, between employee taxes paid, plus an allowance for interest and retirement benefits received). It was not until the 1939 act that monthly survivor benefits were added with respect to deaths of both active workers and retirees, in lieu of the refund benefit.

The term *widow* is used here to include also widowers. Until 1983, the latter did not receive OASDI benefits on the same basis as widows, either being required to prove dependence on the deceased female worker or not being eligible at all. Now, because of legislative changes and court decisions, complete equality of treatment by sex prevails for OASDI survivor benefits.

The minimum eligibility age for aged widows was initially established at age 65. This figure was selected in a purely empirical manner, because it was a round figure (see the earlier discussion about retirement benefits on why this was selected as the minimum retirement age).

Beginning in the 1950s, pressure developed to provide early-retirement benefits, first for widows and spouses and then for insured workers themselves. The minimum early-retirement age was set at 62, again a pragmatic political compromise, rather than a completely logical choice and was later lowered to 60 for widows. The three-year differential, however, did represent about the average difference in age between men and their wives (but, of course, as with any averages, in many cases the actual difference is larger). The benefit amounts were not reduced for widows when they claimed before age 65 under the original amendatory legislation, but this is no longer the case.

Eligibility Conditions for Survivor Benefits

To be eligible for OASDI survivor benefits, individuals must have either fully insured status or currently insured status. The latter requires only six QCs earned in the 13-quarter period ending with the quarter of death.

Survivor Beneficiary Categories

Two general categories of survivors of insured workers can receive monthly benefits. Aged survivors are widows age 60 or over (or at ages 50–59 if disabled) and dependent parents age 62 or over. Young survivors are children under age 18 (or at any age if disabled before age 22), children age 18 who are full-time students in elementary or high school (i.e., defined just the same as in the case of retirement and disability beneficiaries), and the widowed parent of such children who are under age 16 or disabled before age 22. In addition, a death benefit of $255 is payable to widows or, in the absence of a widow, to children eligible for immediate monthly benefits.

The disabled widow receives a benefit at the rate of 71.5 percent of the deceased worker's PIA if claim is first made at ages 50–59.[6] The benefit rate for other widows grades up from 71.5 percent of the PIA if claimed at age 60 to 100 percent if claimed at the NRA, which is age 65 for those attaining age 60 before 2000, grading up to 67 for those attaining age 60 in 2022 and after. Any DRCs that the deceased worker had earned also are applicable to the widow's benefit. Widows, regardless of age, caring for an eligible child (under age 16 or disabled before age 22) have a benefit of 75 percent of the PIA. Divorced spouses, when the marriage lasted at least 10 years, are eligible for benefits under the same conditions as undivorced spouses.

The benefit rate for eligible children is 75 percent of the PIA. The benefit rate for dependent parents is 82.5 percent of the PIA, unless two parents are eligible, in which case it is 75 percent for each one.

The same overall maximum on total family benefits is applicable as is the case for retirement benefits. If a person is eligible for more than one type of benefit (e.g., both as a worker and as a surviving spouse), in essence, only the largest benefit is payable.

Benefit Computation Procedures for Survivor Benefits

In all cases, the monthly survivor benefits are based on the PIA and then are adjusted to reflect the Maximum Family Benefit, both of which are computed in essentially the same manner as is the case for retirement benefits.

---

[6] For individuals who die before age 62, the computation is made as though the individual had attained age 62 in the year of death. In addition, for deferred widow's benefits, an alternative computation based on indexing the deceased's earnings record up to the earlier of age 60 of the worker or age 60 of the widow is used if this produces a more favorable result.

Eligibility Test for Survivor Benefits and Other Restrictions

Marriage (or remarriage) of the survivor beneficiary generally terminates benefit rights. The only exceptions are remarriage of widows after age 60 (or after age 50 for disabled widows) and marriage to another OASDI beneficiary (other than one who is under age 18).

From the inception of the OASDI program, there has been some form of restriction on the payment of benefits to persons who have substantial earnings from employment, the earnings or retirement test. The same test applies to survivor beneficiaries as to retirement benefits for retirees who are under NRA. However, the earnings of one beneficiary (e.g., the widowed mother) do not affect the benefits of the other beneficiaries in the family (e.g., the orphaned children).

If a widow receives a pension from service under a government-employee pension plan under which the members were not covered under OASDI on the last day of her employment, the OASDI widow's benefit is reduced by two-thirds of the amount of such pension. This provision, however, is not applicable to women (or to men who were dependent on their wives) who became eligible for such a pension before December 1982 or to individuals who became first so eligible from December 1982 through June 1983 and who were dependent on their spouses.

Financing Provisions of OASDI Program

From its inception until the 1983 act, the OASDI program has been financed entirely by payroll taxes (and interest earnings on the assets of the trust funds), with only minor exceptions, such as the special benefits at a subminimum level for certain persons without insured status who attained age 72 before 1972. Thus, on a permanent ongoing basis, no payments from general revenues were available to the OASDI system; the contributions for covered federal civilian employees and members of the armed forces are properly considered as "employer" taxes.

The 1983 act introduced two instances of general-revenues financing of the OASDI program. As a one-time matter, the tax rate in 1984 was increased to what had been previously scheduled for 1985 (i.e., for both the employer and employee, from 5.4 percent to 5.7 percent), but the increase for employees was, in essence, rescinded, and the General Fund of the Treasury made up the difference to the OASDI Trust Funds. On an ongoing basis, the General Fund passes on to the trust funds the proceeds of the income taxation of 50 percent of OASDI benefits for upper-middle-income and high-income persons (first effective for 1984), and, in fact, does so somewhat in advance of actual receipt of such moneys.[7]

The payroll taxes for the retirement and survivors benefits go into the OASI Trust Fund, while those for the disability benefits go into the DI Trust Fund, and all benefit payments and administrative expenses for these provisions are paid therefrom. The balances in the trust fund are invested in federal government obligations of various types, with interest rates at the current market values for long-term securities.

---

[7] The income taxes on the next 35 percent of benefits (first effective in 1994) anomalously go to the Hospital Insurance Trust Fund.

The federal government does not guarantee the payments of benefits. If the trust fund were to be depleted, it could not obtain grants, or even loans, from the General Fund of the Treasury. However, a temporary provision (effective only in 1982) permitted the OASI Trust Fund to borrow, repayable with interest, from the DI and HI Trust Funds. A total of $17.5 billion was borrowed ($12.4 billion from HI). The last of such loans were repaid in 1986.

Payroll taxes are levied on earnings up to only a certain annual limit, which is termed the earnings base. This base is applicable to the earnings of an individual from each employer in the year, but the person can obtain a refund (on the income tax form) for all employee taxes paid in excess of those on the earnings base. The self-employed pay OASDI taxes on their self-employment income on no more than the excess of the earnings base over any wages they may have had.

Since 1975, the earnings base for OASDI has been determined by the automatic-adjustment procedure, on the basis of increases in the nationwide average wage. However, for 1979–81, ad hoc increases of a higher amount were legislated; the 1981 base was established at $29,700. The 1982 and subsequent bases were determined under the automatic-adjustment provision. The 2001 base was $80,400, while that for 2002 is $84,900.

The payroll tax rate is a combined one for (OASI), (DI), and (HI), but it is allocated among the three trust funds. The employer and employee rates are equal. The self-employed pay the combined employer-employee rate. In 1984–89, they had an allowance for the reduction in income taxes as if half of the OASDI-HI tax were to be considered as a business expense (as it is for incorporated employers); such allowance was a uniform reduction in the tax rate—2.7 percentage points in 1984, 2.2 percentage points in 1985, and 2.0 percentage points in 1986–89. After 1989, the direct procedure of considering half of the OASDI-HI taxes as a deduction from income is done for the self-employed. Also, until 1991, the earnings base was the same for OASDI and HI, but in 1991, the base for HI was raised to $125,000, and it was $130,200 in 1992 and was eliminated for 1994 and after.

The employer and employee rates were 1 percent each in 1937–49, but have gradually increased over the years, until being 7.15 percent in 1986–87 (the latter subdivided 5.2 percent for OASI, 0.5 percent for DI, and 1.45 percent for HI). These rates increased to 7.51 percent in 1988, and then to 7.65 percent in 1990 (and after), the latter being subdivided 5.3 percent for OASI, 0.9 percent for DI, and 1.45 percent for HI for 2000 and after.

Past Financing Crises of OASDI Program

In the mid-1970s, the OASI and DI trust funds were projected to have serious financing problems over both the long range and the short range. The short-range problem was thought to be remedied by the 1977 act, which raised taxes (both the rates and the earnings bases). At the same time, the long-range problem was partially solved by phased-in significant benefit reductions, by lowering the general benefit level, by freezing the minimum benefit, and by the "spouse government pension" offset, although an estimated deficit situation was still present for the period beginning after about 30 years.

The short-range problem was not really solved. The actuarial cost estimates assumed that earnings would rise at a somewhat more rapid rate than prices in the short range; but the reverse occurred—and to a significant extent—in 1979–81. Because increases in tax income depend on earnings and because increases in benefit outgo depend on prices, the financial result for the OASI Trust Fund was catastrophic. It would have been exhausted in late 1982 if not for legislation enacted in 1981. The DI Trust Fund did not have this problem, because the disability experience, which had worsened significantly in 1970–76, turned around and became relatively favorable—more than offsetting the unfavorable economic experience.

The 1981 act significantly reduced benefit outgo in the short range by a number of relatively small changes, shown in detail in Appendix 1B.

Further action beyond the 1981 amendments was essential to restore both the short-range and long-range solvency of the OASDI program. Because of the difficult political situation, President Reagan established the National Commission on Social Security Reform—a bipartisan group whose members were appointed both by President Reagan and the congressional leadership—to study the problem and make recommendations for its solution. Such recommendations were adopted almost in their entirety in the 1983 act. The most significant changes made by this legislation are described in Appendix 1B.

The changes made by the 1983 act were eminently successful over the short run. In the following years, the assets of the OASDI Trust Funds grew steadily from their very low level then and were about $1.4 trillion at the end of September 2002. Further, they are estimated to increase rapidly for the next two decades and reach a height of $6 trillion in 2025. However, thereafter a decline is estimated, and the balance will be exhausted in 2038 unless changes are made before then (which will most certainly occur). Ideally, the fund balance should be at least equal to one year's outgo at all times during the 75-year valuation period.

Possible Future OASDI Developments

Advisory groups have, over the years, advocated so-called universal coverage. Following the 1983 amendments, relatively little remains to be done in this area, except perhaps to cover compulsorily all new hires in state and local government employment (as was done in the federal area).

The NRA was increased from the present 65 to age 67, phased in over a period of years, by the 1983 act. This was done in recognition of the significant increase in life expectancy that has occurred in the last 40 years, as well as the likely future increases. If life expectancy increases even more rapidly than currently projected, a further increase in such age would reduce the higher long-range future cost of the program resulting from such increase.

The earnings test has always been subject to criticism by many persons, who argue that it is a disincentive to continued employment and that "the benefits have been bought and paid for, and therefore should be available at age 65." The 1983 act, by increasing ultimately (beginning with those who attain age 66 in 2009) the size of the delayed retirement credits (to 8 percent per year) to approximately the actuarial-equivalent level, virtually eliminated the earnings test after the NRA insofar as the cost aspects thereof are concerned. In other words, when the DRC is at an 8 percent level, the individual receives benefits for delayed retirement having approximately the same value as if benefits were paid without regard to the earnings test, beginning at the NRA. Some persons have advocated that the DRC should be at the 8 percent rate as soon as possible. As mentioned earlier, the earnings test was eliminated in 2000 for the month of attaining NRA, although insured workers can waive receipt of benefits and receive DRCs.

As to disability benefits, the definition might be tightened, such as by using "medical only" factors (and not vocational ones). Conversely, the definition could be liberalized so as to be on an occupational basis at age 50 and over. Also, the five-month waiting period could be shortened.

The general benefit level was significantly increased in 1969–72 (by about 23 percent in real terms), but financial problems caused this increase to be partially reversed in subsequent legislation (1974 and 1977). Nonetheless, there will be efforts by many persons to reverse the situation and expand the benefit level.

Over the years, the composition of the OASDI benefit structure—between individual-equity aspects and social-adequacy ones—tended to shift more toward social adequacy. The 1981 amendments, however, moved in the other direction (e.g., by phasing out student benefits and the minimum-benefit provision). There may well be efforts in the future to inject more social adequacy into the program—or, conversely, more individual equity.

It frequently has been advocated that people should be allowed to opt out of the OASDI system and provide their own economic security through private-sector mechanisms, using both their own taxes and those of their employer. Although this approach has certain appealing aspects, it has some significant drawbacks. First, it is not possible to duplicate to any close extent the various features of OASDI, most notably the automatic adjustment of benefits for increases in the CPI.

Second, because the low-cost individuals (young, high-earnings ones) would be the most likely to opt out, there is the question of where the resulting financing short-falls of the OASDI program would be covered. Those who make such proposals (or even the more extreme ones, which involve terminating OASDI for all except those currently covered who are near retirement age) do not answer this question. The only source of financing would be from general revenues, and this means more general taxes, which would be paid to a considerable extent by those who have opted out.

Proposals have been made to means-test (actually, income-test) OASDI benefits. Then, high-income persons would have their benefits sharply reduced (or even eliminated). Although this may seem appealing to solve budget deficits or OASDI financing problems, it has serious faults. Middle-income persons would tend to save less, because they would fear that saving would only mean a reduction in their OASDI benefits. Further, fraud and abuse would occur as people hid their assets and income therefrom or else transferred them to their children and had the income given back secretly.

Many have argued that part of the cost of OASDI should be met from general revenues. At times, an indirect manner of implementing such a funding method has been advocated, such as by moving part of the HI tax rate to OASDI and then partially financing HI from general revenues. The difficulty with this procedure is that no large amounts of general-revenues moneys are available for all future years to come; the General Fund of the Treasury is now estimated to have relatively small deficits for the next 10 to 15 years or so, but large deficits thereafter. In turn, this would mean either that additional taxes of other types would have to be raised or that any budget deficit would become larger, and inflation would be fueled. Those opposed to general-revenues financing of OASDI, and of HI as well, believe that the financing, instead, should be entirely from direct, visible payroll taxes. Nonetheless, it is likely that pressure for general-revenues financing of OASDI will continue.

According to the latest intermediate-cost estimate for present law, the OASDI Trust Funds will have large annual excesses of income over outgo for the next two decades. As a result, mammoth fund balances will accumulate—amounting to about $6.5 trillion in 2025. Under current budgetary procedures, such annual excesses are often considered as meeting the budget-deficit targets, and thus they hide the extent of titanic general-budget deficits. Further, the presence of such large fund balances could well encourage over-liberalization of the OASDI program now—for example, by raising benefit levels or by postponing the scheduled increases in the NRA beginning in about a decade.

To prevent these undesirable results from occurring, Senator Daniel Patrick Moynihan has proposed that the financing basis of the OASDI program be returned to a pay-as-you-go basis. This would be done by an immediate reduction in the contribution rates and the introduction of a graded schedule of increases in the contribution rates, beginning in about 20 years. This proposal produced a vast amount of discussion (and also education of the public). Such a proposal will undoubtedly continue to be raised, although it has strong opposition from those who are concerned with the general-budget deficits and seek to hide them through "counting Social Security surpluses."

In 2001, President Bush established an advisory commission to study partial privatization of OASDI. The commision was unable to agree on a specific plan, but rather only three alternative general proposals. Wide support of these proposals did not develop, at least in part because of the events of September 11 and the subsequent budget consequences.

Supplemental Security Income Program (SSI)

The SSI program replaced the federal/state public assistance programs of aid to the aged, blind, and disabled, except in Guam, Puerto Rico, and the Virgin Islands. Persons must be at least age 65 or be blind or disabled to qualify for the SSI payments.

The basic payment amount, before reduction for other income, for 2002 is $545 per month for one recipient and 50 percent more for an eligible couple. An automatic-adjustment provision closely paralleling that used under OASDI is applicable.

A number of "income disregards" are present. The most important is the disregard of $20 of income per month per family from such sources as OASDI, other pensions, earnings, and investments. The first $65 per month of earned income is disregarded, plus 50 percent of the remainder.

SSI has certain resource exemptions. In order to receive SSI, for 2002, resources cannot exceed $2,000 for an individual and $3,000 for a couple. However, in the calculation of resources, certain items are excluded—the home, household goods, and personal effects (depending on value), an automobile with value of $4,500 or less, burial plots, and property needed for self-support—if these are found to be reasonable. Also, if life insurance policies have a face amount of $1,500 or less for an individual, their cash values are not counted as assets.

Some states pay supplements to SSI.

In addition to SSI, a public assistance program provides payments for widowed mothers (and fathers) with children. This is on a state-by-state basis, with part of the cost borne by the federal government.

Medicare Program

Health (or medical care) benefits for active and retired workers and their dependents in the United States is, in the vast majority of cases, provided through the multiple means of the Medicare portion of Social Security for persons age 65 and over and for long-term disabled persons, private employer-sponsored plans, and individual savings. As mentioned earlier, this is sometimes referred to as a "three-legged stool" or the three pillars of economic security protection. Another view of the situation for persons age 65 and over and for long-term disabled persons is of Medicare providing the floor of protection for certain categories, or, in other cases, providing the basic protection. Supplementing this, private insurance is present, with public assistance programs such as Medicaid, providing a safety net of protection for those whose income is not sufficient to purchase the needed medical care not provided through some form of prepaid insurance.

Private health benefit plans supplement Medicare to some extent. In other instances—essentially for active workers and their families—health benefit protection is provided by the private sector. The net result, however, is a broad network of health benefit protection.

Historical Development of Provisions

Beginning in the early 1950s, efforts were made to provide medical care benefits (primarily for hospitalization) for beneficiaries under the OASDI program. In 1965, such efforts succeeded, and the resulting program is called Medicare.

Initially, Medicare applied only to persons age 65 and over. In 1972, disabled Social Security beneficiaries who had been on the benefit rolls for at least two years were made eligible, as were virtually all persons in the country who have end-stage renal disease (i.e., chronic kidney disease). Since 1972, relatively few changes in coverage or benefit provisions have been made. In 1988, legislation that provided catastrophic-coverage benefits—to be financed largely through a surtax on the income tax of eligible beneficiaries—was enacted. However, as a result of massive protests from those who would be required to pay the surtax, these provisions were repealed in 1989.

Medicare is really two separate programs. One part, Hospital Insurance (HI),[8] is financed primarily from payroll taxes on workers covered under OASDI, including those under the Railroad Retirement system. Beginning in 1983, all civilian employees of the federal government were covered under HI, even though, in general, not covered by OASDI. Also, beginning in April 1986, all newly hired state and local government employees are covered compulsorily (and, at the election of the governmental entity, all employees in service on March 31, 1986, who were not covered under OASDI can be covered for HI). The other part, Supplementary Medical Insurance (SMI), is on an individual voluntary basis and is financed partially by enrollee premiums, with the remainder, currently about 75 percent, coming from general revenues.

As an alternative to "traditional" Medicare, persons eligible under both HI and SMI (except those previously diagnosed with end-stage renal disease) can elect to participate in a Medicare + Choice plan. There are several types of such plans, but generally they must provide at least the same benefits as does Medicare (usually, they provide more, such as some drug benefits and lower cost-sharing payments). These plans receive per capita payments from Medicare (the participant continues paying the SMI premium to Medicare), which hopefully are equitable reimbursement. In theory, these plans are supposed to provide better health care at a lower cost (through managed-care principles), but some critics believe that they do not always provide adequate care, especially because they usually do not allow free choice of physicians to provide the services (and generally little or no choice at all).

Persons Protected by HI

All individuals age 65 and over who are eligible for monthly benefits under OASDI or the Railroad Retirement program also are eligible for HI benefits (as are federal employees and state and local employees who have sufficient earnings credit from their special HI coverage). Persons are "eligible" for OASDI benefits if they could receive them when the person on whose earnings record they are eligible is deceased or receiving disability or retirement benefits, or could be receiving retirement benefits except for having substantial earnings. Thus, the HI eligibles include not only insured workers, but also spouses, disabled children (in the rare cases where they are at least age 65), and survivors, such as widowed spouses and dependent parents. As a specific illustration, HI protection is available for an insured worker and spouse, both at least age 65, even though the worker has such high earnings that OASDI cash benefits are not currently payable because of election to defer receipt of benefits.

In addition, HI eligibility is available for disabled beneficiaries who have been on the benefit roll for at least two years (beyond a five-month waiting period). Such disabled eligibles include not only insured workers but also disabled child beneficiaries age 18 and over who were disabled before age 22, and disabled widowed spouses ages 50–64.

Further, persons under age 65 with end-stage renal disease (ESRD) who require dialysis or renal transplant are eligible for HI benefits if they meet one of a number

---

[8] Sometimes referred to as Part A. Supplementary Medical Insurance is Part B.

of requirements. Such requirements for ESRD benefits include being fully or currently insured, being a spouse or a dependent child of an insured worker or of a monthly beneficiary, or being a monthly beneficiary.

Individuals age 65 and over who are not eligible for HI as a result of their own or some other person's earnings can elect coverage, and then must make premium payments, whereas OASDI eligibles do not. The standard monthly premium rate is $319 for 2002 (but only $175 if they have at least 30 quarters of coverage).

Benefits Provided under HI

The principal benefit provided by the HI program is for hospital services. The full cost for all such services, other than luxury items, is paid by HI during a so-called spell of illness, after an initial deductible has been paid and with daily coinsurance for all hospital days after the 60th one, but with an upper limit on the number of days covered. A spell of illness is a period beginning with the first day of hospitalization and ending when the individual has been out of both hospitals and skilled nursing facilities for 60 consecutive days. The initial deductible is $812 for 2002. The daily coinsurance is $203 for the 61st to 90th days of hospitalization. A nonrenewable lifetime reserve of 60 days is available after the regular 90 days have been used; these lifetime reserve days are subject to daily coinsurance of $406 for 2002. The deductible and coinsurance amounts are adjusted automatically each year after 2002 to reflect past changes in hospital costs.

Benefits also are available for care provided in skilled nursing facilities, following at least three days of hospitalization. Such care is provided only when it is for convalescent or recuperative care and not for custodial care. The first 20 days of such care in a spell of illness are provided without cost to the individual. The next 80 days, however, are subject to a daily coinsurance payment, which is $101.50 in 2002, and it will be adjusted automatically in the future in the same manner as the hospital cost-sharing amounts. No benefits are available after 100 days of care in a skilled nursing facility for a particular spell of illness.

In addition, an unlimited number of home health service benefits are provided by HI and/or SMI without any payment being required from the beneficiary. Also, hospice care for terminally ill persons is covered if all Medicare benefits, other than physician services, are waived; certain cost restrictions and coinsurance requirements apply with respect to prescription drugs.

HI benefit protection is provided only within the United States, with the exception of certain emergency services available when in or near Canada. Not covered by HI are those cases where services are performed in a Department of Veterans Affairs hospital or where the person is eligible for medical services under a workers' compensation program. Furthermore, Medicare is the secondary payor in cases when (a) medical care is payable under any liability policy, especially automobile ones; (b) during the first 30 months of treatment for ESRD cases when private group health insurance provides coverage; (c) for persons age 65 and over (employees and spouses) who are under employer-sponsored group health insurance plans (which is required for all plans of employers with at least 20 employees) unless the employee opts out of it; and (d) for disability beneficiaries under the plan of an employer with at least 100 employees when the beneficiary is either an "active individual" or a family member of an employee.

Financing of HI

With the exception of the small group of persons who voluntarily elect coverage, the HI program is financed by payroll taxes on workers in employment covered by OASDI. This payroll tax rate is combined with that for OASDI. The HI tax rate is the same for employers and employees; self-employed persons pay the combined employer–employee tax rate, but have an offset to allow for the effect of business expenses on income taxes (as described earlier in connection with OASDI taxes). Such HI tax rate for employees was 1.45 percent in 1990 (and in all future years). The maximum taxable earnings base for HI was the same as that for OASDI for all years before 1991, but thereafter was a higher amount, and, beginning in 1994, no limit is applicable. Also, beginning in 1994, part of the income taxes on OASDI benefits is diverted to finance HI. It should be noted that long-range actuarial cost estimates indicate that this rate will not provide adequate financing after about 2025 (or perhaps even sooner).

The vast majority of persons who attained age 65 before 1968, and who were not eligible for HI benefit protection on the basis of an earnings record, were nonetheless given full eligibility for benefits without any charge. The cost for this closed blanketed-in group is met from general revenues, rather than from HI payroll taxes.

The HI Trust Fund receives the income of the program from the various sources and makes the required disbursements for benefits and administrative expenses. The assets are invested and earn interest in the same manner as the OASDI Trust Funds.

Although the federal government is responsible for the administration of the HI program, the actual dealing with the various medical facilities is through fiscal intermediaries, such as Blue Cross and insurance companies, which are reimbursed for their expenses on a cost basis. Beginning in 1988, reimbursement for inpatient hospital services is based on uniform sums for each type of case for about 490 diagnosis-related groups.

Persons Protected under Supplementary Medical Insurance

Individuals age 65 or over can elect SMI coverage on an individual basis regardless of whether they have OASDI insured status. In addition, disabled OASDI and Railroad Retirement beneficiaries eligible for HI and persons with ESRD eligibility under HI can elect SMI coverage. In general, coverage election must be made at about the time of initial eligibility; that is, attainment of age 65 or at the end of the disability-benefit waiting period. Subsequent election during general enrollment periods is possible but with higher premium rates being applicable. Similarly, individuals can terminate coverage and cease premium payment of their own volition.

Benefits Provided under SMI

The principal SMI benefit is partial reimbursement for the cost of physician services, although other medical services, such as diagnostic tests, ambulance services, prosthetic devices, physical therapy, medical equipment, home health services, and drugs not self-administerable are covered. Not covered are out-of-hospital drugs, most dental services, most chiropractic services, routine physical and eye examinations, eyeglasses and hearing aids, and services outside of the United States, except those in connection with HI services that are covered in Canada. Just as for HI, there are limits on SMI coverage in workers' compensation cases, medical care under liability policies, private group health insurance applicable to ESRD, and employer-sponsored group health insurance for employees and their spouses.

SMI pays 80 percent of "recognized" charges, under a complicated determination basis that usually produces a lower charge than the reasonable and prevailing one, after the individual has paid a calendar-year deductible of $100 for 1991 and after. Special limits apply on out-of-hospital mental health care costs and on the services of independent physical and occupational therapists. The cost-sharing payments ($100 deductible and 20 percent coinsurance) are waived for certain services (e.g., home health services, pneumococcal vaccine, and influenza shots, and certain clinical diagnostic laboratory tests). Beginning in 1993, physicians cannot charge Medicare patients more than 115 percent of Medicare "recognized" charges.

Financing of SMI

The standard monthly premium rate is $54 for 2002. The premium is higher for those who fail to enroll as early as they possibly can, with an increase of 10 percent for each full 12 months of delay. The premium is deducted from the OASDI or Railroad Retirement benefits of persons currently receiving them or is paid by direct submittal in other cases.

The remainder of the cost of the program is met by general revenues. In the aggregate, persons age 65 and over pay only about 25 percent of the cost, while for disabled persons such proportion is only about 20 percent. As a result, enrollment in SMI is very attractive, and about 95 percent of those eligible to do so actually enroll.

The enrollee premium rate will be changed every year after 2002, effective for January. According to "permanent" law, the rate of increase in the premium rate is determined by the percentage rise in the level of OASDI cash benefits in the previous year under the automatic adjustment provisions, and in part by the percentage rises in the per capita cost of the program. However, for the premium years 1996–98, the premium rate was set at 25 percent of the cost for persons age 65 or over. (The premium rates for 1992–95 were established by legislation.)

The SMI Trust Fund was established to receive the enrollee premiums and the payments from general revenues. From this fund are paid the benefits and the accompanying administrative expenses. Although the program is under the general supervision of the federal government, most of the administration is accomplished through "carriers," such as Blue Shield or insurance companies, on an actual cost basis for their administrative expenses.

Possible Future Developments of Medicare

Over the years, numerous proposals have been made to modify the Medicare program. Some of these would expand it significantly, while others would curtail it to some extent.

Among the proposals that would expand the program are those to establish some type of national health insurance program, having very comprehensive coverage of medical services applicable to the entire population. Somewhat less broadly, other proposals would extend Medicare coverage to additional categories of OASDI beneficiaries beyond old-age beneficiaries age 65 and over and disabled beneficiaries on the roll for at least two years—such as to early-retirement cases at ages 62–64 and to all disability beneficiaries.

In another direction, liberalizing proposals have been made to add further services, such as out-of-hospital drugs, physical examinations, and dental services. Still other proposals have been made in the direction of reducing the extent of cost-sharing on the part of the beneficiary by lowering or eliminating the deductible and coinsurance provisions and by eliminating the duration-of-stay limits on HI benefit eligibility.

Proposals have been made to reduce the cost of the Medicare program by increasing the cost-sharing payments made by the beneficiary. For example, the cost-sharing in the first 60 days of hospitalization could be changed from a one-time payment of the initial deductible to some type of daily coinsurance that would foster the incentive to shorten hospital stays. Another proposal is to adjust automatically, from year to year, the SMI annual deductible, which, unlike the HI cost-sharing payments, is a fixed amount, although it has been increased by ad hoc changes from the initial $50 in 1966 to $75 in 1982 and to $100 in 1991. Also, it has been proposed that the minimum age for nondisabled persons should rise above 65 when the NRA for OASDI does so.

A major risk for persons age 65 and over that is not covered by Medicare is the cost of long-term custodial nursing-home care and homemaker services for disabled or frail persons. Although many persons recognize the serious nature of this problem, it is currently being met only on a means-test basis by the Medicaid program. Some people believe that the problem should be met on an "insurance" basis under a new part of Medicare, but others think that it is not an "insurable" risk and must be handled on a means-test basis (possibly liberalized somewhat).

Proposals have been enacted to lower the cost of the HI programs as far as reimbursement of hospitals and skilled nursing facilities is concerned, although this would have no effect on the Medicare beneficiary directly.

Medicaid

Over the years, the cost of medical care for recipients of public assistance and for other low-income persons has been met in a variety of ways. Some years ago, these provisions were rather haphazard, and the medical care costs were met by inclusion with the public assistance payments. In 1960, a separate public assistance program in this area was enacted—namely, Medical Assistance for the Aged (MAA), which applied to persons age 65 and over, both those receiving Old-Age Assistance and other persons not having sufficient resources to meet large medical expenses.

Then in 1965, the MAA program and the federal matching for medical vendor payments for other public assistance categories than MAA were combined into the

Medicaid program. This new program covered not only public assistance recipients but also persons of similar demographic characteristics who were medically indigent.

The Medicaid program is operated by the states, with significant federal financing being available. Some states cover only public assistance recipients.

Medicaid programs are required to furnish certain services in order to receive federal financial participation. These services include those for physicians, hospitals (both inpatient and outpatient), laboratory and X-ray tests, home health visits, and nursing home care. Most other medical services, such as drugs, dental care, and eyeglasses, can be included at the option of the state, and then federal matching will be made available. Also, as a result of legislation enacted in 1988, states must pay the SMI premiums and the HI and SMI cost-sharing payments for persons who are eligible for Medicare and who have incomes below the poverty level and have resources of no more than twice the standard under the Supplemental Security Income program. Thus, the states have the advantage of the relatively large general-revenues financing in the Medicaid program.

The federal government pays a proportion of the total cost of the Medicaid expenditures for medical care that varies inversely with the average per capita income of the state. This proportion is 55 percent for a state with the same average per capita income as the nation as a whole. States with above-average income have a lower matching proportion, but never less than 50 percent. Conversely, states with below-average income have a higher federal matching percentage, which can be as much as 83 percent. The federal government also pays part of the administrative costs of the Medicaid programs; generally, this is 50 percent, although for certain types of expenses that are expected to control costs the federal percentage is higher.

Appendix

1A

Detailed Descriptions of Several Social Security Benefit Elements

This appendix describes the features of three complex elements involved in the computation of OASDI benefits.

Computation of Average Indexed Monthly Earnings

The AIME is a career-average earnings basis, but it is determined in such a manner as to closely approximate a final-average basis. In a national social insurance plan, it would be inadvisable to use solely an average of the last few years of employment, because that could involve serious manipulation through the cooperation of both the employee and the employer; whereas in a private pension plan, the employer has a close financial interest not to do so. Furthermore, OASDI benefit computation is not proportionate to years of coverage or proportion of worklife in covered employment, as is the case for private pension plans generally.

The first step in computing the AIME is to determine the number of years over which it must be computed. On the whole, the number depends solely on the year in which the individual attains age 62. The general rule is that the computation period equals the number of years beginning with 1951, or with the year of attaining age 22, if later, up through the year before attainment of age 62, minus the so-called five dropout years. The latter is provided so the very lowest five years of earnings can be eliminated. Also, years of high earnings in or after the year of attaining age 62 can be substituted for earlier, lower years.

As an example, persons attaining age 62 in 1990 have a computation period of 34 years (the 39 years in 1951–89, minus 5). The maximum period is 35 years for those attaining age 62 after 1990. For the infrequent case of an individual who had qualified for OASDI disability benefits and who recovered from the disability, the number of computation years for the AIME for retirement benefits is reduced by the number of full years after age 21 and before age 62 during any part of which the person was under a disability.

The AIME is not computed from the actual covered earnings, but rather after indexing them, to make them more current as compared with the wage level at the time of retirement. Specifically, covered earnings for each year before attainment of age 60 are indexed to that age, while all subsequent covered earnings are used in their actual amount. No earnings before 1951 can be used, but all earnings subsequently, even before age 22 or after age 61, are considered.

The indexing of the earnings record is accomplished by multiplying the actual earnings of each year before the year that age 60 was attained by the increase in earnings from the particular year to the age-60 year. For example, for persons attaining age 62 in 1990 (i.e., age 60 in 1988), any earnings in 1951 would be converted to indexed earnings by multiplying them by 6.90709, which is the ratio of the nationwide average wage in 1988 to that in 1951. Similarly, the multiplying factor for 1952 earnings is 6.50251, and so on. Once the earnings record for each year in the past has been indexed, the earnings for the number of years required to be averaged are selected to include the highest ones possible; if there are not sufficient years with earnings, then zeroes must be used. Then, the AIME is obtained by dividing the total indexed earnings for such years by 12 times such number of years.

Application of Windfall Elimination Provision

Excluded from the operation of this provision are the following categories: (1) persons who attain age 62 before 1986; (2) persons who were *eligible* for a pension from noncovered employment before 1986; (3) disabled-worker beneficiaries who became disabled before 1986 (and were entitled to such benefits in at least one month in the year before attaining age 62); (4) persons who have at least 30 "years of coverage" (as defined hereafter); (5) persons who were employed by the federal government on January 1, 1984, and were then brought into coverage by the 1983 amendments; and (6) persons who were employed on January 1, 1984, by a nonprofit organization that was not covered on December 31, 1983, and had not been so covered at any time in the past.

Under this method of computation of the PIA, beginning with the 1990 cohort of eligibles, the percentage factor applicable to the lowest band of earnings is 40 percent, instead of 90 percent. As a transitional measure, those who became first eligible for OASDI benefits in 1986 have an 80 percent factor, while it is 70 percent for the 1987 cohort, 60 percent for the 1988 cohort, and 50 percent for the 1989 cohort.

For persons who have 21–29 "years of coverage," an alternative phase-in procedure is used (if it produces a larger PIA). The percentage factor applicable to the lowest band of earnings in the PIA formula is 85 percent for 29 years of coverage, 80 percent for 28 years, down to 45 percent for 21 years.

In any event, under any of the foregoing procedures, the PIA as computed in the regular manner will never be reduced by more than 50 percent of the pension based on noncovered employment (or the pro rata portion thereof based on noncovered employment after 1956 if it is based on both covered and noncovered employment).

Determination of "Years of Coverage" for Special Minimum Benefit and for Windfall Elimination Provision

For purposes of the special minimum benefit, for periods before 1991, a "year of coverage" is defined as a year in which earnings are at least 25 percent of the maximum taxable earnings base; while after 1990, a factor of 15 percent is used. However, for 1979 and after, the maximum taxable earnings base is taken to be what would have prevailed if the ad hoc increases in the base provided by the 1977 act had not been applicable, but, instead, the automatic annual increases had occurred.

For the purposes of the Windfall Elimination Provision, a "year of coverage" is defined in the same way, except that the 25 percent factor continues after 1990.

In 2001, a "year of coverage" is $8,955 for purposes of the special minimum benefit and $14,925 for the Windfall Elimination Provision.

Appendix 1B

Changes in Social Security Program Made by Amendments in 1981 and 1983

This appendix describes the most important changes that were made in the OASDI program in 1981 and 1983, when it experienced a significant financial problem, of both a short-range and a long-range nature. The 1981 amendments were of a "stop-gap" nature, while the 1983 amendments were intended to provide a complete solution to the problem.

The 1981 act significantly reduced benefit outgo in the short range by the following actions:

1. The regular minimum benefit (an initial PIA of $122) was eliminated for all new eligibles after 1981, except for certain covered members of religious orders under a vow of poverty.

2. Child school attendance benefits at ages 18–21 were eliminated by a gradual phase-out, except for high school students age 18.

3. Mother's and father's benefits with respect to nondisabled children terminate when the youngest child is age 16 (formerly 18).

4. Lump sum death payments were eliminated, except when a surviving spouse who was living with the deceased worker is present, or when a spouse or child is eligible for immediate monthly benefits.

5. Sick pay in the first six months of illness is considered to be covered wages.

6. Lowering of the exempt age under the earnings test to age 70 in 1982 was delayed until 1983.

7. The Workers' Compensation offset against disability benefits was extended to several other types of governmental disability benefits.

8. Interfund borrowing among the OASI, DI, and HI Trust Funds was permitted, but only until December 31, 1982, and then no more than sufficient to allow payments of OASI benefits through June 1983.

Further action beyond the 1981 amendments was essential to restore both the short-range and long-range solvency of the OASDI program. President Reagan established the National Commission on Social Security Reform—a bipartisan group whose members were appointed both by him and the Congressional leadership—to make recommendations for its solution. Such recommendations were adopted almost in their entirety in the 1983 act.

This legislation made the following significant changes in the OASDI program (as well as some in the HI program):

1. OASDI and HI Coverage Provisions
    a. OASDI-HI coverage of new federal employees and current political appointees, elected officials, and judges. (HI coverage of all federal civilian employees was effective in 1983 under previous law.)
    b. Coverage of all employees of nonprofit charitable, educational, and religious organizations.
    c. State and local employees once covered are prohibited from withdrawing.
    d. Employee contributions to cash-or-deferred arrangements (Sec. 401[k]) and employer contributions under nonqualified deferred-compensation plans when no substantial risk of forfeiture is present are covered.
2. OASDI Benefit Provisions
    a. Cost-of-living adjustments are deferred for six months (i.e., will always be in checks for December payable in early January).
    b. The indexing of benefits in payment status is changed from being based only on the CPI to the lower of CPI or wage increases when the trust funds are relatively low.
    c. Gradual increases will be made in the normal retirement age from the present 65, beginning with those attaining age 62 in 2000—so it will be 66 for those attaining such age in 2009–20, then rising to 67 for those attaining such age in 2027 and after. Age 62 is retained as the early-retirement age, but with appropriate, larger actuarial reductions.
    d. Gradual increases will be made in the credit for postponing claiming (or not receiving) benefits beyond the normal retirement age from 3 percent per year for persons attaining age 65 in 1982–89 to 8 percent for persons attaining normal retirement age in 2009 and after.
    e. The retirement earnings test for persons at the normal retirement age up to age 70 is liberalized, beginning in 1990, by changing the "$1 for $2" reduction in benefits for earnings above the annual exempt amount to a "$1 for $3" basis.

   f. Several minor changes are made to liberalize benefits that primarily affect women (e.g., indexing deferred widow[er]'s benefits by whichever is more favorable, prices or wages, and increasing the benefit rate for disabled widow[er]s age 50 to 59 from 50 percent to 71.5 percent, depending on age at entitlement, to a uniform 71.5 percent).

   g. The situation about windfall benefits for retired and disabled workers, with pensions from noncovered employment and OASDI benefits based on a short period of covered employment, is alleviated.

   h. The offset of government employee pensions based on employment not covered by OASDI against OASDI spouse and widow(er) benefits is reduced from a full offset to a two-thirds offset.

   i. Restrictions are placed on the payment of benefits to prisoners receiving retirement and survivor benefits (previous law related essentially to disability beneficiaries).

   j. Restrictions are placed on the payment of benefits to aliens residing abroad who have, in general, not had at least five years of residence in the United States.

3. Revenue Provisions, OASDI and HI

   a. OASDI tax rate scheduled for 1985 was moved to 1984 for employers, but not employees. Trust funds receive, from general revenues, additional amount of taxes as if employee rate had been increased.

   b. Self-employed pay the combined OASDI-HI employer-employee rate, minus (for 1984–89) a credit (in lieu of a business expense deduction for such taxes). The trust funds receive, from general revenues, the additional amount of taxes as if the full employer-employee rate had been paid.

   c. About 72 percent of the OASDI tax rate increase scheduled for 1990 was moved forward to 1988.

   d. Part of OASDI benefits (but not more than 50 percent) will be subject to income tax for persons with high incomes, with the proceeds going into the OASDI Trust Funds.

   e. A lump sum transfer of general revenues will be made to meet the cost of certain gratuitous military-service wage credits (which, under previous law, would have been paid for in future years).

   f. Interfund borrowing (which, under previous law, was permitted only in 1982) was allowed in 1983–87, with specific repayment provisions (before 1990 at the latest) and with prohibitions against borrowing from a fund that is relatively low.

   g. Operations of OASDI and HI Trust Funds will be removed from Unified Budget after FY 1992 (subsequent legislation moved this up to 1986 for OASDI).

   h. Two public members will be added to the boards of trustees.

4. HI Reimbursement Provisions

   a. A new method of reimbursement of hospitals will be gradually phased in. This will be done on the basis of uniform amounts (but varying among nine geographical areas and as between rural and urban facilities) for each of 467 Diagnosis-Related Groups.

   b. No change is made in the minimum eligibility age for HI benefits for the aged (i.e., it remains at 65).

5. SMI Provisions
   a. The enrollee premium rate is changed to a calendar-year basis (to correspond with the OASDI Cost-of-Living Adjustments (COLAs). The rate for July 1982 through June 1983 was to continue through December 1983.
   b. No change is made in the minimum eligibility age for SMI benefits for the aged (i.e., it remains at 65).

These changes in OASDI were about equally divided, over the long run, between increases in income and reductions in outgo. They were supposed to solve both the short-range problem (the 1980s), which they did, and the long-range problem (of the following 75 years), which, as it turned out, they did not completely do.

Appendix 2

Multiemployer Plans

Cynthia J. Drinkwater[1]

Multiemployer plans provide benefits to employees in unionized industries such as the apparel trades, professional and consumer services, the entertainment industry, transportation, and construction. Often these employees are highly mobile, working for several employers a year. If it were not for multiemployer plans, which are arranged by industry (or related industries) on a local, regional, or national level, such employees would be forced to switch plans as often as they do employment. Benefit coverage would be haphazard and incomplete.

Within the structure of a multiemployer plan, employers contribute to one trust fund from which benefits are paid to all eligible employees. Staff of a separate, centralized office perform administrative functions, such as determination of eligibility, maintenance of participant records, claim processing, and payment of benefits. Contributing employers, thus, avoid the details of administering and delivering benefits. To some extent, contributing employers also enjoy economies of scale inherent in the maintenance of a common plan versus numerous separate ones. This accounts for multiemployer plans maintained even by employers with relatively more permanent workforces, such as those in the retail trade industry.

As with collectively bargained single-employer plans, employer contributions to (or, less frequently, benefits of) multiemployer plans are negotiated between the respective employees and employers and formalized contractually in collective-bargaining agreements. Unlike single-employer collectively bargained plans, which are likely to be administered unilaterally by the employer, multiemployer plan responsibility falls upon a board of trustees equally representative of labor and

---

[1] This appendix originally appeared as Chapter 49 in *The Handbook of Employee Benefits,* 5th ed., Jerry S. Rosenbloom, ed. (Burr Ridge, IL: Irwin Professional Publishing, 2001).

management. The board of trustees is charged with making plan decisions in the interests of plan participants and beneficiaries without regard to the labor or management constituency that designates the board.

It is not always logical or feasible to apply benefit knowledge appropriate for a benefit plan designed, funded, and administered by one employer to a multiemployer plan. In some areas, such as withdrawal liability, plan termination, and plan insolvency, special multiemployer plan rules have been established. In other areas, such as plan qualification, most requirements apply to multiemployer plans as well as single-employer plans, but sometimes multiemployer plan practice is more liberal than what is specified in the requirements, or the requirements are at odds with the multiemployer plan structure. And at times, employee benefits law has been modified to fit the multiemployer plan framework as well as that of the single-employer plan, as evidenced by amendments to the Consolidated Omnibus Budget Reconciliation Act of 1985 (COBRA).

The unique features of a multiemployer plan—mobile employees, numerous contributing employers, a common trust fund with centralized administration, collectively bargained benefits, and a joint board of trustees—have the potential to complicate the responsibilities of trustees, plan administrators, and professionals who carry out the day-to-day tasks of running a plan. Yet, advantages of multiemployer plans to both employees and employers is evidenced by their continued presence in the United States for nearly 45 years. Multiemployer plans in 1992 numbered approximately 7,000 plans, with about 8.5 million total participants in welfare plans and about 10.5 million total participants in pension plans.[2] Multiemployer plans have been and will remain an important part of the employee benefits environment.

Multiemployer Plan Defined

Two characteristics of an employee benefit plan make it multiemployer in nature: the number of contributing employers and a collective-bargaining origin. As indicated by its name, more than one employer contributes to a multiemployer plan. Employers contribute to the plan pursuant to a collective-bargaining agreement (or agreements) with one or more employee organizations. Typically, these employee organizations are unions.

Employer contributions to multiemployer plans are negotiated through the collective-bargaining process and fixed in the collective-bargaining agreement—usually on a dollars-per-hour, unit-of-production, or percentage-of-compensation basis. A distinguishing feature of a multiemployer defined benefit plan is that it actually resembles both a defined benefit and a defined contribution plan—although employer contributions are fixed, participants' benefits are based on a formula. Because contributions to multiemployer plans are calculated on some basis of work performed, a multiemployer

---

[2] Terence Davidson, "Characteristics of Multiemployer Plans," *Employee Benefit Basics,* Second Quarter (Brookfield, WI: International Foundation of Employee Benefit Plans, 1996).

plan's income is dependent on the level of economic activity in participants' industries. Contributions and benefits, therefore, are adjusted periodically to reflect the actual experience of the plan.

The description "multiple employer" plan is sometimes incorrectly interchanged with "multiemployer" plan. A multiple employer plan has only the first feature of a multiemployer plan—more than one employer contributes. There are no collective-bargaining agreements requiring contributions in a multiple-employer plan.

The Taft-Hartley Connection

"Taft-Hartley" plan, too, often is used synonymously with "multiemployer" plan. It is not the number of contributing employers, however, that distinguishes a Taft-Hartley plan but its joint, labor-management administration. Under Section 302(c) of the Taft-Hartley Act of 1947 (also referred to as the Labor-Management Relations Act), it is a criminal act for an employer to give money or anything else of value to employee representatives or a union, including contributions to an employee benefit plan administered solely by the union. An employer is permitted, though, to contribute to a jointly administered employee benefit trust fund for the "sole and exclusive benefit" of employees, their families, and dependents.[3]

Joint labor-management employee benefit plan administration required by the Taft-Hartley Act can be found in either a multiemployer or single-employer plan. Single-employer Taft-Hartley plans, in which an individual employer enters into a collective-bargaining agreement with union employees and administers a benefit plan jointly with the union, are not common. Multiemployer plans always are jointly administered.

Contributions to a jointly administered trust fund are legal under the Taft-Hartley Act only if (1) payments are in accordance with a written agreement with the employer, (2) the agreement provides for employers and employees to agree upon an impartial umpire for disputes (if no neutral persons are authorized to break deadlocks), (3) the trust fund is audited annually, and (4) the employer and employees are represented equally in fund administration. Furthermore, Taft-Hartley plans may be established only to fund certain types of employee benefits. The types of benefits have expanded over the years, generally from just medical/hospital care; pensions; occupational illnesses/injuries; unemployment; and life, disability/sickness, or accident insurance to include vacation, holiday, or severance benefits; apprenticeship and training programs; educational scholarships; child care centers; and legal services. In 1990, Congress added financial assistance for employee housing to the list of valid purposes for establishment of a Taft-Hartley trust fund.

---

[3] LMRA Sec. 302(c)(5). Trust funds established before January 1, 1946, that are unilaterally administered by a union are valid.

Purposes of Taft-Hartley Funds	
Medical/hospital care	Pooled vacation/holiday/severance benefits
Pensions	Apprenticeship/training programs
Occupational illness/injury	Educational scholarships
Unemployment benefits	Child care centers
Life insurance	Legal services
Disability/sickness insurance	Financial assistance for housing
Accident insurance	

"Built-In" Portability of Benefits

One of a multiemployer plan's greatest advantages for a mobile workforce is its built-in portability. Portability refers to the ability to transfer benefits from one employer's plan to another. Although they might work for numerous employers over the course of their work lives, employees covered under collective bargaining agreements that require employer contributions to multiemployer plans usually do not have to be concerned with losing benefits from or transferring benefits among employers' plans. In multiemployer pension plans, for example, employees will be credited years of service for vesting and participation purposes as long as they work for a contributing employer in covered service or in contiguous noncovered service with the same employer. Contiguous noncovered service is nonbargaining unit service, such as supervisory work, preceding or following covered service.[4]

In addition to built-in portability, some multiemployer plans enter into reciprocal agreements with other multiemployer plans—both pension, and health and welfare. Not only, then, are benefits portable from one employer to another through the multiemployer plan, but benefits of employers contributing to different multiemployer plans also are portable among multiemployer plans.

In multiemployer pension plans, reciprocity agreements are arranged in two ways. Among some funds, pension contributions "follow the man." Contributions on behalf of a "traveler" to a local fund are paid to the traveler's home fund, which distributes the entire benefit to the participant based on its own formula. In other reciprocity agreements, no contributions are transferred. Instead, years of service among funds are combined for purposes of plan participation and vesting. Each fund pays benefits based only on its own years of service, or a pro rata share. In health and welfare plans, reciprocity agreements are arranged similarly and used to avoid a period of noncoverage while an employee waits to satisfy another multiemployer plan's eligibility requirements.

First developed in the mid-1960s, reciprocal agreements are most common among the building and construction trades. In 1987, almost one-half of all multi-

---

[4] 29 CFR Sec. 2530.210(c). For benefit accrual purposes, covered service with any employer maintaining the plan will be taken into account.

employer funds were party to reciprocity agreements.[5] In some instances, these agreements extend portability among multiemployer plans to a national level.

Joint Board Of Trustees

A unique feature of multiemployer plans is equal representation of employers and employees in plan administration. Unlike a unilaterally administered single-employer plan, where the employer directly administers the plan without employee participation, a multiemployer plan is administered by a joint board of trustees. The board of trustees is the "plan sponsor" of a multiemployer plan (the equivalent of an employer in a single-employer plan) as well as the plan's "named fiduciary" and has exclusive authority and discretion to manage the assets of the plan.

Multiemployer plan trustees are designated by labor and management and do not necessarily have a background in employee benefits or any specific aspects of plan administration, although professional trustees do exist. How, then, can a politically and economically divided board of trustees administer a plan solely in the interests of plan participants and beneficiaries? Moreover, how can multiemployer plan trustees prudently administer a plan without appropriate skills and experience? The answer lies in the trustees' awareness of and dedication to fulfilling fiduciary duties to plan participants and the trustees' ability to delegate, within limitations, plan responsibilities to experts.

Multiemployer plan trustees, unlike trustees of unilaterally administered single-employer plans who have been selected by management, inevitably face conflicts of interest given their labor or management backgrounds. Often, multiemployer trustees also are officers or agents of either a contributing employer or a union, and therefore have loyalties both to employee benefit plan participants and to the bargaining party they represent.

Working under what is described by many as the "two-hat dilemma," multiemployer plan trustees are inevitably faced with making decisions that promote the interests of plan participants and beneficiaries but conflict with positions they would take if they were not plan trustees. Advising legal action for the collection of delinquent employer contributions, for example, is an area of potential conflict of interest, particularly for management trustees. Despite union or employer selection, the multiemployer plan trustee's labor or management "hat" comes off when administering the plan. "[A]n employee benefit fund trustee is a fiduciary whose duty to the trust beneficiaries must overcome any loyalty to the interest of the party that appointed him," the Supreme Court has declared in an oftrepeated statement.[6]

As with all employee benefit plan fiduciaries, multiemployer plan trustees are charged with administering a plan with the care, skill, prudence, and diligence that a prudent person acting in a similar capacity and familiar with such matters would

---

[5] "Reciprocity and Multiemployer Funds: A Model of Portability," *Employee Benefit Notes,* February 1987, p. 5, contributed by the Martin E. Segal Company.
[6] *NLRB* v. *Amax Coal Co.,* 453 U.S. 322, 323 (1981).

use. Most labor and management trustees have full-time jobs outside of their plan responsibilities, are not paid for their efforts (except for reasonable expenses), and are not necessarily skilled or experienced in employee benefit plan operation. Fiduciary, trustee, and other responsibilities of multiemployer plan trustees, therefore, frequently are delegated to other individuals. This delegation of responsibility is proper as long as it is authorized and prudent.

Under the overview of the joint board of trustees, plan administrators and such professionals as attorneys, accountants, actuaries, consultants, and investment managers handle the daily functions of multiemployer plans. Some multiemployer plan administrators are salaried, working solely for the fund in an employee status. Other plan administrators work under contract for several benefit plans (sometimes both single and multiemployer) at one time. The administrators of most Taft-Hartley funds are salaried.[7]

Through education of multiemployer plan trustees about the two-hat dilemma and prudent delegation of plan responsibilities, potential weaknesses of multiemployer plans can turn into strong points. As a well-known employee benefits attorney has said about the contribution of lay labor and management trustees to multiemployer plan operation: "The greatest strength that the trustee brings to the Taft-Hartley trustee table is his or her knowledge and feeling for the industry and the people in it."[8] The interests of plan participants, when trustees separate labor and management duties from plan duties and prudently delegate responsibilities to other persons better equipped to perform them, are well served by the multiemployer plan.

Withdrawal Liability

In addition to joint labor-management administration and the unique characteristic of built-in portability, the multiemployer plan is notable for a somewhat perpetual existence independent of individual contributing employers. Because other employers participate in a multiemployer plan, an individual employer's withdrawal does not cause the plan to terminate.

This structural aspect of multiemployer plans, specifically of multiemployer pension plans funded for benefits payable far in the future and not on a pay-as-you-go basis, is potentially hazardous to participants. Without some sort of safeguard, employers remaining in a multiemployer defined benefit plan could owe vested benefits earned by employees of employers opting out of the plan. Given this disincentive to remain in a multiemployer plan, particularly one covering employees in a declining industry, many employers would want to withdraw and the plan would be unable to pay participants the retirement benefits they had been promised.

The Employee Retirement Income Security Act of 1974 (ERISA) originally addressed this problem, but did not go far enough in discouraging employers from

[7] Bernard Handel, "Forms and Functions of Administration," chapter in *Trustees Handbook,* 5th ed., Marc Gertner, ed. (Brookfield, WI: International Foundation of Employee Benefit Plans, 1998), p. 323.
[8] Marc Gertner, "Basic Concepts of Trusteeship," chapter in *Trustees Handbook,* p. 19.

withdrawing from a financially weak multiemployer defined benefit plan. Employers faced liability for unfunded vested benefits only if they contributed to a multiemployer plan within five years of the plan's termination. Moreover, liability was limited to 30 percent of the employer's net worth.

In 1980, Congress recognized the precarious financial condition the multiemployer defined benefit plan structure placed on both employers and the Pension Benefit Guaranty Corporation (PBGC) and passed the Multiemployer Pension Plan Amendments Act (MPPAA). The MPPAA amended ERISA's withdrawal liability rules, making withdrawal liability harsher for withdrawing employers but fairer for those remaining in the plan. Under the MPPAA, any employer withdrawing from a multiemployer defined benefit plan that has unfunded, vested benefits is liable for its proportionate share of the benefits—whether the plan terminates or not. Hence, remaining employers no longer shoulder the full burden of the plan's unfunded vested benefits.

Plan Termination and Insolvency

Although an employer's withdrawal from a multiemployer plan does not terminate the plan, a mass withdrawal (all employers withdrawing) will. Also, a multiemployer plan terminates if a plan amendment is adopted to either freeze service credits or change a defined benefit plan to a defined contribution plan. When a multiemployer plan does terminate, no reversion of residual assets to a contributing employer is allowed. In contrast, a single-employer sponsor may recover surplus plan assets upon plan termination (but also will encounter an excise tax of up to 50 percent of the reversion).

Unlike the guarantee of nonforfeitable benefits under a single-employer plan upon plan termination, the PBGC guarantees the nonforfeitable benefits of participants of a multiemployer defined benefit plan only upon plan insolvency—not plan termination. When the available resources of a multiemployer plan are not sufficient to pay benefits for a plan year, the PBGC provides the insolvent plan with a loan.

The PBGC's insolvency insurance program for multiemployer plans is funded and maintained separately from its termination insurance program for single-employer plans. The multiemployer program covers about 9.4 million participants in about 1,700 plans; the single-employer program covers about 35 million participants in about 33,500 plans.[9] The PBGC insolvency insurance premium for multiemployer plans, unlike the termination insurance premium for single-employer plans, is not risk related. The annual premium for each participant of a multiemployer plan is $2.60. In comparison, the annual PBGC premium for single-employer plans is $19 per participant, plus $9 per participant for every $1,000 of unfunded vested benefits.[10]

---

[9] Pension Benefit Guaranty Corporation, *2001 Annual Report to the Congress* (Washington, DC), p. q13.
[10] ERISA Sec. 4006(a)(3).

With the more stringent withdrawal liability provisions MPPAA introduced in 1980, the majority of multiemployer plans are now fully funded and chances of plan insolvency have decreased. In 1994, about 3 percent of multiemployer plans were underfunded by a total of $27.4 billion. In comparison, 55 percent of single-employer plans were underfunded by a total of $64 billion in 1996.[11]

Plan Qualification

Unlike withdrawal liability and PBGC insolvency insurance, which are areas distinct to multiemployer plans, Internal Revenue Code (IRC) plan qualification provisions generally apply to single-employer and multiemployer plans alike. These qualification provisions, such as the minimum participation, minimum coverage, and minimum and full-funding rules, permit tax advantages to pension plans that meet them. As with single-employer plans, if a multiemployer plan is "qualified," contributions are tax deductible for contributing employers, and benefits (including investment income) are tax deferred for employees until distribution.

In some instances, bargaining-unit employees in multiemployer plans are excluded from or easily meet plan qualification rules. For example, a plan of which a qualified trust is a part must benefit the lesser of 50 employees or 40 percent of the employees of an employer. This minimum participation standard does not apply to employees in a multiemployer plan who are covered by collective-bargaining agreements.[12]

Plan qualification provisions designed to prevent discrimination in favor of highly compensated employees similarly call for a disaggregation of a multiemployer plan into a plan covering the bargaining-unit employees and plans covering nonbargaining-unit employees. In the case of the minimum coverage requirements, bargaining-unit employees are excluded from the testing of that portion of the plan covering nonbargaining-unit employees if retirement benefits were the subject of good-faith bargaining. Tested separately and as employees of one employer, the collectively bargained portion of a multiemployer plan should automatically pass the minimum coverage test because all other employees are excluded (i.e., 100 percent of the non-highly compensated and 100 percent of the highly compensated employees in the bargaining unit will be covered).[13]

In nondiscrimination tests that compare the benefits actually provided to highly and non-highly compensated employees, rather than the coverage, such as the 401(k) actual deferral percentage and actual contribution percentage tests, plan qualification requirements become more difficult for multiemployer plans. Bargaining-unit employees, again, are similarly treated as employees of one employer and tested as a separate plan.

---

[11] *Pension Benefit Guaranty Corporation: Financial Condition Improving but Long-Term Risks Remain* (Washington, DC: General Accounting Office, 1999), pp. 8, 12, 13.

[12] IRC Sec. 401(a)(26)(E). A special testing rule for nonbargaining-unit employees allows the plan to meet the minimum participation standard if 50 employees, including those covered by a collectively bargained agreement, benefit from the plan.

[13] Treas. Reg. Sec. 1.410(b)–6(d)(1).

However, multiemployer plan administrators have to rely on contributing employers for identification of highly compensated employees, and it is unclear whether an employer's failure to do so will disqualify the plan. As with other nondiscrimination testing, each employer's nonbargaining-unit employees are treated as a separate plan.[14]

As mentioned earlier, sometimes multiemployer plan practice is more liberal than the plan qualification rules under the IRC, and sometimes plan qualification rules are more liberal for multiemployer plans than for single-employer plans. To constitute a qualified trust, for example, the plan of which it is a part generally cannot require an employee to be over 21 years of age or to complete a period of service longer than one year (if over age 21) to participate. Because most collective-bargaining agreements require contributions for individuals within a bargaining unit or classification—regardless of age—multiemployer plans seldom have an age prerequisite for participation.[15]

Compliance with qualification requirements either intended for single-employer plans or incognizant of multiemployer plans, is, at times, difficult for multiemployer plan trustees and administrators. Compliance with the full funding limitation changes of the Omnibus Budget Reconciliation Act of 1987 (OBRA '87) was particularly problematical. OBRA '87 placed a cap of 150 percent of current liabilities over plan assets on the deductible contributions an employer may make to a pension plan. This full-funding limitation modification, which in 1999 began a phased-in increase to 170 percent by 2005, was intended to prevent the loss of tax revenue through the over-funding of pension plans for liabilities not yet incurred—particularly the overfunding of single-employer plans targeted for recovery of surplus assets upon termination.

Because most multiemployer plans are fully funded, and employer contributions are negotiated over a fixed number of years, contributing employers were concerned about their possible inability to deduct obligatory, negotiated contributions that exceeded the full funding limitation (as well as the related 10 percent excise tax on nondeductible contributions). Options to counter OBRA '87's effects, such as increasing benefits or reopening bargaining, were either impractical or potentially harmful to multiemployer plans. Even more frustrating was the fact that neither unions nor employers had much incentive to overfund a multiemployer plan.[16]

The sometimes arduous application of plan qualification rules and other benefit laws and regulations to multiemployer plans is one contributing factor to a comparatively slow appearance of employee benefit trends, such as flexible benefit plans and 401(k) plans, among multiemployer plans. It is understandable that employers contributing to multiemployer plans for employees who often change jobs with seasons, business cycles, or construction projects are somewhat reluctant to handle

---

[14] See Gerald E. Cole, Jr., and Gregory A. Delamarter, "401(k) for Negotiated Plans," *Employee Benefits Digest,* March 1990, pp. 6, 7.

[15] Daniel F. McGinn, "Minimum Participation and Vesting, Postretirement Age Benefit Adjustments and General Benefit Distribution Rules," chapter in *Trustees Handbook,* p. 233.

[16] "Relentless Pursuit of Fair Funding Treatment: Making Sense of Pension Funding Limitations," *NCCMP Update,* Spring 1989, p. 7. Note that EGTRRA increased the applicable percentage of current full-funding liability in 2002 and 2003 to 165 percent and 170 percent, respectively, then repealed the provision for plan years beginning in 2004.

administrative matters that must be taken care of at the employer level. Salary deferrals to a multiemployer 401(k) plan, for example, have to be withheld from payroll by each employer and forwarded to the plan administrator. Inherent multiemployer plan differences also somewhat impede experimentation with health and welfare benefit plan designs. The extent of employee assistance and wellness programs among multiemployer plans, although increasing, lingers well behind that found among single-employer plans.

COBRA

Multiemployer employee benefit plan regulation by ERISA, the Internal Revenue Code, and other benefits-related law, outside of the plan qualification rules, also sometimes is incongruous with the structure and operation of multiemployer plans. COBRA is an excellent example of a federal statute that, while originally enacted with little acknowledgment of multiemployer plans, has since been interpreted through regulations and amended to clarify and ease the compliance process for multiemployer plans and contributing employers.

One of the first questions COBRA posed for those connected with the administration of multiemployer health plans was its application to contributing employers with fewer than 20 employees. Treasury regulations confirmed the worst: Each of the employers maintaining a multiemployer health plan must have fewer than 20 employees during the preceding calendar year for the plan to be excluded from COBRA. Employers maintaining multiple-employer welfare plans, conversely, are treated as maintaining separate plans, and, therefore, are excluded from COBRA if they have fewer than 20 employees.[17]

Even the intent of COBRA—to allow qualified beneficiaries who lose employer-sponsored group health plan coverage to elect continued coverage at their own expense—was not as relevant in the multiemployer plan context because most multiemployer plans already had continued health coverage options in place. Historically, multiemployer health plans provide an extended period of eligibility to participants during times of temporary unemployment, often based on an hours bank or through a series of self-payments.

Because many multiemployer health plan participants do continue their eligibility for health benefits for a time period despite a reduction in hours or termination (many times without even accessing their hours bank), there often is no loss of coverage upon these events as there is for participants in single-employer plans. Accordingly, employers contributing to multiemployer plans, who are required under

---

[17] Treas. Reg. Sec. 54.4980B-2 Q&A 5(a) (1999). The confusion over the characteristics of a "small employer plan" persists in applying other group health plan statutes to multiemployer plans. For example, the Medicare secondary-payer provisions for group health plans that cover the working aged also, like COBRA, apply to employers with 20 or more employees. But, in the case of the Medicare secondary-payer provisions, employers contributing to multiemployer or multiple-employer plans that have less than 20 employees can elect out if the plan so provides, leaving Medicare as primary payer for employees (and spouses) 65 and older.

COBRA to notify a plan administrator of certain qualifying events, are not always aware whether an employee's reduction in hours or termination has resulted in a loss of coverage, that is, whether a qualifying event has taken place. Advised to err on the side of caution, employers were likely to notify the plan administrator of every reduction in hours and every termination. The plan administrator, in turn, was obliged to notify qualified beneficiaries if continued coverage could not be verified within COBRA's 14-day notification period.

COBRA has since been amended to introduce alternative means of notification for reductions in hours and terminations of employees covered by multiemployer plans, and also longer notification periods for employers contributing to and administrators of multiemployer plans. If a multiemployer plan so provides, the determination of a reduction in hours or termination as a qualifying event may be made by the plan administrator instead of the contributing employer. Also, if the plan so provides, contributing employers may take longer than 30 days to notify the plan administrator of qualifying events, and the plan administrator may take longer than 14 days to notify qualified beneficiaries of their rights. Finally, for any group health plan, notice by the employer to the plan administrator and extension of coverage may begin with the loss of coverage instead of the qualifying event.[18]

COBRA also has been amended since its passage in 1985 to change the entity directly liable for the noncompliance tax burden as well as the form of the sanction. Somewhat atypically placed, the tax penalty for COBRA violations (generally, a $100 excise tax for each day of noncompliance per qualified beneficiary up to a maximum of the lesser of 10 percent paid for medical care or $500,000) now falls on the multiemployer plan, not contributing employers.[19] Prior to amendment by the Technical and Miscellaneous Revenue Act of 1988 (TAMRA), the failure of one contributing employer to comply with COBRA caused all contributing employers to lose their respective tax deductions for contributions to any multiemployer group health plans they maintained and highly compensated employees of all employers to be denied an income exclusion for employer group health coverage.

Conclusion

A multiemployer plan has five basic features: (1) numerous employers contribute to the plan; (2) employees frequently change jobs without loss of benefits (or benefit eligibility); (3) a joint labor-management board of trustees, not contributing employers, manages the plan and its assets, which (4) are placed in a trust fund; and (5) the plan is maintained under a collective-bargaining agreement or agreements. These features have led to separate legislation for multiemployer plans in some instances, such as withdrawal liability and plan insolvency insurance. In other employee benefit

[18] ERISA Sec. 606; IRC Sec. 4980B(f)(6), as amended by the Omnibus Budget Reconciliation Act of 1989, Sec. 7891(d), effective for plan years beginning on or after January 1, 1990.
[19] IRC Sec. 4980B(e). Other persons who are responsible for administering or providing benefits under the plan, such as contributing employers, also can be liable for the excise tax if they cause a COBRA failure.

areas, such as certain plan qualification rules and the continued health care coverage requirements of COBRA, multiemployer plans either have had to adapt to a framework set up for single-employer plans or modify the framework.

In a number of aspects of employee benefit plan design, funding, and administration too numerous to mention in this chapter, application to multiemployer plans differs. In areas even as basic as investment policy, where multiemployer plans historically are more conservative than single-employer plans, multiemployer plans are something of a wrinkle in an otherwise smooth spread of employee benefits. Yet, significantly, multiemployer plans are the only way to provide meaningful benefits to skilled, frequently mobile employees at a cost and level of responsibility acceptable to the industry employers who employ them.

Appendix  3

Section 457 Deferred Compensation Plans

Daniel J. Ryterband*

David Cole

Background

Deferred compensation plans allow employees to postpone receiving income for future service until some later date—most commonly at retirement. Deferred amounts and income earned generally are not taxed until either paid or "made available" to plan participants. Deferred amounts generally are considered made available when participants acquire an immediate, nonforfeitable right to them.

Deferred compensation plans can be structured as pure deferred compensation plans, supplemental benefit arrangements, or a combination of both. In pure deferred compensation plans, employees enter into an agreement with their employer to reduce present compensation or to forgo a raise or bonus in return for the employer's promise to pay benefits at a future date. In supplemental benefit plans, the employer pays an additional, supplemental benefit (sometimes based on a qualified retirement plan benefit formula), without reducing the employee's present compensation, raise, or bonus.

*This appendix originally appeared as Chapter 34 in *The Handbook of Employee Benefits,* 5th ed., Jerry S. Rosenbloom, ed. (Burr Ridge, IL: Irwin Professional Publishing, 2001).

When properly structured, deferred compensation plans shield participants' deferred income from what are termed the tax "doctrines" of economic benefit and constructive receipt. The doctrine of economic benefit generally states that an economic benefit results when an economic or financial benefit, even though not in cash form, is provided to an employee as compensation, such as when an employee receives beneficial ownership of amounts placed with a third party, or when assets are unconditionally and irrevocably paid into a fund to be used for the employee's sole benefit. The doctrine of constructive receipt generally states that income, although not necessarily received in hand by an individual, is considered received and, therefore, currently taxable when it is credited to an account or set aside so it may be drawn upon at any time and amounts receivable are not subject to substantial limitations or restrictions.[1] Generally, events triggering economic benefit or constructive receipt result in deferred amounts becoming available to plan participants, and thus, subject to current taxation. A mere unsecured promise to pay, however, does not constitute receipt of income.[2]

Introduction to Section 457 Plans

Section 457 plans are nonqualified deferred compensation plans available only to state and local government employers (including rural electrical cooperatives) and nongovernment organizations exempt from tax under Internal Revenue Code (IRC) Section 501. Examples of tax-exempt organizations under Section 501 include nongovernmental schools, private hospitals, labor unions, farmers' cooperatives, and certain trade associations, business leagues, private clubs, and fraternal orders. For the most part, they are nonprofit organizations serving their members or a public or charitable cause.

The Revenue Act of 1978 created IRC Section 457, allowing employees of state and local governments to defer a portion of compensation annually in plans meeting specified requirements. The Tax Reform Act of 1986 (TRA '86) extended Section 457's provisions to nonqualified deferred compensation plans of nongovernment tax-exempt employers. Section 457 limits deferral opportunities for employees of eligible employers.

Eligible employers generally use Section 457 plans in two ways:

1. As pure deferred compensation plans that allow participants to reduce their taxable salary in a manner similar to that of private-sector 401(k) plans. (401[k] plans generally are not available to state and local government organizations.)

2. As supplemental benefit plans that provide executives with supplemental retirement income.

Plans meeting the complex requirements of Section 457 as well as related laws and regulations receive favorable federal and state tax treatment (deferral of income tax).[3] Section 457 classifies plans as either "eligible" or "ineligible," each subject to the fol-

---

[1] Reg. Sec. 1.451-2(a).
[2] Rev. Rul. 60-31, 1960-1 CB 174; Rev. Rul. 69-650, 1969-2 CB 106.
[3] IRC Sec. 3121(a)(5)(E), 3121(v)(3), 3306(b)(5)(E).

lowing specific requirements. "Eligible" plans are known as Section 457(b) plans, whereas "ineligible" plans are known as Section 457(f) plans.

Eligible Plan Requirements

In eligible plans of government employers, deferred income and its earnings are tax free until paid to participants or beneficiaries.[4] In eligible plans of nongovernment tax-exempt employers, deferred income and its earnings are tax free until paid or made available to participants or beneficiaries.[5]

Eligibility for Plan Participation

Plan participation must be limited to employees and independent contractors performing service for the employer.[6] Before deferring compensation in any given month, participants must have previously entered into an agreement authorizing the deferrals.[7] Therefore, an active worker must wait until the beginning of the month after entering into an agreement before deferring any income. New employees can make deferrals in their first month of employment if they enter into an agreement on or before their first day of employment.[8] It is not necessary to execute a new agreement for each month.

Maximum Annual Deferral

The Economic Growth and Tax Relief Reconciliation Act of 2001 (EGTRRA) increased the plan ceiling, or maximum annual deferral to $11,000 for 2002 or 100 percent of includable compensation,[9] whichever is less.[10] The $11,000 limit increases each year by $1,000 to $15,000 in 2006, and is subsequently adjusted annually in amounts rounded down to the nearest $500 (based on general cost of living increases).[11] Includable compensation is payment for service performed for the employer which is currently includable in gross income.[12] In general, participants with total compensation in excess of $11,000 (for 2002, to be increased as described above) can defer a maximum of $11,000, and participants with total compensation less than $11,000 can defer up to 100 percent of compensation. Deferred amounts exceeding this limit generally are treated as made available and subject to normal taxation in the taxable year deferred.

For purposes of the plan ceiling, deferred income must be taken into account at its current value (in the plan year deferred, rather than the year received).[13]

---

[4] IRC Sec. 457(a)(1)(A).
[5] IRC Sec. 457(a)(1)(A), 457(a)(1)(B).
[6] IRC Sec. 457(b)(1), Reg. Sec. 1.457-2(d).
[7] IRC Sec. 457(b)(4).
[8] Reg. Sec. 1.457-2(g).
[9] IRC Sec. 457(b)(2).
[10] All provisions of EGTRRA of 2001 will expire on 12/31/2010 unless extended by a future act of Congress.
[11] IRC Sec. 457(e)(15)(A), 457(e)(15)(B).
[12] IRC Sec. 457(e)(5).
[13] IRC Sec. 457(e)(6), Reg. Sec. 1.457-2(e)(3).

Catch-Up Provision

Beginning in 2002, participants age 50 and older at the end of the plan year are allowed to make an additional $1,000 contribution above the dollar limits described earlier (not to exceed 100 percent of includable compensation). The $1,000 catch-up amount increases each year by $1,000 to $5,000 in 2006, and is subsequently adjusted annually in amounts rounded down to the nearest $500 (based on general cost of living increases).[14]

During any or all of the three taxable years ending before the year the participant reaches normal retirement age, the "catch-up" provision described above is superseded by an amount equal to twice the otherwise applicable limit or, if less, the participant's normal ceiling plus aggregate unused annual ceiling amounts for deferrals in prior years.[15] For example, a 62-year-old participant, with gross compensation of $30,000 in an eligible plan with a normal retirement age of 65, who has underutilized deferrals in prior years by $10,000 could elect to defer a maximum of $21,000 for 2002. This amount is computed by adding the underutilized prior year deferrals of $10,000 to the normal limit of $11,000 (which is less than twice the normal limit).

Participants may not use the catch-up provision after the expiration of the three-year period even if it was not fully used in the three years preceding normal retirement age and whether or not the participant or former participant rejoins the plan or participates in another eligible plan after retirement.[16] Normal retirement age may be specified in the plan and defined as a single age or range of ages ending no later than 70½. In plans that do not specify normal retirement age, it is generally age 65 or the latest normal retirement age specified in the employer's pension plan, if later.[17]

Coordination with Other Plans

Prior to EGTRRA, maximum deferrals in eligible 457(b) plans were required to be coordinated with amounts excluded from income under other types of deferral arrangements, such as 401(k) plans, 403(b) plans, savings incentive match plans for employees (SIMPLE plans), and simplified employee pensions (SEPs). Effective in 2002, the requirement to coordinate deferrals no longer applies.[18] Therefore, participants may defer the Section 457(b) plan ceiling irrespective of contributions to other plans.

Funding Requirements

In plans maintained by tax-exempt organizations, deferred amounts and earnings must remain the sole property of the employer until made available to participants, subject only to the claims of the employer's general creditors.[19] However, plans

---

[14] IRC Sec. 414(v)(B), Sec. 414(v)(C).
[15] IRC Sec. 457(b)(3).
[16] Reg. Sec. 1.457-2(f)(3).
[17] Reg. Sec. 1.457-2(f)(4).
[18] EGTRRA Sec. 615(a).
[19] IRC Sec. 457(b)(6).

maintained by government organizations are required to hold all plan assets in a trust, custodial account, or annuity contract for the exclusive benefit of participants and their beneficiaries.[20] The terms of the trust must make it impossible for plan assets or income to be diverted to any purpose other than participant benefits until all liabilities of the plan have been satisfied. The trust requirement is designed to prevent loss of participant retirement benefits to the claims of the government's general creditors. Before the trust requirement was instituted as part of the Small Business Job Protection Act of 1996, participant benefits were held as employer assets and subject to the general claims of the plan sponsor's creditors.

Investment Options Available to Participants

In government plans, which are required to irrevocably set aside assets to pay participant benefits through a formal trust, custodial contract, or annuity contract, participants are generally permitted to choose among various investment alternatives offered under the plan. In plans maintained by tax-exempt organizations, in which deferred amounts and earnings must remain the property of the employer until distributed to the participant, only "informal" funding is permitted. In these plans, employers can earmark assets and allow the participants to direct investment, but they cannot be given a secured interest in the purchased assets. As a result, participants in plans sponsored by tax-exempt organizations can exercise some ownership rights, but remain at risk that the employer may be unable to pay promised benefits.

Most employers that offer eligible 457(b) plans offer participants a variety of investment choices, including equity, bond, and money market funds; guaranteed interest contracts; bank deposit accounts; and fixed- and variable-annuity contracts.

Insurance companies are the predominant investment manager. Other managers include mutual funds, brokerage firms, banks, and investment advisers. In-house investment management is uncommon. Investment managers frequently are responsible for plan implementation, administration and record keeping, and participant enrollment as well, but these functions can be contracted to service providers or performed in-house.

Availability of Loan Provisions

Participant loans are not permitted in eligible 457(b) plans maintained by tax-exempt employers. This is because participants have no secured, nonforfeitable benefit from which to secure the loan and because assets must remain subject to the employer's general creditors until made available. However, in plans maintained by government employers, participant loans may be permitted under the general terms that apply to qualified retirement plans (e.g., 401[k] plans).

Availability of Benefits

Plan benefits generally cannot be made available (other than through a loan feature in a plan maintained by a government employer or a qualified domestic relations

---

[20] IRC Sec. 457(g).

order[21]) until the participant has a severance from employment or is faced with an "unforeseeable emergency," or until the calendar year when the participant attains age 70½, if later.[22] Severance from employment generally occurs at the employee's termination, disability, death, or retirement. Independent contractors are considered separated from service when their contracts expire, assuming the expiration consti-tutes a good-faith and complete termination of the contractual relationship. If the employer expects to renew the contract or hire the independent contractor as an employee, separation from service generally has not occurred.[23] An unforeseeable emergency is a severe financial hardship resulting from a sudden and unexpected ill-ness, loss of property because of casualty, or other similar extraordinary and unfore-seeable circumstance outside participant control. Sending a child to college or pur-chasing a new home are not considered unforeseeable emergencies.[24] In addition, participants may not withdraw money if insurance, liquidation of the participant's assets, or discontinuing plan deferrals will relieve the hardship. Emergency with-drawals are permitted only in amounts necessary to satisfy the emergency need.[25]

An exception to the above rules is available for participants of tax-exempt employers with account balances up to $5,000, excluding the portion of such account balance attributible to rollover contributions (and the earnings allocable thereto), if no amount has been distributed to the participant during the two-year period that precedes the distribution and there has been no prior plan distribution to the participant.[26] Although this provision formerly applied to both governmental and tax-exempt employers, Section 457(e)(9) was amended by EGTRRA so that it now only applies to tax-exempt employers.

Plan Distributions

In general, distributions from eligible plans must begin within 60 days after the later of the close of the plan year in which a participant attains or would have attained the plan's normal retirement age or the day the participant separates from service.[27] Eli-gible 457(b) plans are subject to the same distribution beginning-date requirements as qualified plans. As such, plan distributions must begin no later than April 1 of the calendar year following the calendar year in which an employee either retires or attains age 70½, whichever is later.[28]

Eligible 457(b) plan distributions (and amounts considered made available in plans maintained by tax-exempt organizations) are subject to regular income tax withholding as wages, and payments are reported on Form W-2.[29] However, amounts

---

[21] IRC Sec 414(p)(11).
[22] IRC Sec.457(d)(1).
[23] Reg. Sec. 1.457-2(h)(3).
[24] Reg. Sec. 1.457-2(h)(4).
[25] Reg. Sec. 1.457-2(h)(5).
[26] IRC Sec. 457(a)(2), Sec. 457(e)(9), Sec. 72(t)(9).
[27] IRC Sec. 402(c)(Reg. Sec. 1.457-2(i)(1).
[28] IRC Sec.457(d)(2) and 401(a)(9).
[29] Rev. Rul. 82-46, 1982-1 CB 158.

made available are not taxed if the participant or beneficiary irrevocably elects before distribution to defer payment until a later date.[30] For example, if someone separates from service at age 60 and elects to defer payment until age 65, the amount is not treated as made available (even though the person had the right to receive it) and remains tax deferred until received.

Former participants may have any amount made payable to them transferred to another eligible 457(b) plan without having amounts includible in gross income.[31] Additionally, former government plan participants may roll over plan distributions to an individual retirement plan, a qualified plan, or an annuity plan without having amounts includible in gross income.[32] Conversely, distributions from an individual retirement plan, a qualified plan, or an annuity plan may be rolled over into government 457(b) plans.[33] The rollovers from and into another type of plan must be made within 60 days of distribution.[34] However, the 60-day rollover period is extended where failure to comply is due to casualty, disaster, or other events beyond the reasonable control of the participant.[35] Former participants may elect a trustee-to-trustee transfer of eligible 457(b) plan distributions to a defined benefit governmental plan if such transfer is for the purchase of permissive service credit or a repayment to which Section 415 does not apply without having amounts includible in gross income.[36]

Distributions from 457 plans are exempt from the 10 percent penalty tax on withdrawals made before age 59½ except for portions attributable to rollovers from another type of plan.[37]

IRS Approval

Unlike qualified plans, eligible 457(b) plans need not apply to the Internal Revenue Service (IRS) for approval but can and often apply for private letter rulings indicating the plan meets the requirements of Section 457. Plans not administered according to the law can lose the tax benefit of deferral. State and local government plans that do not comply with the statutory requirements of eligible 457 plans must be amended as of the first plan year beginning more than 180 days after IRS notification of any inconsistencies. A plan not amended within this grace period will be treated as an ineligible plan and becomes subject to the rules of Section 457(f). There is no grace period for plans of nongovernmental tax-exempt employers that must maintain compliance at all times to maintain favorable tax treatment.[38]

---

[30] Reg. Sec. 1.457-1(b).
[31] IRC Sec. 457(e)(10).
[32] IRC Sec. 457(e)(16).
[33] IRC Sec 402(c)(8)(B).
[34] IRC Sec. 402(c)(3)(A).
[35] IRC Sec. 402(c)(3)(B).
[36] IRC Sec. 402(e)(17)(A), 402(e)(17)(B).
[37] IRC Sec. 72(t).
[38] IRC Sec. 457(b) last paragraph, Reg. Sec. 1.457-2(1).

Ineligible Plan Requirements

Ineligible 457 plans are governed by separate rules under Section 457(f). To receive tax-preferred treatment in an ineligible plan, amounts deferred must be subject to a "substantial risk of forfeiture." Unlike eligible plans, ineligible plans place no limits on the amount of deferrals made. Employers, therefore, can use ineligible plans to allow employees a contribution level above the eligible plan limit or to provide supplemental retirement benefits to selected executives. However, ineligible plans are better suited for employer contributions than for salary reduction because of the "substantial risk of forfeiture" provision. If an employer maintains both an eligible and an ineligible plan, it is preferable that they be maintained and administered separately for cost and compliance reasons.

Ineligible 457(f) plan deferred amounts are included in participant or beneficiary gross income in the first taxable year where there is no substantial risk of forfeiture, even if amounts are not received.[39] For a substantial risk of forfeiture to exist, a person's right to receive deferred amounts must be conditioned on future performance of substantial services.[40] Whether the risk of forfeiture is substantial depends on the facts and circumstances of each situation. For example, a substantial risk of forfeiture likely exists when rights to deferred payment are lost at termination of employment for any reason, but a requirement that rights are lost only at termination for cause or committing a crime generally would not create a substantial risk.

Taxation of distributions or amounts made available in ineligible plans is determined under IRC Section 72 annuity rules.[41]

Nondiscrimination Issues

Unlike qualified retirement plans (e.g., 401[k] plans), Section 457 plans are not subject to complex IRS rules that require benefits to be nondiscriminatory. As a result, 457 plans can be offered on a discriminatory basis with participation limited to only a few employees or even to a single employee.

The requirement that 457 plans maintained by tax-exempt employers be unfunded, however, limits availability to certain employee groups in such plans. This is because Title I of the Employee Retirement Income Security Act (ERISA) requires plans be funded, which conflicts with the Section 457 requirement that plans be unfunded. Tax-exempt employers' plans generally are subject to Title I requirements and, therefore, must fall within one of the special Title I exceptions to meet both ERISA and Internal Revenue Code (IRC) requirements. This conflict generally requires nongovernment tax-exempt employer 457 plans to restrict participation to a select group of management or highly compensated employees ("top hat" plans)

---

[39] IRC Sec. 457(f)(1)(A).
[40] IRC Sec. 457(f)(3)(B).
[41] IRC Sec. 72 and 457(f)(1)(B), Reg. Sec. 1.457-3(a)(3).

to avoid ERISA's funding requirements.[42] Nongovernment tax exempt employers have used ineligible 457(f) plans to provide "restoration" plan benefits (i.e., contributions above IRS limits in qualified 401[k] plans or 403[b] plans) for their highly paid employees. Beginning in 2002, nongovernment tax-exempt employers could also use eligible 457(b) plans as an additional executive compensation benefit since eligible 457(b) plans no longer need to coordinate their elective deferral limits with the elective deferrals under other types of plans.

457 Plan Reporting and Disclosure

State and local government employer 457 plans are exempt from ERISA's reporting and disclosure requirements.[43] These employers do not have to comply with requirements for summary plan descriptions; summary annual reports and summary descriptions of material plan modifications; annual registration statements; and plan descriptions, annual reports, and other materials frequently requested by participants. Certain returns and reports (such as Form W-2 and 1099-MISC), however, must be filed with the IRS, and participants and beneficiaries must receive information about their benefits when they terminate employment or receive benefit distributions.

Nongovernmental tax-exempt employer plans must meet ERISA's requirements for reporting and disclosure.[44] However, tax-exempt employer plans maintained for a select group of management or highly compensated employees can satisfy ERISA's reporting and disclosure requirements through an alternative compliance method under Department of Labor regulations. Under this method, a statement must be filed with the Secretary of Labor declaring the plan is maintained primarily to provide deferred compensation for a select group of management or highly compensated employees. Plan documents must be provided upon request to the Department of Labor.[45]

Deferred Arrangements Not Considered Deferred Compensation Plans

A 1987 IRS notice interpreted Section 457 requirements as applying to all deferred arrangements. This was interpreted as meaning benefits such as accrued sick time and vacation not used in the present year (as well as elective deferrals of compensation) would be subject to Section 457 restrictions.[46] The dollar value of these benefits that employees received then would directly reduce their allowable compensation

---

[42] IRS Notice 87-13, 1987-1 CB 432.
[43] ERISA Sec. 4(b)(1).
[44] ERISA Sec. 4(a), 201, 301, and 401.
[45] Labor Reg. Sec. 2520.104-23.
[46] IRS Notice 87-13, 1987-1 CB 432.

deferral amount in eligible plans. Under this interpretation, state and local government and tax-exempt employers were severely restricted in providing deferred compensation and supplemental retirement benefits. Section 457 was later amended so that the following plans generally are excluded from Section 457 restrictions and are not considered as providing compensation deferral:[47]

1. Vacation and sick leave.

2. Compensatory time.

3. Severance pay.

4. Disability pay and death benefits.

To be exempt from Section 457, an arrangement must be legitimate and not an indirect method of deferring cash amounts.

Deferred Compensation Plans Not Subject to Section 457

Certain deferred compensation plans of state and local government and tax-exempt employers generally are not subject to Section 457 restrictions if certain conditions are met.

Nonelective Deferred Compensation of Nonemployees

Plans providing nonelective deferred compensation for services not performed as an employee (e.g., independent contractors) are exempt from Section 457 restrictions for tax years beginning after December 31, 1987. To be considered nonelective, a plan must be uniform for all participants, offer no variations or options, and cover all persons with the same relationship to the employer.[48] For example, if a hospital gives a nonemployee doctor deferred compensation, the deferred compensation is considered nonelective only if all other nonemployee doctors are covered by the same plan.

Church and Judicial Deferred Compensation Plans

Deferred compensation plans of churches and church-controlled organizations for their employees generally are exempt from Section 457 requirements for tax years beginning after December 31, 1987.[49]

State judges' government deferred compensation plans use the tax rules for funded and unfunded nonqualified deferred compensation plans, rather than Section 457 rules, if certain requirements are met. In addition, participants are not subject to the substantial risk of forfeiture rule for ineligible plans.[50] Qualified state judicial plans must have existed continuously since December 31, 1978, and must require:

---

[47] IRC Sec. 457(e)(11).
[48] IRC Sec. 457(e)(12).
[49] IRC Sec. 457(e)(13), 3121(w)(3)(A), 3121(w)(3)(B).
[50] Sec. 1107(c)(4) of P.L. 99-514 (TRA '86).

1. All eligible judges to participate and contribute the same fixed percentage of compensation.

2. The plan to provide no judge with an option that would affect the amount of includible compensation.

3. Retirement benefits to be a percentage of the compensation of judges holding similar positions in the state.

4. Benefits paid in any year not to exceed either 100 percent of a participant's average compensation for the highest three years, or if less, $90,000 adjusted for inflation ($160,000 in 2002).[51]

Nonqualified state judicial plans that do not meet these requirements are taxed as ordinary Section 457 deferred compensation plans.

Nongovernment Tax-Exempt Employer Deferred Compensation Plans

Grandfather provisions may apply to nongovernment tax-exempt employer plans in certain cases. Amounts deferred in tax-exempt employers' plans in taxable years beginning before January 1, 1987, generally are exempt from Section 457 restrictions. Amounts deferred after December 31, 1986, are exempt from Section 457 restrictions if deferrals are based on an agreement that on August 16, 1986, was in writing and stipulated deferrals of a fixed amount (or a fixed percentage of a fixed base amount) or an amount determined by a fixed formula. For example, participants who were deferring 5 percent of compensation according to a written plan on August 16, 1986, must make all subsequent deferrals at 5 percent for the amount to be considered fixed. An example of a fixed formula is a deferred compensation plan designed as a defined benefit plan in which deferrals to be paid in the future are in the form of an annual benefit equal to 1 percent per year of service times final average salary. Changes in the fixed amount or fixed formula result in loss of grandfathered status.[52]

Nonelective Government Employer Deferred Compensation Plans

A grandfather provision also is available to amounts deferred before July 14, 1988, in nonelective government plans by participants covered by a written agreement. To avoid Section 457 restrictions, the agreement must stipulate determination of annual deferrals as a fixed amount or by a fixed formula. Amounts deferred on or after July 14, 1988, are exempt from Section 457 restrictions until the tax year ending after the effective date of an agreement modifying the fixed amount or fixed formula.[53]

Collectively Bargained Deferred Compensation Plans

Collectively bargained plans of both state and local government and nongovernment tax-exempt employers allowing nonelective income deferral may be excluded from

---

[51] Sec. 252 of P.L. 97-248 (TEFRA).
[52] IRS Notice 87-13, 1987-1 CB 432.
[53] Sec. 6064(d)(3) of P.L. 100-647 (TAMRA).

Section 457 restrictions if certain conditions are met. To be grandfathered, a plan must cover a broad group of employees; have a definite, fixed, and uniform benefit structure; and have been in existence on December 31, 1987. A plan loses grandfathered status upon the first material plan modification after December 31, 1987. Modifications to nonelective plans are considered material only if they change the benefit formula or expand the class of participants. This grandfather rule generally applies only to union employees participating in a nonqualified, nonelective plan under a collective bargaining agreement. The rule also is available to nonunion employees if, as of December 31, 1987, participation was extended to a broad group of nonunion employees on the same terms as the union employees and union employees account for at least 25 percent of total participation.[54]

Taxation of Nonelective Deferred Compensation Subject to Section 457

The above discussion on deferred compensation plans not subject to Section 457 indicates that, under certain circumstances, nonelective deferred compensation is exempt from Section 457 rules and current taxation. However, many employees of state and local government and nongovernment tax-exempt employers are taxed on nonelective deferred compensation before they are entitled to receive it. For example:

> A nonprofit organization hires an employee under a five-year employment agreement to pay $50,000 annually. Assuming the employee works the entire five-year period, an additional $10,000 will be paid annually in years six through 10. Under Section 457 rules, the employee would be taxed in year six on the entire present value of all five $10,000 payments. If we assume the discounted present value of the $10,000 payments equals approximately $41,000[55] and the entire amount is subject to 28 percent tax, $11,480 would be paid in tax in Year 6 even though only $10,000 is actually received.

This results in current taxation on amounts the taxpayer:

1. Has not yet received.

2. Has no current right to receive.

3. May not actually ever receive.

Because similar rules do not apply to private-sector employers, this practice places state and local government and nongovernment tax-exempt employers at a disadvantage in recruiting employees. Current congressional efforts aim to correct this inequity by uniformly providing that nonelective deferred compensation is not taxable until actually received.

---

[54] IRS Notice 88-98, 1988-2 CB 421.
[55] Calculated using a 7 percent discount rate, the present value of $10,000 received annually over five years equals $41,001.97.

Conclusion

Most 457 plans are maintained by state and local government employers for the purpose of salary reduction. Without these plans, governmental employers would be precluded from offering salary deferral opportunities that are common among for-profit employers. Section 457 plans used for purposes other than salary reduction are less common but are rapidly gaining in importance. Nongovernment tax-exempt employers can use eligible 457(b) plans to provide supplemental retirement benefits and salary continuation to certain high-paid executives. Amounts deferred under eligible 457(b) plans are no longer coordinated with amounts deferred under other deferral arrangements since the passage of EGTRRA. Nongovernment tax-exempt employers can also use ineligible 457(f) plans to provide supplemental retirement benefits and salary continuation to certain high-paid executives. These plans function to:

1. Provide benefits over IRC Section 415 limits on contributions to, or benefits from, qualified plans.

2. Offset the effect of the $200,000 maximum compensation cap (as of 2002) of IRC Section 401(a)(17) when determining benefits or contributions to qualified plans.

3. Give valued employees additional death and disability benefits.

4. Impose "golden handcuffs" on valued employees or enhance early retirement benefits.

5. Increase benefits for executives recruited in midcareer who are unable to accrue maximum pension benefits in a qualified plan by normal retirement age.

6. Reward key employees for their contributions to the organization.

Keen competition for talented employees forces employers to design plans attractive to an increasingly mobile workforce. For state and local government and nongovernment tax-exempt employers, 457 plans play an important part in meeting overall employee benefit plan objectives. A successful program, however, requires compliance with the complex requirements governing design, operation, and administration of Section 457 plans.

Index